ADAM SMITH

The Theory of
Moral Sentiments

A Liberty Classics Edition

THE GLASGOW EDITION OF THE WORKS AND CORRESPONDENCE OF ADAM SMITH

Commissioned by the University of Glasgow to celebrate the bicentenary of the Wealth of Nations

I
THE THEORY OF MORAL SENTIMENTS
Edited by A. L. MACFIE *and* D. D. RAPHAEL

II
AN INQUIRY INTO THE NATURE AND CAUSES OF THE WEALTH OF NATIONS
Edited by R. H. CAMPBELL *and* A. S. SKINNER; *textual editor* W. B. TODD

III
ESSAYS ON PHILOSOPHICAL SUBJECTS
(and Miscellaneous Pieces)
Edited by W. P. D. WIGHTMAN

IV
LECTURES ON RHETORIC AND BELLES LETTRES
Edited by J. C. BRYCE
This volume includes the *Considerations concerning the First Formation of Languages*

V
LECTURES ON JURISPRUDENCE
Edited by R. L. MEEK, D. D. RAPHAEL, *and* P. G. STEIN
This volume includes two reports of Smith's course together with the 'Early Draft' of the *Wealth of Nations*

VI
CORRESPONDENCE OF ADAM SMITH
Edited by E. C. MOSSNER *and* I. S. ROSS

Associated volumes:
ESSAYS ON ADAM SMITH
Edited by A. S. SKINNER *and* T. WILSON

LIFE OF ADAM SMITH
By I. S. ROSS

The Glasgow Edition of the Works and Correspondence of Adam Smith and the associated volumes are published in hardcover by Oxford University Press. The six titles of the Glasgow Edition, but not the associated volumes, are being published in softcover by Liberty Fund.

ADAM SMITH

The Theory of
Moral Sentiments

EDITED BY

D. D. RAPHAEL

AND

A. L. MACFIE

Liberty Fund

Indianapolis
1984

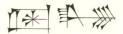
This Liberty Fund edition of 1982 is an exact photographic
reproduction of the edition published by Oxford University
Press in 1976 and reprinted with minor corrections in 1979.

Liberty Fund, Inc.
8335 Allison Pointe Trail #300
Indianapolis, Indiana 46250-1687

This reprint has been authorized by the Oxford University Press.

© Oxford University Press 1976

Library of Congress Cataloging in Publication Data

Smith, Adam, 1723–1790.
The theory of moral sentiments.

Reprint. Originally published: Oxford: Clarendon
Press, 1976. (The Glasgow edition of the works and
correspondence of Adam Smith; 1)
Includes index.
1. Ethics—Early works to 1800. I. Raphael,
D. D. (David Daiches), 1916–   . II. Macfie,
Alec Lawrence. III. Title. IV. Series: Smith,
Adam, 1723–1790. Works. 1976; 1.
AC7.S59 1976a vol. 1 [BJ1005] 330.15'3s 81-23693
ISBN 0-86597-012-2 (pbk.) [170] AACR2

10 9 8 7 6

Cover design by JMH Corporation, Indianapolis.
Printed & bound by
Edwards Brothers, Inc., Ann Arbor, Michigan

Preface

THIS is the first volume of a new edition of the works of Adam Smith undertaken by the University of Glasgow. In editing *The Theory of Moral Sentiments* we have received a great deal of help from the introduction and notes to Walther Eckstein's German translation of the book, published in 1926. Dr. Eckstein kindly added one or two further facts in private correspondence and showed a warm interest in this project of the University of Glasgow. We were sad to learn of his death a few years ago.

We are indebted to a number of other scholars who have given us information or suggestions. They include the late H. B. Acton, W. R. Brock, J. C. Bryce, the late C. J. Fordyce, L. Davis Hammond, K. H. Hennings, Nicholas M. Hope, I. D. Lloyd-Jones, the late W. G. Maclagan, J. C. Maxwell, Ronald L. Meek, W. G. Moore, Ernest C. Mossner, Sylvia Raphael, James Ritchie, Ian Ross, Andrew S. Skinner, Peter Stein, David M. Walker, Derek A. Watts, and W. Gordon Wheeler. All of them were most generous in responding to questions, but a special word of appreciation is due to J. C. Bryce and Andrew Skinner.

D. D. Raphael is grateful to the Warden and Fellows of All Souls College, Oxford, and to the University Court of the University of Glasgow for enabling him to spend more time on editorial work, first as a Visiting Fellow of All Souls for six months in 1967–8, and then as the Stevenson Lecturer in Citizenship at Glasgow in the autumn of 1972.

He also wishes to thank Mrs. Anne S. Walker, his secretary at Glasgow University, and Miss Hilary Burgess, his secretary at Imperial College, for the care with which they have typed the editorial matter.

Appendix II, always intended for this edition, has been published previously, with some minor changes, as an article by D. D. Raphael under the title 'Adam Smith and "the infection of David Hume's society"', in *Journal of the History of Ideas*, xxx (1969), 225–48. (The article contained an error on p. 245, saying that Smith refers to Hume in TMS II.ii.1.5. The reference is in fact to Kames.)

1974

D.D.R.
A.L.M.

Contents

Key to Abbreviations and References

WORKS OF ADAM SMITH

Corr.	*Correspondence*
EPS	*Essays on Philosophical Subjects*, included among which are:
Astronomy	'The History of Astronomy'
Ancient Logics	'The History of the Ancient Logics and Metaphysics'
English and Italian Verses	'Of the Affinity between certain English and Italian Verses'
External Senses	'Of the External Senses'
Stewart	Dugald Stewart, 'Account of the Life and Writings of Adam Smith'
LJ(A)	*Lectures on Jurisprudence*, Report of 1762–3
LJ(B)	*Lectures on Jurisprudence*, Report dated 1766
LRBL	*Lectures on Rhetoric and Belles Lettres*
TMS	*The Theory of Moral Sentiments*
WN	*The Wealth of Nations*

References to Corr. give the number of the letter (as listed in the volume of Smith's *Correspondence* in the present edition), the date, and the name of Smith's correspondent.

References to LJ and to LRBL give the volume (where applicable) and page number of the manuscript (shown in the printed texts of the present edition). References to LJ(B) add the page number in Edwin Cannan (ed.), *Lectures on Justice, Police, Revenue and Arms* by Adam Smith (Oxford, 1896); and references to LRBL add the page number in John M. Lothian (ed.), *Lectures on Rhetoric and Belles Lettres* by Adam Smith (London, etc., 1963).

References to the other works listed above locate the relevant paragraph, not the page, in order that any edition may be consulted. (In the present edition, the paragraph numbers are printed in the margin.) Thus:

Astronomy, II.4 = 'History of Astronomy', Sect.II, § 4

Stewart, I.12 = Dugald Stewart, 'Account of the Life and Writings of Adam Smith', Sect.I, § 12

TMS I.i.5.5 = *The Theory of Moral Sentiments* Part I, Sect.i, Chap.5, § 5

WN V.i.f.26 = *The Wealth of Nations*, Book V, Chap.i, sixth division, § 26

OTHER WORKS

Bonar, *Catalogue 1* [or] *2*	James Bonar, *A Catalogue of the Library of Adam Smith*, ed. 1 (London, 1894) [or] ed. 2 (London, 1932)
Eckstein	Adam Smith, *Theorie der ethischen Gefühle*, translated and edited by Walther Eckstein, 2 vols. (Leipzig, 1926)
Rae, *Life*	John Rae, *Life of Adam Smith* (London, 1895)
Scott, *ASSP*	William Robert Scott, *Adam Smith as Student and Professor* (Glasgow, 1937)

Introduction

1. FORMATION OF *The Theory of Moral Sentiments*

(a) *Adam Smith's lectures on ethics*

The Theory of Moral Sentiments, Adam Smith's first book, was published in 1759 during his tenure of the Chair of Moral Philosophy at the University of Glasgow. A second, revised edition appeared in 1761. Smith left Glasgow at the beginning of 1764. Editions 3 (1767), 4 (1774), and 5 (1781) of TMS differ little from edition 2. Edition 6, however, published shortly before Smith's death in 1790, contains very extensive additions and other significant changes. The original work arose from Smith's lectures to students. The revisions in edition 2 were largely the result of criticism from philosophically minded friends. The new material in edition 6 was the fruit of long reflection by Smith on his wide knowledge of public affairs and his equally wide reading of history.

Adam Smith was appointed to the Chair of Logic at Glasgow in 1751 and moved to the Chair of Moral Philosophy in 1752. His predecessor as Professor of Moral Philosophy, Thomas Craigie, was already ill in 1751, and Smith was asked to substitute for him with lectures on natural jurisprudence and politics[1] in addition to taking the Logic class. Thereafter Smith gave the whole of the Moral Philosophy course, in which he was expected to deal with natural theology and ethics before proceeding to law and government. In view of the speed with which Smith had to prepare his extensive range of teaching at Glasgow, it was inevitable that he should make use of material already available from a series of public lectures which he had delivered in Edinburgh during the years 1748–50. These lectures were sponsored especially by Lord Kames. Both Dugald Stewart in a biography of Smith and A. F. Tytler in one of Kames describe the subject-matter of the Edinburgh lectures simply as rhetoric and belles lettres,[2] but it seems that by 1750 Smith also included political and economic theory, presumably under the title of jurisprudence or civil law.[3] In a later part of his biography (IV.25), Dugald Stewart refers to a short manuscript written by Adam Smith in 1755, listing 'certain leading principles, both political and literary, to which he was anxious to establish his exclusive right'. Stewart says that they included 'many of the most

---

[1] Corr., Letter 9 addressed to William Cullen, dated 3 September 1751.

[2] Dugald Stewart, 'Account of the Life and Writings of Adam Smith, LL.D.' (1793; reprinted in EPS), I.12; A. F. Tytler, *Memoirs of the Life and Writings of Henry Home of Kames* (Edinburgh, 1807), i.190.

[3] W. R. Scott, *Adam Smith as Student and Professor* (Glasgow, 1937), 50, 54–5, cites evidence for lectures on civil law.

important opinions in *The Wealth of Nations*', and then quotes a few sentences from the manuscript itself. These end with a statement from Smith that 'a great part of the opinions enumerated in this paper' had formed 'the constant subjects of my lectures since I first taught Mr. Craigie's class, the first winter I spent in Glasgow, down to this day, without any considerable variation' and that they had also 'been the subjects of lectures which I read at Edinburgh the winter before I left it'.

A report of the content and character of the early Glasgow lectures, both in the Logic and in the Moral Philosophy class, was given to Stewart by John Millar, Professor of Law at Glasgow, originally a pupil and afterwards a close friend of Smith. In his Logic course Smith despatched the traditional logic rather briskly and then 'dedicated all the rest of his time to the delivery of a system of rhetoric and belles lettres'.[4] His Moral Philosophy course could not rely so heavily on the Edinburgh lectures but it will certainly have drawn on them in its latter sections. Millar's report to Dugald Stewart gives a detailed description of it.

His course of lectures on this subject [Moral Philosophy] was divided into four parts. The first contained Natural Theology. . . . The second comprehended Ethics strictly so called, and consisted chiefly of the doctrines which he afterwards published in his Theory of Moral Sentiments. In the third part, he treated at more length of that branch of morality which relates to *justice*, . . .

Upon this subject he followed the plan that seems to be suggested by Montesquieu; endeavouring to trace the gradual progress of jurisprudence, both public and private, from the rudest to the most refined ages, . . . This important branch of his labours he also intended to give to the public; but this intention, which is mentioned in the conclusion of the Theory of Moral Sentiments, he did not live to fulfil.

In the last part of his lectures, he examined those political regulations which are founded, not upon the principle of *justice*, but that of *expediency*, and which are calculated to increase the riches, the power, and the prosperity of a State. . . . What he delivered on these subjects contained the substance of the work he afterwards published under the title of An Inquiry into the Nature and Causes of the Wealth of Nations.[5]

There is no evidence to suggest that the Edinburgh lectures included ethical theory proper, and we must therefore presume that Smith's composition of the subject-matter of TMS began in 1752 at Glasgow.

Millar's statement that both of Smith's books arose from his lectures on Moral Philosophy is confirmed by the evidence of James Wodrow, writing (probably in 1808) to the eleventh Earl of Buchan.

Adam Smith, whose lectures I had the benefit of hearing for a year or two . . . made a laudable attempt at first to follow Hut[cheso]ns animated manner,

---

[4] Stewart, I.16. Stewart identifies his informant as Millar in a note added to the reprint of the 'Account' included in *Works of Adam Smith* (London, 1811), v.412.

[5] Stewart, I.18–20.

lecturing on Ethics without papers, walking up and down his class rooms but not having the same facility in this that Hut[n.] had, ... Dr. Smith soon relinquished the attempt, and read with propriety, all the rest of his valuable lectures from the desk. His Theory of Moral Sentiment founded on sympathy, a very ingenious attempt to account for the principal phenomena in the moral world from this one general principle, like that of gravity in the natural world, did not please Hutcheson's scholars so well as that to which they had been accustomed. The rest of his lectures were admired by them and by all especially those on Money and Commerce, which contained the substance of his book on *the Wealth of Nations*. . . .[6]

Francis Hutcheson was Professor of Moral Philosophy from 1730 to 1746. Smith was his pupil in the late 1730s, Wodrow in the 1740s. Wodrow remained at the University as Keeper of the Library from 1750 to 1755.

It seems, then, that the first published version of TMS was prepared or worked up from the final form of the second part of Smith's lectures on Moral Philosophy. No doubt there was steady development between 1752 and 1758. Although no copy of a student's notes of Smith's lectures on ethics has as yet appeared, there is some evidence from which we can reconstruct his method of improving what he had written. In Appendix II we give reasons for thinking that a fragmentary manuscript of philosophical considerations on justice is a part of Smith's lectures on ethics. Revisions within the manuscript itself and detailed comparison with corresponding passages in TMS show that Smith tended to work over previous composition rather than write a new version. He made minor corrections both of style and of content, he inserted substantial additions, and (when it came to preparing a text for publication) he shuffled passages about like pieces in a jigsaw puzzle. Exactly the same methods of development can be seen in the changes that Smith made when revising the printed book for edition 2 and for edition 6. There is far more evidence for tracing the genesis of *The Wealth of Nations*; we have two Reports by students, apparently from successive sessions, of Smith's lectures on jurisprudence, a fairly long manuscript that has been called 'An early draft of part of *The Wealth of Nations*', and two fragmentary manuscripts that come much nearer to the text of WN itself. From this material Professor Ronald L. Meek and Mr. Andrew S. Skinner have been able to give an extraordinarily precise account of the development of Smith's thought on a central topic of his economic theory.[7] The picture of Smith's working methods that emerges from a comparison of these documents with one another and with WN is similar to that gathered from the more limited evidence for TMS.

---

[6] Taken from transcription in Glasgow Univ. Library, Murray MS. 506, pp. 169 ff.
[7] 'The Development of Adam Smith's Ideas on the Division of Labour', *Economic Journal*, lxxxiii (1973), 1094–1116.

The printed text at times betrays its origin in lectures. At several points Smith refers back to something he has said on a former 'occasion', whereas it would be more natural, in a book, to write of an earlier 'place'. Then again, in the final paragraph of the work he promises to treat of the general theory of jurisprudence in another 'discourse'.

One other piece of internal evidence seems to match part of the description of the original Glasgow lectures given to Dugald Stewart by Millar: 'Each discourse consisted commonly of several distinct propositions, which he successively endeavoured to prove and illustrate.'[8] Much of Part II of TMS can be said to fit this account in a general way, but the first chapter, II.i.1, illustrates it quite strikingly and would seem, if unrelated to Millar's account and the lecture form, a rather odd way of continuing from the more natural mode of discussion in Part I. If this chapter does indeed retain Smith's original method of procedure in his lectures, it is almost unique in this respect and shows that Smith must have commonly recast the actual structure of his lectures for the book, even though he kept most of the words and phrases.

The printed text allows a further conjecture about the lectures. The *last* part of the book seems to originate from material that formed the *first* part of the lectures on ethics in their earliest version. Why otherwise should Smith set out here (VII.i.2) the two main problems of ethical theory, as if by way of introduction, when in fact most of his task is already done? It seems probable (and it would accord with his usual method of approaching a subject) that at first he entered upon ethics with a survey of its history in dealing with the two topics of moral motive and moral judgement. Having carried the history up to the thinkers of his own day, he will have reflected upon the differences between the two theories that impressed him most, those of his teacher Hutcheson and his friend Hume. Whether or not he already had definite views of his own on these matters in 1752, it is impossible to say; in any event his account of sympathy and its place in moral judgement will have developed as he gave more attention to the subject. Once it had developed it became the focus of Smith's own distinctive theory of ethics, and at this stage (if our conjecture about the original form of the lectures is correct) Smith will have recast his thoughts, starting off with sympathy, building up his theory from that base, and making the historical survey a sort of appendix.

An examination of changes in style might perhaps give some guidance about alterations from the original lecture notes. There is a clear difference in style between much of what Smith wrote for edition 1 and the considerable additions, including the whole of Part VI, which he composed late in life for edition 6. The earlier matter tends to be rhetorical, in tune with the style accepted for lectures in the mid-eighteenth century, while the

[8] Stewart, I.21.

later writing is in the more urbane style of WN. Both WN and the additions to TMS were of course written with a direct view to publication. When one remembers the type of classes that Smith addressed as a Professor in Glasgow, the style of the original material can be better understood. Most of the students were of the age of secondary schoolboys today. The number attending the class of public lectures on Moral Philosophy in Smith's time was probably about eighty, many of them being destined for the Church. To hold the attention of his class Smith used rhetorical language and made humorous references to manners of the day in a way likely to interest young people.

Of the lectures that Smith delivered in his last four years at Glasgow after the publication of TMS, Stewart (III.1) writes:

During that time, the plan of his lectures underwent a considerable change. His ethical doctrines, of which he had now published so valuable a part, occupied a smaller portion of the course than formerly: and accordingly, his attention was naturally directed to a more complete illustration of the principles of jurisprudence and of political oeconomy.

The last statement appears to be borne out by the two surviving Reports of the lectures on jurisprudence as delivered in sessions 1762-3 and 1763-4. It would be wrong, however, to infer from Stewart's account that Smith's thought on ethics stood still at this time. There is substantial development of his theory in edition 2 of TMS, especially of his notion of the impartial spectator. He can also be seen to apply that concept in the lectures on jurisprudence, so that there is a continuity in his thinking, as indeed Smith himself makes plain at the end of TMS.

(b) Influence of Stoic philosophy

Stoic philosophy is the primary influence on Smith's ethical thought. It also fundamentally affects his economic theory. Like other scholars of his day Smith was well versed in ancient philosophy, and in TMS he often refers as a matter of course to Plato, Aristotle, and Cicero (the last sometimes, but not always, as a source of information about Stoicism). In his survey of the history of moral philosophy in Part VII, however, Stoicism is given far more space than any other 'system', ancient or modern, and is illustrated by lengthy passages from Epictetus and Marcus Aurelius. (The *Discourses* of Epictetus seem to have been chiefly responsible for Smith's early fascination with Stoicism.) In editions 1-5 of TMS some of this material on the Stoics appears separately in Part I, but the separation does not produce a lesser impact on the reader; on the contrary, it shows up more clearly the pervasive character of Stoic influence. Even in edition 6 there remain in the earlier Parts of the book enough direct references to and quotations from Stoic doctrine to indicate this. Stoicism never lost its hold over Smith's mind. When revising his book for edition 6 in his last years, he not only moved two of the earlier passages on 'that famous sect' (as he calls it in the Advertisement) to the historical survey in Part VII. He also added further reflections, especially on the Stoic view of suicide, stimulated no doubt by the posthumous publication of an essay by Hume arguing that suicide was sometimes admirable.

More important, however, is the influence of Stoic principles on Smith's own views, again something that persisted to his latest writings. In the fresh material added to edition 6 of TMS, Smith's elaboration of his account of Stoicism in Part VII is less significant than the clearly Stoic tone of much that he wrote for Part III on the sense of duty and for the new Part VI on the character of virtue. Part VI deals with the three virtues of prudence, beneficence, and self-command. The third of these, which also figures in the additions to Part III, is distinctively Stoic. The first, though common to many systems of ethics, is interpreted by Smith in a Stoic manner. He departs from Stoicism in his views on beneficence, but even there, when he comes to discuss universal benevolence in VI.ii.3, he introduces Stoic ideas and Stoic language to a remarkable degree.

Smith's ethical doctrines are in fact a combination of Stoic and Christian virtues—or, in philosophical terms, a combination of Stoicism and Hutcheson. Hutcheson resolved all virtue into benevolence, a philosophical version of the Christian ethic of love. At an early stage in TMS, Adam Smith supplements this with Stoic self-command.

And hence it is, that to feel much for others and little for ourselves, that to restrain our selfish, and to indulge our benevolent affections, constitutes the perfection of human nature; . . . As to love our neighbour as we love ourselves is the great law of Christianity, so it is the great precept of nature to love ourselves only as we love our neighbour, or what comes to the same thing, as our neighbour is capable of loving us. (I.i.5.5)

Smith emphasizes self-command again when supplementing for edition 6 his treatment of the sense of duty in Part III. He there repeats the dual character of his ideal. 'The man of the most perfect virtue . . . is he who joins, to the most perfect command of his own original and selfish feelings, the most exquisite sensibility both to the original and sympathetic feelings of others' (II.3.34). In Part VI Smith goes farther, making self-command a necessary condition for the exercise of other virtues. Great merit in the practice of any virtue presupposes that there has been temptation to the contrary and that the temptation has been overcome; that is to say, it presupposes self-command. 'Self-command is not only itself a great virtue, but from it all the other virtues seem to derive their principal lustre' (VI.iii.11). For Adam Smith, self-command has come to permeate the whole of virtue, an indication of the way in which Stoicism permeated his reflection over the whole range of ethics and social science.

When Smith sets Stoic self-command beside Christian love in the first of the quotations given above, he calls it 'the great precept of nature'. Life according to nature was the basic tenet of Stoic ethics, and a Stoic idea of nature and the natural forms a major part of the philosophical foundations of TMS and WN alike. The Stoic doctrine went along with a view of nature as a cosmic harmony. Phrases that occur in Smith's account of this Stoic conception are echoed when he expresses his own opinions. The correspondence is most striking in the chapter on universal bene-volence, where Marcus Aurelius is recalled by name as well as in phrase: 'the great Conductor' whose 'benevolence and wisdom have . . . contrived and conducted the immense machine of the universe' (in the new material of edition 6 at VI.ii.3.4–5) is a recollection of the 'all-wise Architect and Conductor' of 'one immense and connected system', 'the whole machine of the world', (quoted from Marcus Aurelius in VII.ii.1.37). Essentially similar turns of speech are to be found in a number of passages, both early and late, of TMS. Indeed, the frequency of such phrases leads one to think that commentators have laid too much stress on the 'invisible hand', which appears only once in each of Smith's two books. On both occasions the context is the Stoic idea of harmonious system, seen in the working of society.

The Stoics themselves applied the notion to society no less than to the physical universe, and used the Greek word *sympatheia* (in the sense of organic connection) of both. This is not the sympathy that figures in Adam Smith's ethics. Sympathy and the impartial spectator, as Smith interprets them, are the truly original features of his theory. Yet it is quite likely that in his own mind each of these two ideas was intimately related to the Stoic outlook. Like the Stoics he thought of the social bond in terms of 'sympathy', and he describes the Stoic view of world citizenship and self-command as if it implied the impartial spectator.

Man, according to the Stoics, ought to regard himself . . . as a citizen of the world, a member of the vast commonwealth of nature. . . . We should view our-selves . . . in the light in which any other citizen of the world would view us. What befalls ourselves we should regard as what befalls our neighbour, or, what comes to the same thing, as our neighbour regards what befalls us. (III.3.11)

In WN the Stoic concept of natural harmony appears especially in 'the obvious and simple system of natural liberty' (IV.ix.51). We should remember that the three writers on whom Smith chiefly draws for Stoic doctrine—Epictetus, Marcus Aurelius, and Cicero—were all Roman, and that the practical bent of the Romans closely connected men's moral duties with their legal obligations as citizens. The universalist ethic of Stoicism became enshrined in the 'law' of nature. This tradition Smith accepted, understandably in his setting. Ethics for him implied a 'natural jurisprudence', and his economic theories arose out of, indeed were originally part of, his lectures on jurisprudence.

The Stoic concept of social harmony, as Smith understood it, did not mean that everyone behaved virtuously. Stoic ethics said it was wrong to injure others for one's own advantage, but Stoic metaphysics said that good could come out of evil.

> The ancient stoics were of opinion, that as the world was governed by the all-ruling providence of a wise, powerful, and good God, every single event ought to be regarded, as making a necessary part of the plan of the universe, and as tending to promote the general order and happiness of the whole: that the vices and follies of mankind, therefore, made as necessary a part of this plan as their wisdom or their virtue; and by that eternal art which educes good from ill, were made to tend equally to the prosperity and perfection of the great system of nature. (I.ii.3.4)

This doctrine anticipates the better-known statement of Smith's own opinion that the selfish rich 'are led by an invisible hand' to help the poor and to serve the interest of society at large (IV.1.10). Smith has added the idea of a 'deception' by nature and the phrase 'an invisible hand'. The famous phrase may have sprung from an uneasiness about the reconciliation of selfishness with the perfection of the system. In itself the idea of deception by an invisible hand is unconvincing. It gains its plausibility from the preceding account of aesthetic pleasure afforded by power and riches, a pleasure that is reinforced by the admiration of spectators. Smith himself clearly set most store by the psychological explanation. But the invisible hand, through its reappearance in WN, has captured the attention, especially of economists.

In the TMS passage Smith writes disparagingly of the 'natural selfishness and rapacity' of the rich, but this does not mean that he regards all self-interested action as bad in itself and redeemable only by the deception of nature. He does not even accept the view of Hutcheson that self-love is morally neutral. Smith follows the Stoics once again in holding that self-preservation is the first task committed to us by nature and that prudence is a virtue so long as it does not injure others. His explicit account of Stoicism in Part VII begins with the doctrine that 'every animal was by nature recommended to its own care, and was endowed with the principle of self-love', for the sake of preserving its existence and perfection (VII.ii.1.15). This is echoed by an expression of Smith's own view in Part II, 'Every man is, no doubt, by nature, first and principally recommended to his own care' (II.ii.2.1), and then again in the new Part VI, where it is reaffirmed with acknowledgement, 'Every man, as the Stoics used to say, is first and principally recommended to his own care' (VI.ii.1.1).

Smith does appear to give rather more scope to prudence in the new Part VI than in the earlier material, no doubt reflecting a change of emphasis in the thought of the more mature man who had written WN. Essentially, however, TMS and WN are at one. For example, Smith writes in TMS of 'that great purpose of human life which we call bettering our condition' (I.iii.2.1). This reappears in WN in vivid form: 'But the principle which prompts to save, is the desire of bettering our condition, a desire which, though generally calm and dispassionate, comes with us from the womb, and never leaves us till we go into the grave' (II.iii.28).[9] In WN this is of course worked out in its economic aspect, as the drive to employ one's stock and industry to one's best advantage. In TMS the desire to better our condition is related to class distinction and is attributed to 'vanity', the desire 'to be observed, to be attended to, to be taken notice of with sympathy, complacency, and approbation'. There is a difference of tone, but both books treat the desire to better our condition as natural and proper.

The consistency and the Stoic character of Smith's views of prudence may be brought out by comparing two passages, one written for edition 6, the other for edition 1. In VI.i.11 Smith says: 'In the steadiness of his industry and frugality, in his steadily sacrificing the ease and enjoyment of the present moment for the probable expectation of the still greater ease and enjoyment of a more distant but more lasting period of time, the prudent man is always both supported and rewarded by the entire approbation of the impartial spectator. . . .' The reference to industry and frugality immediately recalls WN. The other passage, in IV.2.8, written thirty years earlier, contains a similar reference when discussing self-command: from the spectator's approval of self-command 'arises that eminent esteem with which all men naturally regard a steady perseverance in the practice of frugality, industry, and application, though directed to no other purpose than the acquisition of fortune'. The passage in Part VI appears to take a more charitable view of prudence as such, but in fact there is no real change of doctrine, for in the Part VI passage Smith goes on to explain that the approval of the impartial spectator is really directed at 'that proper exertion of self-command' which enables the prudent man to attach almost as much importance to future enjoyment as to present. There is no reason to suppose that Smith departs in any way from this view when he gives similar praise to industry and frugality in WN. The moral quality of prudence depends on its association with the Stoic virtue of self-command.

Smith's respect for Stoicism was not unqualified, and he ends his account of it, as of other 'systems', with some firm criticisms. Apart from the particular question of suicide, which he says is contrary to nature 'in her sound and healthful state', Smith finds fault with two features of the Stoic philosophy. First, he rejects the Stoic 'paradoxes' that all virtuous actions are

[9] Cf. also WN III.iii.12; IV.v.b.43; IV.ix.28.

equally good and all failings equally bad. Second, while accepting the idea of world citizenship, he rejects the Stoic view that this should obliterate stronger ties of feeling for smaller groups. On the contrary, Smith argues, it is nature that teaches us to put family, friends, and nation first, while also providing us with the judgements of the impartial spectator to check any excessive attachment. Despite the criticisms, however, it is not too much to say that Adam Smith's ethics and natural theology are predominantly Stoic.

(c) *Influence of contemporary thinkers*

Among contemporary thinkers Hume had the greatest influence on the formation of Smith's ethical theory. Smith rejects or transforms Hume's ideas far more often than he follows them, but his own views would have been markedly different if he had not been stimulated to disagreement with Hume. Second in order of importance is the influence of Hutcheson, whose teaching directed Smith's general approach to moral philosophy and enabled him to appreciate the progress in that approach made by Hume. The particular doctrines of TMS, however, owe little to Hutcheson's actual theory, which Smith probably took to be superseded by Hume's more complex account.

The relation of Smith's ethics to the thought of Hutcheson and Hume needs to be described in some detail, but first let us note the extent to which Smith was influenced by other moral philosophers of his time. It is remarkably small. Smith was well informed about ancient philosophy, keenly interested in the history of science and the evolution of society, and widely read in the culture of his own time, especially its literature, history, and nascent social science. He was anything but insular: his reading of recent books was almost as extensive in French as in English, and it was not negligible in Italian. Yet he was not closely acquainted with much of the ethical theory of the eighteenth century. Perhaps the very breadth of his interests and outlook was responsible for this. In his 'Letter to the Editors of the *Edinburgh Review*', July 1755, Smith could describe, from his own reading, not only Rousseau's *Discourse on Inequality* but also 'the Theory of agreeable sentiments by Mr. De Pouilly'; yet his ignorance of recent works in English comparable with the latter is shown by his remark that the characteristic English approach to philosophy, taken over by France, 'now seems to be intirely neglected by the English themselves'. In fact there were several English contributions to mental and moral philosophy in the 1740s and early 1750s at least as valuable as Lévesque de Pouilly's little book on the psychology of pleasure. Smith's statement in the 'Letter' that England had until then been pre-eminent for originality in philosophy is simply a repetition of what Hume had said in the Introduction to the *Treatise of Human Nature*, and Smith's list of 'English' thinkers

(Hobbes, Locke, Mandeville, Shaftesbury, Butler, Clarke, Hutcheson) differs little from Hume's. It follows Hume in including Hutcheson, although the point of the 'Letter', unlike that of Hume's Introduction, is to urge the *Edinburgh Review* to look beyond Scotland.

There are a few particular issues on which Smith was affected by contemporary thinkers other than Hutcheson and Hume. When he distinguishes justice from beneficence he refers to the work of Lord Kames, 'an author of very great and original genius' (II.ii.1.5), but perhaps Smith's view of the distinction was reinforced rather than suggested by that of Kames since the theories of the two men do not have much in common. (The tone of homage in Smith's allusion to Kames may owe something to gratitude for promoting the Edinburgh lectures, which in turn led to the Glasgow appointment.) At I.iii.1.1 Smith refers, rather inaccurately, to a passage of Bishop Butler about sympathy, though not so as to suggest any indebtedness. In another place, III.5.5–6, Smith unconsciously recalls some of Butler's phrases about the authority of conscience. Here Smith is as much influenced by Hutcheson as by Butler himself, for Hutcheson's lectures (posthumously published as *A System of Moral Philosophy*) had adopted Butler's language on this topic. The passage in TMS probably survives from the earliest version of Smith's lectures, in which he will have followed the example of Hutcheson more closely than in later years when he had developed his own theory of conscience as the imagined impartial spectator. The unconscious repetition of phrases, both from his own earlier work and from that of other writers who had moved him to agreement or disagreement, is a characteristic feature of Adam Smith's writings, and Butler is not the only contemporary philosopher to leave such traces in his mind. Faint echoes of Mandeville and of Rousseau can be heard in the passage about the deception of nature (IV.1.8 and 10). But all these are nothing to the echoes of Stoicism and of Hume that appear so often in both the language and the doctrine of TMS.

In Part VII of the book Smith discusses recent as well as ancient philosophy. Apart from Hutcheson, the only contemporary philosopher who is considered at length is Mandeville in VII.ii.4. (In editions 1–5 his name was coupled with that of La Rochefoucauld, but Smith's actual exposition and criticism of 'licentious systems' in this chapter were always confined to the work of Mandeville.) There are short accounts of Hume's views in VII.ii.3.21 and in VII.iii.3.3 and 17. There are references to Hobbes in VII.iii.1 and 2, a glance at Clarke, Wollaston, and Shaftesbury in VII.ii.1.48, a perfunctory mention of the Cambridge Platonists in VII.ii.3.3, and a more definite reference in VII.iii.2.4 to one of them, Cudworth, as a representative of ethical rationalism.

The ethical writings of both Hutcheson and Hume contain important criticism of opposing views. Hutcheson attacked egoistic theory, notably as expounded by Mandeville, and theories of ethical rationalism, especially those of Samuel Clarke and William Wollaston. Hume redoubled the assault on rationalism with a veritable barrage of subtle argument, but he did not repeat Hutcheson's criticism of egoism, doubtless thinking that this was now dead. Adam Smith evidently felt the same about ethical rationalism. His chapter on the rationalists (VII.iii.2) is brief and summary. He takes it for granted that moral rules are inductive generalizations and that moral concepts must arise in the first place from feeling. In the last paragraph of the chapter he refers to Hutcheson's criticism of ethical rationalism in *Illustrations upon the Moral Sense* as being quite decisive. (It is noteworthy that he does not explicitly mention Hume's more finely directed series of arguments in the *Treatise of Human Nature*, though there is presumably an implicit reference to Hume in the statement that Hutcheson was 'the first' to distinguish 'with any degree of precision' the respective roles of reason and feeling in morals.) Smith writes as if he had little knowledge or appreciation of the carefully argued counter-attacks on Hutcheson in writers such as John Balguy and Richard Price. Unlike Hume, however, Smith evidently thought that egoistic theory was still a force to be reckoned with, as is shown by the length of his chapter on Mandeville. Perhaps this was because he had seen the strength of Mandeville's position in economic affairs. At any rate he treats it more seriously than ethical rationalism. Mandeville's system, he says, could not have 'imposed upon' so many people or have caused 'alarm' to so many others 'had it not in some respects bordered upon the truth' (VII.ii.4.14).

Hutcheson held (against egoism) that moral action and moral judgement are both disinterested, and (against rationalism) that they both depend on natural feelings. Moral action is motivated by the disinterested feeling of benevolence, and moral judgement expresses the disinterested feeling of approval or disapproval that Hutcheson called 'the moral sense'. Since benevolence aims at producing happiness or preventing unhappiness, and since a wide benevolence is approved more than a narrow, the morally best action is that which 'procures the greatest happiness for the greatest numbers'.[10] The approval of virtue is like the appreciation of beauty, a feeling aroused in a spectator.

Hume agreed with Hutcheson that benevolence is a motive natural to man and that it naturally evokes approval. But he did not agree that benevolence is the sole motive of virtuous action or that moral approval is an innate basic feeling. He distinguished natural from artificial virtue; benevolence is the chief example of the former, justice of the latter. Moral approval can be explained by sympathy. The spectator takes sympathetic

---

[10] *Inquiry concerning Moral Good and Evil*, III.viii; D. D. Raphael, *British Moralists 1650–1800*, § 333.

pleasure in the happiness that natural virtue, such as benevolence, tends to produce, and his approval is an expression of that sympathetic pleasure. Artificial virtue depends indirectly on utility, the utility of its rules, and the approval of artificial virtue depends ultimately on sympathy with the happiness of society. Hume therefore retained the view that all virtue is connected with beneficial effects. He also retained from Hutcheson the analogy between ethics and aesthetics and an emphasis on the role of the spectator in moral judgement.

Hume's theory is superior to Hutcheson's in explaining more. It recognizes a complexity in moral motivation and tries to account for our adherence to moral rules. It is not satisfied with the bare existence of disinterested approval and gives an explanation in terms of sympathy. Adam Smith follows up Hume's advance by pointing out a greater complexity and offering different explanations. Sympathy is central in Smith's account but is itself more complex than Hume's concept of sympathy. For Hume, sympathy is a sharing of the pleasure or pain produced in a person affected by an action. For Smith, sympathy can be a sharing of *any* feeling and its first role in moral approbation concerns the motive of the agent. The spectator who sympathizes with the agent's motive approves of the action as proper. Sympathy with the feelings of the person affected by the action comes in to help form the more complex judgement of merit. A benevolent action is not only proper but meritorious. The judgement of merit expresses a double sympathy, both with the benevolent motive of the agent and with the gratitude felt by the person benefited. The second element in double sympathy has some affinity with Hume's concept but is not quite the same. Hume thinks of the spectator as sharing by sympathy the pleasure of the benefit itself; Smith thinks of the spectator as sharing by sympathy the gratitude that the benefit evokes.

This difference points to a sharper difference between the two philosophers on justice and on the place of utility in moral judgement. Although Hume distinguishes justice from benevolence, he connects both with utility and relates the approval of both to sympathy with beneficial effects. Smith's explanation of justice is built in the first instance on sympathy with resentment for harm (as merit is built on sympathy with gratitude for benefit). Smith continually insists that considerations of utility are the last, not the first, determinants of moral judgement. Our basic judgement of right and wrong is concerned with the agent's motive, not with the effect of his action. Our more complex judgements of merit and demerit, justice and injustice, depend on the reactions of gratitude and resentment to benefit and harm respectively, not simply on the benefit and harm themselves. And even though the pleasant or painful effects of action are relevant to the moral judgement passed upon it, they are primarily the effects of this particular action upon particular individuals, not the more remote effects upon society at large. Considerations of general social utility are an afterthought, not a foundation.

This is not to say that utility is of little importance in Smith's thought. It is of course crucial for his economic theory. One feature that comes out more clearly in TMS is the place of aesthetic pleasure in the value attached to utility. Useful means are valued first for the ends at which they aim, but then we are charmed by the beauty of their own sheer efficiency, and this pleasure, Smith believes, plays a major part in sustaining economic activity and political planning. Smith legitimately took pride in his originality on this last point (IV.i.3) but derived the more general idea from Hume. Both Hume and Smith learned from Hutcheson to keep aesthetics in mind when thinking about ethics. In *Treatise of Human Nature*, II.ii.5, Hume wrote of the effect of sympathy in forming esteem for the rich and powerful (a thesis followed by Smith in TMS I.iii.2), and then went on to compare with this the role of sympathy in the communication of aesthetic pleasure, including the aesthetic pleasure afforded by convenience or utility. Smith seized on the last remark and emphasized its social importance.

It seems likely that the title of Lévesque de Pouilly's book, *Théorie des sentiments agréables*, suggested to Smith that a suitable name for the philosophy of morals, as he understood it, would be the theory of moral sentiments. This is a description of the subject, not of Smith's individual theory (for which the word 'sympathy' is virtually essential). Smith took it as established by Hutcheson and Hume that morals depend on 'sentiment' or feeling. He differed from them, however, in insisting upon the plurality of moral feelings. Hutcheson postulated a single 'moral sense' or capacity to feel approval, analogous to the sense of beauty and the sense of honour. Hume likewise wrote in the *Treatise of Human Nature* (III.i.2) of approbation as a 'particular' or 'peculiar' kind of pleasant feeling, but in the *Enquiry concerning the Principles of Morals* (appendix iv) he distinguished different kinds of approbation for different kinds of virtue. Smith followed the distinction drawn by Hume in the *Enquiry* between the 'amiable' and the 'awful' virtues, each arousing a different type of approval. For Smith this meant that there are different forms of the 'sense of propriety'. He then further distinguished the sense of propriety from the sense of merit and the sense of duty. Smith accordingly took the view that there are several kinds of moral approbation, a variety of moral feelings or sentiments. The philosophy of morals may therefore be called the theory of moral sentiments. Nothing of all this can be found in Lévesque de Pouilly's book, which is mainly concerned with the psychology of pleasant feeling in general. The content of TMS owes nothing to it, but Smith seems to have adapted Lévesque de Pouilly's title to suit his own more specific subject. Lévesque de Pouilly's book appeared in English translation in 1749 as *The Theory of Agreeable Sensations*, but Smith's reference to it as the 'Theory of agreeable sentiments' shows that he had read the original French version, first published in 1747 and then reprinted in 1749 and 1750 (the 1750 edition in London). His use of the phrase 'the Theory of moral Sentiments' as a name for the subject of ethics appears already in the manuscript fragment of his lecture on justice, presumably written in the early 1750s (see Appendix II).

2. EVOLUTION

(a) *Development between editions*

SMITH made substantial changes to TMS in editions 2 and 6. The most important feature of these changes is a development of his concept of the impartial spectator. An account of this is given by D. D. Raphael in the volume of *Essays on Adam Smith* (edited by Andrew S. Skinner and Thomas Wilson) accompanying the present edition of Smith's Works. A summary of salient points will therefore suffice here.

Both Hutcheson and Hume gave prominence, in their ethical theories, to the approval of 'a spectator' or of 'every spectator', even of 'a judicious spectator'. This conception helps to bring out the disinterested character of the moral standpoint; the spectator is not personally involved, as is the agent or a person affected by the action. A spectator theory of moral judgement implies impartiality, even though Hutcheson and Hume did not use the adjective 'impartial'[11] in this connection. The originality of Adam Smith's impartial spectator lies in his development of the idea so as to explain the source and nature of conscience, i.e. of a man's capacity to judge his own actions and especially of his sense of duty. On this aspect of ethics the theories of Hutcheson and Hume were undoubtedly lame, as was clear to their rationalist critics. Hutcheson himself must have seen the force of the criticism when he accepted, in his later work, the view of Bishop Butler that conscience has 'authority', though he did not attempt to explain this in terms of his theory of approval. Smith did, in terms of his own theory.

According to Smith, conscience is a product of social relationship. Our first moral sentiments are concerned with the actions of other people. Each of us judges as a spectator and finds himself judged by spectators. Reflection upon our own conduct begins later in time and is inevitably affected by the more rudimentary experience. 'Reflection' is here a live metaphor, for the thought process mirrors the judgement of a hypothetical observer. 'We suppose ourselves the spectators of our own behaviour, and

[11] It may have been suggested to Smith by Addison's dedication of vol. i of *The Spectator*, which begins: 'I should not act the part of an impartial spectator, if I directed the following papers to one who is not of the most consummate and most acknowledged merit.'

endeavour to imagine what effect it would, in this light, produce upon us. This is the only looking-glass by which we can, in some measure, with the eyes of other people, scrutinize the propriety of our own conduct' (III.1.5). The looking-glass requires imagination; Smith's impartial spectator is not the actual 'man without' but an imagined 'man within'. When I judge my own conduct I do not simply observe what an actual spectator has to say; I imagine what I should feel if I myself were a spectator of the proposed action.

There is an important difference between this view and the more straight-forward idea that conscience reflects the feelings of real external spectators. If I imagine myself as a spectator, I may on the one hand fail to overcome my natural partiality for myself as the actual agent, and in this respect 'the man within' may be an inferior witness. But on the other hand 'the man without' is liable to lack relevant information that I possess, and in that way the judgement of conscience can be superior to that of actual spectators.

This feature of Smith's account was not made sufficiently clear in edition 1 of TMS. Smith was led to clarify it for his readers, and perhaps also for himself, as the result of an objection put to him by Sir Gilbert Elliot. Elliot's letter has not survived but we can infer the point of it from Smith's reply,[12] which was accompanied by a draft of a revision that was introduced (with some changes of detail) in edition 2. Elliot's objection must have come to this: if conscience is a reflection of social attitudes, how can it ever differ from, or be thought superior to, popular opinion? In the revision for edition 2 Smith showed how the imagined impartial spectator can reach a more objective opinion than actual spectators, who are liable to be misled by ignorance or the distortions of perspective. Imagination can conjure up a spectator free from those limitations, just as it can enable us to reach objective judgements of perception.

At this stage Smith still retained the view that conscience begins with popular opinion. He says, in the revision for edition 2, that the jurisdiction of conscience 'is in a great measure derived from the authority of that very tribunal, whose decisions it so often and so justly reverses'. But by the time he came to revise the work again for edition 6, Smith had become even more sceptical of popular opinion and replaced the passage just quoted by the statement that 'the jurisdictions of those two tribunals are founded upon principles which, though in some respects resembling and akin, are, however, in reality different and distinct' (III.2.32). The judgement of the real spectator depends on the desire for actual praise, that of the imagined impartial spectator on the desire for praiseworthiness. Smith maintains the distinction in other parts of the new material added to edition 6, especially in his treatment of self-command.

[12] Corr., Letter 40, dated 10 October 1759.

Although Smith's special concept of the impartial spectator was developed to explain a man's moral judgements about himself, the general idea is of course used for other moral judgements too. In Smith's view, the main stream of ethical theory, which holds that virtue consists in 'propriety', has offered only two suggestions for a firm criterion of right action; one is utility, the other is the impartial spectator. Throughout the work he gives reasons for preferring the second. Its central importance for him is underlined by his adding to edition 6 a short paragraph in criticism of modern theories of propriety (VII.ii.1.49).

None of those systems either give, or even pretend to give, any precise or distinct measure by which this fitness or propriety of affection can be ascertained or judged of. That precise and distinct measure can be found nowhere but in the sympathetic feelings of the impartial and well-informed spectator.

Sir Gilbert Elliot was not the only critic to be answered in edition 2. Smith also deals, at I.iii.1.9, with an objection put to him by Hume in Letter 36, dated 28 July 1759. Hume's objection concerned sympathy and approval. According to Hume's own theory, the feeling of approval is a special sort of pleasure and arises from sympathy with the pleasure produced by a virtuous action. Smith likewise connected approbation with sympathy but did not limit this to sympathy with pleasure. He wrote of sympathizing with grief and thereby approving it as proper in the circumstances. Sympathy with grief is of course a sharing of a painful feeling. But Smith also wrote, in I.i.2.6, that we are always pleased when we can sympathize. Hume thought there was an inconsistency here. In his reply Smith makes clearer the relation between sympathetic feeling and the feeling of approval. Sympathetic feeling can be either pleasurable or painful. When a spectator does sympathize, in either way, he can also note the correspondence between his own feeling and that of the person observed, and this perception of correspondence is always pleasurable. The sentiment of approval is the second, necessarily pleasurable, feeling, not the first.

A distinction between sympathy and approval is all the more necessary for a passage added to edition 6. As has already been mentioned in section 1(*c*) above (p. *14*), Smith followed Hume in using sympathy to explain 'the distinction of ranks' (I.iii.2). We admire the rich and the great because we take sympathetic pleasure in their enjoyments. The admiration or respect is perfectly natural and contributes to the stability of society. By 1789, however, when revising the book for edition 6, Smith was less complacent and followed that discussion with a new chapter (I.iii.3) on 'the corruption of our moral sentiments' by the disposition to admire the rich and the great. In it he says that while wealth and power commonly receive respect, they do not deserve it, as do wisdom and virtue. Yet he still thinks that the respect for the rich and the great is both natural and useful. In VI.ii.1.20, again a passage written for edition 6, Smith returns briefly to the rich and the great as contrasted with the wise and the virtuous. He there commends 'the benevolent wisdom of nature' in leading us to admire the former so much, his reason being the old one that our natural tendency to respect wealth and power helps to maintain social order. Despite the connection with sympathy and utility, Smith does not wish to class this respect as a form of moral approbation. It is, he says, similar to and apt to be mistaken for the moral respect that we feel for wisdom and virtue, but nonetheless it is not the same (I.iii.3.3).

A major change in edition 6 was the inclusion of an entirely new Part VI. In general this rounds out and clarifies, rather than changes, Smith's ethical theory. It describes a division of virtue into three categories: prudence; benevolence and justice (both of which concern the effects of conduct on other people); and self-command. Smith always included all of these in his idea of virtue, but the earlier version of his views did not set out so clearly their relative place in the scheme of things and did not say much about prudence. The increased attention to prudence in edition 6 is natural from the more mature Adam Smith who had pondered on economics for so long. The prudent man of TMS VI.i. is the frugal man of WN.II.iii. The Stoic virtue of self-command was highlighted even in edition 1. Edition 6 devotes a substantial section (iii) to self-command in the new Part VI and also adds further reflections in III.3, where self-command is compared with conscience in the fully developed concept of the impartial spectator. The more extensive treatment given to self-command in edition 6 suggests that Smith had now acquired an even warmer regard for Stoicism than he felt in earlier days. This is confirmed both by the more elaborate treatment of Stoic philosophy as such, in VII.ii.1, and by the account of universal benevolence, in VII.ii.3, in terms of Stoic rather than of Christian doctrine.

Other features of the new Part VI reflect the interests and experience of an older man. Descriptions of different characters—the prudent man, the man of system, the magnanimous, the proud, the vain man—follow the model of Aristotle and Theophrastus but also declare Smith's own scale of values. Unlike Aristotle he did not think that theorizing was necessarily the best form of human life. Indeed he despised the pure theorist who pursued dogma with no regard for practice, and he seems to have admired heroic characters most.

In his strictures on civil faction and the spirit of system (VI.ii.2.12–18), Smith appears to be reacting to the French Revolution. This has led Walther Eckstein, in the Introduction (xlii f.) to his edition of TMS, to attribute to Smith's old age a conservatism that was not there before. If we did not know from other evidence that Smith was a lifelong Whig,

Eckstein says, we might suppose from this section of TMS that he was a Tory. It seems to us, however, that Eckstein's interpretation is dubious. Most men grow more cautious with advancing years, and Smith was no exception. But his general position in politics does not seem to have changed substantially. He was always a staunch republican in spirit (as Eckstein agrees). There is at first sight some substance in a specific point made by Eckstein. In VI.ii.2.16 Smith commends 'the divine maxim of Plato' that a man should not 'use violence' against his country any more than against his parents. Eckstein notes (xliii) that this is recalled in LJ(B) 15 (Cannan ed., 11), where Smith says the Tory principle of authority declares that 'to offend' against government is as bad as 'to rebel' against a parent. (LJ(A) v.124 contains a similar statement.) There is, however, a difference between the two formulations; one does not have to be a Tory to take the TMS view that it is wrong to use 'violence' against the state. Eckstein also cites as evidence Smith's view in VI.ii.1.20 that respect for rank contributes to social stability, and his comparable statements in VI.ii.2.9–10 that attachment to one's own particular order also helps stability and 'checks the spirit of innovation'. But such support for the existing social structure is nothing new in Smith. We have already noted that he approved of the respect for rank even more warmly (i.e. without qualification) in edition 1. Further, his approval is on grounds of utility, which in the LJ passage is said to be the principle of Whig, as contrasted with Tory, politics. Smith believed in a careful balance between order and innovation. There is a strong conservative strain in his thinking, but it is not markedly stronger in the edition 6 material of TMS than in the earlier writing. That he should be shocked by the events of 1789 is entirely what we would expect.

There is more of a case for Eckstein's further suggestion (intro. xlv ff.) that a change in Smith's religious views can be inferred from revisions in edition 6, especially from the omission of a passage on the Atonement and from the sceptical sound of a single dry sentence that took its place (II.ii.3.12). Less striking indications of such a change can in fact be seen in earlier revisions of the passage. This matter is dealt with fully in Appendix II. Other passages added in edition 6 show that Smith was still imbued with a religious spirit (as Eckstein notes), but it seems reasonable to conclude that he had moved away from orthodox Christianity. There is additional evidence pointing in the same direction, e.g. Letter 163 addressed to Alexander Wedderburn, dated 14 August 1776, which says: 'Poor David Hume is dying very fast, but with great chearfulness and good humour and with more real resignation to the necessary course of things, than any Whining Christian ever dyed with pretended resignation to the will of God.' Smith did not, however, follow Hume into scepticism. All the evidence points rather to a trend towards natural religion, an attitude shown also in the sympathy with which he rearranged and expanded the Stoic passages of TMS.

(b) Relation of TMS to WN

In the light of what has been said in the preceding section about changes in edition 6, there is no need to add much to discussions in the past about the relation of TMS to WN. The so-called 'Adam Smith problem' was a pseudo-problem based on ignorance and misunderstanding. Anybody who reads TMS, first in one of the earlier editions and then in edition 6, will not have the slightest inclination to be puzzled that the same man wrote this book and WN, or to suppose that he underwent any radical change of view about human conduct. Smith's account of ethics and of human behaviour is basically the same in edition 6 of 1790 as in edition 1 of 1759. There is development but no fundamental alteration. It is also perfectly obvious that TMS is not isolated from WN (1776). Some of the content of the new material added to edition 6 of TMS clearly comes from the author of WN. No less clearly, a little of the content of edition 1 of TMS comes from the potential author of WN. Of course WN is narrower in scope and far more extensive in the working out of details than is TMS. It is largely, though by no means wholly, about economic activity and so, when it refers to motivation, concentrates on self-interest. There is nothing surprising in Adam Smith's well known statement (WN I.ii.2): 'It is not from the benevolence of the butcher, the brewer, or the baker, that we expect our dinner, but from their regard to their own interest.' Who would suppose this to imply that Adam Smith had come to disbelieve in the very existence or the moral value of benevolence? Nobody with any sense. But this does not necessarily exclude scholars, some of whom have adopted the *Umschwungstheorie*, the hypothesis that the moral philosopher who made sympathy the basis of social behaviour in TMS did an about-turn from altruistic to egoistic theory in WN owing to the influence of the French 'materialist' thinkers whom he met in Paris in 1766.

The charge of 'materialism' (meaning an egoistic theory of human nature) in WN was made by Bruno Hildebrand as early as 1848 in *Die Nationalökonomie der Gegenwart und Zukunft* (Frankfurt). It was followed up by Carl G. A. Knies in *Die Politische Oekonomie vom Standpunkte der geschichtlichen Methode* (Braunschweig, 1853), where the suggestion was first made that Smith changed his views between writing TMS and WN, and that the change was a result of his visit to France. The full-blown version of the *Umschwungstheorie*, however, was produced by Witold von Skarżyński in *Adam Smith als Moralphilosoph und Schoepfer der National-oekonomie* (Berlin, 1878). Skarżyński's ideas were sparked off by those of H. T. Buckle in vol. ii of his *History of Civilization in England* (London, 1861). Buckle put forward a theory of a peculiar relationship between

Smith's two books. Skarżyński saw that this was questionable, but in re-acting against it (and against Buckle's high praise of Smith) he adopted one of Buckle's chief errors and then added some of his own. Buckle's view needs to be considered first.

Buckle's interpretation of Adam Smith is in Chapter 6 of his book, dealing with Scottish thought in the eighteenth century. Buckle had a curious obsession with methodology, and in this chapter he insists that all Scottish philosophers of that period proceeded by the method of deduction and would have nothing to do with induction. Adam Smith conformed to the pattern, according to Buckle, except for one thing; he followed 'a peculiar form of deduction' (p. 437) in arguing from premises that deliberately left out part of the relevant data. The procedure, based on the method of geometry (so Buckle says), was to select one set of premises and reason from them in one context, and then to take the remaining data as another set of premises for inference in a different context. Each piece of reasoning, Buckle continues, is incomplete on its own; they need to be seen as supplementing each other. That is how we must view TMS and WN.

To understand the philosophy of this, by far the greatest of all the Scotch thinkers, both works must be taken together, and considered as one; since they are, in reality, the two divisions of a single subject. In the *Moral Sentiments*, he investigates the sympathetic part of human nature; in the *Wealth of Nations*, he investigates its selfish part. And as all of us are sympathetic as well as selfish . . . and as this classification is a primary and exhaustive division of our motives to action, it is evident, that if Adam Smith had completely accomplished his vast design, he would at once have raised the study of human nature to a science, . . . (432–3)

The general theme of this passage has point, but it is distorted by Buckle's assumption that sympathy and selfishness can be set side by side as motives, indeed as an 'exhaustive division' of motives. After asserting that Smith 'soon perceived that an inductive investigation was impossible' and therefore adopted his 'peculiar form of deduction', Buckle repeats his view of how Smith proceeded in the two books.

In the *Moral Sentiments*, he ascribes our actions to sympathy; in his *Wealth of Nations*, he ascribes them to selfishness. A short view of these two works will prove the existence of this fundamental difference, and will enable us to perceive that each is supplementary to the other; so that, in order to understand either, it is necessary to study both. (437)

It is indeed true that the two books complement each other and that the understanding of either is helped by studying both. But Buckle has not taken his own advice. He cannot have 'studied' TMS if he thinks that it 'ascribes our actions to sympathy'. Sympathy is the core of Smith's explanation of moral *judgement*. The motive to action is an entirely different matter. Smith recognizes a variety of motives, not only for action in general but also for virtuous action. These motives include self-interest or, to use the eighteenth-century term, self-love. It is this, not 'selfishness', that comes to the fore in WN. Smith distinguished the two expressions, using 'selfishness' in a pejorative sense for such self-love as issues in harm or neglect of other people. While Smith is ready to couple selfishness with 'rapacity' (TMS IV.1.10), he also insists, against Hutcheson, that a proper 'regard to our own private happiness and interest' is a necessary element in virtue (VII.ii.3.16). It is therefore impossible to accept the view that there is any difference of substance between TMS and WN on self-interest as a motive.

As for methodology, Buckle may have been misled by WN V.i.f.26, the one paragraph about logic in that work. In describing the divisions of ancient philosophy, Smith says that logic arose from considering 'the difference between a probable and a demonstrative argument, between a fallacious and a conclusive one'. Buckle may have taken this to imply that probable or inductive argument should be wholly rejected. Smith has something more to say about methodology in LRBL and in the essay on the History of Astronomy in EPS. In LRBL ii.133–5 (Lothian ed., 139–40) he prefers the 'Newtonian' method of 'didactic' discourse to 'that of Aristotle'. The first connects together all the relevant phenomena and their explanatory principles, while the latter, 'the unconnected method', explains each phenomenon *ad hoc*. But it is not at all clear that this is a distinction between deduction and induction. For in Astronomy, II.12, Smith represents scientific explanation, including that of Newton, as addressing itself to the imagination by showing regularities in the apparently irregular, and here he is following Hume's view of *inductive* reasoning. There is no good reason to suppose that Smith thought 'inductive investigation was impossible', let alone that he pursued a special form of deduction, with a 'peculiar artifice', derived from geometry. His own habits of reasoning include both deduction and induction, as one would expect. Buckle's suggestion that he followed the analogy of geometry is particularly inept because it allies Smith with the method of rationalism. Smith was in fact a firm empiricist and had little sympathy with rationalist philosophy. The 'peculiar artifice' of distorting the premises of an argument is Buckle's own invention, designed to explain the existence of two allegedly inconsistent accounts of human nature.

Skarżyński rightly rejected the idea that an artifice of logic could make inconsistency consistent, but he mistakenly accepted Buckle's assumption that Smith's two books gave contrary accounts of conduct. He therefore was led to the conclusion that Smith changed his views between writing them. To this was added the conviction that Smith was not an original thinker: according to Skarżyński, Smith learned all his moral philosophy from Hutcheson and Hume, and all his economics from French scholars.

So Smith's change of mind between 1759 and 1776 was attributed to his visit to France in 1764–6.

Skarżyński knew Dugald Stewart's 'Account of the Life and Writings of Adam Smith', which contains two important pieces of evidence against the thesis that Smith learned all his economics in France. We have already noted these in section 1(*a*) above. First, Stewart gives us the report of John Millar that Smith's lectures on Moral Philosophy included a section on economics that 'contained the substance' of WN; and second, Stewart describes a manuscript of 1755 in which Smith claims to have dictated before 1749, and to have delivered from 1750 onwards, lectures that incorporated certain of his leading principles in political economy. For Skarżyński, however, this is not evidence. How unfortunate, he says ironically, that 'these valuable lectures' were burned shortly before Smith's death; mere assertion without written evidence is worthless (pp. 6–7). And when he quotes Millar's statement that the lectures contained the substance of WN, he adds two exclamation marks to show his incredulity (53).

What Skarżyński would have called genuine evidence came to light eighteen years after the appearance of his book. A Report, copied in 1766, of Adam Smith's lectures on jurisprudence was brought to the attention of Edwin Cannan and published by him in 1896. We can now say with some certainty that it relates to lectures given in 1763–4. A further Report of the lectures given in 1762–3 has been discovered more recently. Skarżyński would (or should) have found these Reports even more effective than the original notes that Adam Smith asked his friends to burn as he lay dying. If Smith's manuscripts had not been burned, Skarżyński might have said that they were not necessarily the same as the manuscripts used for lectures in the 1760s; and indeed they may well have been altered. The Reports that we now have are less authentic in one sense, but there is no question of their having been revised by Smith after his visit to France.

A comparison of the two Reports shows that Smith was actively developing and varying his treatment of the subject-matter in the period 1762–4. We also have a manuscript that W. R. Scott called 'An early draft of part of *The Wealth of Nations*' and published in his *Adam Smith as Student and Professor*. It must have been written before April 1763.[13] These documents show that Smith had gone a considerable way in his economic thinking by the time he left Scotland for France in 1764, and that this early material provided a sound foundation for developments which were certainly stimulated by the visit to France but which occupied his mind throughout the period 1764–76. What he took from the Physiocrats is clear, as are his criticisms.

[13] Ronald L. Meek and Andrew S. Skinner, 'The Development of Adam Smith's Ideas on the Division of Labour', *Economic Journal*, lxxxiii (1973), 1103.

Although Skarżyński did not have access to the manuscripts known today, he could have informed himself more adequately of facts that were available. He says on p. 166 of his book, truly enough, that Smith did not publish anything on political economy before 1776, but he then goes on to assert, in defiance of the testimony of Dugald Stewart, that Smith had 'probably not once applied himself definitely to the study of political economy' before his visit to France. Skarżyński evidently had no notion that lectures on economic matters were a recognized part of Moral Philosophy as taught in the Scottish Universities at that time. The tradition stemmed from the treatment of natural law by Roman and medieval writers, and more immediately from the jurisprudence of Grotius and Pufendorf. At Glasgow, Hutcheson's predecessor in the Chair of Moral Philosophy, Gerschom Carmichael, used his own annotated edition of Pufendorf's *De Officio Hominis et Civis*. Hutcheson continued the practice. Smith draws on Grotius in TMS (and on both Grotius and Pufendorf in LJ, though Skarżyński could not have known that). The tradition is common to all the Scottish teachers of Moral Philosophy in the eighteenth century. Skarżyński's study of TMS seems to have been concentrated on noting Smith's indebtedness to Hume. He treats the book as merely reproducing from Hume and at times doing it badly (76-7, 94-5). He even says (88) that Smith's 'twists and turns', 'sophistries and confusions', could serve very well to obtain for TMS 'the approval of three bishops and numerous literati' (*Schöngeister*), an ironic reference to Hume's teasing account (Letter 31, dated 12 April 1759) of the success of the book. If Skarżyński had studied TMS more thoroughly, he might have learned that Smith's ethical theory differs substantially from Hume's, despite indebtedness. He might even have come to see that Buckle's interpretation of it was mistaken.

Smith himself provides the best evidence against any idea that there is a conflict between his two works. In the Advertisement to edition 6 of TMS he refers to the final paragraph of the book, which promises another one on law and government, and says that he has 'partly executed this promise' in WN. Clearly therefore he regards WN as continuing the sequence of thought set out in TMS. Moreover, as we have said at the beginning of this section, any reader can see that the new material in edition 6 is simply a development of Smith's earlier position and at the same time reflects some of the interests of WN. Skarżyński was presumably unaware of the Advertisement and the additional matter in edition 6 of TMS. The references on pp. 36 and 48 of his book show that he used the Rautenberg translation (1770) of edition 3, although the main additions to edition 6 were in fact available in the later German translation by Kosegarten (1791-5).

Commentators who have taken the trouble to read TMS with more care reject the view that there was a 'swing' or that there is any radical inconsistency between TMS and WN. The scholars who show the most thorough knowledge of the book and of its Scottish background are: Wilhelm Hasbach, *Untersuchungen über Adam Smith und die Entwicklung der Politischen Ökonomie* (Leipzig, 1891); Ludovico Limentani, *La morale della simpatia* (Genoa, 1914); Walther Eckstein in the Introduction to his translation (1926); and T. D. Campbell, *Adam Smith's Science of Morals* (London, 1971). To these can be added, for acute treatment of the *Umschwungstheorie*: Richard Zeyss, *Adam Smith und der Eigennutz* (Tübingen, 1889); and August Oncken, 'The Consistency of Adam Smith', *Economic Journal*, vii (London, 1897), 443–50, and in more detail, 'Das Adam Smith-Problem', *Zeitschrift für Socialwissenschaft*, ed. Julius Wolf, I Jahrgang (Berlin, 1898), 25–33, 101–8, 276–87. See also A. L. Macfie, *The Individual in Society* (London, 1967).

3. RECEPTION

(a) *Early comment and foreign translations*

SMITH's reputation in Scotland was already established before 1759. The publication of TMS made him known and esteemed both in England and abroad. The immediate success of the book is delightfully described by Hume, writing from London in Letter 31, dated 12 April 1759. After a teasing tale of alleged interruptions to his letter, he finally reaches the point, prefacing it with a reminder that popular opinion is worthless, as if to console Smith for a coming disappointment.

Supposing, therefore, that you have duely prepard yourself for the worst by all these Reflections; I proceed to tell you the melancholy News, that your Book has been very unfortunate: For the Public seem disposed to applaud it extremely. It was looked for by the foolish People with some Impatience; and the Mob of Literati are beginning already to be very loud in its Praises. Three Bishops calld yesterday at Millar's[14] Shop in order to buy Copies, and to ask Questions about the Author: The Bishop of Peterborough said he had passd the Evening in a Company, where he heard it extolld above all Books in the World. You may conclude what Opinion true Philosophers will entertain of it, when these Retainers to Superstition praise it so highly. The Duke of Argyle is more decisive than he uses to be in its Favour: . . . Lord Lyttleton says, that Robertson and Smith and Bower are the Glories of English Literature. Oswald[15] protests he does not know whether he has reap'd more Instruction or Entertainment from it: . . . Millar exults and brags that two thirds of the Edition are already sold, and that he is now sure of Success. . . .

Charles Townsend, who passes for the cleverest Fellow in England, is so taken with the Performance, that he said to Oswald he wou'd put the Duke of

[14] Andrew Millar, the publisher.
[15] James Oswald, a friend of Smith's from boyhood.

Buccleugh under the Authors Care, and woud endeavour to make it worth his while to accept of that Charge. . . .

At the beginning of the letter Hume says that he sent copies of the book to the Duke of Argyll, Lord Lyttelton, Horace Walpole, Soame Jenyns, and Edmund Burke ('an Irish Gentleman, who wrote lately a very pretty Treatise on the Sublime'). Their names, and also those of Charles Towns-hend and 'Mr. Solicitor General' (i.e. Charles Yorke, referred to in Hume's second letter below), are included in a list of recipients of complimentary copies that heads Letter 33, sent by Andrew Millar to Adam Smith on 26 April 1759. Hume wrote again to Smith on 28 July (Letter 36) to report further reactions.

I am very well acquainted with Bourke, who was much taken with your Book. He got your Direction from me with a View of writing to you, and thanking you for your Present: For I made it pass in your Name. I wonder he has not done it: . . . I am not acquainted with Jennyns; but he spoke very highly of the Book to Oswald, . . . Millar show'd me a few days ago a Letter from Lord Fitz-maurice; where he tells him, that he had carryd over a few Copies to the Hague for Presents. Mr. Yorke was much taken with it as well as several others who had read it.

I am told that you are preparing a new Edition, and propose to make some Additions and Alterations, in order to obviate Objections.

Hume then proceeds to give Smith his own objection about sympathy, which we have discussed in section 2(a) above. The contemplation by Smith (and presumably Millar) of a second edition so soon after the publication of the first is a further mark of the book's success.

Burke did write to Smith, but not until the autumn. Meanwhile Smith had received additional testimony of the warm reception in London. William Robertson wrote to him from Edinburgh on 14 June (Letter 34):

Our friend John Home arrived here from London two days ago. Tho' I dare say you have heard of the good reception of the *Theory* from [m]any different people, I must acquaint you with the intelligence Home brings. He assures me that it is in the hands of all persons of the best fashion; that it meets with great approbation both on account of the matter and stile; and that it is impossible for any book on so serious a subject to be received in a more gracious manner. It comforts the English a good deal to hear that you were bred at Oxford, they claim some part of you on that account.

In July 1759 a notice of the book appeared in the *Monthly Review* (xxi.1–18). It was unsigned, as was customary, but it has been identified as the work of William Rose.[16] After some general introductory remarks on moral philosophy, he writes:

[16] Benjamin C. Nangle, *The Monthly Review, First Series, 1749–1789, Indexes of Contributors and Articles* (Oxford, 1934), 199.

The Author of the work now before us, however, bids fairer for a favourable hearing than most other moral Writers; his language is always perspicuous and forcible, and often elegant; his illustrations are beautiful and pertinent; and his manner lively and entertaining. Even the superficial and careless Reader, though incapable of forming a just judgment of our Author's system, and entering into his peculiar notions, will be pleased with his agreeable manner of illustrating his argument, by the frequent appeals he makes to fact and experience; and those who are judges of the subject, whatever opinion they may entertain of his peculiar sentiments, must, if they have any pretensions to candor, readily allow, that he has supported them with a great deal of ingenuity.

The principle of Sympathy, on which he founds his system, is an unquestionable principle in human nature; but whether his reasonings upon it are just and satisfactory or not, we shall not take upon us to pronounce: it is sufficient to say, that they are extremely ingenious and plausible. He is, besides, a nice and delicate observer of human nature; seems well acquainted with the systems both of antient and modern moralists; and possesses the happy talent of treating the most intricate subjects not only with perspicuity but with elegance.—We now proceed to give some account of what he has advanced.

Then follows extensive quotation or summary of Smith's argument covering all six Parts of the book. When the reviewer gives Smith's criticism of utilitarian theory in Part IV, he names Hume as the target. A concluding paragraph reverts from quotation to appraisal and ends as follows:

The last part of the Theory will be peculiarly agreeable to the learned reader, who will there find a clear and distinct view of the several systems of moral philosophy, which have gained any considerable degree of reputation either in antient or modern times; with many pertinent and ingenious reflections upon them. The whole work, indeed, shews a delicacy of sentiment, and acuteness of understanding, that are seldom to be met with; and what ought particularly to be mentioned, there is the strictest regard preserved, throughout, to the principles of religion, so that the serious reader will find nothing that can give him any just ground of offence.—In a word, without any partiality to the author, he is one of the most elegant and agreeable writers, upon morals, that we are acquainted with.

The *Monthly Review* was owned and edited by Ralph Griffiths. In Letter 48 addressed to William Strahan, dated 4 April 1760, Smith asks to be remembered to Griffiths and adds: 'I am greatly obliged to him for the very handsom character he gave of my book in his review.'

Burke wrote a review that was more handsome still, for his periodical, the *Annual Register*. But first he sent a letter to Smith on 10 September 1759 (Letter 38), in which he gave his opinion at greater length and added some criticism. It will be remembered that Hume had expected Burke to thank Smith for a complimentary copy of TMS. In his letter Burke apologizes for the delay, pleading business and saying that he wanted to read the book 'with proper care and attention' before writing. He then shows that he has indeed read it and reflected on it with care.

I am not only pleased with the ingenuity of your Theory; I am convinced of its solidity and Truth; and I do not know that it ever cost me less trouble to admit so many things to which I had been a stranger before. I have ever thought that the old Systems of morality were too contracted and that this Science could never stand well upon any narrower Basis than the whole of Human Nature. All the writers who have treated this Subject before you were like those Gothic Architects who were fond of turning great Vaults upon a single slender Pillar; There is art in this, and there is a degree of ingenuity without doubt; but it is not sensible, and it cannot long be pleasing. A theory like yours founded on the Nature of man, which is always the same, will last, when those that are founded on his opinions, which are always changing, will and must be forgotten. I own I am particularly pleased with those easy and happy illustrations from common Life and manners in which your work abounds more than any other that I know by far. They are indeed the fittest to explain those natural movements of the mind with which every Science relating to our Nature ought to begin. . . . Besides so much powerful reasoning as your Book contains, there is so much elegant Painting of the manners and passions, that it is highly valuable even on that account. The stile is every where lively and elegant, and what is, I think equally important in a work of that kind, it is well varied; it is often sublime too, particularly in that fine Picture of the Stoic Philosophy towards the end of your first part which is dressed out in all the grandeur and Pomp that becomes that magnificent delusion. I have mentioned something of what affected me as Beauties in your work. I will take the Liberty to mention too what appeared to me as a sort of Fault. You are in some few Places, what Mr Locke is in most of his writings, rather a little too diffuse. This is however a fault of the generous kind, and infinitely preferable to the dry sterile manner, which those of dull imaginations are apt to fall into. To another I should apologise for a freedom of this Nature.

Burke's review in the *Annual Register* (year 1759, pp. 484 ff.) repeats some of the comments made in the private letter. After some general introductory remarks about 'this excellent work' in which 'the parts grow so naturally and gracefully out of each other', the review goes on:

There have been of late many books written on our moral duties, and our moral sanctions. One would have thought the matter had been exhausted. But this author has struck out a new, and at the same time a perfectly natural road of speculation on this subject. . . . We conceive, that here the theory is in all its essential parts just, and founded on truth and nature. The author seeks for the foundation of the just, the fit, the proper, the decent, in our most common and most allowed passions; and making approbation and disapprobation the tests of virtue and vice, and shewing that those are founded on sympathy, he raises from this simple truth, one of the most beautiful fabrics of moral theory, that has perhaps ever appeared. The illustrations are numerous and happy, and shew the author to be a man of uncommon observation. His language is easy and spirited, and puts things before you in the fullest light; it is rather painting than writing.

Charles Townshend, referred to in Hume's first letter, had married the widowed Countess of Dalkeith and was therefore the stepfather of the young Duke of Buccleuch. Townshend did eventually carry out the plan that Hume describes, of asking Smith to act as tutor to the Duke, on terms tempting enough for Smith to give up his Professorship at Glasgow. That is how Smith visited France and Geneva in 1764–6, and how he was able to retire thereafter to Kirkcaldy and devote himself to writing WN.

Townshend was not alone in being led by TMS to think of using Smith's services as a teacher. Lord Buchan says he went to Glasgow after St. Andrews, Edinburgh, and Oxford in order to learn from Smith and John Millar; but since this was in 1760 and since Millar's appointment at Glasgow began in 1761, Buchan must in fact have been attracted in the first place by the reputation of Smith alone.[17] Another student who came from Oxford, in 1762, was Henry Herbert, later Lord Porchester.[18] Some came from farther afield. Théodore Tronchin, the celebrated physician of Geneva who attended Voltaire among others, sent his son to Glasgow in 1761, expressly 'to study under Mr. Smith'.[19]

The international reputation of TMS is borne out by part of the resolution adopted by the University of Glasgow on 1 March 1764 accepting the resignation of Adam Smith, 'whose uncommon Genius, great Abilities and extensive Learning did so much Honour to this Society; His elegant and ingenious Theory of Moral Sentiments having recommended him to the esteem of Men of Taste and Literature thro'out Europe'.[20] The last two words are a pardonable exaggeration, but certainly in France the book was soon applauded.

The *Journal encyclopédique* for October 1760 carried a notice consisting of a short extract followed by some favourable comment, perhaps echoing that of the *Monthly Review*.

Cet Ouvrage Nous a paru recommandable par la force et la chaleur de son style, par la beauté et la noblesse des sentimens, par la nouveauté et la justesse des réflexions, par le ton imposant des raisonnemens; mais ce qui le rend encore plus précieux, c'est que tout y respire la vertu la plus pure, et que la Religion y est par-tout respectée.[21]

Hume went to France in 1763 as Secretary to the British Embassy, and shortly after his arrival he wrote to Smith from Fontainebleau in Letter 77,

---

[17] Cf. John Rae, *Life of Adam Smith* (London, 1895), 51–2. Rae is, however, mistaken when he says (58) that admiration for TMS induced the future Earl of Shelburne (Lord Fitzmaurice) to send his brother Thomas to study under Smith. Lord Fitzmaurice advised his father to do this in 1758 on the suggestion of Sir Gilbert Elliot, and Thomas Fitzmaurice was in residence at Glasgow early in 1759 before TMS appeared (see Letter 27 to Smith from Elliot, dated 14 November 1758, and Letter 28 from Smith to Lord Fitzmaurice, dated 21 February 1759).

[18] Scott, *ASSP*, 68, 293 n.3.   [19] Rae, *Life*, 59.   [20] Scott, *ASSP*, 221.

[21] Quoted by the Abbé Blavet in the preface (vii–viii) of his translation of TMS.

dated 28 October 1763: 'The Baron d'Holbac, whom I saw at Paris, told me, that there was one under his Eye that was translating your Theory of moral Sentiments; and desird me to inform you of it: . . .' This was Marc-Antoine Eidous, who had also translated Hutcheson's *Inquiry into Beauty and Virtue*. His rendering of TMS appeared in 1764 under the title *Métaphysique de l'âme*. A contemporary note in F.-M. de Grimm's *Correspondance littéraire* (Part I, vol. iv, 291 f.) says that the work did not have any success in Paris to match its reputation in Britain, but that this was due to the defects of the translation and was no argument against its merit.[22]

However, Parisians of literary tastes were perfectly capable of reading TMS in English. The Abbé Morellet records that he did so.[23] The Comtesse de Boufflers-Rouverel wrote in a letter of 6 May 1766 to Hume that she had begun to read TMS and thought she would like it.[24] There is another record, a few years later, of the interest of Madame de Boufflers and of other Parisians in TMS. Gilbert and Hugh Elliot, the young sons of Sir Gilbert Elliot, were in Paris in 1770, and a letter from Hugh describes a visit to Madame de Boufflers.

She received us very kindly, and spoke about all our Scotch and English authors; if she had time, she would set about translating Mr. Smith's Moral Sentiments— 'Il a des idées si justes de la sympathie.' This book is now in great vogue here; this doctrine of sympathy bids fair for cutting out David Hume's Immaterialism, especially with the ladies, ever since they heard of his marriage.[25]

Another member of the French nobility who contemplated, and indeed began, a translation of TMS was Louis-Alexandre, Duc de La Rochefoucauld-d'Anville, a descendant of the author of the *Maximes*. He abandoned the task after completing Part I, because of the appearance of a translation by the Abbé Blavet.[26] Blavet's translation was of edition 3 (1767) and was published in 1774–5. Yet another French translation, of edition 7 (1792), appeared in 1798. This was by Sophie de Grouchy, widow of Condorcet, who appended some essays of her own (in the form of letters) on the topic of sympathy.

Eckstein (intro. xxxii ff.) has brought together evidence of the reception of TMS in Germany. Lessing mentions the book in his celebrated work on aesthetics, *Laokoon* (1766), quoting a passage, in his own translation, from I.ii.1. Herder makes several references to it, the earliest one being in his aesthetic work, *Kritische Wälder* (1769). The first German translation

[22] Eckstein, intro. xxi *n.* 1; cf. Rae, *Life*, 196.

[23] Rae, *Life*, 197.

[24] J. H. Burton (ed.), *Letters of Eminent Persons addressed to David Hume* (Edinburgh and London, 1849), 237–8; cf. Rae, *Life*, 198.

[25] Countess of Minto, *A Memoir of Hugh Elliot* (Edinburgh, 1868), 13; cf. Rae, *Life*, 199. The report of Hume's marriage was an unfounded rumour.

[26] Corr., Letter 194 from the Duc de La Rochefoucauld to Smith, dated 3 March 1778.

was of edition 3 and appeared in 1770. The name of the translator is not stated but he was in fact Christian Günther Rautenberg, who had already translated Lord Kames's *Principles of Morality and Natural Religion.*

It seems that Kant knew and valued TMS, judging from a letter of 1771 written to him by one Markus Herz. A passage in this letter speaks of 'the Englishman Smith, who, Mr. Friedländer tells me, is your favourite' (*Liebling*), and then goes on to compare the work of Smith with 'the first part' of 'Home, Kritik', no doubt meaning *Elements of Criticism* by Henry Home, Lord Kames. As Eckstein points out, the date of 1771 (too early for WN and one year after the publication of the first German translation of TMS) and the comparison with Kames show that the writer must have had TMS in mind. The passage also suggests that Herz at least, like Lessing and Herder, was interested in the relevance of TMS to aesthetics. It is unlikely, however, that Kant's own regard for the work will have been thus confined. Eckstein goes on to note that there is a passage in Kant's *Reflections on Anthropology* where Kant writes of 'the man who goes to the root of things' and who looks at every subject 'not just from his own point of view but from that of the community' and then adds, in brackets, 'the Impartial Spectator' (*der Unpartheyische Zuschauer*).

A second German translation, by Ludwig Theobul Kosegarten, was published in 1791, presumably made from edition 4 or 5. Kosegarten produced a supplementary volume in 1795, containing a translation of the main additions of edition 6, and of the whole of Part III as revised for that edition.

A third German translation, that of Walther Eckstein, appeared in 1926. This is more than a translation. It contains a careful record of practically all the revisions of substance that were made in the different editions of TMS; it is annotated in detail; and its long Introduction is a valuable contribution to knowledge. The work is indeed the first scholarly edition of TMS, and its scholarship is of a high order. We are greatly indebted to it as the starting-point for many of our own notes and for some of the information given in our Introduction.

A further German translation by Elisa von Loeschebrand-Horn was published in 1949 as the first volume of selections from the works of Adam Smith, edited by Hans Georg Schachtschabel. We have not seen this version, but the description of the edition and the length of the volume concerned (338 pp.) suggest that it does not include the whole of TMS.

In Russia Smith was well known as an economist, little as a moral philosopher. One of his Russian pupils, however, Semyon Desnitsky, who later became a Professor of Law at Moscow University, made some use of TMS (and much of LJ) in his lectures. In a work of 1770 he said that he hoped to publish a Russian translation of TMS, but for some reason he did not carry out the intention.[27] A Russian translation by P. A. Bibikov appeared in 1868.

A Spanish translation by Edmund O'Gorman was published in Mexico in 1941. A Japanese translation by Tomio Yonebayashi was published in 1948–9 and was reprinted in 1954. See also p. 402 below.

(b) Select bibliography

1. Editions of TMS

Editions authorized by Adam Smith (all imprinted London and Edinburgh):

Ed. 1, 1759; ed. 2, 1761; ed. 3, 1767; ed. 4, 1774; ed. 5, 1781; ed. 6, 2 vols., 1790.

Other editions (this list is almost certainly incomplete):

Dublin, 1777 (called 'the sixth edition'); ed. 7, 2 vols., London and Edinburgh, 1792; Basel, 1793; ed. 8, 2 vols., London, 1797; ed. 9, 2 vols., London, 1801; ed. 10, 2 vols., London, 1804; 2 vols., Edinburgh, 1808; Glasgow, 1809; London, 1812; 2 vols., Edinburgh, 1813; Boston, 1817; Philadelphia, 1817; New York, 1821; 2 vols., New York, 1822; 2 vols., London, 1825; London, 1846; Edinburgh, 1849; London, 1853; London, 1861; London, 1871; Boston, New York, and Philadelphia, in or before 1876; London, 1880; Boston and New York, 1887; London, 1887; London, 1892; Edinburgh, 1894; London, 1907; London, 1911; Kyoto, 1961; New York, 1966; New Rochelle, N.Y., 1969.

TMS is also published in vol. i of *The Works of Adam Smith*, London, 1812; reprinted, Aalen, 1963; in vol. i of *The Whole Works of Adam Smith*, London, 1822; in vols. iv–v of *The Works of Adam Smith*, London, 1825; and in *Essays, Philosophical and Literary*, London, 1869; reprinted, New York, in or before 1876; reprinted, London, 1880.

2. Translations

French:

1. *Métaphysique de l'âme: ou Théorie des sentimens moraux* [translated by Marc-Antoine Eidous]; 2 vols., Paris, 1764.

2. *Théorie des sentimens moraux*, translated by l'Abbé Blavet; 2 vols., Paris, 1774–5; reprinted, Paris, 1782.

3. *Théorie des sentimens moraux*, translated from ed. 7 by Sophie de Grouchy, Marquise de Condorcet; 2 vols., Paris, 1798; reprinted, Paris,

---

[27] A. H. Brown, 'Adam Smith's First Russian Followers', in the volume of *Essays on Adam Smith* (edited by Andrew S. Skinner and Thomas Wilson) accompanying the present edition of Smith's Works.

1820; revised ed., Paris, 1830; republished with introduction and notes by Henri Baudrillart, Paris, 1860.

German:

1. *Theorie der moralischen Empfindungen*, translated from ed. 3 [by Christian Günther Rautenberg]; Braunschweig, 1770.
2. *Theorie der sittlichen Gefühle*, translated and edited by Ludwig Theobul Kosegarten; Leipzig, 1791: vol. ii, containing the additions to ed. 6; Leipzig, 1795.
3. *Theorie der ethischen Gefühle*, translated (from ed. 6 but including variants in earlier eds.) and edited by Walther Eckstein; 2 vols., Leipzig, 1926.
4. *Theorie der ethischen Gefühle*, translated by Elisa von Loeschebrand-Horn (vol. i of Smith, *Werke*, selected and edited by Hans Georg Schachtschabel); Frankfurt, 1949.

Russian:

Teoriya Nravstvennykh Chuvstv, translated by P. A. Bibikov; St. Petersburg, 1868.

Spanish:

Teoria de los sentimientos morales, translated by Edmund O'Gorman, introduced by Edward Nicol; Pánuco, Mexico, 1941.

Japanese:

Dōtoku Jōsō Ron, translated by Tomio Yonebayashi; 2 vols., Tokyo, 1948–9; reprinted, Tokyo, 1954. See also p. 402 below.

3. *Discussion*

This list is restricted to books and published theses that contain a substantial treatment of Smith's ethical thought. (Even as such it is no doubt incomplete.) It does not include articles nor, except incidentally, books dealing with his other writings. Readers who wish to supplement it should consult the bibliographies in: Eckstein, i.lxxiv ff; *The Vanderblue Memorial Collection of Smithiana* (Baker Library, Harvard Graduate School of Business Administration; Boston, 1939): Burt Franklin and Francesco G. M. Cordasco, *Adam Smith: A Bibliographical Checklist; critical writings and scholarship on Smith, 1876–1950* (New York, 1950); and Keitaro Amano, *Bibliography of the Classical Economics*, Part I (Science Council of Japan, Economic Series No. 27; Tokyo, 1961).

The most important works concerned with the 'Adam Smith problem' have been listed in section 2(*b*) above.

Thomas Brown, *Lectures on the Philosophy of the Human Mind*, vol. iv; Edinburgh, 1820. Reprinted in *Lectures on Ethics*; Edinburgh, 1846.

Victor Cousin, *Cours d'histoire de la philosophie morale aux dix-huitième siècle*, vol. iii, *École écossaise*; Paris, 1840.

August Oncken, *Adam Smith und Immanuel Kant*; Leipzig, 1877.

Witold von Skarżyński, *Adam Smith als Moralphilosoph und Schoepfer der Nationaloekonomie*; Berlin, 1878.

James Anson Farrer, *Adam Smith*; London, 1881.

Richard Zeyss, *Adam Smith und der Eigennutz*; Tübingen, 1889.

Wilhelm Paszkowski, *Adam Smith als Moralphilosoph*; Halle, 1890.

Johannes Schubert, *Adam Smith's Moralphilosophie*; Leipzig, 1890 and 1891.

Ethel Muir, *The Ethical System of Adam Smith*; Halifax, Nova Scotia, 1898.

Johan Gerrit Appeldoorn, *De Leer der Sympathie bij David Hume en Adam Smith*; Drachten, 1903.

Albion Woodbury Small, *Adam Smith and Modern Sociology*; Chicago, 1907.

Ludovico Limentani, *La morale della simpatia*; Genoa, 1914.

Giovanni Pioli, *L'etica della simpatia nella 'Teoria dei Sentimenti Morali' di Adamo Smith*; Rome, 1920.

Glen Raymond Morrow, *The Ethical and Economic Theories of Adam Smith*; New York, 1923.

James Bonar, *Moral Sense*; London and New York, 1930.

Manuel Fuentes Irurozqui, *El moralista Adam Smith, economista*; Madrid, 1944.

Luigi Bagolini, *La simpatia nella morale e nel diritto*; Bologna, 1952; ed. 2, revised and extended, Turin, 1966.

Giulio Preti, *Alle origini dell' etica contemporeana: Adamo Smith*; Bari, 1957.

Alec Lawrence Macfie, *The Individual in Society*; London, 1967.

Thomas Douglas Campbell, *Adam Smith's Science of Morals*; London, 1971.

4. THE TEXT

(a) Account of editions 1–7

SIX authorized editions of TMS were published in Adam Smith's lifetime. Edition 6, which incorporated extensive additions and substantial revision of other kinds, appeared in 1790, a few weeks before his death. In Letter 295 addressed to Thomas Cadell, his publisher, dated 25 May 1790,

Smith acknowledges the receipt of his twelve copies of this edition. Glasgow University Library possesses one of them, presented by Smith to a friend and inscribed in his own hand. We have collated copies of all these six editions, and also of edition 7 (published in 1792) since it is in principle possible that some of the minor changes in edition 7 were corrections made by the author after going through edition 6. This is in fact unlikely, because Smith was already very ill by the time that edition 6 appeared. There is also some internal evidence against it: in VII.ii.4.3, editions 6 and 7 intelligibly but mistakenly print 'lawful' instead of 'awful', and if Smith had corrected edition 6 he would almost certainly have picked up this error, while a printer, less familiar with the doctrines of the book as a whole, would not have recognized it as an error. Nevertheless there are a few places in which edition 7 does correct errors (as well as some where it introduces new ones, and a number where it revises punctuation or spelling), so that it is as well to include the variants of edition 7 in the collation.

John Rae's account, in his *Life of Adam Smith*, of the different editions of TMS is erroneous in several respects. On p. 141 he says that edition 1 was published in two volumes, while in fact it was a single volume. On pp. 148–9 he writes:

The second edition of the *Theory*, which Hume was anticipating immediately in 1759, did not appear till 1761, and it contained none of the alterations or additions he expected; but the *Dissertation on the Origin of Languages* was for the first time published along with it. The reason for the omission of the other additions is difficult to discover, for the author had not only prepared them, but gone the length of placing them in the printer's hands in 1760, as appears from the following letter [Letter 50 addressed to William Strahan, the printer, dated 4 April 1760]. They did not appear either in the third edition in 1767, or the fourth in 1774, or the fifth in 1781; nor till the sixth, which was published, with considerable additions and corrections, immediately before the author's death in 1790.

On p. 425 Rae repeats the gist of this by saying of the projected edition 6: 'The book had been thirty years before the world and had passed through five editions, but it had never undergone any revision or alteration whatever.' In fact edition 2 is considerably revised when compared with edition 1. Although the alterations and additions are not as extensive as in edition 6, they are very substantial and are perfectly consistent with Letter 50. The particular addition which Hume was expecting in answer to his criticism made in Letter 36 addressed to Smith, dated 28 July 1759, appears as a footnote to I.iii.1.9. The Dissertation on the Origin of Languages, however, was first appended, not to edition 2 of TMS, but to edition 3, having previously been published in the *Philological Miscellany*, vol. i, in 1761. Editions 3, 4, and 5 of TMS each contain some minor revision by the author.

We have used two copies of edition 1, one belonging to Glasgow University Library, the other to the Bodleian Library, and have found no differences between them. Edition 1 is a single octavo volume of [xii] + 552 pages, the last page containing a list of Errata (two of which, being respectively on the first and last lines of a page, have in fact already been corrected in the text). The title-page describes the work simply as 'The Theory of Moral Sentiments' and the author as 'Adam Smith, Professor of Moral Philosophy in the University of Glasgow'. The book is imprinted 1759, London and Edinburgh. In Letter 33 addressed to Smith, dated 26 April 1759, the London publisher, Andrew Millar, wrote: 'I recd the errata which are printed, . . . I have no Sort of doubt of this Impression being Soon gone tho' it will not be published till next Week, . . .'

We have used three copies of edition 2, two from Glasgow University Library and one from the Bodleian. One of the Glasgow copies is defective, lacking the final Part; but since this particular volume is not in its original binding, it is likely that it was complete when first issued. In other respects (e.g. broken letters and misprints) it is identical with the other two copies. Edition 2, like edition 1, is a single octavo volume, but is completely reset in a new form. The pages are slightly longer than those of edition 1, the type is a little smaller, and there is less space between the lines. This edition contains [x] + 436 pages, with no list of Errata. The title-page follows that of edition 1 in its description of the book and author, and is likewise imprinted as being published at London and Edinburgh. It bears the date 1761, but copies must have been available, at least to the author if not to the public, at the end of 1760, since Smith sent a list of Errata with Letter 54 addressed to William Strahan, dated 30 December 1760. The letter begins:

My Dear Strahan
The opposite leaf will set before your eyes the manifold sins and iniquities you have been guilty of in printing my book. The first six, at least the first, third and fourth and sixth are what you call sins against the holy Ghost which cannot upon any account be pardoned. The Remainder are capable of remission in case of repentance, humiliation and contrition.

W. R. Scott printed this letter in his book, *Adam Smith as Student and Professor*, but without the list of Errata that accompanied it. The sheet of Errata was traced by Professor Ernest C. Mossner in the course of preparing the volume of *Correspondence* for the present edition of Smith's Works. The Errata relate to edition 2 of TMS. They are divided into two groups. The first group of six is preceded by the statement, 'The following Errata must be corrected as totally disfiguring the sense', which is why the letter calls them sins against the Holy Ghost. Some indeed not only disfigure but flatly contradict the sense required: 'approbation' for 'disapprobation', 'utility' for 'inutility', and 'pleased' for 'displeased'. All six of this first group of errors are corrected in edition 3. The second group consists of twenty-five errors, seven of which are corrected in edition 3, three in edition 4, and four in edition 6; one further error is avoided in edition 6 by a new form of correction (Smith had evidently forgotten the original list by this time); the remaining ten have never been corrected before the present edition. Since the list of Errata was no doubt intended to be printed with any further impressions of edition 2, we have treated it as if it had been, incorporating Smith's revisions (apart from the one which he rephrased for edition 6) in our text.

Edition 2 contains substantial revisions of edition 1. A couple of the changes are merely formal: Section ii of Part I in edition 1 becomes Chapters 2–5 of Section i, and the 'Sections' of Parts III–V become 'Chapters'. Throughout the book there are quite a large number of minor stylistic improvements. The footnote at I.iii.1.9, in reply to Hume's criticism, is added. After III.1.4, edition 1 had three paragraphs; edition 2 transfers the first to a later position, withdraws the second (substituting for it, in the present § 6, an improved version of the same thought), and retains the third with slight revision but in a new position. At the end of III.1.5, edition 2 withdraws a paragraph that was in edition 1, and adds § 6, the improved version of the paragraph withdrawn earlier. In what was III.ii of edition 1, and III.2 of editions 2–5 (see the present III.2.31 and III.3.1–5, 7–9, 11), edition 2 adds sixteen new paragraphs; these include an important development of the theory of the impartial spectator so as to provide a genetic explanation of conscience. Consequently, edition 2 is not quite the same book as edition 1, though the changes are not on the scale of those made in edition 6.

Smith mentioned the changes in Letter 50 addressed to William Strahan, dated 4 April 1760, to which Rae refers in the passage quoted earlier from *Life*, 148–9. We give part of the first paragraph of this letter.

I sent up to Mr Millar four or five Posts ago the same additions, which I had formerly sent to you, with a good many corrections and improvements which occurred to me since. If there are any typographical errors remaining in the last edition which had escaped me, I hope you will correct them. In other respects I could wish it was printed pretty exactly according to the copy which I delivered to you. . . . To desire you to read my book over and mark all the corrections you would wish me to make upon a sheet of paper and send it to me, would, I fear, be giving you too much trouble. If, however, you could induce yourself to take this trouble, you would oblige me greatly: I know how much I shall be benefitted and I shall at the same time preserve the pretious right of private judgement for the sake of which our forefathers kicked out the Pope and the Pretender. I believe you to be much more infallible than the Pope, but as I am a Protestant my conscience makes me scruple to submit to any unscriptural authority.

Apart from changes in 'substantives' (i.e. in the words as conveyors of meaning), there are in edition 2 numerous revisions of 'accidentals' (i.e. of punctuation, spelling, division of words, and use of capital or lower-case letters and of roman or italic type). Many of them will have been introduced by the printer, but it cannot be assumed that all were. Some of the changes in punctuation, such as the substitution of a full point and new sentence for a semi-colon, are almost certainly due to the author. The revision of chapter headings, so as to replace roman by italic type, is likely at least to have had Smith's approval, since in Letter 276 addressed to Thomas Cadell (Millar's successor as publisher), dated 15 March 1788, he himself uses this style to refer to chapter headings. Letter 50 addressed to Strahan, dated 4 April 1760 and quoted above, shows the care that Smith took in revising the work and in giving instructions to the printer.

Editions 3, 4, and 5 have the same size, format, pagination, and (in general) division of lines as edition 2, but with the Dissertation on the Origin of Languages added. None of them, however, is a reprint from standing type. Each has been composed anew, but following the pages and (mostly) the line divisions of the previous edition, a frequent printing practice of the time, used in order to allow different parts of a book to be set up in type by different compositors working simultaneously. Our evidence for saying that no edition is a reprint is twofold. The mere fact that there is sometimes a different division of lines is of course not conclusive, since a compositor using standing type would reset some lines in order to accommodate revisions or to improve bad spacing. But, in the first place, misprints in these particular editions have been introduced when the compositor had no reason whatever to reset a line. Secondly, a test suggested by R. B. McKerrow, of laying a ruler across two full points and seeing whether it always cuts the same letters, shows conclusively that even when there is no change in the text, the later edition has been recomposed.

We have used two copies of edition 3, one from Glasgow University Library, the other from the Bodleian, and have found no differences between them. Edition 3 is a single octavo volume of [viii] + 478 pages, with no list of Errata. The text of TMS ends at p. 436, and pp. 437–78 contain the Dissertation on the Origin of Languages. There is in consequence a new form of title-page, which describes the contents of the book as: 'The Theory of Moral Sentiments. To which is added A Dissertation on the Origin of Languages.' The author is now called 'Adam Smith, L.L.D.' with no reference to his former Professorship at the University of Glasgow, which Smith had resigned in 1764. In Letter 100 addressed to William Strahan (undated but probably written in the winter of 1766-7), Smith refers to the forthcoming edition 3 and asks that he be called 'simply Adam Smith without any addition before or behind'. Presumably he would have preferred to dispense even with the insertion of his LL.D. Edition 3 was published at London and Edinburgh in 1767.

As is to be expected in a line-by-line repetition of an earlier edition, the revision of substantives in edition 3 is light, though not negligible. Two groups of these minor changes are of interest and have a related character. In a theological passage at II.ii.3.12 and the paragraph that then followed it, the categorical tone of certain phrases is softened to a problematic one; for example, 'religion authorises' becomes 'religion, we suppose, authorises', and 'neither can he [man] see any reason' becomes 'and he thinks he can see no reason'. Similarly, in   passage at V.2.5 about the character of the clergyman, two instances of 'is are altered to 'seems to be' and 'is supposed to be'. Since the treatment in edition 6 of the former passage became the subject of controversy after Smith's death, the change of tone in 1767 is of some significance.

There is also in edition 3 a fair amount of revision in accidentals, probably due in the main to the printer on this occasion. As has already been stated, some of the mistakes (including all of the first group) listed in the draft Errata page for edition 2 are corrected, but many are left uncorrected. The printer has corrected a few further misprints of edition 2, has introduced a number of new ones, and has changed the punctuation quite often and the spelling occasionally.

The Dissertation on the Origin of Languages was evidently set up, not from manuscript, but from a copy of the printed version that had already appeared in the *Philological Miscellany*, vol. i (London, 1761), for in Letter 100 addressed to Strahan, Smith wrote:

The *Dissertation upon the Origin of Languages* is to be printed at the end of the *Theory*. There are some literal errors in the printed copy of it which I should have been glad to have corrected, but have not the opportunity as I have no copy by me. They are of no great consequence. In the titles, both of the *Theory* and *Dissertation*, call me simply Adam Smith without any addition either before or behind.

In fact there is no separate title-page for the Dissertation. The reference in the letter to 'the printed copy' may have confirmed Rae's mistaken impression (shared by Dugald Stewart in his 'Account of the Life and Writings of Adam Smith', II.44) that the Dissertation was first printed in edition 2 of TMS, for he repeats the statement on p. 233 of his *Life*, before giving the text of the letter.

In the present edition of Smith's Works the Dissertation on the Origin of Languages is being published together with LRBL. The relevant volume will include a collation of the text of the Dissertation in the *Philological Miscellany* and in the different editions of TMS.

We have used one copy of edition 4, belonging to the Aberdeen Public Library. Edition 4 is, like edition 3, a single octavo volume of [viii] + 478 pages, but these are followed on this occasion by two pages of advertisement. The title-page is different, however, in adding to the description of the main work: 'The Theory of Moral Sentiments, or An Essay towards an Analysis of the Principles by which Men naturally judge concerning the Conduct and Character, first of their Neighbours, and afterwards of themselves.' The author remains 'Adam Smith, LL.D.' Edition 4 was published in 1774 at London and Edinburgh.

Edition 4 was set up from a copy of edition 3. It includes the latter's intentional revisions, both in substantives and in accidentals, but it corrects most of the misprints introduced in edition 3. In fact, whereas the compositors of edition 3 were rather careless, the printer evidently took great pains with edition 4 to secure accuracy and consistency. There are very few misprints, and the many revisions of accidentals are made with intelligence. They include modernization of such words as 'compleat' (though only from what was then I.iii.3), 'meer', 'antient', 'falshood', 'vitious'; relative consistency in the spelling of words (e.g. 'sympathize', 'entire') which had previously been spelt inconsistently; and the removal of nearly all the remaining instances (usually at the end of a line) of the contracted form 'tho''. There are again, as in edition 3, a few minor changes in substantives, and some at least of these are such that they must have been made by the author.

We have used two copies of edition 5, both belonging to Glasgow University Library, and have found no differences between them. Edition 5 is, like edition 4, a single octavo volume of [viii] + 478 pages together with the same two pages of advertisement. The title-page follows that of its predecessor. Edition 5 was published in 1781 at London and Edinburgh. It contains a fair number of revisions of accidentals, chiefly in punctuation, but occasionally in spelling; e.g. it reverts from the spelling 'blamable' of edition 4 to the spelling 'blameable' of editions 1–3. Nevertheless it must have been set up from a copy of edition 4 and not from one of the earlier editions, since it includes all the revisions of substantives, and most of the revisions of accidentals, that were made in edition 4. It also includes a few further revisions in substantives, of a minor character.

The changes in accidentals, especially in punctuation, are usually sensible, though sometimes pernickety, and are such as one would expect to be carried over by the printer of the next edition. In fact, however, most of the revisions of accidentals in edition 5, and all of its revisions of substantives, are *not* carried over to edition 6, though a minority of the accidentals are. This must mean that the printer of edition 6 worked from a revised copy of edition 4, and not from one of edition 5.

Why, then, it may be asked, are certain of the revisions of accidentals in edition 5 carried over? It is conceivable that the printer of edition 6 had at hand an unrevised copy of edition 5 also, but since edition 6 does not contain the substantive revisions of edition 5, this is most improbable. It is more likely that those revisions of accidentals which are repeated in edition 6 were introduced anew by the printer or the author for the same sort of reasons that had caused them to be inserted in edition 5. We say 'the printer or the author' because it is quite likely that some of the changes in accidentals were made by Adam Smith himself. There is at least one instance (the last sentence of I.iii.1) where the substitution of an exclamation mark in edition 5 for a question mark in edition 4 is essential to restore the required sense (editions 1–3 had printed an innocuous full point), but this would not be perceived by a printer, who would not know whether the Duke of Biron's tears did or did not disgrace his memory. In this instance, the revision is not repeated in edition 6, which reverts to the misleading question mark of edition 4.

Most of the revisions of accidentals which are carried over from edition 5 to edition 6 are in fact of a kind that one could expect to be reintroduced in a later revision of edition 4. There is, however, one place (VII.ii.1.16–18) where, for a few pages, edition 6 follows the accidentals of edition 5, as against those of edition 4, to an extent that suggests more than coincidence. It looks as if the printer were using, at this point, printed copy from pages of edition 5. Significantly, the passage is one (on the Stoics) that has been transposed from Part I, with some cancellation. It seems probable that the particular circumstances of revision of this passage made it necessary for Smith to use a second set of the printed pages, and that he took these from a copy of edition 5.

What of the minor changes of substantives in edition 5, none of which is carried over to edition 6? It cannot be assumed mechanically that changes in substantives are due to the author. Indeed one of those in edition 5 (at VII.iii.3.17) cannot have been made by the author since it is clearly an error, giving a sense opposite to that required. On the other hand, two of the changes in substantives, though of a minor character like the rest, could not possibly have been introduced by the printer. We can therefore be certain that Adam Smith himself made some light revision of edition 4 for the printing of edition 5. He must, however, have forgotten this when he again used a copy of edition 4 in revising for edition 6. This supposition is confirmed by the conclusion already reached, that he was ready to substitute a few pages of edition 5 for those of edition 4 when working out his transposition and partial cancellation of the passage on the Stoics. He must have thought that the two editions were identical.

The hypothesis that Smith had forgotten his light revision for edition 5 is less implausible than it sounds. During these years he was heavily preoccupied with more important matters than imperfections of detail in TMS. Furthermore, we can infer with certainty an analogous lapse of memory. We know that Smith compiled a long list of minor errata (as well as a few major ones) in edition 2; and since ten of his corrections were never introduced into the later editions, we are entitled to conclude that Smith had forgotten all about the list. This is especially clear from the one instance (II.iii.intro.1) where he saw, when revising for edition 6, that a mistake had been made, but corrected it in a different manner.

We have used four copies of edition 6, three from Glasgow University Library and one from the Bodleian. One of the Glasgow copies had pp. 145–58 of Volume I bound up between pp. 128 and 129. This particular copy is not in its original binding, and the error is likely to have occurred when the volume was rebound. Otherwise there is no difference between the four copies, except in details of the gilt design on the covers of those that still have their original binding.

Edition 6 is in two volumes octavo. Volume I has xvi + 488 pages, and contains Parts I–IV of TMS. Volume II has viii + 462 pages; it contains Parts V–VII of TMS, which ends on p. 399, and the Dissertation on Languages, which occupies pp. 401–62. Edition 6 is of course completely reset and is quite different typographically from its predecessors. The actual type is of the same size as that used for editions 2–5, but there is more space between the lines, as there was in edition 1. But since edition 1 also had slightly larger type, edition 6 has the neatest appearance of all and is the easiest to read. There are line spaces between the paragraphs in edition 6, but not in any of the earlier editions. The title-page of each volume of edition 6 follows editions 4 and 5 in its description of the contents, but the author is now called 'Adam Smith, LL.D. Fellow of the Royal Societies of London and Edinburgh; One of the Commissioners of his Majesty's Customs in Scotland; and formerly Professor of Moral Philosophy in the University of Glasgow'. The title-pages also state that edition 6 is 'with considerable additions and corrections'. The edition was published in 1790 at London and Edinburgh.

Two letters of Adam Smith to Thomas Cadell speak of his work of revising TMS for the enlarged edition. In Letter 276, dated 15 March 1788, he wrote:

... I am at present giving the most intense application. My subject is *the theory of moral Sentiments*, to all parts of which I am making many additions and corrections. The chief and the most important additions will be to the third part, that concerning *the sense of Duty* and to the last part concerning *the History of moral Philosophy*. . . . I am a slow a very slow workman, who do and undo everything I write at least half a dozen of times before I can be tolerably pleased with it; and tho' I have now, I think, brought my work within compass, yet it will be the month of June before I shall be able to send it to you.

In fact the work took even longer than he anticipated, and on 31 March 1789 (Letter 287) he wrote again:

Ever since I wrote to you last I have been labouring very hard in preparing the proposed new edition of the Theory of Moral Sentiments. . . . Besides the

Additions and Improvements I mentioned to you; I have inserted, immediately after the fifth part, a compleat new sixth part containing a practical system of Morality, under the title of the Character of Virtue. The Book now will consist of seven Parts and will make two pretty large 8 vo. Volumes. After all my labours, however, I am afraid it will be Midsummer before I can get the whole Manuscript in such proper order as to send it to you. I am very much ashamed of this delay; but the subject has grown upon me.

Smith's estimate that he would be ready by the summer of 1789 was again over-optimistic. Stewart, V.9, says of the publication of edition 6 in 1790 that the additions had been sent to the press 'in the beginning of the preceding winter', presumably about December 1789.

Edition 6 begins with an added Advertisement, which appears to say that the revisions had been contemplated over a long period, and briefly mentions the main changes made. A more detailed account of the major changes is as follows. In the footnote to I.iii.1.9, which had been added in edition 2, edition 6 omits the final sentence. At I.iii.2.9, editions 1–5 began a fresh chapter on the Stoical Philosophy; in edition 6, part of the material is transferred to VII.ii.1.23 and 20, part is withdrawn, and a sentence is added at the beginning of I.iii.2.9 so as to connect the preceding discussion with what follows. I.iii.3 is a new chapter, in which the social advantages of admiration for 'the rich and the great' are qualified by its corrupting effect on moral approbation. At the conclusion of II.ii.3.12, a sentence is added to replace a paragraph which had previously followed § 12 and which is now withdrawn; this particular revision, as we have already mentioned in our account of edition 3, was later the subject of controversy; we discuss it in Appendix II, where we also give new information about a manuscript fragment that has been supposed to be connected with Smith's revision of the passage. At II.iii.3.4–5, one and a half paragraphs are added on the concept of 'piacular' guilt, a topic referred to again in new material at VII.iv.30. At III.1.2, the major part of what was Chapter 1 in editions 2–5 (Section i in edition 1) is transferred to become part of Chapter 2, and what was formerly Chapter 2 (Section ii in edition 1) becomes Chapter 1, with a few linking sentences. Most of III.2 is new, but three paragraphs (§§ 4, 5, and the major part of § 9) have been transferred from what was III.1 in editions 2–5; the new material includes a further development of the theory of conscience so as to distinguish the sense of praiseworthiness from the consciousness of being actually praised by others; at the same time some caution is introduced about the reliability and the efficacy of the judgements of conscience in the face of erroneous judgement by the outside world. At III.3, a fresh chapter, with an addition to the beginning of § 1, is begun, taking up material which in editions 2–5 was part of III.2; one and a half paragraphs are added at §§ 5–6; § 10 is new; one and a half paragraphs are withdrawn at § 11; and there is a lengthy addition at §§ 12–45, mainly on self-command, with some further development again of the theory of the impartial spectator and conscience. III.4 is largely a revised version of what was the latter part of III.2 in editions 2–5. The whole of Part VI is new; it deals with certain practical and political applications of moral theory, and especially with the virtues of prudence, benevolence, and self-command (already the subject of new material in III.3), and the vices of pride and vanity. In VII.ii.1, there is rearrangement and development of Smith's account of Stoicism: at § 17, a passage is withdrawn; at the end of § 18, a sentence is added; after § 19, one paragraph is withdrawn, § 20 has been transferred from Part I, §§ 21–2 are added, and § 23 is another insertion of a passage formerly in Part I; §§ 24–47 are new, dealing mainly with the Stoic view of suicide. Edition 6 then reverts to the text of editions 1–5 at § 48, but adds a short paragraph at § 49. At VII.ii.4, where the earlier editions had linked La Rochefoucauld with Mandeville as the authors of 'licentious systems', all references to La Rochefoucauld are withdrawn. In VII.4, a new passage is added at §§ 23–7 and the beginning of § 28, developing Smith's views on veracity and deceit; a passage that had formed the latter part of § 28 is withdrawn; and three new paragraphs are added at §§ 29–31, again on deceit and with a further reference to 'piacular' guilt.

Edition 6 also contains many minor revisions, both of substantives and of accidentals. Some of the changes in accidentals appear to be due to the author himself. Quite frequently, punctuation which has been left unchanged in all the editions from 1 to 5 is revised in edition 6; and while one cannot be certain that this is not the work of the printer, anxious to do his part in producing a highly superior edition, it seems likely that Smith himself will have paid attention to these details, as to others.

We have already given, in our account of edition 5, the evidence for believing that both author and printer used a revised copy of edition 4 in preparing most of the older material for incorporation in edition 6. In matters of spelling and the use of initial capital letters, edition 6 generally follows and takes farther the revisions of edition 4, which had made fairly radical changes from the practice of the earlier editions. There are some exceptions. For example, editions 1–3 tended, though not uniformly, to print the word 'nature' with a lower-case initial letter, even when Smith personifies nature, as he frequently does. Edition 4 uses a capital letter for most instances of personification or near-personification. Edition 6 follows edition 4 in the old material, but in the new material it sometimes uses a capital letter, more commonly a lower-case. Another example is the use of a capital initial letter for the word 'gods' when referring to pagan deities. Editions 1–3 had done this at times. Edition 4 changed the capital letter to lower-case. Edition 6 prints a capital letter both in old and in new material, but a lower-case initial for the one instance of 'goddess'. This simply means that the printers were accustomed to use the capital letter for the word 'God' and did not stop to distinguish, as the reviser for edition 4 did, between the Christian God and pagan gods.

We have used two copies of edition 7, one from Glasgow University Library, the other from the Bodleian, and have found no differences between them. Edition 7 resembles edition 6 very closely. Like its predecessor, it is in two octavo volumes, the first of xvi + 488 pages, the second of viii + 462 pages. The title-pages follow those of edition 6, except that the words 'with considerable additions and corrections' are properly omitted since the revisions are not new in this edition. The Advertisement, however, is repeated without any indication that it was written for edition 6, and in consequence some of its words appear incongruous in 1792, the year in which edition 7 was published at London and Edinburgh.

Edition 7 has the same pagination, and generally the same division of lines, as edition 6. It is not a reprint, but has been set up so as to follow edition 6 line by line, in the same way as editions 3–5 were each set up to follow their predecessors. The tests that establish this for editions 3–5 show it to be true of edition 7 also. Edition 7 corrects a few misprints of edition 6, introduces some new misprints or other errors, and resets a few lines so as to improve spacing. There are some changes in accidentals, chiefly punctuation. For the reasons given at the beginning of this section, it is practically certain that the compositors of edition 7 did not have any author's corrections of edition 6 to guide them.

An unauthorized edition of TMS was published in Dublin, bearing the date 1777 and calling itself 'the sixth edition'. The Library of Trinity College, Dublin, possesses a copy (another is in the Goldsmiths' Library, London) and we have examined a Xerox of it. The Dublin edition seems clearly to have been set up from a copy of edition 4 but it is quite different from editions 3, 4, and 5 in format, pagination, and division of lines. It is a single octavo volume of [viii] + 426 pages. The text of TMS occupies pp. 1–388, and the Dissertation on Languages pp. 389–426. On the title-page the account of the contents is the same as in editions 4 and 5, but the author is differently described as 'Adam Smith, L.L.D. F.R.S. Formerly Professor of Philosophy in the University of Glasgow; and Author of the Nature and Cause of the Wealth of Nations'. The date of 1777 is consonant with the mention, albeit incorrect ('Cause' instead of 'Causes'), of the title of WN, which first appeared in 1776 and named its author as 'Adam Smith, LL.D. and F.R.S. Formerly Professor of Moral Philosophy in the University of Glasgow'. The text of the Dublin edition departs at times from that of editions 4 and 5 in accidentals. It commonly agrees with edition 4 where that differs from edition 5, so there is little doubt that the Dublin printer followed edition 4 (1774) and not edition 5 (1781), and this again fits the date of 1777. There is no reason to suppose that

Adam Smith consented to, or even knew of, the publication of the Dublin edition, and therefore we have ignored it in our collation of variants.

(b) *Editorial policy*

In the preparation of a critical edition of a work from printed books, bibliographical scholars of the present day attach great importance to the principles laid down by Sir Walter Greg in his paper, 'The Rationale of Copy-Text', first published in *Studies in Bibliography* (University of Virginia), vol. iii (1950), and reprinted in W. W. Greg, *Collected Papers*, edited by J. C. Maxwell (Oxford, 1966). In that paper Greg drew, and explained the importance of, the distinction between the two kinds of variants to be found in the different editions of a book, changes in substantives and changes in accidentals. So long as one is dealing with editions which can be assumed to have received revision by the author, changes in substantives can usually, though not always, be attributed to him, while changes in accidentals (of books printed some considerable time ago) can often, but again certainly not always, be attributed to the printer. Consequently, bibliographical scholars recommend that, in order to elicit a text that gives the nearest possible approach to the author's intentions, the editor of a critical edition should, in the absence of a manuscript, make the first edition of a work his copy-text; he should then proceed, through each successive edition that appeared during the author's lifetime, to the first of the posthumous editions, if there are any such, keeping in mind the distinction between substantives and accidentals when introducing revisions. As a general rule, but one to be applied with judgement and discretion, they advise an editor, in the absence of evidence to the contrary, to include changes in substantives, provided that such changes make good sense, and to exclude changes in accidentals, on the ground that these were probably due to the printer.

To this general rule there are naturally exceptions. One class of works that cannot easily be subjected to it are those for which an edition later than the first is known to have been extensively and carefully revised by the author. TMS falls into this class. To follow the usual rule for this book would in fact produce a curious patchwork.

There is no doubt that the printers of edition 1 of TMS followed their manuscript copy fairly closely. Edition 1 frequently, though not consistently, uses antique spellings such as 'compleat', 'antient', 'chearful', 'cloaths', 'intire', and the contractions 'tho'' and 'thro'', all of which we know were used by Adam Smith or his amanuenses. These older or abbreviated forms were gradually removed in later editions, especially in 4 and 6. We can also be fairly sure that many of the revisions in punctuation were made by the printers, though there is good evidence that some of them were made by the author. While it is a hazardous business to judge which revisions of accidentals are due to the author, and which to the printer, that is insufficient reason for refusing to make the attempt, and it can be done. But the new material added in edition 6 does not go back to the antique spellings; its usage on accidentals is, generally speaking, closely consistent with the usage that edition 6 follows in the older material. It would be quite unwarrantable for an editor to introduce the antique spellings into the new material of edition 6, especially since even edition 1 does not use them consistently, and since there is evidence from certain idiosyncrasies in the new passages that the printers of edition 6 kept reasonably close to their manuscript copy. In the added material, therefore, the accidentals of edition 6 must generally be accepted. But if, at the same time, the accidentals of edition 1 were retained for the older material, the result would be a patchwork text, which would indeed show up immediately some features of the history of the editions, but which would undoubtedly be contrary to the intentions of the author. Adam Smith took great care over the preparation of edition 6, and he would not thank us if we replaced its general appearance of neat consistency by a mixture of ancient and modern forms. In a sense, of course, every revised version of a book is a patchwork in its substantives; but when the author has tried to present it as a seamless fabric, an editor has no business to disclose the seams, in the text itself, by printing the differing accidentals of the original versions of old and new matter.

It follows that the copy-text for TMS must be edition 6 and not edition 1. There is no virtue in making a fetish of retaining the accidentals of the first edition. Mr. J. C. Maxwell has pointed out to us that the main purpose of Greg's article was not to insist that editors should exclude changes of accidentals and include those of substantives, but to show the need to test the credentials of each change in a substantive before accepting it as due to the author. This of course implies that one should equally not assume without consideration that changes in accidentals are due to the printer or that the accidentals of the first edition are the nearest approach one can make to the work of the author. Sometimes one can be fairly certain that a revision of an accidental was made by the author; we have given examples in 4(a) above (pp. *38, 41*). Sometimes one can be even more certain that an inconsistency in the accidentals of a first printed version is not a reflection of the manuscript but simply an indication that different parts of the book were set up by different compositors; in edition 1 of TMS, the first few chapters use the spelling 'sympathize', the next few, 'sympathise', and the next again go back to 'sympathize'; similarly, in the new Part VI of edition 6, Chapter 1 of Section ii regularly uses the spelling 'connection', while Chapters 2–3 regularly use 'connexion'. Furthermore, the actual writing of the author on accidentals does not always represent his intentions for the printed text. Edition 1 of TMS very often has the contracted forms 'tho'' and 'thro''. These are commonly used by Adam Smith in letters written in his own hand, but we cannot assume that he intended this labour-saving device to be reproduced in print. He often used the contracted form '&', but nobody would suppose that he wanted that to be reproduced in the printed versions of his books. So when later editions of TMS replace 'tho'' by 'though', it is reasonable to think that Smith would have approved. Likewise, if the printer adds a comma where its absence impedes the reader from seeing at once the sense of a passage, one must again suppose that the author would have approved.

The view that all changes in accidentals should normally be rejected assumes that the author will not have had much opportunity or determination to attend to these details in proofs. This is in fact not true of Adam Smith. While he will not have been quite so meticulous as a modern scholar might be, he evidently took particular pains over the correction of proofs. This has already been illustrated in quotations from some of his letters to his publishers, especially Letter 50 addressed to William Strahan, dated 4 April 1760. There is further evidence to the same effect in three of his letters about WN. In Letter 227 addressed to William Strahan, dated 22 May 1783, he wrote: 'I must correct the press myself and you must, therefor, frank me the sheets as they are printed. I would even rather than not correct it myself come up to London in the beginning of next winter and attend the Press myself.' Letter 237 addressed to William Strahan, dated 10 June 1784, confirms the impression which can be formed independently, from internal evidence, that Smith gave his personal attention to punctuation: 'I return you the Proof which, indeed, requires little correction, except in the pointing and not much in that.' William Strahan died in 1785. The third letter (No. 256) is addressed to his son, Andrew Strahan, and is dated 13 February 1786: 'I beg you will employ one of your best compositors in printing the new edition of my book. I must, likewise beg that a compleat copy be sent to me before it is published, that I may revise and correct it. You may depend upon my not detaining you above a week.'

We are not suggesting that Smith himself was responsible for most of the changes in accidentals. Plainly he was not. But since he went over his proofs so carefully and was ready to revise even punctuation, we must assume that he was prepared to approve such revisions as he left unaltered. This applies particularly to edition 6, on which he worked so long. If he had wanted to go back, for example, to the antique spellings of editions 1–3, he had the opportunity at this time to do so. Since edition 6 in fact repeats the modernized spellings of edition 4 both in the old and in the new material, and often introduces them in places where edition 4 had omitted to do so, we are bound to suppose that this procedure had Smith's approval.

If we did revert to the forms of edition 1 on accidentals, it is by no means certain that we should be reproducing what Smith himself had written. Writing in his own hand was very irksome to him, and he was in the habit of employing amanuenses for any extensive piece of work. The manuscript of WN was almost certainly written by an amanuensis, and it will be seen from Appendix II that Smith evidently used an amanuensis for his lectures in Glasgow at quite an early stage of his Professorship. This would suggest that the manuscript of TMS was probably not in the hand of Smith himself. As it happens, edition 1 of WN contains far more antique spellings than does edition 1 of TMS, and would give a quite false impression if taken to illustrate Smith's own practice. For example, edition 1 of WN usually adds 'k' to many words that we now commonly end with 'c', such as 'public', 'republic', 'mechanic', 'Catholic', 'physic', 'academic', 'stoic', 'metallic', 'authentic', 'characteristic', 'domestic', 'rustic', 'politic'. Not many of these words are to be found in letters written in Smith's own hand, but 'public' and 'mechanic' do occur and are spelt without a 'k'. Quite a number of the words listed occur in TMS also, and in edition 1 of that work none of them, except 'public' occasionally and 'republic' once, is spelt with an added 'k'. In so far as direct comparison can be made between edition 1 of TMS and Smith's usage in letters written in his own hand, there is a fair degree of correspondence, and certainly nothing like the extent of discrepancy that exists between the letters and edition 1 of WN. Both the letters and edition 1 of TMS commonly use the forms 'inconveniency', 'cloaths', 'antient', 'compleat', 'chearful', and 'chuse'. (The last, which is not universal in the earlier editions, is generally retained in the old material of edition 6 and is quite commonly used in the new material too.) The letters tend to use the contracted forms 'tho''' and 'thro''', which occur usually, but by no means universally, in edition 1 of the book. On the other side, the letters have 'Nature' with a capital initial and 'public' without a 'k', while edition 1 of TMS prints 'nature' almost always and 'publick' from time to time. Both the letters and the book are inconsistent in using the two forms 'entire' and 'intire', but 'e' is more common in the letters, while 'i' is far more common in edition 1 of the book. In his letters and in inscribing presentation copies of his books, Smith showed a marked preference for the spelling 'authour', while the book always uses the form 'author'. The correspondences between the letters and the book are not at all strong evidence that Smith himself wrote the manuscript for edition 1, since these correspondences are equally consistent with the hypothesis that the manuscript of TMS was written by an amanuensis, though not the one who wrote the manuscript of WN. On the other hand, the discrepancies in this instance do not add up to any strong evidence that Smith did not write the manuscript. It remains an open question. Comparison with the letters is inconclusive. The fact that Smith used an amanuensis for his lectures suggests that he is likely to have done so for the book. J. R.

McCulloch is reported by Rae (*Life*, 260-1) to have said that Smith wrote TMS in his own hand, but it seems that McCulloch was going simply on his own impression that the style of the book was less diffuse than that of WN. (This point is further discussed in Appendix II.)

We have, then, taken edition 6 as our copy-text. We have departed from it in a small number of instances. First, we have corrected misprints. Second, we have incorporated those corrections of the Errata lists for editions 1 and 2 which were overlooked. Third, we have included those revisions in edition 5 which can reasonably be attributed to the author and which were forgotten in the preparation of edition 6. Fourth, there are some instances where the reading of an earlier edition is to be preferred on the ground that the later reading is an error that was overlooked. Fifth, there are a few places where we have ourselves introduced an emendation which we believe represents the author's own intention. With one exception, these emendations are a necessary consequence of nearby revisions that the author himself has made. The exception concerns the words 'convenience(s)' and 'inconvenience(s)'. In editions 1–5, the forms 'conveniency', etc., are always used, except for a lapse on a single occasion in edition 4. Edition 6 retains these forms in the old material, apart from one paragraph of Part VII. In its new material it uses the alternative forms 'convenience', etc., in Part VI (several instances), but 'conveniency', etc., in new passages of III.3 and of VII.ii.1. Now in the case of this particular set of words, we can say with confidence that Smith had an insistent preference for 'conveniency' and its cognates. Apart from the fact that he always uses these forms in letters written in his own hand, there is an interesting piece of evidence in the manuscript that W. R. Scott called 'An early draft of part of *The Wealth of Nations*'. This manuscript was written by an .amanuensis, but some of the revisions, written over original material, are in Adam Smith's own hand. Scott (*ASSP*, 325) notes an instance of the word 'conveniencies' where the last three letters are in Smith's hand, and Scott conjectures that the amanuensis may originally have written 'conveniences' There is another instance of the word 'conveniencies' (331) where the second 'i' is due to revision, probably for the same reason. Consequently we have judged that Adam Smith would have wanted the word (and its cognates) to be spelt in this way throughout his book, and that it was probably so spelt in the manuscript of the new material for edition 6. The instances of the alternative spelling in the text of edition 6 were probably due to a particular compositor.

One could argue that our editorial emendation of 'convenience' to 'conveniency' might have been extended to certain other forms of words for which Smith is known to have had a preference, such as 'authour', 'compleat', 'cloaths', and 'chearful'. But these words do not stand on all fours with 'conveniency' and its cognates, which are the forms regularly used in editions 1–5 and carried over to edition 6 in all instances but one of the old material, as well as being used sometimes in the new material. By contrast, 'authour' is never used in any of the editions; 'compleat' is generally, though not consistently, used in editions 1–3, but is replaced by 'complete' for the major part of edition 4 and throughout edition 6; 'cloaths' and its cognates, and likewise 'chearful', are regularly used in editions 1–5 but not at all in edition 6.

At any rate we have decided to be fairly conservative in our departures from the text of edition 6. We have given the reader some indication of the changes in accidentals, as between the different editions, that are most important for this purpose, and the apparatus of variants will enable him to go farther if he wishes. The critical apparatus is divided into two sections, one appearing as footnotes to the text, the other forming Appendix I. The character of the two sections needs some explanation.

The variants in the textual footnotes are referred to by alphabetical indicators in the text itself. They consist of two quite distinct groups. (1) Since edition 6 is our copy-text, the reader ought to be told immediately whenever our text departs from that of edition 6. Every such departure is indicated in the text by being enclosed within superscribed letters of the alphabet; the reading of edition 6, and the variants, if any, in other editions, are given in the footnote, together with reasons for the emendation if these are not at once obvious. (2) We have also printed as footnotes, with alphabetical indicators in the text, all variants that disclose a change or addition of thought by the author, as contrasted with revisions of substantives that constitute merely an improvement in the expression of the same thought. (Occasionally there may be difference of opinion whether a revision of words does or does not have a slight effect on the sense conveyed, and in such instances we have thought it best to allow for a possible change of thought and to include the variant in the footnotes to the text pages.) This class of variants is the really important one for most readers. TMS is a book on a philosophical subject, and a proper understanding of it requires an awareness of the respects in which the author's thought developed. We have therefore thought it right to bring these changes directly to the reader's attention by the same method of immediate presentation as has been used for emendations.

Other variants that are at all worthy of record have been included in Appendix I. They include both substantives and accidentals. The variants in substantives that appear in Appendix I are those which the author has revised simply in order to improve the expression of his thought, without changing the thought itself. Appendix I also contains the vast majority of variants in accidentals, but not all, since a few changes of accidentals are involved in one or other of the two classes of variants that are printed on the text pages.

One small group of trivial variants has not been recorded, on the ground that they are practically of no significance, except to students of the history of printing, who would in any event want to make their own record of such matters. These are the introduction of a misprint, or the addition or omission of a mark of punctuation, in one intermediate edition only, when the next edition restores the original reading. We have, however, excluded edition 5 from our rule of ignoring such trivia. Because of the unusual relationship of edition 5 to its predecessor and successor, there is some interest in noting all the variants that it affords.

Editions 1–7 all conclude the headings and titles of Parts, Sections, and chapters with full points. There is no reason why a modern edition should reproduce this particular piece of early printing practice, and we have not done so either in the text or in the relevant variants.

In the textual apparatus, the numerals in italic type following an entry stand for the editions containing it, *1E* and *2E* being used for the Errata lists of editions 1 and 2. The numerals in roman type preceding an entry in Appendix I stand for the page and line in which the passage is located. A caret below the line (ʌ) stands for the omission of a mark of punctuation. A wavy dash (~) stands for a repetition of all the words up to a mark of punctuation or a caret.

The numerals printed in the margin at the beginning of each paragraph are not in the original editions. The practice of numbering the paragraphs within each chapter, or similar segment, will be followed also for WN and EPS in this edition of the Works of Adam Smith, in order that cross-references may be made from one work to another by means of paragraphs instead of pages, and so without confining the reader to the present edition.

THE

THEORY

OF

MORAL SENTIMENTS.

By ADAM SMITH,
Professor of Moral Philosophy in the
University of Glasgow.

LONDON:
Printed for A. Millar, in the Strand;
And A. Kincaid and J. Bell, in Edinburgh.
MDCCLIX.

Title-page of edition 1

1 SINCE the first publication of the THEORY OF MORAL SENTIMENTS, which was so long ago as the beginning of the year 1759, several corrections, and a good many illustrations of the doctrines contained in it, have occurred to me. But the various occupations in which the different accidents of my life necessarily involved me, have till now prevented me from revising this work with the care and attention which I always intended. The reader will find the principal alterations which I have made in this New Edition, in the last Chapter of the third Section of Part First; and in the four first Chapters of Part Third. Part Sixth, as it stands in this New Edition, is altogether new. In Part Seventh, I have brought together the greater part of the different passages concerning the Stoical Philosophy, which, in the former Editions, had been scattered about in different parts of the work.[1] I have likewise endeavoured to explain more fully, and examine more distinctly, some of the doctrines of that famous sect. In the fourth and last Section of the same Part, I have thrown together a few additional observations concerning the duty and principle of veracity. There are, besides, in other parts of the work, a few other alterations and corrections of no great moment.

2 In the last paragraph of the first Edition of the present work, I said, that I should in another discourse endeavour to give an account of the general principles of law and government, and of the different revolutions which they had undergone in the different ages and periods of society; not only in what concerns justice, but in what concerns police, revenue, and arms, and whatever else is the object of law. In the *Enquiry concerning*[2] *the Nature and Causes of the Wealth of Nations*, I have partly executed this promise; at least so far as concerns police, revenue, and arms. What remains, the theory of jurisprudence, which I have long projected, I have hitherto been hindered from executing, by the same occupations which had till now prevented me from revising the present work. Though my very advanced age leaves me, I acknowledge, very little expectation of ever being able to execute this great work to my own satisfaction; yet, as I have not altogether abandoned the design, and as I wish still to continue under the obligation of doing what I can, I have allowed the paragraph to remain as it was published more than thirty years ago, when I entertained no doubt of being able to execute every thing which it announced.

---

a *The* Advertisement *was added in ed. 6.*

[1] An exaggeration. See Introduction, pp. *5–6, 43–4.*
[2] The title of WN as published is *An Inquiry into. . .*

Contents

PART II

Of MERIT and DEMERIT; or of the Objects of REWARD and PUNISHMENT

PART III

PART IV

PART V

PART VI

SECTION I

SECTION II

SECTION III

8 *Contents*

PART VII

PART I
Of the PROPRIETY of ACTION
Consisting of Three Sections

SECTION I
Of the SENSE of PROPRIETY

CHAP. I
Of SYMPATHY

1 How selfish soever man may be supposed, there are evidently some principles in his nature, which interest him in the fortune of others, and render their happiness necessary to him, though he derives nothing from it except the pleasure of seeing it. Of this kind is pity or compassion, the emotion which we feel for the misery of others, when we either see it, or are made to conceive it in a very lively manner. That we often derive sorrow from the sorrow of others, is a matter of fact too obvious to require any instances to prove it; for this sentiment, like all the other original passions of human nature, is by no means confined to the virtuous and humane, though they perhaps may feel it with the most exquisite sensibility. The greatest ruffian, the most hardened violator of the laws of society, is not altogether without it.

2 As we have no immediate experience of what other men feel, we can form no idea of the manner in which they are affected, but by conceiving what we ourselves should feel in the like situation. Though our brother is upon the rack, as long as we ourselves are at our ease, our senses will never inform us of what he suffers. They never did, and never can, carry us beyond our own person, and it is by the imagination only that we can form any conception of what are his sensations. Neither can that faculty help us to this any other way, than by representing to us what would be our own, if we were in his case. It is the impressions of our own senses only, not those of his, which our imaginations copy. By the imagination we place ourselves in his situation, we conceive ourselves enduring all the same torments, we enter as it were into his body, and become in some measure the same person with him, and thence form some idea of his sensations, and even feel something which, though weaker in degree, is not altogether unlike them. His agonies, when they are thus brought home to ourselves, when we have thus adopted and made them our own, begin at last to affect us, and we then tremble and shudder at the thought of what he feels. For as to be in pain or distress of any kind excites the most excessive sorrow, so to conceive or to imagine that we are in it, excites some degree of the same emotion, in proportion to the vivacity or dulness of the conception.

3   That this is the source of our fellow-feeling for the misery of others, that
it is by changing places in fancy with the sufferer, that we come either to
conceive or to be affected by what he feels, may be demonstrated by many
obvious observations, if it should not be thought sufficiently evident of itself.
When we see a stroke aimed and just ready to fall upon the leg or arm of
another person, we naturally shrink and draw back our own leg or our
own arm; and when it does fall, we feel it in some measure, and are hurt
by it as well as the sufferer. The mob, when they are gazing at a dancer
on the slack rope, naturally writhe and twist and balance their own bodies,
as they see him do, and as they feel that they themselves must do if in his
situation. Persons of delicate fibres and a weak constitution of body complain, that in looking on the sores and ulcers which are exposed by beggars
in the streets, they are apt to feel an itching or uneasy sensation in the correspondent part of their own bodies. The horror which they conceive at
the misery of those wretches affects that particular part in themselves
more than any other; because that horror arises from conceiving what they
themselves would suffer, if they really were the wretches whom they are
looking upon, and if that particular part in themselves was actually affected
in the same miserable manner. The very force of this conception is sufficient, in their feeble frames, to produce that itching or uneasy sensation
complained of. Men of the most robust make, observe that in looking upon
sore eyes they often feel a very sensible soreness in their own, which proceeds from the same reason; that organ being in the strongest man more
delicate, than any other part of the body is in the weakest.

4   Neither is it those circumstances only, which create pain or sorrow, that
call forth our fellow-feeling. Whatever is the passion which arises from any
object in the person principally concerned, an analogous emotion springs
up, at the thought of his situation, in the breast of every attentive spectator.
Our joy for the deliverance of those heroes of tragedy or romance who interest us, is as sincere as our grief for their distress, and our fellow-feeling
with their misery is not more real than that with their happiness. We enter
into their gratitude towards those faithful friends who did not desert
them in their difficulties; and we heartily go along with their resentment
against those perfidious traitors who injured, abandoned, or deceived them.
In every passion of which the mind of man is susceptible, the emotions
of the by-stander always correspond to what, by bringing the case home to
himself, he imagines should be the sentiments of the sufferer.

5   Pity and compassion are words appropriated to signify our fellow-feeling
with the sorrow of others. Sympathy, though its meaning was, perhaps,
originally the same, may now, however, without much impropriety, be
made use of to denote our fellow-feeling with any passion whatever.[1]

---

[1] Smith's unusually wide definition of 'sympathy' needs to be noted because some
scholars, more familiar with his economics than his moral philosophy, have mistakenly

6   Upon some occasions sympathy may seem to arise merely from the view of a certain emotion in another person. The passions, upon some occasions, may seem to be transfused from one man to another, instantaneously, and antecedent to any knowledge of what excited them in the person principally concerned. Grief and joy, for example, strongly expressed in the look and gestures of any one, at once affect the spectator with some degree of a like painful or agreeable emotion. A smiling face is, to every body that sees it, a cheerful object; as a sorrowful countenance, on the other hand, is a melancholy one.

7   This, however, does not hold universally, or with regard to every passion. There are some passions of which the expressions excite no sort of sympathy, but before we are acquainted with what gave occasion to them, serve rather to disgust and provoke us against them. The furious behaviour of an angry man is more likely to exasperate us against himself than against his enemies. As we are unacquainted with his provocation, we cannot bring his case home to ourselves, nor conceive any thing like the passions which it excites. But we plainly see what is the situation of those with whom he is angry, and to what violence they may be exposed from so enraged an adversary. We readily, therefore, sympathize with their fear or resentment, and are immediately disposed to take part against the man from whom they appear to be in so much danger.

8   If the very appearances of grief and joy inspire us with some degree of the like emotions, it is because they suggest to us the general idea of some good or bad fortune that has befallen the person in whom we observe them: and in these passions this is sufficient to have some little influence upon us. The effects of grief and joy terminate in the person who feels those emotions, of which the expressions do not, like those of resentment, suggest to us the idea of any other person for whom we are concerned, and whose interests are opposite to his. The general idea of good or bad fortune, therefore, creates some concern for the person who has met with it, but the general idea of provocation excites no sympathy with the anger of the man who has received it. Nature, it seems, teaches us to be more averse to enter into this passion, and, till informed of its cause, to be disposed rather to take part against it.

9   Even our sympathy with the grief or joy of another, before we are informed of the cause of either, is always extremely imperfect. General lamentations, which express nothing but the anguish of the sufferer, create rather a curiosity to inquire into his situation, along with some disposition to sympathize with him, than any actual sympathy that is very sensible. The first question which we ask is, What has befallen you? Till this be answered, though we are uneasy both from the vague idea of his misfor-

equated sympathy with benevolence and have inferred that TMS deals with the altruistic side of human conduct and WN with its egoistic side. See Introduction, section 2(*b*).

tune, and still more from torturing ourselves with conjectures about what it may be, yet our fellow-feeling is not very considerable.

10   Sympathy, therefore, does not arise so much from the view of the passion, as from that of the situation which excites it. We sometimes feel for another, a passion of which he himself seems to be altogether incapable; because, when we put ourselves in his case, that passion arises in our breast from the imagination, though it does not in his from the reality. We blush for the impudence and rudeness of another, though he himself appears to have no sense of the impropriety of his own behaviour; because we cannot help feeling with what confusion we ourselves should be covered, had we behaved in so absurd a manner.

11   Of all the calamities to which the condition of mortality exposes mankind, the loss of reason appears, to those who have the least spark of humanity, by far the most dreadful, and they behold that last stage of human ᵃwretchednessᵃ with deeper commiseration than any other. But the poor wretch, who is in it, laughs and sings perhaps, and is altogether insensible of his own misery. The anguish which humanity feels, therefore, at the sight of such an object, cannot be the reflection of any sentiment of the sufferer. The compassion of the spectator must arise altogether from the consideration of what he himself would feel if he was reduced to the same unhappy situation, and, what perhaps is impossible, was at the same time able to regard it with his present reason and judgment.

12   What are the pangs of a mother, when she hears the moanings of her infant that during the agony of disease cannot express what it feels? In her idea of what it suffers, she joins, to its real helplessness, her own consciousness of that helplessness, and her own terrors for the unknown consequences of its disorder; and out of all these, forms, for her own sorrow, the most complete image of misery and distress. The infant, however, feels only the uneasiness of the present instant, which can never be great. With regard to the future, it is perfectly secure, and in its thoughtlessness and want of foresight, possesses an antidote against fear and anxiety, the great tormentors of the human breast, from ᵇwhichᵇ reason and philosophy will, in vain, attempt to defend it, when it grows up to a man.

13   We sympathize even with the dead, and overlooking what is of real importance in their situation, that awful futurity which awaits them, we are chiefly affected by those circumstances which strike our senses, but can have no influence upon their happiness. It is miserable, we think, to be deprived of the light of the sun; to be shut out from life and conversation; to be laid in the cold grave, a prey to corruption and the reptiles of the earth; to be no more thought of in this world, but to be obliterated, in a little time, from the affections, and almost from the memory, of their dearest friends and relations. Surely, we imagine, we can never feel too much for

ᵃ⁻ᵃ *1–5* wretchedness, *6 7*   ᵇ⁻ᵇ *1–5* which, *6 7*

those who have suffered so dreadful a calamity. The tribute of our fellow-feeling seems doubly due to them now, when they are in danger of being forgot by every body; and, by the vain honours which we pay to their memory, we endeavour, for our own misery, artificially to keep alive our melancholy remembrance of their misfortune. That our sympathy can afford them no consolation seems to be an addition to their calamity; and to think that all we can do is unavailing, and that, what alleviates all other distress, the regret, the love, and the lamentations of their friends, can yield no comfort to them, serves only to exasperate our sense of their misery. The happiness of the dead, however, most assuredly, is affected by none of these circumstances; nor is it the thought of these things which can ever disturb the ᶜprofoundᶜ security of their repose. The idea of that dreary and endless melancholy, which the fancy naturally ascribes to their condition, arises altogether from our joining to the change which has been produced upon them, our own consciousness of that change, from our putting ourselves in their situation, and from our lodging, if I may be allowed to say so, our own living souls in their inanimated bodies, and thence conceiving what would be our emotions in this case. It is from this very illusion of the imagination, that the foresight of our own dissolution is so terrible to us, and that the idea of those circumstances, which undoubtedly can give us no pain when we are dead, makes us miserable while we are alive. And from thence arises one of the most important principles in human nature, the dread of death, the great poison to the happiness, but the great restraint upon the injustice of mankind, which, while it afflicts and mortifies the individual, guards and protects the society.

ᵃCHAP. II

Of the Pleasure of mutual Sympathy

1 BUT whatever may be the cause of sympathy, or however it may be excited, nothing pleases us more than to observe in other men a fellow-feeling with all the emotions of our own breast; nor are we ever so much shocked as by the appearance of the contrary. Those who are fond of deducing all our sentiments from certain refinements of self-love, think themselves at no loss to account, according to their own principles, both for this pleasure and this pain. Man, say they, conscious of his own weakness, and of the need which he has for the assistance of others, rejoices whenever he observes that they adopt his own passions, because he is then assured of that assistance; and grieves whenever he observes the contrary, because he

ᶜ⁻ᶜ *om. 1*

ᵃ *Chapters 2–5 form a separate Section in ed. 1.*

is then assured of their opposition.[1] But both the pleasure and the pain
are always felt so instantaneously, and often upon such frivolous occasions,
that it seems evident that neither of them can be derived from any such
self-interested consideration. A man is mortified when, after having endeavoured to divert the company, he looks round and sees that nobody
laughs at his jests but himself. On the contrary, the mirth of the company
is highly agreeable to him, and he regards this correspondence of their
sentiments with his own as the greatest applause.

2   Neither does his pleasure seem to arise altogether from the additional
vivacity which his mirth may receive from sympathy with theirs, nor his
pain from the disappointment he meets with when he misses this pleasure;
though both the one and the other, no doubt, do in some measure. When
we have read a book or poem so often that we can no longer find any amusement in reading it by ourselves, we can still take pleasure in reading it to a
companion. To him it has all the graces of novelty; we enter into the surprise and admiration which it naturally excites in him, but which it is no
longer capable of exciting in us; we consider all the ideas which it presents
rather in the light in which they appear to him, than in that in which they
appear to ourselves, and we are amused by sympathy with his amusement
which thus enlivens our own. On the contrary, we should be vexed if he
did not seem to be entertained with it, and we could no longer take any
pleasure in reading it to him. It is the same case here. The mirth of the
company, no doubt, enlivens our own mirth, and their silence, no doubt,
disappoints us. But though this may contribute both to the pleasure which
we derive from the one, and to the pain which we feel from the other, it is
by no means the sole cause of either; and this correspondence of the
sentiments of others with our own appears to be a cause of pleasure, and
the want of it a cause of pain, which cannot be accounted for in this manner.
The sympathy, which my friends express with my joy, might, indeed, give
me pleasure by enlivening that joy: but that which they express with my
grief could give me none, if it served only to enliven that grief. Sympathy,
however, enlivens joy and alleviates grief. It enlivens joy by presenting
another source of satisfaction; and it alleviates grief by insinuating into the
heart almost the only agreeable sensation which it is at that time capable
of receiving.

[1] Smith presumably has Hobbes and Mandeville in mind as the leading exponents of
the view that all sentiments depend on self-love, but in fact neither of them gives this, or
any, account of the pleasure and pain felt on observing sympathy and antipathy. Smith
may simply be making a reasonable conjecture of what an egoistic theorist would say.
It is also possible that, as in I.iii.1.1 below, he is misremembering a passage in Joseph
Butler, *Fifteen Sermons*, v, para. 2 (D. D. Raphael, *British Moralists 1650–1800*, § 412),
where compassion as a distinct feeling is explained by connecting it with the want of
assistance. Butler's explanation is of course not given from an egoistic standpoint, but it
follows a lengthy and penetrating criticism of Hobbes's egoistic account of pity, so that
Smith might in memory have confused Butler's own account with that of Hobbes.

3   It is to be observed accordingly, that we are still more anxious to communicate to our friends our disagreeable than our agreeable passions, that we derive still more satisfaction from their sympathy with the former than from that with the latter, and that we are still more shocked by the want of it.

4   How are the unfortunate relieved when they have found out a person to whom they can communicate the cause of their sorrow? Upon his sympathy they seem to disburthen themselves of a part of their distress: he is not improperly said to share it with them. He not only feels a sorrow of the same kind with that which they feel, but as if he had derived a part of it to himself, what he feels seems to alleviate the weight of what they feel. Yet by relating their misfortunes they in some measure renew their grief. They awaken in their memory the remembrance of those circumstances which *b*occasioned*b* their affliction. Their tears accordingly flow faster than before, and they are apt to abandon themselves to all the weakness of sorrow. They take pleasure, however, in all this, and, it is evident, are sensibly relieved by it; because the sweetness of his sympathy more than compensates the bitterness of that sorrow, which, in order to excite this sympathy, they had thus enlivened and renewed. The cruelest insult, on the contrary, which can be offered to the unfortunate, is to appear to make light of their calamities. To seem not to be affected with the joy of our companions is but want of politeness; but not to wear a serious countenance when they tell us their afflictions, is real and gross inhumanity.

5   Love is an agreeable; resentment, a disagreeable passion; and accordingly we are not half so anxious that our friends should adopt our friendships, as that they should enter into our resentments. We can forgive them though they seem to be little affected with the favours which we may have received, but lose all patience if they seem indifferent about the injuries which may have been done to us: nor are we half so angry with them for not entering into our gratitude, as for not sympathizing with our resentment. They can easily avoid being friends to our friends, but can hardly avoid being enemies to those with whom we are at variance. We seldom resent their being at enmity with the first, though upon that account we may sometimes affect to make an awkward quarrel with them; but we quarrel with them in good earnest if they live in friendship with the last. The agreeable passions of love and joy can satisfy and support the heart without any auxiliary pleasure. The bitter and painful emotions of grief and resentment more strongly require the healing consolation of sympathy.

6   As the person who is principally interested in any event is pleased with our sympathy, and hurt by the want of it, so we, too, seem to be pleased when we are able to sympathize with him, and to be hurt when we are unable to do so. We run not only to congratulate the successful, but to condole

b-b *1 2E* occasion 2–7

with the afflicted; and the pleasure which we find in the conversation of one whom in all the passions of his heart we can entirely sympathize with, seems to do more than compensate the painfulness of that sorrow with which the view of his situation affects us. On the contrary, it is always disagreeable to feel that we cannot sympathize with him, and instead of being pleased with this exemption from sympathetic pain, it hurts us to find that we cannot share his uneasiness. If we hear a person loudly lamenting his misfortunes, ᶜwhich,ᶜ however, upon bringing the case home to ourselves, we feel, can produce no such violent effect upon us, we are shocked at his grief; and, because we cannot enter into it, call it pusillanimity and weakness. It gives us the spleen, on the other hand, to see another too happy or too much elevated, as we call it, with any little piece of good fortune. We are disobliged even with his joy; and, because we cannot go along with it, call it levity and folly. We are even put out of humour if our companion laughs louder or longer at a joke than we think it deserves; that is, than we feel that we ourselves could laugh at it.

CHAP. III

Of the manner in which we judge of the propriety or impropriety of the affections of other men, by their concord or dissonance with our own

1 WHEN the original passions of the person principally concerned are in perfect concord with the sympathetic emotions of the spectator, they necessarily appear to this last just and proper, and suitable to their objects; and, on the contrary, when, upon bringing the case home to himself, he finds that they do not coincide with what he feels, they necessarily appear to him unjust and improper, and unsuitable to the causes which excite them. To approve of the passions of another, therefore, as suitable to their objects, is the same thing as to observe that we entirely sympathize with them; and not to approve of them as such, is the same thing as to observe that we do not entirely sympathize with them. The man who resents the injuries that have been done to me, and observes that I resent them precisely as he does, necessarily approves of my resentment. The man whose sympathy keeps time to my grief, cannot but admit the reasonableness of my sorrow. He who admires the same poem, or the same picture, and admires them exactly as I do, must surely allow the justness of my admiration. He who laughs at the same joke, and laughs along with me, cannot well deny the propriety of my laughter. On the contrary, the person who, upon these different occasions, either feels no such emotion as that which I feel, or feels none that bears any proportion to mine, cannot avoid disapproving my sentiments on account of their dissonance with his own. If my animosity goes

ᶜ⁻ᶜ *1-5* ~ₐ *6 7*

beyond what the indignation of my friend can correspond to; if my grief exceeds what his most tender compassion can go along with; if my admiration is either too high or too low to tally with his own; if I laugh loud and heartily when he only smiles, or, on the contrary, only smile when he laughs loud and heartily; in all these cases, as soon as he comes from considering the object, to observe how I am affected by it, according as there is more or less disproportion between his sentiments and mine, I must incur a greater or less degree of his disapprobation: and upon all occasions his own sentiments are the standards and measures by which he judges of mine.

2   To approve of another man's opinions is to adopt those opinions, and to adopt them is to approve of them. If the same arguments which convince you convince me likewise, I necessarily approve of your conviction; and if they do not, I necessarily disapprove of it: neither can I possibly conceive that I should do the one without the other. To approve or disapprove, therefore, of the opinions of others is acknowledged, by every body, to mean no more than to observe their agreement or disagreement with our own. But this is equally the case with regard to our approbation or disapprobation of the sentiments or passions of others.

3   There are, indeed, some cases in which we seem to approve without any sympathy or correspondence of sentiments, and in which, consequently, the sentiment of approbation would seem to be different from the perception of this coincidence. A little attention, however, will convince us that even in these cases our approbation is ultimately founded upon a sympathy or correspondence of this kind. I shall give an instance in things of a very frivolous nature, because in them the judgments of mankind are less apt to be perverted by wrong systems. We may often approve of a jest, and think the laughter of the company quite just and proper, though we ourselves do not laugh, because, perhaps, we are in a grave humour, or happen to have our attention engaged with other objects. We have learned, however, from experience, what sort of pleasantry is upon most occasions capable of making us laugh, and we observe that this is one of that kind. We approve, therefore, of the laughter of the company, and feel that it is natural and suitable to its object; because, though in our present mood we cannot easily enter into it, we are sensible that upon most occasions we should very heartily join in it.

4   The same thing often happens with regard to all the other passions. A stranger passes by us in the street with all the marks of the deepest affliction; and we are immediately told that he has just received the news of the death of his father. It is impossible that, in this case, we should not approve of his grief. Yet it may often happen, without any defect of humanity on our part, that, so far from entering into the violence of his sorrow, we should scarce conceive the first movements of concern upon his account.

Both he and his father, perhaps, are entirely unknown to us, or we happen to be employed about other things, and do not take time to picture out in our imagination the different circumstances of distress which must occur to him. We have learned, however, from experience, that such a misfortune naturally excites such a degree of sorrow, and we know that if we took time to consider his situation, fully and in all its parts, we should, without doubt, most sincerely sympathize with him. It is upon the consciousness of this conditional sympathy, that our approbation of his sorrow is founded, even in those cases in which that sympathy does not actually take place; and the general rules derived from our preceding experience of what our sentiments would commonly correspond with, correct upon this, as upon many other occasions, the impropriety of our present emotions.

5 The sentiment or affection of the heart from which any action proceeds, and upon which its whole virtue or vice must ultimately depend, may be considered under two different aspects, or in two different relations; first, in relation to the cause which excites it, or the motive which gives occasion to it; and secondly, in relation to the end which it proposes, or the effect which it tends to produce.

6 In the suitableness or unsuitableness, in the proportion or disproportion which the affection seems to bear to the cause or object which excites it, consists the propriety or impropriety, the decency or ungracefulness of the consequent action.

7 In the beneficial or hurtful nature of the effects which the affection aims at, or tends to produce, consists the merit or demerit of the action, the qualities by which it is entitled to reward, or is deserving of punishment.

8 Philosophers have, of late years, considered chiefly the tendency of affections, and have given little attention to the relation which they stand in to the cause which excites them. In common life, however, when we judge of any person's conduct, and of the sentiments which directed it, we constantly consider them under both these aspects. When we blame in another man the excesses of love, of grief, of resentment, we not only consider the ruinous effects which they tend to produce, but the little occasion which was given for them. The merit of his favourite, we say, is not so great, his misfortune is not so dreadful, his provocation is not so extraordinary, as to justify so violent a passion. We should have indulged, we say; perhaps, have approved of the violence of his emotion, had the cause been in any respect proportioned to it.

9 When we judge in this manner of any affection, as proportioned or disproportioned to the cause which excites it, it is scarce possible that we should make use of any other rule or canon but the correspondent affection in ourselves. If, upon bringing the case home to our own breast, we find that the sentiments which it gives occasion to, coincide and tally with

our own, we necessarily approve of them as proportioned and suitable to their objects; if otherwise, we necessarily disapprove of them, as extravagant and out of proportion.

10 Every faculty in one man is the measure by which he judges of the like faculty in another. I judge of your sight by my sight, of your ear by my ear, of your reason by my reason, of your resentment by my resentment, of your love by my love. I neither have, nor can have, any other way of judging about them.

CHAP. IV

The same subject continued

1 WE may judge of the propriety or impropriety of the sentiments of another person by their correspondence or disagreement with our own, upon two different occasions; either, first, when the objects which excite them are considered without any peculiar relation, either to ourselves or to the person whose sentiments we judge of; or, secondly, when they are considered as peculiarly affecting one or other of us.

2 1. With regard to those objects which are considered without any peculiar relation either to ourselves or to the person whose sentiments we judge of; wherever his sentiments entirely correspond with our own, we ascribe to him the qualities of taste and good judgment. The beauty of a plain, the greatness of a mountain, the ornaments of a building, the expression of a picture, the composition of a discourse, the conduct of a third person, the proportions of different quantities and numbers, the various appearances which the great machine of the universe is perpetually exhibiting, with the secret wheels and springs which produce them; all the general subjects of science and taste, are what we and our *a*companion*a* regard as having no peculiar relation to either of us. We both look at them from the same point of view, and we have no occasion for sympathy, or for that imaginary change of situations from which it arises, in order to produce, with regard to these, the most perfect harmony of sentiments and affections. If, notwithstanding, we are often differently affected, it arises either from the different degrees of attention, which our different habits of life allow us to give easily to the several parts of those complex objects, or from the different degrees of natural acuteness in the faculty of the mind to which they are addressed.

3 When the sentiments of our companion coincide with our own in things of this kind, which are obvious and easy, and in which, perhaps, we never

a-a 1 companions 2–7 *The singular form is supported by other phrases in the context and especially by* our companion *at the beginning of § 3.*

found a single person who differed from us, though we, no doubt, must approve of them, yet he seems to deserve no praise or admiration on account of them. But when they not only coincide with our own, but lead and direct our own; when in forming them he appears to have attended to many things which we had overlooked, and to have adjusted them to all the various circumstances of their objects; we not only approve of them, but wonder and are surprised at their uncommon and unexpected acuteness and comprehensiveness, and he appears to deserve a very high degree of admiration and applause. For approbation heightened by wonder and surprise, constitutes the sentiment which is properly called admiration,[1] and of which applause is the natural expression. The decision of the man who judges that exquisite beauty is preferable to the grossest deformity, or that twice two are equal to four, must certainly be approved of by all the world, but will not, surely, be much admired. It is the acute and delicate discernment of the man of taste, who distinguishes the minute, and scarce perceptible differences of beauty and deformity; it is the comprehensive accuracy of the experienced mathematician, who unravels, with ease, the most intricate and perplexed proportions; it is the great leader in science and taste, the man who directs and conducts our own sentiments, the extent and superior justness of whose talents astonish us with wonder and surprise, who excites our admiration, and seems to deserve our applause: and upon this foundation is grounded the greater part of the praise which is bestowed upon what are called the intellectual virtues.

4   The utility of those qualities, it may be thought,[2] is what first recommends them to us; and, no doubt, the consideration of this, when we come to attend to it, gives them a new value. Originally, however, we approve of another man's judgment, not as something useful, but as right, as accurate, as agreeable to truth and reality: and it is evident we attribute those qualities to it for no other reason but because we find that it agrees with our own. Taste, in the same manner, is originally approved of, not as useful, but as just, as delicate, and as precisely suited to its object. The idea of the utility of all qualities of this kind, is plainly an after-thought, and not what first recommends them to our approbation.

5   2. With regard to those objects, which affect in a particular manner either ourselves or the person whose sentiments we judge of, it is at once more difficult to preserve this harmony and correspondence, and at the same time, vastly more important. My companion does not naturally

---

[1] In Astronomy, intro. 1, probably written earlier than TMS, Smith regards admiration as distinct from wonder and surprise. 'What is new and singular, excites that sentiment which, in strict propriety, is called Wonder; what is unexpected, Surprise; and what is great or beautiful, Admiration.' He goes on to say that we can admire what is neither novel nor unexpected, implying that admiration can exist apart from wonder and surprise.

[2] Smith has Hume in mind. Cf. IV.2.3–7, where § 3 refers directly to Hume and § 7 refers back to the present passage.

look upon the misfortune that has befallen me, or the injury that has been done me, from the same point of view in which I consider them. They affect me much more nearly. We do not view them from the same station, as we do a picture, or a poem, or a system of philosophy, and are, therefore, apt to be very differently affected by them. But I can much more easily overlook the want of this correspondence of sentiments with regard to such indifferent objects as concern neither me nor my companion, than with regard to what interests me so much as the misfortune that has befallen me, or the injury that has been done me. Though you despise that picture, or that poem, or even that system of philosophy, which I admire, there is little danger of our quarrelling upon that account. Neither of us can reasonably be much interested about them. They ought all of them to be matters of great indifference to us both; so that, though our opinions may be opposite, our affections may still be very nearly the same. But it is quite otherwise with regard to those objects by which either you or I are particularly affected. Though your judgments in matters of speculation, though your sentiments in matters of taste, are quite opposite to mine, I can easily overlook this opposition; and if I have any degree of temper, I may still find some entertainment in your conversation, even upon those very subjects. But if you have either no fellow-feeling for the misfortunes I have met with, or none that bears any proportion to the grief which distracts me; or if you have either no indignation at the injuries I have suffered, or none that bears any proportion to the resentment which transports me, we can no longer converse upon these subjects. We become intolerable to one another. I can neither support your company, nor you mine. You are confounded at my violence and passion, and I am enraged at your cold insensibility and want of feeling.

6   In all such cases, that there may be some correspondence of sentiments between the spectator and the person principally concerned, the spectator must, first of all, endeavour, as much as he can, to put himself in the situation of the other, and to bring home to himself every little circumstance of distress which can possibly occur to the sufferer. He must adopt the whole case of his companion with all its minutest incidents; and strive to render as perfect as possible, that imaginary change of situation upon which his sympathy is founded.

7   After all this, however, the emotions of the spectator will still be very apt to fall short of the violence of what is felt by the sufferer. Mankind, though naturally sympathetic, never conceive, for what has befallen another, that degree of passion which naturally animates the person principally concerned. That imaginary change of situation, upon which their sympathy is founded, is but momentary. The thought of their own safety, the thought that they themselves are not really the sufferers, continually intrudes itself upon them; and though it does not hinder them from con-

ceiving a passion somewhat analogous to what is felt by the sufferer, hinders them from conceiving any thing that approaches to the same degree of violence. The person principally concerned is sensible of this, and at the same time passionately desires a more complete sympathy. He longs for that relief which nothing can afford him but the entire concord of the affections of the spectators with his own. To see the emotions of their hearts, in every respect, beat time to his own, in the violent and disagreeable passions, constitutes his sole consolation. But he can only hope to obtain this by lowering his passion to that pitch, in which the spectators are capable of going along with him. He must flatten, if I may be allowed to say so, the sharpness of its natural tone, in order to reduce it to harmony and concord with the emotions of those who are about him. What they feel, will, indeed, always be, in some respects, different from what he feels, and compassion can never be exactly the same with original sorrow; because the secret consciousness that the change of situations, from which the sympathetic sentiment arises, is but imaginary, not only lowers it in degree, but, in some measure, varies it in kind, and gives it a quite different modification. These two sentiments, however, may, it is evident, have such a correspondence with one another, as is sufficient for the harmony of society. Though they will never be unisons, they may be concords, and this is all that is wanted or required.

8   In order to produce this concord, as nature teaches the spectators to assume the circumstances of the person principally concerned, so she teaches this last in some measure to assume those of the spectators. As they are continually placing themselves in his situation, and thence conceiving emotions similar to what he feels; so he is as constantly placing himself in theirs, and thence conceiving some degree of that coolness about his own fortune, with which he is sensible that they will view it. As they are constantly considering what they themselves would feel, if they actually were the sufferers, so he is as constantly led to imagine in what manner he would be affected if he was only one of the spectators of his own situation. As their sympathy makes them look at it, in some measure, with his eyes, so his sympathy makes him look at it, in some measure, with theirs, especially when in their presence and acting under their observation: and as the reflected passion, which he thus conceives, is much weaker than the original one, it necessarily abates the violence of what he felt before he came into their presence, before he began to recollect in what manner they would be affected by it, and to view his situation in this candid and impartial light.

9   The mind, therefore, is rarely so disturbed, but that the company of a friend will restore it to some degree of tranquillity and sedateness. The breast is, in some measure, calmed and composed the moment we come into his presence. We are immediately put in mind of the light in which he will

view our situation, and we begin to view it ourselves in the same light; for the effect of sympathy is instantaneous. We expect less sympathy from a common acquaintance than from a friend: we cannot open to the former all those little circumstances which we can unfold to the latter: we assume, therefore, more tranquillity before him, and endeavour to fix our thoughts upon those general outlines of our situation which he is willing to consider. We expect still less sympathy from an assembly of strangers, and we assume, therefore, still more tranquillity before them, and always endeavour to bring down our passion to that pitch, which the particular company we are in may be expected to go along with. Nor is this only an assumed appearance: for if we are at all masters of ourselves, the presence of a mere acquaintance will really compose us, still more than that of a friend; and that of an assembly of strangers still more than that of an acquaintance.

10   Society and conversation, therefore, are the most powerful remedies for restoring the mind to its tranquillity, if, at any time, it has unfortunately lost it; as well as the best preservatives of that equal and happy temper, which is so necessary to self-satisfaction and enjoyment. Men of retirement and speculation, who are apt to sit brooding at home over either grief or resentment, though they may often have more humanity, more generosity, and a nicer sense of honour, yet seldom possess that equality of temper which is so common among men of the world.

CHAP. V

Of the amiable and respectable virtues

1   UPON these two different efforts, upon that of the spectator to enter into the sentiments of the person principally concerned, and upon that of the person principally concerned, to bring down his emotions to what the spectator can go along with, are founded two different sets of virtues. The soft, the gentle, the amiable virtues, the virtues of candid condescension and indulgent humanity, are founded upon the one: the great, the awful and respectable, the virtues of self-denial, of self-government, of that command of the passions which subjects all the movements of our nature to what our own dignity and honour, and the propriety of our own conduct require, take their origin from the other.[1]

[1] Smith's distinction between the 'amiable' and the 'awful' or 'respectable' virtues is influenced, at least in the words used, by some remarks of Hume: 'The characters of *Caesar* and *Cato*, as drawn by *Sallust*, are both of them virtuous, in the strictest sense of the word; but in a different way: Nor are the sentiments entirely the same, which arise from them. The one produces love; the other esteem: The one is amiable; the other awful: We cou'd wish to meet with the one character in a friend; the other character we wou'd be ambitious of in ourselves.' (*Treatise of Human Nature*, III.iii.4; ed. L. A. Selby-Bigge,

2   How amiable does he appear to be, whose sympathetic heart seems to re-echo all the sentiments of those with whom he converses, who grieves for their calamities, who resents their injuries, and who rejoices at their good fortune! When we bring home to ourselves the situation of his companions, we enter into their gratitude, and feel what consolation they must derive from the tender sympathy of so affectionate a friend. And for a contrary reason, how disagreeable does he appear to be, whose hard and obdurate heart feels for himself only, but is altogether insensible to the happiness or misery of others! We enter, in this case too, into the pain which his presence must give to every mortal with whom he converses, to those especially with whom we are most apt to sympathize, the unfortunate and the injured.

3   On the other hand, what noble propriety and grace do we feel in the conduct of those who, in their own case, exert that recollection and self-command which constitute the dignity of every passion, and which bring it down to what others can enter *into!*ᵃ We are disgusted with that clamorous grief, which, without any delicacy, calls upon our compassion with sighs and tears and importunate lamentations. But we reverence that reserved, that silent and majestic sorrow, which discovers itself only in the swelling of the eyes, in the quivering of the lips and cheeks, and in the distant, but affecting, coldness of the whole behaviour. It imposes the like silence upon us. We regard it with respectful attention, and watch with anxious concern over our whole behaviour, lest by any impropriety we should disturb that concerted tranquillity, which it requires so great an effort to support.

4   The insolence and brutality of anger, in the same ᵇmanner,ᵇ when we indulge its fury without check or restraint, is, of all objects, the most detestable. But we admire that noble and generous resentment which governs its pursuit of the greatest injuries, not by the rage which they are apt to excite in the breast of the sufferer, but by the indignation which they naturally call forth in that of the impartial spectator; which allows no word, no gesture, to escape it beyond what this more equitable sentiment would dictate; which never, even in thought, attempts any greater vengeance, nor desires to inflict any greater punishment, than what every indifferent person would rejoice to see executed.

ᵃ⁻ᵃ *5*   ~. *1–3*   ~? *4 6 7*   *The exclamation mark of ed. 5, which produces consistency with the preceding paragraph, was overlooked when ed. 6 was prepared from a copy of ed. 4.*
  ᵇ⁻ᵇ *1–3*   ~^ *4–7*

607–8. Cf. *Enquiry concerning the Principles of Morals*, appendix iv; ed. Selby-Bigge, § 265.) The distinction is, however, far more important for Smith than for Hume. Smith gives the second type of virtue an equal place with benevolence or humanity in constituting human perfection and sets 'the great precept of nature' on a par with 'the great law of Christianity' (§ 5 below); he combines the Christian ethic of love with the Stoic ethic of self-command. This feature of Smith's moral philosophy marks a striking divergence from the position of Hutcheson and Hume.

5   And hence it is, that to feel much for others and little for ourselves, that to restrain our selfish, and to indulge our benevolent affections, constitutes the perfection of human nature; and can alone produce among mankind that harmony of sentiments and passions in which consists their whole grace and propriety. As to love our neighbour as we love ourselves is the great law of Christianity, so it is the great precept of nature to love ourselves only as we love our neighbour, or what comes to the same thing, as our neighbour is capable of loving us.

6   As taste and good judgment, when they are considered as qualities which deserve praise and admiration, are supposed to imply a delicacy of sentiment and an acuteness of understanding not commonly to be met with; so the virtues of sensibility and self-command are not apprehended to consist in the ordinary, but in the uncommon degrees of those qualities. The amiable virtue of humanity requires, surely, a sensibility, much beyond what is possessed by the rude vulgar of mankind. The great and exalted virtue of magnanimity undoubtedly demands much more than that degree of self-command, which the weakest of mortals is capable of exerting. As in the common degree of the intellectual qualities, there is no abilities; so in the common degree of the moral, there is no virtue. Virtue is excellence, something uncommonly great and beautiful, which rises far above what is vulgar and ordinary. The amiable virtues consist in that degree of sensibility which surprises by its exquisite and unexpected delicacy and tenderness. The awful and respectable, in that degree of self-command which astonishes by its amazing superiority over the most ungovernable passions of human nature.

7   There is, in this respect, a considerable difference between virtue and mere propriety; between those qualities and actions which deserve to be admired and celebrated, and those which simply deserve to be approved of. Upon many occasions, to act with the most perfect propriety, requires no more than that common and ordinary degree of sensibility or self-command which the most worthless of mankind are possest of, and sometimes even that degree is not necessary. Thus, to give a very low instance, to eat when we are hungry, is certainly, upon ordinary occasions, perfectly right and proper, and cannot miss being approved of as such by every body. Nothing, however, could be more absurd than to say it was virtuous.

8   On the contrary, there may frequently be a considerable degree of virtue in those actions which fall short of the most perfect propriety; because they may still approach nearer to perfection than could well be expected upon occasions in which it was so extremely difficult to attain it: and this is very often the case upon those occasions which require the greatest exertions of self-command. There are some situations which bear so hard upon human nature, that the greatest degree of self-government, which can belong to so imperfect a creature as man, is not able to stifle, altogether,

the voice of human weakness, or reduce the violence of the passions to that pitch of moderation, in which the impartial spectator can entirely enter into them. Though in those cases, therefore, the behaviour of the sufferer fall short of the most perfect propriety, it may still deserve some applause, and even in a certain sense, may be denominated virtuous. It may still manifest an effort of generosity and magnanimity of which the greater part of men are incapable; and though it fails of absolute perfection, it may be a much nearer approximation towards perfection, than what, upon such trying occasions, is commonly either to be found or to be expected.

9   In cases of this kind, when we are determining the degree of blame or applause which seems due to any action, we very frequently make use of two different standards. The first is the idea of complete propriety and perfection, which, in those difficult situations, no human conduct ever did, or ever can come up to; and in comparison with which the actions of all men must for ever appear blameable and imperfect. The second is the idea of that degree of proximity or distance from this complete perfection, which the actions of the greater part of men commonly arrive at. Whatever goes beyond this degree, how far soever it may be removed from absolute perfection, seems to deserve applause; and whatever falls short of it, to deserve blame.

10   It is in the same manner that we judge of the productions of all the arts which address themselves to the imagination. When a critic examines the work of any of the great masters in poetry or painting, he may sometimes examine it by an idea of perfection, in his own mind, which neither that nor any other human work will ever come up to; and as long as he compares it with this standard, he can see nothing in it but faults and imperfections. But when he comes to consider the rank which it ought to hold among other works of the same kind, he necessarily compares it with a very different standard, the common degree of excellence which is usually attained in this particular art; and when he judges of it by this new measure, it may often appear to deserve the highest applause, upon account of its approaching much nearer to perfection than the greater part of those works which can be brought into competition with it.

SECTION II
Of the Degrees of the different Passions which are consistent with Propriety

INTRODUCTION

1 THE propriety of every passion excited by objects peculiarly related to ourselves, the pitch which the spectator can go along with, must lie, it is evident, in a certain mediocrity. If the passion is too high, or if it is too low, he cannot enter into it. Grief and resentment for private misfortunes and injuries may easily, for example, be too high, and in the greater part of mankind they are so. They may likewise, though this more rarely happens, be too low. We denominate the excess, weakness and fury: and we call the defect stupidity, insensibility, and want of spirit. We can enter into neither of them, but are astonished and confounded to see them.

2 This mediocrity, however, in which the point of propriety consists, is different in different passions. It is high in some, and low in others. There are some passions which it is indecent to express very strongly, even upon those occasions, in which it is acknowledged that we cannot avoid feeling them in the highest degree. And there are others of which the strongest expressions are upon many occasions extremely graceful, even though the passions themselves do not, perhaps, arise so necessarily. The first are those passions with which, for certain reasons, there is little or no sympathy: the second are those with which, for other reasons, there is the greatest. And if we consider all the different passions of human nature, we shall find that they are regarded as decent, or indecent, just in proportion as mankind are more or less disposed to sympathize with them.

CHAP. I
Of the Passions which take their origin from the body

1 1. IT is indecent to express any strong degree of those passions which arise from a certain situation or disposition of the body; because the company, not being in the same disposition, cannot be expected to sympathize with them. Violent hunger, for example, though upon many occasions not only natural, but unavoidable, is always indecent, and to eat voraciously is universally regarded as a piece of ill manners. There is, however, some degree of sympathy, even with hunger. It is agreeable to see our companions eat with a good appetite, and all expressions of loathing are offensive. The disposition of body which is habitual to a man in health, makes his stomach easily keep time, if I may be allowed so coarse an expression,

with the one, and not with the other. We can sympathize with the distress which excessive hunger occasions when we read the description of it in the journal of a siege, or of a sea voyage. We imagine ourselves in the situation of the sufferers, and thence readily conceive the grief, the fear and consternation, which must necessarily distract them. We feel, ourselves, some degree of those passions, and therefore sympathize with them: but as we do not grow hungry by reading the description, we cannot properly, even in this case, be said to sympathize with their hunger.

2   It is the same case with the passion by which Nature unites the two sexes. Though naturally the most furious of all the passions, all strong expressions of it are upon every occasion indecent, even between persons in whom its most complete indulgence is acknowledged by all laws, both human and divine, to be perfectly innocent. There seems, however, to be some degree of sympathy even with this passion. To talk to a woman as we *would* to a man is improper: it is expected that their company should inspire us with more gaiety, more pleasantry, and more attention; and an intire insensibility to the fair sex, renders a man contemptible in some measure even to the men.

3   Such is our aversion for all the appetites which take their origin from the body: all strong expressions of them are loathsome and disagreeable. According to some ancient philosophers, these are the passions which we share in common with the brutes, and which having no connexion with the characteristical qualities of human nature, are upon that account beneath its dignity. But there are many other passions which we share in common with the brutes, such as resentment, natural affection, even gratitude, which do not, upon that account, appear to be so brutal. The true cause of the peculiar disgust which we conceive for the appetites of the body when we see them in other men, is that we cannot enter into them. To the person himself who feels them, as soon as they are gratified, the object that excited them ceases to be agreeable: even its presence often becomes offensive to him; he looks round to no purpose for the charm which transported him the moment before, and he can now as little enter into his own passion as another person. When we have dined, we order the covers to be removed; and we should treat in the same manner the objects of the most ardent and passionate desires, if they were the objects of no other passions but those which take their origin from the body.

4   In the command of those appetites of the body consists that virtue which is properly called temperance. To restrain them within those bounds, which regard to health and fortune prescribes, is the part of prudence. But to confine them within those limits, which grace, which propriety, which delicacy, and modesty, require, is the office of temperance.

a-a *1E* should *1-7*

5   2. It is for the same reason that to cry out with bodily pain, how intolerable soever, appears always unmanly and unbecoming. There is, however, a good deal of sympathy even with bodily pain. If, as has already
been observed,[1] I see a stroke aimed, and just ready to fall upon the leg,
or arm, of another person, I naturally shrink and draw back my own leg,
or my own arm: and when it does fall, I feel it in some measure, and am
hurt by it as well as the sufferer. My hurt, however, is, no doubt, excessively slight, and, upon that account, if he makes any violent out-cry, as I
cannot go along with him, I never fail to despise him. And this is the case
of all the passions which take their origin from the body: they excite either
no sympathy at all, or such a degree of it, as is altogether disproportioned to
the violence of what is felt by the sufferer.

6   It is quite otherwise with those passions which take their origin from
the imagination. The frame of my body can be but little affected by the
alterations which are brought about upon that of my companion: but my
imagination is more ductile, and more readily assumes, if I may say so,
the shape and configuration of the imaginations of those with whom I am
familiar. A disappointment in love, or ambition, will, upon this account, call
forth more sympathy than the greatest bodily evil. Those passions arise
altogether from the imagination. The person who has lost his whole
fortune, if he is in health, feels nothing in his body. What he suffers is from
the imagination only, which represents to him the loss of his dignity,
neglect from his friends, contempt from his enemies, dependance, want,
and misery, coming fast upon him; and we sympathize with him more
strongly upon this account, because our imaginations can more readily
mould themselves upon his imagination, than our bodies can mould themselves upon his body.

7   The loss of a leg may generally be regarded as a more real calamity than
the loss of a mistress. It would be a ridiculous tragedy, however, of which
the catastrophe was to turn upon a loss of that kind. A misfortune of the
other kind, how frivolous soever it may appear to be, has given occasion
to many a fine one.

8   Nothing is so soon forgot as pain. The moment it is gone the whole
agony of it is over, and the thought of it can no longer give us any sort of
disturbance. We ourselves cannot then enter into the anxiety and anguish
which we had before conceived. An unguarded word from a friend will
occasion a more durable uneasiness. The agony which this creates is by
no means over with the word. What at first disturbs us is not the object
of the senses, but the idea of the imagination. As it is an idea, therefore,
which occasions our uneasiness, till time and other accidents have in some
measure effaced it from our memory, the imagination continues to fret
and rankle within, from the thought of it.

[1] I.i.1.3

9   Pain never calls forth any very lively sympathy unless it is accompanied with danger. We sympathize with the fear, though not with the agony of the sufferer. Fear, however, is a passion derived altogether from the imagination, which represents, with an uncertainty and fluctuation that increases our anxiety, not what we really feel, but what we may hereafter possibly suffer. The gout or the tooth-ach, though exquisitely painful, excite very little sympathy; more dangerous diseases, though accompanied with very little pain, excite the highest.

10   Some people faint and grow sick at the sight of a chirurgical operation, and that bodily pain which is occasioned by tearing the flesh, seems, in them, to excite the most excessive sympathy. We conceive in a much more lively and distinct manner the pain which proceeds from an external cause, than we do that which arises from an internal disorder. I can scarce form an idea of the agonies of my neighbour when he is tortured with the gout, or the stone; but I have the clearest conception of what he must suffer from an incision, a wound, or a fracture. The chief cause, however, why such objects produce such violent effects upon us, is their novelty. One who has been witness to a dozen dissections, and as many amputations, sees, ever after, all operations of this kind with great indifference, and often with perfect insensibility. Though we have read or seen represented more than five hundred tragedies, we shall seldom feel so entire an abatement of our sensibility to the objects which they represent to us.

11   In some of the Greek tragedies there is an attempt to excite compassion, by the representation of the agonies of bodily pain. Philoctetes[2] cries out and faints from the extremity of his sufferings. Hippolytus[3] and Hercules[4] are both introduced as expiring under the severest tortures, which, it seems, even the fortitude of Hercules was incapable of supporting. In all these cases, however, it is not the pain which interests us, but some other circumstances. It is not the sore foot, but the solitude, of Philoctetes which affects us, and diffuses over that charming tragedy, that romantic wildness, which is so agreeable to the imagination. The agonies of Hercules and Hippolytus are interesting only because we foresee that death is to be the consequence. If those heroes were to recover, we should think the representation of their sufferings perfectly ridiculous. What a tragedy would that be of which the distress consisted in a colic! Yet no pain is more exquisite. These attempts to excite compassion by the representation of bodily pain, may be regarded as among the greatest breaches of decorum of which the Greek theatre has set the example.

12   The little sympathy which we feel with bodily pain is the foundation of the propriety of constancy and patience in enduring it. The man, who under the severest tortures allows no weakness to escape him, vents no groan, gives way to no passion which we do not entirely enter into, com-

---

[2] In Sophocles' *Philoctetes*.   [3] In Euripides' *Hippolytus*.   [4] In Sophocles' *Trachiniae*.

mands our highest admiration. His firmness enables him to keep time with
our indifference and insensibility. We admire and entirely go along with
the magnanimous effort which he makes for this purpose. We approve of
his behaviour, and from our experience of the common weakness of human
nature, we are surprised, and wonder how he should be able to act so as
to deserve approbation. Approbation, mixed and animated by wonder
and surprise, constitutes the sentiment which is properly called admiration, of which, applause is the natural expression, as has already been
observed.[5]

CHAP. II

*Of those Passions which take their origin from a particular turn or habit of the
Imagination*

1 EVEN of the passions derived from the imagination, those which take their
origin from a peculiar turn or habit it has acquired, though they may be
acknowledged to be perfectly natural, are, however, but little sympathized
with. The imaginations of mankind, not having acquired that particular
turn, cannot enter into them; and such passions, though they may be allowed to be almost unavoidable in some part of life, are always, in some
measure, ridiculous. This is the case with that strong attachment which
naturally grows up between two persons of different sexes, who have long
fixed their thoughts upon one another. Our imagination not having run
in the same channel with that of the lover, we cannot enter into the
eagerness of his emotions. If our friend has been injured, we readily
sympathize with his resentment, and grow angry with the very person with
whom he is angry. If he has received a benefit, we readily enter into his
gratitude, and have a very high sense of the merit of his benefactor. But if
he is in love, though we may think his passion just as reasonable as any of
the kind, yet we never think ourselves bound to conceive a passion of the
same kind, and for the same person for whom he has conceived it. The
passion appears to every body, but the man who feels it, entirely disproportioned to the value of the object; and love, though it is pardoned in a
certain age because we know it is natural, is always laughed at, because we
cannot enter into it. All serious and strong expressions of it appear ridiculous to a third person; *a*and though a lover may be good company to
his mistress, he is so to nobody else.*a* He himself is sensible of this; and as
long as he continues in his sober senses, endeavours to treat his own passion with raillery and ridicule. It is the only style in which we care to hear

a-a and if the lover is not good company to his mistress, he is to no body else. *1-3* and
if the lover is not . . . he is so to no body else. *4 5*

----

[5] I.i.4.3

of it; because it is the only style in which we ourselves are disposed to talk of it. We grow weary of the grave, pedantic, and long-sentenced love of Cowley and ᵇPetrarca,ᵇ who never have done with exaggerating the violence of their attachments; but the gaiety of Ovid, and the gallantry of Horace, are always agreeable.

2   But though we feel no proper sympathy with an attachment of this kind, though we never approach even in imagination towards conceiving a passion for that particular person, yet as we either have conceived, or may be disposed to conceive, passions of the same kind, we readily enter into those high hopes of happiness which are proposed from its gratification, as well as into that exquisite distress which is feared from its disappointment. It interests us not as a passion, but as a situation that gives occasion to other passions which interest us; to hope, to fear, and to distress of every kind: in the same manner as in a description of a sea voyage, it is not the hunger which interests us, but the distress which that hunger occasions. Though we do not properly enter into the attachment of the lover, we readily go along with those expectations of romantic happiness which he derives from it. We feel how natural it is for the mind, in a certain situation, relaxed with indolence, and fatigued with the violence of desire, to long for serenity and quiet, to hope to find them in the gratification of that passion which distracts it, and to frame to itself the idea of that life of pastoral tranquillity and retirement which the elegant, the tender, and the passionate Tibullus takes so much pleasure in describing; a life like what the poets describe in the Fortunate Islands,[1] a life of friendship, liberty, and repose; free from labour, and from care, and from all the turbulent passions which attend them. Even scenes of this kind interest us most, when they are painted rather as what is hoped, than as what is enjoyed. The grossness of that passion, which mixes with, and is, perhaps, the foundation of love, disappears when its gratification is far off and at a distance; but renders the whole offensive, when described as what is immediately possessed. The happy passion, upon this account, interests us much less than the fearful and the melancholy. We tremble for whatever can disappoint such natural and agreeable hopes: and thus enter into all the anxiety, and concern, and distress of the lover.

3   Hence it is, that, in some modern tragedies and romances, this passion appears so wonderfully interesting. It is not so much the love of Castalio and Monimia which attaches us in the Orphan,[2] as the distress which that love occasions. The author who should introduce two lovers, in a scene

ᵇ⁻ᵇ Propertius, *1–5*

---

[1] In ancient Greek myth the Fortunate Islands or Islands of the Blessed were the abode of the virtuous in the life after death. Hesiod (*Works and Days*, 170 ff.) and Pindar (*Olympian Odes*, 2.61 ff.) both describe it as a life free from toil and care.
[2] *The Orphan* by Thomas Otway.

of perfect security, expressing their mutual fondness for one another,
would excite laughter, and not sympathy. If a scene of this kind is ever
admitted into a tragedy, it is always, in some measure, improper, and is
endured, not from any sympathy with the passion that is expressed in it,
but from concern for the dangers and difficulties with which the audience
foresee that its gratification is likely to be attended.

4   The reserve which the laws of society impose upon the fair sex, with
regard to this weakness, renders it more peculiarly distressful in them, and,
upon that very account, more deeply interesting. We are charmed with the
love of Phaedra, as it is expressed in the French tragedy of that name,[3] notwithstanding all the extravagance and guilt which attend it. That very extravagance and guilt may be said, in some measure, to recommend it to us.
Her fear, her shame, her remorse, her horror, her despair, become thereby
more natural and interesting. All the secondary passions, if I may be allowed to call them so, which arise from the situation of love, become necessarily more furious and violent; and it is with these secondary passions only
that we can properly be said to sympathize.

5   Of all the passions, however, which are so extravagantly disproportioned to the value of their objects, love is the only one that appears, even
to the weakest minds, to have any thing in it that is either graceful or agreeable. In itself, first of all, though it may be ridiculous, it is not naturally
odious; and though its consequences are often fatal and dreadful, its intentions are seldom mischievous. And then, though there is little propriety
in the passion itself, there is a good deal in some of those which always
accompany it. There is in love a strong mixture of humanity, generosity,
kindness, friendship, esteem; passions with which, of all others, for reasons
which shall be explained immediately, we have the greatest propensity to
sympathize, even notwithstanding we are sensible that they are, in some
measure, excessive. The sympathy which we feel with them, renders the
passion which they accompany less disagreeable, and supports it in our
imagination, notwithstanding all the vices which commonly go along with it;
though in the one sex it necessarily leads to the last ruin and infamy; and
though in the other, where it is apprehended to be least fatal, it is almost
always attended with an incapacity for labour, a neglect of duty, a contempt
of fame, and even of common reputation. Notwithstanding all this, the degree
of sensibility and generosity with which it is supposed to be accompanied,
renders it to many the object of vanity; and they are fond of appearing
capable of feeling what would do them no honour if they had really felt
it.

6   It is for a reason of the same kind, that a certain reserve is necessary
when we talk of our own friends, our own studies, our own professions.
All these are objects which we cannot expect should interest our com-

---

[3] Racine's *Phèdre*.

panions in the same degree in which they interest us. And it is for want of this reserve, that the one half of mankind make bad company to the other. A philosopher is company to a philosopher only; the member of a club, to his own little knot of companions.

CHAP. III

Of the unsocial Passions

1 THERE is another set of passions, which, though derived from the imagination, yet before we can enter into them, or regard them as graceful or becoming, must always be brought down to a pitch much lower than that to which undisciplined nature would raise them. These are, hatred and resentment, with all their different modifications. With regard to all such passions, our sympathy is divided between the person who feels them, and the person who is the object of them. The interests of these two are directly opposite. What our sympathy with the person who feels them would prompt us to wish for, our fellow-feeling with the other would lead us to fear. As they are both men, we are concerned for both, and our fear for what the one may suffer, damps our resentment for what the other has suffered. Our sympathy, therefore, with the man who has received the provocation, necessarily falls short of the passion which naturally animates him, not only upon account of those general causes which render all sympathetic passions inferior to the original ones, but upon account of that particular cause which is peculiar to itself, our opposite sympathy with another person. Before resentment, therefore, can become graceful and agreeable, it must be more humbled and brought down below that pitch to which it would naturally rise, than almost any other passion.

2 Mankind, at the same time, have a very strong sense of the injuries that are done to another. The villain, in a tragedy or romance, is as much the object of our indignation, as the hero is that of our sympathy and affection. We detest Iago as much as we esteem Othello; and delight as much in the punishment of the one, as we are grieved at the distress of the other. But though mankind have so strong a fellow-feeling with the injuries that are done to their brethren, they do not always resent them the more that the sufferer appears to resent them. Upon most occasions, the greater his patience, his mildness, his humanity, provided it does not appear that he wants spirit, or that fear was the motive of his forbearance, the higher *their* resentment against the person who injured him. The amiableness of the character exasperates their sense of the atrocity of the injury.

3 *Those* passions, however, are regarded as necessary parts of the character of human nature. A person becomes contemptible who tamely sits

a-a 2E the 1–7   *b-b* 1E These 1–7

still, and submits to insults, without attempting either to repel or to revenge
them. We cannot enter into his indifference and insensibility: we call his
behaviour mean-spiritedness, and are as really provoked by it as by the
insolence of his adversary. Even the mob are enraged to see any man submit patiently to affronts and ill usage. They desire to see this insolence
resented, and resented by the person who suffers from it. They cry to
him with fury, to defend, or to revenge himself. If his indignation rouses at
last, they heartily applaud, and sympathize with it. It enlivens their own
indignation against his enemy, whom they rejoice to see him attack ᶜin
his turn,ᶜ and are as really gratified by his revenge, provided it is not im-
moderate, as if the injury had been done to themselves.

4   But though the utility of those passions to the individual, by rendering
it dangerous to insult or injure him, be acknowledged; and though their
utility to the public, as the guardians of justice, and of the equality of its
administration, be not less considerable, as shall be shewn hereafter;[1] yet
there is still something disagreeable in the passions themselves, which
makes the appearance of them in other men the natural object of our
aversion. The expression of anger towards any body present, if it exceeds
a bare intimation that we are sensible of his ill usage, is regarded not only
as an insult to that particular person, but as a rudeness to the whole company. Respect for them ought to have restrained us from giving way to so
boisterous and offensive an emotion. It is the remote effects of these passions which are agreeable; the immediate effects are mischief to the person
against whom they are directed. But it is the immediate, and not the remote
effects of objects which render them agreeable or disagreeable to the imagination. A prison is certainly more useful to the public than a palace;
and the person who founds the one is generally directed by a much juster
spirit of patriotism, than he who builds the other. But the immediate effects
of a prison, the confinement of the wretches shut up in it, are disagreeable;
and the imagination either does not take time to trace out the remote ones,
or sees them at too great a distance to be much affected by them. A prison,
therefore, will always be a disagreeable object; and the fitter it is for the
purpose for which it was intended, it will be the more so. A palace, on the
contrary, will always be agreeable; yet its remote effects may often be
inconvenient to the public. It may serve to promote luxury, and set the
example of the dissolution of manners. Its immediate effects, however, the
conveniency, the pleasure, and the gaiety of the people who live in it, being
all agreeable, and suggesting to the imagination a thousand agreeable ideas,
that faculty generally rests upon them, and seldom goes further in tracing
its more distant consequences. Trophies of the instruments of music or
of agriculture, imitated in painting or in stucco, make a common and an

---

ᶜ⁻ᶜ *1 2E*   in turn, *2–7*
[1] II.ii.3

agreeable ornament of our halls and dining-rooms. A trophy of the same kind, composed of the instruments of surgery, of dissecting and amputation-knives, of saws for cutting the bones, of trepanning instruments, etc. would be absurd and shocking. Instruments of surgery, however, are always more finely polished, and generally more nicely adapted to the purposes for which they are intended, than instruments of agriculture. The remote effects of them too, the health of the patient, is agreeable; yet as the immediate effect of them is pain and suffering, the sight of them always displeases us. Instruments of war are agreeable, though their immediate effect may seem to be in the same manner pain and suffering. But then it is the pain and suffering of our enemies, with whom we have no sympathy. With regard to us, they are immediately connected with the agreeable ideas of courage, victory, and honour. They are themselves, therefore, supposed to make one of the noblest parts of dress, and the imitation of them one of the finest ornaments of architecture. It is the same case with the qualities of the mind. The ancient stoics were of opinion, that as the world was governed by the all-ruling providence of a wise, powerful, and good God, every single event ought to be regarded, as making a necessary part of the plan of the universe, and as tending to promote the general order and happiness of the whole: that the vices and follies of mankind, therefore, made as necessary a part of this plan as their wisdom or their virtue; and by that eternal art which educes good from ill, were made to tend equally to the prosperity and perfection of the great system of nature. No speculation of this kind, however, how deeply soever it might be rooted in the mind, could diminish our natural abhorrence for vice, whose immediate effects are so destructive, and whose remote ones are too distant to be traced by the imagination.

5   It is the same case with those passions we have been just now considering. Their immediate effects are so disagreeable, that even when they are most justly provoked, there is still something about them which disgusts us. These, therefore, are the only passions of which the expressions, as I formerly observed, do not dispose and prepare us to sympathize with them, before we are informed of the cause which excites them. The plaintive voice of misery, when heard at a distance, will not allow us to be indifferent about the person from whom it comes. As soon as it strikes our ear, it interests us in his fortune, and, if continued, forces us almost involuntarily to fly to his assistance. The sight of a smiling countenance, in the same manner, elevates even the pensive into that gay and airy mood, which disposes him to sympathize with, and share the joy which it expresses; and he feels his heart, which with thought and care was before that shrunk and depressed, instantly expanded and elated. But it is quite otherwise with the expressions of hatred and resentment. The hoarse, boisterous, and discordant voice of anger, when heard at a distance, inspires us either

with fear or aversion. We do not fly towards it, as to one who cries out with
pain and agony. Women, and men of weak nerves, tremble and are overcome with fear, though sensible that themselves are not the objects of the
anger. They conceive fear, however, by putting themselves in the situation
of the person who is so. Even those of stouter hearts are disturbed; not
indeed enough to make them afraid, but enough to make them angry;
for anger is the passion which they would feel in the situation of the other
person. It is the same case with hatred. Mere expressions of spite inspire
it against nobody, but the man who uses them. Both these passions are
by nature the objects of our aversion. Their disagreeable and boisterous
appearance never excites, never prepares, and often disturbs our sympathy.
Grief does not more powerfully engage and attract us to the person in
whom we observe it, than these, while we are ignorant of their cause, disgust and detach us from him. It was, it seems, the intention of Nature, that
those rougher and more unamiable emotions, which drive men from one
another, should be less easily and more rarely communicated.

6   When music imitates the modulations of grief or joy, it either actually
inspires us with those passions, or at least puts us in the mood which disposes us to conceive them. But when it imitates the notes of anger, it inspires us with fear. Joy, grief, love, admiration, devotion, are all of them
passions which are naturally musical. Their natural tones are all soft,
clear, and melodious; and they naturally express themselves in periods
which are distinguished by regular pauses, and which upon that account
are easily adapted to the regular returns of the correspondent airs of a
tune. The voice of anger, on the contrary, and of all the passions which are
akin to it, is harsh and discordant. Its periods too are all irregular, sometimes very long, and sometimes very short, and distinguished by no
regular pauses. It is with difficulty, therefore, that music can imitate any of
those passions; and the music which does imitate them is not the most
agreeable. A whole entertainment may consist, without any impropriety,
of the imitation of the social and agreeable passions. It would be a strange
entertainment which consisted altogether of the imitations of hatred and
resentment.

7   If those passions are disagreeable to the spectator, they are not less so to
the person who feels them. Hatred and anger are the greatest poison to the
happiness of a good mind. There is, in the very feeling of those passions,
something harsh, jarring, and convulsive, something that tears and distracts the breast, and is altogether destructive of that composure and tranquillity of mind which is so necessary to happiness, and which is best promoted by the contrary passions of gratitude and love. It is not the value of
what they lose by the perfidy and ingratitude of those they live with, which
the generous and humane are most apt to regret. Whatever they may have
lost, they can generally be very happy without it. What most disturbs them

is the idea of perfidy and ingratitude exercised towards themselves; and the discordant and disagreeable passions which this excites, constitute, in their own opinion, the chief part of the injury which they suffer.

8   How many things are requisite to render the gratification of resentment completely agreeable, and to make the spectator thoroughly sympathize with our revenge? The provocation must first of all be such that we should become contemptible, and be exposed to perpetual insults, if we did not, in some measure, resent it. Smaller offences are always better neglected; nor is there any thing more despicable than that froward and captious humour which takes fire upon every slight occasion of quarrel. We should resent more from a sense of the propriety of resentment, from a sense that mankind expect and require it of us, than because we feel in ourselves the furies of that disagreeable passion. There is no passion, of which the human mind is capable, concerning whose justness we ought to be so doubtful, concerning whose indulgence we ought so carefully to consult our natural sense of propriety, or so diligently to consider what will be the sentiments of the cool and impartial spectator. Magnanimity, or a regard to maintain our own rank and dignity in society, is the only motive which can ennoble the expressions of this disagreeable passion. This motive must characterize our whole stile and deportment. These must be plain, open, and direct; determined without positiveness, and elevated without insolence; not only free from petulance and low scurrility, but generous, candid, and full of all proper regards, even for the person who has offended us. It must appear, in short, from our whole manner, without our labouring affectedly to express it, that passion has not extinguished our humanity; and that if we yield to the dictates of revenge, it is with reluctance, from necessity, and in consequence of great and repeated provocations. When resentment is guarded and qualified in this manner, it may be admitted to be even generous and noble.

CHAP. IV

Of the social Passions

1 As it is a divided sympathy which renders the whole set of passions just now mentioned, upon most occasions, so ungraceful and disagreeable; so there is another set opposite to these, which a redoubled sympathy renders almost always peculiarly agreeable and becoming. Generosity, humanity, kindness, compassion, mutual friendship and esteem, all the social and benevolent affections, when expressed in the countenance or behaviour, even towards those who are *a*not*a* peculiarly connected with ourselves,

***

a-a om. 1-5   Presumably emended by the author; but since the earlier reading too makes good sense, it may originally have been intentional.

please the indifferent spectator upon almost every occasion. His sympathy with the person who feels those passions, exactly coincides with his concern for the person who is the object of them. The interest, which, as a man, he is obliged to take in the happiness of this last, enlivens his fellow-feeling with the sentiments of the other, whose emotions are employed about the same object. We have always, therefore, the strongest disposition to sympathize with the benevolent affections. They appear in every respect agreeable to us. We enter into the satisfaction both of the person who feels them, and of the person who is the object of them. For as to be the object of hatred and indignation gives more pain than all the evil which a brave man can fear from his enemies; so there is a satisfaction in the consciousness of being beloved, which, to a person of delicacy and sensibility, is of more importance to happiness, than all the advantage which he can expect to derive from it. What character is so detestable as that of one who takes pleasure to sow dissension among friends, and to turn their most tender love into mortal hatred? Yet wherein does the atrocity of this so much abhorred injury consist? Is it in depriving them of the frivolous good offices, which, had their friendship continued, they might have expected from one another? It is in depriving them of that friendship itself, in robbing them of each other's affections, from which both derived so much satisfaction; it is in disturbing the harmony of their hearts, and putting an end to that happy commerce which had before subsisted between them. These affections, that harmony, this commerce, are felt, not only by the tender and the delicate, but by the rudest vulgar of mankind, to be of more importance to happiness than all the little services which could be expected to flow from them.

2   The sentiment of love is, in itself, agreeable to the person who feels it. It sooths and composes the breast, seems to favour the vital motions, and to promote the healthful state of the human constitution; and it is rendered still more delightful by the consciousness of the gratitude and satisfaction which it must excite in him who is the object of it. Their mutual regard renders them happy in one another, and sympathy, with this mutual regard, makes them agreeable to every other person. With what pleasure do we look upon a family, through the whole of which reign mutual love and esteem, where the parents and children are companions for one another, without any other difference than what is made by respectful affection on the one side, and kind indulgence on the other; where freedom and fondness, mutual raillery and mutual kindness, show that no opposition of interest divides the brothers, nor any rivalship of favour sets the sisters at variance, and where every thing presents us with the idea of peace, cheerfulness, harmony, and contentment? On the contrary, how uneasy are we made when we go into a house in which jarring contention sets one half of those who dwell in it against the other; where amidst affected

smoothness and complaisance, suspicious looks and sudden starts of passion betray the mutual jealousies which burn within them, and which are every moment ready to burst out through all the restraints which the presence of the company imposes?

3   Those amiable passions, even when they are acknowledged to be excessive, are never regarded with aversion. There is something agreeable even in the weakness of friendship and humanity. The too tender mother, the too indulgent father, the too generous and affectionate friend, may sometimes, perhaps, on account of the softness of their natures, be looked upon with a species of pity, in which, however, there is a mixture of love, but can never be regarded with hatred and aversion, nor even with contempt, unless by the most brutal and worthless of mankind. It is always with concern, with sympathy and kindness, that we blame them for the extravagance of their attachment. There is a helplessness in the character of extreme humanity which more than any thing interests our pity. There is nothing in itself which renders it either ungraceful or disagreeable. We only regret that it is unfit for the world, because the world is unworthy of it, and because it must expose the person who is endowed with it as a prey to the perfidy and ingratitude of insinuating falsehood, and to a thousand pains and uneasinesses, which, of all men, he the least deserves to feel, and which generally too he is, of all men, the least capable of supporting. It is quite otherwise with hatred and resentment. Too violent a propensity to those detestable passions, renders a person the object of universal dread and abhorrence, who, like a wild beast, ought, we think, to be hunted out of all civil society.

CHAP. V

Of the selfish Passions

1 BESIDES those two opposite sets of passions, the social and unsocial, there is another which holds a sort of middle place between them; is never either so graceful as is sometimes the one set, nor is ever so odious as is sometimes the other. Grief and joy, when conceived upon account of our own private good or bad fortune, constitute this third set of passions. Even when excessive, they are never so disagreeable as excessive resentment, because no opposite sympathy can ever interest us against them: and when most suitable to their objects, they are never so agreeable as impartial humanity and just benevolence; because no double sympathy can ever interest us for them. There is, however, this difference between grief and joy, that we are generally most disposed to sympathize with small joys and great sorrows. The man who, by some sudden revolution of fortune, is lifted up all

at once into a condition of life, greatly above what he had formerly lived
in, may be assured that the congratulations of his best friends are not all
of them perfectly sincere. An upstart, though of the greatest merit, is
generally disagreeable, and a sentiment of envy commonly prevents us
from heartily sympathizing with his joy. If he has any judgment, he is
sensible of this, and instead of appearing to be elated with his good fortune,
he endeavours, as much as he can, to smother his joy, and keep down that
elevation of mind with which his new circumstances naturally inspire him.
He affects the same plainness of dress, and the same modesty of behaviour,
which became him in his former station. He redoubles his attention to his
old friends, and endeavours more than ever to be humble, assiduous, and
complaisant. And this is the behaviour which in his situation we most
approve of; because we expect, it seems, that he should have more sympathy with our envy and aversion to his happiness, than we have with his
happiness. It is seldom that with all this he succeeds. We suspect the sincerity of his humility, and he grows weary of this constraint. In a little
time, therefore, he generally leaves all his old friends behind him, some
of the meanest of them excepted, who may, perhaps, condescend to become his dependents: nor does he always acquire any new ones; the pride
of his new connections is as much affronted at finding him their equal, as
that of his old ones had been by his becoming their superior: and it requires
the most obstinate and persevering modesty to atone for this mortification to either. He generally grows weary too soon, and is provoked, by the
sullen and suspicious pride of the one, and by the saucy contempt of the
other, to treat the first with neglect, and the second with petulance, till at
last he grows habitually insolent, and forfeits the esteem of all. If the chief
part of human happiness arises from the consciousness of being beloved, as
I believe it does, those sudden changes of fortune seldom contribute much
to happiness. He is happiest who advances more gradually to greatness,
whom the public destines to every step of his preferment long before he
arrives at it, in whom, upon that account, when it comes, it can excite no
extravagant joy, and with regard to whom it cannot reasonably create either
any jealousy in those he overtakes, or any envy in those he leaves
behind.

2   Mankind, however, more readily sympathize with those smaller joys
which flow from less important causes. It is decent to be humble amidst
great prosperity; but we can scarce express too much satisfaction in all the
little occurrences of common life, in the company with which we spent the
evening last night, in the entertainment that was set before us, in what was
said and what was done, in all the little incidents of the present conversation, and in all those frivolous nothings which fill up the void of human life.
Nothing is more graceful than habitual cheerfulness, which is always
founded upon a peculiar relish for all the little pleasures which common

occurrences afford. We readily sympathize with it: it inspires us with the same joy, and makes every trifle turn up to us in the same agreeable aspect in which it presents itself to the person endowed with this happy disposition. Hence it is that youth, the season of gaiety, so easily engages our affections. That propensity to joy which seems even to animate the bloom, and to sparkle from the eyes of youth and beauty, though in a person of the same sex, exalts, even the aged, to a more joyous mood than ordinary. They forget, for a time, their infirmities, and abandon themselves to those agreeable ideas and emotions to which they have long been strangers, but which, when the presence of so much happiness recalls them to their breast, take their place there, like old acquaintance, from whom they are sorry to have ever been parted, and whom they embrace more heartily upon account of this long separation.

3   It is quite otherwise with grief. Small vexations excite no sympathy, but deep affliction calls forth the greatest. The man who is made uneasy by every little disagreeable incident, who is hurt if either the cook or the butler have failed in the least article of their duty, who feels every defect in the highest ceremonial of politeness, whether it be shewn to himself or to any other person, who takes it amiss that his intimate friend did not bid him good-morrow when they met in the forenoon, and that his brother hummed a tune all the time he himself was telling a story; who is put out of humour by the badness of the weather when in the country, by the badness of the roads when upon a journey, and by the want of company, and dulness of all public diversions when in town; such a person, I say, though he should have some reason, will seldom meet with much sympathy. Joy is a pleasant emotion, and we gladly abandon ourselves to it upon the slightest occasion. We readily, therefore, sympathize with it in others, whenever we are not prejudiced by envy. But grief is painful, and the mind, even when it is our own misfortune, naturally resists and recoils from it. We would endeavour either not to conceive it at all, or to shake it off as soon as we have conceived it. Our aversion to grief will not, indeed, always hinder us from conceiving it in our own case upon very trifling occasions, but it constantly prevents us from sympathizing with it in others when excited by the like frivolous causes: for our sympathetic passions are always less irresistible than our original ones. There is, besides, a malice in mankind, which not only prevents all sympathy with little uneasinesses, but renders them in some measure diverting. Hence the delight which we all take in raillery, and in the small vexation which we observe in our companion, when he is pushed, and urged, and teased upon all sides. Men of the most ordinary good-breeding dissemble the pain which any little incident may give them; and those who are more thoroughly formed to society, turn, of their own accord, all such incidents into raillery, as they know their companions will do for them. The habit which a man, who lives in the

world, has acquired of considering how every thing that concerns himself
will appear to others, makes those frivolous calamities turn up in the same
ridiculous light to him, in which he knows they will certainly be considered
by them.

4   Our sympathy, on the contrary, with deep distress, is very strong and
very sincere. It is unnecessary to give an instance. We weep even at the
feigned representation of a tragedy. If you labour, therefore, under any
signal calamity, if by some extraordinary misfortune you are fallen into
poverty, into diseases, into disgrace and disappointment; even though
your own fault may have been, in part, the occasion, yet you may generally
depend upon the sincerest sympathy of all your friends, and, as far as
interest and honour will permit, upon their kindest assistance too. But if
your misfortune is not of this dreadful kind, if you have only been a little
baulked in your ambition, if you have only been jilted by your mistress,
or are only hen-pecked by your wife, lay your account with the raillery of all
your acquaintance.

SECTION III

Of the Effects of Prosperity and Adversity upon the Judgment of Mankind with
regard to the Propriety of Action; and why it is more easy to obtain their
Approbation in the one state than in the other

CHAP. I

*That though our sympathy with sorrow is generally a more lively sensation than our
sympathy with joy, it commonly falls much more short of the violence of what is
naturally felt by the person principally concerned*

1   OUR sympathy with sorrow, though not more real, has been more taken
notice of than our sympathy with joy. The word sympathy, in its most
proper and primitive signification, denotes our fellow-feeling with the sufferings, not that with the enjoyments, of others. A late ingenious and subtile
philosopher thought it necessary to prove, by arguments, that we had a real
sympathy with joy, and that congratulation was a principle of human
nature.[1] Nobody, I believe, ever thought it necessary to prove that compassion was such.

2   First of all, our sympathy with sorrow is, in some sense, more universal

a-a om. 1

[1] Joseph Butler (d. 1752), *Fifteen Sermons*, v, para. 2; Raphael, *British Moralists
1650–1800*, § 412: 'Though men do not universally rejoice with all whom they see rejoice,
yet . . . they naturally compassionate all . . . whom they see in distress . . . insomuch that
words expressing this latter, pity, compassion, frequently occur; whereas we have scarce

than that with joy. Though sorrow is excessive, we may still have some fellow-feeling with it. What we feel does not, indeed, in this case, amount to that complete sympathy, to that perfect harmony and correspondence of sentiments which constitutes approbation. We do not weep, and exclaim, and lament, with the sufferer. We are sensible, on the contrary, of his weakness and of the extravagance of his passion, and yet often feel a very sensible concern upon his account. But if we do not entirely enter into, and go along with, the joy of another, we have no sort of regard or fellow-feeling for it. The man who skips and dances about with that intemperate and senseless joy which we cannot accompany him in, is the object of our contempt and indignation.

3   Pain besides, whether of mind or body, is a more pungent sensation than pleasure, and our sympathy with pain, though it falls greatly short of what is naturally felt by the sufferer, is generally a more lively and distinct perception than our sympathy with pleasure, though this last often approaches more nearly, as I shall shew immediately, to the natural vivacity of the original passion.

4   Over and above all this, we often struggle to keep down our sympathy with the sorrow of others. Whenever we are not under the observation of the sufferer, we endeavour, for our own sake, to suppress it as much as we can, and we are not always successful. The opposition which we make to it, and the reluctance with which we yield to it, necessarily oblige us to take more particular notice of it. But we never have occasion to make this opposition to our sympathy with joy. If there is any envy in the case, we never feel the least propensity towards it; and if there is none, we give way to it without any reluctance. On the contrary, as we are always ashamed of our own envy, we often pretend, and sometimes really wish to sympathize with the joy of others, when by that disagreeable sentiment we are disqualified from doing so. We are glad, we say, on account of our neighbour's good fortune, when in our hearts, perhaps, we are really sorry. We often feel a sympathy with sorrow when we would wish to be rid of it; and we often miss that with joy when we would be glad to have it. The obvious observation, therefore, which it naturally falls in our way to make, is, that our propensity to sympathize with sorrow must be very strong, and our inclination to sympathize with joy very weak.

any single one, by which the former is distinctly expressed. Congratulation indeed answers condolence: but both these words are intended to signify certain forms of civility, rather than any inward sensation or feeling. This difference or inequality is so remarkable, that we plainly consider compassion as itself an original, distinct, particular affection in human nature; whereas to rejoice in the good of others, is only a consequence of the general affection of love and good-will to them.' Adam Smith's memory has misled him into thinking that Butler gave arguments for the existence of sympathetic joy as a separate principle. In fact Butler proceeds to explain why, unlike compassion, it is not considered a separate principle. Hence Eckstein (i.284–5), while believing that the reference is probably to Butler, adds, implausibly, that it might be to Hutcheson or Hume.

5   Notwithstanding this prejudice, however, I will venture to affirm, that, when there is no envy in the case, our propensity to sympathize with joy is much stronger than our propensity to sympathize with sorrow; and that our fellow-feeling for the agreeable emotion approaches much more nearly to the vivacity of what is naturally felt by the persons principally concerned, than that which we conceive for the painful one.

6   We have some indulgence for that excessive grief which we cannot entirely go along with. We know what a prodigious effort is requisite before the sufferer can bring down his emotions to complete harmony and concord with those of the spectator. Though he fails, therefore, we easily pardon him. But we have no such indulgence for the intemperance of joy; because we are not conscious that any such vast effort is requisite to bring it down to what we can entirely enter into. The man who, under the greatest calamities, can command his sorrow, seems worthy of the highest admiration; but he who, in the fulness of prosperity, can in the same manner master his joy, seems hardly to deserve any praise. We are sensible that there is a much wider interval in the one case than in the other, between what is naturally felt by the person principally concerned, and what the spectator can entirely go along with.

7   What can be added to the happiness of the man who is in health, who is out of debt, and has a clear conscience? To one in this situation, all accessions of fortune may properly be said to be superfluous; and if he is much elevated upon account of them, it must be the effect of the most frivolous levity. This situation, however, may very well be called the natural and ordinary state of mankind. Notwithstanding the present misery and depravity of the world, so justly lamented, this really is the state of the greater part of men. The greater part of men, therefore, cannot find any great difficulty in elevating themselves to all the joy which any accession to this situation can well excite in their companion.

8   But though little can be added to this state, much may be taken from it. Though between this condition and the highest pitch of human prosperity, the interval is but a trifle; between it and the lowest depth of misery the distance is immense and prodigious. Adversity, on this account, necessarily depresses the mind of the sufferer much more below its natural state, than prosperity can elevate him above it. The spectator, therefore, must find it much more difficult to sympathize entirely, and keep perfect time, with his sorrow, than thoroughly to enter into his joy, and must depart much further from his own natural and ordinary temper of mind in the one case than in the other. It is on this account, that though our sympathy with sorrow is often a more pungent sensation than our sympathy with joy, it always falls much more short of the violence of what is naturally felt by the person principally concerned.

9   It is agreeable to sympathize with joy; and wherever envy does not

oppose it, our heart abandons itself with satisfaction to the highest transports of that delightful sentiment. But it is painful to go along with grief,
and we always enter into it with reluctance*. When we attend to the representation of a tragedy, we struggle against that sympathetic sorrow which
the entertainment inspires as long as we can, and we give way to it at
last only when we can no longer avoid it: we even then endeavour to cover
our concern from the company. If we shed any tears, we carefully conceal
them, and are afraid, lest the spectators, not entering into this excessive
tenderness, should regard it as effeminacy and weakness. The wretch whose
misfortunes call upon our compassion feels with what reluctance we are
likely to enter into his sorrow, and therefore proposes his grief to us with
fear and hesitation: he even smothers the half of it, and is ashamed, upon
account of this hard-heartedness of mankind, to give vent to the fulness
of his affliction. It is otherwise with the man who riots in joy and success.
Wherever envy does not interest us against him, he expects our completest
sympathy. He does not fear, therefore, to announce himself with shouts of
exultation, in full confidence that we are heartily disposed to go along with
him.

   *b** It has been objected[2] to me that as I found the sentiment of approbation, which is
always agreeable, upon sympathy, it is inconsistent with my system to admit any disagreeable sympathy. I answer, that in the sentiment of approbation there are two things to be
taken notice of; first, the sympathetic passion of the spectator; and, secondly, the emotion
which arises from his observing the perfect coincidence between this sympathetic passion
in himself, and the original passion in the person principally concerned. This last emotion,
in which the sentiment of approbation properly consists, is always agreeable and delightful. The other may either be agreeable or disagreeable, according to the nature of the
original passion, whose features it must always, in some measure, retain.*c*

   *b The footnote was added in ed. 2. An earlier draft of it was enclosed by Smith with Letter
40 addressed to Sir Gilbert Elliot, dated 10 October 1759. The draft is in the hand of an
amanuensis with minor revision in the hand of Smith. Variants from the above text in this
draft are given in Appendix I.*
   c Two sounds, I suppose, may, each of them [them, *4 5*] taken singly, be austere, and
yet, if they are perfect concords, the perception of their [this *draft*] harmony and coincidence may be agreeable. [agreable. *draft*] *add draft-of-1759 2–5*

   [2] By Hume in Letter 36, dated 28 July 1759: 'I am told that you are preparing a new
Edition, and propose to make some Additions and Alterations, in order to obviate Objec-
tions. . . . I wish you had more particularly and fully prov'd, that all kinds of Sympathy
are necessarily Agreeable. This is the Hinge of your System, and yet you only mention
the Matter cursorily in p. 20 [I.i.2.6]. Now it woud appear that there is a disagreeable
Sympathy, as well as an agreeable. And indeed, as the Sympathetic Passion is a reflex
Image of the principal, it must partake of its Qualities, and be painful where that is so. . . .
It is always thought a difficult Problem to account for the Pleasure, receivd from the
Tears and Grief and Sympathy of Tragedy; which woud not be the Case, if all Sympathy
was agreeable. An Hospital woud be a more entertaining Place than a Ball. I am afraid
that in p. 99 and 111 [I.ii.5.4 and I.iii.1.9] this Proposition has escapd you, or rather is
interwove with your Reasonings in that place. You say expressly, *it is painful to go along
with Grief and we always enter into it with Reluctance*. It will probably be requisite for you
to modify or explain this Sentiment, and reconcile it to your System.'
   Rae, *Life*, 148, mistakenly says that the second edition of TMS 'contained none of the
alterations or additions [Hume] expected'.

10   Why should we be more ashamed to weep than to laugh before company?
We may often have as real occasion to do the one as to do the other: but we
always feel that the spectators are more likely to go along with us in the
agreeable, than in the painful emotion. It is always miserable to complain,
even when we are oppressed by the most dreadful calamities. But the
triumph of victory is not always ungraceful. Prudence, indeed, would often
advise us to bear our prosperity with more moderation; because prudence
would teach us to avoid that envy which this very triumph is, more than
any thing, apt to excite.

11   How hearty are the acclamations of the mob, who never bear any envy
to their superiors, at a triumph or a public entry? And how sedate and
moderate is commonly their grief at an execution? Our sorrow at a funeral
generally amounts to no more than an affected gravity; but our mirth at a
christening or a marriage, is always from the heart, and without any
affectation. Upon these, and all such joyous occasions, our satisfaction,
though not so durable, is often as lively as that of the persons principally
concerned. Whenever we cordially congratulate our friends, which, however, to the disgrace of human nature, we do but seldom, their joy literally
becomes our joy: we are, for the moment, as happy as they are: our heart
swells and overflows with real pleasure: joy and complacency sparkle from
our eyes, and animate every feature of our countenance, and every gesture
of our body.

12   But, on the contrary, when we condole with our friends in their afflictions, how little do we feel, in comparison of what they feel? We sit down
by them, we look at them, and while they relate to us the circumstances of
their misfortune, we listen to them with gravity and attention. But while
their narration is every moment interrupted by those natural bursts of
passion which often seem almost to choak them in the midst of it; how far are
the languid emotions of our hearts from keeping time to the transports of
theirs? We may be sensible, at the same time, that their passion is natural,
and no greater than what we ourselves might feel upon the like occasion.
We may even inwardly reproach ourselves with our own want of sensibility, and perhaps, on that account, work ourselves up into an artificial
sympathy, which, however, when it is raised, is always the slightest and
most transitory imaginable; and generally, as soon as we have left the room,
vanishes, and is gone for ever. Nature, it seems, when she loaded us with
our own sorrows, thought that they were enough, and therefore did not
command us to take any further share in those of others, than what was
necessary to prompt us to relieve them.

13   It is on account of this dull sensibility to the afflictions of others, that
magnanimity amidst great distress appears always so divinely graceful.
His behaviour is genteel and agreeable who can maintain his cheerfulness
amidst a number of frivolous disasters. But he appears to be more than

mortal who can support in the same manner the most dreadful calamities. We feel what an immense effort is requisite to silence those violent emotions which naturally agitate and distract those in his situation. We are amazed to find that he can command himself so entirely. His firmness, at the same time, perfectly coincides with our insensibility. He makes no demand upon us for that more exquisite degree of sensibility which we find, and which we are mortified to find, that we do not possess. There is the most perfect correspondence between his sentiments and ours, and on that account the most perfect propriety in his behaviour. It is a propriety too, which, from our experience of the usual weakness of human nature, we could not reasonably have expected he should be able to maintain. We wonder with surprise and astonishment at that strength of mind which is capable of so noble and generous an effort. The sentiment of complete sympathy and approbation, mixed and animated with wonder and surprise, constitutes what is properly called admiration, as has already been more than once taken notice of. Cato, surrounded on all sides by his enemies, unable to resist them, disdaining to submit to them, and reduced, by the proud maxims of that age, to the necessity of destroying himself; yet never shrinking from his misfortunes, never supplicating with the lamentable voice of wretchedness, those miserable sympathetic tears which we are always so unwilling to give; but on the contrary, arming himself with manly fortitude, and the moment before he executes his fatal resolution, giving, with his usual tranquillity, all necessary orders for the safety of his friends; appears to Seneca, that great preacher of insensibility, a spectacle which even the gods themselves might behold with pleasure and admiration.[3]

14   Whenever we meet, in common life, with any examples of such heroic magnanimity, we are always extremely affected. We are more apt to weep and shed tears for such as, in this manner, seem to feel nothing for themselves, than for those who give way to all the weakness of sorrow: and in this particular case, the sympathetic grief of the spectator appears to go beyond the original passion in the person principally concerned. The friends of Socrates all wept when he drank the last potion, while he himself expressed the gayest and most cheerful tranquillity.[4] Upon all such occasions the spectator makes no effort, and has no occasion to make any, in order to conquer his sympathetic sorrow. He is under no fear that it will transport him to any thing that is extravagant and improper; he is rather pleased with the sensibility of his own heart, and gives way to it with complacence and self-approbation. He gladly indulges, therefore, the most melancholy views which can naturally occur to him, concerning the calamity of his friend, for whom, perhaps, he never felt so exquisitely before,

---

[3] Seneca, *De Providentia* (*Dialogues*, Book I), ii.9.
[4] Plato, *Phaedo*, 117 b–e.

the tender and tearful passion of love. But it is quite otherwise with the person principally concerned. He is obliged, as much as possible, to turn away his eyes from whatever is either naturally terrible or disagreeable in his situation. Too serious an attention to those circumstances, he fears, might make so violent an impression upon him, that he could no longer keep within the bounds of moderation, or render himself the object of the complete sympathy and approbation of the spectators. He fixes his thoughts, therefore, upon those only which are agreeable, the applause and admiration which he is about to deserve by the heroic magnanimity of his behaviour. To feel that he is capable of so noble and generous an effort, to feel that in this dreadful situation he can still act as he would desire to act, animates and transports him with joy, and enables him to support that triumphant gaiety which seems to exult in the victory he thus gains over his misfortunes.

15   On the contrary, he always appears, in some measure, mean and despicable, who is sunk in sorrow and dejection upon account of any calamity of his own. We cannot bring ourselves to feel for him what he feels for himself, and what, perhaps, we should feel for ourselves if in his situation: we, therefore, despise him; unjustly, perhaps, if any sentiment could be regarded as unjust, to which we are by nature irresistibly determined. The weakness of sorrow never appears in any respect agreeable, except when it arises from what we feel for others more than from what we feel for ourselves. A son, upon the death of an indulgent and respectable father, may give way to it without much blame. His sorrow is chiefly founded upon a sort of sympathy with his departed parent; and we readily enter into this humane emotion. But if he should indulge the same weakness upon account of any misfortune which affected himself only, he would no longer meet with any such indulgence. If he should be reduced to beggary and ruin, if he should be exposed to the most dreadful dangers, if he should even be led out to a public execution, and there shed one single tear upon the scaffold, he would disgrace himself for ever in the opinion of all the gallant and generous part of mankind. Their compassion for him, however, would be very strong, and very sincere; but as it would still fall short of this excessive weakness, they would have no pardon for the man who could thus expose himself in the eyes of the world. His behaviour would affect them with shame rather than with sorrow; and the dishonour which he had thus brought upon himself would appear to them the most lamentable circumstance in his misfortune. How did it disgrace the memory of the intrepid Duke of Biron,[5] who had so often braved death in the field, that he wept upon the scaffold, when he beheld the state to which he was

[5] Charles de Gontaut (1562–1602), son of the Baron de Biron, was made Duc de Biron and Marshal of France by Henri IV for his courage and success in war, but was later found guilty of treason. He was executed on 31 July 1602.

fallen, and remembered the favour and the glory from which his own rashness had so unfortunately thrown *d*him!*d*

CHAP. II
Of the origin of Ambition, and of the distinction of Ranks

1　It is because mankind are disposed to sympathize more entirely with our
joy than with our sorrow, that we make parade of our riches, and conceal
our poverty. Nothing is so mortifying as to be obliged to expose our distress to the view of the public, and to feel, that though our situation is
open to the eyes of all mankind, no mortal conceives for us the half of
what we suffer. Nay, it is chiefly from this regard to the sentiments of
mankind, that we pursue riches and avoid poverty. For to what purpose
is all the toil and bustle of this world? what is the end of avarice and ambition, of the pursuit of wealth, of power, and preheminence? Is it to supply
the necessities of nature? The wages of the meanest labourer can supply
them. We see that they afford him food and clothing, the comfort of a
house, and of a family. *a*If we examined his oeconomy with rigour, we
should find*a* that he spends a great part of them upon conveniencies, which
may be regarded as superfluities, and that, upon extraordinary occasions,
he can give something even to vanity and distinction. What then is the
cause of our aversion to his situation, and why should those who have been
educated in the higher ranks of life, regard it as worse than death, to be
reduced to live, even without labour, upon the same simple fare with him,
to dwell under the same lowly roof, and to be clothed in the same humble
attire? Do they imagine that their stomach is better, or their sleep sounder
in a palace than in a cottage? The contrary has been so often observed,
and, indeed, is so very obvious, though it had never been observed, that
there is nobody ignorant of it. From whence, then, arises that emulation
which runs through all the different ranks of men, and what are the advantages which we propose by that great purpose of human life which we
call bettering our condition? To be observed, to be attended to, to be taken
notice of with sympathy, complacency, and approbation, are all the advantages which we can propose to derive from it. It is the vanity, not the ease,
or the pleasure, which interests us. But vanity is always founded upon the
belief of our being the object of attention and approbation. The rich man

---

d-d 5　～. *1–3*　～? *4 6 7　The question-mark gives the wrong sense, as inviting a negative
answer.*

---

a-a If we examine ... with rigor, we shall find *1*　If we examine ... with rigor, we
should find *2–5*　If we examine ... with rigour, we should find *6–7　We have emended
examine to examined, as presumably intended by the revision of shall to should.*

glories in his riches, because he feels that they naturally draw upon him the attention of the world, and that mankind are disposed to go along with him in all those agreeable emotions with which the advantages of his situation so readily inspire him. At the thought of this, his heart seems to swell and dilate itself within him, and he is fonder of his wealth, upon this account, than for all the other advantages it procures him. The poor man, on the contrary, is ashamed of his poverty. He feels that it either places him out of the sight of mankind, or, that if they take any notice of him, they have, however, scarce any fellow-feeling with the misery and distress which he suffers. He is mortified upon both accounts; for though to be overlooked, and to be disapproved of, are things entirely different, yet as obscurity covers us from the daylight of honour and approbation, to feel that we are taken no notice of, necessarily damps the most agreeable hope, and disappoints the most ardent desire, of human nature. The poor man goes out and comes in unheeded, and when in the midst of a crowd is in the same obscurity as if shut up in his own hovel. Those humble cares and painful attentions which occupy those in his situation, afford no amusement to the dissipated and the gay. They turn away their eyes from him, or if the extremity of his distress forces them to look at him, it is only to spurn so disagreeable an object from among them. The fortunate and the proud wonder at the insolence of human wretchedness, that it should dare to present itself before them, and with the loathsome aspect of its misery presume to disturb the serenity of their happiness. The man of rank and distinction, on the contrary, is observed by all the world. Every body is eager to look at him, and to conceive, at least by sympathy, that joy and exultation with which his circumstances naturally inspire him. His actions are the objects of the public care. Scarce a word, scarce a gesture, can fall from him that is altogether neglected. In a great assembly he is the person upon whom all direct their eyes; it is upon him that their passions seem all to wait with expectation, in order to receive that movement and direction which he shall impress upon them; and if his behaviour is not altogether absurd, he has, every moment, an opportunity of interesting mankind, and of rendering himself the object of the observation and fellow-feeling of every body about him. It is this, which, notwithstanding the restraint it imposes, notwithstanding the loss of liberty with which it is attended, renders greatness the object of envy, and compensates, in the opinion of mankind, all that toil, all that anxiety, all those mortifications which must be undergone in the pursuit of it; and what is of yet more consequence, all that leisure, all that ease, all that careless security, which are forfeited for ever by the acquisition.

2   When we consider the condition of the great, in those delusive colours in which the imagination is apt to paint it, it seems to be almost the abstract idea of a perfect and happy state. It is the very state which, in all our

waking dreams and idle reveries, we had sketched out to ourselves as the
final object of all our desires. We feel, therefore, a peculiar sympathy with
the satisfaction of those who are in it. We favour all their inclinations,
and forward all their wishes. What pity, we think, that any thing should
spoil and corrupt so agreeable a situation! We could even wish them immortal; and it seems hard to us, that death should at last put an end to such
perfect enjoyment. It is cruel, we think, in Nature to compel them from
their exalted stations to that humble, but hospitable home, which she has
provided for all her children. Great King, live for ever! is the compliment,
which, after the manner of eastern adulation, we should readily make them,
if experience did not teach us its absurdity. Every calamity that befals them,
every injury that is done them, excites in the breast of the spectator ten
times more compassion and resentment than he would have felt, had the
same things happened to other men. It is the misfortunes of Kings only
which afford the proper subjects for tragedy. They resemble, in this respect, the misfortunes of lovers. Those two situations are the chief which
interest us upon the theatre; because, in spite of all that reason and experience can tell us to the contrary, the prejudices of the imagination
attach to these two states a happiness superior to any other. To disturb,
or to put an end to such perfect enjoyment, seems to be the most atrocious
of all injuries. The traitor who conspires against the life of his monarch,
is thought a greater monster than any other murderer. All the innocent
blood that was shed in the civil wars, provoked less indignation than the
death of Charles I. A stranger to human nature, who saw the indifference
of men about the misery of their inferiors, and the regret and indignation
which they feel for the misfortunes and sufferings of those above them,
would be apt to imagine, that pain must be more agonizing, and the convulsions of death more terrible to persons of higher rank, than to those of
meaner stations.

3   Upon this disposition of mankind, to go along with all the passions of
the rich and the powerful, is founded the distinction of ranks, and the
order of society. Our obsequiousness to our superiors more frequently
arises from our admiration for the advantages of their situation, than from
any private expectations of benefit from their good-will.[1] Their benefits
can extend but to a few; but their fortunes interest almost every body.
We are eager to assist them in completing a system of happiness that approaches so near to perfection; and we desire to serve them for their own
sake, without any other recompense but the vanity or the honour of obliging them. Neither is our deference to their inclinations founded chiefly,
or altogether, upon a regard to the utility of such submission, and to the
order of society, which is best supported by it. Even when the order of
society seems to require that we should oppose them, we can hardly bring

[1] Cf. Hume, *Treatise of Human Nature*, II.iii.5; ed. Selby-Bigge, 360–2.

ourselves to do it. That kings are the servants of the people, to be obeyed, resisted, deposed, or punished, as the public conveniency may require, is the doctrine of reason and philosophy; but it is not the doctrine of Nature. Nature would teach us to submit to them for their own sake, to tremble and bow down before their exalted station, to regard their smile as a reward sufficient to compensate any services, and to dread their displeasure, though no other evil were to follow from it, as the severest of all mortifications. To treat them in any respect as men, to reason and dispute with them upon ordinary occasions, requires such resolution, that there are few men whose magnanimity can support them in it, unless they are likewise assisted by familiarity and acquaintance. The strongest motives, the most furious passions, fear, hatred, and resentment, are scarce sufficient to balance this natural disposition to respect them: and their conduct must, either justly or unjustly, have excited the highest degree of all those passions, before the bulk of the people can be brought to oppose them with violence, or to desire to see them either punished or deposed. Even when the people have been brought this length, they are apt to relent every moment, and easily relapse into their habitual state of deference to those whom they have been accustomed to look upon as their natural superiors. They cannot stand the mortification of their monarch. Compassion soon takes the place of resentment, they forget all past provocations, their old principles of loyalty revive, and they run to re-establish the ruined authority of their old masters, with the same violence with which they had opposed it. The death of Charles I. brought about the Restoration of the royal family. Compassion for James II. when he was seized by the populace in making his escape on ship-board,[2] had almost prevented the Revolution, and made it go on more heavily than before.

4   Do the great seem insensible of the easy price at which they may acquire the public admiration; or do they seem to imagine that to them, as to other men, it must be the purchase either of sweat or of blood? By what important accomplishments is the young nobleman instructed to support the dignity of his rank, and to render himself worthy of that superiority over his fellow-citizens, to which the virtue of his ancestors had raised them? Is it by knowledge, by industry, by patience, by self-denial, or by virtue of any kind? As all his words, as all his motions are attended to, he learns an habitual regard to every circumstance of ordinary behaviour, and studies to perform all those small duties with the most exact propriety. As he is conscious how much he is observed, and how much mankind are disposed to favour all his inclinations, he acts, upon the most indifferent occasions, with that freedom and elevation which the thought of this

---

[2] James II left for France during the night of 11–12 December 1688, but his ship was delayed by adverse winds. He was captured and badly treated by a group of fishermen from Faversham.

naturally inspires. His air, his manner, his deportment, all mark that elegant and graceful sense of his own superiority, which those who are born to inferior stations can hardly ever arrive at. These are the arts by which he proposes to make mankind more easily submit to his authority, and to govern their inclinations according to his own pleasure: and in this he is seldom disappointed. These arts, supported by rank and preheminence, are, upon ordinary occasions, sufficient to govern the world. Lewis XIV. during the greater part of his reign, was regarded, not only in France, but over all Europe, as the most perfect model of a great prince. But what were the talents and virtues by which he acquired this great reputation? Was it by the scrupulous and inflexible justice of all his undertakings, by the immense dangers and difficulties with which they were attended, or by the unwearied and unrelenting application with which he pursued them? Was it by his extensive knowledge, by his exquisite judgment, or by his heroic valour? It was by none of these qualities. But he was, first of all, the most powerful prince in Europe, and consequently held the highest rank among kings; and ᵇthen,ᵇ says his historian,[3] 'he surpassed all his courtiers in the gracefulness of his shape, and the majestic beauty of his features. The sound of his voice, noble and affecting, gained those hearts which his presence intimidated. He had a step and a deportment which could suit only him and his rank, and which would have been ridiculous in any other person. The embarrassment which he occasioned to those who spoke to him, flattered that secret satisfaction with which he felt his own superiority. The old officer, who was confounded and faultered in asking him a favour, and not being able to conclude his discourse, said to him: Sir, your majesty, I hope, will believe that I do not tremble thus before your enemies: had no difficulty to obtain what he demanded.' These frivolous accomplishments, supported by his rank, and, no doubt too, by a degree of other talents and virtues, which seems, however, not to have been much above mediocrity, established this prince in the esteem of his own age, and have drawn, even from posterity, a good deal of respect for his memory. Compared with these, in his own times, and in his own presence, no other virtue, it seems, appeared to have any merit. Knowledge, industry, valour, and beneficence, trembled, were abashed, and lost all dignity before them.

5   But it is not by accomplishments of this kind, that the man of inferior rank must hope to distinguish himself. Politeness is so much the virtue of the great, that it will do little honour to any body but themselves. The coxcomb, who imitates their manner, and affects to be eminent by the

---

ᵇ⁻ᵇ *1-5*   ∼ ∧ *6 7*

---

[3] Voltaire, *Siècle de Louis XIV*, ch. 25. Smith is probably giving his own translation from the French.

superior propriety of his ordinary behaviour, is rewarded with a double share of contempt for his folly and presumption. Why should the man, whom nobody thinks it worth while to look at, be very anxious about the manner in which he holds up his head, or disposes of his arms while he walks through a room? He is occupied surely with a very superfluous attention, and with an attention too that marks a sense of his own importance, which no other mortal can go along with. The most perfect modesty and plainness, joined to as much negligence as is consistent with the respect due to the company, ought to be the chief characteristics of the behaviour of a private man. If ever he hopes to distinguish himself, it must be by more important virtues. He must acquire dependants to balance the dependants of the great, and he has no other fund to pay them from, but the labour of his body, and the activity of his mind. He must cultivate these therefore: he must acquire superior knowledge in his profession, and superior industry in the exercise of it. He must be patient in labour, resolute in danger, and firm in distress. These talents he must bring into public view, by the difficulty, importance, and, at the same time, good judgment of his undertakings, and by the severe and unrelenting application with which he pursues them. Probity and prudence, generosity and frankness, must characterize his behaviour upon all ordinary occasions; and he must, at the same time, be forward to engage in all those situations, in which it requires the greatest talents and virtues to act with propriety, but in which the greatest applause is to be acquired by those who can acquit themselves with honour. With what impatience does the man of spirit and ambition, who is depressed by his situation, look round for some great opportunity to distinguish himself? No circumstances, which can afford this, appear to him undesirable. He even looks forward with satisfaction to the prospect of foreign war, or civil dissension; and, with secret transport and delight, sees through all the confusion and bloodshed which attend them, the probability of those wished-for occasions presenting themselves, in which he may draw upon himself the attention and admiration of mankind. The man of rank and distinction, on the contrary, whose whole glory consists in the propriety of his ordinary behaviour, who is contented with the humble renown which this can afford him, and has no talents to acquire any other, is unwilling to embarrass himself with what can be attended either with difficulty or distress. To figure at a ball is his great triumph, and to succeed in an intrigue of gallantry, his highest exploit. He has an aversion to all public confusions, not from the love of mankind, for the great never look upon their inferiors as their fellow-creatures; nor yet from want of courage, for in that he is seldom defective; but from a consciousness that he possesses none of the virtues which are required in such situations, and that the public attention will certainly be drawn away from him by others. He may be willing to expose himself to some little danger, and to make a campaign when it happens to be the fashion. But he shudders with horror at the thought of any situation which demands the continual and long exertion of patience, industry, fortitude, and application of thought. These virtues are hardly ever to be met with in men who are born to those high stations. In all governments accordingly, even in monarchies, the highest offices are generally possessed, and the whole detail of the administration conducted, by men who were educated in the middle and inferior ranks of life, who have been carried forward by their own industry and abilities, though loaded with the jealousy, and opposed by the resentment, of all those who were born their superiors, and to whom the great, after having regarded them first with contempt, and afterwards with envy, are at last contented to truckle with the same abject meanness with which they desire that the rest of mankind should behave to themselves.

6   It is the loss of this easy empire over the affections of mankind which renders the fall from greatness so insupportable. When the family of the king of Macedon was led in triumph by Paulus Aemilius, their misfortunes, it is said, made them divide with their conqueror the attention of the Roman people. The sight of the royal children, whose tender age rendered them insensible of their situation, struck the spectators, amidst the public rejoicings and prosperity, with the tenderest sorrow and compassion. The king appeared next in the procession; and seemed like one confounded and astonished, and bereft of all sentiment, by the greatness of his calamities. His friends and ministers followed after him. As they moved along, they often cast their eyes upon their fallen sovereign, and always burst into tears at the sight; their whole behaviour demonstrating that they thought not of their own misfortunes, but were occupied entirely by the superior greatness of his. The generous Romans, on the contrary, beheld him with disdain and indignation, and regarded as unworthy of all compassion the man who could be so mean-spirited as to bear to live under such calamities.[4] Yet what did those calamities amount to? According to the greater part of historians, he was to spend the remainder of his days, under the protection of a powerful and humane people, in a state which in itself should seem worthy of envy, a state of plenty, ease, leisure, and security, from which it was impossible for him even by his own folly to fall. But he was no longer to be surrounded by that admiring mob of fools, flatterers, and dependants, who had formerly been accustomed to attend upon all his motions. He was no longer to be gazed upon by multitudes, nor to have it in his power to render himself the object of their respect, their gratitude, their love, their admiration. The passions of nations were no longer to mould themselves upon his inclinations. This was that insupportable calamity which bereaved the king of all sentiment; which made his friends forget their own misfortunes; and which the Roman magnanimity could

---

[4] Cf. Plutarch, *Lives*, Aemilius Paulus, 33-4.

scarce conceive how any man could be so mean-spirited as to bear to survive.

7   'Love,' says my Lord Rochfaucault, 'is commonly succeeded by ambition; but ambition is hardly ever succeeded by love.'[5] That passion, when once it has got entire possession of the breast, will admit neither a rival nor a successor. To those who have been accustomed to the possession, or even to the hope of public admiration, all other pleasures sicken and decay. Of all the discarded statesmen who for their own ease have studied to get the better of ambition, and to despise those honours which they could no longer arrive at, how few have been able to succeed? The greater part have spent their time in the most listless and insipid indolence, chagrined at the thoughts of their own insignificancy, incapable of being interested in the occupations of private life, without enjoyment, except when they talked of their former greatness, and without satisfaction, except when they were employed in some vain project to recover it. Are you in earnest resolved never to barter your liberty for the lordly servitude of a court, but to live free, fearless, and independent? There seems to be one way to continue in that virtuous resolution; and perhaps but one. Never enter the place from whence so few have been able to return; never come within the circle of ambition; nor ever bring yourself into comparison with those masters of the earth who have already engrossed the attention of half mankind before you.

8   Of such mighty importance does it appear to be, in the imaginations of men, to stand in that situation which sets them most in the view of general sympathy and attention. And thus, place, that great object which divides the wives of aldermen, is the end of half the labours of human life; and is the cause of all the tumult and bustle, all the rapine and injustice, which avarice and ambition have introduced into this world. People of sense, it is said, indeed despise place; that is, they despise sitting at the head of the table, and are indifferent who it is that is pointed out to the company by that frivolous circumstance, which the smallest advantage is capable of overbalancing. But rank, distinction pre-eminence, no man despises, unless he is either raised very much above, or sunk very much below, the ordinary standard of human nature; unless he is either so confirmed in wisdom and real philosophy, as to be satisfied that, while the propriety of his conduct renders him the just object of approbation, it is of little consequence though he be neither attended to, nor approved of; or so habituated to the idea of his own meanness, so sunk in slothful and sottish indifference, as entirely to have forgot the desire, and almost the very wish, for superiority.

[5] La Rochefoucauld, *Maximes*, 490. Smith's (slightly free) English translation is again probably his own.

9   ᶜAs to become the natural object of the joyous congratulations and sympathetic attentions of mankind is, in this manner, the circumstance which gives to prosperity all its dazzling splendour; so nothing darkens so much the gloom of adversity as to feel that our misfortunes are the objects, not of the fellow-feeling, but of the contempt and aversion of our brethren. It is upon this account thatᶜ the most dreadful calamities are not always

---

ᶜ⁻ᶜ *om. 1–5, which here begin a new chapter. The third paragraph of that chapter leads into what follows* ᶜ⁻ᶜ *in ed. 6. We give the text of ed. 1 with the variants of eds. 2–5 below. Part of this material reappears in ed. 6 at VII.ii.1.23 and 20.*

CHAP. III

Of the stoical philosophy [*ital. 2–5*]

WHEN we examine in this manner into the ground of the different degrees of estimation which mankind are apt to bestow upon the different conditions of life, we shall find, that the excessive preference, which they generally give to some of them above others, is in a great measure without any foundation. If to be able to act with propriety, and to render ourselves the proper objects of the approbation of mankind, be, as we have been endeavouring to show, what chiefly recommends to us one condition above another, this may be equally [equally be *2–5*] attained in them all. The noblest propriety of conduct may be supported in adversity, as well as in prosperity; and tho' [though *2–5*] it is somewhat more difficult in the first, it is upon that very account more admirable. Perils and misfortunes are not only the proper school of heroism, they are the only proper theatre which can exhibit its virtue to advantage, and draw upon it the full applause of the world. The man, whose whole life has been one even and uninterrupted course of prosperity, who never braved any danger, who never encountered any difficulty, who never surmounted any distress, can excite but an inferior degree of admiration. When poets and romance-writers endeavour to invent a train of adventures, which shall give the greatest lustre to those characters for whom they mean to interest us, they are all of a different kind. They are rapid and sudden changes of fortune, situations the most apt to drive those who are in them to frenzy and distraction, or to abject despair; but in which their heroes act with so much propriety, or at least with so much spirit and undaunted resolution, as still to command our esteem. Is not the unfortunate magnanimity of Cato, Brutus, and Leonidas, as much the object of admiration, as that of the successful Caesar or Alexander? To a generous mind, therefore, ought it not to be as much the object of envy? If a more dazzling splendor seems to attend the fortunes of successful conquerors, it is because they join together the advantages of both situations, the lustre of prosperity to the high admiration which is excited by dangers encountered, and difficulties surmounted, with intrepidity and valour.

It was upon this account that, according to the stoical philosophy, to a wise man all the different conditions of life were equal. Nature, they said, had recommended some objects to our choice, and others to our disapprobation. Our primary appetites directed us to the pursuit of health, strength, ease, and perfection, in all the qualities of mind and body; and of whatever could promote or secure these, riches, power, authority: and the same original principle taught us to avoid the contrary. But in chusing or rejecting, in preferring or postponing, those first objects of original appetite and aversion, nature [Nature *4 5*] had likewise taught us, that there was a certain order, propriety, and grace, to be observed, of infinitely greater consequence to happiness and perfection, than the attainment of those objects themselves. The objects of our primary appetites or aversions were to be pursued or avoided, chiefly because a regard to this grace and propriety required such conduct. In directing all our actions according to these, consisted the happiness and glory of human nature. In departing from those rules which they prescribed to us, its greatest wretchedness and most compleat [complete *4 5*] depravity. The outward appearance of this order and propriety was indeed more easily maintained in some circumstances than in others.

To a fool, however, to one whose passions were subjected to no proper controul, to act with real grace and propriety, was equally impossible in every situation. Tho' [Though *2–5*] the giddy multitude might admire him, tho' [though *2–5*] his vanity might sometimes be elated by their ignorant praises into something that resembled self-approbation, yet still when he turned his view to what passed within his own breast, he was secretly conscious to himself of the absurdity and meanness of all his motives, and inwardly blushed and trembled at the thoughts of the contempt which he knew he deserved, and which mankind would certainly bestow upon him if they saw his conduct in the light in which in his own heart he was obliged to regard it. [6]To a wise man, on the contrary, to one whose passions were all brought under perfect subjection to the ruling principles of his nature, to reason and the love of propriety, to act so as to deserve approbation was equally easy upon all occasions. Was he in prosperity, he returned thanks to Jupiter for having joined him with circumstances which were easily mastered, and in which there was little temptation to do wrong. Was he in adversity, he equally returned thanks to the director of this spectacle of human life, for having opposed to him a vigorous athlete, over whom, tho' [though *2–5*] the contest was likely to be more violent, the victory was more glorious, and equally certain. Can there be any shame in that distress which is brought upon us without any fault of our own, and in which we behave with perfect propriety? There can, therefore, be no evil, but, on the contrary, the greatest good and advantage. A brave man exults in those dangers, in which, from no rashness of his own, his fortune has involved him. They afford an opportunity of exercising that heroic intrepidity, whose exertion gives the exalted delight which flows from the consciousness of superior propriety and deserved admiration. One who is master of all his exercises has no aversion to measure his strength and activity with the strongest. And in the same manner, one who is master of all his passions, does not dread any circumstance [circumstances *2–5*] in which the superintendent [superintendant *4 5*] of the universe may think proper to place him. The bounty of that divine being [Divine Being *4 5*] has provided him with virtues which render him superior to every situation. If it is pleasure, he has temperance to refrain from it; if it is pain, he has constancy to bear it; if it is danger or death, he has magnanimity and fortitude to despise it. He [7]never complains of the destiny of providence, nor thinks the universe in confusion when he is out of order. He does not look upon himself, according to what self-love would suggest, as a whole, separated and detached from every other part of nature, to be taken care of by itself, and for itself. He regards himself in the light in which he imagines the great Genius of human nature, and of the world [world, *4 5*] regards him. He enters, if I may say so, into the sentiments of that Divine Being, and considers himself as an atom, a particle, of an immense and infinite system, which must, and ought to be disposed of, according to the conveniency of the whole. Assured of the wisdom which directs all the events of human life, whatever lot befalls [befals *5*] him, he accepts it with joy, satisfied that, if he had known all the connexions and dependencies of the different parts of the universe, it is the very lot which he himself would have wished for. If it is life, he is contented to live: and if it is death, as nature [Nature *4 5*] must have no further occasion for his presence here, he willingly goes where he is appointed. I accept, said a stoical philosopher, with equal joy and satisfaction, whatever fortune can befal me. Riches or poverty, pleasure or pain, health or sickness, all is alike: nor would I desire that the Gods [gods *4 5*] should in any respect change my destination. If I was to ask of them any thing, beyond what their bounty has already bestowed, it would [should *2–5*] be that they would inform me beforehand what it was their pleasure should be done with me, that I might of my own accord place myself in this situation, and demonstrate the chearfulness with which I embraced their allotment. If I am going to sail, says Epictetus, I chuse the best ship, and the best pilot, and I wait for the fairest weather that my circumstances and duty will allow. Prudence and propriety, the principles which the Gods [gods *4 5*] have given me for the direction of my conduct, require this of me; but they require no more: and if, notwithstanding, a storm arises, which neither the strength of the vessel, nor the skill of the pilot are likely to withstand, I give myself no trouble about the consequence. All that I had to do, is done already. [*2–5* already, *1*] The directors of my con-

---

[6] For the next eleven sentences cf. VII.ii.1.23.
[7] For the next fifteen sentences cf. VII.ii.1.20.

those which it is most difficult to support. It is often more mortifying to appear in public under small disasters, than under great misfortunes. The first excite no sympathy; but the second, though they may excite none that approaches to the anguish of the sufferer, call forth, however, a very lively compassion. The sentiments of the spectators are, in this last case, less wide of those of the sufferer, and their imperfect fellow-feeling lends him some assistance in supporting his misery. Before a gay assembly, a gentleman would be more mortified to appear covered with filth and rags than with blood and wounds. This last situation would interest their pity; the other would provoke their laughter. The judge who orders a criminal to be set in the pillory, dishonours him more than if he had condemned him to the scaffold. The great prince, who, some years ago, caned a general officer at the head of his army, disgraced him irrecoverably.[8] The punishment would have been much less had he shot him through the body. By the laws of honour, to strike with a cane dishonours, to strike with a sword does not, for an obvious reason. Those slighter punishments, when inflicted on a gentleman, to whom dishonour is the greatest of all evils, come to be regarded among a humane and generous people, as the most dreadful of any. With regard to persons of that rank, therefore, they are universally laid aside, and the law, while it takes their life upon many occasions, respects their honour upon almost all. To scourge a person of quality, or to set him in the pillory, upon account of any crime whatever, is a brutality of which no European government, except that of Russia, is capable.

10   A brave man is not rendered contemptible by being brought to the scaffold; he is, by being set in the pillory. His behaviour in the one situation may gain him universal esteem and admiration. No behaviour in the other can render him agreeable. The sympathy of the spectators supports him in the one case, and saves him from that shame, that consciousness that

duct never command me to be miserable, to be anxious, desponding, or afraid. Whether we are to be drowned, or to come to a harbour, is the business of Jupiter, not mine. I leave it intirely [entirely *4 5*] to his determination, nor ever break my rest with considering which way he is likely to decide it, but receive whatever comes with equal indifference and security.

Such was the philosophy of the stoics. A [stoics; a *2–5*] philosophy which affords the noblest lessons of magnanimity, is the best school of heroes and patriots, and to the greater part of whose precepts there can be no other objection, except that honourable one, that they teach us to aim at a perfection altogether beyond the reach of human nature. I shall not at present stop to examine it. I shall only observe, in confirmation of what has formerly been said, that. . . .

---

[8] We cannot identify this incident. Even Frederick William I of Prussia, who was inordinately fond of using the cane, drew the line at officers, let alone generals. An anecdote about Frederick the Great has a whiff of similarity. Once in a fit of anger he struck with his cane the horse of an officer of the hussars; the officer immediately shot the horse dead, declaring that he could not ride a horse that had been caned: Reinhold Koser, *Geschichte Friedrichs des Grossen*, ed. 4–5 (Stuttgart and Berlin, 1912–14), ii.288. But a horse is not a general.

his misery is felt by himself only, which is of all sentiments the most un-supportable. There is no sympathy in the other; or, if there is any, it is not with his pain, which is a trifle, but with his consciousness of the want of sympathy with which this pain is attended. It is with his shame, not with his sorrow. Those who pity him, blush and hang down their heads for him. He droops in the same manner, and feels himself irrecoverably degraded by the punishment, though not by the crime. The man, on the contrary, who dies with resolution, as he is naturally regarded with the erect aspect of esteem and approbation, so he wears himself the same undaunted coun-tenance; and, if the crime does not deprive him of the respect of others, the punishment never will. He has no suspicion that his situation is the object of contempt or derision to any body, and he can, with propriety, assume the air, not only of perfect serenity, but of triumph and exultation.

11   'Great dangers,' says the Cardinal de Retz, 'have their charms, because there is some glory to be got, even when we miscarry. But moderate dan-gers have nothing but what is horrible, because the loss of reputation al-ways attends the want of success.'⁹ His maxim has the same foundation with what we have been just now observing with regard to punishments.

12   Human virtue is superior to pain, to poverty, to danger, and to death; nor does it even require its utmost efforts do despise them. But to have its misery exposed to insult and derision, to be led in triumph, to be set up for the hand of scorn to point at, is a situation in which its constancy is much more apt to fail. Compared with the contempt of mankind, all other ᵈexternalᵈ evils are easily supported.

ᵃCHAP. III

Of the corruption of our moral sentiments, which is occasioned by this disposition to admire the rich and the great, and to despise or neglect persons of poor and mean condition

1   THIS disposition to admire, and almost to worship, the rich and the power-ful, and to despise, or, at least, to neglect persons of poor and mean con-dition, though necessary both to establish and to maintain the distinction of ranks and the order of society, is, at the same time, the great and most universal cause of the corruption of our moral sentiments. That wealth and greatness are often regarded with the respect and admiration which are

ᵈ⁻ᵈ *om. 1–5*

ᵃ *This chapter was added in ed. 6.*

---

⁹ Cardinal de Retz, *Mémoires*, under Sept. 1648: Pléiade ed. (Paris, 1956), 108 (110 in recent printings); *Oeuvres*, ed. A. Feillet and others (Paris, 1870–1920), ii.68. The English translation is probably Smith's own. Smith refers to the maxim again, with a slightly different form of translation, in LRBL ii.42 (Lothian ed., 98).

due only to wisdom and virtue; and that the contempt, of which vice and folly are the only proper objects, is often most unjustly bestowed upon poverty and weakness, has been the complaint of moralists in all ages.

2   We desire both to be respectable and to be respected. We dread both to be contemptible and to be contemned. But, upon coming into the world, we soon find that wisdom and virtue are by no means the sole objects of respect; nor vice and folly, of contempt. We frequently see the respectful attentions of the world more strongly directed towards the rich and the great, than towards the wise and the virtuous. We see frequently the vices and follies of the powerful much less despised than the poverty and weakness of the innocent. To deserve, to acquire, and to enjoy the respect and admiration of mankind, are the great objects of ambition and emulation. Two different roads are presented to us, equally leading to the attainment of this so much desired object; the one, by the study of wisdom and the practice of virtue; the other, by the acquisition of wealth and greatness. Two different characters are presented to our emulation; the one, of proud ambition and ostentatious avidity; the other, of humble modesty and equitable justice. Two different models, two different pictures, are held out to us, according to which we may fashion our own character and behaviour; the one more gaudy and glittering in its colouring; the other more correct and more exquisitely beautiful in its outline: the one forcing itself upon the notice of every wandering eye; the other, attracting the attention of scarce any body but the most studious and careful observer. They are the wise and the virtuous chiefly, a select, though, I am afraid, but a small party, who are the real and steady admirers of wisdom and virtue. The great mob of mankind are the admirers and worshippers, and, what may seem more extraordinary, most frequently the disinterested admirers and worshippers, of wealth and greatness.

3   The respect which we feel for wisdom and virtue is, no doubt, different from that which we conceive for wealth and greatness; and it requires no very nice discernment to distinguish the difference. But, notwithstanding this difference, those sentiments bear a very considerable resemblance to one another. In some particular features they are, no doubt, different, but, in the general air of the countenance, they seem to be so very nearly the same, that inattentive observers are very apt to mistake the one for the other.

4   In equal degrees of merit there is scarce any man who does not respect more the rich and the great, than the poor and the humble. With most men the presumption and vanity of the former are much more admired, than the real and solid merit of the latter. It is scarce agreeable to good morals, or even to good language, perhaps, to say, that mere wealth and greatness, abstracted from merit and virtue, deserve our respect. We must acknowledge, however, that they almost constantly obtain it; and that they may, therefore, be considered as, in some respects, the natural objects of it.

Those exalted stations may, no doubt, be completely degraded by vice and folly. But the vice and folly must be very great, before they can operate this complete degradation. The profligacy of a man of fashion is looked upon with much less contempt and aversion, than that of a man of meaner condition. In the latter, a single transgression of the rules of temperance and propriety, is commonly more resented, than the constant and avowed contempt of them ever is in the former.

5   In the middling and inferior stations of life, the road to virtue and that to fortune, to such fortune, at least, as men in such stations can reasonably expect to acquire, are, happily in most cases, very nearly the same. In all the middling and inferior professions, real and solid professional abilities, joined to prudent, just, firm, and temperate conduct, can very seldom fail of success. Abilities will even sometimes prevail where the conduct is by no means correct. Either habitual imprudence, however, or injustice, or weakness, or profligacy, will always cloud, and sometimes depress altogether, the most splendid professional abilities. Men in the inferior and middling stations of life, besides, can never be great enough to be above the law, which must generally overawe them into some sort of respect for, at least, the more important rules of justice. The success of such people, too, almost always depends upon the favour and good opinion of their neighbours and equals; and without a tolerably regular conduct these can very seldom be obtained. The good old proverb, therefore, That honesty is the best policy, holds, in such situations, almost always perfectly true. In such situations, therefore, we may generally expect a considerable degree of virtue; and, fortunately for the good morals of society, these are the situations of by far the greater part of mankind.

6   In the superior stations of life the case is unhappily not always the same. In the courts of princes, in the drawing-rooms of the great, where success and preferment depend, not upon the esteem of intelligent and well-informed equals, but upon the fanciful and foolish favour of ignorant, presumptuous, and proud superiors; flattery and falsehood too often prevail over merit and abilities. In such societies the abilities to please, are more regarded than the abilities to serve. In quiet and peaceable times, when the storm is at a distance, the prince, or great man, wishes only to be amused, and is even apt to fancy that he has scarce any occasion for the service of any body, or that those who amuse him are sufficiently able to serve him. The external graces, the frivolous accomplishments of that impertinent and foolish thing called a man of fashion, are commonly more admired than the solid and masculine virtues of a warrior, a statesman, a philosopher, or a legislator. All the great and awful virtues, all the virtues which can fit, either for the council, the senate, or the field, are, by the insolent and insignificant flatterers, who commonly figure the most in such corrupted societies, held in the utmost contempt and derision. When

the duke of Sully was called upon by Lewis the Thirteenth, to give his advice in some great emergency, he observed the favourites and courtiers whispering to one another, and smiling at his unfashionable appearance. 'Whenever your majesty's father,' said the old warrior and statesman, 'did me the honour to consult me, he ordered the buffoons of the court to retire into the antechamber.'[1]

7   It is from our disposition to admire, and consequently to imitate, the rich and the great, that they are enabled to set, or to lead what is called the fashion. Their dress is the fashionable dress; the language of their conversation, the fashionable style; their air and deportment, the fashionable behaviour. Even their vices and follies are fashionable; and the greater part of men are proud to imitate and resemble them in the very qualities which dishonour and degrade them. Vain men often give themselves airs of a fashionable profligacy, which, in their hearts, they do not approve of, and of which, perhaps, they are really not guilty. They desire to be praised for what they themselves do not think praise-worthy, and are ashamed of unfashionable virtues which they sometimes practise in secret, and for which they have secretly some degree of real veneration. There are hypocrites of wealth and greatness, as well as of religion and virtue; and a vain man is as apt to pretend to be what he is not, in the one way, as a cunning man is in the other. He assumes the equipage and splendid way of living of his superiors, without considering that whatever may be praise-worthy in any of these, derives its whole merit and propriety from its suitableness to that situation and fortune which both require and can easily support the expence. Many a poor man places his glory in being thought rich, without considering that the duties (if one may call such follies by so very venerable a name) which that reputation imposes upon him, must soon reduce him to beggary, and render his situation still more unlike that of those whom he admires and imitates, than it had been originally.

8   To attain to this envied situation, the candidates for fortune too frequently abandon the paths of virtue; for unhappily, the road which leads to the one, and that which leads to the other, lie sometimes in very opposite directions. But the ambitious man flatters himself that, in the splendid situation to which he advances, he will have so many means of commanding the respect and admiration of mankind, and will be enabled to act with such superior propriety and grace, that the lustre of his future conduct will entirely cover, or efface, the foulness of the steps by which he arrived at that elevation. In many governments the candidates for the highest stations are above the law; and, if they can attain the object of their ambition, they have no fear of being called to account for the means by which they acquired it. They often endeavour, therefore, not only by fraud and falsehood, the ordinary and vulgar arts of intrigue and cabal; but sometimes

----

[1] *Mémoires du Duc de Sully*, Supplément: in ed. of 1822 (Ledoux, Paris), vi.186.

by the perpetration of the most enormous crimes, by murder and assassina-
tion, by rebellion and civil war, to supplant and destroy those who oppose
or stand in the way of their greatness. They more frequently miscarry
than succeed; and commonly gain nothing but the disgraceful punishment
which is due to their crimes. But, though they should be so lucky as to
attain that wished-for greatness, they are always most miserably disappointed
in the happiness which they expect to enjoy in it. It is not ease or pleasure,
but always honour, of one kind or another, though frequently an honour
very ill understood, that the ambitious man really pursues. But the honour
of his exalted station appears, both in his own eyes and in those of other
people, polluted and defiled by the baseness of the means through which
he rose to it. Though by the profusion of every liberal expence; though by
excessive indulgence in every profligate pleasure, the wretched, but usual,
resource of ruined characters; though by the hurry of public business, or
by the prouder and more dazzling tumult of war, he may endeavour to
efface, both from his own memory and from that of other people, the
remembrance of what he has done; that remembrance never fails to pursue
him. He invokes in vain the dark and dismal powers of forgetfulness and
oblivion. He remembers himself what he has done, and that remembrance
tells him that other people must likewise remember it. Amidst all the gaudy
pomp of the most ostentatious greatness; amidst the venal and vile
adulation of the great and of the learned; amidst the more innocent, though
more foolish, acclamations of the common people; amidst all the pride of
conquest and the triumph of successful war, he is still secretly pursued by
the avenging furies of shame and remorse; and, while glory seems to sur-
round him on all sides, he himself, in his own imagination, sees black and
foul infamy fast pursuing him, and every moment ready to overtake
him from behind. Even the great Caesar, though he had the magnanimity
to dismiss his guards, could not dismiss his suspicions. The remembrance
of Pharsalia still haunted and pursued him. When, at the request of the
senate, he had the generosity to pardon Marcellus, he told that assembly,
that he was not unaware of the designs which were carrying on against
his life; but that, as he had lived long enough both for nature and for glory,
he was contented to die, and therefore despised all conspiracies.[2] He had,

[2] Marcus Claudius Marcellus was a Roman aristocrat hostile to Julius Caesar. His most
notorious act as consul in 51 B.C. was to scourge a magistrate of Como, a colony founded
by Caesar. Marcellus supported Pompey against Caesar in their struggle for power, and
after Caesar had won a decisive victory at the battle of Pharsalus in 48 B.C. Marcellus
retired to Mytilene. In September 46 Caesar pardoned Marcellus at the request of leading
members of the Senate. This was the most notable example of Caesar's 'clemency', aimed
at conciliating the aristocracy to his rule. Cicero was moved to deliver his speech *Pro
Marcello*, expressing appreciation of Caesar's magnanimity. Adam Smith is recalling a
passage from that speech (viii.25), in which Cicero quotes Caesar as having said 'I have
lived long enough either for nature or for glory'. Cicero's own comment (very different
from Smith's) is that Caesar may have lived long enough for nature and perhaps also for
glory, but is far from having lived long enough for the good of Rome.

perhaps, lived long enough for nature. But the man who felt himself the object of such deadly resentment, from those whose favour he wished to gain, and whom he still wished to consider as his friends, had certainly lived too long for real glory; or for all the happiness which he could ever hope to enjoy in the love and esteem of his equals.

PART II

Of MERIT and DEMERIT; or, of the Objects of REWARD and PUNISHMENT
Consisting of Three Sections

SECTION I
Of the SENSE of MERIT and DEMERIT

INTRODUCTION

1 THERE is another set of qualities ascribed to the actions and conduct of mankind, distinct from their propriety or impropriety, their decency or ungracefulness, and which are the objects of a distinct species of approbation and disapprobation. These are Merit and Demerit, the qualities of deserving reward, and of deserving punishment.

2 It has already been observed,[1] that the sentiment or affection of the heart, from which any action proceeds, and upon which its whole virtue or vice depends, may be considered under two different aspects, or in two different relations: first, in relation to the cause or object which excites it; and, secondly, in relation to the end which it proposes, or to the effect which it tends to produce: that upon the suitableness or unsuitableness, upon the proportion or disproportion, which the affection seems to bear to the cause or object which excites it, depends the propriety or impropriety, the decency or ungracefulness of the consequent action; and that upon the beneficial or hurtful effects which the affection proposes or tends to produce, depends the merit or demerit, the good or ill desert of the action to which it gives occasion. Wherein consists our sense of the propriety or impropriety of actions, has been explained in the former part of this discourse. We come now to consider, wherein consists that of their good or ill desert.

CHAP. I[1]

That whatever appears to be the proper object of gratitude, appears to deserve reward; and that, in the same manner, whatever appears to be the proper object of resentment, appears to deserve punishment

1 To us, therefore, that action must appear to deserve reward, which appears to be the proper and approved object of that sentiment, which most immediately and directly prompts us to reward, or to do good to another.

---

[1] I.i.3.5–7

[1] The mode of exposition in this chapter of TMS seems to retain, more than most, the original form of Smith's lecturing method, which John Millar described as follows: 'Each discourse consisted commonly of several distinct propositions, which he successively endeavoured to prove and illustrate' (Stewart, I.21).

And in the same manner, that action must appear to deserve punishment, which appears to be the proper and approved object of that sentiment which most immediately and directly prompts us to punish, or to inflict evil upon another.

2 The sentiment which most immediately and directly prompts us to reward, is gratitude; that which most immediately and directly prompts us to punish, is resentment.

3 To us, therefore, that action must appear to deserve reward, which appears to be the proper and approved object of gratitude; as, on the other hand, that action must appear to deserve punishment, which appears to be the proper and approved object of resentment.

4 To reward, is to recompense, to remunerate, to return good for good received. To punish, too, is to recompense, to remunerate, though in a different manner; it is to return evil for evil that has been done.

5 There are some other passions, besides gratitude and resentment, which interest us in the happiness or misery of others; but there are none which so directly excite us to be the instruments of either. The love and esteem which grow upon acquaintance and habitual approbation, necessarily lead us to be pleased with the good fortune of the man who is the object of such agreeable emotions, and consequently, to be willing to lend a hand to promote it. Our love, however, is fully satisfied, though his good fortune should be brought about without our assistance. All that this passion desires is to see him happy, without regarding who was the author of his prosperity. But gratitude is not to be satisfied in this manner. If the person to whom we owe many obligations, is made happy without our assistance, though it pleases our love, it does not content our gratitude. Till we have recompensed him, till we ourselves have been instrumental in promoting his happiness, we feel ourselves still loaded with that debt which his past services have laid upon us.

6 The hatred and dislike, in the same manner, which grow upon habitual disapprobation, would often lead us to take a malicious pleasure in the misfortune of the man whose conduct and character excite so painful a passion. But though dislike and hatred harden us against all sympathy, and sometimes dispose us even to rejoice at the distress of another, yet, if there is no resentment in the case, if neither we nor our friends have received any great personal provocation, these passions would not naturally lead us to wish to be instrumental in bringing it about. Though we could fear no punishment in consequence of our having had some hand in it, we would rather that it should happen by other means. To one under the dominion of violent hatred it would be agreeable, perhaps, to hear, that the person whom he abhorred and detested was killed by some accident. But if he had the least spark of justice, which, though this passion is not very favourable to virtue, he might still have, it would hurt him excessively

to have been himself, even without design, the occasion of this misfortune. Much more would the very thought of voluntarily contributing to it shock him beyond all measure. He would reject with horror even the imagination of so execrable a design; and if he could imagine himself capable of such an enormity, he would begin to regard himself in the same odious light in which he had considered the person who was the object of his dislike. But it is quite otherwise with resentment: if the person who had done us some great injury, who had murdered our father or our brother, for example, should soon afterwards die of a fever, or even be brought to the scaffold upon account of some other crime, though it might sooth our hatred, it would not fully gratify our resentment. Resentment would prompt us to desire, not only that he should be punished, but that he should be punished by our means, and upon account of that particular injury which he had done to us. Resentment cannot be fully gratified, unless the offender is not only made to grieve in his turn, but to grieve for that particular wrong which we have suffered from him. He must be made to repent and be sorry for this very action, that others, through fear of the like punishment, may be terrified from being guilty of the like offence. The natural gratification of this passion tends, of its own accord, to produce all the political ends of punishment; the correction of the criminal, and the example to the public.

7   Gratitude and resentment, therefore, are the sentiments which most immediately and directly prompt to reward and to punish. To us, therefore, he must appear to deserve reward, who appears to be the proper and approved object of gratitude; and he to deserve punishment, who appears to be that of resentment.

CHAP. II

Of the proper objects of gratitude and resentment

1   To be the proper and approved object either of gratitude or resentment, can mean nothing but to be the object of that gratitude, and of that resentment, which naturally seems proper, and is approved of.

2   But these, as well as all the other passions of human nature, seem proper and are approved of, when the heart of every impartial spectator entirely sympathizes with them, when every indifferent by-stander entirely enters into, and goes along with them.

3   He, therefore, appears to deserve reward, who, to some person or persons, is the natural object of a gratitude which every human heart is disposed to beat time to, and thereby applaud: and he, on the other hand, appears to deserve punishment, who in the same manner is to some person or persons the natural object of a resentment which the breast of every

reasonable man is ready to adopt and sympathize with. To us, surely, that action must appear to deserve reward, which every body who knows of it would wish to reward, and therefore delights to see rewarded: and that action must as surely appear to deserve punishment, which every body who hears of it is angry with, and upon that account rejoices to see punished.

4 1. As we sympathize with the joy of our companions when in prosperity, so we join with them in the complacency and satisfaction with which they naturally regard whatever is the cause of their good fortune. We enter into the love and affection which they conceive for it, and begin to love it too. We should be sorry for their sakes if it was destroyed, or even if it was placed at too great a distance from them, and out of the reach of their care and protection, though they should lose nothing by its absence except the pleasure of seeing it. If it is man who has thus been the fortunate instrument of the happiness of his brethren, this is still more peculiarly the case. When we see one man assisted, protected, relieved by another, our sympathy with the joy of the person who receives the benefit serves only to animate our fellow-feeling with his gratitude towards him who bestows it. When we look upon the person who is the cause of his pleasure with the eyes with which we imagine he must look upon him, his benefactor seems to stand before us in the most engaging and amiable light. We readily therefore sympathize with the grateful affection which he conceives for a person to whom he has been so much obliged; and consequently applaud the returns which he is disposed to make for the good offices conferred upon him. As we entirely enter into the affection from which these returns proceed, they necessarily seem every way proper and suitable to their object.

5 2. In the same manner, as we sympathize with the sorrow of our fellow-creature whenever we see his distress, so we likewise enter into his abhorrence and aversion for whatever has given occasion to it. Our heart, as it adopts and beats time to his grief, so is it likewise animated with that spirit by which he endeavours to drive away or destroy the cause of it. The indolent and passive fellow-feeling, by which we accompany him in his sufferings, readily gives way to that more vigorous and active sentiment by which we go along with him in the effort he makes, either to repel them, or to gratify his aversion to what has given occasion to them. This is still more peculiarly the case, when it is man who has caused them. When we see one man oppressed or injured by another, the sympathy which we feel with the distress of the sufferer seems to serve only to animate our fellow-feeling with his resentment against the offender. We are rejoiced to see him attack his adversary in his turn, and are eager and ready to assist him whenever he exerts himself for defence, or even for vengeance within a

certain degree. If the injured should perish in the quarrel, we not only sympathize with the real resentment of his friends and relations, but with the imaginary resentment which in fancy we lend to the dead, who is no longer capable of feeling that or any other human sentiment. But as we put ourselves in his situation, as we enter, as it were, into his body, and in our imaginations, in some measure, animate anew the deformed and mangled carcass of the slain, when we bring home in this manner his case to our own bosoms, we feel upon this, as upon many other occasions, an emotion which the person principally concerned is incapable of feeling, and which yet we feel by an illusive sympathy with him. The sympathetic tears which we shed for that immense and irretrievable loss, which in our fancy he appears to have sustained, seem to be but a small part of the duty which we owe him. The injury which he has suffered demands, we think, a principal part of our attention. We feel that resentment which we imagine he ought to feel, and which he would feel, if in his cold and lifeless body there remained any consciousness of what passes upon earth. His blood, we think, calls aloud for vengeance. The very ashes of the dead seem to be disturbed at the thought that his injuries are to pass unrevenged. The horrors which are supposed to haunt the bed of the murderer, the ghosts which, superstition imagines, rise from their graves to demand vengeance upon those who brought them to an untimely end, all take their origin from this natural sympathy with the imaginary resentment of the slain. And with regard, at least, to this most dreadful of all crimes, Nature, antecedent to all reflections upon the utility of punishment, has in this manner stamped upon the human heart, in the strongest and most indelible characters, an immediate and instinctive approbation of the sacred and necessary law of retaliation.

CHAP. III

That where there is no approbation of the conduct of the person who confers the benefit, there is little sympathy with the gratitude of him who receives it: and that, on the contrary, where there is no disapprobation of the motives of the person who does the mischief, there is no sort of sympathy with the resentment of him who suffers it

1   IT is to be observed, however, that, how beneficial soever on the one hand, or how hurtful soever on the other, the actions or intentions of the person who acts may have been to the person who is, if I may say so, acted upon, yet if in the one case there appears to have been no propriety in the motives of the agent, if we cannot enter into the affections which influenced his conduct, we have little sympathy with the gratitude of the person who receives the benefit: or if, in the other case, there appears to have been no impropriety in the motives of the agent, if, on the contrary, the affections which influenced his conduct are such as we must necessarily enter into, we can have no sort of sympathy with the resentment of the person who

suffers. Little gratitude seems due in the one case, and all sort of resentment seems unjust in the other. The one action seems to merit little reward, the other to deserve no punishment.

2   1.   First, I say, *a*That*a* wherever we cannot sympathize with the affections of the agent, wherever there seems to be no propriety in the motives which influenced his conduct, we are less disposed to enter into the gratitude of the person who received the benefit of his actions. A very small return seems due to that foolish and profuse generosity which confers the greatest benefits from the most trivial motives, and gives an estate to a man merely because his name and sirname happen to be the same with those of the giver. Such services do not seem to demand any proportionable recompense. Our contempt for the folly of the agent hinders us from thoroughly entering into the gratitude of the person to whom the good office has been done. His benefactor seems unworthy of it. As when we place ourselves in the situation of the person obliged, we feel that we could conceive no great reverence for such a benefactor, we easily absolve him from a great deal of that submissive veneration and esteem which we should think due to a more respectable character; and provided he always treats his weak friend with kindness and humanity, we are willing to excuse him from many attentions and regards which we should demand to a worthier patron. Those Princes, who have heaped, with the greatest profusion, wealth, power, and honours, upon their favourites, have seldom excited that degree of attachment to their persons which has often been experienced by those who were more frugal of their favours. The well-natured, but injudicious prodigality of James the First of Great Britain seems to have attached nobody to his person; and that Prince, notwithstanding his social and harmless disposition, appears to have lived and died without a friend. The whole gentry and nobility of England exposed their lives and fortunes in the cause of his more frugal and distinguishing son, notwithstanding the coldness and distant severity of his ordinary deportment.

3   2.   Secondly, I say, That wherever the conduct of the agent appears to have been entirely directed by motives and affections which we thoroughly enter into and approve of, we can have no sort of sympathy with the resentment of the sufferer, how great soever the mischief which may have been done to him. When two people quarrel, if we take part with, and entirely adopt the resentment of one of them, it is impossible that we should enter into that of the other. Our sympathy with the person whose motives we go along with, and whom therefore we look upon as in the right, cannot but harden us against all fellow-feeling with the other, whom we necessarily regard as in the wrong. Whatever this last, therefore, may have

a-a *1-3 7* that *4-6* Cf. § 3, *line 1, where all eds. retain* That

suffered, while it is no more than what we ourselves should have wished him to suffer, while it is no more than what our own sympathetic indignation would have prompted us to inflict upon him, it cannot either displease or provoke us. When an inhuman murderer is brought to the scaffold, though we have some compassion for his misery, we can have no sort of fellow-feeling with his resentment, if he should be so absurd as to express any against either his prosecutor or his judge. The natural tendency of their just indignation against so vile a criminal is indeed the most fatal and ruinous to him. But it is impossible that we should be displeased with the tendency of a sentiment, which, when we bring the case home to ourselves, we feel that we cannot avoid adopting.

CHAP. IV

Recapitulation of the foregoing chapters

1 1. WE do not, therefore, thoroughly and heartily sympathize with the gratitude of one man towards another, merely because this other has been the cause of his good fortune, unless he has been the cause of it from motives which we entirely go along with. Our heart must adopt the principles of the agent, and go along with all the affections which influenced his conduct, before it can entirely sympathize with, and beat time to, the gratitude of the person who has been benefited by his actions. If in the conduct of the benefactor there appears to have been no propriety, how beneficial soever its effects, it does not seem to demand, or necessarily to require, any proportionable recompense.

2   But when to the beneficent tendency of the action is joined the propriety of the affection from which it proceeds, when we entirely sympathize and go along with the motives of the agent, the love which we conceive for him upon his own account, enhances and enlivens our fellow-feeling with the gratitude of those who owe their prosperity to his good conduct. His actions seem then to demand, and, if I may say so, to call aloud for a proportionable recompense. We then entirely enter into that gratitude which prompts to bestow it. The benefactor seems then to be the proper object of reward, when we thus entirely sympathize with, and approve of, that sentiment which prompts to reward him. When we approve of, and go along with, the affection from which the action proceeds, we must necessarily approve of the action, and regard the person towards whom it is directed, as its proper and suitable object.

3   2. In the same manner, we cannot at all sympathize with the resentment of one man against another, merely because this other has been the

cause of his misfortune, unless he has been the cause of it from motives which we cannot enter into. Before we can adopt the resentment of the sufferer, we must disapprove of the motives of the agent, and feel that our heart renounces all sympathy with the affections which influenced his conduct. If there appears to have been no impropriety in these, how fatal soever the tendency of the action which proceeds from them to those against whom it is directed, it does not seem to deserve any punishment, or to be the proper object of any resentment.

4   But when to the hurtfulness of the action is joined the impropriety of the affection from whence it proceeds, when our heart rejects with abhorrence all fellow-feeling with the motives of the agent, we then heartily and entirely sympathize with the resentment of the sufferer. Such actions seem then to deserve, and, if I may say so, to call aloud for, a proportionable punishment; and we entirely enter into, and thereby approve of, that resentment which prompts to inflict it. The offender necessarily seems then to be the proper object of punishment, when we thus entirely sympathize with, and thereby approve of, that sentiment which prompts to punish. In this case too, when we approve, and go along with, the affection from which the action proceeds, we must necessarily approve of the action, and regard the person against whom it is directed, as its proper and suitable object.

CHAP. V

The analysis of the sense of Merit and Demerit

1   1.   As our sense, therefore, of the propriety of conduct arises from what I shall call a direct sympathy with the affections and motives of the person who acts, so our sense of its merit arises from what I shall call an indirect sympathy with the gratitude of the person who is, if I may say so, acted upon.

2   As we cannot indeed enter thoroughly into the gratitude of the person who receives the benefit, unless we beforehand approve of the motives of the benefactor, so, upon this account, the sense of merit seems to be a compounded sentiment, and to be made up of two distinct emotions; a direct sympathy with the sentiments of the agent, and an indirect sympathy with the gratitude of those who receive the benefit of his actions.

3   We may, upon many different occasions, plainly distinguish those two different emotions combining and uniting together in our sense of the good desert of a particular character or action. When we read in history concerning actions of proper and beneficent greatness of mind, how eagerly do we enter into such designs? How much are we animated by that high-spirited generosity which directs them? How keen are we for their success?

How grieved at their disappointment? In imagination we become the very person whose actions are represented to us: we transport ourselves in fancy to the scenes of those distant and forgotten adventures, and imagine ourselves acting the part of a Scipio or a Camillus, a Timoleon or an Aristides.[1] So far our sentiments are founded upon the direct sympathy with the person who acts. Nor is the indirect sympathy with those who receive the benefit of such actions less sensibly felt. Whenever we place ourselves in the situation of these last, with what warm and affectionate fellow-feeling do we enter into their gratitude towards those who served them so essentially? We embrace, as it were, their benefactor along with them. Our heart readily sympathizes with the highest transports of their grateful affection. No honours, no rewards, we think, can be too great for them to bestow upon him. When they make this proper return for his services, we heartily applaud and go along with them; but are shocked beyond all measure, if by their conduct they appear to have little sense of the obligations conferred upon them. Our whole sense, in short, of the merit and good desert of such actions, of the propriety and fitness of recompensing them, and making the person who performed them rejoice in his turn, arises from the sympathetic emotions of gratitude and love, with which, when we bring home to our own breast the situation of those principally concerned, we feel ourselves naturally transported towards the man who could act with such proper and noble beneficence.

4   2.   In the same manner as our sense of the impropriety of conduct arises from a want of sympathy, or from a direct antipathy to the affections and motives of the agent, so our sense of its demerit arises from what I shall here too call an indirect sympathy with the resentment of the sufferer.

5   As we cannot indeed enter into the resentment of the sufferer, unless our heart beforehand disapproves the motives of the agent, and renounces all fellow-feeling with them; so upon this account the sense of demerit, as well as that of merit, seems to be a compounded sentiment, and to be made up of two distinct emotions; a direct antipathy to the sentiments of the agent, and an indirect sympathy with the resentment of the sufferer.

[1] Smith thinks of all four as men of great military prowess and patriotism whose services were not properly appreciated. Publius Cornelius Scipio Africanus led the Romans to victory against Hannibal in the Second Punic War. He later retired from public life embittered by attacks on his family. Marcus Furius Camillus delivered Rome from invasion by the Gauls and is called by Livy the 'second founder' of the city. Tradition has it that after an earlier military success he was accused of having unfairly distributed the booty and so he went into voluntary exile. Timoleon of Corinth overthrew the despotic rule of his brother and then, many years later, was sent by the Corinthians to liberate Sicily from tyrants and invaders. Between these two exploits he lived in retirement because his mother and his kinsmen blamed him for having allowed his brother to be put to death. Aristides 'the Just' was an Athenian statesman and general who took a leading part in the defeat of the Persian invaders of Greece at the battles of Salamis and Plataea. He was ostracized for a time owing to political rivalry with Themistocles.

6   We may here too, upon many different occasions, plainly distinguish those two different emotions combining and uniting together in our sense of the ill desert of a particular character or action. When we read in history concerning the perfidy and cruelty of a Borgia or a Nero, our heart rises up against the detestable sentiments which influenced their conduct, and renounces with horror and abomination all fellow-feeling with such execrable motives. So far our sentiments are founded upon the direct antipathy to the affections of the agent: and the indirect sympathy with the resentment of the sufferers is still more sensibly felt. When we bring home to ourselves the situation of the persons whom those scourges of mankind insulted, murdered, or betrayed, what indignation do we not feel against such insolent and inhuman oppressors of the earth? Our sympathy with the unavoidable distress of the innocent sufferers is not more real nor more lively, than our fellow-feeling with their just and natural resentment: The former sentiment only heightens the latter, and the idea of their distress serves only to inflame and blow up our animosity against those who occasioned it. When we think of the anguish of the sufferers, we take part with them more earnestly against their oppressors; we enter with more eagerness into all their schemes of vengeance, and feel ourselves every moment wreaking, in imagination, upon such violators of the laws of society, that punishment which our sympathetic indignation tells us is due to their crimes. Our sense of the horror and dreadful atrocity of such conduct, the delight which we take in hearing that it was properly punished, the indignation which we feel when it escapes this due retaliation, our whole sense and feeling, in short, of its ill desert, of the propriety and fitness of inflicting evil upon the person who is guilty of it, and of making him grieve in his turn, arises from the sympathetic indignation which naturally boils up in the breast of the spectator, whenever he thoroughly brings home to himself the case of the sufferer*.

7   * To ascribe in this manner our natural sense of the ill desert of human actions to a sympathy with the resentment of the sufferer, may seem, to the greater part of people, to be a degradation of that sentiment. Resentment is commonly regarded as so odious a passion, that they will be apt to think it impossible that so laudable a principle, as the sense of the ill desert of vice, should in any respect be founded upon it. They will be more willing, perhaps, to admit that our sense of the merit of good actions is founded upon a sympathy with the gratitude of the persons who receive the benefit of them; because gratitude, as well as all the other benevolent passions, is regarded as an amiable principle, which can take nothing from the worth of whatever is founded upon it. Gratitude and resentment, however, are in every respect, it is evident, counterparts to one another; and if our sense of merit arises from a sympathy with the one, our sense of demerit can scarce miss to proceed from a fellow-feeling with the other.

8   Let it be considered too that resentment, though, in the degrees in which we too often see it, the most odious, perhaps, of all the passions, is not disapproved of when properly humbled and entirely brought down to the level of the sympathetic indignation of the spectator. When we, who are the bystanders, feel that our own animosity entirely corresponds with that of the sufferer, when the resentment of this last does not in any respect go beyond our own, when no word, no gesture, escapes him that denotes an emotion more

violent than what we can keep time to, and when he never aims at inflicting any punishment beyond what we should rejoice to see inflicted, or what we ourselves would upon this account even desire to be the instruments of inflicting, it is impossible that we should not entirely approve of his sentiments. Our own emotion in this case must, in our eyes, undoubtedly justify his. And as experience teaches us how much the greater part of mankind are incapable of this moderation, and how great an effort must be made in order to bring down the rude and undisciplined impulse of resentment to this suitable temper, we cannot avoid conceiving a considerable degree of esteem and admiration for one who appears capable of exerting so much self-command over one of the most ungovernable passions of his nature. When indeed the animosity of the sufferer exceeds, as it almost always does, what we can go along with, as we cannot enter into it, we necessarily disapprove of it. We even disapprove of it more than we should of an equal excess of almost any other passion derived from the imagination. And this too violent resentment, instead of carrying us along with it, becomes itself the object of our resentment and indignation. We enter into the opposite resentment of the person who is the object of this unjust emotion, and who is in danger of suffering from it. Revenge, therefore, the excess of resentment, appears to be the most detestable of all the passions, and is the object of the horror and indignation of every body. And as in the way in which this passion commonly discovers itself among mankind, it is excessive a hundred times for once that it is moderate, we are very apt to consider it as altogether odious and detestable, because in its most ordinary appearances it is so. Nature, however, even in the present depraved state of mankind, does not seem to have dealt so unkindly with us, as to have endowed us with any principle which is wholly and in every respect evil, or which, in no degree and in no direction, can be the proper object of praise and approbation. Upon some occasions we are sensible that this passion, which is generally too strong, may likewise be too weak. We sometimes complain that a particular person shows too little spirit, and has too little sense of the injuries that have been done to him; and we are as ready to despise him for the defect, as to hate him for the excess of this passion.

9   The inspired writers would not surely have talked so frequently or so strongly of the wrath and anger of God, if they had regarded every degree of those passions as vicious and evil, even in so weak and imperfect a creature as man.

10   Let it be considered too, that the present inquiry is not concerning a matter of right, if I may say so, but concerning a matter of fact. We are not at present examining upon what principles a perfect being would approve of the punishment of bad actions; but upon what principles so weak and imperfect a creature as man actually and in fact approves of it. The principles which I have just now mentioned, it is evident, have a very great effect upon his sentiments; and it seems wisely ordered that it should be so. The very existence of society requires that unmerited and unprovoked malice should be restrained by proper punishments; and consequently, that to inflict those punishments should be regarded as a proper and laudable action. Though man, therefore, be naturally endowed with a desire of the welfare and preservation of society, yet the Author of nature has not entrusted it to his reason to find out that a certain application of punishments is the proper means of attaining this end; but has endowed him with an immediate and instinctive approbation of that very application which is most proper to attain it. The oeconomy of nature is in this respect exactly of a piece with what it is upon many other occasions. With regard to all those ends which, upon account of their peculiar importance, may be regarded, if such an expression is allowable, as the favourite ends of nature, she has constantly in this manner not only endowed mankind with an appetite for the end which she proposes, but likewise with an appetite for the means by which alone this end can be brought about, for their own sakes, and independent of their tendency to produce it. Thus self-preservation, and the propagation of the species, are the great ends which Nature seems to have proposed in the formation of all animals. Mankind are endowed with a desire of those ends, and an aversion to the contrary; with a love of life, and a dread of dissolution; with a desire of the continuance and perpetuity of the species, and with an aversion to the thoughts of its intire extinction. But though we are in this manner endowed with a very strong desire of those ends, it has not been intrusted to the slow and uncertain determinations of our reason, to find out the proper means of bringing them about. Nature has directed us to the greater

part of these by original and immediate instincts. Hunger, thirst, the passion which unites the two sexes, the love of pleasure, and the dread of pain, prompt us to apply those means for their own sakes, and without any consideration of their tendency to those beneficent ends which the great Director of nature intended to produce by them.

11   Before I conclude this note, I must take notice of a difference between the approbation of propriety and that of merit or beneficence. Before we approve of the sentiments of any person as proper and suitable to their objects, we must not only be affected in the same manner as he is, but we must perceive this harmony and correspondence of sentiments between him and ourselves. Thus, though upon hearing of a misfortune that had befallen my friend, I should conceive precisely that degree of concern which he gives way to; yet till I am informed of the manner in which he behaves, till I perceive the harmony between his emotions and mine, I cannot be said to approve of the sentiments which influence his behaviour. The approbation of propriety therefore requires, not only that we should entirely sympathize with the person who acts, but that we should perceive this perfect concord between his sentiments and our own. On the contrary, when I hear of a benefit that has been bestowed upon another person, let him who has received it be affected in what manner he pleases, if, by bringing his case home to myself, I feel gratitude arise in my own breast, I necessarily approve of the conduct of his benefactor, and regard it as meritorious, and the proper object of reward. Whether the person who has received the benefit conceives gratitude or not, cannot, it is evident, in any degree alter our sentiments with regard to the merit of him who has bestowed it. No actual correspondence of sentiments, therefore, is here required. It is sufficient that if he was grateful, they would correspond; and our sense of merit is often founded upon one of those illusive sympathies, by which, when we bring home to ourselves the case of another, we are often affected in a manner in which the person principally concerned is incapable of being affected. There is a similar difference between our disapprobation of demerit, and that of impropriety.

SECTION II
Of Justice and Beneficence

CHAP. I
Comparison of those two virtues

1   ACTIONS of a beneficent tendency, which proceed from proper motives, seem alone to require reward; because such alone are the approved objects of gratitude, or excite the sympathetic gratitude of the spectator.

2   Actions of a hurtful tendency, which proceed from improper motives, seem alone to deserve punishment; because such alone are the approved objects of resentment, or excite the sympathetic resentment of the spectator.

3   Beneficence is always free, it cannot be extorted by force, the mere want of it exposes to no punishment; because the mere want of beneficence tends to do no real positive evil. It may disappoint of the good which might reasonably have been expected, and upon that account it may justly excite dislike and disapprobation: it cannot, however, provoke any resentment which mankind will go along with. The man who does not recompense his benefactor, when he has it in his power, and when his benefactor needs his assistance, is, no doubt, guilty of the blackest ingratitude. The heart of every impartial spectator rejects all fellow-feeling with the selfishness of his motives, and he is the proper object of the highest disapprobation.

But still he does no positive hurt to any body. He only does not do that good which in propriety he ought to have done. He is the object of hatred, a passion which is naturally excited by impropriety of sentiment and behaviour; not of resentment, a passion which is never properly called forth but by actions which tend to do real and positive hurt to some particular persons. His want of gratitude, therefore, cannot be punished. To oblige him by force to perform what in gratitude he ought to perform, and what every impartial spectator would approve of him for performing, would, if possible, be still more improper than his neglecting to perform it. His benefactor would dishonour himself if he attempted by violence to constrain him to gratitude, and it would be impertinent for any third person, who was not the superior of either, to intermeddle. But of all the duties of beneficence, those which gratitude recommends to us approach nearest to what is called a perfect and complete obligation. What friendship, what generosity, what charity, would prompt us to do with universal approbation, is still more free, and can still less be extorted by force than the duties of gratitude. We talk of the debt of gratitude, not of charity, or generosity, nor even of friendship, when friendship is mere esteem, and has not been enhanced and complicated with gratitude for good offices.

4   Resentment seems to have been given us by nature for defence, and for defence only. It is the safeguard of justice and the security of innocence. It prompts us to beat off the mischief which is attempted to be done to us, and to retaliate that which is already done; that the offender may be made to repent of his injustice, and that others, through fear of the like punishment, may be terrified from being guilty of the like offence. It must be reserved therefore for these purposes, nor can the spectator ever go along with it when it is exerted for any other. But the mere want of the beneficent virtues, though it may disappoint us of the good which might reasonably be expected, neither does, not attempts to do, any mischief from which we can have occasion to defend ourselves.

5   There *is, however,* another virtue, of which the observance is not left to the freedom of our own wills, which may be extorted by force, and of which the violation exposes to resentment, and consequently to punishment. This virtue is justice: the violation of justice is injury: it does real and positive hurt to some particular persons, from motives which are naturally disapproved of. It is, therefore, the proper object of resentment, and of punishment, which is the natural consequence of resentment. As mankind go along with, and approve of the violence employed to avenge the hurt which is done by injustice, so they much more go along with, and approve of, that which is employed to prevent and beat off the injury, and to restrain the offender from hurting his neighbours. The person himself who meditates an injustice is sensible of this, and feels that force

may, with the utmost propriety, be made use of, both by the person whom he is about to injure, and by others, either to obstruct the execution of his crime, or to punish him when he has executed it. And upon this is founded that remarkable distinction between justice and all the other social virtues, which has of late been particularly insisted upon by an author of very great and original genius,[1] that we feel ourselves to be under a stricter obligation to act according to justice, than agreeably to friendship, charity, or generosity; that the practice of these last mentioned virtues seems to be left in some measure to our own choice, but that, somehow or other, we feel ourselves to be in a peculiar manner tied, bound, and obliged to the observation of justice. We feel, that is to say, that force may, with the utmost propriety, and with the approbation of all mankind, be made use of to constrain us to observe the rules of the one, but not to follow the precepts of the other.

6   We must always, however, carefully distinguish what is only blamable, or the proper object of disapprobation, from what force may be employed either to punish or to prevent. That seems blamable which falls short of that ordinary degree of proper beneficence which experience teaches us to expect of every body; and on the contrary, that seems praise-worthy which goes beyond it. The ordinary degree itself seems neither blamable nor praise-worthy. A father, a son, a brother, who behaves to the correspondent relation neither better nor worse than the greater part of men commonly do, seems properly to deserve neither praise nor blame. He who surprises us by extraordinary and unexpected, though still proper and suitable kindness, or on the contrary by extraordinary and unexpected, as well as unsuitable unkindness, seems praise-worthy in the one case, and blamable in the other.

7   Even the most ordinary degree of kindness or beneficence, however, cannot, among equals, be extorted by force. Among equals each individual is naturally, and antecedent to the institution of civil government, regarded as having a right both to defend himself from injuries, and to exact a certain degree of punishment for those which have been done to him.

---

[1] Henry Home, Lord Kames, in *Essays on the Principles of Morality and Natural Religion* (1751), Part I, essay ii ('Of the Foundation and Principles of the Law of Nature'), chaps. 3–4. To call him 'an author of very great and original genius' seems extravagant but no doubt reflects Smith's gratitude to Kames, who was one of three friends responsible for arranging Smith's Edinburgh lectures in 1748 and who probably also recommended him for the Chair of Logic at Glasgow in 1751. Smith cannot be referring here to Hume, whose distinctions between justice and benevolence (*Enquiry concerning the Principles of Morals* (1751), II–III and appendix iii: *Treatise of Human Nature*, III (1740), ii.1–2 and 6; iii.1) are drawn quite differently. Eckstein (i.290) thinks, with others, that the flattering description probably refers to Hume, but notes that Hume does not speak of a 'stricter obligation' to justice than to other virtues, and therefore adds that the reference may be to Kames. Bonar, *Catalogue 1*, 52, attributes the reference to Hume, but acknowledges in *Catalogue 2*, 97–8, that Eckstein's alternative suggestion is correct. Apart from stressing the stricter obligation of justice as a 'primary virtue', Kames writes that justice 'is considered as less free than generosity' (p. 71); cf. Smith here and in § 3 above.

Every generous spectator not only approves of his conduct when he does this, but enters so far into his sentiments as often to be willing to assist him. When one man attacks, or robs, or attempts to murder another, all the neighbours take the alarm, and think that they do right when they run, either to revenge the person who has been injured, or to defend him who is in danger of being so. But when a father fails in the ordinary degree of parental affection towards a son; when a son seems to want that filial reverence which might be expected to his father; when brothers are without the usual degree of brotherly affection; when a man shuts his breast against compassion, and refuses to relieve the misery of his fellow-creatures, when he can with the greatest ease; in all these cases, though every body blames the conduct, nobody imagines that those who might have reason, perhaps, to expect more kindness, have any right to extort it by force. The sufferer can only complain, and the spectator can intermeddle no other way than by advice and persuasion. Upon all such occasions, for equals to use force against one another, would be thought the highest degree of insolence and presumption.

8   A superior may, indeed, sometimes, with universal approbation, oblige those under his jurisdiction to behave, in this respect, with a certain degree of propriety to one another. The laws of all civilized nations oblige parents to maintain their children, and children to maintain their parents, and impose upon men many other duties of beneficence. The civil magistrate is entrusted with the power not only of preserving the public peace by restraining injustice, but of promoting the prosperity of the commonwealth, by establishing good discipline, and by discouraging every sort of vice and impropriety; he may prescribe rules, therefore, which not only prohibit mutual injuries among fellow-citizens, but command mutual good offices to a certain degree. When the sovereign commands what is merely indifferent, and what, antecedent to his orders, might have been omitted without any blame, it becomes not only blamable but punishable to disobey him. When he commands, therefore, what, antecedent to any such order, could not have been omitted without the greatest blame, it surely becomes much more punishable to be wanting in obedience. Of all the duties of a law-giver, however, this, perhaps, is that which it requires the greatest delicacy and reserve to execute with propriety and judgment. To neglect it altogether exposes the commonwealth to many gross disorders and shocking enormities, and to push it too far is destructive of all liberty, security, and justice.

9   Though the mere want of beneficence seems to merit no punishment from equals, the greater exertions of that virtue appear to deserve the highest reward. By being productive of the greatest good, they are the natural and approved objects of the liveliest gratitude. Though the breach of justice, on the contrary, exposes to punishment, the observance of the

rules of that virtue seems scarce to deserve any reward. There is, no doubt, a propriety in the practice of justice, and it merits, upon that account, all the approbation which is due to propriety. But as it does no real positive good, it is entitled to very little gratitude. Mere justice is, upon most occasions, but a negative virtue, and only hinders us from hurting our neighbour. The man who barely abstains from violating either the person, or the estate, or the reputation of his neighbours, has surely very little positive merit. He fulfils, however, all the rules of what is peculiarly called justice, and does every thing which his equals can with propriety force him to do, or which they can punish him for not doing. We may often fulfil all the rules of justice by sitting still and doing nothing.

10 As every man doth, so shall it be done to him, and retaliation seems to be the great law which is dictated to us by Nature. Beneficence and generosity we think due to the generous and beneficent. Those whose hearts never open to the feelings of humanity, should, we think, be shut *out,* in the same manner, from the affections of all their fellow-creatures, and be allowed to live in the midst of society, as in a great desert where there is nobody to care for them, or to inquire after them. The violator of the laws of justice ought to be made to feel himself that evil which he has done to another; and since no regard to the sufferings of his brethren is capable of restraining him, he ought to be over-awed by the fear of his own. The man who is barely innocent, who only observes the laws of justice with regard to others, and merely abstains from hurting his neighbours, can merit only that his neighbours in their turn should respect his innocence, and that the same laws should be religiously observed with regard to him.

CHAP. II
Of the sense of Justice, of Remorse, and of the consciousness of Merit

1 THERE can be no proper motive for hurting our neighbour, there can be no incitement to do evil to another, which mankind will go along with, except just indignation for evil which that other has done to us. To disturb his happiness merely because it stands in the way of our own, to take from him what is of real use to him merely because it may be of equal or of more use to us, or to indulge, in this manner, at the expence of other people, the natural preference which every man has for his own happiness above that of other people, is what no impartial spectator can go along with. Every man is, no doubt, by nature, first and principally recommended to his own care; and as he is fitter to take care of himself than of any other person, it is fit and right that it should be so. Every man, therefore, is

much more deeply interested in whatever immediately concerns himself, than in what concerns any other man: and to hear, perhaps, of the death of another person, with whom we have no particular connexion, will give us less concern, will spoil our stomach, or break our rest much less than a very insignificant disaster which has befallen ourselves. But though the ruin of our neighbour may affect us much less than a very small misfortune of our own, we must not ruin him to prevent that small misfortune, nor even to prevent our own ruin. We must, here, as in all other cases, view ourselves not so much according to that light in which we may naturally appear to ourselves, as according to that in which we naturally appear to others. Though every man may, according to the proverb, be the whole world to himself, to the rest of mankind he is a most insignificant part of it. Though his own happiness may be of more importance to him than that of all the world besides, to every other person it is of no more consequence than that of any other man. Though it may be true, therefore, that every individual, in his own breast, naturally prefers himself to all mankind, yet he dares not look mankind in the face, and avow that he acts according to this principle. He feels that in this preference they can never go along with him, and that how natural soever it may be to him, it must always appear excessive and extravagant to them. When he views himself in the light in which he is conscious that others will view him, he sees that to them he is but one of the multitude in no respect better than any other in it. If he would act so as that the impartial spectator may enter into the principles of his conduct, which is what of all things he has the greatest desire to do, he must, upon this, as upon all other occasions, humble the arrogance of his self-love, and bring it down to something which other men can go along with. They will indulge it so far as to allow him to be more anxious about, and to pursue with more earnest assiduity, his own happiness than that of any other person. Thus far, whenever they place themselves in his situation, they will readily go along with him. In the race for wealth, and honours, and preferments, he may run as hard as he can, and strain every nerve and every muscle, in order to outstrip all his competitors. But if he should justle, or throw down any of them, the indulgence of the spectators is entirely at an end. It is a violation of fair play, which they cannot admit of. This man is to them, in every respect, as good as he: they do not enter into that self-love by which he prefers himself so much to this other, and cannot go along with the motive from which he hurt him. They readily, therefore, sympathize with the natural resentment of the injured, and the offender becomes the object of their hatred and indignation. He is sensible that he becomes so, and feels that those sentiments are ready to burst out from all sides against him.

2   As the greater and more irreparable the evil that is done, the resentment of the sufferer runs naturally the higher; so does likewise the sympathetic

indignation of the spectator, as well as the sense of guilt in the agent. Death is the greatest evil which one man can inflict upon another, and excites the highest degree of resentment in those who are immediately connected with the slain. Murder, therefore, is the most atrocious of all crimes which affect individuals only, in the sight both of mankind, and of the person who has committed it. To be deprived of that which we are possessed of, is a greater evil than to be disappointed of what we have only the expectation. Breach of property, therefore, theft and robbery, which take from us what we are possessed of, are greater crimes than breach of contract, which only disappoints us of what we expected. The most sacred laws of justice, therefore, those whose violation seems to call loudest for vengeance and punishment, are the laws which guard the life and person of our neighbour; the next are those which guard his property and possessions; and last of all come those which guard what are called his personal rights, or what is due to him from the promises of others.

3   The violator of the more sacred laws of justice can never reflect on the sentiments which mankind must entertain with regard to him, without feeling all the agonies of shame, and horror, and consternation. When his passion is gratified, and he begins coolly to reflect on his past conduct, he can enter into none of the motives which influenced it. They appear now as detestable to him as they did always to other people. By sympathizing with the hatred and abhorrence which other men must entertain for him, he becomes in some measure the object of his own hatred and abhorrence. The situation of the person, who suffered by his injustice, now calls upon his pity. He is grieved at the thought of it; regrets the unhappy effects of his own conduct, and feels at the same time that they have rendered him the proper object of the resentment and indignation of mankind, and of what is the natural consequence of resentment, vengeance and punishment. The thought of this perpetually haunts him, and fills him with terror and amazement. He dares no longer look society in the face, but imagines himself as it were rejected, and thrown out from the affections of all mankind. He cannot hope for the consolation of sympathy in this his greatest and most dreadful distress. The remembrance of his crimes has shut out all fellow-feeling with him from the hearts of his fellow-creatures. The sentiments which they entertain with regard to him, are the very thing which he is most afraid of. Every thing seems hostile, and he would be glad to fly to some inhospitable desert, where he might never more behold the face of a human creature, nor read in the countenance of mankind the condemnation of his crimes. But solitude is still more dreadful than society. His own thoughts can present him with nothing but what is black, unfortunate, and disastrous, the melancholy forebodings of incomprehensible misery and ruin. The horror of solitude drives him back into society, and he comes again into the presence of mankind, astonished to appear before

them, loaded with shame and distracted with fear, in order to supplicate
some little protection from the countenance of those very judges, who he
knows have already all unanimously condemned him. Such is the nature of
that sentiment, which is properly called remorse; of all the sentiments which
can enter the human breast the most dreadful.[1] It is made up of shame from
the sense of the impropriety of past conduct; of grief for the effects of it;
of pity for those who suffer by it; and of the dread and terror of punishment from the consciousness of the justly provoked resentment of all
rational creatures.

4   The opposite behaviour naturally inspires the opposite sentiment. The
man who, not from frivolous fancy, but from proper motives, has performed a generous action, when he looks forward to those whom he has
served, feels himself to be the natural object of their love and gratitude, and,
by sympathy with them, of the esteem and approbation of all mankind.
And when he looks backward to the motive from which he acted, and surveys it in the light in which the indifferent spectator will survey it, he still
continues to enter into it, and applauds himself by sympathy with the
approbation of this supposed impartial judge. In both these points of view
his own conduct appears to him every way agreeable. His mind, at the
thought of it, is filled with cheerfulness, serenity, and composure. He is in
friendship and harmony with all mankind, and looks upon his fellow-
creatures with confidence and benevolent satisfaction, secure that he has
rendered himself worthy of their most favourable regards. In the combination of all these sentiments consists the consciousness of merit, or of deserved reward.

CHAP. III
Of the utility of this constitution of Nature

1   IT is thus that man, who can subsist only in society, was fitted by nature
to that situation for which he was made. All the members of human society
stand in need of each others assistance, and are likewise exposed to mutual
injuries. Where the necessary assistance is reciprocally afforded from love,
from gratitude, from friendship, and esteem, the society flourishes and is
happy. All the different members of it are bound together by the agreeable
bands of love and affection, and are, as it were, drawn to one common
centre of mutual good offices.

2   But though the necessary assistance should not be afforded from such

[1] Smith may here again be influenced by Kames, who also writes vividly of remorse,
including the words 'Hence that remorse of conscience, the most severe of all tortures . . .'
(*Principles of Morality and Natural Religion*, I.ii.3; ed. 1, 64; L. A. Selby-Bigge, *British
Moralists*, § 932). Cf. R. F. Brissenden in *Texas Studies in Lit. and Lang.* xi (1969), 961.

generous and disinterested motives, though among the different members of the society there should be no mutual love and affection, the society, though less happy and agreeable, will not necessarily be dissolved. Society may subsist among different men, as among different merchants, from a sense of its utility, without any mutual love or affection; and though no man in it should owe any obligation, or be bound in gratitude to any other, it may still be upheld by a mercenary exchange of good offices according to an agreed valuation.

3   Society, however, cannot subsist among those who are at all times ready to hurt and injure one another. The moment that injury begins, the moment that mutual resentment and animosity take place, all the bands of it are broke asunder, and the different members of which it consisted are, as it were, dissipated and scattered abroad by the violence and opposition of their discordant affections. If there is any society among robbers and murderers, they must at least, according to the trite observation, abstain from robbing and murdering one another. Beneficence, therefore, is less essential to the existence of society than justice. Society may subsist, though not in the most comfortable state, without beneficence; but the prevalence of injustice must utterly destroy it.

4   Though Nature, therefore, exhorts mankind to acts of beneficence, by the pleasing consciousness of deserved reward, she has not thought it necessary to guard and enforce the practice of it by the terrors of merited punishment in case it should be neglected. It is the ornament which embellishes, not the foundation which supports the building, and which it was, therefore, sufficient to recommend, but by no means necessary to impose. Justice, on the contrary, is the main pillar that upholds the whole edifice. If it is removed, the great, the immense fabric of human society, that fabric which to raise and support seems in this world, if I may say so, to have been the peculiar and darling care of Nature, must in a moment crumble into atoms. In order to enforce the observation of justice, therefore, Nature has implanted in the human breast that consciousness of ill-desert, those terrors of merited punishment which attend upon its violation, as the great safe-guards of the association of mankind, to protect the weak, to curb the violent, and to chastise the guilty. Men, though naturally sympathetic, feel so little for another, with whom they have no particular connexion, in comparison of what they feel for themselves; the misery of one, who is merely their fellow-creature, is of so little importance to them in comparison even of a small conveniency of their own; they have it so much in their power to hurt him, and may have so many temptations to do so, that if this principle did not stand up within them in his defence, and overawe them into a respect for his innocence, they would, like wild beasts, be at all times ready to fly upon him; and a man would enter an assembly of men as he enters a den of lions.

5   In every part of the universe we observe means adjusted with the nicest
artifice to the ends which they are intended to produce; and in the mechanism of a plant, or animal body, admire how every thing is contrived for
advancing the two great purposes of nature, the support of the individual,
and the propagation of the species. But in these, and in all such objects,
we still distinguish the efficient from the final cause of their several motions
and organizations. The digestion of the food, the circulation of the blood,
and the secretion of the several juices which are drawn from it, are
operations all of them necessary for the great purposes of animal life. Yet
we never endeavour to account for them from those purposes as from their
efficient causes, nor imagine that the blood circulates, or that the food
digests of its own accord, and with a view or intention to the purposes of
circulation or digestion. The wheels of the watch are all admirably adjusted to the end for which it was made, the pointing of the hour. All their
various motions conspire in the nicest manner to produce this effect. If
they were endowed with a desire and intention to produce it, they could
not do it better. Yet we never ascribe any such desire or intention to them,
but to the watch-maker, and we know that they are put into motion by a
spring, which intends the effect it produces as little as they do. But though,
in accounting for the operations of bodies, we never fail to distinguish in
this manner the efficient from the final cause, in accounting for those of
the mind we are very apt to confound these two different things with one
another. When by natural principles we are led to advance those ends,
which a refined and enlightened reason would recommend to us, we are
very apt to impute to that reason, as to their efficient cause, the sentiments and
actions by which we advance those ends, and to imagine that to be the wisdom
of man, which in reality is the wisdom of God. Upon a superficial view, this
cause seems sufficient to produce the effects which are ascribed to it; and
the system of human nature seems to be more simple and agreeable when all
its different operations are in this manner deduced from a single principle.

6   As society cannot subsist unless the laws of justice are tolerably observed,
as no social intercourse can take place among men who do not generally
abstain from injuring one another; the consideration of this necessity, it has
been thought, was the ground upon which we approved of the enforcement of the laws of justice by the punishment of those who violated them.[1]

[1] Like Eckstein (i.290), we think that Smith has Hume in mind here. Hume's *Enquiry
concerning the Principles of Morals* (1751), III, argues forcibly that 'public utility is the
sole origin of justice'; cf. *Enquiry*, appendix iii. (In the earlier *Treatise of Human Nature*,
III.ii.2, the account of justice is essentially the same, but Hume does not give all the emphasis to utility.) Although Hume is largely concerned with the civil law of property, he speaks
of 'justice' and 'equity' generally and in one place (*Enquiry*, III.i; ed. Selby-Bigge, § 148)
includes a reference to the equity of punishment as depending on utility. At the beginning
of § 7 below Smith writes of § 6 as the account of punishment 'commonly given', and in
LJ(A) ii.90 he says that utilitarian theories of punishment have been held by 'Grotius
and other writers'. Nevertheless he must surely have had Hume's *Enquiry* at the forefront

Man, it has been said, has a natural love for society, and desires that the union of mankind should be preserved for its own sake, and though he himself was to derive no benefit from it. The orderly and flourishing state of society is agreeable to him, and he takes delight in contemplating it. Its disorder and confusion, on the contrary, is the object of his aversion, and he is chagrined at whatever tends to produce it. He is sensible too that his own interest is connected with the prosperity of society, and that the happiness, perhaps the preservation of his existence, depends upon its preservation. Upon every account, therefore, he has an abhorrence at whatever can tend to destroy society, and is willing to make use of every means, which can hinder so hated and so dreadful an event. Injustice necessarily tends to destroy it. Every appearance of injustice, therefore, alarms him, and he runs, if I may say so, to stop the progress of what, if allowed to go on, would quickly put an end to every thing that is dear to him. If he cannot restrain it by gentle and fair means, he must *ᵃbeatᵃ* it down by force and violence, and at any rate must put a stop to its further progress. Hence it is, they say, that he often approves of the enforcement of the laws of justice even by the capital punishment of those who violate them. The disturber of the public peace is hereby removed out of the world, and others are terrified by his fate from imitating his example.

7   Such is the account commonly given of our approbation of the punishment of injustice. And so far this account is undoubtedly true, that we frequently have occasion to confirm our natural sense of the propriety and fitness of punishment, by reflecting how necessary it is for preserving the order of society. When the guilty is about to suffer that just retaliation, which the natural indignation of mankind tells them is due to his crimes; when the insolence of his injustice is broken and humbled by the terror of his approaching punishment; when he ceases to be an object of fear, with the generous and humane he begins to be an object of pity. The thought of what he is about to suffer extinguishes their resentment for the sufferings of others to which he has given occasion. They are disposed to pardon and forgive him, and to save him from that punishment, which in all their cool hours they had considered as the retribution due to such crimes. Here, therefore, they have occasion to call to their assistance the consideration of the general interest of society. They counterbalance the impulse of this weak and partial humanity by the dictates of a humanity that is more generous and comprehensive. They reflect that mercy to the guilty is cruelty to the innocent, and oppose to the emotions of compassion which

ᵃ⁻ᵃ *1 2* bear *3–7* bear *is probably a printer's error.*

of his thoughts when he prepared the present chapter for publication in 1759. The sentences that follow in § 6 seem to refer particularly to Hume's view that utility pleases through sympathy.

they feel for a particular person, a more enlarged compassion which they feel for mankind.

8   Sometimes too we have occasion to defend the propriety of observing the general rules of justice by the consideration of their necessity to the support of society. We frequently hear the young and the licentious ridiculing the most sacred rules of morality, and professing, sometimes from the corruption, but more frequently from the vanity of their hearts, the most abominable maxims of conduct. Our indignation rouses, and we are eager to refute and expose such detestable principles. But though it is their intrinsic hatefulness and detestableness, which originally inflames us against them, we are unwilling to assign this as the sole reason why we condemn them, or to pretend that it is merely because we ourselves hate and detest them. The reason, we think, would not appear to be conclusive. Yet why should it not; if we hate and detest them because they are the natural and proper objects of hatred and detestation? But when we are asked why we should not act in such or such a manner, the very question seems to suppose that, to those who ask it, this manner of acting does not appear to be for its own sake the natural and proper object of those sentiments. We must show them, therefore, that it ought to be so for the sake of something else. Upon this account we generally cast about for other arguments, and the consideration which first occurs to us, is the disorder and confusion of society which would result from the universal prevalence of such practices. We seldom fail, therefore, to insist upon this topic.

9   But though it commonly requires no great discernment to see the destructive tendency of all licentious practices to the welfare of society, it is seldom this consideration which first animates us against them. All men, even the most stupid and unthinking, abhor fraud, perfidy, and injustice, and delight to see them punished. But few men have reflected upon the necessity of justice to the existence of society, how obvious soever that necessity may appear to be.

10   That it is not a regard to the preservation of society, which originally interests us in the punishment of crimes committed against individuals, may be demonstrated by many obvious considerations. The concern which we take in the fortune and happiness of individuals does not, in common cases, arise from that which we take in the fortune and happiness of society. We are no more concerned for the destruction or loss of a single man, because this man is a member or part of society, and because we should be concerned for the destruction of society, than we are concerned for the loss of a single guinea, because this guinea is a part of a thousand guineas, and because we should be concerned for the loss of the whole sum. In neither case does our regard for the individuals arise from our regard for the multitude: but in both cases our regard for the multitude is compounded and made up of the particular regards which we feel for the different indivi-

duals of which it is composed. As when a small sum is unjustly taken from us, we do not so much prosecute the injury from a regard to the preservation of our whole fortune, as from a regard to that particular sum which we have lost; so when a single man is injured, or destroyed, we demand the punishment of the wrong that has been done to him, not so much from a concern for the general interest of society, as from a concern for that very individual who has been injured. It is to be observed, however, that this concern does not necessarily include in it any degree of those exquisite sentiments which are commonly called love, esteem, and affection, and by which we distinguish our particular friends and acquaintance. The concern which is requisite for this, is no more than the general fellow-feeling which we have with every man merely because he is our fellow-creature. We enter into the resentment even of an odious person, when he is injured by those to whom he has given no provocation. Our disapprobation of his ordinary character and conduct does not in this case altogether prevent our fellow-feeling with his natural indignation; though with those who are not either extremely candid, or who have not been accustomed to correct and regulate their natural sentiments by general rules, it is very apt to damp it.

11   Upon some occasions, indeed, we both punish and approve of punishment, merely from a view to the general interest of society, which, we imagine, cannot otherwise be secured. Of this kind are all the punishments inflicted for breaches of what is called either civil police, or military discipline. Such crimes do not immediately or directly hurt any particular person; but their remote consequences, it is supposed, do produce, or might produce, either a considerable inconveniency, or a great disorder in the society. A centinel, for example, who falls asleep upon his watch, suffers death by the laws of war, because such carelessness might endanger the whole army. This severity may, upon many occasions, appear necessary, and, for that reason, just and proper. When the preservation of an individual is inconsistent with the safety of a multitude, nothing can be more just than that the many should be preferred to the one. Yet this punishment, how necessary soever, always appears to be excessively severe. The natural atrocity of the crime seems to be so little, and the punishment so great, that it is with great difficulty that our heart can reconcile itself to it. Though such carelessness appears very blamable, yet the thought of this crime does not naturally excite any such resentment, as would prompt us to take such dreadful revenge. A man of humanity must recollect himself, must make an effort, and exert his whole firmness and resolution, before he can bring himself either to inflict it, or to go along with it when it is inflicted by others. It is not, however, in this manner, that he looks upon the just punishment of an ungrateful murderer or parricide. His heart, in this case, applauds with ardour, and even with transport, the just retaliation

which seems due to such detestable crimes, and which, if, by any accident, they should happen to escape, he would be highly enraged and disappointed. The very different sentiments with which the spectator views those different punishments, is a proof that his approbation of the one is far from being founded upon the same principles with that of the other. He looks upon the centinel as an unfortunate victim, who, indeed, must, and ought to be, devoted to the safety of numbers, but whom still, in his heart, he would be glad to save; and he is only sorry, that the interest of the many should oppose it. But if the murderer should escape from punishment, it would excite his highest indignation, and he would call upon God to avenge, in another world, that crime which the injustice of mankind had neglected to chastise upon earth.

12   For it well deserves to be taken notice of, that we are so far from imagining that injustice ought to be punished in this life, merely on account of the order of society, which cannot otherwise be maintained, that Nature teaches us to hope, and *b*religion, we suppose, authorises*b* us to expect, that it will be punished, even in a life to come. Our sense of its ill desert pursues it, if I may say so, even beyond the grave, though the example of its punishment there cannot serve to deter the rest of mankind, who see it not, who know it not, from being guilty of the like practices here. The justice of God, however, we think, still requires, that he should hereafter avenge the injuries of the widow and the fatherless, who are here so often insulted with impunity. *c*In every religion, and in every superstition that the world has ever beheld, accordingly, there has been a Tartarus as well as an Elysium; a place provided for the punishment of the wicked, as well as one for the reward of the just.*c*

---

b–b religion authorises *1 2 See Appendix II.*
    c–c This sentence was added in ed. 6, replacing a concluding paragraph that had appeared in eds. 1–5. We give below the text of the paragraph as printed in ed. 1, with the variants of later editions. See also Appendix II.

That the Deity loves virtue and hates vice, as a voluptuous man loves riches and hates poverty, not for their own sakes, but for the effects which they tend to produce; that he loves the one, only because it promotes the happiness of society, which his benevolence prompts him to desire; and that he hates the other, only because it occasions the misery of mankind, which the same divine quality renders the object of his aversion; is not the doctrine of nature, but of an artificial, though ingenious, refinement of philosophy. All our natural sentiments [of untaught nature but of an artificial refinement of reason and philosophy. Our untaught, natural sentiments, all *3–5*] prompt us to believe, that as perfect virtue is supposed necessarily to appear to the Deity, as it does to us, for its own sake, and without any further view, the natural and proper object of love and reward, so must vice, of hatred and punishment. That the gods neither resent nor hurt, was the general maxim of all the different sects of the ancient philosophy: and if, by resenting, be understood, that violent and disorderly perturbation, which often distracts and confounds the human breast; or if, by hurting, be understood, the doing mischief wantonly, and without regard to propriety or justice, such weakness is undoubtedly unworthy of the divine perfection. But if it be meant, that vice does not appear to the Deity to be, for its own sake, the object of abhorrence and aversion, and what, for its own sake, it is fit and right should be punished,

SECTION III

Of the Influence of Fortune upon the Sentiments of Mankind, with regard to the Merit or Demerit of Actions

INTRODUCTION

1 WHATEVER praise or blame can be due to any action, must belong either, first, to the intention or affection of the heart, from which it proceeds; or, secondly, to the external action or movement of the body, which this affection gives occasion to; or, lastly, to the good or bad consequences, which actually, and in fact, proceed from it. These three different things constitute the whole nature and circumstances of the action, and must be the foundation of whatever quality can belong to it.

2 That the two last of these three circumstances cannot be the foundation of any praise or blame, is abundantly evident; nor has the contrary ever been asserted by any body. The external action or movement of the body is often the same in the most innocent and in the most blameable

the truth of this maxim can, by no means, be so easily admitted. [maxim seems repugnant to some very natural feelings. *3–5*] If we consult our natural sentiments, we are apt [are even apt *3–5*] to fear, lest [lest, *2–5*] before the holiness of God, vice should appear to be more worthy of punishment than the weakness and imperfection of human virtue can ever seem to be of reward. Man, when about to appear before a being of infinite perfection, can feel but little confidence in his own merit, or in the imperfect propriety of his own conduct. In the presence of his fellow-creatures, he may often [may even *2–5*] justly elevate himself, and may often have reason to think highly of his own character and conduct, compared to the still greater imperfection of theirs. But the case is quite different when about to appear before his infinite Creator. To such a being, he can scarce imagine, that his littleness and weakness should ever seem to be [being, he fears, that his littleness and weakness can scarce ever appear *3–5*] the proper object, either of esteem or of reward. But he can easily conceive, how the numberless violations of duty, of which he has been guilty, should render him the proper object of aversion and punishment; neither can he see any [and he thinks he can see no *3–5*] reason why the divine indignation should not be let loose without any restraint, upon so vile an insect, as he is sensible [he imagines *3–5*] that he himself must appear to be. If he would still hope for happiness, he is conscious [he suspects *3–5*] that he cannot demand it from the justice, but that he must entreat it from the mercy of God. Repentance, sorrow, humiliation, contrition at the thought of his past conduct, are, [seem, *3–5*] upon this account, the sentiments which become him, and seem to [and to *3–5*] be the only means which he has left for appeasing that wrath which, he knows, he has justly provoked. He even distrusts the efficacy of all these, and naturally fears, lest the wisdom of God should not, like the weakness of man, be prevailed upon to spare the crime, by the most importunate lamentations of the criminal. Some other intercession, some other sacrifice, some other atonement, he imagines, [imagines *2–5*] must be made for him, beyond what he himself is capable of making, before the purity of the divine justice can be reconciled to his manifold offences. The doctrines of revelation coincide, in every respect, with those original anticipations of nature; and, as they teach us how little we can depend upon the imperfection of our own virtue, so they show us, at the same time, that the most powerful intercession has been made, and that the most dreadful atonement has been paid for our manifold transgressions and iniquities.

actions. He who shoots a bird, and he who shoots a man, both of them perform the same external movement: each of them draws the trigger of a gun. The consequences which actually, and in fact, happen to proceed from any action, are, if possible, still more indifferent either to praise or blame, than even the external movement of the body. As they depend, not upon the agent, but upon fortune, they cannot be the proper foundation for any sentiment, of which his character and conduct are the objects.

3   The only consequences for which he can be answerable, or by which he can deserve either approbation or disapprobation of any kind, are those which were someway or other intended, or those which, at least, show some agreeable or disagreeable quality in the intention of the heart, from which he acted. To the intention or affection of the heart, therefore, to the propriety or impropriety, to the beneficence or hurtfulness of the design, all praise or blame, all approbation or disapprobation, of any kind, which can justly be bestowed upon any action, must ultimately belong.

4   When this maxim is thus proposed, in abstract and general terms, there is nobody who does not agree to it. Its self-evident justice is acknowledged by all the world, and there is not a dissenting voice among all mankind. Every body allows, that how different soever the accidental, the unintended and unforeseen consequences of different actions, yet, if the intentions or affections from which they arose were, on the one hand, equally proper and equally beneficent, or, on the other, equally improper and equally malevolent, the merit or demerit of the actions is still the same, and the agent is equally the suitable object either of gratitude or of resentment.

5   But how well soever we may seem to be persuaded of the truth of this equitable maxim, when we consider it after this manner, in abstract, yet when we come to particular cases, the actual consequences which happen to proceed from any action, have a very great effect upon our sentiments concerning its merit or demerit, and almost always either enhance or diminish our sense of both. Scarce, in any one instance, perhaps, will our sentiments be found, after examination, to be entirely regulated by this rule, which we all acknowledge ought entirely to regulate them.

6   This irregularity of sentiment, which every body feels, which scarce any body is sufficiently aware of, and which nobody is willing to acknowledge, I proceed now to explain; and I shall consider, first, the cause which gives occasion to it, or the mechanism by which nature produces it; secondly, the extent of its influence; and, last of all, the end which it answers, or the purpose which the Author of nature seems to have intended by it.

CHAP. I

Of the causes of this Influence of Fortune

1   THE causes of pain and pleasure, whatever they are, or however they operate, seem to be the objects, which, in all animals, immediately excite those two passions of gratitude and resentment. They are excited by in-animated, as well as by animated objects. We are angry, for a moment, even at the stone that hurts us. A child beats it, a dog barks at it, a choleric man is apt to curse it. The least reflection, indeed, corrects this sentiment, and we soon become sensible, that what has no feeling is a very improper object of revenge. When the mischief, however, is very great, the object which caused it becomes disagreeable to us ever after, and we take pleasure to burn or destroy it. We should treat, in this manner, the instrument which had accidentally been the cause of the death of a friend, and we should often think ourselves guilty of a sort of inhumanity, if we neglected to vent this absurd sort of vengeance upon it.[1]

2   We conceive, in the same manner, a sort of gratitude for those inani-mated objects, which have been the causes of great, or frequent pleasure to us. The sailor, who, as soon as he got ashore, should mend his fire with the plank upon which he had just escaped from a shipwreck, would seem to be guilty of an unnatural action. We should expect that he would rather preserve it with care and affection, as a monument that was, in some measure, dear to him. A man grows fond of a snuff-box, of a pen-knife, of a staff which he has long made use of, and conceives something like a real love and affection for them. If he breaks or loses them, he is vexed out of all proportion to the value of the damage. The house which we have long lived in, the tree, whose verdure and shade we have long enjoyed, are both looked upon with a sort of respect that seems due to such benefactors. The decay of the one, or the ruin of the other, affects us with a kind of melancholy, though we should sustain no loss by it. The Dryads and the Lares of the ancients, a sort of genii of trees and houses, were probably first suggested by this sort of affection, which the authors of those supersti-tions felt for such objects, and which seemed unreasonable, if there was nothing animated about them.

3   But, before any thing can be the proper object of gratitude or resentment, it must not only be the cause of pleasure or pain, it must likewise be cap-able of feeling them. Without this other quality, those passions cannot vent themselves with any sort of satisfaction upon it. As they are excited by the causes of pleasure and pain, so their gratification consists in retaliat-ing those sensations upon what gave occasion to them; which it is to no purpose to attempt upon what has no sensibility. Animals, therefore, are

---

[1] Smith is no doubt thinking not only of natural attitudes but also of their reflection in ancient systems of law. Cf. LJ(A) ii. 118–20 and LJ(B) 188 (Cannan ed., 141–2).

less improper objects of gratitude and resentment than inanimated objects. The dog that bites, the ox that gores, are both of them punished. If
they have been the causes of the death of any person, neither the public,
nor the relations of the slain, can be satisfied, unless they are put to death
in their turn: nor is this merely for the security of the living, but, in some
measure, to revenge the injury of the dead.[2] Those animals, on the contrary,
that have been remarkably serviceable to their masters, become the objects
of a very lively gratitude. We are shocked at the brutality of that officer,
mentioned in the Turkish Spy, who stabbed the horse that had carried
him across an arm of the sea, lest that animal should afterwards distinguish
some other person by a similar adventure.[3]

4   But, though animals are not only the causes of pleasure and pain, but
are also capable of feeling those sensations, they are still far from being
complete and perfect objects, either of gratitude or resentment; and those
passions still feel, that there is something wanting to their entire gratification. What gratitude chiefly desires, is not only to make the benefactor
feel pleasure in his turn, but to make him conscious that he meets with
this reward on account of his past conduct, to make him pleased with that
conduct, and to satisfy him that the person upon whom he bestowed his
good offices was not unworthy of them. What most of all charms us in our
benefactor, is the concord between his sentiments and our own, with regard to what interests us so nearly as the worth of our own character, and
the esteem that is due to us. We are delighted to find a person who values
us as we value ourselves, and distinguishes us from the rest of mankind,
with an attention not unlike that with which we distinguish ourselves. To
maintain in him these agreeable and flattering sentiments, is one of the
chief ends proposed by the returns we are disposed to make to him. A
generous mind often disdains the interested thought of extorting new
favours from its benefactor, by what may be called the importunities of its
gratitude. But to preserve and to increase his esteem, is an interest which
the greatest mind does not think unworthy of its attention. And this is the
foundation of what I formerly observed, that when we cannot enter into
the motives of our benefactor, when his conduct and character appear
unworthy of our approbation, let his services have been ever so great, our
gratitude is always sensibly diminished. We are less flattered by the distinction; and to preserve the esteem of so weak, or so worthless a patron,
seems to be an object which does not deserve to be pursued for its own sake.

5   The object, on the contrary, which resentment is chiefly intent upon,
is not so much to make our enemy feel pain in his turn, as to make him

[2] Smith is again thinking of ancient law. 'The ox that gores' is a reference to Exodus
21:28, 'If an ox gore a man or a woman, that they die: then the ox shall be surely stoned,
and his flesh shall not be eaten; but the owner of the ox shall be quit.' Cf. LJ(A) ii.118.
[3] [G. P. Marana,] *Letters writ by a Turkish Spy*, vol. iv, Book III, letter 10. Marana tells
the story of 'a certain French nobleman', not of an 'officer'.

conscious that he feels it upon account of his past conduct, to make him repent of that conduct, and to make him sensible, that the person whom he injured did not deserve to be treated in that manner. What chiefly enrages us against the man who injures or insults us, is the little account which he seems to make of us, the unreasonable preference which he gives to himself above us, and that absurd self-love, by which he seems to imagine, that other people may be sacrificed at any time, to his conveniency or his humour. The glaring impropriety of this conduct, the gross insolence and injustice which it seems to involve in it, often shock and exasperate us more than all the mischief which we have suffered. To bring him back to a more just sense of what is due to other people, to make him sensible of what he owes us, and of the wrong that he has done to us, is frequently the principal end proposed in our revenge, which is always imperfect when it cannot accomplish this. When our enemy appears to have done us no injury, when we are sensible that he acted quite properly, that, in his situation, we should have done the same thing, and that we deserved from him all the mischief we met with; in that case, if we have the least spark either of candour or justice, we can entertain no sort of resentment.

6   Before any thing, therefore, can be the complete and proper object, either of gratitude or resentment, it must possess three different qualifications. First, it must be the cause of pleasure in the one case, and of pain in the other. Secondly, it must be capable of feeling those sensations. And, thirdly, it must not only have produced those sensations, but it must have produced them from design, and from a design that is approved of in the one case, and disapproved of in the other. It is by the first qualification, that any object is capable of exciting those passions: it is by the second, that it is in any respect capable of gratifying them: the third qualification is not only necessary for their complete satisfaction, but as it gives a pleasure or pain that is both exquisite and peculiar, it is likewise an additional exciting cause of those passions.

7   As what gives pleasure or pain, either in one way or another, is the sole exciting cause of gratitude and resentment; though the intentions of any person should be ever so proper and *ª*beneficent*ª* on the one hand, or ever so improper and malevolent on the other; yet, if he has failed in producing either the good or the evil which he intended, as one of the exciting causes is wanting in both cases, less gratitude seems due to him in the one, and less resentment in the other. And, on the contrary, though in the intentions of any person, there was either no laudable degree of benevolence on the one hand, or no blameable degree of malice on the other; yet, if his actions should produce either great good or great evil, as one of the exciting causes takes place upon both these occasions, some gratitude is apt to arise to-

---

ª–ª 5 beneficent, *1–4 6 7* Cf. malevolent, *in the next line, and cf. also the following sentence where ed. 1 alone inserts a comma after* benevolence.

wards him in the one, and some resentment in the other. A shadow of merit seems to fall upon him in the first, a shadow of demerit in the second. And, as the consequences of actions are altogether under the empire of Fortune, hence arises her influence upon the sentiments of mankind with regard to merit and demerit.

CHAP. II

Of the extent of this Influence of Fortune

1 THE effect of this influence of fortune is, first, to diminish our sense of the merit or demerit of those actions which arose from the most laudable or blamable intentions, when they fail of producing their proposed effects: and, secondly, to increase our sense of the merit or demerit of actions, beyond what is due to the motives or affections from which they proceed, when they accidentally give occasion either to extraordinary pleasure or pain.

2   1. First, I say, though the intentions of any person should be ever so proper and beneficent, on the one hand, or ever so improper and malevolent, on the other, yet, if they fail in producing their effects, his merit seems imperfect in the one case, and his demerit incomplete in the other. Nor is this irregularity of sentiment felt only by those who are immediately affected by the consequences of any action. It is felt, in some measure, even by the impartial spectator. The man who solicits an office for another, without obtaining it, is regarded as his friend, and seems to deserve his love and affection. But the man who not only solicits, but procures it, is more peculiarly considered as his patron and benefactor, and is entitled to his respect and gratitude. The person obliged, we are apt to think, may, with some justice, imagine himself on a level with the first: but we cannot enter into his sentiments, if he does not feel himself inferior to the second. It is common indeed to say, that we are equally obliged to the man who has endeavoured to serve us, as to him who actually did so. It is the speech which we constantly make upon every unsuccessful attempt of this kind; but which, like all other fine speeches, must be understood with a grain of allowance. The sentiments which a man of generosity entertains for the friend who fails, may often indeed be nearly the same with those which he conceives for him who succeeds: and the more generous he is, the more nearly will those sentiments approach to an exact level. With the truly generous, to be beloved, to be esteemed by those whom they themselves think worthy of esteem, gives more pleasure, and thereby excites more gratitude, than all the advantages which they can ever expect from those

sentiments. When they lose those advantages therefore, they seem to lose but a trifle, which is scarce worth regarding. They still however lose something. Their pleasure therefore, and consequently their gratitude, is not perfectly complete: and accordingly if, between the friend who fails and the friend who succeeds, all other circumstances are equal, there will, even in the noblest and the best mind, be some little difference of affection in favour of him who succeeds. Nay, so unjust are mankind in this respect, that though the intended benefit should be procured, yet if it is not procured by the means of a particular benefactor, they are apt to think that less gratitude is due to the man, who with the best intentions in the world could do no more than help it a little forward. As their gratitude is in this case divided among the different persons who contributed to their pleasure, a smaller share of it seems due to any one. Such a person, we hear men commonly say, intended no doubt to serve us; and we really believe exerted himself to the utmost of his abilities for that purpose. We are not, however, obliged to him for this benefit; since, had it not been for the concurrence of others, all that he could have done would never have brought it about. This consideration, they imagine, should, even in the eyes of the impartial spectator, diminish the debt which they owe to him. The person himself who has unsuccessfully endeavoured to confer a benefit, has by no means the same dependency upon the gratitude of the man whom he meant to oblige, nor the same sense of his own merit towards him, which he would have had in the case of success.

3   Even the merit of talents and abilities which some accident has hindered from producing their effects, seems in some measure imperfect, even to those who are fully convinced of their capacity to produce them. The general who has been hindered by the envy of ministers from gaining some great advantage over the enemies of his country, regrets the loss of the opportunity for ever after. Nor is it only upon account of the public that he regrets it. He laments that he was hindered from performing an action which would have added a new lustre to his character in his own eyes, as well as in those of every other person. It satisfies neither himself nor others to reflect that the plan or design was all that depended on him, that no greater capacity was required to execute it than what was necessary to concert it: that he was allowed to be every way capable of executing it, and that had he been permitted to go on, success was infallible. He still did not execute it; and though he might deserve all the approbation which is due to a magnanimous and great design, he still wanted the actual merit of having performed a great action. To take the management of any affair of public concern from the man who has almost brought it to a conclusion, is regarded as the most invidious injustice. As he had done so much, he should, we think, have been allowed to acquire the complete merit of putting an end to it. It was objected to Pompey, that he came in upon the

victories of Lucullus, and gathered those laurels which were due to the fortune and valour of another. The glory of Lucullus, it seems, was less complete even in the opinion of his own friends, when he was not permitted to finish that conquest which his conduct and courage had put in the power of almost any man to finish.[1] It mortifies an architect when his plans are either not executed at all, or when they are so far altered as to spoil the effect of the building. The plan, however, is all that depends upon the architect. The whole of his genius is, to good judges, as completely discovered in that as in the actual execution. But a plan does not, even to the most intelligent, give the same pleasure as a noble and magnificent building. They may discover as much both of taste and genius in the one as in the other. But their effects are still vastly different, and the amusement derived from the first, never approaches to the wonder and admiration which are sometimes excited by the second. We may believe of many men, that their talents are superior to those of Caesar and Alexander; and that in the same situations they would perform still greater actions. In the mean time, however, we do not behold them with that astonishment and admiration with which those two heroes have been regarded in all ages and nations. The calm judgments of the mind may approve of them more, but they want the splendour of great actions to dazzle and transport it. The superiority of virtues and talents has not, even upon those who acknowledge that superiority, the same effect with the superiority of atchievements.

4   As the merit of an unsuccessful attempt to do good seems thus, in the eyes of ungrateful mankind, to be diminished by the miscarriage, so does likewise the demerit of an unsuccessful attempt to do evil. The design to commit a crime, how clearly soever it may be proved, is scarce ever punished with the same severity as the actual commission of it. The case of treason is perhaps the only exception.[2] That crime immediately affecting the being of the government itself, the government is naturally more jealous of it than of any other. In the punishment of treason, the sovereign resents the injuries which are immediately done to himself: in the punishment of other crimes, he resents those which are done to other men. It is his own resentment which he indulges in the one case: it is that of his subjects which by sympathy he enters into in the other. In the first case, therefore, as he judges in his own cause, he is very apt to be more violent and sanguinary in his punishments than the impartial spectator can approve of. His resentment too rises here upon smaller occasions, and does not always, as in other cases, wait for the perpetration of the crime, or even

[1] Lucius Licinius Lucullus commanded the Roman army against Mithridates from 74 to 66 B.C. Brilliant successes in the early years were followed by failure of the compaign of 68, and Lucullus lost control of his troops. He was required to hand over the command to Pompey in 66. Smith is probably recalling Plutarch, *Lives*, Lucullus, 35–6, in the remarks about laurels and the opinion of Lucullus' friends.

[2] Cf. LJ(A) v.61–2 and LJ(B) 80 (Cannan ed., 56).

for the attempt to commit it. A treasonable concert, though nothing has been done, or even attempted in consequence of it, nay, a treasonable conversation, is in many countries punished in the same manner as the actual commission of treason. With regard to all other crimes, the mere design, upon which no attempt has followed, is seldom punished at all, and is never punished severely. A criminal design, and a criminal action, it may be said indeed, do not necessarily suppose the same degree of depravity, and ought not therefore to be subjected to the same punishment. We are capable, it may be said, of resolving, and even of taking measures to execute, many things which, when it comes to the point, we feel ourselves altogether incapable of executing. But this reason can have no place when the design has been carried the length of the last attempt. The man, however, who fires a pistol at his enemy but misses him, is punished with death by the laws of scarce any country. By the old law of Scotland, though he should wound him, yet, unless death ensues within a certain time, the assassin is not liable to the last punishment.[3] The resentment of mankind, however, runs so high against this crime, their terror for the man who shows himself capable of committing it, is so great, that the mere attempt to commit it ought in all countries to be capital. The attempt to commit smaller crimes is almost always punished very lightly, and sometimes is not punished at all. The thief, whose hand has been caught in his neighbour's pocket before he had taken any thing out of it, is punished with ignominy only. If he had got time to take away an handkerchief, he would have been put to death. The house-breaker, who has been found setting a ladder to his neighbour's window, but had not got into it, is not exposed to the capital punishment. The attempt to ravish is not punished as a rape. The attempt to seduce a married woman is not punished at all, though seduction is punished severely. Our resentment against the person who only attempted to do a mischief, is seldom so strong as to bear us out in inflicting the same punishment upon him, which we should have thought due if he had actually done it. In the one case, the joy of our deliverance alleviates our sense of the atrocity of his conduct; in the other, the grief of our misfortune increases it. His real demerit, however, is undoubtedly the same in both cases, since his intentions were equally criminal; and there is in this respect, therefore, an irregularity in the sentiments of all men, and a consequent relaxation of discipline in the laws of, I believe, all nations, of the most civilized, as well as of the most barbarous. The

---

[3] We are advised by Professor David M. Walker that Scots law has never had any rule to this effect. Sir George Mackenzie, *Laws and Customs of Scotland in Matters Criminal* (1678), I.xi.10, wrote that he would like to see a fixed period of forty days, but neither this nor any other stated interval ever became the rule. A fixed period of a year is, however, the rule in several other European systems of law, including the law of England. As Eckstein notes (i.293), such a rule is not intended to express leniency towards a less heinous act but is simply an attempt to draw a line for attributing causal connection.

humanity of a civilized people disposes them either to dispense with, or to mitigate punishments wherever their natural indignation is not goaded on by the consequences of the crime. Barbarians, on the other hand, when no actual consequence has happened from any action, are not apt to be very delicate or inquisitive about the motives.

5   The person himself who either from passion, or from the influence of bad company, has resolved, and perhaps taken measures to perpetrate some crime, but who has fortunately been prevented by an accident which put it out of his power, is sure, if he has any remains of conscience, to regard this event all his life after as a great and signal deliverance. He can never think of it without returning thanks to Heaven for having been thus graciously pleased to save him from the guilt in which he was just ready to plunge himself, and to hinder him from rendering all the rest of his life a scene of horror, remorse, and repentance. But though his hands are innocent, he is conscious that his heart is equally guilty as if he had actually executed what he was so fully resolved upon. It gives great ease to his conscience, however, to consider that the crime was not executed, though he knows that the failure arose from no virtue in him. He still considers himself as less deserving of punishment and resentment; and this good fortune either diminishes, or takes away altogether, all sense of guilt. To remember how much he was resolved upon it, has no other effect than to make him regard his escape as the greater and more miraculous: for he still fancies that he has escaped, and he looks back upon the danger to which his peace of mind was exposed, with that terror, with which one who is in safety may sometimes remember the hazard he was in of falling over a precipice, and shudder with horror at the thought.

6   2.   The second effect of this influence of fortune, is to increase our sense of the merit or demerit of actions beyond what is due to the motives or affection from which they proceed, when they happen to give occasion to extraordinary pleasure or pain. The agreeable or disagreeable effects of the action often throw a shadow of merit or demerit upon the agent, though in his intention there was nothing that deserved either praise or blame, or at least that deserved them in the degree in which we are apt to bestow them. Thus, even the messenger of bad news is disagreeable to us, and, on the contrary, we feel a sort of gratitude for the man who brings us good tidings. For a moment we look upon them both as the authors, the one of our good, the other of our bad fortune, and regard them in some measure as if they had really brought about the events which they only give an account of. The first author of our joy is naturally the object of a transitory gratitude: we embrace him with warmth and affection, and should be glad, during the instant of our prosperity, to reward him as for some signal service. By the custom of all courts, the officer, who brings the news of a

victory, is entitled to considerable preferments, and the general always chuses one of his principal favourites to go upon so agreeable an errand. The first author of our sorrow is, on the contrary, just as naturally the object of a transitory resentment. We can scarce avoid looking upon him with chagrin and uneasiness; and the rude and brutal are apt to vent upon him that spleen which his intelligence gives occasion to. Tigranes, king of Armenia, struck off the head of the man who brought him the first account of the approach of a formidable enemy.[4] To punish in this manner the author of bad tidings, seems barbarous and inhuman: yet, to reward the messenger of good news, is not disagreeable to us; we think it suitable to the bounty of kings. But why do we make this difference, since, if there is no fault in the one, neither is there any merit in the other? It is because any sort of reason seems sufficient to authorize the exertion of the social and benevolent affections; but it requires the most solid and substantial to make us enter into that of the unsocial and malevolent.

7   But though in general we are averse to enter into the unsocial and malevolent affections, though we lay it down for a rule that we ought never to approve of their gratification, unless so far as the malicious and unjust intention of the person, against whom they are directed, renders him their proper object; yet, upon some occasions, we relax of this severity. When the negligence of one man has occasioned some unintended damage to another, we generally enter so far into the resentment of the sufferer, as to approve of his inflicting a punishment upon the offender much beyond what the offence would have appeared to deserve, had no such unlucky consequence followed from it.

8   There is a degree of negligence, which would appear to deserve some chastisement though it should occasion no damage to any body. Thus, if a person should throw a large stone over a wall into a public street without giving warning to those who might be passing by, and without regarding where it was likely to fall, he would undoubtedly deserve some chastisement. A very accurate police would punish so absurd an action, even though it had done no mischief. The person who has been guilty of it, shows an insolent contempt of the happiness and safety of others. There is real injustice in his conduct. He wantonly exposes his neighbour to what no man in his senses would chuse to expose himself, and evidently wants that sense of what is due to his fellow-creatures which is the basis of justice and of society. Gross negligence therefore is, in the law, said to be almost equal to malicious design*. When any unlucky consequences happen from such

*Lata culpa prope dolum est.[5]

---

[4] Plutarch, *Lives*, Lucullus, 25. The 'formidable enemy' was Lucullus.

[5] Smith is misquoting from memory. The *Corpus Iuris Civilis* does not contain the phrase precisely as Smith gives it. He is probably thinking either of *lata culpa plane dolo comparabitur* (*Digest*, XI.6.1.1) or of *magna culpa dolus est* (*Digest*, L.16.226).

carelessness, the person who has been guilty of it is often punished as if
he had really intended those consequences; and his conduct, which was
only thoughtless and insolent, and what deserved some chastisement, is
considered as atrocious, and as liable to the severest punishment. Thus if,
by the imprudent action above-mentioned, he should accidentally kill a
man, he is, by the laws of many countries, particularly by the old law of
Scotland,[6] liable to the last punishment. And though this is no doubt
excessively severe, it is not altogether inconsistent with our natural sentiments. Our just indignation against the folly and inhumanity of his conduct
is exasperated by our sympathy with the unfortunate sufferer. Nothing,
however, would appear more shocking to our natural sense of equity, than
to bring a man to the scaffold merely for having thrown a stone carelessly
into the street without hurting any body. The folly and inhumanity of his
conduct, however, would in this case be the same; but still our sentiments
would be very different. The consideration of this difference may satisfy
us how much the indignation, even of the spectator, is apt to be animated
by the actual consequences of the action. In cases of this kind there will,
if I am not mistaken, be found a great degree of severity in the laws of
almost all nations; as I have already observed that in those of an opposite
kind there was a very general relaxation of discipline.

9   There is another degree of negligence which does not involve in it any
sort of injustice. The person who is guilty of it treats his neighbours as he
treats himself, means no harm to any body, and is far from entertaining any
insolent contempt for the safety and happiness of others. He is not,
however, so careful and circumspect in his conduct as he ought to be, and
deserves upon this account some degree of blame and censure, but no
sort of punishment. Yet ᵃifᵃ by a negligence* of this kind he should occasion some damage to another person, he is by the laws of, I believe, all
countries, obliged to compensate it. And though this is no doubt a real
punishment, and what no mortal would have thought of inflicting upon
him, had it not been for the unlucky accident which his conduct gave
occasion to; yet this decision of the law is approved of by the natural sentiments of all mankind. Nothing, we think, can be more just than that one
man should not suffer by the carelessness of another; and that the damage
occasioned by blamable negligence, should be made up by the person who
was guilty of it.

10   There is another species of negligence†, which consists merely in a want
of the most anxious timidity and circumspection, with regard to all the

*Culpa levis.   †Culpa levissima.

ᵃ⁻ᵃ *1–5* if, *6 7*

[6] In LJ Smith notes that Scots law made no distinction between murder and man-
slaughter. See LJ(A) ii.112 and LJ(B) 187 (Cannan ed., 140).

possible consequences of our actions. The want of this painful attention, when no bad consequences follow from it, is so far from being regarded as blamable, that the contrary quality is rather considered as such. That timid circumspection which is afraid of every thing, is never regarded as a virtue, but as a quality which more than any other incapacitates for action and business. Yet when, from a want of this excessive care, a person happens to occasion some damage to another, he is often by the law obliged to compensate it. Thus, by the Aquilian law, the man, who not being able to manage a horse that had accidentally taken fright, should happen to ride down his neighbour's slave, is obliged to compensate the damage.[7] When an accident of this kind happens, we are apt to think that he ought not to have rode such a horse, and to regard his attempting it as an unpardonable levity; though without this accident we should not only have made no such reflection, but should have regarded his refusing it as the effect of timid weakness, and of an anxiety about merely possible events, which it is to no purpose to be aware of. The person himself, who by an accident even of this kind has involuntarily hurt another, seems to have some sense of his own ill desert, with regard to him. He naturally runs up to the sufferer to express his concern for what has happened, and to make every acknowledgment in his power. If he has any sensibility, he necessarily desires to compensate the damage, and to do every thing he can to appease that animal resentment, which he is sensible will be apt to arise in the breast of the sufferer. To make no apology, to offer no atonement, is regarded as the highest brutality. Yet why should he make an apology more than any other person? Why should he, since he was equally innocent with any other bystander, be thus singled out from among all mankind, to make up for the bad fortune of another? This task would surely never be imposed upon him, did not even the impartial spectator feel some indulgence for what may be regarded as the unjust resentment of that other.

CHAP. III

Of the final cause of this Irregularity of Sentiments

1 SUCH is the effect of the good or bad ªconsequencesª of actions upon the sentiments both of the person who performs them, and of others; and thus, Fortune, which governs the world, has some influence where we should be least willing to allow her any, and directs in some measure the sentiments of mankind, with regard to the character and conduct both of themselves and others. That the world judges by the event, and not by the design,

ª-ª *1 2E* consequence *2-7*

---

[7] Cf. Justinian, *Institutes*, IV.iii.8.

has been in all ages the complaint, and is the great discouragement of virtue. Every body agrees to the general maxim, that as the event does not depend on the agent, it ought to have no influence upon our sentiments, with regard to the merit or propriety of his conduct. But when we come to particulars, we find that our sentiments are scarce in any one instance exactly conformable to what this equitable maxim would direct. The happy or unprosperous event of any action, is not only apt to give us a good or bad opinion of the prudence with which it was conducted, but almost always too animates our gratitude or resentment, our sense of the merit or demerit of the design.

2   Nature, however, when she implanted the seeds of this irregularity in the human breast, seems, as upon all other occasions, to have intended the happiness and perfection of the species. If the hurtfulness of the design, if the malevolence of the affection, were alone the causes which excited our resentment, we should feel all the furies of that passion against any person in whose breast we suspected or believed such designs or affections were harboured, though they had never broke out into any *b*action.*b* Sentiments, thoughts, intentions, would become the objects of punishment; and if the indignation of mankind run as high against them as against actions; if the baseness of the thought which had given birth to no action, seemed in the eyes of the world as much to call aloud for vengeance as the baseness of the action, every court of judicature would become a real inquisition. There would be no safety for the most innocent and circumspect conduct. Bad wishes, bad views, bad designs, might still be suspected; and while these excited the same indignation with bad conduct, while bad intentions were as much resented as bad actions, they would equally expose the person to punishment and resentment. Actions, therefore, which either produce actual evil, or attempt to produce it, and thereby put us in the immediate fear of it, are by the Author of nature rendered the only proper and approved objects of human punishment and resentment. Sentiments, designs, affections, though it is from these that according to cool reason human actions derive their whole merit or demerit, are placed by the great Judge of hearts beyond the limits of every human jurisdiction, and are reserved for the cognizance of his own unerring tribunal. That necessary rule of justice, therefore, that men in this life are liable to punishment for their actions only, not for their designs and intentions, is founded upon this salutary and useful irregularity in human sentiments concerning merit or demerit, which at first sight appears so absurd and unaccountable. But every part of nature, when attentively surveyed, equally demonstrates the providential care of its Author, and

b-b *1 2* actions. *3-7* *The change in ed. 3 was probably a printer's revision, perhaps influenced by* actions *in the next sentence.*

we may admire the wisdom and goodness of God even in the weakness and folly of ᶜman.ᶜ

3   Nor is that irregularity of sentiments altogether without its utility, by which the merit of an unsuccessful attempt to serve, and much more that of mere good inclinations and kind wishes, appears to be imperfect. Man was made for action, and to promote by the exertion of his faculties such changes in the external circumstances both of himself and others, as may seem most favourable to the happiness of all. He must not be satisfied with indolent benevolence, nor fancy himself the friend of mankind, because in his heart he wishes well to the prosperity of the world. That he may call forth the whole vigour of his soul, and strain every nerve, in order to produce those ends which it is the purpose of his being to advance, Nature has taught him, that neither himself nor mankind can be fully satisfied with his conduct, nor bestow upon it the full measure of applause, unless he has actually produced them. He is made to know, that the praise of good intentions, without the merit of good offices, will be but of little avail to excite either the loudest acclamations of the world, or even the highest degree of self-applause. The man who has performed no single action of importance, but whose whole conversation and deportment express the justest, the noblest, and most generous sentiments, can be entitled to demand no very high reward, even though his inutility should be owing to nothing but the want of an opportunity to serve. We can still refuse it him without blame. We can still ask him, What have you done? What actual service can you produce, to entitle you to so great a recompense? We esteem you, and love you; but we owe you nothing. To reward indeed that latent virtue which has been useless only for want of an opportunity to serve, to bestow upon it those honours and preferments, which, though in some measure it may be said to deserve them, it could not with propriety have insisted upon, is the effect of the most divine benevolence. To punish, on the contrary, for the affections of the heart only, where no crime has been committed, is the most insolent and barbarous tyranny. The benevolent affections seem to deserve most praise, when they do not wait till it becomes almost a crime for them not to exert themselves. The malevolent, on the contrary, can scarce be too tardy, too slow, or deliberate.

4   It is even of ᵈconsiderable importance, thatᵈ the evil which is done without design should be regarded as a misfortune to the doer as well as to the sufferer. Man is thereby taught to reverence the happiness of his brethren, to tremble lest he should, even unknowingly, do any thing that can hurt them, and to dread that animal resentment which, he feels, is ready to burst out against him, if he should, without design, be the unhappy instrument

---

ᶜ⁻ᶜ 2E men. *1-7 Cf. VI.iii.30, a passage added in ed. 6, where the phrase is introduced again, with the correct reading* man.
ᵈ⁻ᵈ use that *1-5*

of their calamity. ᵉAs, in the ancient heathen religion, that holy ground which had been consecrated to some god, was not to be trod upon but upon solemn and necessary occasions, and the man who had even ignorantly violated it, became piacular from that moment, and, until proper atonement should be made, incurred the vengeance of that powerful and invisible being to whom it had been set apart;[1] so, by the wisdom of Nature, the happiness of every innocent man is, in the same manner, rendered holy, consecrated, and hedged round against the approach of every other man; not to be wantonly trod upon, not even to be, in any respect, ignorantly and involuntarily violated, without requiring some expiation, some atonement in proportion to the greatness of such undesigned violation. A man of humanity, who accidentally, and without the smallest degree of blamable negligence, has been the cause of the death of another man, feels himself piacular, though not guilty. During his whole life he considers this accident as one of the greatest misfortunes that could have befallen him. If the family of the slain is poor, and he himself in tolerable circumstances, he immediately takes them under his protection, and, without any other merit, thinks them entitled to every degree of favour and kindness. If they are in better circumstances, he endeavours by every submission, by every expression of sorrow, by rendering them every good office which he can devise or they accept of, to atone for what has happened, and to propitiate, as much as possible, their, perhaps natural, though no doubt most unjust resentment, for the great, though involuntary, offence which he has given them.

5   The distress which an innocent person feels, who, by some accident, has been led to do something which, if it had been done with knowledge and design, would have justly exposed him to the deepest reproach, has given occasion to some of the finest and most interesting scenes both of the ancient and of the modern drama. It is this fallacious sense of guilt, if I may call it so, which constitutes the whole distress of Oedipus and Jocasta upon the Greek, of Monimia and Isabella upon the English, theatre.[2] They are all of them in the highest degree piacular, though not one of them is in the smallest degree guilty.

ᵉ *The passage from* As, in the ancient . . . *to the end of* § 5 *was added in ed. 6.*

---

[1] Smith is thinking of the religion of ancient Rome. A person who had unwittingly violated certain religious laws was required to make atonement, and the word *piaculum* was used both for the trespass and for the act of expiation. The laws were especially stringent about encroachment upon sacred precincts.

Smith refers again to the concept of the piacular at VII.iv.30, another passage added in ed. 6.

[2] All four unwittingly violated sacred rules of marriage. Oedipus and his mother Jocasta, who appear in Sophocles' *Oedipus Rex*, formed an incestuous marriage in ignorance of their blood relationship. Monimia, in Otway's *The Orphan* (cf. I.ii.2.3 above), admitted her brother-in-law to her bed, thinking he was her husband. Isabella, in Thomas

6   Notwithstanding, however, all these seeming irregularities of sentiment,
if man should unfortunately either give occasion to those evils which he
did not intend, or fail in producing that good which he intended, Nature
has not left his innocence altogether without consolation, nor his virtue
altogether without reward. He then calls to his assistance that just and
equitable maxim, That those events which did not depend upon our conduct, ought not to diminish the esteem that is due to us. He summons
up his whole magnanimity and firmness of soul, and strives to regard himself, not in the light in which he at present appears, but in that in which
he ought to appear, in which he would have appeared had his generous
designs been crowned with success, and in which he would still appear, notwithstanding their miscarriage, if the sentiments of mankind were either
altogether candid and equitable, or even perfectly consistent with themselves. The more candid and humane part of mankind entirely go along
with the ʳeffortʳ which he thus makes to support himself in his own
opinion. They exert their whole generosity and greatness of mind, to correct in themselves this irregularity of human nature, and endeavour to
regard his unfortunate magnanimity in the same light in which, had it been
successful, they would, without any such generous exertion, have naturally
been disposed to consider it.

ʳ⁻ʳ *1* 2E   efforts 2–7

Southerne's *The Fatal Marriage, or The Innocent Adultery*, made a bigamous marriage
through believing mistakenly that her husband was dead.

PART III

Of the Foundation of our Judgments concerning our own Sentiments and Conduct, and of the Sense of Duty

^aConsisting of One Section^a

^bCHAP. I^b

^cOf the Principle of Self-approbation and of Self-disapprobation^c

1 In the two foregoing parts of this discourse, I have chiefly considered the origin and foundation of our judgments concerning the sentiments and conduct of others. I come now to consider ^dmore particularly^d the origin of those concerning our own.

2 ^eThe principle by which we naturally either approve or disapprove of our own conduct, seems to be altogether the same with that by which we exercise the like judgments concerning the conduct of other people. We either approve or disapprove of the conduct of another man according as we feel that, when we bring his case home to ourselves, we either can or cannot entirely sympathize with the sentiments and motives which directed it. And, in the same manner, we either approve or disapprove of our own conduct, according as we feel that, when we place ourselves in the situation

^{a–a} *om. 1 6 7* Consisting of one SECTION *2–5*
^{b–b} SECT. I *1*
^{c–c} Of the consciousness of merited praise or blame *1 idem ital. 2–5 Apart from the first paragraph, the content of Sect. i in ed. 1 (Chap. 1 in eds. 2–5) is largely what became part of Chap. 2 in ed. 6.*
^{d–d} *om. 1–5*
^{e–e} *These five sentences were added in ed. 6. After the end of § 1, ed. 1 (followed by eds. 2–5 with variants as indicated) proceeds:*

> The desire of the approbation and esteem of those we live with, which is of so much [of such *2–5*] importance to our happiness, cannot be fully and intirely [entirely *4 5*] contented but by rendering ourselves the just and proper objects of those sentiments, and by adjusting our own character and conduct according to those measures and rules by which esteem and approbation are naturally bestowed. It is not sufficient, that from ignorance or mistake, . . .

The passage continues as in III.2.4 (second sentence) to the end of III.2.5, and then proceeds to give the major part of III.2.9. Sect. i in ed. 1 (Chap. 1 in eds. 2–5) ends there, and Sect. ii (Chap. 2 in eds. 2–5) begins as follows:

SECT. II [CHAP. II *2–5*]

In what manner our own judgments refer to what ought to be the judgments of others: And [*and 2–5*] of the origin of general rules [*ital. 2–5*]

> A Great part, perhaps the greatest part [part, *2*] of human happiness and misery arises from the view of our past conduct, and from the degree of approbation or disapprobation which we feel from the consideration of it. But in whatever manner it may affect us, our sentiments of this kind have always some secret reference. . . .

Sect. ii of ed. 1 (Chap. 2 of eds. 2–5) then proceeds more or less as in the text of ed. 6 at the end of the five new sentences.

of another man, and view it, as it were, with his eyes and from his station, we either can or cannot entirely enter into and sympathize with the sentiments and motives which influenced it. We can never survey our own sentiments and motives, we can never form any judgment concerning them; unless we remove ourselves, as it were, from our own natural station, and endeavour to view them as at a certain distance from us. But we can do this in no other way than by endeavouring to view them with the eyes of other people, or as other people are likely to view them.*e* *f*Whatever judgment we can form concerning them, accordingly, must always bear*f* some secret reference, either to what are, or to what, upon a certain condition, would be, or to what, we imagine, ought to be the *g*judgment*g* of others. *h*We endeavour to examine our own conduct as we imagine any other fair and impartial spectator*h* would examine it. If, upon placing ourselves in his situation, we thoroughly enter into all the passions and motives which influenced it, we approve of it, by sympathy with the approbation of this supposed equitable judge. If otherwise, we enter into his disapprobation, and condemn it.

3   Were it possible that a human creature could grow up to manhood in some solitary place, without any communication with his own species, he could no more think of his own character, of the propriety or demerit of his own sentiments and conduct, of the beauty or deformity of his own mind, than of the beauty or deformity of his own face. All these are objects which he cannot easily see, which naturally he does not look at, *j*and with regard to which he is provided with no mirror which can present them to his view.*j* Bring him into society, and he is immediately provided with the mirror which he wanted before.[1] It is placed in the countenance and behaviour of those he lives with, which always mark when they enter into, and when they disapprove of his sentiments; and it is here that he first views the propriety and impropriety of his own passions, the beauty and deformity of his own mind. To a man who from his birth was a stranger to society, the objects of his passions, the external bodies which either pleased or hurt him, would occupy his whole attention. The passions themselves, the desires or aversions, the joys or sorrows, which those objects excited, though of all things the most immediately present to him, could scarce ever be the objects of his thoughts. The idea of them could never interest

j-j But in whatever manner it [*i.e. our past conduct*] may affect us, our sentiments of this kind have always *1–5*
g-g sentiments *1–5*
h-h We examine it as we imagine an impartial spectator *1–5*
j-j and upon which he is provided with no mirror to enable him to turn his eyes. *1*

[1] Cf. Hume, *Treatise of Human Nature*, II.ii.5; ed. Selby-Bigge, 365; (after speaking of sympathy in relation to personal beauty): 'the minds of men are mirrors to one another, not only because they reflect each others emotions, but also because those rays of passions, sentiments and opinions may be often reverberated . . .'.

him so much as to call upon his attentive consideration. The consideration
of his joy could in him excite no new joy, nor that of his sorrow any new
sorrow, though the consideration of the causes of those passions might
often excite both. Bring him into society, and all his own passions will
immediately become the causes of new passions. He will observe that mankind approve of some of them, and are disgusted by others. He will be
elevated in the one case, and cast down in the other; his desires and aversions, his joys and sorrows, will now often become the causes of new
desires and new aversions, new joys and new sorrows: they will now, therefore, interest him deeply, and often call upon his most attentive consideration.*k*

4   Our first ideas of personal beauty and deformity, are drawn from the
shape and appearance of others, not from our own. We soon become sensible, however, that others exercise the same criticism upon us. We are
pleased when they approve of our figure, and are disobliged when they seem
to be disgusted. We become anxious to know how far our appearance
deserves either their blame or approbation. We examine our persons limb

*k Between § 3 and § 4, ed. 1 inserts three further paragraphs. [1]—To be amiable . . .
deserve to be hated?—was transferred in ed. 2 so as to follow what is now § 6; it remained
there in the subsequent editions, and is now § 7. [2] and [3] are given below. [2] was withdrawn
in ed. 2, which substituted an improved expression of its thought in the paragraph that is now
§ 6. [3] was retained, with slight revision (noted in the variants below), in ed. 2, but was transferred so as to follow the present § 7; it remained there in eds. 3–5, but was withdrawn in ed. 6.
We show variants not only of eds. 2–5 but also of the draft revision for ed. 2 enclosed with
Letter 40 addressed to Sir Gilbert Elliot, dated 10 October 1759. The draft is in the hand of an
amanuensis with light revision in Smith's own hand. The commas that the draft adds to the
text of ed. 1 were inserted by Smith himself.*

[2] To judge of ourselves as we judge of others, to approve and condemn in ourselves
what we approve and condemn in others, is the greatest exertion of candour and impartiality. In order to do this, we must look at ourselves with the same eyes with which we
look at others: we must imagine ourselves not the actors, but the spectators of our own
character and conduct, and consider how these would affect us when viewed from this
new station, in which their excellencies and imperfections can alone be discovered. We
must enter, in short, either into what are, or into what ought to be, or into what, if the
whole circumstances of our conduct were known, we imagine would be the sentiments
of others, before we can either applaud or condemn it.

[3] A moral being is an accountable being. An [Man is considered as a moral, because
he is regarded as an accountable being. But an *draft 2–5*] accountable being, as the word
expresses, is a being that must give an account of its actions to some other, and that consequently [that, consequently, *draft*] must regulate them according to the good-liking
[good liking *draft 2–5*] of this other. Man is accountable to God and his fellow creatures.
[fellow-creatures. *2–5*] But tho' [though *2–5*] he is, no doubt, principally accountable
to God, [God; *3–5*] in the order of time, [time *3*] he must necessarily conceive himself as
accountable to his fellow creatures, [fellow-creatures, *2–5*] before he can form any idea
of the Deity, or of the rules by which that Divine Being [divine being *2–5*] will judge of
his conduct. A child surely [child, surely, *draft*] conceives itself as accountable to its
parents, and is elevated or cast down by the thought of their merited approbation or disapprobation, long before it forms any idea of its accountableness to the Deity, or of the
rules by which that Divine Being [Divine being *draft* divine being *2–5*] will judge of its
conduct.

by limb, and by placing ourselves before a looking-glass, or by some such expedient, endeavour, as much as possible, to view ourselves at the distance and with the eyes of other people. If, after this examination, we are satisfied with our own appearance, we can more easily support the most disadvantageous judgments of others. If, on the contrary, we are sensible that we are the natural objects of distaste, every appearance of their disapprobation mortifies us beyond all measure. A man who is tolerably handsome, will allow you to laugh at any little irregularity in his person; but all such jokes are commonly unsupportable to one who is really deformed. It is evident, however, that we are anxious about our own beauty and deformity, only upon account of its effect upon others. If we had no connexion with society, we should be altogether indifferent about either.

5   In the same manner our first moral criticisms are exercised upon the characters and conduct of other people; and we are all very forward to observe how each of these affects us. But we soon learn, that other people are equally frank with regard to our own. We become anxious to know how far we deserve their censure or applause, and whether to them we must necessarily appear those agreeable or disagreeable creatures which they represent us. We begin, upon this account, to examine our own passions and conduct, and to consider how these must appear to them, by considering how they would appear to us if in their situation. We suppose ourselves the spectators of our own behaviour, and endeavour to imagine what effect it would, in this light, produce upon us. This is the only looking-glass by which we can, in some measure, with the eyes of other people, scrutinize the propriety of our own conduct. If in this view it pleases us, we are tolerably satisfied. We can be more indifferent about the applause, and, in some measure, despise the censure of ᶦthe world;ᶦ secure that, however misunderstood or misrepresented, we are the natural and proper objects of approbation. On the contrary, if we are ᵐdoubtful aboutᵐ it, we are often, upon that very account, more anxious to gain their approbation, and, provided we have not already, as they say, shaken hands with infamy, we are altogether distracted at the thoughts of their censure, which then strikes us with double severity.ⁿ

ᶦ⁻ᶦ others; *1–5*
ᵐ⁻ᵐ displeased with *1 3–5*   pleased with *2 (corr. 2E)*
ⁿ *After the end of § 5, ed. 1 adds a further paragraph:*

Unfortunately this moral looking-glass is not always a very good one. Common looking-glasses, it is said, are extremely deceitful, and by the glare which they throw over the face, conceal from the partial eyes of the person many deformities which are obvious to every body besides. But there is not in the world such a smoother of wrinkles as is every man's imagination, with regard to the blemishes of his own character.

    Ed. 1 then proceeds to a passage which in ed. 6 became the major part of Chapter 4, There are two different occasions . . . *(III.4.2) to the end of that chapter.*
    In ed. 2 (followed by eds. 3–5), the short paragraph quoted above was withdrawn, and § 6 was added.

6 [o]When I endeavour to examine my own conduct, when I endeavour to pass sentence upon it, and either to approve or condemn it, it is evident that, in all such cases, I divide myself, as it were, into two persons; and that I, the examiner and judge, represent a different character from that other I, the person whose conduct is examined into and judged of. The first is the spectator, whose sentiments with regard to my own conduct I endeavour to enter into, by placing myself in his situation, and by considering how it would appear to me, when seen from that particular point of view. The second is the agent, the person whom I properly call myself, and of whose conduct, under the character of a spectator, I was endeavouring to form some opinion. The first is the judge; the second the [p]person judged of.[p] But that the judge should, in every respect, be the same with the [q]person judged of,[q] is as impossible, as that the cause should, in every respect, be the same with the effect.

7 [r]To be amiable and to be meritorious; that is, to deserve love and to deserve reward, are the great characters of virtue; and to be odious and punishable, of vice. But all these characters have an immediate reference to the sentiments of others. Virtue is not said to be amiable, or to be meritorious, because it is the object of its own love, or of its own gratitude; but because it excites those sentiments in other men. The consciousness that it is the object of such favourable regards, is the source of that inward tranquillity and self-satisfaction with which it is naturally attended, as the suspicion of the contrary gives occasion to the torments of vice. What so great happiness as to be beloved, and to know that we deserve to be beloved? What so great misery as to be hated, and to know that we deserve to be hated?[s]

[a]CHAP II

Of the love of Praise, and of that of Praise-worthiness; and of the dread of Blame, and of that of Blame-worthiness

1 MAN naturally desires, not only to be loved, but to be lovely; or to be that thing which is the natural and proper object of love. He naturally dreads,

[o] *§ 6 was added in the draft revision of 1759 and in ed. 2. It is an improved expression of the thought contained in paragraph* [2] *of the variants noted at § 3*[k].

[p–p] pannel. *draft 2–5 'The panel' is a Scots term for 'the accused' in a criminal law trial.*

[q–q] pannel, *draft 2–5*

[r] *See note* [k] *to § 3.*

[s] *After the end of § 7, the draft of 1759 and eds. 2–5 proceed with the slightly revised version of paragraph* [3] *given in the variants at § 3*[k]. *They then follow this with several paragraphs that give an earlier view of the thought contained in III.2.31–2. These paragraphs are printed in the textual note at III.2.31*[r]. *Eds. 2–5 next proceed more or less as in III.3.1–5, 7–9, and 11. (The draft has part of this material.) Thereafter they revert to the text of ed. 1 at what is now III.4.3. In all, ed. 2 has here added sixteen paragraphs to what was contained in ed. 1.*

[a] *Most of the content of this chapter was added or re-written for ed. 6. §§ 1–3, §§ 6–8, the*

not only to be hated, but to be hateful; or to be that thing which is the natural and proper object of hatred. He desires, not only praise, but praise-worthiness; or to be that thing which, though it should be praised by nobody, is, however, the natural and proper object of praise. He dreads, not only blame, but blame-worthiness; or to be that thing which, though it should be blamed by nobody, is, however, the natural and proper object of blame.

2   The love of praise-worthiness is by no means derived altogether from the love of praise. Those two principles, though they resemble one another, though they are connected, and often blended with one another, are yet, in many respects, distinct and independent of one another.

3   The love and admiration which we naturally conceive for those whose character and conduct we approve of, necessarily dispose us to desire to become ourselves the objects of the like agreeable sentiments, and to be as amiable and as admirable as those whom we love and admire the most. Emulation, the anxious desire that we ourselves should excel, is originally founded in our admiration of the excellence of others. Neither can we be satisfied with being merely admired for what other people are admired. We must at least believe ourselves to be admirable for what they are admirable. But, in order to attain this satisfaction, we must become the impartial spectators of our own character and conduct. We must endeavour to view them with the eyes of other people, or as other people are likely to view them. When seen in this light, if they appear to us as we wish, we are happy and contented. But it greatly confirms this happiness and contentment when we find that other people, viewing them with those very eyes with which we, in imagination only, were endeavouring to view them, see them precisely in the same light in which we ourselves had seen them. Their approbation necessarily confirms our own self-approbation. Their praise necessarily strengthens our own sense of our own praise-worthiness. In this case, so far is the love of praise-worthiness from being derived altogether from that of praise; that the love of praise seems, at least in a great measure, to be derived from that of praise-worthiness.

4   The most sincere praise can give little pleasure when it cannot be con-sidered as some sort of proof of praise-worthiness. [b]It is [c]by no means[c] sufficient that, from ignorance or mistake, esteem and [d]admiration[d] should, in some way or other, be bestowed upon us. If we are conscious

---

beginning of § 9, §§ 10–30, and §§ 33–5 are quite new, while §§ 31–2 re-state in a new form the thought of several paragraphs that were added in the draft revision of 1759 and in ed. 2 and were then withdrawn in ed. 6. §§ 4–5 and most of § 9 repeat, with light revision, what formed the major part of Section i in ed. 1 and of Chapter 1 in ed. 2. See note [e–e] at III.1.2.
   [b] *The passage from this point to the end of § 5 formed part of Sect. i in ed. 1, and of Chap. 1 in ed. 2.*
   [c–c] not *1–5*
   [d–d] approbation *1–5*

that we do not deserve to be so favourably thought of, and that if the truth were known, we should be regarded with very different sentiments, our satisfaction is far from being complete. The man who applauds us either for actions which we did not perform, or for motives which had no sort of influence upon our conduct, applauds not us, but another person. We can derive no sort of satisfaction from his praises. To us they should be more mortifying than any censure, and should perpetually call to our minds, the most humbling of all reflections, the reflection of what we ought to be, but what we are not. A woman who *e*paints, could derive, one should imagine, but little vanity from the compliments that are paid to her complexion.*e* These, we should expect, ought rather to put her in mind of the sentiments which her real complexion would excite, and mortify her the more by the contrast. To be pleased with such groundless applause is a proof of the most superficial levity and weakness. It is what is properly called vanity, and is the foundation of the most ridiculous and contemptible vices, the vices of affectation and common lying; follies which, if experience did not teach us how common they are, one should imagine the least spark of common sense would save us from. The foolish liar, who endeavours to excite the admiration of the company by the relation of adventures which never had any existence; the important coxcomb, who gives himself airs of rank and distinction which he well knows he has no just pretensions to; are both of them, no doubt, pleased with the applause which they fancy they meet with. But their vanity arises from so gross an illusion of the imagination, that it is difficult to conceive how any rational creature should be imposed upon by it. When they place themselves in the situation of those whom they fancy they have deceived, they are struck with the highest admiration for their own persons. They look upon themselves, not in that light in which, they know, they ought to appear to their companions, but in that in which they believe their companions actually look upon them. Their superficial weakness and trivial folly hinder them from ever turning their eyes inwards, or from seeing themselves in that despicable point of view in which their own consciences *f*must*f* tell them that they would appear to every body, if the real truth should ever come to be known.

5   As ignorant and groundless praise can give no solid joy, no satisfaction that will bear any serious examination, so, on the contrary, it often gives real comfort to reflect, that though no praise should actually be bestowed upon us, our conduct, however, has been such as to deserve it, and has been in every respect suitable to those measures and rules by which praise and approbation are naturally and commonly bestowed. We are pleased, not only with praise, but with having done what is praise-worthy. We are

e-e paints to conceal her ugliness, could derive, . . . paid to her beauty. *1–5*
f-f should *1–5*

pleased to think that we have rendered ourselves the natural objects of
approbation, though no approbation should ever actually be bestowed upon
us: and we are mortified to reflect that we have justly *ᵍmeritedᵍ* the blame
of those we live with, though that sentiment should never actually be exerted against us. The man who is conscious to himself that he has exactly
observed those measures of conduct which experience informs him are
generally agreeable, reflects with satisfaction on the propriety of his own
behaviour. When he views it in the light in which the impartial spectator
would view it, he thoroughly enters into all the motives which influenced
it. He looks back upon every part of it with pleasure and approbation,
and though mankind should never be acquainted with what he has done,
he regards himself, not so much according to the light in which they actually regard him, as according to that in which they would regard him if
they were better informed. He anticipates the applause and admiration
which in this case would be bestowed upon him, and he applauds and admires himself by sympathy with sentiments, which do not indeed actually
take place, but which the ignorance of the public alone hinders from taking
place, which he knows are the natural and ordinary effects of such conduct,
which his imagination strongly connects with it, and which he has acquired
a habit of conceiving as something that naturally and in propriety ought to
follow from it. Men *ʰhaveʰ* voluntarily thrown away life to acquire after
death a renown which they could no longer enjoy. Their imagination, in
the mean time, anticipated that fame which was in future times to be
bestowed upon them. Those applauses which they were never to hear
rung in their ears; the thoughts of that admiration, whose effects they were
never to feel, played about their hearts, banished from their breasts the
strongest of all natural fears, and transported them to perform actions
which seem almost beyond the reach of human nature. But in point of
reality there is surely no great difference between that approbation which
is not to be bestowed till we can no longer enjoy it, and that which, indeed,
is never to be bestowed, but which would be bestowed, if the world was
ever made to understand properly the real circumstances of our behaviour.
If the one often produces such violent effects, we cannot wonder that the
other should always be highly regarded.*ʲ*

6   Nature, when she formed man for society, endowed him with an
original desire to please, and an original aversion to offend his brethren.
She taught him to feel pleasure in their favourable, and pain in their unfavourable regard. She rendered their approbation most flattering and
most agreeable to him for its own sake; and their disapprobation most
mortifying and most offensive.

ᵍ⁻ᵍ incurred *1–5*   *ʰ⁻ʰ* have often *1–5*
ʲ After the end of § 5, eds. 1–5 proceed with a paragraph which begins On the contrary,
the man who has broke . . . *and which continues as at § 9ᵏ.*

7   But this desire of the approbation, and this aversion to the disapprobation of his brethren, would not alone have rendered him fit for that society
for which he was made. Nature, accordingly, has endowed him, not only
with a desire of being approved of, but with a desire of being what ought
to be approved of; or of being what he himself approves of in other men.
The first desire could only have made him wish to appear to be fit for
society. The second was necessary in order to render him anxious to be
really fit. The first could only have prompted him to the affectation of
virtue, and to the concealment of vice. The second was necessary in order
to inspire him with the real love of virtue, and with the real abhorrence of
vice. In every well-formed mind this second desire seems to be the strongest
of the two. It is only the weakest and most superficial of mankind who can
be much delighted with that praise which they themselves know to be altogether unmerited. A weak man may sometimes be pleased with it, but a
wise man rejects it upon all occasions. But, though a wise man feels little
pleasure from praise where he knows there is no praise-worthiness, he
often feels the highest in doing what he knows to be praise-worthy,
though he knows equally well that no praise is ever to be bestowed upon
it. To obtain the approbation of mankind, where no approbation is due,
can never be an object of any importance to him. To obtain that approbation where it is really due, may sometimes be an object of no great importance to him. But to be that thing which deserves approbation, must
always be an object of the highest.

8   To desire, or even to accept of praise, where no praise is due, can be
the effect only of the most contemptible vanity. To desire it where it is
really due, is to desire no more than that a most essential act of justice
should be done to us. The love of just fame, of true glory, even for its own
sake, and independent of any advantage which he can derive from it, is
not unworthy even of a wise man. He sometimes, however, neglects, and
even despises it; and he is never more apt to do so than when he has the
most perfect assurance of the perfect propriety of every part of his own
conduct. His self-approbation, in this case, stands in need of no confirmation from the approbation of other men. It is alone sufficient, and he is
contented with it. This self-approbation, if not the only, is at least the
principal object, about which he can or ought to be anxious. The love of it,
is the love of virtue.

9   As the love and admiration which we naturally conceive for some characters, dispose us to wish to become ourselves the proper objects of such
agreeable sentiments; so the hatred and contempt which we as naturally
conceive for others, dispose us, perhaps still more strongly, to dread the
very thought of resembling them in any respect. Neither is it, in this case,
too, so much the thought of being hated and despised that we are afraid
of, as that of being hateful and despicable. We dread the thought of doing

any thing which can render us the just and proper objects of the hatred and contempt of our fellow-creatures; even though we had the most perfect security that those sentiments were never actually to be exerted against us. *k*The man who has broke through all those measures of conduct, which can alone render him agreeable to mankind, though he should have the most perfect assurance that what he had done was for ever to be concealed from every human eye, it is all to no purpose. When he looks back upon it, and views it in the light in which the impartial spectator would view it, he finds that he can enter into none of the motives which influenced it. He is abashed and confounded at the thoughts of it, and necessarily feels a very high degree of that shame which he would be exposed to, if his actions should ever come to be generally known. His imagination, in this case too, anticipates the contempt and derision from which nothing saves him but the ignorance of those he lives with. He still feels that he is the natural object of these sentiments, and still trembles at the thought of what he would suffer, if they were ever actually exerted against him. But if what he had been guilty of was not merely one of those improprieties which are the objects of simple disapprobation, but one of those enormous crimes which excite detestation and resentment, he could never think of it, as long as he had any sensibility left, without feeling all the agony of horror and remorse; and though he could be assured that no man was ever to know it, and could even bring himself to believe that there was no God to revenge it, he would still feel enough of both these sentiments to embitter the whole of his life: he would still regard himself as the natural object of the hatred and indignation of all his fellow-creatures; and, if his heart was not grown callous by the habit of crimes, he could not think without terror and astonishment even of the manner in which mankind would look upon him, of what would be the expression of their countenance and of their eyes, if the dreadful truth should ever come to be known. These natural pangs of an affrighted conscience are the daemons, the avenging furies, which, in this life, haunt the guilty, which allow them neither quiet nor repose, which often drive them to despair and distraction, from which no assurance of secrecy can protect them, from which no principles of irreligion can entirely deliver them, and from which nothing can free them but the vilest and most abject of all states, a complete insensibility to honour and infamy, to vice and virtue. Men of the most detestable characters, who, in the execution of the most dreadful crimes, had taken their measures so coolly as to avoid even the suspicion of guilt, have sometimes been driven, by the horror of their situation, to discover, of their own accord, what no human sagacity could ever have investigated. By acknowledging their guilt, by submitting themselves to the resentment of their offended fellow-citizens, and, by thus satiating that vengeance of which

k In eds. 1–5, a new paragraph, following § 5, begins here: On the contrary, the man . . .

they were sensible that they had become the proper objects, they hoped, by their death to reconcile themselves, at least in their own imagination, to the natural sentiments of mankind; to be able to consider themselves as less worthy of hatred and resentment; to atone, in some measure, for their crimes, and *l*by thus becoming the objects, rather of compassion than of horror,*l* if *m*possible*m* to die in peace and with the forgiveness of all their fellow-creatures. Compared to what they felt before the discovery, even the thought of this, it seems, was happiness.*n*

10   *o*In such cases, the horror of blame-worthiness seems, even in persons who cannot be suspected of any extraordinary delicacy or sensibility of character, completely to conquer the dread of blame. In order to allay that horror, in order to pacify, in some degree, the remorse of their own consciences, they voluntarily submitted themselves both to the reproach and to the punishment which they knew were due to their crimes, but which, at the same time, they might easily have avoided.

11   They are the most frivolous and superficial of mankind only who can be much delighted with that praise which they themselves know to be altogether unmerited. Unmerited reproach, however, is frequently capable of mortifying very severely even men of more than ordinary constancy. Men of the most ordinary constancy, indeed, easily learn to despise those foolish tales which are so frequently circulated in society, and which, from their own absurdity and falsehood, never fail to die away in the course of a few weeks, or of a few days. But an innocent man, though of more than ordinary constancy, is often, not only shocked, but most severely mortified by the serious, though false, imputation of a crime; especially when that imputation happens unfortunately to be supported by some circumstances which give it an air of probability. He is humbled to find that any body should think so meanly of his character as to suppose him capable of being guilty of it. Though perfectly conscious of his own innocence, the very imputation seems often, even in his own imagination, to throw a shadow of disgrace and dishonour upon his character. His just indignation, too, at so very gross an injury, which, however, it may frequently be improper, and sometimes even impossible to revenge, is itself a very painful sensation. There is no greater tormentor of the human breast than violent resentment which cannot be gratified. An innocent man, brought to the scaffold by the false imputation of an infamous or odious crime, suffers the most cruel misfortune which it is possible for innocence to suffer. The agony of his mind may, in this case, frequently be greater than that of

l-l om. *1-5*

m-m 7 possible, *1-6*   *The addition of* *l-l* *in ed. 6 rendered this comma unintentionally ambiguous.*

n At this point, ed. 1 ends Sect. i and begins Sect. ii as shown in note *e-e* *to III.1.2. Eds. 2-5 follow ed. 1 but with chapters instead of sections.*

o The remainder of this chapter was added in ed. 6. But see also note *r* *at § 31.*

those who suffer for the like crimes, of which they have been actually
guilty. Profligate criminals, such as common thieves and highwaymen,
have frequently little sense of the baseness of their own conduct, and consequently no remorse. Without troubling themselves about the justice or injustice of the punishment, they have always been accustomed to look upon
the gibbet as a lot very likely to fall to them. When it does fall to them,
therefore, they consider themselves only as not quite so lucky as some of
their companions, and submit to their fortune, without any other uneasiness than what may arise from the fear of death; a fear which, even by such
worthless wretches, we frequently see, can be so easily, and so very completely conquered. The innocent man, on the contrary, over and above the
uneasiness which this fear may occasion, is tormented by his own indignation at the injustice which has been done to him. He is struck with horror
at the thoughts of the infamy which the punishment may shed upon his
memory, and foresees, with the most exquisite anguish, that he is hereafter to be remembered by his dearest friends and relations, not with regret
and affection, but with shame, and even with horror for his supposed disgraceful conduct: and the shades of death appear to close round him with a
darker and more melancholy gloom than naturally belongs to them. Such
fatal accidents, for the tranquillity of mankind, it is to be hoped, happen
very rarely in any country; but they happen sometimes in all countries,
even in those where justice is in general very well administered. The unfortunate Calas, a man of much more than ordinary constancy (broke upon
the wheel and burnt at Tholouse[1] for the supposed murder of his own son,
of which he was perfectly innocent), seemed, with his last breath, to depre-
cate, not so much the cruelty of the punishment, as the disgrace which the
imputation might bring upon his memory. After he had been broke, and
was just going to be thrown into the fire, the monk, who attended the
execution, exhorted him to confess the crime for which he had been condemned. My Father, said Calas, can you yourself bring yourself to believe
that I am guilty?

12   To persons in such unfortunate circumstances, that humble philosophy
which confines its views to this life, can afford, perhaps, but little consolation. Every thing that could render either life or death respectable is taken
from them. They are condemned to death and to everlasting infamy.
Religion can alone afford them any effectual comfort. She alone can tell

---

[1] On 10 March 1762. Jean Calas was a Calvinist, whose eldest son decided to renounce
the family faith for Roman Catholicism in order to be eligible for the bar but then committed suicide in a fit of remorse. The father was accused of murdering him and was found
guilty with no shred of proof. Owing to the efforts of Voltaire a new trial was eventually
held on 9 March 1765. Calas was declared innocent and his family was granted compensation.

Adam Smith will have heard much of this *cause célèbre* when he resided at Toulouse for
eighteen months in 1764–5, and his anecdote of Calas's last words to the monk is doubtless
recalled from conversations at that time.

them, that it is of little importance what man may think of their conduct, while the all-seeing Judge of the world approves of it. She alone can present to them the view of another world; a world of more candour, humanity, and justice, than the present; where their innocence is in due time to be declared, and their virtue to be finally rewarded: and the same great principle which can alone strike terror into triumphant vice, affords the only effectual consolation to disgraced and insulted innocence.

13   In smaller offences, as well as in greater crimes, it frequently happens that a person of sensibility is much more hurt by the unjust imputation, than the real criminal is by the actual guilt. A woman of gallantry laughs even at the well-founded surmises which are circulated concerning her conduct. The worst founded surmise of the same kind is a mortal stab to an innocent virgin. The person who is deliberately guilty of a disgraceful action, we may lay it down, I believe, as a general rule, can seldom have much sense of the disgrace; and the person who is habitually guilty of it, can scarce ever have any.

14   When every man, even of middling understanding, so readily despises unmerited applause, how it comes to pass that unmerited reproach should often be capable of mortifying so severely men of the soundest and best judgment, may, perhaps, deserve some consideration.

15   Pain, I have already had occasion to observe,[2] is, in almost all cases, a more pungent sensation than the opposite and correspondent pleasure. The one, almost always, depresses us much more below the ordinary, or what may be called the natural state of our happiness, than the other ever raises us above it. A man of sensibility is apt to be more humiliated by just censure than he is ever elevated by just applause. Unmerited applause a wise man rejects with contempt upon all occasions; but he often feels very severely the injustice of unmerited censure. By suffering himself to be applauded for what he has not performed, by assuming a merit which does not belong to him, he feels that he is guilty of a mean falsehood, and deserves, not the admiration, but the contempt of those very persons who, by mistake, had been led to admire him. It may, perhaps, give him some well-founded pleasure to find that he has been, by many people, thought capable of performing what he did not perform. But, though he may be obliged to his friends for their good opinion, he would think himself guilty of the greatest baseness if he did not immediately undeceive them. It gives him little pleasure to look upon himself in the light in which other people actually look upon him, when he is conscious that, if they knew the truth, they would look upon him in a very different light. A weak man, however, is often much delighted with viewing himself in this false and delusive light. He assumes the merit of every laudable action that is ascribed

[2] I.iii.1.3

to him, and pretends to that of many which nobody ever thought of ascribing to him. He pretends to have done what he never did, to have written what another wrote, to have invented what another discovered; and is led into all the miserable vices of plagiarism and common lying. But though no man of middling good sense can derive much pleasure from the imputation of a laudable action which he never performed, yet a wise man may suffer great pain from the serious imputation of a crime which he never committed. Nature, in this case, has rendered the pain, not only more pungent than the opposite and correspondent pleasure, but she has rendered it so in a much greater than the ordinary degree. A denial rids a man at once of the foolish and ridiculous pleasure; but it will not always rid him of the pain. When he refuses the merit which is ascribed to him, nobody doubts his veracity. It may be doubted when he denies the crime which he is accused of. He is at once enraged at the falsehood of the imputation, and mortified to find that any credit should be given to it. He feels that his character is not sufficient to protect him. He feels that his brethren, far from looking upon him in that light in which he anxiously desires to be viewed by them, think him capable of being guilty of what he is accused of. He knows perfectly that he has not been guilty. He knows perfectly what he has done; but, perhaps, scarce any man can know perfectly what he himself is capable of doing. What the peculiar constitution of his own mind may or may not admit of, is, perhaps, more or less a matter of doubt to every man. The trust and good opinion of his friends and neighbours, tends more than any thing to relieve him from this most disagreeable doubt; their distrust and unfavourable opinion to increase it. He may think himself very confident that their unfavourable judgment is wrong: but this confidence can seldom be so great as to hinder that judgment from making some impression upon him; and the greater his sensibility, the greater his delicacy, the greater his worth in short, this impression is likely to be the greater.

16   The agreement or disagreement both of the sentiments and judgments of other people with our own, is, in all cases, it must be observed, of more or less importance to us, exactly in proportion as we ourselves are more or less uncertain about the propriety of our own sentiments, about the accuracy of our own judgments.

17   A man of sensibility may sometimes feel great uneasiness lest he should have yielded too much even to what may be called an honourable passion; to his just indignation, perhaps, at the injury which may have been done either to himself or to his friend. He is anxiously afraid lest, meaning only to act with spirit, and to do justice, he may, from the too great vehemence of his emotion, have done a real injury to some other person; who, though not innocent, may not have been altogether so guilty as he at first apprehended. The opinion of other people becomes, in this case, of the

utmost importance to him. Their approbation is the most healing balsam; their disapprobation, the bitterest and most tormenting poison that can be poured into his uneasy mind. When he is perfectly satisfied with every part of his own conduct, the judgment of other people is often of less importance to him.

18   There are some very noble and beautiful arts, in which the degree of excellence can be determined only by a certain nicety of taste, of which the decisions, however, appear always, in some measure, uncertain. There are others, in which the success admits, either of clear demonstration, or very satisfactory proof. Among the candidates for excellence in those different arts, the anxiety about the public opinion is always much greater in the former than in the latter.

19   The beauty of poetry is a matter of such nicety, that a young beginner can scarce ever be certain that he has attained it. Nothing delights him so much, therefore, as the favourable judgments of his friends and of the public; and nothing mortifies him so severely as the contrary. The one establishes, the other shakes, the good opinion which he is anxious to entertain concerning his own performances. Experience and success may in time give him a little more confidence in his own judgment. He is at all times, however, liable to be most severely mortified by the unfavourable judgments of the public. Racine was so disgusted by the indifferent success of his Phaedra, the finest tragedy, perhaps, that is extant in any language, that, though in the vigour of his life, and at the height of his abilities, he resolved to write no more for the stage. That great poet used frequently to tell his son, that the most paltry and impertinent criticism had always given him more pain, than the highest and justest eulogy had ever given him pleasure.[3] The extreme sensibility of Voltaire to the slightest censure of the same kind is well known to every body.[4] The Dunciad of Mr. Pope is an everlasting monument of how much the most correct, as well as the most elegant and harmonious of all the English poets, had been hurt by the criticisms of the lowest and most contemptible authors.[5] Gray (who joins to the sublimity of Milton the elegance and

[3] Racine's *Phèdre* was first produced on 1 January 1677. Its lack of success was partly due to the plot of a hostile faction who engaged Nicolas Pradon to treat of the same subject in a play called *Phèdre et Hippolyte*, produced two days later. Modern scholars take the view that Racine's withdrawal from dramatic poetry for twelve years had more than one cause, his appointment as a royal historiographer, his return to religion, and his resentment of the plot against the success of *Phèdre*. They attach least weight to the third of these.

[4] An instance that Smith will have had in mind was Voltaire's pique at Lord Kames's disapproval, in *Elements of Criticism*, of the *Henriade*. Not content with ridiculing the *Elements* in a review, Voltaire showed on several subsequent occasions that he could neither forgive nor forget Kames's criticism.

[5] Alexander Pope's satiric poem, *The Dunciad*, is directed against a number of his critics but especially (in its first version, 1728) against Lewis Theobald, who had attacked Pope's edition of Shakespeare.

harmony of Pope, and to whom nothing is wanting to render him, perhaps, the first poet in the English language, but to have written a little more) is said to have been so much hurt, by a foolish and impertinent parody of two of his finest odes, that he never afterwards attempted any considerable work.[6] Those men of letters who value themselves upon what is called fine writing in prose, approach somewhat to the sensibility of poets.

20   Mathematicians, on the contrary, who may have the most perfect assurance, both of the truth and of the importance of their discoveries, are frequently very indifferent about the reception which they may meet with from the public. The two greatest mathematicians that I ever have had the honour to be known to, and, I believe, the two greatest that have lived in my time, Dr. Robert Simpson of Glasgow, and Dr. Matthew Stewart of Edinburgh,[7] never seemed to feel even the slightest uneasiness from the neglect with which the ignorance of the public received some of their most valuable works. The great work of Sir Isaac Newton, *p*his*p* *Mathematical Principles of Natural Philosophy*, I have been told, was for several years neglected by the public. The tranquillity of that great man, it is probable, never suffered, upon that account, the interruption of a single quarter of an hour. Natural philosophers, in their independency upon the public opinion, approach nearly to mathematicians, and, in their judgments concerning the merit of their own discoveries and observations, enjoy some degree of the same security and tranquillity.

21   The morals of those different classes of men of letters are, perhaps, sometimes somewhat affected by this very great difference in their situation with regard to the public.

---

p-p his 6 7

[6] Thomas Gray's two Pindaric odes, 'The Progress of Poesy' and 'The Bard' (1757), were parodied by Robert Lloyd and George Colman the elder in an ode 'To Obscurity', published in 1760 together with a second ode 'To Oblivion' parodying the 'Ode to Memory' (1756) by Gray's friend William Mason. Mason was indeed hurt but there is doubt whether Gray was. Overtly at least, Gray took the parody in good part. See R. Halsband, 'A Parody of Thomas Gray', *Philological Quarterly*, xxii (1943), 255–66. (On p. 264, note 42, Mr. Halsband says that Adam Smith's account of the matter was first printed in ed. 7 of TMS, 'which was revised by Smith and published posthumously in 1792'. This is incorrect. It appeared in ed. 6, and there is no reason to believe that Smith did any revision for ed. 7.)

For Smith's praise of Gray, cf. LRBL ii.96 (Lothian ed., 123), where Smith says that the best of Horace's Odes are inferior to Gray's. Cf. also a report in *The Bee*, iii (11 May 1791), 6, of views expressed by Smith in an interview given in 1780: 'At the same time, he mentioned Gray's odes, which Johnson has damned so completely, and in my humble opinion with so much justice, as the standard of lyric excellence.' Smith uses a line from 'The Progress of Poesy' ('Yet oft, before his infant eyes, would run') as an illustration in English and Italian Verses, 21, written after 1781 (and published in EPS).

[7] Robert Simson (1687–1768), Professor of Mathematics at the University of Glasgow, 1711–61. Matthew Stewart (1717–85), Professor of Mathematics at the University of Edinburgh, 1747–75. Matthew Stewart, the father of Dugald Stewart, was a fellow-student of Smith when both were pupils of Simson. Rae (*Life*, 11) reminds us that when Smith wrote that these two men were the greatest mathematicians to whom he had been known, he had also been for many years a friend of d'Alembert.

22   Mathematicians and natural philosophers, from their independency
upon the public opinion, have little temptation to form themselves into
factions and cabals, either for the support of their own reputation, or for the
depression of that of their rivals. They are almost always men of the most
amiable simplicity of manners, who live in good harmony with one another,
are the friends of one another's reputation, enter into no intrigue in order
to secure the public applause, but are pleased when their works are approved of, without being either much vexed or very angry when they are
neglected.

23   It is not always the same case with poets, or with those who value themselves upon what is called fine writing. They are very apt to divide themselves into a sort of literary factions; each cabal being often avowedly,
and almost always secretly, the mortal enemy of the reputation of every
other, and employing all the mean arts of intrigue and solicitation to pre-
occupy the public opinion in favour of the works of its own members,
and against those of its enemies and rivals. In France, Despreaux and
Racine did not think it below them to set themselves at the head of a literary
cabal, in order to depress the reputation, first of Quinault and Perreault,
and afterwards of Fontenelle and La Motte, and even to treat the good La
Fontaine with a species of most disrespectful kindness.[8] In England, the
amiable Mr. Addison did not think it unworthy of his gentle and modest
character to set himself at the head of a little cabal of the same kind, in
order to keep down the rising reputation of Mr. Pope.[9] Mr. Fontenelle,
in writing the lives and characters of the members of the academy of
sciences, a society of mathematicians and natural philosophers, has frequent opportunities of celebrating the amiable simplicity of their manners; a
quality which, he observes, was so universal among them as to be characteristical, rather of that whole class of men of letters, than of any individual[10] Mr. D'Alembert, in writing the lives and characters of the mem-

---

[8] Boileau (Nicolas Boileau-Despréaux) and Racine, who were close friends, espoused
the cause of the ancients in the 'Querelle des anciens et des modernes'. Philippe Quinault,
dramatist, was parodied by Boileau. Charles Perrault, Fontenelle, and Houdar de La
Motte were advocates of modernism in the 'Querelle'. Perrault's poem *Siècle de Louis le
Grand* was attacked by Boileau; Fontenelle's election to the Académie française was
blocked on four occasions by Racine, Boileau, and their friends; La Motte incautiously
showed his 'modern' adaptation of Homer's *Iliad* to Boileau, who made fun of it. La
Fontaine supported the ancients and was a fellow-member with Racine, Boileau, and
Molière of a famous literary circle; Smith is probably thinking of a report, in Louis
Racine's *Mémoires* of his father, that Molière once protested when the others were teasing
La Fontaine and that they all used to call him 'le bonhomme' because of his ingenuous-
ness: *Oeuvres de J. Racine*, ed. Mesnard (Paris, 1912), i.270.

[9] Pope quarrelled with Addison in 1715 for describing Thomas Tickell's verse translation of Homer as more accurate than Pope's. His resentment was shown in some verses,
written at this time but published later (and best known from the revised version in 'An
Epistle to Dr. Arbuthnot'), satirizing Addison and his 'little senate'. There is no justifica-
tion for Smith's view that Addison's literary circle was set up in order to decry Pope.

[10] Fontenelle was Secretary of the Académie des Sciences from 1699 to 1740 and wrote

bers of the French academy, a society of poets and fine writers, or of those who are supposed to be such, seems not to have had such frequent opportunities of making any remark of this kind, and nowhere pretends to represent this amiable quality as characteristical of that class [q]of[q] men of letters whom he celebrates.[11]

24 Our uncertainty concerning our own merit, and our anxiety to think favourably of it, should together naturally enough make us desirous to know the opinion of other people concerning it; to be more than ordinarily elevated when that opinion is favourable, and to be more than ordinarily mortified when it is otherwise: but they should not make us desirous either of obtaining the favourable, or of avoiding the unfavourable opinion, by intrigue and cabal. When a man has bribed all the judges, the most unanimous decision of the court, though it may gain him his law-suit, cannot give him any assurance that he was in the right: and had he carried on his law-suit merely to satisfy himself that he was in the right, he never would have bribed the judges. But though he wished to find himself in the right, he wished likewise to gain his law-suit; and therefore he bribed the judges. If praise were of no consequence to us, but as a proof of our own praise-worthiness, we never should endeavour to obtain it by unfair means. But, though to wise men it is, at least in doubtful cases, of principal consequence upon this account; it is likewise of some consequence upon its own account: and therefore (we cannot, indeed, upon such occasions, call them wise men, but) men very much above the common level have sometimes attempted both to obtain praise, and to avoid blame, by very unfair means.

25 Praise and blame express what actually are; praise-worthiness and blame-worthiness, what naturally ought to be the sentiments of other people with regard to our character and conduct. The love of praise is the desire of obtaining the favourable sentiments of our brethren. The love of praise-worthiness is the desire of rendering ourselves the proper objects of those sentiments. So far those two principles resemble and are akin to one another. The like affinity and resemblance take place between the dread of blame and that of blame-worthiness.

26 The man who desires to do, or who actually does, a praise-worthy action, may likewise desire the praise which is due to it, and sometimes, perhaps, more than is due to it. The two principles are in this case blended together. How far his conduct may have been influenced by the one, and how far by the other, may frequently be unknown even to himself. It must almost

q–q *om.* 6 7

finely styled *éloges* of its deceased members. The general observation quoted by Smith comes at the end of the *éloge* of Lemery.

[11] D'Alembert became Secretary of the Académie française in 1772 and wrote *éloges* of members who had died between 1700 and 1772.

always be so to other people. They who are disposed to lessen the merit of his conduct, impute it chiefly or altogether to the mere love of praise, or to what they call mere vanity. They who are disposed to think more favourably of it, impute it chiefly or altogether to the love of praise-worthiness; to the love of what is really honourable and noble in human conduct; to the desire, not merely of obtaining, but of deserving the approbation and applause of his brethren. The imagination of the spectator throws upon it either the one colour or the other, according either to his habits of thinking, or to the favour or dislike which he may bear to the person whose conduct he is considering.

27   Some splenetic philosophers, in judging of human nature, have done as peevish individuals are apt to do in judging of the conduct of one another, and have imputed to the love of praise, or to what they call vanity, every action which ought to be ascribed to that of praise-worthiness. I shall hereafter have occasion to give an account of some of their systems, and shall not at present stop to examine them.[12]

28   Very few men can be satisfied with their own private consciousness that they have attained those qualities, or performed those actions, which they admire and think praise-worthy in other people; unless it is, at the same time, generally acknowledged that they possess the one, or have performed the other; or, in other words, unless they have actually obtained that praise which they think due both to the one and to the other. In this respect, however, men differ considerably from one another. Some seem indifferent about the praise, when, in their own minds, they are perfectly satisfied that they have attained the praise-worthiness. Others appear much less anxious about the praise-worthiness than about the praise.

29   No man can be completely, or even tolerably satisfied, with having avoided every thing blame-worthy in his conduct; unless he has likewise avoided the blame or the reproach. A wise man may frequently neglect praise, even when he has best deserved it; but, in all matters of serious consequence, he will most carefully endeavour so to regulate his conduct as to avoid, not only blame-worthiness, but, as much as possible, every probable imputation of blame. He will never, indeed, avoid blame by doing any thing which he judges blame-worthy; by omitting any part of his duty, or by neglecting any opportunity of doing any thing which he judges to be really and greatly praise-worthy. But, with these modifications, he will most anxiously and carefully avoid it. To show much anxiety about praise, even for praise-worthy actions, is seldom a mark of great wisdom, but

[12] Smith has Mandeville mainly in mind. Cf. VII.ii.4, especially § 7. Smith writes here in the plural, no doubt recalling the plural title of VII.ii.4, which in eds. 1–5 classed La Rochefoucauld together with Mandeville. But when Smith wrote the present passage for ed. 6, he was already committed to deleting the references to La Rochefoucauld; and indeed § 7, on the doctrine that moral motives can be reduced to vanity, always had reference to Mandeville alone.

generally of some degree of weakness. But, in being anxious to avoid the shadow of blame or reproach, there may be no weakness, but frequently the most praise-worthy prudence.

30   'Many people,' says Cicero, 'despise glory, who are yet most severely mortified by unjust reproach; and that most inconsistently.'[13] This inconsistency, however, seems to be founded in the unalterable principles of human nature.

31   ʳThe all-wise Author of Nature has, in this manner, taught man to respect the sentiments and judgments of his brethren; to be more or less

ʳ §§ *31–2 were added in ed. 6, like the preceding and succeeding paragraphs of this chapter, but these two paragraphs revise the thought of the following passage, which was added in ed.* 2 *(and in the draft revision of 1759) after the paragraph that is now III.1.7 and the one that is printed as [3] in the variants at III.1.3ᵏ. Eds. 3–5 follow ed.* 2 *with minor variants, which we note below together with variants in the draft of 1759.*

The great judge [Great Judge *draft*] of the world, has, for the wisest reasons, thought proper to interpose, between the weak eye of human reason, [reason *draft*] and the throne of his eternal justice, a degree of obscurity and darkness, which though [darkness which, tho *draft* darkness, which, though 5] it does not intirely [entirely *draft*] cover that great tribunal from the view of mankind, yet renders the impression of it faint and feeble in comparison of what might be expected from the grandeur and importance of so mighty an object. If those infinite rewards and punishments [punishments, *draft*] which the Almighty has prepared for those who obey or transgress his will, were perceived as distinctly as we foresee the frivolous and temporary retaliations [relations 2 *corr.* 2E] which we may expect from one another, the weakness of human nature, astonished at the immensity of objects so little fitted to its comprehension, could no longer attend to the little affairs of this world; and it is absolutely impossible that the business of society could have been carried on, if, in this respect, there had been a fuller revelation of the intentions of providence [Providence *4 5*] than that which has already been made. That men, however, might never be without a rule to direct their conduct by, nor without a judge whose authority should enforce its observation, the author [Author *4 5*] of nature has made man the immediate judge of mankind, and has, in this respect, as in many others, created him after his own image, and appointed him his vicegerent upon earth to superintend the behaviour of his brethren. [bretheren. *draft*] They are taught by nature [Nature *draft*] to acknowledge that power and jurisdiction which has thus been conferred upon him, and to tremble and [or *draft*] exult according as they imagine that they have either merited his censure, [censure *draft*] or deserved his applause.

But whatever may be the authority of this inferiour tribunal [inferior tribunal, *draft*] which is continually before their eyes, if at any time it should decide contrary to those principles and rules, [these rules and principles *draft*] which nature [Nature *4 5*] has established for regulating its judgments, [judgements, *draft* 4] men feel that they may appeal [men appeal *draft*] from this unjust decision, and call upon a superiour [superior *draft*] tribunal, the tribunal established in their own breasts, [own minds, *draft*] to redress the injustice of this weak or partial judgment. [judgement. *draft*]

There are certain principles established by nature [Nature *4 5*] for governing our judgments [judgements *draft* judgment *3–5*] concerning the conduct of those we live with. As long as we decide according to those principles, and neither applaud nor condemn any thing which nature [Nature *4 5*] has not rendered the proper object of applause or condemnation, nor any further than she has rendered it such, as our sentence is, in this case, if I may say so, quite agreeable to law, it is liable neither to repeal nor to correction of any kind. The person [than she has rendered them such, the person, *draft*] concerning whom we form these judgments, [judgements *draft*] must himself necessarily approve of them. When he puts himself into our situation, he cannot avoid viewing his own conduct

[13] Cicero, *De Officiis*, I.xxi.71. Smith's translation is somewhat free.

[he cannot avoid entering into those views of his own conduct which, he feels, must naturally occur to us, and he is obliged to consider it himself *draft*] in the very same light in which we appear to view it. He is sensible, that to us, and to every impartial spectator, he must necessarily appear the natural and proper object of those sentiments which we express with regard to him. Those [same light in which we represent it. Our *draft*] sentiments, therefore, must necessarily produce their full effect upon him, and he cannot fail [faill *draft*] to conceive all the triumph of self-approbation [self approbation *draft*] from, what appears to him, [from what appears to him *draft 5*] such merited applause, as well as all the horrors of shame from, [from *draft 5*] what, he is sensible, is such deserved condemnation. [*Draft runs on.*]

But it is otherwise, [otherwise *draft*] if we have either applauded or condemned him, contrary to those principles and rules which nature [Nature *4 5*] has established for the direction of our judgments [judgements *draft*] concerning every thing of this kind. If we have either applauded or condemned him for what, when he puts himself into [in *draft*] our situation, does not appear to him to be the object either of applause or condemnation; as in this case [as, in this case, *draft*] he cannot enter into our sentiments, provided [if *draft*] he has any constancy or firmness, he is but little affected by them, and can neither be much elevated [be elevated *draft*] by the favourable, nor greatly mortified [favourable nor mortified *draft*] by the unfavourable decision. The applause of the whole world will avail but little, [little *draft*] if our own conscience condemn [condemns *draft*] us; and the disapprobation of all mankind is not capable of oppressing us, [us *draft*] when we are absolved by the tribunal within our own breast, and when our own mind tells us that mankind are in the wrong.

But though [tho *draft*] this tribunal within the breast be thus the supreme arbiter of all our actions, though [tho' *draft*] it can reverse the decisions of all mankind with regard to our character and conduct, and [conduct, tho it can *draft*] mortify us amidst the applause, or [applauses and *draft*] support us under the censure of the world; yet, [world, yet *draft*] if we enquire [inquire *4 5*] into the origin of its institution, its jurisdiction we shall find [jurisdiction, we shall find, *draft*] is in a great measure derived from the authority of that very tribunal, whose decisions it so often and so justly reverses. [*Draft runs on.*]

When we first come into the world, from the natural desire to please, we accustom ourselves [world, being desireous to please those we live with, we are accustomed *draft*] to consider what behaviour is likely to be agreeable [agreable *draft*] to every person we converse with, to our parents, to our masters, to our companions. We address ourselves to individuals, and for some time fondly pursue the impossible and absurd project of gaining [project of rendering ourselves universally agreable, and of gaining *draft*] the good-will [good will *draft*] and approbation of every body. We are soon taught by experience, however, [We soon learn, however, from experience *draft*] that this universal approbation is altogether unattainable. As soon as we come to have more important interests to manage, we find, that by pleasing one man, [man *draft*] we almost certainly disoblige another, and that by humouring an individual, we may often irritate a whole people. The fairest and most equitable conduct must frequently obstruct the interests, [interests *draft*] or thwart the inclinations of particular persons, who will seldom [seldome *draft*] have candour enough to enter into the propriety of our motives, or to see that this [that our *draft*] conduct, how disagreeable [disagreable *draft*] soever to them, is perfectly suitable to our situation. In order to defend ourselves from such partial judgments, we soon learn to set [situation. We soon learn, therefore, to sett *draft*] up in our own minds a judge between ourselves and those we live with. We conceive ourselves as acting in the presence of a person quite candid and equitable, of one who has no particular relation [relation, *draft*] either to ourselves, or to those whose interests are affected by our conduct, [conduct; *draft*] who is neither father, nor brother, nor friend [friend, *draft*] either to them [them, *draft*] or to us, [us; *draft*] but is merely [meerly *draft*] a man in general, an impartial spectator who considers our conduct with the same indifference with which we regard that of other people. If, [If *draft*] when we place ourselves in the situation of such a person, our own actions appear to us under an agreeable [agreable *draft*] aspect, if we feel that such a spectator cannot avoid entering into all the motives which influenced us, whatever may be the judgments [judgements *draft*] of the world, we must still be [we cannot help being *draft*] pleased when they approve of his conduct, and to be more or less hurt when they disapprove of it. He has made man, if I may say so, the immediate judge of mankind; and has, in this respect, as in many others, created him after his own image, and appointed him his vicegerent upon earth, to super-intend the behaviour of his brethren. They are taught by nature, to ack-nowledge that power and jurisdiction which has thus been conferred upon him, to be more or less humbled and mortified when they have incurred his censure, and to be more or less elated when they have obtained his applause.

32   But though man has, in this manner, been rendered the immediate judge of mankind, he has been rendered so only in the first instance; and an appeal lies from his sentence to a much higher tribunal, to the tribunal of their own consciences, to that of the supposed impartial and well-informed spec-tator, to that of the man within the breast, the great judge and arbiter of their conduct. The jurisdictions of those two tribunals are founded upon principles which, though in some respects resembling and akin, are, how-ever, in reality different and distinct. The jurisdiction of the man without,

pleased with our own behaviour, and regard [regarding *draft*] ourselves, in spite of the censure of our companions, as the just and proper objects of approbation. [*Draft runs on.*]

On the contrary, if the man within condemns us, the loudest acclamations of mankind appear but as the noise of ignorance and folly, and whenever we assume the character of this impartial judge, we cannot avoid viewing our own actions with his distaste and dis-satisfaction. The weak, the vain, [vain *draft*] and the frivolous, indeed, may be mortified by the most groundless censure, [censure *draft*] or elated by the most absurd applause. Such persons are not accustomed to consult the judge within concerning the opinion [oppinion *draft*] which they ought to form of their own conduct. This inmate of the breast, this abstract man, the representative of mankind, [mankind *draft*] and substitute of the Deity, whom nature [Nature *draft 4*] has constituted [has appointed *draft*] the supreme judge [supreme arbiter *draft*] of all their actions, [actions *draft*] is seldom [seldome *draft*] appealed to by them. They are contented with the decision of the inferiour [inferior *draft*] tribunal. The approbation of their companions, of the particular persons whom they have lived and conversed with, has generally been the ultimate object of all their wishes. If they obtain this, [If they succeed in this *draft*] their joy is compleat; [complete; *4 5*] and if they fail, [faill *draft*] they are entirely disappointed. They never think of appealing to the superior court. They have seldom [seldome *draft*] enquired [inquired *4 5*] after its decisions, [decisions *draft*] and are altogether unacquainted with the rules and forms of its procedure. When the world injures them, therefore, they are incapable of doing themselves justice, and are, in consequence, [justice and are in consequence *draft*] neces-sarily the slaves of the world. But it is otherwise with the man who has, upon all occasions, been accustomed to have recourse to the judge within, [within *draft 3*] and to consider, not what the world approves or disapproves of, but what appears to this impartial spec-tator, [spectator *draft*] the natural and proper object of approbation or [and *draft*] disapprobation. The judgment [judgement *draft*] of this supreme arbiter of his conduct, [conduct *draft*] is the applause, [applause *draft*] which he has been accustomed principally to court, is the censure which he has been accustomed principally to fear. Compared with this final decision, the sentiments of all mankind, though [tho' *draft*] not altogether indifferent, appear to be but of small moment; and he is incapable of being either much elevated by their favourable, or greatly depressed by their most disadvantageous [dis-advantageous, *5*] judgment. [judgement. *draft*]

The draft and eds. 2–5 then continue as in III.3.1: It is only by consulting this judge within, [within *draft*] . . .

is founded altogether in the desire of actual praise, and in the aversion to
actual blame. The jurisdiction of the man within, is founded altogether in
the desire of praise-worthiness, and in the aversion to blame-worthiness;
in the desire of possessing those qualities, and performing those actions,
which we love and admire in other people; and in the dread of possessing
those qualities, and performing those actions, which we hate and despise
in other people. If the man without should applaud us, either for actions
which we have not performed, or for motives which had no influence
upon us; the man within can immediately humble that pride and elevation of mind which such groundless acclamations might otherwise occasion,
by telling us, that as we know that we do not deserve them, we render ourselves despicable by accepting them. If, on the contrary, the man without
should reproach us, either for actions which we never performed, or for
motives which had no influence upon those which we may have performed;
the man within may immediately correct this false judgment, and assure
us, that we are by no means the proper objects of that censure which has so
unjustly been bestowed upon us. But in this and in some other cases, the
man within seems sometimes, as it were, astonished and confounded by the
vehemence and clamour of the man without. The violence and loudness,
with which blame is sometimes poured out upon us, seems to stupify and
benumb our natural sense of praise-worthiness and blame-worthiness;
and the judgments of the man within, though not, perhaps, absolutely
altered or perverted, are, however, so much shaken in the steadiness and
firmness of their decision, that their natural effect, in securing the tranquillity of the mind, is frequently in a great measure destroyed. We scarce
dare to absolve ourselves, when all our brethren appear loudly to condemn
us. The supposed impartial spectator of our conduct seems to give his
opinion in our favour with fear and hesitation; when that of all the real
spectators, when that of all those with whose eyes and from whose station
he endeavours to consider it, is unanimously and violently against us. In
such cases, this demigod within the breast appears, like the demigods of the
poets, though partly of immortal, yet partly too of mortal extraction.
When his judgments are steadily and firmly directed by the sense of praise-
worthiness and blame-worthiness, he seems to act suitably to his divine
extraction: But when he suffers himself to be astonished and confounded
by the judgments of ignorant and weak man, he discovers his connexion
with mortality, and appears to act suitably, rather to the human, than to the
divine, part of his origin.

33   In such cases, the only effectual consolation of humbled and afflicted
man lies in an appeal to a still higher tribunal, to that of the all-seeing Judge
of the world, whose eye can never be deceived, and whose judgments can
never be perverted. A firm confidence in the unerring rectitude of this
great tribunal, before which his innocence is in due time to be declared,

and his virtue to be finally rewarded, can alone support him under the weakness and despondency of his own mind, under the perturbation and astonishment of the man within the breast, whom nature has set up as, in this life, the great guardian, not only of his innocence, but of his tranquillity. Our happiness in this life is thus, upon many occasions, dependent upon the humble hope and expectation of a life to come: a hope and expectation deeply rooted in human nature; which can alone support its lofty ideas of its own dignity; can alone illumine the dreary prospect of its continually approaching mortality, and maintain its cheerfulness under all the heaviest calamities to which, from the disorders of this life, it may sometimes be exposed. That there is a world to come, where exact justice will be done to every man, where every man will be ranked with those who, in the moral and intellectual qualities, are really his equals; where the owner of those humble talents and virtues which, from being depressed by fortune, had, in this life, no opportunity of displaying themselves; which were unknown, not only to the public, but which he himself could scarce be sure that he possessed, and for which even the man within the breast could scarce venture to afford him any distinct and clear testimony; where that modest, silent, and unknown merit, will be placed upon a level, and sometimes above those who, in this world, had enjoyed the highest reputation, and who, from the advantage of their situation, had been enabled to perform the most splendid and dazzling actions; is a doctrine, in every respect so venerable, so comfortable to the weakness, so flattering to the grandeur of human nature, that the virtuous man who has the misfortune to doubt of it, cannot possibly avoid wishing most earnestly and anxiously to believe it. It could never have been exposed to the derision of the scoffer, had not the distributions of rewards and punishments, which some of its most zealous assertors have taught us was to be made in that world to come, been too frequently in direct opposition to all our moral sentiments.

34   That the assiduous courtier is often more favoured than the faithful and active servant; that attendance and adulation are often shorter and surer roads to preferment than merit or service; and that a campaign at Versailles or St. James's[14] is often worth two either in Germany or Flanders, is a complaint which we have all heard from many a venerable, but discontented, old officer. But what is considered as the greatest reproach even to the weakness of earthly sovereigns, has been ascribed, as an act of justice, to divine perfection; and the duties of devotion, the public and private worship of the Deity, have been represented, even by men of virtue and abilities, as the sole virtues which can either entitle to reward or exempt from punishment in the life to come. They were the virtues,

[14] St. James's Palace. Ambassadors to the United Kingdom are still said to be accredited to the Court of St. James.

perhaps, most suitable to their station, and in which they themselves chiefly excelled; and we are all naturally disposed to over-rate the excellencies of our own characters. In the discourse which the eloquent and philosophical Massillon[15] pronounced, on giving his benediction to the standards of the regiment of Catinat, there is the following address to the officers: 'What is most deplorable in your situation, Gentlemen, is, that in a life hard and painful, in which the services and the duties sometimes go beyond the rigour and severity of the most austere cloisters; you suffer always in vain for the life to come, and frequently even for this life. Alas! the solitary monk in his cell, obliged to mortify the flesh and to subject it to the spirit, is supported by the hope of an assured recompence, and by the secret unction of that grace which softens the yoke of the Lord. But you, on the bed of death, can you dare to represent to Him your fatigues and the daily hardships of your employment? can you dare to solicit Him for any re-compence? and in all the exertions that you have made, in all the violences that you have done to yourselves, what is there that He ought to place to His own account? The best days of your life, however, have been sacrificed to your profession, and ten years service has more worn out your body, than would, perhaps, have done a whole life of repentance and mortifica-tion. Alas! my brother, one single day of those sufferings, consecrated to the Lord, would, perhaps, have obtained you an eternal happiness. One single action, painful to nature, and offered up to Him, would, perhaps, have secured to you the inheritance of the Saints. And you have done all this, and in vain, for this world.'

[15] Jean Baptiste Massillon (1663–1742), Bishop of Clermont. The passage occurs in 'Discours prononcé à une bénédiction des drapeaux du régiment de Catinat', usually bound up with 'Le Petit Carême'; *Oeuvres complètes* (Paris 1821), i.273–4.

The English translation is probably Smith's own. It departs from the French in certain minor details: (1) 'in all the exertions that you have made' is an addition in the English version; (2) Massillon twice writes of 'le Seigneur' followed shortly by 'Jésus-Christ', and on both occasions Smith's English translation is 'the Lord . . . Him'; (3) where Smith's translation has 'a whole life of repentance and mortification', Massillon says simply 'une vie entière de pénitence' (though he does use the word 'mortifier' earlier of the monk, as in the English translation). The first of these changes does not seem significant; the second and third are.

As regards the third, Smith picks up his added word 'mortification' at the beginning of § 35, 'the futile mortifications of a monastery'. The whole of the present passage was added in ed. 6. Cf. a passage written earlier in WN V.i.e.29: 'But when moral, as well as natural philosophy, came to be taught only as subservient to theology, . . . heaven was to be earned only by penance and mortification, by the austerities and abasement of a monk; not by the liberal, generous, and spirited conduct of a man.' Both passages may recall Hume, *Enquiry concerning the Principles of Morals*, IX.i; ed. Selby-Bigge, § 219: 'penance, mortification, . . . and the whole train of monkish virtues . . . are . . . everywhere rejected by men of sense'.

The printing of this extract shows that the compositors followed their copy closely. An initial capital for 'He' and 'Him', referring to God, is unusual in printed texts of this period, and 'recompence' is at variance with the spelling of this word elsewhere in ed. 6. Smith probably had the translated extract by him from an earlier date and inserted it into his manuscript of the new material for ed. 6.

35   To compare, in this manner, the futile mortifications of a monastery, to the ennobling hardships and hazards of war; to suppose that one day, or one hour, employed in the former should, in the eye of the great Judge of the world, have more merit than a whole life spent honourably in the latter, is surely contrary to all our moral sentiments; to all the principles by which nature has taught us to regulate our contempt or admiration. It is this spirit, however, which, while it has reserved the celestial regions for monks and friars, or for those whose conduct and conversation resembled those of monks and friars, has condemned to the infernal all the heroes, all the statesmen and lawgivers, all the poets and philosophers of former ages; all those who have invented, improved, or excelled in the arts which contribute to the subsistence, to the conveniency, or to the ornament of human life; all the great protectors, instructors, and benefactors of mankind; all those to whom our natural sense of praise-worthiness forces us to ascribe the highest merit and most exalted virtue. Can we wonder that so strange an application of this most respectable doctrine should sometimes have exposed it to contempt and derision; with those at least who had themselves, perhaps, no great taste or turn for the devout and contemplative virtues*?

^aCHAP. III

Of the Influence and Authority of Conscience

1   BUT though the approbation of his own conscience can scarce, upon some extraordinary occasions, content the weakness of man; though the testimony of the supposed impartial ^bspectator,^b of the great inmate of the breast, cannot always alone support him; yet the influence and authority of this principle is, upon all occasions, very great; and ^cit is only by consulting this judge within, that we can ^dever see what^d relates to ourselves in its proper shape and dimensions; or that we can ^eever^e make any proper comparison between our own interests and those of other people.

2   As to the eye of the body, objects appear great or small, not so much

---

* See Voltaire.

> Vous y grillez sage et docte Platon,
> Divin Homere, eloquent Ciceron, etc.[16]

---

^a *This chapter is not in ed. 1. In eds. 2–6, the latter part of § 1 and §§ 2–5, 7–9, and 11, with some change, appear as additions to III.2. Some, but not all, of these additions are included also, with variation, in the draft revision of 1759. Most of § 4, the whole of §§ 5–9, and the first half of § 10 are not in the draft.*

^{b–b} ∼ ∧ 6 7 *Comma added by present editors; cf. VI. concl. 1, likewise written for ed. 6.*

^c *In the draft of 1759 and in eds. 2–5, the paragraph begins at this point, following the long passage that is printed in note* ^r *at III.2.31.*

^{d–d} see whatever *draft 2–5*   ^{e–e} om. *draft 2–5*

---

¹⁶ Voltaire, *La Pucelle d'Orléans*, chant 5; *Oeuvres complètes*, ed. Besterman and others (Genève, 1968–), 7.348.

according to their real dimensions, as according to the nearness or distance of their situation; so do they likewise to what may be called the natural eye of the mind: and we remedy the defects of both these organs pretty much in the same manner. In my present situation an immense landscape of lawns, and woods, and distant mountains, seems to do no more than cover the little window which I write by,[1] and to be out of all proportion less than the chamber in which I am sitting. I can form a just comparison between those great objects and the little objects around me, in no other way, than by transporting myself, at least in fancy, to a different station, from whence I can survey both at nearly equal distances, and thereby form some judgment of their real proportions. Habit and experience have taught me to do this so easily and so readily, that I am scarce sensible that I do it; and a man must be, in some measure, acquainted with the philosophy of vision,[2] before he can be thoroughly convinced, how little those distant objects would appear to the eye, if the imagination, from a knowledge of their real magnitudes, did not swell and dilate them.

3   [3]In the same manner, to the selfish and original passions of human nature, the loss or gain of a very small interest of our own, appears to be of vastly more importance, excites a much more passionate joy or sorrow, a much more ardent desire or aversion, than the greatest concern of another with whom we have no particular connexion. His interests, as long as they are surveyed from this station, can never be put into the balance with our own, can never restrain us from doing whatever may tend to promote our own, how ruinous soever to him. Before we can make any proper comparison of those opposite interests, we must change our position. We must view them, neither from our own place nor yet from his, neither with our own eyes nor yet with his, but from the place and with the eyes of a third person, who has no particular connexion with either, and who judges with impartiality between us.*f* Here, too, habit and experience have taught us *g*to

---

f This is the only station from which both can be seen at equal distances, or from which any proper comparison can be made between them. *adds draft*
    g–g to assume this station *draft*

[1] Cf. External Senses, 54: 'If you shut one eye, and hold immediately before the other a small circle of plain glass, of not more than half an inch in diameter, you may see through that circle the most extensive prospects; lawns and woods, and arms of the sea, and distant mountains. . . . If . . . you could conceive a fairy hand and a fairy pencil to come between your eye and the glass, that pencil could delineate upon that little glass the outline of all those extensive lawns and woods, and arms of the sea, and distant mountains, . . .'
    [2] Smith praises and follows Berkeley's *New Theory of Vision* when discussing the sense of seeing in his essay on the External Senses, § 54 of which is recalled here.
    [3] The comparison between the work of the imagination in visual perception and in moral judgement is derived from Hume, *Enquiry concerning the Principles of Morals*, V.ii; ed. Selby-Bigge, § 185. In §§ 3–4 Smith is recalling further features of Hume's ethical theory, and in parts of § 4 he is criticizing Hume's view that moral judgement is never an exercise of reason. Smith's general position here is nonetheless a development of Hume's; cf. especially *Treatise of Human Nature*, III.iii.1; ed. Selby-Bigge, 580–4.

do this*g* so easily and so readily, that we are scarce sensible that we *h*do*h* it; and it requires, in this case too, some degree of reflection, and even of philosophy, to convince us, how little interest we should take in the greatest concerns of our neighbour, how little we should be affected by whatever relates to him, if the sense of propriety and justice did not correct the otherwise natural inequality of our sentiments.

4 *j*Let us suppose that the great empire of China, with all its myriads of inhabitants, was suddenly swallowed up by an earthquake,[4] and let us consider how a man of humanity in Europe, who had no sort of connexion with that part of the world, would be affected upon receiving intelligence of this dreadful calamity. He would, I imagine, first of all, express very strongly his sorrow for the misfortune of that unhappy people, he would make many melancholy reflections upon the precariousness of human life, and the vanity of all the labours of man, which could thus be annihilated in a moment. He would too, perhaps, if he was a man of speculation, enter into many reasonings concerning the effects which this disaster might produce upon the commerce of Europe, and the trade and business of the world in general.[5] And when all this fine philosophy was over, when all these humane sentiments had been once fairly expressed, he would pursue his business or his pleasure, take his repose or his diversion, with the same ease and tranquillity, as if no such accident had happened. The most frivolous disaster which could befal himself would occasion a more real disturbance. If he was to lose his little finger to-morrow, he would not sleep to-night; but, provided he never saw them, he will snore with the most profound security over the ruin of a hundred millions of his brethren, and the destruction of that immense multitude seems plainly an object

---

h-h assume *draft (revision, in Smith's own hand, of* do)

j *Most of § 4, the whole of §§ 5–9, and the first half of § 10 are not in the draft of 1759, which instead reads here (running on from preceding sentence):*

It is from this station only that we can see the propriety of generosity and the deformity of injustice; the propriety of resigning the greatest interests of our own for the yet more important interests of others, and the deformity of doing the smallest injury to another in order to obtain the greatest benefite to ourselves. The real littleness of ourselves and of whatever relates to ourselves can be seen from this station only; and it is here only that we can learn the great lesson of Stoical magnanimity and firmness, to be no more affected by what befalls ourselves than by what befalls our neighbour, or, what comes to the same thing, than our neighbour is capable of being affected by what befalls us. 'When our neighbour, says Epictetus, . . .

The draft continues as in § 11. For the first sentence and the first half of the second sentence in the above passage cf. *k-k* *of the text of § 4, and for the remainder of the passage cf.* *x* *of § 11.*

---

[4] Perhaps suggested by the great Lisbon earthquake of 1755.

[5] It is significant that for Smith, writing this passage in 1760, 'a man of speculation' would be liable to reflect on the economic consequences, not the theological implications, of the disaster.

less interesting to him, than this paltry misfortune of his own.[6] To prevent, therefore, this paltry misfortune to himself, would a man of humanity be willing to sacrifice the lives of a hundred millions of his brethren, provided he had never seen them? Human nature startles with horror at the thought, and the world, in its greatest depravity and corruption, never produced such a villain as could be capable of entertaining it. But what makes this difference? When our passive feelings are almost always so sordid and so selfish, how comes it that our active principles should often be so generous and so noble? When we are always so much more deeply affected by whatever concerns ourselves, than by whatever concerns other men; what is it which prompts the generous, upon all occasions, and the mean upon many, to sacrifice their own interests to the greater interests of others? It is not the soft power of humanity, it is not that feeble spark of benevolence which Nature has lighted up in the human heart, that is thus capable of counteracting the strongest impulses of self-love.[7] It is a stronger power, a more forcible motive, which exerts itself upon such occasions. It is reason, principle, conscience, the inhabitant of the breast, the man within, the great judge and arbiter of our conduct. It is he who, whenever we are about to act so as to affect the happiness of others, calls to us, with a voice capable of astonishing the most presumptuous of our passions, that we are but one of the multitude, in no respect better than any other in it; and that when we prefer ourselves so shamefully and so blindly to others, we become the proper objects of resentment, abhorrence, and execration. *k*It is from him only that we learn the real littleness of ourselves, and of whatever relates to ourselves, and the natural misrepresentations of self-love can be corrected only by the eye of this impartial spectator. It is he who shows us the propriety of generosity and the deformity of injustice; the propriety of resigning the greatest interests of our own, for the yet greater interests of others, and the deformity of doing the smallest injury to another, in order to obtain the greatest benefit to ourselves.*k* It is not the love of our neighbour, it is not the love of mankind, which upon many occasions prompts us to the practice of those divine virtues. It is a stronger love, a more powerful affection, which generally takes place upon such occasions; the love of what is honourable and noble, of the grandeur, and dignity, and superiority of our own characters.

5   When the happiness or misery of others depends in any respect upon our

---

k-k See note ¹ above on the reading of the draft of 1759.

   [6] The example may possibly recall Hume, *Treatise*, II.iii.3; ed. Selby-Bigge, 416: ''Tis not contrary to reason to prefer the destruction of the whole world to the scratching of my finger.'

   [7] Hume (*Enquiry*, IX.i; ed. Selby-Bigge, §§ 221–3) contrasts the sentiments of self-love with those of 'humanity' and treats the latter as the foundation of disinterested moral judgement. Smith's further reference to 'benevolence' is probably intended to include Hutcheson with Hume in the object of his criticism.

conduct, we dare not, [l]as self-love might suggest to us, prefer the interest of one to that of many. The man within immediately calls to us, that we value ourselves too much and other people too little, and that, by doing so, we render ourselves the proper object of the contempt and indignation of our brethren.[l] [m]Neither is this sentiment confined to men of extraordinary magnanimity and virtue. It is deeply impressed upon every tolerably good soldier, who feels that he would become the scorn of his companions, if he could be supposed capable of shrinking from danger, or of hesitating, either to expose or to throw away his life, when the good of the service required it.

6   One individual must never prefer himself so much even to any other individual, as to hurt or injure that other, in order to benefit himself, though the benefit to the one should be much greater than the hurt or injury to the other. The poor man must neither defraud nor steal from the rich, though the acquisition might be much more beneficial to the one than the loss could be hurtful to the other. The man within immediately calls to him, in this case too, that he is no better than his neighbour, and that by this unjust preference he renders himself the proper object of the contempt and indignation of mankind; as well as of the punishment which that contempt and indignation must naturally dispose them to inflict, for having thus violated one of those sacred rules, upon the tolerable observation of which depend the whole security and peace of human society. There is no commonly honest man who does not more dread the inward disgrace of such an action, the indelible stain which it would for ever stamp upon his own mind, than the greatest external calamity which, without any fault of his own, could possibly befal him; and who does not inwardly feel the truth of that great stoical maxim, that for one man to deprive another unjustly of any thing, or unjustly to promote his own advantage by the loss or disadvantage of another, is more contrary to nature, than death, than poverty, than pain, than all the misfortunes which can affect him, either in his body, or in his external circumstances.

7   [n]When the happiness or misery of others, indeed,[n] in no respect depends upon our conduct, when our interests are altogether separated and detached from theirs, so that there is neither connexion nor competition between them, [o]we do not always think it so necessary to restrain, either our natural

---

[l-l] as self-love would suggest to us, prefer any little interest of our own, to the yet greater interest of our neighbour. We feel that we should become the proper objects of the resentment and indignation of our brethren, and the sense of the impropriety of this affection is supported and enlivened by the yet stronger sense of the demerit of the action, which it would in this case give occasion to. But when the happiness or misery of others in no respect depends . . . *2–5 See note* [n-n] *at § 7.*

[m] *The latter half of § 5 and the whole of § 6 were added in ed. 6.*

[n-n] . . . But when the happiness or misery of others *2–5 See note* [l-l] *at § 5.*

[o-o] as the sense of demerit does not in this case interpose, the meer [mere *4 5*] sense of impropriety is seldom able to restrain us from abandoning ourselves to our natural anxiety about our own affairs, and to our natural indifference about those of other men. *2–5*

and, perhaps, improper anxiety about our own affairs, or our natural and, perhaps, equally improper indifference about those of other men.[o] The most vulgar education teaches us to act, upon all important occasions, with some sort of impartiality between ourselves and others, and even the ordinary commerce of the world is capable of adjusting our active principles to some degree of propriety. But it is the most artificial and refined education [p]only, it has been said, which can correct[p] the inequalities of our passive feelings; and we must for this [q]purpose, it has been pretended, have[q] recourse to the severest, as well as to the profoundest philosophy.

8   Two different sets of philosophers have attempted to teach us this hardest of all the lessons of morality. One set have laboured to increase our sensibility to the interests of others; another, to diminish that to our own. The first would have us feel for others as we naturally feel for ourselves. The second would have us feel for ourselves as we naturally feel for others. [r]Both, perhaps, have carried their doctrines a good deal beyond the just standard of nature and propriety.[r]

9   The first are those [s]whining and[s] melancholy moralists, who are perpetually reproaching us with our happiness, while so many of our brethren are in [t]misery, *who[t] regard as impious the natural joy of prosperity, which does not think of the many wretches that are at every instant labouring under all sorts of calamities, in the languor of poverty, in the agony of disease, in the horrors of death, under the insults and oppression of their enemies. Commiseration for those miseries which we never saw, which we never heard of, but which we may be assured are at all times infesting such numbers of our fellow-creatures, ought, they think, to damp the pleasures of the fortunate, and to render a certain melancholy dejection habitual to

---

* See Thomson's Seasons, Winter:
                    'Ah! little think the gay licentious proud,' etc.
See also Pascal.[8]

[p-p] only, which pretends to correct *2–5*   [q-q] purpose have *2–5*
[r-r] *om. 2–5*   [s-s] *om. 2–5*
[t-t] *2–5* misery*, who *6 7*   *The note applies to* who, *not to* misery.

---

[8] James Thomson, *The Seasons*, Winter, 322–8:

> Ah! little think the gay licentious proud,
> Whom pleasure, power, and affluence surround—
> They, who their thoughtless hours in giddy mirth,
> And wanton, often cruel, riot waste—
> Ah! little think they, while they dance along,
> How many feel, this very moment, death
> And all the sad variety of pain;

In his reference to Pascal Smith is presumably thinking of the *Pensées*, in which one leading theme is the wretchedness (*la misère*) of the human condition and our readiness to be 'diverted' from it by so-called happiness. This does not, however, properly illustrate the text, as does the extract from Thomson's poem.

all men. But first of all, this extreme sympathy with misfortunes which we know nothing about, seems altogether absurd and unreasonable. Take the whole earth at an average, for one man who suffers pain or misery, you will find twenty in prosperity and joy, or at least in tolerable circumstances. No reason, surely, can be assigned why we should rather weep with the one than rejoice with the twenty. This artificial commiseration, besides, is not only absurd, but seems altogether unattainable; and those who affect this character have commonly nothing but a certain ᵘaffected and sentimentalᵘ sadness, which, without reaching the heart, serves only to render the countenance and conversation impertinently dismal and disagreeable. And last of all, this disposition of mind, though it could be attained, would be perfectly useless, and could serve no other purpose than to render miserable the person who possessed it. Whatever interest we take in the fortune of those with whom we have no acquaintance or connexion, and who are placed altogether out of the sphere of our activity, can produce only anxiety to ourselves, without any manner of advantage to them. To what purpose should we trouble ourselves about the world in the moon? All men, even those at the greatest distance, are no doubt entitled to our good wishes, and our good wishes we naturally give them. But if, notwithstanding, they should be unfortunate, to give ourselves any anxiety upon that account, seems to be no part of our duty. That we should be but little interested, therefore, in the fortune of those whom we can neither serve nor hurt, and who are in every respect so very remote from us, seems wisely ordered by Nature; and if it were possible to alter in this respect the original constitution of our frame, we could yet gain nothing by the change.

10   ᵛIt is never objected to us that we have too little fellow-feeling with the joy of success. Wherever envy does not prevent it, the favour which we bear to prosperity is rather apt to be too great; and the same moralists who blame us for want of sufficient sympathy with the miserable, reproach us for the levity with which we are too apt to admire and almost to worship the fortunate, the powerful, and the rich.

11   Among the moralists who endeavour to correct the natural inequality of our passive feelings by diminishing our sensibility to what peculiarly concerns ourselves, we may count all the ancient sects of philosophers, but particularly the ancient Stoics. Man, according to the Stoics, ought to regard himself, not as something separated and detached, but as a citizen of the world, a member of the vast commonwealth of nature. To the interest of this great community, he ought at all times to be willing that his own little interest should be sacrificed. Whatever concerns himself, ought to affect him no more than whatever concerns any other equally important part of this immense system. We should view ourselves, not in the light in which our own selfish passions are apt to place us, but in the light in

ᵘ⁻ᵘ hypocritical 2–5   ᵛ § *10 was added in ed. 6.*

which any other citizen of the world would view us. ^wWhat befalls ourselves
we should regard as what befalls our neighbour, or, what comes to the same
thing, as our neighbour regards what befalls us. 'When our neighbour,'
says Epictetus,⁹ 'loses his wife, or his son, there is nobody who is not
sensible that this is a human calamity, a natural event altogether according
to the ordinary course of things; but, when the same thing happens to
ourselves, then we cry out, as if we had suffered the most dreadful misfortune. We ought, however, to remember how we were affected when this
accident happened to another, and such as we were in his case, such ought
we to be in our own.'^x

12   ^yThose private misfortunes, for which our feelings are apt to go beyond
the bounds of propriety, are of two different kinds. They are either such as

^w *See note ¹ to § 4 on the reading of the draft of 1759.*
^x *At this point the draft of 1759 continues with a short paragraph:*

It is not upon all occasions, however, that we are capable of judging with this perfect
impartiality between ourselves and others. Even the judge within is often in danger of
being corrupted by the violence and injustice of our selfish passions, and is often induced
to make a report very different from what the real circumstances of the case are capable
of authorizing.

*Ed. 2 revises and expands the paragraph and precedes it with the addition of several sen-
tences to what is now the text of § 11. Eds. 3–5 follow ed. 2, with variants as noted.*

How difficult soever it may be to attain this supreme degree of magnanimity and firmness,
it is by no means either absurd or useless to attempt it. Though few men have the stoical
idea of what this perfect propriety requires, yet all men endeavour in some measure to
command themselves, and to bring down their selfish passions to something which their
neighbour can go along with. But this can never be done so effectually as by viewing whatever befals [befalls 4 5] themselves in the light in which their neighbours are apt to view
it. The stoical philosophy, in this respect, does little more than unfold our natural ideas
of perfection. There is nothing absurd or improper, therefore, in aiming at this perfect
self-command. Neither would the attainment of it be useless, but, on the contrary, the
most advantageous of all things, as establishing our happiness upon the most solid and
secure foundation, a firm confidence in that wisdom and justice which governs the world,
and an intire [entire 4 5] resignation of ourselves, and of whatever relates to ourselves
[ourselves, 5] to the all-wise disposal of this ruling principle in nature.

It scarce ever happens, however, that we are capable of adjusting our passive feelings to
this perfect propriety. We indulge ourselves, and even the world indulges us, in some
degree of irregularity in this respect. Though we should be too much affected by what
concerns ourselves, and too little by what concerns other men, yet, if we always act with
impartiality between ourselves and others, if we never actually sacrifice any great interest
of others, [others 5] to any little interest of our own, we are easily pardoned: and it were
well, if [if, 4 5] upon all occasions, those who desire to do their duty [duty, 5] were capable
of maintaining even this [this even 2   *corr.* 2E] degree of impartiality between themselves
and others. But this is very far from being the case. Even in good men, the judge within
us is often in danger of being corrupted by the violence and injustice of their selfish passions, and is often induced to make a report very different from what the real circumstances
of the case are capable of authorising. [authorizing. 4 5]

*The draft and eds. 2–5 next proceed to what is now III.4.2, reverting there to what was
contained in ed. 1. The last words of the above passage reappear at the end of III.4.1.*
^y *§§ 12–45 were added in ed. 6.*

⁹ *Encheiridion*, 26. As usual, Smith's translation is somewhat free.

affect us only indirectly, by affecting, in the first place, some other persons who are particularly dear to us; such as our parents, our children, our brothers and sisters, our intimate friends; or they are such as affect ourselves immediately and directly, either in our body, in our fortune, or in our reputation; such as pain, sickness, approaching death, poverty, disgrace, etc.[10]

13   In misfortunes of the first kind, our emotions may, no doubt, go very much beyond what exact propriety will admit of; but they may likewise fall short of it, and they frequently do so. The man who should feel no more for the death or distress of his own father, or son, than for those of any other man's father or son, would appear neither a good son nor a good father. Such unnatural indifference, far from exciting our applause, would incur our highest disapprobation. Of those domestic affections, however, some are most apt to offend by their excess, and others by their defect. Nature, for the wisest purposes, has rendered, in most men, perhaps in all men, parental tenderness a much stronger affection than filial piety. The continuance and propagation of the species depend altogether upon the former, and not upon the latter. In ordinary cases, the existence and preservation of the child depend altogether upon the care of the parents. Those of the parents seldom depend upon that of the child. Nature, therefore, has rendered the former affection so strong, that it generally requires not to be excited, but to be moderated; and moralists seldom endeavour to teach us how to indulge, but generally how to restrain our fondness, our excessive attachment, the unjust preference which we are disposed to give to our own children above those of other people. They exhort us, on the contrary, to an affectionate attention to our parents, and to make a proper return to them, in their old age, for the kindness which they had shown to us in our infancy and youth. In the Decalogue we are commanded to honour our fathers and mothers. No mention is made of the love of our children. Nature had sufficiently prepared us for the performance of this latter duty. Men are seldom accused of affecting to be fonder of their children than they really are. They have sometimes been suspected of displaying their piety to their parents with too much ostentation. The ostentatious sorrow of widows has, for a like reason, been suspected of insincerity. We should respect, could we believe it sincere, even the excess of such kind affections; and though we might not perfectly approve, we should not severely condemn it. That it appears praise-worthy, at least in the eyes of those who affect it, the very affectation is a proof.

14   Even the excess of those kind affections which are most apt to offend by

---

[10] Near the beginning of his lectures on jurisprudence Smith distinguishes injuries that a man may receive as an individual, as a member of a family, and as a citizen. He then specifies the first group as injuries to body, reputation, or estate. LJ(A) i.10, 12; LJ(B) 6 (Cannan ed., 5).

their excess, though it may appear blameable, never appears odious. We blame the excessive fondness and anxiety of a parent, as something which may, in the end, prove hurtful to the child, and which, in the mean time, is excessively inconvenient to the parent; but we easily pardon it, and never regard it with hatred and detestation. But the defect of this usually excessive affection appears always peculiarly odious. The man who appears to feel nothing for his own children, but who treats them upon all occasions with unmerited severity and harshness, seems of all brutes the most detestable. The sense of propriety, so far from requiring us to eradicate altogether that extraordinary sensibility, which we naturally feel for the misfortunes of our nearest connections, is always much more offended by the defect, than it ever is by the excess of that sensibility. The stoical apathy[11] is, in such cases, never agreeable, and all the metaphysical sophisms by which it is supported can seldom serve any other purpose than to blow up the hard insensibility of a coxcomb to ten times its native impertinence. The poets and romance writers, who best paint the refinements and delicacies of love and friendship, and of all other private and domestic affections, Racine and Voltaire; Richardson, Maurivaux, and Riccoboni;[12] are, in such cases, much better instructors than Zeno, Chrysippus, or Epictetus.[13]

15   That moderated sensibility to the misfortunes of others, which does not disqualify us for the performance of any duty; the melancholy and affectionate remembrance of our departed friends; *the pang*, as Gray says, *to secret sorrow dear;*[14] are by no means undelicious sensations. Though they outwardly wear the features of pain and grief, they are all inwardly stamped with the ennobling characters of virtue and self-approbation.

16   It is otherwise in the misfortunes which affect ourselves immediately and directly, either in our body, in our fortune, or in our reputation. The sense of propriety is much more apt to be offended by the excess, than by the defect of our sensibility, and there are but very few cases in which we can approach too near to the stoical apathy and indifference.

17   That we have very little fellow-feeling with any of the passions which take their origin from the body, has already been observed.[15] That pain which is occasioned by an evident cause; such as, the cutting or tearing of the flesh; is, perhaps, the affection of the body with which the spectator

[11] The Stoics made a virtue of 'apathy' (ἀπάθεια), the absence of feeling or passion, for the sake of mental tranquillity.

[12] Samuel Richardson (1689–1761), author of *Pamela* and *Clarissa*. Marivaux (1688–1763), French writer of comedies and novels, noted for his delicate analysis of feelings. Marie-Jeanne Riccoboni (1713–92), also a French author, wrote sentimental novels in the form of letters, like Richardson; Smith met her in Paris in 1766 (Rae, *Life*, 210–12).

[13] All Stoics. Zeno of Citium founded the Stoic school of philosophy; Chrysippus was its third head.

[14] 'Epitaph on Mrs. Clerke', but Gray wrote 'A pang, . . .'.

[15] I.ii.1

feels the most lively sympathy. The approaching death of his neighbour, too, seldom fails to affect him a good deal. In both cases, however, he feels so very little in comparison of what the person principally concerned feels, that the latter can scarce ever offend the former by appearing to suffer with too much ease.

18   The mere want of fortune, mere poverty, excites little compassion. Its complaints are too apt to be the objects rather of contempt than of fellow-feeling.[16] We despise a beggar; and, though his importunities may extort an alms from us, he is scarce ever the object of any serious commiseration. The fall from riches to poverty, as it commonly occasions the most real distress to the sufferer, so it seldom fails to excite the most sincere commiseration in the spectator. Though, in the present state of society, this misfortune can seldom happen without some misconduct, and some very considerable misconduct too, in the sufferer; yet he is almost always so much pitied that he is scarce ever allowed to fall into the lowest state of poverty; but by the means of his friends, frequently by the indulgence of those very creditors who have much reason to complain of his imprudence, is almost always supported in some degree of decent, though humble, mediocrity. To persons under such misfortunes, we could, perhaps, easily pardon some degree of weakness; but, at the same time, they who carry the firmest countenance, who accommodate themselves with the greatest ease to their new situation, who seem to feel no humiliation from the change, but to rest their rank in the society, not upon their fortune, but upon their character and conduct, are always the most approved of, and never fail to command our highest and most affectionate admiration.

19   As, of all the external misfortunes which can affect an innocent man immediately and directly, the undeserved loss of reputation is certainly the greatest; so a considerable degree of sensibility to whatever can bring on so great a calamity, does not always appear ungraceful or disagreeable. We often esteem a young man the more, when he resents, though with some degree of violence, any unjust reproach that may have been thrown upon his character or his honour. The affliction of an innocent young lady, on account of the groundless surmises which may have been circulated concerning her conduct, appears often perfectly amiable. Persons of an advanced age, whom long experience of the folly and injustice of the world, has taught to pay little regard, either to its censure or to its applause, neglect and despise obloquy, and do not even deign to honour its futile authors with any serious resentment. This indifference, which is founded altogether on a firm confidence in their own well-tried and well-established characters, would be disagreeable in young people, who neither can nor

---

[16] Cf. I.iii.3.1, likewise added in ed. 6. Cf. also Hume, *Treatise of Human Nature*, II.ii.5; ed. Selby-Bigge, 357: 'Nothing has a greater tendency to give us an esteem for any person, than his power and riches; or a contempt, than his poverty and meanness'.

ought to have any such confidence. It might in them be supposed to fore-
bode, in their advancing years, a most improper insensibility to real
honour and infamy.

20   In all other private misfortunes which affect ourselves immediately and
directly, we can very seldom offend by appearing to be too little affected.
We frequently remember our sensibility to the misfortunes of others with
pleasure and satisfaction. We can seldom remember that to our own,
without some degree of shame and humiliation.

21   If we examine the different shades and gradations of weakness and self-
command, as we meet with them in common life, we shall very easily
satisfy ourselves that this control of our passive feelings must be acquired,
not from the abstruse syllogisms of a quibbling dialectic, but from that
great discipline which Nature has established for the acquisition of this
and of every other virtue; a regard to the sentiments of the real or supposed
spectator of our conduct.

22   A very young child has no self-command; but, whatever are its emotions,
whether fear, or grief, or anger, it endeavours always, by the violence of its
outcries, to alarm, as much as it can, the attention of its nurse, or of its
parents. While it remains under the custody of such partial protectors,
its anger is the first and, perhaps, the only passion which it is taught to
moderate. By noise and threatening they are, for their own ease, often
obliged to frighten it into good temper; and the passion which incites it to
attack, is restrained by that which teaches it to attend to its own safety.
When it is old enough to go to school, or to mix with its equals, it soon
finds that they have no such indulgent partiality. It naturally wishes to gain
their favour, and to avoid their hatred or contempt. Regard even to its own
safety teaches it to do so; and it soon finds that it can do so in no other
way than by moderating, not only its anger, but all its other passions, to the
degree which its play-fellows and companions are likely to be pleased with.
It thus enters into the great school of self-command, it studies to be more
and more master of itself, and begins to exercise over its own feelings a discipline which the practice of the longest life is very seldom sufficient to
bring to complete perfection.

23   In all private misfortunes, in pain, in sickness, in sorrow, the weakest
man, when his friend, and still more when a stranger visits him, is immediately impressed with the view in which they are likely to look upon his
situation. Their view calls off his attention from his own view; and his breast
is, in some measure, becalmed the moment they come into his presence.
This effect is produced instantaneously and, as it were, mechanically;
but, with a weak man, it is not of long continuance. His own view of his
situation immediately recurs upon him. He abandons himself, as before,
to sighs and tears and lamentations; and endeavours, like a child that has
not yet gone to school, to produce some sort of harmony between his own

grief and the compassion of the spectator, not by moderating the former, but by importunately calling upon the latter.

24   With a man of a little more firmness, the effect is somewhat more permanent. He endeavours, as much as he can, to fix his attention upon the view which the company are likely to take of his situation. He feels, at the same time, the esteem and approbation which they naturally conceive for him when he thus preserves his tranquillity; and, though under the pressure of some recent and great calamity, appears to feel for himself no more than what they really feel for him. He approves and applauds himself by sympathy with their approbation, and the pleasure which he derives from this sentiment supports and enables him more easily to continue this generous effort. In most cases he avoids mentioning his own misfortune; and his company, if they are tolerably well bred, are careful to say nothing which can put him in mind of it. He endeavours to entertain them, in his usual way, upon indifferent subjects, or, if he feels himself strong enough to venture to mention his misfortune, he endeavours to talk of it as, he thinks, they are capable of talking of it, and even to feel it no further than they are capable of feeling it. If he has not, however, been well inured to the hard discipline of self-command, he soon grows weary of this restraint. A long visit fatigues him; and, towards the end of it, he is constantly in danger of doing, what he never fails to do the moment it is over, of abandoning himself to all the weakness of excessive sorrow. Modern good manners, which are extremely indulgent to human weakness, forbid, for some time, the visits of strangers to persons under great family distress, and permit those only of the nearest relations and most intimate friends. The presence of the latter, it is thought, will impose less restraint than that of the former; and the sufferers can more easily accommodate themselves to the feelings of those, from whom they have reason to expect a more indulgent sympathy. Secret enemies, who fancy that they are not known to be such, are frequently fond of making those charitable visits as early as the most intimate friends. The weakest man in the world, in this case, endeavours to support his manly countenance, and, from indignation and contempt of their malice, to behave with as much gaiety and ease as he can.

25   The man of real constancy and firmness, the wise and just man who has been thoroughly bred in the great school of self-command, in the bustle and business of the world, exposed, perhaps, to the violence and injustice of faction, and to the hardships and hazards of war, maintains this control of his passive feelings upon all occasions; and whether in solitude or in society, wears nearly the same countenance, and is affected very nearly in the same manner. In success and in disappointment, in prosperity and in adversity, before friends and before enemies, he has often been under the necessity of supporting this manhood. He has never dared to forget for one moment the judgment which the impartial spectator would pass upon his

sentiments and conduct. He has never dared to suffer the man within the breast to be absent one moment from his attention. With the eyes of this great inmate he has always been accustomed to regard whatever relates to himself. This habit has become perfectly familiar to him. He has been in the constant practice, and, indeed, under the constant necessity, of modelling, or of endeavouring to model, not only his outward conduct and behaviour, but, as much as he can, even his inward sentiments and feelings, according to those of this awful and respectable judge. He does not merely affect the sentiments of the impartial spectator. He really adopts them. He almost identifies himself with, he almost becomes himself that impartial spectator, and scarce even feels but as that great arbiter of his conduct directs him to feel.

26   The degree of the self-approbation with which every man, upon such occasions, surveys his own conduct, is higher or lower, exactly in proportion to the degree of self-command which is necessary in order to obtain that self-approbation. Where little self-command is necessary, little self-approbation is due. The man who has only scratched his finger, cannot much applaud himself, though he should immediately appear to have forgot this paltry misfortune. The man who has lost his leg by a cannon shot, and who, the moment after, speaks and acts with his usual coolness and tranquillity, as he exerts a much higher degree of self-command, so he naturally feels a much higher degree of self-approbation. With most men, upon such an accident, their own natural view of their own misfortune would force itself upon them with such a vivacity and strength of colouring, as would entirely efface all thought of every other view. They would feel nothing, they could attend to nothing, but their own pain and their own fear; and not only the judgment of the ideal man within the breast, but that of the real spectators who might happen to be present, would be entirely overlooked and disregarded.

27   The reward which Nature bestows upon good behaviour under misfortune, is thus exactly proportioned to the degree of that good behaviour. The only compensation she could possibly make for the bitterness of pain and distress is thus too, in equal degrees of good behaviour, exactly proportioned to the degree of that pain and distress. In proportion to the degree of the self-command which is necessary in order to conquer our natural sensibility, the pleasure and pride of the conquest are so much the greater; and this pleasure and pride are so great that no man can be altogether unhappy who completely enjoys them. Misery and wretchedness can never enter the breast in which dwells complete self-satisfaction; and though it may be too much, perhaps, to say, with the Stoics, that, under such an accident as that above mentioned, the happiness of a wise man is in every respect equal to what it could have been under any other circumstances; yet it must be acknowledged, at least, that this

complete enjoyment of his own self-applause, though it may not altogether extinguish, must certainly very much alleviate his sense of his own sufferings.

28   In such paroxysms of distress, if I may be allowed to call them so, the wisest and firmest man, in order to preserve his equanimity, is obliged, I imagine, to make a considerable, and even a painful exertion. His own natural feeling of his own distress, his own natural view of his own situation, presses hard upon him, and he cannot, without a very great effort, fix his attention upon that of the impartial spectator. Both views present themselves to him at the same time. His sense of honour, his regard to his own dignity, directs him to fix his whole attention upon the one view. His natural, his untaught and undisciplined feelings, are continually calling it off to the other. He does not, in this case, perfectly identify himself with the ideal man within the breast, he does not become himself the impartial spectator of his own conduct. The different views of both characters exist in his mind separate and distinct from one another, and each directing him to a behaviour different from that to which the other directs him. When he follows that view which honour and dignity point out to him, Nature does not, indeed, leave him without a recompense. He enjoys his own complete self-approbation, and the applause of every candid and impartial spectator. By her unalterable laws, however, he still suffers; and the recompense which she bestows, though very considerable, is not sufficient completely to compensate the sufferings which those laws inflict. Neither is it fit that it should. If it did completely compensate them, he could, from self-interest, have no motive for avoiding an accident which must necessarily diminish his utility both to himself and to society; and Nature, from her parental care of both, meant that he should anxiously avoid all such accidents. He suffers, therefore, and though, in the agony of the paroxysm, he maintains, not only the manhood of his countenance, but the sedateness and sobriety of his judgment, it requires his utmost and most fatiguing exertions, to do so.

29   By the constitution of human nature, however, agony can never be permanent; and, if he survives the paroxysm, he soon comes, without any effort, to enjoy his ordinary tranquillity. A man with a wooden leg suffers, no doubt, and foresees that he must continue to suffer during the remainder of his life, a very considerable inconveniency. He soon comes to view it, however, exactly as every impartial spectator views it; as an inconveniency under which he can enjoy all the ordinary pleasures both of solitude and of society. He soon identifies himself with the ideal man within the breast, he soon becomes himself the impartial spectator of his own situation. He no longer weeps, he no longer laments, he no longer grieves over it, as a weak man may sometimes do in the beginning. The view of the impartial spectator becomes so perfectly habitual to him, that, without any effort,

without any exertion, he never thinks of surveying his misfortune in any other view.

30   The never-failing certainty with which all men, sooner or later, accommodate themselves to whatever becomes their permanent situation, may, perhaps, induce us to think that the Stoics were, at least, thus far very nearly in the right; that, between one permanent situation and another, there was, with regard to real happiness, no essential difference: or that, if there were any difference, it was no more than just sufficient to render some of them the objects of simple choice or preference; but not of any earnest or anxious desire: and others, of simple rejection, as being fit to be set aside or avoided; but not of any earnest or anxious aversion. Happiness consists in tranquillity and enjoyment. Without tranquillity there can be no enjoyment; and where there is perfect tranquillity there is scarce any thing which is not capable of amusing. But in every permanent situation, where there is no expectation of change, the mind of every man, in a longer or shorter time, returns to its natural and usual state of tranquillity. In prosperity, after a certain time, it falls back to that state; in adversity, after a certain time, it rises up to it. In the confinement and solitude of the Bastile, after a certain time, the fashionable and frivolous Count de Lauzun recovered tranquillity enough to be capable of amusing himself with feeding a spider.[17] A mind better furnished would, perhaps, have both sooner recovered its tranquillity, and sooner found, in its own thoughts, a much better amusement.

31   The great source of both the misery and disorders of human life, seems to arise from over-rating the difference between one permanent situation and another. Avarice over-rates the difference between poverty and riches: ambition, that between a private and a public station: vain-glory, that between obscurity and extensive reputation. The person under the influence of any of those extravagant passions, is not only miserable in his actual situation, but is often disposed to disturb the peace of society, in order to arrive at that which he so foolishly admires. The slightest observation, however, might satisfy him, that, in all the ordinary situations of human life, a well-disposed mind may be equally calm, equally cheerful, and equally contented. Some of those situations may, no doubt, deserve to be preferred to others: but none of them can deserve to be pursued with that passionate ardour which drives us to violate the rules either of prudence or of justice; or to corrupt the future tranquillity of our minds, either by shame from the remembrance of our own folly, or by remorse from the horror of our own injustice. Wherever prudence does not direct, wherever

---

[17] Antonin Nompar de Caumont, Comte (later Duc) de Lauzun, 1633–1723, was imprisoned in the Bastille for six months in 1665 for insolence to Louis XIV. He was afterwards imprisoned for ten years, 1671–81, but in the fortress of Pignerol, not the Bastille. We cannot trace the source of Smith's anecdote.

justice does not permit, the attempt to change our situation, the man who does attempt it, plays at the most unequal of all games of hazard, and stakes every thing against scarce any thing. What the favourite of the king of Epirus said to his master, may be applied to men in all the ordinary situations of human life. When the King had recounted to him, in their proper order, all the conquests which he proposed to make, and had come to the last of them; And what does your Majesty propose to do then? said the Favourite.—I propose then, said the King, to enjoy myself with my friends, and endeavour to be good company over a bottle.—And what hinders your Majesty from doing so now? replied the Favourite.[18] In the most glittering and exalted situation that our idle fancy can hold out to us, the pleasures from which we propose to derive our real happiness, are almost always the same with those which, in our actual, though humble station, we have at all times at hand, and in our power. Except the frivolous pleasures of vanity and superiority, we may find, in the most humble station, where there is only personal liberty, every other which the most exalted can afford; and the pleasures of vanity and superiority are seldom consistent with perfect ²tranquillity,² the principle and foundation of all real and satisfactory enjoyment. Neither is it always certain that, in the splendid situation which we aim at, those real and satisfactory pleasures can be enjoyed with the same security as in the humble one which we are so very eager to abandon. Examine the records of history, recollect what has happened within the circle of your own experience, consider with attention what has been the conduct of almost all the greatly unfortunate, either in private or public life, whom you may have either read of, or heard of, or remember; and you will find that the misfortunes of by far the greater part of them have arisen from their not knowing when they were well, when it was proper for them to sit still and to be contented. The inscription upon the tomb-stone of the man who had endeavoured to mend a tolerable constitution by taking physic; '*I was well, I wished to be better; here I am;*'[19] may generally be applied with great justness to the distress of disappointed avarice and ambition.

32   It may be thought a singular, but I believe it to be a just observation, that, in the misfortunes which admit of some remedy, the greater part of men do not either so readily or so universally recover their natural and usual tranquillity, as in those which plainly admit of none. In misfortunes of the

²⁻² 7   ~ ∧ 6

---

[18] Plutarch, *Lives*, Pyrrhus, 14. The king was Pyrrhus, the favourite Cineas.

[19] Cf. Dryden, 'The Dedication of the Aeneis' (1697): 'Like him, who being in good Health, lodg'd himself in a Physician's House, and was over-perswaded by his Landlord to take Physick, of which he dyed, for the benefit of his Doctor. *Stavo ben* (was written on his Monument) *ma, per star meglio, sto qui.*' *Poems of John Dryden*, ed. Kinsley (Oxford, 1958), iii.1013. The Italian epitaph is quoted also in *The Spectator*, 25 (29 March 1711), where it is simply attributed to a valetudinarian.

latter kind, it is chiefly in what may be called the paroxysm, or in the first attack, that we can discover any sensible difference between the sentiments and behaviour of the wise and those of the weak man. In the end, Time, the great and universal comforter, gradually composes the weak man to the same degree of tranquillity which a regard to his own dignity and manhood teaches the wise man to assume in the beginning. The case of the man with the wooden leg is an obvious example of this. In the irreparable misfortunes occasioned by the death of children, or of friends and relations, even a wise man may for some time indulge himself in some degree of moderated sorrow. An affectionate, but weak woman, is often, upon such occasions, almost perfectly distracted. Time, however, in a longer or shorter period, never fails to compose the weakest woman to the same degree of tranquillity as the strongest man. In all the irreparable calamities which affect himself immediately and directly, a wise man endeavours, from the beginning, to anticipate and to enjoy before-hand, that tranquillity which he foresees the course of a few months, or a few years, will certainly restore to him in the end.

33   In the misfortunes for which the nature of things admits, or seems to admit, of a remedy, but in which the means of applying that remedy are not within the reach of the sufferer, his vain and fruitless attempts to restore himself to his former situation, his continual anxiety for their success, his repeated disappointments upon their miscarriage, are what chiefly hinder him from resuming his natural tranquillity, and frequently render miserable, during the whole of his life, a man to whom a greater misfortune, but which plainly admitted of no remedy, would not have given a fortnight's disturbance. In the fall from royal favour to disgrace, from power to insignificancy, from riches to poverty, from liberty to confinement, from strong health to some lingering, chronical, and perhaps incurable disease, the man who struggles the least, who most easily and readily acquiesces in the fortune which has fallen to him, very soon recovers his usual and natural tranquillity, and surveys the most disagreeable circumstances of his actual situation in the same light, or, perhaps, in a much less unfavourable light, than that in which the most indifferent spectator is disposed to survey them. Faction, intrigue, and cabal, disturb the quiet of the unfortunate statesman. Extravagant projects, visions of gold mines, interrupt the repose of the ruined bankrupt. The prisoner, who is continually plotting to escape from his confinement, cannot enjoy that careless security which even a prison can afford him. The medicines of the physician are often the greatest torment of the incurable patient. The monk who, in order to comfort Joanna of Castile, upon the death of her husband Philip, told her of a King, who, fourteen years after his decease, had been restored to life again, by the prayers of his afflicted queen, was not likely, by his legendary tale, to restore sedateness to the distempered mind of that unhappy Princess.

She endeavoured to repeat the same experiment in hopes of the same success; resisted for a long time the burial of her husband, soon after raised his body from the grave, attended it almost constantly herself, and watched, with all the impatient anxiety of frantic expectation, the happy moment when her wishes were to be gratified by the revival of her beloved Philip*.

34   Our sensibility to the feelings of others, so far from being inconsistent with the manhood of self-command, is the very principle upon which that manhood is founded. The very same principle or instinct which, in the misfortune of our neighbour, prompts us to compassionate his sorrow; in our own misfortune, prompts us to restrain the abject and miserable lamentations of our own sorrow. The same principle or instinct which, in his prosperity and success, prompts us to congratulate his joy; in our own prosperity and success, prompts us to restrain the levity and intemperance of our own joy. In both cases, the propriety of our own sentiments and feelings seems to be exactly in proportion to the vivacity and force with which we enter into and conceive his sentiments and feelings.

35   The man of the most perfect virtue, the man whom we naturally love and revere the most, is he who joins, to the most perfect command of his own original and selfish feelings, the most exquisite sensibility both to the original and sympathetic feelings of others. The man who, to all the soft, the amiable, and the gentle virtues, joins all the great, the awful, and the respectable, must surely be the natural and proper object of our highest love and admiration.[20]

36   The person best fitted by nature for acquiring the former of those two sets of virtues, is likewise best fitted for acquiring the latter. The man who feels the most for the joys and sorrows of others, is best fitted for acquiring the most complete control of his own joys and sorrows. The man of the most exquisite humanity, is naturally the most capable of acquiring the highest degree of self-command. He may not, however, always have acquired it; and it very frequently happens that he has not. He may have lived too much in ease and tranquillity. He may have never been exposed to the violence of faction, or to the hardships and hazards of war. He may have never experienced the insolence of his superiors, the jealous and malignant envy of his equals, or the pilfering injustice of his inferiors. When, in an advanced age, some accidental change of fortune exposes him to all these, they all make too great an impression upon him. He has the disposition which fits him for acquiring the most perfect self-command; but he has never had the opportunity of acquiring it. Exercise and practice have been wanting; and without these no habit can ever be tolerably established.

* See Robertson's Charles V. vol. ii. pp. 14 and 15. first edition. [William Robertson, *History of the Reign of the Emperor Charles V*. The passage comes early in Book I.]

[20] Cf. I.i.5, especially §§ 1 and 5.

Hardships, dangers, injuries, misfortunes, are the only masters under whom we can learn the exercise of this virtue. But these are all masters to whom nobody willingly puts himself to school.

37   The situations in which the gentle virtue of humanity can be most happily cultivated, are by no means the same with those which are best fitted for forming the austere virtue of self-command. The man who is himself at ease can best attend to the distress of others. The man who is himself exposed to hardships is most immediately called upon to attend to, and to control his own feelings. In the mild sunshine of undisturbed tranquillity, in the calm retirement of undissipated and philosophical leisure, the soft virtue of humanity flourishes the most, and is capable of the highest improvement. But, in such situations, the greatest and noblest exertions of self-command have little exercise. Under the boisterous and stormy sky of war and faction, of public tumult and confusion, the sturdy severity of self-command prospers the most, and can be the most successfully cultivated. But, in such situations, the strongest suggestions of humanity must frequently be stifled or neglected; and every such neglect necessarily tends to weaken the principle of humanity. As it may frequently be the duty of a soldier not to take, so it may sometimes be his duty not to give quarter; and the humanity of the man who has been several times under the necessity of submitting to this disagreeable duty, can scarce fail to suffer a considerable diminution. For his own ease, he is too apt to learn to make light of the misfortunes which he is so often under the necessity of occasioning; and the situations which call forth the noblest exertions of self-command, by imposing the necessity of violating sometimes the property, and sometimes the life of our neighbour, always tend to diminish, and too often to extinguish altogether, that sacred regard to both, which is the foundation of justice and humanity. It is upon this account, that we so frequently find in the world men of great humanity who have little self-command, but who are indolent and irresolute, and easily disheartened, either by difficulty or danger, from the most honourable pursuits; and, on the contrary, men of the most perfect self-command, whom no difficulty can discourage, no danger appal, and who are at all times ready for the most daring and desperate enterprises, but who, at the same time, seem to be hardened against all sense either of justice or humanity.

38   In solitude, we are apt to feel too strongly whatever relates to ourselves: we are apt to over-rate the good offices we may have done, and the injuries we may have suffered: we are apt to be too much elated by our own good, and too much dejected by our own bad fortune. The conversation of a friend brings us to a better, that of a stranger to a still better temper. The man within the breast, the abstract and ideal spectator of our sentiments and conduct, requires often to be awakened and put in mind of his duty, by the presence of the real spectator: and it is always from that spec-

tator, from whom we can expect the least sympathy and indulgence, that we are likely to learn the most complete lesson of self-command.

39   Are you in adversity? Do not mourn in the darkness of solitude, do not regulate your sorrow according to the indulgent sympathy of your intimate friends; return, as soon as possible, to the day-light of the world and of society. Live with strangers, with those who know nothing, or care nothing about your misfortune; do not even shun the company of enemies; but give yourself the pleasure of mortifying their malignant joy, by making them feel how little you are affected by your calamity, and how much you are above it.

40   Are you in prosperity? Do not confine the enjoyment of your good fortune to your own house, to the company of your own friends, perhaps of your flatterers, of those who build upon your fortune the hopes of mending their own; frequent those who are independent of you, who can value you only for your character and conduct, and not for your fortune. Neither seek nor shun, neither intrude yourself into nor run away from the society of those who were once your superiors, and who may be hurt at finding you their equal, or, perhaps, even their superior. The impertinence of their pride may, perhaps, render their company too disagreeable: but if it should not, be assured that it is the best company you can possibly keep; and if, by the simplicity of your unassuming demeanour, you can gain their favour and kindness, you may rest satisfied that you are modest enough, and that your head has been in no respect turned by your good fortune.

41   The propriety of our moral sentiments is never so apt to be corrupted, as when the indulgent and partial spectator is at hand, while the indifferent and impartial one is at a great distance.

42   Of the conduct of one independent nation towards another, neutral nations are the only indifferent and impartial spectators. But they are placed at so great a distance that they are almost quite out of sight. When two nations are at variance, the citizen of each pays little regard to the sentiments which foreign nations may entertain concerning his conduct. His whole ambition is to obtain the approbation of his own fellow-citizens; and as they are all animated by the same hostile passions which animate himself, he can never please them so much as by enraging and offending their enemies. The partial spectator is at hand: the impartial one at a great distance. In war and negotiation, therefore, the laws of justice are very seldom observed. Truth and fair dealing are almost totally disregarded. Treaties are violated; and the violation, if some advantage is gained by it, sheds scarce any dishonour upon the violator. The ambassador who dupes the minister of a foreign nation, is admired and applauded. The just man who disdains either to take or to give any advantage, but who would think it less dishonourable to give than to take one; the man who, in all private transactions, would be the most beloved and the most esteemed; in those

public transactions is regarded as a fool and an idiot, who does not understand his business; and he incurs always the contempt, and sometimes even
the detestation of his fellow-citizens. In war, not only what are called the
laws of nations, are frequently violated, without bringing (among his own
fellow-citizens, whose judgments he only regards) any considerable dishonour upon the violator; but those laws themselves are, the greater part
of them, laid down with very little regard to the plainest and most obvious
rules of justice. That the innocent, though they may have some connexion
or dependency upon the guilty (which, perhaps, they themselves cannot
help), should not, upon that account, suffer or be punished for the guilty,
is one of the plainest and most obvious rules of justice. In the most unjust
war, however, it is commonly the sovereign or the rulers only who are
guilty. The subjects are almost always perfectly innocent. Whenever it
suits the conveniency of a public enemy, however, the goods of the peaceable citizens are seized both at land and at sea; their lands are laid waste,
their houses are burnt, and they themselves, if they presume to make any
resistance, are murdered or led into captivity; and all this in the most perfect conformity to what are called the laws of nations.

43   The animosity of hostile factions, whether civil or ecclesiastical, is often
still more furious than that of hostile nations; and their conduct towards
one another is often still more atrocious. What may be called the laws of
faction have often been laid down by grave authors with still less regard
to the rules of justice than what are called the laws of nations. The most
ferocious patriot never stated it as a serious question, Whether faith
ought to be kept with public enemies?—Whether faith ought to be kept
with rebels? Whether faith ought to be kept with heretics? are questions
which have been often furiously agitated by celebrated doctors both civil
and ecclesiastical. It is needless to observe, I presume, that both rebels
and heretics are those unlucky persons, who, when things have come to a
certain degree of violence, have the misfortune to be of the weaker party.
In a nation distracted by faction, there are, no doubt, always a few, though
commonly but a very few, who preserve their *aa*judgment*aa* untainted by the
general contagion. They seldom amount to more than, here and there,
a solitary individual, without any influence, excluded, by his own candour,
from the confidence of either party, and who, though he may be one of
the wisest, is necessarily, upon that very account, one of the most insignificant men in the society. All such people are held in contempt and derision,
frequently in detestation, by the furious zealots of both parties. A true
party-man hates and despises candour; and, in reality, there is no vice
which could so effectually disqualify him for the trade of a party-man as
that single virtue. The real, revered, and impartial spectator, therefore, is,

---

aa-aa judgement 6 7 *Probably an inadvertent slip by the printer. Cf. III.4.4 and 11.
Elsewhere the spelling* judgment *is always used.*

upon no occasion, at a greater distance than amidst the violence and rage of contending parties. To them, it may be said, that such a spectator scarce exists any where in the universe. Even to the great Judge of the universe, they impute all their own prejudices, and often view that Divine Being as animated by all their own vindictive and implacable passions. Of all the corrupters of moral sentiments, therefore, faction and fanaticism have always been by far the greatest.

44   Concerning the subject of self-command, I shall only observe further, that our admiration for the man who, under the heaviest and most unexpected misfortunes, continues to behave with fortitude and firmness, always supposes that his sensibility to those misfortunes is very great, and such as it requires a very great effort to conquer or command. The man who was altogether insensible to bodily pain, could deserve no applause from enduring the torture with the most perfect patience and equanimity. The man who had been created without the natural fear of death, could claim no merit from preserving his coolness and presence of mind in the midst of the most dreadful dangers. It is one of the extravagancies of Seneca,[21] that the Stoical wise man was, in this respect, superior even to a God; that the security of the God was altogether the benefit of nature, which had exempted him from suffering; but that the security of the wise man was his own benefit, and derived altogether from himself and from his own exertions.

45   The sensibility of some men, however, to some of the objects which immediately affect themselves, is sometimes so strong as to render all self-command impossible. No sense of honour can control the fears of the man who is weak enough to faint, or to fall into convulsions, upon the approach of danger. Whether such weakness of nerves, as it has been called, may not, by gradual exercise and proper discipline, admit of some cure, may, perhaps, be doubtful. It seems certain that it ought never to be trusted or employed.

[a]CHAP. IV

Of the Nature of Self-deceit, and of the Origin and Use of general Rules

1   IN order to pervert the rectitude of our own judgments concerning the propriety of our own conduct, it is not always necessary that the real and impartial spectator should be at a great distance. When he is at hand, when

---

[a] *This chapter is a revised version of what was the latter part of Sect. ii in ed. 1 and Chap. 2 in eds. 2–5. See note* [n] *at III.1.5 and note* [x] *at III.3.11. § 1 is not in ed. 1, but the latter part of it, from* the violence and injustice of our own selfish passions . . ., *is a revision of a passage added in the draft revision of 1759 and in ed. 2.*

[21] *De Providentia* (*Dialogues*, Book I), vi.6.

he is present, the violence and injustice of our own selfish passions are sometimes sufficient to induce the man within the breast to make a report very different from what the real circumstances of the case are capable of authorising.

2   There are two different occasions upon which we examine our own conduct, and endeavour to view it in the light in which the impartial spectator would view it: first, when we are about to act; and secondly, after we have acted. Our views are *ᵇapt to beᵇ* very partial in both cases; but they are *ᶜapt to be most partialᶜ* when it is of most importance that they should be otherwise.

3   When we are about to act, the eagerness of passion will seldom allow us to consider what we are doing, with the candour of an indifferent person. The violent emotions which at that time agitate us, discolour our views of *ᵈthings;ᵈ* even when we are endeavouring to place ourselves in the situation of another, and to regard the objects that interest us in the light in which they will naturally appear to *ᵉhim, theᵉ* fury of our own passions constantly calls us back to our own place, where every thing appears magnified and misrepresented by self-love. Of the manner in which those objects would appear to another, of the view which he would take of them, we can obtain, if I may say so, but instantaneous glimpses, which vanish in a moment, and which, even while they last, are not altogether just. We cannot even for that moment divest ourselves entirely of the heat and keenness with which our peculiar situation inspires us, nor consider what we are about to do with the complete impartiality of an equitable judge. The passions, upon this account, as father Malebranche says, all justify themselves, and seem reasonable and proportioned to their objects, as long as we continue to feel them.[1]

4   When the action is over, indeed, and the passions which prompted it have subsided, we can enter more coolly into the sentiments of the indifferent spectator. What before interested us is now become almost as indifferent to us as it always was to him, and we can now examine our own conduct with his candour and impartiality. *ᶠThe man of to-day is no longer agitated by*

ᵇ⁻ᵇ *om.* *1–5*

ᶜ⁻ᶜ most so, *1–5*

ᵈ⁻ᵈ ~, *1–7   The semi-colon is an editors' emendation, required by the correction at* ᵉ⁻ᵉ *in* *1E.*

ᵉ⁻ᵉ *1E* ~. The *1–7   The correction by 1E requires a stronger mark of punctuation than a comma at* ᵈ⁻ᵈ, *and we have presumed that the MS. had, or was intended to have, a semicolon there. The apodosis to the clause,* even when . . . appear to him, *is the* fury . . . by self-love, *and not* The violent emotions . . . views of things, *which would make less good sense.*

ᶠ⁻ᶠ *om.* *1–5*

[1] *Recherche de la vérité*, V.11. Hutcheson also cites with approval this dictum of Malebranche; *Inquiry concerning Moral Good and Evil*, II.4; Raphael, *British Moralists 1650–1800*, § 322.

the same passions which distracted the man of yesterday: and when the paroxysm of emotion, in the same manner as when the paroxysm of distress, is fairly over, we can identify ourselves, as it were, with the ideal man within the breast, and, in our own character, view, as in the one case, our own situation, so in the other, our own conduct, with the severe eyes of the most impartial spectaᵗor.*ᶠ* But our judgments now are *ᵍ*often*ᵍ* of little importance in comparison of what they were before; *ʰ*and can frequently produce*ʰ* nothing but vain regret and unavailing repentance; without *ʲ*always*ʲ* securing us from the like errors in time to come. It is seldom, however, that they are quite candid even in this case. The opinion which we entertain of our own character depends entirely on our *ᵏ*judgments*ᵏ* concerning our past conduct. It is so disagreeable to think ill of ourselves, that we often purposely turn away our view from those circumstances which might render that *ˡ*judgment*ˡ* unfavourable. He is a bold surgeon, they say, whose hand does not tremble when he performs an operation upon his own person; and he is often equally bold who does not hesitate to pull off the mysterious veil of self-delusion, which covers from his view the deformities of his own conduct. Rather than see our own behaviour under so disagreeable an aspect, we too often, foolishly and weakly, endeavour to exasperate anew those unjust passions which had formerly misled us; we endeavour by artifice to awaken our old hatreds, and irritate afresh our almost forgotten resentments: we even exert ourselves for this miserable purpose, and thus persevere in injustice, merely because we once were unjust, and because we are ashamed and afraid to see that we were so.

5 So partial are the views of mankind with regard to the propriety of their own conduct, both at the time of action and after it; and so difficult is it for them to view it in the light in which any indifferent spectator would consider it. But if it was by a peculiar faculty, such as the moral sense is supposed to be, that they judged of their own conduct, if they were endued with a particular power of perception, which distinguished the beauty or deformity of passions and affections; as their own passions would be more immediately exposed to the view of this faculty, it would judge with more accuracy concerning them, than concerning those of other men, of which it had only a more distant prospect.[2]

6 This self-deceit, this fatal weakness of mankind, is the source of half the disorders of human life. If we saw ourselves in the light in which others

---

ᵍ⁻ᵍ om. *1–5*
ʰ⁻ʰ and when they are most severely impartial, can commonly produce *1–5*
ʲ⁻ʲ om. *1–5*
ᵏ⁻ᵏ *1*E judgment *1–7*
ˡ⁻ˡ *1–5* judgement *6 7 See note* *ᵃᵃ⁻ᵃᵃ* at III.3.43.

---

[2] A criticism of Hutcheson. Cf. VII.iii.3.5–10.

see us, or in which they would see us if they knew all, a reformation would generally be unavoidable. We could not otherwise endure the sight.

7   Nature, however, has not left this weakness, which is of so much importance, altogether without a remedy; nor has she abandoned us entirely to the delusions of self-love. Our continual observations upon the conduct of others, insensibly lead us to form to ourselves certain general rules concerning what is fit and proper either to be done or to be avoided. Some of their actions shock all our natural sentiments. We hear every body about us express the like detestation against them. This still further confirms, and even exasperates our natural sense of their deformity. It satisfies us that we view them in the proper light, when we see other people view them in the same light. We resolve never to be guilty of the like, nor ever, upon any account, to render ourselves in this manner the objects of universal disapprobation. We thus naturally lay down to ourselves a general rule, that all such actions are to be avoided, as tending to render us odious, contemptible, or punishable, the objects of all those sentiments for which we have the greatest dread and aversion. Other actions, on the contrary, call forth our approbation, and we hear every body around us express the same favourable opinion concerning them. Every body is eager to honour and reward them. They excite all those sentiments for which we have by nature the strongest desire; the love, the gratitude, the admiration of mankind. We become ambitious of performing the like; and thus naturally lay down to ourselves a rule of another kind, that every opportunity of acting in this manner is carefully to be sought after.

8   It is thus that the general rules of morality are formed. They are ultimately founded upon experience of what, in particular instances, our moral faculties, our natural sense of merit and propriety, approve, or disapprove of. We do not originally approve or condemn particular actions; because, upon examination, they appear to be agreeable or inconsistent with a certain general rule. The general rule, on the contrary, is formed, by finding from experience, that all actions of a certain kind, or circumstanced in a certain manner, are approved or disapproved of. To the man who first saw an inhuman murder, committed from avarice, envy, or unjust resentment, and upon one too that loved and trusted the murderer, who beheld the last agonies of the dying person, who heard him, with his expiring breath, complain more of the perfidy and ingratitude of his false friend, than of the violence which had been done to him, there could be no occasion, in order to conceive how horrible such an action was, that he should reflect, that one of the most sacred rules of conduct was what prohibited the taking away the life of an innocent person, that this was a plain violation of that rule, and consequently a very blamable action. His detestation of this crime, it is evident, would arise instantaneously and antecedent to his having formed to himself any such general rule. The general rule, on the contrary,

which he might afterwards form, would be founded upon the detestation which he felt necessarily arise in his own breast, at the thought of this, and every other particular action of the same kind.

9   When we read in history or romance, the account of actions either of generosity or of baseness, the admiration which we conceive for the one, and the contempt which we feel for the other, neither of them arise from reflecting that there are certain general rules which declare all actions of the one kind admirable, and all actions of the other contemptible. Those general rules, on the contrary, are all formed from the experience we have had of the effects which actions of all different kinds naturally produce upon us.

10   An amiable action, a respectable action, an horrid action, are all of them actions which naturally excite for the person who performs them, the love, the respect, or the horror of the spectator. The general rules which determine what actions are, and what are not, the objects of each of those sentiments, can be formed no other way than by observing what actions actually and in fact excite them.

11   When these general rules, indeed, have been formed, when they are universally acknowledged and established, by the concurring sentiments of mankind, we frequently appeal to them as to the standards of ᵐjudgment,ᵐ in debating concerning the degree of praise or blame that is due to certain actions of a complicated and dubious nature. They are upon these occasions commonly cited as the ultimate foundations of what is just and unjust in human conduct; and this circumstance seems to have misled several very eminent authors, to draw up their systems in such a manner, as if they had supposed that the original judgments of mankind with regard to right and wrong, were formed like the decisions of a court of judicatory, by considering first the general rule, and then, secondly, whether the particular action under consideration fell properly within its comprehension.

12   Those general rules of conduct, when they have been fixed in our mind by habitual reflection, are of great use in correcting the misrepresentations of self-love concerning what is fit and proper to be done in our particular situation. The man of furious resentment, if he was to listen to the dictates of that passion, would perhaps regard the death of his enemy, as but a small compensation for the wrong, he imagines, he has received; which, however, may be no more than a very slight provocation. But his observations upon the conduct of others, have taught him how horrible all such sanguinary revenges appear. Unless his education has been very singular, he has laid it down to himself as an inviolable rule, to abstain from them upon all occasions. This rule preserves its authority with him, and renders him incapable of being guilty of such a violence. Yet the fury of his own temper may be such, that had this been the first time in which he considered such an action, he would undoubtedly have determined it to be quite just and

ᵐ⁻ᵐ *1–5* judgement, *6 7 See note* ᵃᵃ⁻ᵃᵃ *at III.3.43.*

proper, and what every impartial spectator would approve of. But that reverence for the rule which past experience has impressed upon him, checks the impetuosity of his passion, and helps him to correct the too partial views which self-love might otherwise suggest, of what was proper to be done in his situation. If he should allow himself to be so far transported by passion as to violate this rule, yet, even in this case, he cannot throw off altogether the awe and respect with which he has been accustomed to regard it. At the very time of acting, at the moment in which passion mounts the highest, he hesitates and trembles at the thought of what he is about to do: he is secretly conscious to himself that he is breaking through those measures of conduct which, in all his cool hours, he had resolved never to infringe, which he had never seen infringed by others without the highest disapprobation, and of which the infringement, his own mind forebodes, must soon render him the object of the same disagreeable sentiments. Before he can take the last fatal resolution, he is tormented with all the agonies of doubt and uncertainty; he is terrified at the thought of violating so sacred a rule, and at the same time is urged and goaded on by the fury of his desires to violate it. He changes his purpose every moment; sometimes he resolves to adhere to his principle, and not indulge a passion which may corrupt the remaining part of his life with the horrors of shame and repentance; and a momentary calm takes possession of his breast, from the prospect of that security and tranquillity which he will enjoy when he thus determines not to expose himself to the hazard of a contrary conduct. But immediately the passion rouses anew, and with fresh fury drives him on to commit what he had the instant before resolved to abstain from. Wearied and distracted with those continual irresolutions, he at length, from a sort of despair, makes the last fatal and irrecoverable step; but with that terror and amazement with which one flying from an enemy, throws himself over a precipice, where he is sure of meeting with more certain destruction than from any thing that pursues him from behind. Such are his sentiments even at the time of acting; though he is then, no doubt, less sensible of the impropriety of his own conduct than afterwards, when his passion being gratified and palled, he begins to view what he has done in the light in which others are apt to view it; and actually feels, what he had only foreseen very imperfectly before, the stings of remorse and repentance begin to agitate and torment him.

[a]CHAP. V[a]

Of the influence and authority of the general Rules of Morality, and that they are justly regarded as the Laws of the Deity

1   THE regard to those general rules of conduct, is what is properly called a

[a-a] SECT. III *1*   CHAP. III *2-5*

sense of duty, a principle of the greatest consequence in human life, and the only principle by which the bulk of mankind are capable of directing their actions. Many men behave very decently, and through the whole of their lives avoid any considerable degree of blame, who yet, perhaps, never felt the sentiment upon the propriety of which we found our approbation of their conduct, but acted merely from a regard to what they saw were the established rules of behaviour. The man who has received great benefits from another person, may, by the natural coldness of his temper, feel but a very small degree of the sentiment of gratitude. If he has been virtuously educated, however, he will often have been made to observe how odious those actions appear which denote a want of this sentiment, and how amiable the contrary. Though his heart therefore is not warmed with any grateful affection, he will strive to act as if it was, and will endeavour to pay all those regards and attentions to his patron which the liveliest gratitude could suggest. He will visit him regularly; he will behave to him respectfully; he will never talk of him but with expressions of the highest esteem, and of the many obligations which he owes to him. And what is more, he will *b*carefully*b* embrace every opportunity of making a proper return for past services. He may do all this too without any hypocrisy or blamable dissimulation, without any selfish intention of obtaining new favours, and without any design of imposing either upon his benefactor or the public. The motive of his actions may be no other than a reverence for the established rule of duty, a serious and earnest desire of acting, in every respect, according to the law of gratitude. A wife, in the same manner, may sometimes not feel that tender regard for her husband which is suitable to the relation that subsists between them. If she has been virtuously educated, however, she will endeavour to act as if she felt it, to be careful, officious, faithful, and sincere, and to be deficient in none of those attentions which the sentiment of conjugal affection could have prompted her to perform. Such a friend, and such a wife, are neither of them, undoubtedly, the very best of their kinds; and though both of them may have the most serious and earnest desire to fulfil every part of their duty, yet they will fail in many nice and delicate regards, they will miss many opportunities of obliging, which they could never have overlooked if they had possessed the sentiment that is proper to their situation. Though not the very first of their kinds, however, they are perhaps the second; and if the regard to the general rules of conduct has been very strongly impressed upon them, neither of them will fail in any very essential part of their duty. None but those of the happiest mould are capable of suiting, with exact justness, their sentiments and behaviour to the smallest difference of situation, and of acting upon all occasions with the most delicate and accurate propriety. The coarse clay of

---

b–b chearfully *1*   carefully *was probably intended even for ed. 1.*

which the bulk of mankind are formed, cannot be wrought up to such perfection. There is scarce any man, however, who by discipline, education,
and example, may not be so impressed with a regard to general rules, as to
act upon almost every occasion with tolerable decency, and through the
whole of his life to avoid any considerable degree of blame.

2   Without this sacred regard to general rules, there is no man whose
conduct can be much depended upon. It is this which constitutes the most
essential difference between a man of principle and honour and a worthless fellow. The one adheres, on all occasions, steadily and resolutely to his
maxims, and preserves through the whole of his life one even tenour of
conduct. The other, acts variously and accidentally, as humour, inclination,
or interest chance to be uppermost. Nay, such are the inequalities of humour to which all men are subject, that without this principle, the man who,
in all his cool hours, had the most delicate sensibility to the propriety of
conduct, might often be led to act absurdly upon the most frivolous occasions, and when it was scarce possible to assign any serious motive for his
behaving in this manner. Your friend makes you a visit when you happen to
be in a humour which makes it disagreeable to receive him: in your present
mood his civility is very apt to appear an impertinent intrusion; and if you
were to give way to the views of things which at this time occur, though
civil in your temper, you would behave to him with coldness and contempt.
What renders you incapable of such a rudeness, is nothing but a regard
to the general rules of civility and hospitality, which prohibit it. That
habitual reverence which your former experience has taught you for these,
enables you to act, upon all such occasions, with nearly equal propriety,
and hinders those inequalities of temper, to which all men are subject,
from influencing your conduct in any very sensible degree. But if without
regard to these general rules, even the duties of politeness, which are so
easily observed, and which one can scarce have any serious motive to violate,
would yet be so frequently violated, what would become of the duties of
justice, of truth, of chastity, of fidelity, which it is often so difficult to observe, and which there may be so many strong motives to violate? But
upon the tolerable observance of these duties, depends the very existence
of human society, which would crumble into nothing if mankind were not
generally impressed with a reverence for those important rules of conduct.

3   This reverence is still further enhanced by an opinion which is first
impressed by nature, and afterwards confirmed by reasoning and philosophy,
that those important rules of morality are the commands and laws of the
Deity, who will finally reward the obedient, and punish the transgressors
of their duty.

4   This opinion or apprehension, I say, seems first to be impressed by
nature. Men are naturally led to ascribe to those mysterious beings,
whatever they are, which happen, in any country, to be the objects of

religious fear, all their own sentiments and passions. They have no other, they can conceive no other to ascribe to them. Those unknown intelligences which they imagine but see not, must necessarily be formed with some sort of resemblance to those intelligences of which they have experience. During the ignorance and darkness of pagan superstition, mankind seem to have formed the ideas of their divinities with so little delicacy, that they ascribed to them, indiscriminately, all the passions of human nature, those not excepted which do the least honour to our species, such as lust, hunger, avarice, envy, revenge. They could not fail, therefore, to ascribe to those beings, for the excellence of whose nature they still conceived the highest admiration, those sentiments and qualities which are the great ornaments of humanity, and which seem to raise it to a resemblance of divine perfection, the love of virtue and beneficence, and the abhorrence of vice and injustice. The man who was injured, called upon Jupiter to be witness of the wrong that was done to him, and could not doubt, but that divine being would behold it with the same indignation which would animate the meanest of mankind, who looked on when injustice was committed. The man who did the injury, felt himself to be the proper object of the detestation and resentment of mankind; and his natural fears led him to impute the same sentiments to those awful beings, whose presence he could not avoid, and whose power he could not resist. These natural hopes and fears, and suspicions, were propagated by sympathy, and confirmed by education; and the gods were universally represented and believed to be the rewarders of humanity and mercy, and the avengers of perfidy and injustice. And thus religion, even in its rudest form, gave a sanction to the rules of morality, long before the age of artificial reasoning and philosophy. That the terrors of religion should thus enforce the natural sense of duty, was of too much importance to the happiness of mankind, for nature to leave it dependent upon the slowness and uncertainty of philosophical researches.

5   [1]These researches, however, when they came to take place, confirmed those original anticipations of nature. Upon whatever we suppose that our

---

[1] Several phrases in this paragraph recall Bishop Butler. Cf. *Dissertation of the Nature of Virtue*, para. 1; Raphael, *British Moralists 1650–1800*, § 429: '... upon supposition of such a moral faculty; whether called conscience, moral reason, moral sense, or divine reason; ...' *Fifteen Sermons*, preface, para. 24; Raphael, § 379: 'conscience ... plainly bears upon it marks of authority over all the rest, and claims the absolute direction of them all, ...' sermon ii, paras. 14–15; Raphael, § 402: 'you cannot form a notion of this faculty, conscience, without taking in judgment, direction, superintendency. ... This is its right and office. ...'

The paragraph probably formed part of an early version of Smith's lectures, for his statement that the moral faculties 'may be considered as a sort of senses' is not consistent with his criticism of Hutcheson's moral sense theory at III.4.5 and VII.iii.3.5–10. Lord Kames, who readily uses the expression 'moral sense', quotes the 'marks of authority' passage from Butler in *Essays on the Principles of Morality and Natural Religion* (1751), I.ii.3; Selby-Bigge, *British Moralists*, § 931.

moral faculties are founded, whether upon a certain modification of reason, upon an original instinct, called a moral sense, or upon some other principle of our nature, it cannot be doubted, that they were given us for the direction of our conduct in this life. They carry along with them the most evident badges of this authority, which denote that they were set up within us to be the supreme arbiters of all our actions, to superintend all our senses, passions, and appetites, and to judge how far each of them was either to be indulged or restrained. Our moral faculties are by no means, as some have pretended, upon a level in this respect with the other faculties and appetites of our nature, endowed with no more right to restrain these last, than these last are to restrain them. No other faculty or principle of action judges of any other. Love does not judge of resentment, nor resentment of love. Those two passions may be opposite to one another, but cannot, with any propriety, be said to approve or disapprove of one another. But it is the peculiar office of those faculties now under our consideration to judge, to bestow censure or applause upon all the other principles of our nature. They may be considered as a sort of senses of which those principles are the objects. Every sense is supreme over its own objects. There is no appeal from the eye with regard to the beauty of colours, nor from the ear with regard to the harmony of sounds, nor from the taste with regard to the agreeableness of flavours. Each of those senses judges in the last resort of its own objects. Whatever gratifies the taste is sweet, whatever pleases the eye is beautiful, whatever soothes the ear is harmonious. The very essence of each of those qualities consists in its being fitted to please the sense to which it is addressed. It belongs to our moral faculties, in the same manner to determine when the ear ought to be soothed, when the eye ought to be indulged, when the taste ought to be gratified, when and how far every other principle of our nature ought either to be indulged or restrained. What is agreeable to our moral faculties, is fit, and right, and proper to be done; the contrary wrong, unfit, and improper. The sentiments which they approve of, are graceful and becoming: the contrary, ungraceful and unbecoming. The very words, right, wrong, fit, improper, graceful, unbecoming, mean only what pleases or displeases those faculties.

6   Since these, therefore, were plainly intended to be the governing principles of human nature, the rules which they prescribe are to be regarded as the commands and laws of the Deity, promulgated by those vicegerents which he has thus set up within us. All general rules are commonly denominated laws: thus the general rules which bodies observe in the communication of motion, are called the laws of motion. But those general rules which our moral faculties observe in approving or condemning whatever sentiment or action is subjected to their examination, may much more justly be denominated such. They have a much greater resemblance to

what are properly called laws, those general rules which the sovereign lays down to direct the conduct of his subjects. Like them they are rules to direct the free actions of men: they are prescribed most surely by a lawful superior, and are attended too with the sanction of rewards and punishments. Those vicegerents of God within us, never fail to punish the violation of them, by the torments of inward shame, and self-condemnation; and on the contrary, always reward obedience with tranquillity of mind, with contentment, and self-satisfaction.

7   There are innumerable other considerations which serve to confirm the same conclusion. The happiness of mankind, as well as of all other rational creatures, seems to have been the original purpose intended by the Author of nature, when he brought them into existence. No other end seems worthy of that supreme wisdom and divine benignity which we necessarily ascribe to him; and this opinion, which we are led to by the abstract consideration of his infinite perfections, is still more confirmed by the examination of the works of nature, which seem all intended to promote happiness, and to guard against misery. But by acting according to the dictates of our moral faculties, we necessarily pursue the most effectual means for promoting the happiness of mankind, and may therefore be said, in some sense, to co-operate with the Deity, and to advance as far as in our power the plan of Providence. By acting otherways, on the contrary, we seem to obstruct, in some measure, the scheme which the Author of nature has established for the happiness and perfection of the world, and to declare ourselves, if I may say so, in some measure the enemies of God. Hence we are naturally encouraged to hope for his extraordinary favour and reward in the one case, and to dread his vengeance and punishment in the other.

8   There are besides many other reasons, and many other natural principles, which all tend to confirm and inculcate the same salutary doctrine. If we consider the general rules by which external prosperity and adversity are commonly distributed in this life, we shall find, that notwithstanding the disorder in which all things appear to be in this world, yet even here every virtue naturally meets with its proper reward, with the recompense which is most fit to encourage and promote it; and this too so surely, that it requires a very extraordinary concurrence of circumstances entirely to disappoint it. What is the reward most proper for encouraging industry, prudence, and circumspection? Success in every sort of business. And is it possible that in the whole of life these virtues should fail of attaining it? Wealth and external honours are their proper recompense, and the recompense which they can seldom fail of acquiring. What reward is most proper for promoting the practice of truth, justice, and humanity? The confidence, the esteem, and love of those we live with. Humanity does not desire to be great, but to be beloved. It is not in being rich that truth and justice would rejoice, but in being trusted and believed, recompenses which

those virtues must almost always acquire. By some very extraordinary and unlucky circumstance, a good man may come to be suspected of a crime of which he was altogether incapable, and upon that account be most unjustly exposed for the remaining part of his life to the horror and aversion of mankind. By an accident of this kind he may be said to lose his all, notwithstanding his integrity and justice; in the same manner as a cautious man, notwithstanding his utmost circumspection, may be ruined by an earthquake or an inundation. Accidents of the first kind, however, are perhaps still more rare, and still more contrary to the common course of things than those of the second; and it still remains true, that the practice of truth, justice, and humanity is a certain and almost infallible method of acquiring what those virtues chiefly aim at, the confidence and love of those we live with. A person may be very easily misrepresented with regard to a particular action; but it is scarce possible that he should be so with regard to the general tenor of his conduct. An innocent man may be believed to have done wrong: this, however, will rarely happen. On the contrary, the established opinion of the innocence of his manners, will often lead us to absolve him where he has really been in the fault, notwithstanding very strong presumptions. A knave, in the same manner, may escape censure, or even meet with applause, for a particular knavery, in which his conduct is not understood. But no man was ever habitually such, without being almost universally known to be so, and without being even frequently suspected of guilt, when he was in reality perfectly innocent. And so far as vice and virtue can be either punished or rewarded by the sentiments and opinions of mankind, they both, according to the common course of things, meet even here with something more than exact and impartial justice.

9　　But though the general rules by which prosperity and adversity are commonly distributed, when considered in this cool and philosophical light, appear to be perfectly suited to the situation of mankind in this life, yet they are by no means suited to some of our natural sentiments. Our natural love and admiration for some virtues is such, that we should wish to bestow on them all sorts of honours and rewards, even those which we must acknowledge to be the proper recompenses of other qualities, with which those virtues are not always accompanied. Our detestation, on the contrary, for some vices is such, that we should desire to heap upon them every sort of disgrace and disaster, those not excepted which are the natural consequences of very different qualities. Magnanimity, generosity, and justice, command so high a degree of admiration, that we desire to see them crowned with wealth, and power, and honours of every kind, the natural consequences of prudence, industry, and application; qualities with which those virtues are not inseparably connected. Fraud, falsehood, brutality, and violence, on the other hand, excite in every human breast such scorn and abhorrence, that our indignation rouses to see them possess those advantages which they may in some sense be said to have merited, by the diligence and industry with which they are sometimes attended. The industrious knave cultivates the soil; the indolent good man leaves it uncultivated. Who ought to reap the harvest? ᶜwhoᶜ starve, and who live in plenty? The natural course of things decides it in favour of the knave: the natural sentiments of mankind in favour of the man of virtue. Man judges, that the good qualities of the one are greatly over-recompensed by those advantages which they tend to procure him, and that the omissions of the other are by far too severely punished by the distress which they naturally bring upon him; and human laws, the consequences of human sentiments, forfeit the life and the estate of the industrious and cautious traitor, and reward, by extraordinary recompenses, the fidelity and public spirit of the improvident and careless good citizen. Thus man is by Nature directed to correct, in some measure, that distribution of things which she herself would otherwise have made. The rules which for this purpose she prompts him to follow, are different from those which she herself observes. She bestows upon every virtue, and upon every vice, that precise reward or punishment which is best fitted to encourage the one, or to restrain the other. She is directed by this sole consideration, and pays little regard to the different degrees of merit and demerit, which they may seem to possess in the sentiments and passions of man. Man, on the contrary, pays regard to this only, and would endeavour to render the state of every virtue precisely proportioned to that degree of love and esteem, and of every vice to that degree of contempt and abhorrence, which he himself conceives for it. The rules which she follows are fit for her, those which he follows for him: but both are calculated to promote the same great end, the order of the world, and the perfection and happiness of human nature.

10   But though man is thus employed to alter that distribution of things which natural events would make, if left to themselves; though, like the gods of the poets, he is perpetually interposing, by extraordinary means, in favour of virtue, and in opposition to vice, and, like them, endeavours to turn away the arrow that is aimed at the head of the righteous, but to ac-celerate the sword of destruction that is lifted up against the wicked; yet he is by no means able to render the fortune of either quite suitable to his own sentiments and wishes. The natural course of things cannot be entirely controlled by the impotent endeavours of man: the current is too rapid and too strong for him to stop it; and though the rules which direct it appear to have been established for the wisest and best purposes, they some-times produce effects which shock all his natural sentiments. That a great combination of men should prevail over a small one; that those who engage

ᶜ⁻ᶜ *1* 5 Who 2–4 *6* 7

in an enterprise with forethought and all necessary preparation, should prevail over such as oppose them without any; and that every end should be acquired by those means only which Nature has established for acquiring it, seems to be a rule not only necessary and unavoidable in itself, but even useful and proper for rousing the industry and attention of mankind. Yet, when, in consequence of this rule, violence and artifice prevail over sincerity and justice, what indignation does it not excite in the breast of every human spectator? What sorrow and compassion for the sufferings of the innocent, and what furious resentment against the success of the oppressor? We are equally grieved and enraged at the wrong that is done, but often find it altogether out of our power to redress it. When we thus despair of finding any force upon earth which can check the triumph of injustice, we naturally appeal to heaven, and hope, that the great Author of our nature will himself execute hereafter, what all the principles which he has given us for the direction of our conduct, prompt us to attempt even here; that he will complete the plan which he himself has thus taught us to begin; and will, in a life to come, render to every one according to the works which he has performed in this world. And thus we are led to the belief of a future state, not only by the weaknesses, by the hopes and fears of human nature, but by the noblest and best principles which belong to it, by the love of virtue, and by the abhorrence of vice and injustice.

11   'Does it suit the greatness of God,' says the eloquent and philosophical bishop of Clermont,[2] with that passionate and exaggerating force of imagination, which seems sometimes to exceed the bounds of decorum; 'does it suit the greatness of God, to leave the world which he has created in so universal a disorder? To see the wicked prevail almost always over the just; the innocent dethroned by the usurper; the father become the victim of the ambition of an unnatural son; the husband expiring under the stroke of a barbarous and faithless wife? From the height of his greatness ought God to behold those melancholy events as a fantastical amusement, without taking any share in them? Because he is great, should he be weak, or unjust, or barbarous? Because men are little, ought they to be allowed either to be dissolute without punishment, or virtuous without reward? O God! if this is the character of your Supreme Being; if it is you whom we adore under such dreadful ideas; I can no longer acknowledge you for my father, for my protector, for the comforter of my sorrow, the support of my weakness, the rewarder of my fidelity. You would then be no more than an indolent and fantastical tyrant, who sacrifices mankind to his insolent vanity, and who has brought them out of nothing, only to make them serve for the sport of his leisure and of his caprice.'

[2] Massillon, Sermon pour le lundi de la première semaine de carême: 'Sur la vérité d'un avenir', deuxième partie; *Oeuvres complètes* (Paris, 1821), ii.221–2. The English translation is probably Smith's own.

12   When the general rules which determine the merit and demerit of
actions, come thus to be regarded as the laws of an All-powerful Being,
who watches over our conduct, and who, in a life to come, will reward
the observance, and punish the breach of them; they necessarily acquire a
new sacredness from this consideration. That our regard to the will of the
Deity ought to be the supreme rule of our conduct, can be doubted of by
nobody who believes his existence. The very thought of disobedience
appears to involve in it the most shocking impropriety. How vain, how
absurd would it be for man, either to oppose or to neglect the commands
that were laid upon him by Infinite Wisdom, and Infinite Power! How unnatural, how impiously ungrateful not to reverence the precepts that were
prescribed to him by the infinite goodness of his Creator, even though no
punishment was to follow their violation. The sense of propriety too is here
well supported by the strongest motives of self-interest. The idea that,
however we may escape the observation of man, or be placed above the
reach of human punishment, yet we are always acting under the eye, and
exposed to the punishment of God, the great avenger of injustice, is a
motive capable of restraining the most headstrong passions, with those at
least who, by constant *d*reflection,*d* have rendered it familiar to them.

13   It is in this manner that religion enforces the natural sense of duty: and
hence it is, that mankind are generally disposed to place great confidence
in the probity of those who seem deeply impressed with religious sentiments. Such persons, they imagine, act under an additional tie, besides
those which regulate the conduct of other men. The regard to the propriety
of action, as well as to reputation, the regard to the applause of his own
breast, as well as to that of others, are motives which they suppose have the
same influence over the religious man, as over the man of the world. But
the former lies under another restraint, and never acts deliberately but as
in the presence of that Great Superior who is finally to recompense him
according to his deeds. A greater trust is reposed, upon this account, in the
regularity and exactness of his conduct. And wherever the natural principles
of religion are not corrupted by the factious and party zeal of some worthless cabal; wherever the first duty which it requires, is to fulfil all the
obligations of morality; wherever men are not taught to regard frivolous
observances, as more immediate duties of religion, than acts of justice and
beneficence; and to imagine, that by sacrifices, and ceremonies, and vain
supplications, they can bargain with the Deity for fraud, and perfidy, and
violence, the world undoubtedly judges right in this respect, and justly
places a double confidence in the rectitude of the religious man's behaviour.

d-d *1-5* ~∧ *6 7*

[a]CHAP. VI[a]

In what cases the Sense of Duty ought to be the sole principle of our conduct; and in what cases it ought to concur with other motives

1 RELIGION affords such strong motives to the practice of virtue, and guards us by such powerful restraints from the temptations of vice, that many have been led to suppose, that religious principles were the sole laudable motives of action. We ought neither, they said, to reward from gratitude, nor punish from resentment; we ought neither to protect the helplessness of our children, nor afford support to the infirmities of our parents, from natural affection. All affections for particular objects, ought to be extinguished in our breast, and one great affection take the place of all others, the love of the Deity, the desire of rendering ourselves agreeable to him, and of directing our conduct, in every respect, according to his will. We ought not to be grateful from gratitude, we ought not to be charitable from humanity, we ought not to be public-spirited from the love of our country, nor generous and just from the love of mankind. The sole principle and motive of our conduct in the performance of all those different duties, ought to be a sense that God has commanded us to perform them. I shall not at present take time to examine this opinion particularly; I shall only observe, that we should not have expected to have found it entertained by any sect, who professed themselves of a religion in which, as it is the first precept to love the Lord our God with all our heart, with all our soul, and with all our strength, so it is the second to love our neighbour as we love ourselves; and we love ourselves surely for our own sakes, and not merely because we are commanded to do so. That the sense of duty should be the sole principle of our conduct, is no where the precept of Christianity; but that it should be the ruling and the governing one, as philosophy, and as, indeed, common sense directs. It may be a question, however, in what cases our actions ought to arise chiefly or entirely from a sense of duty, or from a regard to general rules; and in what cases some other sentiment or affection ought to concur, and have a principal influence.

2 The decision of this question, which cannot, perhaps, be given with any very great accuracy, will depend upon two different circumstances; first, upon the natural agreeableness or deformity of the sentiment or affection which would prompt us to any action independent of all regard to general rules; and, secondly, upon the precision and exactness, or the looseness and inaccuracy, of the general rules themselves.

3   I.   First, I say, it will depend upon the natural agreeableness or de-

[a-a] CHAP. IV *1-5* SECT. IV *1E*

formity of the affection itself, how far our actions ought to arise from it, or entirely proceed from a regard to the general rule.

4   All those graceful and admired actions, to which the benevolent affections would prompt us, ought to proceed as much from the passions themselves, as from any regard to the general rules of conduct. A benefactor thinks himself but ill requited, if the person upon whom he has bestowed his good offices, repays them merely from a cold sense of duty, and without any affection to his person. A husband is dissatisfied with the most obedient wife, when he imagines her conduct is animated by no other principle besides her regard to what the relation she stands in requires. Though a son should fail in none of the offices of filial duty, yet if he wants that affectionate reverence which it so well becomes him to feel, the parent may justly complain of his indifference. Nor could a son be quite satisfied with a parent who, though he performed all the duties of his situation, had nothing of that fatherly fondness which might have been expected from him. With regard to all such benevolent and social affections, it is agreeable to see the sense of duty employed rather to restrain than to enliven them, rather to hinder us from doing too much, than to prompt us to do what we ought. It gives us pleasure to see a father obliged to check his own fondness, a friend obliged to set bounds to his natural generosity, a person who has received a benefit, obliged to restrain the too sanguine gratitude of his own temper.

5   The contrary maxim takes place with regard to the malevolent and unsocial passions. We ought to reward from the gratitude and generosity of our own hearts, without any reluctance, and without being obliged to reflect how great the propriety of rewarding: but we ought always to punish with reluctance, and more from a sense of the propriety of punishing, than from any savage disposition to revenge. Nothing is more graceful than the behaviour of the man who appears to resent the greatest injuries, more from a sense that they deserve, and are the proper objects of resentment, than from feeling himself the furies of that disagreeable passion; who, like a judge, considers only the general rule, which determines what vengeance is due for each particular offence; who, in executing that rule, feels less for what himself has suffered, than for what the offender is about to suffer; who, though in *wrath,* remembers mercy, and is disposed to interpret the rule in the most gentle and favourable manner, and to allow all the alleviations which the most candid humanity could, consistently with good sense, admit of.

6   As the selfish passions, according to what has formerly been observed, hold, in other respects, a sort of middle place, between the social and unsocial affections, so do they likewise in this. The pursuit of the objects of

private interest, in all common, little, and ordinary cases, ought to flow
rather from a regard to the general rules which prescribe such conduct, than
from any passion for the objects themselves; but upon more important
and extraordinary occasions, we should be awkward, insipid, and ungraceful, if the objects themselves did not appear to animate us with a considerable degree of passion. To be anxious, or to be laying a plot either to gain
or to save a single shilling, would degrade the most vulgar tradesman in the
opinion of all his neighbours. Let his circumstances be ever so mean, no
attention to any such small matters, for the sake of the things themselves,
must appear in his conduct. His situation may require the most severe
oeconomy and the most exact assiduity: but each particular exertion of that
oeconomy and assiduity must proceed, not so much from a regard for that
particular saving or gain, as for the general rule which to him prescribes,
with the utmost rigour, such a tenor of conduct. His parsimony to-day must
not arise from a desire of the particular three-pence which he will save by
it, nor his attendance in his shop from a passion for the particular ten-
pence which he will acquire by it: both the one and the other ought to
proceed solely from a regard to the general rule, which prescribes, with
the most unrelenting severity, this plan of conduct to all persons in his
way of life. In this consists the difference between the character of a miser
and that of a person of exact oeconomy and assiduity. The one is anxious
about small matters for their own sake; the other attends to them only in
consequence of the scheme of life which he has laid down to himself.

7   It is quite otherwise with regard to the more extraordinary and important
objects of self-interest. A person appears mean-spirited, who does not
pursue these with some degree of earnestness for their own sake. We
should despise a prince who was not anxious about conquering or defend-
ing a province. We should have little respect for a private gentleman who
did not exert himself to gain an estate, or even a considerable office, when
he could acquire them without either meanness or injustice. A member of
parliament who shews no keenness about his own election, is abandoned by
his friends, as altogether unworthy of their attachment. Even a tradesman is
thought a poor-spirited fellow among his neighbours, who does not bestir
himself to get what they call an extraordinary job, or some uncommon
advantage. This spirit and keenness constitutes the difference between
the man of enterprise and the man of dull regularity. Those great objects
of self-interest, of which the loss or acquisition quite changes the rank of
the person, are the objects of the passion properly called ambition; a passion, which when it keeps within the bounds of prudence and justice, is
always admired in the world, and has even sometimes a certain irregular
greatness, which dazzles the imagination, when it passes the limits of both
these virtues, and is not only unjust but extravagant. Hence the general
admiration for heroes and conquerors, and even for statesmen, whose

projects have been very daring and extensive, though altogether devoid of justice; such as those of the Cardinals of Richlieu and of Retz. The objects of avarice and ambition differ only in their greatness. A miser is as furious about a halfpenny, as a man of ambition about the conquest of a kingdom.

8 II. Secondly, I say, it will depend partly upon the precision and exactness, or the looseness and inaccuracy of the general rules themselves, how far our conduct ought to proceed entirely from a regard to them.

9 The general rules of almost all the virtues, the general rules which determine what are the offices of prudence, of charity, of generosity, of gratitude, of friendship, are in many respects loose and inaccurate, admit of many exceptions, and require so many modifications, that it is scarce possible to regulate our conduct entirely by a regard to them. The common proverbial maxims of prudence, being founded in universal experience, are perhaps the best general rules which can be given about it. To affect, however, a very strict and literal adherence to them would evidently be the most absurd and ridiculous pedantry. Of all the virtues I have just now mentioned, gratitude is that, perhaps, of which the rules are the most precise, and admit of the fewest exceptions. That as soon as we can we should make a return of equal, and if possible of superior value to the services we have received, would seem to be a pretty plain rule, and one which admitted of scarce any exceptions. Upon the most superficial examination, however, this rule will appear to be in the highest degree loose and inaccurate, and to admit of ten thousand exceptions. If your benefactor attended you in your sickness, ought you to attend him in his? or can you fulfil the obligation of gratitude, by making a return of a different kind? If you ought to attend him, how long ought you to attend him? The same time which he attended you, or longer, and how much longer? If your friend lent you money in your distress, ought you to lend him money in his? How much ought you to lend him? When ought you to lend him? Now, or to-morrow, or next month? And for how long a time? It is evident, that no general rule can be laid down, by which a precise answer can, in all cases, be given to any of these questions. The difference between his character and yours, between his circumstances and yours, may be such, that you may be perfectly grateful, and justly refuse to lend him a halfpenny: and, on the contrary, you may be willing to lend, or even to give him ten times the sum which he lent you, and yet justly be accused of the blackest ingratitude, and of not having fulfilled the hundredth part of the obligation you lie under. As the duties of gratitude, however, are perhaps the most sacred of all those which the beneficent virtues prescribe to us, so the general rules which determine them are, as I said before, the most accurate. Those which ascertain the actions required by friendship, humanity, hospitality, generosity, are still more vague and indeterminate.

10   There is, however, one virtue of which the general rules determine with
the greatest exactness every external action which it requires. This virtue
is justice. The rules of justice are accurate in the highest degree, and admit
of no exceptions or modifications, but such as may be ascertained as
accurately as the rules themselves, and which generally, indeed, flow from
the very same principles with them. If I owe a man ten pounds, justice
requires that I should precisely pay him ten pounds, either at the time
agreed upon, or when he demands it. What I ought to perform, how
much I ought to perform, when and where I ought to perform it, the whole
nature and circumstances of the action prescribed, are all of them precisely
fixt and determined. Though it may be awkward and pedantic, therefore,
to affect too strict an adherence to the common rules of prudence or generosity, there is no pedantry in sticking fast by the rules of justice. On the
contrary, the most sacred regard is due to them; and the actions which this
virtue requires are never so properly performed, as when the chief motive
for performing them is a reverential and religious regard to those general
rules which require them. In the practice of the other virtues, our conduct
should rather be directed by a certain idea of propriety, by a certain taste
for a particular tenor of conduct, than by any regard to a precise maxim
or rule; and we should consider the end and foundation of the rule, more
than the rule itself. But it is otherwise with regard to justice: the man who
in that refines the least, and adheres with the most obstinate stedfastness
to the general rules themselves, is the most commendable, and the most to
be depended upon. Though the end of the rules of justice be, to hinder us
from hurting our neighbour, it may frequently be a crime to violate them,
though we could pretend, with some pretext of reason, that this particular
violation could do no hurt. A man often becomes a villain the moment he
begins, even in his own heart, to chicane in this manner. The moment
he thinks of departing from the most staunch and positive adherence to
what those inviolable precepts prescribe to him, he is no longer to be
trusted, and no man can say what degree of guilt he may not arrive at.
The thief imagines he does no evil, when he steals from the rich, what he
supposes they may easily want, and what possibly they may never even
know has been stolen from them. The adulterer imagines he does no evil,
when he corrupts the wife of his friend, provided he covers his intrigue
from the suspicion of the husband, and does not disturb the peace of the
family. When once we begin to give way to such refinements, there is no
enormity so gross of which we may not be capable.

11   The rules of justice may be compared to the rules of grammar; the rules
of the other virtues, to the rules which critics lay down for the attainment
of what is sublime and elegant in composition. The one, are precise,
accurate, and indispensable. The other, are loose, vague, and indeterminate,
and present us rather with a general idea of the perfection we ought to aim

at, than afford us any certain and infallible directions for acquiring it. A man may learn to write grammatically by rule, with the most absolute infallibility; and so, perhaps, he may be taught to act justly. But there are no rules whose observance will infallibly lead us to the attainment of elegance or sublimity in writing; though there are some which may help us, in some measure, to correct and ascertain the vague ideas which we might otherwise have entertained of those perfections. And there are no rules by the knowledge of which we can infallibly be taught to act upon all occasions with prudence, with just magnanimity, or proper beneficence: though there are some which may enable us to correct and ascertain, in several respects, the imperfect ideas which we might otherwise have entertained of those virtues.

12   It may sometimes happen, that with the most serious and earnest desire of acting so as to deserve approbation, we may mistake the proper rules of conduct, and thus be misled by that very principle which ought to direct us. It is in vain to expect, that in this case mankind should entirely approve of our behaviour. They cannot enter into that absurd idea of duty which influenced us, nor go along with any of the actions which follow from it. There is still, however, something respectable in the character and behaviour of one who is thus betrayed into vice, by a wrong sense of duty, or by what is called an erroneous conscience. How fatally soever he may be misled by it, he is still, with the generous and humane, more the object of commiseration than of hatred or resentment. They lament the weakness of human nature, which exposes us to such unhappy delusions, even while we are most sincerely labouring after perfection, and endeavouring to act according to the best principle which can possibly direct us. False notions of religion are almost the only causes which can occasion any very gross perversion of our natural sentiments in this way; and that principle which gives the greatest authority to the rules of duty, is alone capable of distorting our ideas of them in any considerable degree. In all other cases common sense is sufficient to direct us, if not to the most exquisite propriety of conduct, yet to something which is not very far from it; and provided we are in earnest desirous to do well, our behaviour will always, upon the whole, be praise-worthy. That to obey the will of the Deity, is the first rule of duty, all men are agreed. But concerning the particular commandments which that will may impose upon us, they differ widely from one another. In this, therefore, the greatest mutual forbearance and toleration is due; and though the defence of society requires that crimes should be punished, from whatever motives they proceed, yet a good man will always punish them with reluctance, when they evidently proceed from false notions of religious duty. He will never feel against those who commit them that indignation which he feels against other criminals, but will rather regret, and sometimes even admire their unfortunate firmness

and magnanimity, at the very time that he punishes their crime. In the tragedy of Mahomet, one of the finest of Mr. Voltaire's,[1] it is well represented, what ought to be our sentiments for crimes which proceed from such motives. In that tragedy, two young people of different sexes, of the most innocent and virtuous dispositions, and without any other weakness except what endears them the more to us, a mutual fondness for one another, are instigated by the strongest motives of a false religion, to commit a horrid murder, that shocks all the principles of human nature. A venerable old man, who had expressed the most tender affection for them both, for whom, notwithstanding he was the avowed enemy of their religion, they had both conceived the highest reverence and esteem, and who was in reality their father, though they did not know him to be such, is pointed out to them as a sacrifice which God had expressly required at their hands, and they are commanded to kill him. While they are about executing this crime, they are tortured with all the agonies which can arise from the struggle between the idea of the indispensableness of religious duty on the one side, and compassion, gratitude, reverence for the age, and love for the humanity and virtue of the person whom they are going to destroy, on the other. The representation of this exhibits one of the most interesting, and perhaps the most instructive spectacle that was ever introduced upon any theatre. The sense of duty, however, at last prevails over all the amiable weaknesses of human nature. They execute the crime imposed upon them; but immediately discover their error, and the fraud which had deceived them, and are distracted with horror, remorse, and resentment. Such as are our sentiments for the unhappy Seid and Palmira, such ought we to feel for every person who is in this manner misled by religion, when we are sure that it is really religion which misleads him, and not the pretence of it, which is made a cover to some of the worst of human passions.

13   As a person may act wrong by following a wrong sense of duty, so nature may sometimes prevail, and lead him to act right in opposition to it. We cannot in this case be displeased to see that motive prevail, which we think ought to prevail, though the person himself is so weak as to think otherwise. As his conduct, however, is the effect of weakness, not principle, we are far from bestowing upon it any thing that approaches to complete approbation. A bigoted Roman Catholic, who, during the massacre of St. Bartholomew, had been so overcome by compassion, as to save some unhappy Protestants, whom he thought it his duty to destroy, would not seem to be entitled to that high applause which we should have bestowed upon him, had he exerted the same generosity with complete self-approbation.

---

[1] *Mahomet* was first produced in 1741. The report in *The Bee*, iii (11 May 1791), 7, of an interview with Smith in 1780 says that he regarded *Mahomet* as 'the very climax of dramatic excellence'.

We might be pleased with the humanity of his temper, but we should still regard him with a sort of pity which is altogether inconsistent with the admiration that is due to perfect virtue. It is the same case with all the other passions. We do not dislike to see them exert themselves properly, even when a false notion of duty would direct the person to restrain them. A very devout Quaker, who upon being struck upon one cheek, instead of turning up the other, should so far forget his literal interpretation of our Saviour's precept, as to bestow some good discipline upon the brute that insulted him, would not be disagreeable to us. We should laugh and be diverted with his spirit, and rather like him the better for it. But we should by no means regard him with that respect and esteem which would seem due to one who, upon a like occasion, had acted properly from a just sense of what was proper to be done. No action can properly be called virtuous, which is not accompanied with the sentiment of self-approbation.

PART IV

Of the EFFECT of UTILITY upon the Sentiment of Approbation
ᵃConsisting of One Sectionᵃ

ᵇCHAP. Iᵇ

*Of the beauty which the appearance of UTILITY bestows upon all the productions of art,
and of the extensive influence of this species of Beauty*

1 THAT utility is one of the principal sources of beauty has been observed by every body, who has considered with any attention what constitutes the nature of beauty. The conveniency of a house gives pleasure to the spectator as well as its regularity, and he is as much hurt when he observes the contrary defect, as when he sees the correspondent windows of different forms, or the door not placed exactly in the middle of the building. That the fitness of any system or machine to produce the end for which it was intended, bestows a certain propriety and beauty upon the whole, and renders the very thought and contemplation of it agreeable, is so very obvious that nobody has overlooked it.

2 The cause too, why utility pleases, has of late been assigned by an ingenious and agreeable philosopher,[1] who joins the greatest depth of thought to the greatest elegance of expression, and possesses the singular and happy talent of treating the abstrusest subjects not only with the most perfect perspicuity, but with the most lively eloquence. The utility of any object, according to him, pleases the master by perpetually suggesting to him the pleasure or conveniency which it is fitted to promote. Every time he looks at it, he is put in mind of this pleasure; and the object in this manner becomes a source of perpetual satisfaction and enjoyment. The spectator enters by sympathy into the sentiments of the master, and necessarily views the object under the same agreeable aspect. When we visit the palaces of the great, we cannot help conceiving the satisfaction we should enjoy if we ourselves were the masters, and were possessed of so much artful and ingeniously contrived accommodation. A similar account is given why the appearance of inconveniency should render any object disagreeable both to the owner and to the spectator.

3 But that this fitness, this happy contrivance of any production of art, should often be more valued, than the very end for which it was intended; and that the exact adjustment of the means for attaining any conveniency or pleasure, should frequently be more regarded, than that very conveniency

---

ᵃ⁻ᵃ *om. I* Consisting of One SECTION *2–7*
ᵇ⁻ᵇ SECT. I *I*

[1] David Hume. *Treatise of Human Nature*, II.ii.5; ed. Selby-Bigge, 363–5: III.iii.I; Selby-Bigge, 576–7: *Enquiry concerning the Principles of Morals*, V.ii; ed. Selby-Bigge, § 179. Section V of the *Enquiry* is entitled 'Why Utility pleases', but Smith seems to be thinking more of *Treatise*, II.ii.5.

or pleasure, in the attainment of which their whole merit would seem to
consist, has not, so far as I know, been yet taken notice of by any body.[2]
That this however is very frequently the case, may be observed in a thousand instances, both in the most frivolous and in the most important concerns of human life.

4   When a person comes into his chamber, and finds the chairs all standing
in the middle of the room, he is angry with his servant, and rather than see
them continue in that disorder, perhaps takes the trouble himself to set them
all in their places with their backs to the wall. The whole propriety of this
new situation arises from its superior conveniency in leaving the floor free
and disengaged. To attain this conveniency he voluntarily puts himself to
more trouble than all he could have suffered from the want of it; since
nothing was more easy, than to have set himself down upon one of them,
which is probably what he does when his labour is over. What he wanted
therefore, it seems, was not so much this conveniency, as that arrangement
of things which promotes it. Yet it is this conveniency which ultimately
recommends that arrangement, and bestows upon it the whole of its propriety and beauty.

5   A watch, in the same manner, that falls behind above two minutes in a
day, is despised by one curious in watches. He sells it perhaps for a couple
of guineas, and purchases another at fifty, which will not lose above a
minute in a fortnight. The sole use of watches however, is to tell us what
o'clock it is, and to hinder us from breaking any engagement, or suffering
any other inconveniency by our ignorance in that particular point. But the
person so nice with regard to this machine, will not always be found either
more scrupulously punctual than other men, or more anxiously concerned
upon any other account, to know precisely what time of day it is. What
interests him is not so much the attainment of this piece of knowledge, as
the perfection of the machine which serves to attain it.

6   How many people ruin themselves by laying out money on trinkets of
frivolous utility? What pleases these lovers of toys is not so much the
utility, as the aptness of the machines which are fitted to promote it.
All their pockets are stuffed with little conveniencies. They contrive
new pockets, unknown in the clothes of other people, in order to
carry a greater number. They walk about loaded with a multitude
of baubles, in weight and sometimes in value not inferior to an
ordinary Jew's-box,[3] some of which may sometimes be of some little use,
but all of which might at all times be very well spared, and of which the
whole utility is certainly not worth the fatigue of bearing the burden.

[2] Smith sets great store by this observation not only for its originality but also because
it forms a link, in his view, between ethics and political economy, as may be seen from
§§ 8–11, especially § 10. See also Introduction, *14*.

[3] Presumably a box of wares carried by a Jewish pedlar.

7   Nor is it only with regard to such frivolous objects that our conduct is influenced by this principle; it is often the secret motive of the most serious and important pursuits of both private and public life.

8   The poor man's son, whom heaven in its anger has visited with ambition, when he begins to look around him, admires the condition of the rich. He finds the cottage of his father too small for his accommodation, and fancies he should be lodged more at his ease in a palace. He is displeased with being obliged to walk a-foot, or to endure the fatigue of riding on horseback. He sees his superiors carried about in machines, and imagines that in one of these he could travel with less inconveniency. He feels himself naturally indolent, and willing to serve himself with his own hands as little as possible; and judges, that a numerous retinue of servants would save him from a great deal of trouble. He thinks if he had attained all these, he ᶜwouldᶜ sit still contentedly, and be quiet, enjoying himself in the thought of the happiness and tranquillity of his situation. He is enchanted with the distant idea of this felicity. It appears in his fancy like the life of some superior rank of beings, and, in order to arrive at it, he devotes himself for ever to the pursuit of wealth and greatness. To obtain the conveniencies which these afford, he submits in the first year, nay in the first month of his application, to more fatigue of body and more uneasiness of mind than he could have suffered through the whole of his life from the want of them. He studies to distinguish himself in some laborious profession. With the most unrelenting industry he labours night and day to acquire talents superior to all his competitors. He endeavours next to bring those talents into public view, and with equal assiduity solicits every opportunity of employment. For this purpose he makes his court to all mankind; he serves those whom he hates, and is obsequious to those whom he despises. Through the whole of his life he pursues the idea of a certain artificial and elegant *r*epose which he may never arrive at, for which he sacrifices a real tranquillity that is at all times in his power, and which, if in the extremity of old age he should at last attain to it, he will find to be in no respect preferable to that humble security and contentment which he had abandoned for it. It is then, in the last dregs of life, his body wasted with toil and diseases, his mind galled and ruffled by the memory of a thousand injuries and disappointments which he imagines he has met with from the injustice of his enemies, or from the perfidy and ingratitude of his friends, that he begins at last to find that wealth and greatness are mere trinkets of frivolous utility, no more adapted for procuring ease of body or tranquillity of mind than the tweezer-cases of the lover of toys; and like them too, more troublesome to the person who carries them about with him than all the advantages they can afford him are commodious. There is no other real difference between them, except that the conveniencies of the one are somewhat more observable than those

ᶜ⁻ᶜ could 1-3

of the other. The palaces, the gardens, the equipage, the retinue of the great, are objects of which the obvious conveniency strikes every body. They do not require that their masters should point out to us wherein consists their utility. Of our own accord we readily enter into it, and by sympathy enjoy and thereby applaud the satisfaction which they are fitted to afford him. But the curiosity of a tooth-pick, of an ear-picker, of a machine for cutting the nails, or of any other trinket of the same kind, is not so obvious. Their conveniency may perhaps be equally great, but it is not so striking, and we do not so readily enter into the satisfaction of the man who possesses them. They are therefore less reasonable subjects of vanity than the magnificence of wealth and greatness; and in this consists the sole advantage of these last. They more effectually gratify that love of distinction so natural to man. To one who was to live alone in a desolate island it might be a matter of doubt, perhaps, whether a palace, or a collection of such small conveniencies as are commonly contained in a tweezer-case, would contribute most to his happiness and enjoyment. If he is to live in society, indeed, there can be no comparison, because in this, as in all other cases, we constantly pay more regard to the sentiments of the spectator, than to those of the person principally concerned, and consider rather how his situation will appear to other people, than how it will appear to himself. If we examine, however, why the spectator distinguishes with such admiration the condition of the rich and the great, we shall find that it is not so much upon account of the superior ease or pleasure which they are supposed to enjoy, as of the numberless artificial and elegant contrivances for promoting this ease or pleasure. He does not even imagine that they are really happier than other people: but he imagines that they possess more means of happiness. And it is the ingenious and artful adjustment of those means to the end for which they were intended, that is the principal source of his admiration. But in the languor of disease and the weariness of old age, the pleasures of the vain and empty distinctions of greatness disappear. To one, in this situation, they are no longer capable of recommending those toilsome pursuits in which they had formerly engaged him. In his heart he curses ambition, and vainly regrets the ease and the indolence of youth, pleasures which are fled for ever, and which he has foolishly sacrificed for what, when he has got it, can afford him no real satisfaction. In this miserable aspect does greatness appear to every man when reduced either by spleen or disease to observe with attention his own situation, and to consider what it is that is really wanting to his happiness. Power and riches appear then to be, what they are, enormous and operose machines contrived[4] to produce a few trifling conveniencies to

---

[4] Probably recalls 'operose Contrivances' in Mandeville, *Fable of the Bees*, Remark (L) on luxury; ed. F. B. Kaye, i.119.

the body, consisting of springs the most nice and delicate, which must be kept in order with the most anxious attention, and which in spite of all our care are ready every moment to burst into pieces, and to crush in their ruins their unfortunate possessor. They are immense fabrics, which it requires the labour of a life to raise, which threaten every moment to overwhelm the person that dwells in them, and which while they stand, though they may save him from some smaller inconveniencies, can protect him from none of the severer inclemencies of the season. They keep off the summer shower, not the winter storm, but leave him always as much, and sometimes more exposed than before, to anxiety, to fear, and to sorrow; to diseases, to danger, and to death.

9   But though this splenetic philosophy, which in time of sickness or low spirits is familiar to every man, thus entirely depreciates those great objects of human desire, when in better health and in better humour, we never fail to regard them under a more agreeable aspect. Our imagination, which in pain and sorrow seems to be confined and cooped up within our own persons, in times of ease and prosperity expands itself to every thing around us. We are then charmed with the beauty of that accommodation which reigns in the palaces and oeconomy of the great; and admire how every thing is adapted to promote their ease, to prevent their wants, to gratify their wishes, and to amuse and entertain their most frivolous desires. If we consider the real satisfaction which all these things are capable of affording, by itself and separated from the beauty of that arrangement which is fitted to promote it, it will always appear in the highest degree contemptible and trifling. But we rarely view it in this abstract and philosophical light. We naturally confound it in our imagination with the order, the regular and harmonious movement of the system, the machine or oeconomy by means of which it is produced. The pleasures of wealth and greatness, when considered in this complex view, strike the imagination as something grand and beautiful and noble, of which the attainment is well worth all the toil and anxiety which we are so apt to bestow upon it.

10   And it is well that nature imposes upon us in this manner. It is this deception which rouses and keeps in continual motion the industry of mankind. It is this which first prompted them to cultivate the ground, to build houses, to found cities and commonwealths, and to invent and improve all the sciences and arts, which ennoble and embellish human life; which have entirely changed the whole face of the globe, have turned the rude forests of nature into agreeable and fertile plains,[5] and made the track-

---

[5] Recalls Smith's translation, in his 'Letter to the Editors of the *Edinburgh Review*' (now published in EPS), 13, of a passage from Rousseau, *Discours sur l'origine de l'inégalité*: 'and the vast forrests of nature were changed into agreeable plains'. Rousseau's own words were: 'les vastes forêts se changèrent en des campagnes riantes'. Smith's repetition of the phrase here may be mere coincidence, but it is also possible (as was suggested to us by

less and barren ocean a new fund of subsistence, and the great high road of communication to the different nations of the earth. The earth by these labours of mankind has been obliged to redouble her natural fertility, and to maintain a greater multitude of inhabitants. It is to no purpose, that the proud and unfeeling landlord views his extensive fields, and without a thought for the wants of his brethren, in imagination consumes himself the whole harvest that grows upon them. The homely and vulgar proverb, that the eye is larger than the belly, never was more fully verified than with regard to him. The capacity of his stomach bears no proportion to the immensity of his desires, and will receive no more than that of the meanest peasant.[6] The rest he is obliged to distribute among those, who prepare, in the nicest manner, that little which he himself makes use of, among those who fit up the palace in which this little is to be consumed, among those who provide and keep in order all the different baubles and trinkets, which are employed in the oeconomy of greatness; all of whom thus derive from his luxury and caprice, that share of the necessaries of life, which they would in vain have expected from his humanity or his justice. The produce of the soil maintains at all times nearly that number of inhabitants which it is capable of maintaining. The rich only select from the heap what is most precious and agreeable. They consume little more than the poor, and in spite of their natural selfishness and rapacity, though they mean only their own conveniency, though the sole end which they propose from the labours of all the thousands whom they employ, be the gratification of their own vain and insatiable desires, they divide with the poor the produce of all their improvements. They are led by an invisible hand[7] to make nearly

H. B. Acton) that Smith is implicitly contesting Rousseau's view that the acquisition of property causes inequality. The phrase about the forests is preceded, in the translation from Rousseau, by '. . . equality disappeared, property was introduced, labour became necessary, . . .' In the present paragraph of TMS Smith proceeds to argue that the rich are led by an invisible hand to make a distribution of necessities that is nearly the same as would exist in a state of natural equality. In the 'Letter' Smith introduced Rousseau as a critic of Mandeville, and he may well have both writers in mind here also (cf. preceding note).

[6] Cf. WN I.xi.c.7: 'The rich man consumes no more food than his poor neighbour. . . . The desire of food is limited in every man by the narrow capacity of the human stomach; but the desire of the conveniencies and ornaments . . . seems to have no limit or certain boundary.' See A. L. Macfie, *Individual in Society*, III–VI, for relation of TMS to WN.

[7] The phrase recurs in WN IV.ii.9: 'every individual necessarily labours to render the annual revenue of the society as great as he can. He generally, indeed, neither intends to promote the public interest, nor knows how much he is promoting it. . . . he intends only his own gain, and he is . . . led by an invisible hand to promote an end which was no part of his intention.' In both places Smith says that the end unintentionally promoted is the interest of society, but there is a difference: the TMS passage refers to the distribution of means to happiness, the WN passage to maximization.

Smith first used the expression 'invisible hand' in Astronomy, III.2, when writing of early religious thought, in which only irregular events were attributed to supernatural agency. 'Fire burns, and water refreshes; heavy bodies descend, and lighter substances fly upwards, by the necessity of their own nature; nor was the invisible hand of Jupiter ever

the same distribution of the necessaries of life, which would have been made, had the earth been divided into equal portions among all its inhabitants, and thus without intending it, without knowing it, advance the interest of the society, and afford means to the multiplication of the species. When Providence divided the earth among a few lordly masters, it neither forgot nor abandoned those who seemed to have been left out in the partition. These last too enjoy their share of all that it produces. In what constitutes the real happiness of human life, they are in no respect inferior to those who would seem so much above them. In ease of body and peace of mind, all the different ranks of life are nearly upon a level, and the beggar, who suns himself by the side of the highway, possesses that security which kings are fighting for.

11   The same principle, the same love of system, the same regard to the beauty of order, of art and contrivance, frequently serves to recommend those institutions which tend to promote the public welfare. When a patriot exerts himself for the improvement of any part of the public police, his conduct does not always arise from pure sympathy with the happiness of those who are to reap the benefit of it. It is not commonly from a fellow-feeling with carriers and waggoners that a public-spirited man encourages the mending of high roads. When the legislature establishes premiums and other encouragements to advance the linen or woollen manufactures, its conduct seldom proceeds from pure sympathy with the wearer of cheap or fine cloth, and much less from that with the manufacturer or merchant. The perfection of police, the extension of trade and manufactures, are noble and magnificent objects. The contemplation of them pleases us, and we are interested in whatever can tend to advance them. They make part of the great system of government, and the wheels of the political machine seem to move with more harmony and ease by means of them. We take pleasure in beholding the perfection of so beautiful and grand a system, and we are uneasy till we remove any obstruction that can in the least disturb or encumber the regularity of its motions. All constitutions of government, however, are valued only in proportion as they tend to promote the happiness of those who live under them. This is their sole use and end. From a certain spirit of system, however, from a certain love of art and contrivance, we sometimes seem to value the means more than the end, and to be eager to promote the happiness of our fellow-creatures, rather from a view to perfect and improve a certain beautiful and orderly system, than from any immediate sense or feeling of what they either suffer or enjoy. There have been men of the greatest public spirit, who have shown themselves in other respects not very sensible to the feelings of humanity. And on the contrary, there have been men of the greatest humanity, who seem to have

apprehended to be employed in those matters.' See A. L. Macfie, 'The Invisible Hand of Jupiter', *Journal of the History of Ideas*, xxxii (1971), 595-9.

been entirely devoid of public spirit. Every man may find in the circle of
his acquaintance instances both of the one kind and the other. Who had
ever less humanity, or more public spirit, than the celebrated legislator of
Muscovy?[8] The social and well-natured James the First of Great Britain
seems, on the contrary, to have had scarce any passion, either for the glory
or the interest of his country. Would you awaken the industry of the man
who seems almost dead to ambition, it will often be to no purpose to describe to him the happiness of the rich and the great; to tell him that they
are generally sheltered from the sun and the rain, that they are seldom
hungry, that they are seldom cold, and that they are rarely exposed to
weariness, or to want of any kind. The most eloquent exhortation of this
kind will have little effect upon him. If you would hope to succeed, you
must describe to him the conveniency and arrangement of the different
apartments in their palaces; you must explain to him the propriety of their
equipages, and point out to him the number, the order, and the different
offices of all their attendants. If any thing is capable of making impression
upon him, this will. Yet all these things tend only to keep off the sun and
the rain, to save them from hunger and cold, from want and weariness. In
the same manner, if you would implant public virtue in the breast of him
who seems heedless of the interest of his country, it will often be to no
purpose to tell him, what superior advantages the subjects of a well-
governed state enjoy; that they are better lodged, that they are better
clothed, that they are better fed. These considerations will commonly
make no great impression. You will be more likely to persuade, if you
describe the great system of public police which procures these advantages,
if you explain the connexions and dependencies of its several parts, their
mutual subordination to one another, and their general subserviency to the
happiness of the society; if you show how this system might be introduced
into his own country, what it is that hinders it from taking place there at
present, how those obstructions might be removed, and all the several
wheels of the machine of government be made to move with more harmony
and smoothness, without grating upon one another, or mutually retarding
one another's motions. It is scarce possible that a man should listen to a
discourse of this kind, and not feel himself animated to some degree of
public spirit. He will, at least for the moment, feel some desire to remove
those obstructions, and to put into motion so beautiful and so orderly a
machine. Nothing tends so much to promote public spirit as the study of
politics, of the several systems of civil government, their advantages and
disadvantages, of the constitution of our own country, its situation, and
interest with regard to foreign nations, its commerce, its defence, the disadvantages it labours under, the dangers to which it may be exposed, how
to remove the one, and how to guard against the other. Upon this account

[8] Peter the Great.

political disquisitions, if just, and reasonable, and practicable, are of all the works of speculation the most useful. Even the weakest and the worst of them are not altogether without their utility. They serve at least to animate the public passions of men, and rouse them to seek out the means of promoting the happiness of the society.

^aCHAP. II^a

Of the beauty which the appearance of Utility bestows upon the characters and actions of men; and how far the perception of this beauty may be regarded as one of the original principles of approbation

1   THE characters of men, as well as the contrivances of art, or the institutions of civil government, may be fitted either to promote or to disturb the happiness both of the individual and of the society. The prudent, the equitable, the active, resolute, and sober character promises prosperity and satisfaction, both to the person himself and to every one connected with him. The rash, the insolent, the slothful, effeminate, and voluptuous, on the contrary, forebodes ruin to the individual, and misfortune to all who have any thing to do with him. The first turn of mind has at least all the beauty which can belong to the most perfect machine that was ever invented for promoting the most agreeable purpose: and the second, all the deformity of the most awkward and clumsy contrivance. What institution of government could tend so much to promote the happiness of mankind as the general prevalence of wisdom and virtue? All government is but an imperfect remedy for the deficiency of these. Whatever beauty, therefore, can belong to civil government upon account of its utility, must in a far superior degree belong to these. On the contrary, what civil policy can be so ruinous and destructive as the vices of men? The fatal effects of bad government arise from nothing, but that it does not sufficiently guard against the mischiefs which human wickedness gives occasion to.

2   This beauty and deformity which characters appear to derive from their usefulness or inconveniency, are apt to strike, in a peculiar manner, those who consider, in an abstract and philosophical light, the actions and conduct of mankind. When a philosopher goes to examine why humanity is approved of, or cruelty condemned, he does not always form to himself, in a very clear and distinct manner, the conception of any one particular action either of cruelty or of humanity, but is commonly contented with the vague and indeterminate idea which the general names of those qualities suggest to him. But it is in particular instances only that the propriety or

^{a-a} SECT. II *1*

impropriety, the merit or demerit of actions is very obvious and discernible. It is only when particular examples are given that we perceive distinctly either the concord or disagreement between our own affections and those of the agent, or feel a social gratitude arise towards him in the one case, or a sympathetic resentment in the other. When we consider virtue and vice in an abstract and general manner, the qualities by which they excite these several sentiments seem in a great measure to disappear, and the sentiments themselves become less obvious and discernible. On the contrary, the happy effects of the one and the fatal consequences of the other seem then to rise up to the view, and as it were to stand out and distinguish themselves from all the other qualities of either.

3   The same ingenious and agreeable author who first explained why utility pleases, has been so struck with this view of things, as to resolve our whole approbation of virtue into a perception of this species of beauty which results from the appearance of utility. No qualities of the mind, he observes, are approved of as virtuous, but such as are useful or agreeable either to the person himself or to others;[1] and no qualities are disapproved of as vicious but such as have a contrary tendency. And Nature, indeed, seems to have so happily adjusted our sentiments of approbation and disapprobation, to the conveniency both of the individual and of the society, that after the strictest examination it will be found, I believe, that this is universally the case. But still I affirm, that it is not the view of this utility or hurtfulness which is either the first or principal source of our approbation and disapprobation. These sentiments are no doubt enhanced and enlivened by the perception of the beauty or deformity which results from this utility or hurtfulness. But still, I say, they are originally and essentially different from this perception.

4   For first of all, it seems impossible that the approbation of virtue should be a sentiment of the same kind with that by which we approve of a convenient and well-contrived building; or that we should have no other reason for praising a man than that for which we commend a chest of drawers.[2]

5   And secondly, it will be found, upon examination, that the usefulness of any disposition of mind is seldom the first ground of our approbation; and that the sentiment of approbation always involves in it a sense of propriety quite distinct from the perception of utility. We may observe this with regard to all the qualities which are approved of as virtuous, both those which, according to this system, are originally valued as useful to ourselves,

---

[1] Hume, *Treatise of Human Nature*, III.iii.1; ed. Selby-Bigge, 591: *Enquiry concerning the Principles of Morals*, especially IX.i; ed. Selby-Bigge, §§ 217, 219, 226.

[2] Hume must have had an objection of this character put to him, for he attempts to reply to it in a footnote appended to *Enquiry concerning the Principles of Morals*, V.i, first paragraph; ed. Selby-Bigge, § 172. The footnote is in all editions of the *Enquiry*, including the first (1751).

as well as those which are esteemed on account of their usefulness to others.

6   The qualities most useful to ourselves are, first of all, superior reason and understanding, by which we are capable of discerning the remote consequences of all our actions, and of foreseeing the advantage or detriment which is likely to result from them: and secondly, self-command, by which we are enabled to abstain from present pleasure or to endure present pain, in order to obtain a greater pleasure or to avoid a greater pain in some future time. In the union of those two qualities consists the virtue of prudence, of all the virtues that which is most useful to the individual.

7   With regard to the first of those qualities, it has been observed on a former occasion,[3] that superior reason and understanding are originally approved of as just and right and accurate, and not merely as useful or advantageous. It is in the abstruser sciences, particularly in the higher parts of mathematics, that the greatest and most admired exertions of human reason have been displayed. But the utility of those sciences, either to the individual or to the public, is not very obvious, and to prove it, requires a discussion which is not always very easily comprehended. It was not, therefore, their utility which first recommended them to the public admiration. This quality was but little insisted upon, till it became necessary to make some reply to the reproaches of those, who, having themselves no taste for such sublime discoveries, endeavoured to depreciate them as useless.

8   That self-command, in the same manner, by which we restrain our present appetites, in order to gratify them more fully upon another occasion, is approved of, as much under the aspect of propriety, as under that of utility. When we act in this manner, the sentiments which influence our conduct seem exactly to coincide with those of the spectator. The spectator does not feel the solicitations of our present appetites. To him the pleasure which we are to enjoy a week hence, or a year hence, is just as interesting as that which we are to enjoy this moment. When for the sake of the present, therefore, we sacrifice the future, our conduct appears to him absurd and extravagant in the highest degree, and he cannot enter into the principles which influence it. On the contrary, when we abstain from present pleasure, in order to secure greater pleasure to come, when we act as if the remote object interested us as much as that which immediately presses upon the senses, as our affections exactly correspond with his own, he cannot fail to approve of our behaviour: and as he knows from experience, how few are capable of this self-command, he looks upon our conduct with a considerable degree of wonder and admiration. Hence arises that eminent esteem with which all men naturally regard a steady perseverance in the

---

[3] I.i.4.4. The word 'occasion' is a relic of the original lecture form of Smith's material. Cf. § 9 below and VII.iii.1.2.

practice of frugality, industry, and application, though directed to no other purpose than the acquisition of fortune. The resolute firmness of the person who acts in this manner, and in order to obtain a great though remote advantage, not only gives up all present pleasures, but endures the greatest labour both of mind and body, necessarily commands our approbation. That view of his interest and happiness which appears to regulate his conduct, exactly tallies with the idea which we naturally form of it. There is the most perfect correspondence between his sentiments and our own, and at the same time, from our experience of the common weakness of human nature, it is a correspondence which we could not reasonably have expected. We not only approve, therefore, but in some measure admire his conduct, and think it worthy of a considerable degree of applause. It is the consciousness of this merited approbation and esteem which is alone capable of supporting the agent in this tenour of conduct. The pleasure which we are to enjoy ten years hence interests us so little in comparison with that which we may enjoy to-day, the passion which the first excites, is naturally so weak in comparison with that violent emotion which the second is apt to give occasion to, that the one could never be any balance to the other, unless it was supported by the sense of propriety, by the consciousness that we merited the esteem and approbation of every body, by acting in the one way, and that we became the proper objects of their contempt and derision by behaving in the other.

9   Humanity, justice, generosity, and public spirit, are the qualities most useful to others. Wherein consists the propriety of humanity and justice has been explained upon a former occasion,[4] where it was shewn how much our esteem and approbation of those qualities depended upon the concord between the affections of the agent and those of the spectators.

10   The propriety of generosity and public spirit is founded upon the same principle with that of justice. Generosity is different from humanity. Those two qualities, which at first sight seem so nearly allied, do not always belong to the same person. Humanity is the virtue of a woman, generosity of a man. The fair-sex, who have commonly much more tenderness than ours, have seldom so much generosity. That women rarely make considerable donations, is an observation of the civil law*. Humanity consists merely in the exquisite fellow-feeling which the spectator entertains with the sentiments of the persons principally concerned, so as to grieve for their

* Raro mulieres donare solent.[5]

---

[4] I.i.3.1. The word 'occasion' again shows the original lecture form of the material (cf. § 7 above and VII.iii.1.2), but in the lecture the next word 'where' will have been 'when'.

[5] We are advised by Professor Peter Stein that although this phrase does not occur in the *Corpus Iuris Civilis*, it was a maxim coined by later commentators in the light of passages on the miserly character of women to be found in the Great Gloss of Accursius (thirteenth century), which came to be regarded as an authoritative part of the civil law. The phrase is given in S. Daoyz, *Iuris Civilis Summa seu Index* (1742), under *mulier*.

sufferings, to resent their injuries, and to rejoice at their good fortune. The most humane actions require no self-denial, no self-command, no great exertion of the sense of propriety. They consist only in doing what this exquisite sympathy would of its own accord prompt us to do. But it is otherwise with generosity. We never are generous except when in some respect we prefer some other person to ourselves, and sacrifice some great and important interest of our own to an equal interest of a friend or of a superior. The man who gives up his pretensions to an office that was the great object of his ambition, because he imagines that the services of another are better entitled to it; the man who exposes his life to defend that of his friend, which he judges to be of more *b*importance;*b* neither of them act from humanity, or because they feel more exquisitely what concerns that other person than what concerns themselves. They both consider those opposite interests, not in the light in which they naturally appear to themselves, but in that in which they appear to others. To every bystander, the success or preservation of this other person may justly be more interesting than their own; but it cannot be so to themselves. When to the interest of this other person, therefore, they sacrifice their own, they accommodate themselves to the sentiments of the spectator, and by an effort of magnanimity act according to those views of things *c*which, they feel,*c* must naturally occur to any third person. The soldier who throws away his life in order to defend that of his officer, would perhaps be but little affected by the death of that officer, if it should happen without any fault of his own; and a very small disaster which had befallen himself might excite a much more lively sorrow. But when he endeavours to act so as to deserve applause, and to make the impartial spectator enter into the principles of his conduct, he feels, that to every body but himself, his own life is a trifle compared with that of his officer, and that when he sacrifices the one to the other, he acts quite properly and agreeably to what would be the natural apprehensions of every impartial bystander.

11   It is the same case with the greater exertions of public spirit. When a young officer exposes his life to acquire some inconsiderable addition to the dominions of his sovereign, it is not because the acquisition of the new territory is, to himself, an object more desireable than the preservation of his own life. To him his own life is of infinitely more value than the conquest of a whole kingdom for the state which he serves. But when he compares those two objects with one another, he does not view them in the light in which they naturally appear to himself, but in that in which they appear to the nation he fights for. To them the success of the war is of the highest importance; the life of a private person of scarce any consequence. When he puts himself in their situation, he immediately feels that he cannot be too prodigal of his blood, if, by shedding it, he can promote so valuable a

b–b 5 ∼, *1–4* 6 7   *c–c* 2 ∼∧ ∼, *1 3 4* 6 7 ∼∧ ∼∧ 5 purpose. In thus thwarting, from a sense of duty and propriety, the strongest of all natural propensities, consists the heroism of his conduct. There is many an honest Englishman, who, in his private station, would be more seriously disturbed by the loss of a guinea, than by the national loss of Minorca, who yet, had it been in his power to defend that fortress, would have sacrificed his life a thousand times rather than, through his fault, have let it fall into the hands of the enemy.[6] When the first Brutus led forth his own sons to a capital punishment, because they had conspired against the rising liberty of Rome,[7] he sacrificed what, if he had consulted his own breast only, would appear to be the stronger to the weaker affection. Brutus ought naturally to have felt much more for the death of his own sons, than for all that probably Rome could have suffered from the want of so great an example. But he viewed them, not with the eyes of a father, but with those of a Roman citizen. He entered so thoroughly into the sentiments of this last character, that he paid no regard to that tie, by which he himself was connected with them; and to a Roman citizen, the sons even of Brutus seemed contemptible, when put into the balance with the smallest interest of Rome. In these and in all other cases of this kind, our admiration is not so much founded upon the utility, as upon the unexpected, and on that account the great, the noble, and exalted propriety of such actions. This utility, when we come to view it, bestows upon them, undoubtedly, a new beauty, and upon that account still further recommends them to our approbation. This beauty, however, is chiefly perceived by men of reflection and speculation, and is by no means the quality which first recommends such actions to the natural sentiments of the bulk of mankind.

12   It is to be observed, that so far as the sentiment of approbation arises from the perception of this beauty of utility, it has no reference of any kind to the sentiments of others. If it was possible, therefore, that a person should grow up to manhood without any communication with society, his own actions might, notwithstanding, be agreeable or disagreeable to him on account of their tendency to his happiness or disadvantage. [d]He[d] might perceive a beauty of this kind in prudence, temperance, and good conduct, and a deformity in the opposite behaviour: he might view his own temper and character with that sort of satisfaction with which we consider a well-contrived machine, in the one case; or with that sort of distaste and dissatisfaction with which we regard a very awkward and clumsy contrivance,

[d-d] *1–5* 7   he 6

---

[6] Smith is doubtless referring to the ignominious failure of Admiral Byng in May 1756 to defeat the French fleet blockading Minorca, then a British possession.

[7] Lucius Junius Brutus is called the founder of the Roman Republic because he led the Romans in the expulsion of their tyrannical king Tarquinius Superbus. Brutus was then elected consul in 509 B.C. Tradition has it that he condemned his two sons to death for joining a conspiracy to restore the Tarquins.

in the other. As these perceptions, however, are merely a matter of taste, and have all the feebleness and delicacy of that species of perceptions, upon the justness of which what is properly called taste is founded, they probably would not be much attended to by one in ᵉthisᵉ solitary and miserable condition. Even though they should occur to him, they would by no means have the same effect upon him, antecedent to his connexion with society, which they would have in consequence of that connexion. He would not be cast down with inward shame at the thought of this deformity; nor would he be elevated with secret triumph of mind from the consciousness of the contrary beauty. He would not exult from the notion of deserving reward in the one case, nor tremble from the suspicion of meriting punishment in the other. All such sentiments suppose the idea of some other being, who is the natural judge of the person that feels them; and it is only by sympathy with the decisions of this arbiter of his conduct, that he can conceive, either the triumph of self-applause, or the shame of self-condemnation.

ᵉ⁻ᵉ *1 2E* his *2–7*

PART V

Of the INFLUENCE of CUSTOM and FASHION upon the Sentiments of Moral Approbation and Disapprobation
*a*Consisting of One Section*a*

*b*CHAP. I*b*

Of the Influence of Custom and Fashion upon our Notions of Beauty and Deformity

1 THERE are other principles besides those already enumerated, which have a considerable influence upon the moral sentiments of mankind, and are the chief causes of the many irregular and discordant opinions which prevail in different ages and nations concerning what is blameable or praise-worthy. These principles are custom and fashion, principles which extend their dominion over our judgments concerning beauty of every kind.

2 When two objects have frequently been seen together, the imagination acquires a habit of passing easily from the one to the other. If the first appear, we lay our account that the second is to follow. Of their own accord they put us in mind of one another, and the attention glides easily along them. Though, independent of custom, there should be no real beauty in their union, yet when custom has thus connected them together, we feel an impropriety in their separation. The one we think is awkward when it appears without its usual companion. We miss something which we expected to find, and the habitual arrangement of our ideas is disturbed by the disappointment. A suit of clothes, for example, seems to want something if they are without the most insignificant ornament which usually accompanies them, and we find a meanness or awkwardness in the absence even of a haunch button. When there is any natural propriety in the union, custom increases our sense of it, and makes a different arrangement appear still more disagreeable than it would otherwise seem to be. Those who have been accustomed to see things in a good taste, are more disgusted by whatever is clumsy or awkward. Where the conjunction is improper, custom either diminishes, or takes away altogether, our sense of the impropriety. Those who have been accustomed to slovenly disorder lose all sense of neatness or elegance. The modes of furniture or dress which seem ridiculous to strangers, give no offence to the people who are used to them.

3 Fashion is different from custom, or rather is a particular species of it. That is not the fashion which every body wears, but which those wear who are of a high rank, or character. The graceful, the easy, and commanding

a–a om. 1 Consisting of one Section *2 3* Consisting of one SECTION *4 5*
b–b SECT. I *1*

manners of the great, joined to the usual richness and magnificence of their dress, give a grace to the very form which they happen to bestow upon it. As long as they continue to use this form, it is connected in our imaginations with the idea of something that is genteel and magnificent, and though in itself it should be indifferent, it seems, on account of this relation, to have something about it that is genteel and magnificent too. As soon as they drop it, it loses all the grace, which it had appeared to possess before, and being now used only by the inferior ranks of people, seems to have something of their meanness and awkwardness.

4   Dress and furniture are allowed by all the world to be entirely under the dominion of custom and fashion. The influence of those principles, however, is by no means confined to so narrow a sphere, but extends itself to whatever is in any respect the object of taste, to music, to poetry, to architecture. The modes of dress and furniture are continually changing, and that fashion appearing ridiculous to-day which was admired five years ago, we are experimentally convinced that it owed its vogue chiefly or entirely to custom and fashion. Clothes and furniture are not made of very durable materials. A well-fancied coat is done in a twelve-month, and cannot continue longer to propagate, as the fashion, that form according to which it was made. The modes of furniture change less rapidly than those of dress; because furniture is commonly more durable. In five or six years, however, it generally undergoes an entire revolution, and every man in his own time sees the fashion in this respect change many different ways. The productions of the other arts are much more lasting, and, when happily imagined, may continue to propagate the fashion of their make for a much longer time. A well-contrived building may endure many centuries: a beautiful air may be delivered down by a sort of tradition, through many successive generations: a well-written poem may last as long as the world; and all of them continue for ages together, to give the vogue to that particular style, to that particular taste or manner, according to which each of them was composed. Few men have an opportunity of seeing in their own times the fashion in any of these arts change very considerably. Few men have so much experience and acquaintance with the different modes which have obtained in remote ages and nations, as to be thoroughly reconciled to them, or to judge with impartiality between them, and what takes place in their own age and country. Few men therefore are willing to allow, that custom or fashion have much influence upon their judgments concerning what is beautiful, or otherwise, in the productions of any of those arts; but imagine, that all the rules, which they think ought to be observed in each of them, are founded upon reason and nature, not upon habit or prejudice. A very little attention, however, may convince them of the contrary, and satisfy them, that the influence of custom and fashion over dress and furniture, is not more absolute than over architecture, poetry, and music.

5   Can any reason, for example, be assigned why the Doric capital should be appropriated to a pillar, whose height is equal to eight diameters; the Ionic volute to one of nine; and the Corinthian foliage to one of ten? The propriety of each of those appropriations can be founded upon nothing but habit and custom. The eye having been used to see a particular proportion connected with a particular ornament, would be offended if they were not joined together. Each of the five orders has its peculiar ornaments, which cannot be changed for any other, without giving offence to all those who know any thing of the rules of architecture. According to some architects, indeed, such is the exquisite judgment with which the ancients have assigned to each order its proper ornaments, that no others can be found which are equally suitable. It seems, however, a little difficult to be conceived that these forms, though, no doubt, extremely agreeable, should be the only forms which can suit those proportions, or that there should not be five hundred others which, antecedent to established custom, would have fitted them equally well. When custom, however, has established particular rules of building, provided they are not absolutely unreasonable, it is absurd to think of altering them for others which are only equally good, or even for others which, in point of elegance and beauty, have naturally some little advantage over them. A man would be ridiculous who should appear in public with a suit of clothes quite different from those which are commonly worn, though the new dress should in itself be ever so graceful or convenient. And there seems to be an absurdity of the same kind in ornamenting a house after a quite different manner from that which custom and fashion have prescribed; though the new ornaments should in themselves be somewhat superior to the common ones.

6   According to the ancient rhetoricians, a certain measure ᶜofᶜ verse was by nature appropriated to each particular species of writing, as being naturally expressive of that character, sentiment, or passion, which ought to predominate in it. One verse, they said, was fit for grave and another for gay works, which could not, they thought, be interchanged without the greatest impropriety.[1] The experience of modern times, however, seems to contradict this principle, though in itself it would appear to be extremely probable. What is the burlesque verse in English, is the heroic verse in French. The tragedies of Racine and the Henriad of Voltaire, are ᵈnearlyᵈ in the same verse with,

ᵉLet me have your advice in a weighty affair.ᵉ

ᶜ⁻ᶜ *1 2E* or *2–7*   ᵈ⁻ᵈ om. *1–5*   ᵉ⁻ᵉ *Thus said to my lady the knight full of care. 1–5*

---

[1] e.g. Aristotle, *Poetics*, 1459ᵇ31–1460ᵃ4; Horace, *Ars Poetica*, 73–98. Smith's subsequent remarks about 'the heroic verse' suggest that he has in mind especially Aristotle's statement that it would be 'improper' to compose an epic poem in any metre other than 'the heroic', which is 'the most grave and weighty' of metres, while the iambic and the trochaic are 'lively'.

The burlesque verse in French, on the contrary, is pretty much the same with the heroic verse of ten syllables in English. Custom has made the one nation associate the ideas of gravity, sublimity, and seriousness, to that measure which the other has connected with whatever is gay, flippant, and ludicrous. Nothing would appear more absurd in English, than a tragedy written in the Alexandrine verses of the French; or in French, than a work of the same kind in verses of ten syllables.[2]

7   An eminent artist will bring about a considerable change in the established modes of each of those arts, and introduce a new fashion of writing, music, or architecture. As the dress of an agreeable man of high rank recommends itself, and how peculiar and fantastical soever, comes soon to be admired and imitated; so the excellencies of an eminent master recommend his peculiarities, and his manner becomes the fashionable style in the art which he practises. The taste of the Italians in music and architecture has, within these fifty years, undergone a considerable change, from imitating the peculiarities of some eminent masters in each of those arts. Seneca is accused by Quintilian[3] of having corrupted the taste of the Romans, and of having introduced a frivolous prettiness in the room of majestic reason and masculine eloquence. Sallust and Tacitus have by others been charged with the same accusation, though in a different manner. They gave reputation, it is pretended, to a style, which though in the highest degree concise, elegant, expressive, and even poetical, wanted, however, ease, simplicity, and nature, and was evidently the production of the most laboured and studied affectation. How many great qualities must that writer possess, who can thus render his very faults agreeable? After the praise of refining the taste of a nation, the highest eulogy, perhaps, which can be bestowed upon

[2] The plays of Racine and the *Henriade* of Voltaire are both written in Alexandrines, i.e. lines of twelve syllables. The earlier and the later variants of the line of English verse are, respectively, the first and the second line of a burlesque poem of 1729 by Swift, 'The Grand Question debated. Whether *Hamilton's Bawn* should be turned into a *Barrack* or a *Malt-House*.' By 'the burlesque verse in French' Smith means the line of ten syllables, which was in fact little used in the eighteenth century except by Voltaire in his comedies and in his mock-heroic poem *La Pucelle d'Orléans*, and by J.-B. Rousseau in his *Épîtres*. Smith is undoubtedly thinking of its use by Voltaire; cf. the close of III.2, where he quotes a couplet from *La Pucelle*. By 'the heroic verse of ten syllables in English' Smith means Miltonic blank verse.

Smith's comparison between French and English verses here depends entirely on counting the number of syllables in a line, a criterion that is appropriate for French verse but quite inappropriate for English. (Eckstein, i.575, observes that Smith's replacement in ed. 6 of the first by the second line of Swift's poem must have been because he noticed that the first line has only eleven syllables. Hence also the insertion of 'nearly' in ed. 6.) Smith is equally mistaken in supposing that the French necessarily associate the Alexandrine with 'the ideas of gravity, sublimity, and seriousness'. From Corneille onwards it has been the standard line also for verse comedy.

In English and Italian Verses, Smith compares 'English heroic verse' with Italian. He again writes of the number of syllables in a line, but recognizes in the last paragraph that this is less significant than the number of feet.

[3] Cf. *Institutio Oratoria*, X.i.125–31.

any author, is to say, that he corrupted it. In our own language, Mr. Pope and Dr. Swift have each of them introduced a manner different from what was practised before, into all works that are written in rhyme, the one in long verses, the other in short. The quaintness of Butler[4] has given place to the plainness of Swift. The rambling freedom of Dryden, and the correct but often tedious and prosaic languor of Addison, are no longer the objects of imitation, but all long verses are now written after the manner of the nervous precision of Mr. Pope.

8   Neither is it only over the productions of the arts, that custom and fashion exert their dominion. They influence our judgments, in the same manner, with regard to the beauty of natural objects. What various and opposite forms are deemed beautiful in different species of things? The proportions which are admired in one animal, are altogether different from those which are esteemed in another. Every class of things has its own peculiar conformation, which is approved of, and has a beauty of its own, distinct from that of every other species. It is upon this account that a learned Jesuit, father Buffier,[5] has determined that the beauty of every object consists in that form and colour, which is most usual among things of that particular sort to which it belongs. Thus, in the human form, the beauty of each feature lies in a certain middle, equally removed from a variety of other forms that are ugly. A beautiful nose, for example, is one that is neither very long, nor very short, neither very straight, nor very crooked, but a sort of middle among all these extremes, and less different from any one of them, than all of them are from one another. It is the form which Nature seems to have aimed at in them all, which, however, she deviates from in a great variety of ways, and very seldom hits exactly; but to which all those deviations still bear a very strong resemblance. When a number of drawings are made after one pattern, though they may all miss it in some respects, yet they will all resemble it more than they resemble one another; the general character of the pattern will run through them all; the most singular and odd will be those which are most wide of it; and though very few will copy it exactly, yet the most accurate delineations will bear a greater resemblance to the most careless, than the careless ones will bear to one another. In the same manner, in each species of creatures, what is most beautiful bears the strongest characters of the general fabric of the species, and has the strongest resemblance to the greater part of the individuals with which it is classed. Monsters, on the contrary, or what is perfectly deformed, are always most singular and odd, and have the least resemblance to the generality of that species to which they belong. And thus the beauty of each species, though in one sense the rarest of all things, because

---

[4] Samuel Butler, author of *Hudibras*.

[5] Claude Buffier, *Traité des premières vérités et de la source de nos jugements*, Part I, ch. 13.

few individuals hit this middle form exactly, yet in another, is the most
common, because all the deviations from it resemble it more than they
resemble one another. The most customary form, therefore, is in each
species of things, according to him, the most beautiful. And hence it is
that a certain practice and experience in contemplating each species
of objects is requisite, before we can judge of its beauty, or know
wherein the middle and most usual form consists. The nicest judgment
concerning the beauty of the human species, will not help us to judge of
that of flowers, or horses, or any other species of things. It is for the same
reason that in different climates, and where different customs and ways of
living take place, as the generality of any species receives a different conformation from those circumstances, so different ideas of its beauty prevail.
The beauty of a Moorish is not exactly the same with that of an English
horse. What different ideas are formed in different nations concerning the
beauty of the human shape and countenance? A fair complexion is a shocking deformity upon the coast of Guinea. Thick lips and a flat nose are a
beauty. In some nations long ears that hang down upon the shoulders are
the objects of universal admiration. In China if a lady's foot is so large as
to be fit to walk upon, she is regarded as a monster of ugliness. Some of
the savage nations in North-America tie four boards round the heads of
their children, and thus squeeze them, while the bones are tender and
gristly, into a form that is almost perfectly square. Europeans are astonished
at the absurd barbarity of this practice, to which some missionaries have
imputed the singular stupidity of those nations among whom it prevails.
But when they condemn those savages, they do not reflect that the ladies
in Europe had, till within these very few years, been endeavouring, for near
a century past, to squeeze the beautiful roundness of their natural shape
into a square form of the same kind. And that, notwithstanding the many
distortions and diseases which this practice was known to occasion,
custom had rendered it agreeable among some of the most civilized nations
which, perhaps, the world ever beheld.

9   Such is the system of this learned and ingenious Father, concerning the
nature of beauty; of which the whole charm, according to him, would
thus seem to arise from its falling in with the habits which custom had
impressed upon the imagination, with regard to things of each particular
kind. I cannot, however, be induced to believe that our sense even of
external beauty is founded altogether on custom. The utility of any form,
its fitness for the useful purposes for which it was intended, evidently
recommends it, and renders it agreeable to us, independent of custom.
Certain colours are more agreeable than others, and give more delight to
the eye the first time it ever beholds them. A smooth surface is more agreeable than a rough one. Variety is more pleasing than a tedious undiversified
uniformity. Connected variety, in which each new appearance seems to be

introduced by what went before it, and in which all the adjoining parts seem to have some natural relation to one another, is more agreeable than a disjointed and disorderly assemblage of unconnected objects. But though I cannot admit that custom is the sole principle of beauty, yet I can so far allow the truth of this ingenious system as to grant, that there is scarce any one external form so beautiful as to please, if quite contrary to custom and unlike whatever we have been used to in that particular species of things: or so deformed as not to be agreeable, if custom uniformly supports it, and habituates us to see it in every single individual of the kind.

^aCHAP. II^a

Of the Influence of Custom and Fashion upon Moral Sentiments

1 SINCE our sentiments concerning beauty of every kind, are so much influenced by custom and fashion, it cannot be expected, that those, concerning the beauty of conduct, should be entirely exempted from the dominion of those principles. Their influence here, however, seems to be much less than it is every where else. There is, perhaps, no form of external objects, how absurd and fantastical soever, to which custom will not reconcile us, or which fashion will not render even agreeable. But the characters and conduct of a Nero, or a Claudius, are what no custom will ever reconcile us to, what no fashion will ever render agreeable; but the one will always be the object of dread and hatred; the other of scorn and derision. The principles of the imagination, upon which our sense of beauty depends, are of a very nice and delicate nature, and may easily be altered by habit and education: but the sentiments of moral approbation and disapprobation, are founded on the strongest and most vigorous passions of human nature; and though they may be somewhat warpt, cannot be entirely perverted.

2 But though the influence of custom and fashion upon moral sentiments, is not altogether so ^bgreat,^b it is however perfectly similar to what it is every where else. When custom and fashion coincide with the natural principles of right and wrong, they heighten the delicacy of our sentiments, and increase our abhorrence for every thing which approaches to evil. Those who have been educated in what is really good company, not in what is commonly called such, who have been accustomed to see nothing in the persons whom they esteemed and lived with, but justice, modesty, humanity, and good order; are more shocked with whatever seems to be inconsistent with the rules which those virtues prescribe. Those, on the contrary, who have had the misfortune to be brought up amidst violence, licentiousness, falsehood, and injustice; lose, though not all sense

of the impropriety of such conduct, yet all sense of its dreadful enormity, or of the vengeance and punishment due to it. They have been familiarized with it from their infancy, custom has rendered it habitual to them, and they are very apt to regard it as, what is called, the way of the world, something which either may, or must be practised, to hinder us from being the dupes of our own integrity.

3   Fashion too will sometimes give reputation to a certain degree of disorder, and, on the contrary, discountenance qualities which deserve esteem. In the reign of Charles II. a degree of licentiousness was deemed the characteristic of a liberal education. It was connected, according to the notions of those times, with generosity, sincerity, magnanimity, loyalty, and proved that the person who acted in this manner, was a gentleman, and not a puritan. Severity of manners, and regularity of conduct, on the other hand, were altogether unfashionable, and were connected, in the imagination of that age, with cant, cunning, hypocrisy, and low manners. To superficial minds, the vices of the great seem at all times agreeable. They connect them, not only with the splendour of fortune, but with many superior virtues, which they ascribe to their superiors; with the spirit of freedom and independency, with frankness, generosity, humanity, and politeness. The virtues of the inferior ranks of people, on the contrary, their parsimonious frugality, their painful industry, and rigid adherence to rules, seem to them mean and disagreeable. They connect them, both with the meanness of the station to which those qualities commonly belong, and with many great vices, which, they suppose, usually accompany them; such as an abject, cowardly, ill-natured, lying, pilfering disposition.

4   The objects with which men in the different professions and states of life are conversant, being very different, and habituating them to very different passions, naturally form in them very different characters and manners. We expect in each rank and profession, a degree of those manners, which, experience has taught us, belong to it. But as in each species of things, we are particularly pleased with the middle conformation, which, in every part and feature, agrees most exactly with the general standard which nature seems to have established for things of that kind; so in each rank, or, if I may say so, in each species of men, we are particularly pleased, if they have neither too much, nor too little of the character which usually accompanies their particular condition and situation. A man, we say, should look like his trade and profession; yet the pedantry of every profession is disagreeable. The different periods of life have, for the same reason, different manners assigned to them. We expect in old age, that gravity and sedateness which its infirmities, its long experience, and its worn-out sensibility seem to render both natural and respectable; and we lay our account to find in youth that sensibility, that gaiety and sprightly vivacity which experience teaches us to expect from the lively impressions that all

interesting objects are apt to make upon the tender and unpractised senses of that early period of life. Each of those two ages, however, may easily have too much of ᶜthᶜe peculiarities which belong to it. The flirting levity of youth, and the immovable insensibility of old age, are equally disagreeable. The young, according to the common saying, are most agreeable when in their behaviour there is something of the manners of the old, and the old, when they retain something of the gaiety of the young. Either of them, however, may easily have too much of the manners of the other. The extreme coldness, and dull formality, which are pardoned in old age, make youth ridiculous. The levity, the carelessness, and the vanity, which are indulged in youth, render old age contemptible.

5   The peculiar character and manners which we are led by custom to appropriate to each rank and profession, have sometimes perhaps a propriety independent of custom; and are what we should approve of for their own sakes, if we took into consideration all the different circumstances which naturally affect those in each different state of life. The propriety of a person's behaviour, depends not upon its suitableness to any one circumstance of his situation, but to all the circumstances, which, when we bring his case home to ourselves, we feel, should naturally call upon his attention. If he appears to be so much occupied by any one of them, as entirely to neglect the rest, we disapprove of his conduct, as something which we cannot entirely go along with, because not ᵈproperlyᵈ adjusted to all the circumstances of his situation: ᵉyet,ᵉ perhaps, the emotion he expresses for the object which principally interests him, does not exceed what we should entirely sympathize with, and approve of, in one whose attention was not required by any other thing. A parent in private life might, upon the loss of an only son, express without blame a degree of grief and tenderness, which would be unpardonable in a general at the head of an army, when glory, and the public safety, demanded so great a part of his attention. As different objects ought, upon common occasions, to occupy the attention of men of different professions, so different passions ought naturally to become habitual to them; and when we bring home to ourselves their situation in this particular respect, we must be sensible, that every occurrence should naturally affect them more or less, according as the emotion which it excites, coincides or disagrees with the fixt habit and temper of their minds. We cannot expect the same sensibility to the gay pleasures and amusements of life in a clergyman, which we lay our account with in an officer. The man whose peculiar occupation it is to keep the world in mind of that awful futurity which awaits them, who is to announce what may be the fatal consequences of every deviation from the rules of duty, and who is himself to set the example of the most

ᶜ⁻ᶜ *1 2E*   these *2–7*   ᵈ⁻ᵈ perfectly *1*   ᵉ⁻ᵉ *1–5* Yet, *6 7* exact conformity, *'seems to be'* the messenger of tidings, which cannot, in propriety, be delivered either with levity or indifference. His mind *⁹is supposed to be⁹* continually occupied with what is too grand and solemn, to leave any room for the impressions of those frivolous objects, which fill up the attention of the dissipated and the gay. We readily feel therefore, that, independent of custom, there is a propriety in the manners which custom has allotted to this profession; and that nothing can be more suitable to the character of a clergyman than that grave, that austere and abstracted severity, which we are habituated to expect in his behaviour. These reflections are so very obvious, that there is scarce any man so inconsiderate, as not, at some time, to have made them, and to have accounted to himself in this manner for his approbation of the usual character of this order.

6   The foundation of the customary character of some other professions is not so obvious, and our approbation of it is founded entirely in habit, without being either confirmed, or enlivened by any reflections of this kind. We are led by custom, for example, to annex the character of gaiety, levity, and sprightly freedom, as well as of some degree of dissipation, to the military profession. Yet, if we were to consider what mood or tone of temper would be most suitable to this situation, we should be apt to determine, perhaps, that the most serious and thoughtful turn of mind would best become those whose lives are continually exposed to uncommon danger, and who should therefore be more constantly occupied with the thoughts of death and its consequences than other men. It is this very circumstance, however, which is not improbably the occasion why the contrary turn of mind prevails so much among men of this profession. It requires so great an effort to conquer the fear of death, when we survey it with steadiness and attention, that those who are constantly exposed to it, find it easier to turn away their thoughts from it altogether, to wrap themselves up in careless security and indifference, and to plunge themselves, for this purpose, into every sort of amusement and dissipation. A camp is not the element of a thoughtful or a melancholy man: persons of that cast, indeed, are often abundantly determined, and are capable, by a great effort, of going on with inflexible resolution to the most unavoidable death. But to be exposed to continual, though less imminent danger, to be obliged to exert, for a long time, a degree of this effort, exhausts and depresses the mind, and renders it incapable of all happiness and enjoyment. The gay and careless, who have occasion to make no effort at all, who fairly resolve never to look before them, but to lose in continual pleasures and amusements all anxiety about their situation, more easily support such circumstances. Whenever, by any peculiar circumstances, an officer has no reason to lay his account with being exposed to any uncommon danger, he is very apt to lose the gaiety and dissipated thoughtlessness of his character. The

'–' is *I 2*   *⁹–⁹* is *I 2*

captain of a city guard is commonly as sober, careful, and penurious an animal as the rest of his fellow-citizens.[1] A long peace is, for the same reason, very apt to diminish the difference between the civil and the military character. The ordinary situation, however, of men of this profession, renders gaiety, and a degree of dissipation, so much their usual character; and custom has, in our imagination, so strongly connected this character with this state of life, that we are very apt to despise any man, whose peculiar humour or situation, renders him incapable of acquiring it. We laugh at the grave and careful faces of a city guard, which so little resemble those of their profession. They themselves seem often to be ashamed of the regularity of their own manners, and, not to be out of the fashion of their trade, are fond of affecting that levity, which is by no means natural to them. Whatever is the deportment which we have been accustomed to see in a respectable order of men, it comes to be so associated in our imagination with that order, that whenever we see the one, we lay our account that we are to meet with the other, and when disappointed, miss something which we expected to find. We are embarrassed, and put to a stand, and know not how to address ourselves to a character, which plainly affects to be of a different species from those with which we should have been disposed to class it.

7   The different situations of different ages and countries are apt, in the same manner, to give different characters to the generality of those who live in them, and their sentiments concerning the particular degree of each quality, that is either blamable or praise-worthy, vary, according to that degree which is usual in their own country, and in their own times. That degree of politeness, which would be highly esteemed, *ᵸperhapsᵸ* would be thought effeminate adulation, in Russia, would be regarded as rudeness and barbarism at the court of France. That degree of order and frugality, which, in a Polish nobleman, would be considered as excessive parsimony, would be regarded as extravagance in a citizen of Amsterdam. Every age and country look upon that degree of each quality, which is commonly to be met with in those who are esteemed among themselves, as the golden mean of that particular talent or virtue. And as this varies, according as their different circumstances render different qualities more or less habitual to them, their sentiments concerning the exact propriety of character and behaviour vary accordingly.

8   Among civilized nations, the virtues which are founded upon humanity,

---

ᵸ⁻ᵸ *1* ~, *2–7 The comma makes the sense unnecessarily doubtful.*

[1] By a pleasant irony of fate Smith himself came to wear this well-fitting cap. Eckstein (ii.576) aptly recalls Rae, *Life*, 374: 'One of the duties of a citizen which he undertook will perhaps occasion surprise—he became a Captain of the City Guard. He was made Honorary Captain of the Trained Bands of Edinburgh—the City Guard—on the 4th of June 1781 . . .' The passage in the text was written long before that, for edition 1.

are more cultivated than those which are founded upon self-denial and the command of the passions. Among rude and barbarous nations, it is quite otherwise, the virtues of self-denial are more cultivated than those of humanity. The general security and happiness which prevail in ages of civility and politeness, afford little exercise to the contempt of danger, to patience in enduring labour, hunger, and pain. Poverty may easily be avoided, and the contempt of it therefore almost ceases to be a virtue. The abstinence from pleasure becomes less necessary, and the mind is more at liberty to unbend itself, and to indulge its natural inclinations in all those particular respects.

9   Among savages and barbarians it is quite otherwise. Every savage undergoes a sort of Spartan discipline, and by the necessity of his situation is inured to every sort of hardship. He is in continual danger: he is often exposed to the greatest extremities of hunger, and frequently dies of pure want. His circumstances not only habituate him to every sort of distress, but teach him to give way to none of the passions which that distress is apt to excite. He can expect from his countrymen no sympathy or indulgence for such weakness. Before we can feel much for others, we must in some measure be at ease ourselves. If our own misery pinches us very severely, we have no leisure to attend to that of our neighbour: and all savages are too much occupied with their own wants and necessities, to give much attention to those of another person. A savage, therefore, whatever be the nature of his distress, expects no sympathy from those about him, and disdains, upon that account, to expose himself, by allowing the least weakness to escape him. His passions, how furious and violent soever, are never permitted to disturb the serenity of his countenance or the composure of his conduct and behaviour. The savages in North America, we are told, assume upon all occasions the greatest indifference, and would think themselves degraded if they should ever appear in any respect to be overcome, either by love, or grief, or resentment. Their magnanimity and self-command, in this respect, are almost beyond the conception of Europeans. In a country in which all men are upon a level, with regard to rank and fortune, it might be expected that the mutual inclinations of the two parties should be the only thing considered in marriages, and should be indulged without any sort of control. This, however, is the country in which all marriages, without exception, are made up by the parents, and in which a young man would think himself disgraced for ever, if he shewed the least preference of one woman above another, or did not express the most complete indifference, both about the time when, and the person to whom, he was to be married. The weakness of love, which is so much indulged in ages of humanity and politeness, is regarded among savages as the most unpardonable effeminacy. Even after the marriage, the two parties seem to be ashamed of a connexion which is founded upon so sordid a necessity.

They do not live together. They see one another by stealth only. They both continue to dwell in the houses of their respective fathers, and the open cohabitation of the two sexes, which is permitted without blame in all other countries, is here considered as the most indecent and unmanly sensuality. Nor is it only over this agreeable passion that they exert this absolute self-command. They often bear, in the sight of all their country-men, with injuries, reproach, and the grossest insults, with the appearance of the greatest insensibility, and without expressing the smallest resentment. When a savage is made prisoner of war, and receives, as is usual, the sentence of death from his conquerors, he hears it without expressing any emotion, and afterwards submits to the most dreadful torments, without ever bemoaning himself, or discovering any other passion but contempt of his enemies. While he is hung by the shoulders over a slow fire, he derides his tormentors, and tells them with how much more ingenuity he himself had tormented such of their countrymen as had fallen into his hands. After he has been scorched and burnt, and lacerated in all the most tender and sensible parts of his body for several hours together, he is often allowed, in order to prolong his misery, a short respite, and is taken down from the stake: he employs this interval in talking upon all indifferent subjects, inquires after the news of the country, and seems indifferent about nothing but his own situation. The spectators express the same insensibility; the sight of so horrible an object seems to make no impression upon them; they scarce look at the prisoner, except when they lend a hand to torment him. At other times they smoke tobacco, and amuse themselves with any common object, as if no such matter was going on. Every savage is said to prepare himself from his earliest youth for this dreadful end. He composes, for this purpose, what they call the song of death, a song which he is to sing when he has fallen into the hands of his enemies, and is expiring under the tortures which they inflict upon him. It consists of insults upon his tormentors, and expresses the highest contempt of death and pain. He sings this song upon all extraordinary occasions, when he goes out to war, when he meets his enemies in the field, or whenever he has a mind to show that he has familiarised his imagination to the most dreadful misfortunes, and that no human event can daunt his resolution, or alter his purpose. The same contempt of death and torture prevails among all other savage nations. There is not a negro from the coast of Africa who does not, in this respect, possess a degree of magnanimity which the soul of his sordid master is *too often* scarce capable of conceiving. Fortune never exerted more cruelly her empire over mankind, than when she subjected those nations of heroes to the refuse of the jails of Europe, to wretches who possess the virtues neither of the countries which they

¹⁻¹ om. 1 2

come from, nor of those which they go to, and whose levity, brutality, and baseness, so justly expose them to the contempt of the vanquished.

10   This heroic and unconquerable firmness, which the custom and education of his country demand of every savage, is not required of those who are brought up to live in civilized societies. If these last complain when they are in pain, if they grieve when they are in distress, if they allow themselves either to be overcome by love, or to be discomposed by anger, they are easily pardoned. Such weaknesses are not apprehended to affect the essential parts of their character. As long as they do not allow themselves to be transported to do any thing contrary to justice or humanity, they lose but little reputation, though the serenity of their countenance, or the composure of their discourse and behaviour, should be somewhat ruffled and disturbed. A humane and polished people, who have more sensibility to the passions of others, can more readily enter into an animated and passionate behaviour, and can more easily pardon some little excess. The person principally concerned is sensible of this; and being assured of the equity of his judges, indulges himself in stronger expressions of passion, and is less afraid of exposing himself to their contempt by the violence of his emotions. We can venture to express more emotion in the presence of a friend than in that of a stranger, because we expect more indulgence from the one than from the other. And in the same manner the rules of decorum among civilized nations, admit of a more animated behaviour, than is approved of among barbarians. The first converse together with the openness of friends; the second with the reserve of strangers. The emotion and vivacity with which the French and the Italians, the two most polished nations upon the continent, express themselves on occasions that are at all interesting, surprise at first those strangers who happen to be travelling among them, and who, having been educated among a people of duller sensibility, cannot enter into this passionate behaviour, of which they have never seen any example in their own country. A young French nobleman will weep in the presence of the whole court upon being refused a regiment. An Italian, says the abbot Dû Bos, expresses more emotion on being condemned in a fine of twenty shillings, than an Englishman on receiving the sentence of death.[2] Cicero, in the times of the highest Roman politeness, could, without degrading himself, weep with all the bitterness of sorrow in the sight of the whole senate and the whole people; as it is evident he must have done in the end of almost every oration. The orators of the earlier and ruder ages of Rome could not probably, consistent with the manners of the times, have expressed themselves with so much emotion. It would have been regarded, I suppose, as a violation of nature and propriety

[2] Jean-Baptiste (l'Abbé) Du Bos discusses differences of national character in *Réflexions critiques sur la poésie et sur la peinture*, Part II, sect. 15, but we cannot trace, either there or elsewhere in his writings, the statement attributed to him by Smith.

in the Scipios, in the Leliuses, and in the elder Cato,[3] to have exposed so much tenderness to the view of the public. Those ancient warriors could express themselves with order, gravity, and good judgment; but are said to have been strangers to that sublime and passionate eloquence which was first introduced into Rome, not many years before the birth of Cicero, by the two Gracchi, by Crassus, and by Sulpitius.[4] This animated eloquence, which has been long practised, with or without success, both in France and Italy, is but just beginning to be introduced into England. So wide is the difference between the degrees of self-command which are required in civilized and in barbarous nations, and by such different standards do they judge of the propriety of behaviour.

11   This difference gives occasion to many others that are not less essential. A polished people being accustomed to give way, in some measure, to the movements of nature, become frank, open, and sincere. Barbarians, on the contrary, being obliged to smother and conceal the appearance of every passion, necessarily acquire the habits of falsehood and dissimulation. It is observed by all those who have been conversant with savage nations, whether in Asia, Africa, or America, that they are all equally impenetrable, and that, when they have a mind to conceal the truth, no examination is capable of drawing it from them. They cannot be trepanned by the most artful questions. The torture itself is incapable of making them confess any thing which they have no mind to tell. The passions of a savage too, though they never express themselves by any outward emotion, but lie concealed in the breast of the sufferer, are, notwithstanding, all mounted to the highest pitch of fury. Though he seldom shows any symptoms of anger, yet his vengeance, when he comes to give way to it, is always sanguinary and dreadful. The least affront drives him to despair. His countenance and discourse indeed are still sober and composed, and express nothing but the most perfect tranquillity of mind: but his actions are often the most furious and violent. Among the North-Americans it is not uncommon for persons of the tenderest age and more fearful sex to drown themselves upon receiving only a slight reprimand from their mothers, and this too without expressing any passion, or saying any thing, except, *you shall no longer have a daughter.* In civilized nations the passions

---

[3] The most illustrious of the Scipios were Publius Cornelius Scipio Africanus (236–184/3 B.C.) and his grandson by adoption, Publius Cornelius Scipio Aemilianus Numantinus (185/4–129 B.C.). The latter was noted for his stern character. Gaius Laelius the elder was a friend of Scipio Africanus; his son, Gaius Laelius Sapiens, was a friend of Scipio Aemilianus and is the central character in Cicero's *De Amicitia.* Marcus Porcius Cato the elder (234–149 B.C.) became known as 'Censorius' for his severity as censor in 184 B.C.

[4] Tiberius Sempronius Gracchus (tribune of the *plebs* in 133 B.C.), his brother Gaius (tribune in 123 and 122), Lucius Licinius Crassus (140–91), and Publius Sulpicius Rufus (124–88) all appear in Cicero's account of earlier orators in *Brutus.* Cicero admired Crassus especially for his *gravitas* and says (lv. 203) that Sulpicius, who took Crassus as his model, furnished the best example of the grand style in oratory.

of men are not commonly so furious or so desperate. They are often clamorous and noisy, but are seldom very hurtful; and seem frequently to aim at no other satisfaction, but that of convincing the spectator, that they are in the right to be so much moved, and of procuring his sympathy and approbation.

12 All these effects of custom and fashion, however, upon the moral sentiments of mankind, are inconsiderable, in comparison of those which they give occasion to in some other cases; and it is not concerning the general style of character and behaviour, that those principles produce the greatest perversion of judgment, but concerning the propriety or impropriety of particular usages.

13 The different manners which custom teaches us to approve of in the different professions and states of life, do not concern things of the greatest importance. We expect truth and justice from an old man as well as from a young, from a clergyman as well as from an officer; and it is in matters of small moment only that we look for the distinguishing marks of their respective characters. With regard to these too, there is often some unobserved circumstance which, if it was attended to, would show us, that, independent of custom, there was a propriety in the character which custom had taught us to allot to each profession. We cannot complain, therefore, in this case, that the perversion of natural sentiment is very great. Though the manners of different nations require different degrees of the same quality, in the character which they think worthy of esteem, yet the worst that can be said to happen even here, is that the duties of one virtue are sometimes extended so as to encroach a little upon the precincts of some other. The rustic hospitality that is in fashion among the Poles encroaches, perhaps, a little upon oeconomy and good order; and the frugality that is esteemed in Holland, upon generosity and good-fellowship. The hardiness demanded of savages diminishes their humanity; and, perhaps, the delicate sensibility required in civilized nations sometimes destroys the masculine firmness of the character. In general, the style of manners which takes place in any nation, may commonly upon the whole be said to be that which is most suitable to its situation. Hardiness is the character most suitable to the circumstances of a savage; sensibility to those of one who lives in a very civilized society. Even here, therefore, we cannot complain that the moral sentiments of men are very grossly perverted.

14 It is not therefore in the general style of conduct or behaviour that custom authorises the widest departure from what is the natural propriety of action. With regard to particular usages, its influence is often much more destructive of good morals, and it is capable of establishing, as lawful and blameless, particular actions, which shock the plainest principles of right and wrong.

15 Can there be greater barbarity, for example, than to hurt an infant?

Its helplessness, its innocence, its amiableness, call forth the compassion, even of an enemy, and not to spare that tender age is regarded as the most furious effort of an enraged and cruel conqueror. What then should we imagine must be the heart of a parent who could injure that weakness which even a furious enemy is afraid to violate? Yet the exposition, that is, the murder of new-born infants, was a practice allowed of in almost all the states of Greece, even among the polite and civilized Athenians; and whenever the circumstances of the parent rendered it inconvenient to bring up the child, to abandon it to hunger, or to wild beasts, was regarded without blame or censure. This practice had probably begun in times of the most savage barbarity. The imaginations of men had been first made familiar with it in that earliest period of society, and the uniform continuance of the custom had hindered them afterwards from perceiving its enormity. We find, at this day, that this practice prevails among all savage nations; and in that rudest and lowest state of society it is undoubtedly more pardonable than in any other. The extreme indigence of a savage is often such that he himself is frequently exposed to the greatest extremity of hunger, he often dies of pure want, and it is frequently impossible for him to support both himself and his child. We cannot wonder, therefore, that in this case he should abandon it. One who, in flying from an enemy, whom it was impossible to resist, should throw down his infant, because it retarded his flight, would surely be excusable; since, by attempting to save it, he could only hope for the consolation of dying with it. That in this state of society, therefore, a parent should be allowed to judge whether he can bring up his child, ought not to surprise us so greatly. In the latter ages of Greece, however, the same thing was permitted from views of remote interest or conveniency, which could by no means excuse it. Uninterrupted custom had by this time so thoroughly authorised the practice, that not only the loose maxims of the world tolerated this barbarous prerogative, but even the doctrine of philosophers, which ought to have been more just and accurate, was led away by the established custom, and upon this, as upon many other occasions, instead of censuring, supported the horrible abuse, by far-fetched considerations of public utility. Aristotle[5] talks of it as of what the magistrate ought upon many occasions to encourage. The humane Plato[6] is of the same opinion, and, with all that love of mankind which seems to animate all his writings, no where marks this practice with disapprobation. When custom can give sanction to so dreadful a violation of humanity, we may well imagine that there is scarce any particular practice so gross which it cannot authorise. Such a thing, we hear men every day saying, is commonly done, and they seem to think this a sufficient apology for what, in itself, is the most unjust and unreasonable conduct.

---

[5] *Politics*, 1335^{b}20–1. [6] *Republic*, 460 c, 461 c.

16   There is an obvious reason why custom should never pervert our sentiments with regard to the general style and character of conduct and
behaviour, in the same degree as with regard to the propriety or unlawful-
ness of particular usages. There never can be any such custom. No society
could subsist a moment, in which the usual strain of men's conduct and
behaviour was of a piece with the horrible practice I have just now mentioned.

^aPART VI
Of the CHARACTER of VIRTUE
Consisting of Three Sections

INTRODUCTION

1 WHEN we consider the character of any individual, we naturally view it under two different aspects; first, as it may affect his own happiness; and secondly, as it may affect that of other people.

^aSECTION I

Of the Character of the Individual, so far as it affects his own Happiness; or of Prudence^a

1 THE preservation and healthful state of the body seem to be the objects which Nature first recommends to the care of every individual. The appetites of hunger and thirst, the agreeable or disagreeable sensations of pleasure and pain, of heat and cold, etc. may be considered as lessons delivered by the voice of Nature herself, directing him what he ought to chuse, and what he ought to avoid, for this purpose. The first lessons which he is taught by those to whom his childhood is entrusted, tend, the greater part of them, to the *same* purpose. Their principal object is to teach him how to keep out of harm's way.

2 As he grows up, he soon learns that some care and foresight are necessary for providing the means of gratifying those natural appetites, of procuring pleasure and avoiding pain, of procuring the agreeable and avoiding the disagreeable temperature of heat and cold. In the proper direction of this care and foresight consists the art of preserving and increasing what is called his external fortune.

3 Though it is in order to supply the necessities and ^bconveniencies^b of the body, that the advantages of external fortune are originally recommended to us, yet we cannot live long in the world without perceiving that the respect of our equals, our credit and rank in the society we live in, depend

---

^a *Part VI was added in ed. 6.*

^{a–a} SECT. I/*Of...Prudence 6 7*

^{b–b} conveniences *6 7 See Introduction, 50.*

very much upon the degree in which we possess, or are supposed to possess, those advantages. The desire of becoming the proper objects of this respect, of deserving and obtaining this credit and rank among our equals, is, perhaps, the strongest of all our desires, and our anxiety to obtain the advantages of fortune is accordingly much more excited and irritated by this desire, than by that of supplying all the necessities and ᶜconvenienciesᶜ of the body, which are always very easily supplied.

4   Our rank and credit among our equals, too, depend very much upon, what, perhaps, a virtuous man would wish them to depend entirely, our character and conduct, or upon the confidence, esteem, and good-will, which these naturally excite in the people we live with.

5   The care of the health, of the fortune, of the rank and reputation of the individual, the objects upon which his comfort and happiness in this life are supposed principally to depend, is considered as the proper business of that virtue which is commonly called Prudence.

6   We suffer more, it has already been observed,[1] when we fall from a better to a worse situation, than we ever enjoy when we rise from a worse to a better. Security, therefore, is the first and the principal object of prudence. It is averse to expose our health, our fortune, our rank, or reputation, to any sort of hazard. It is rather cautious than enterprising, and more anxious to preserve the advantages which we already possess, than forward to prompt us to the acquisition of still greater advantages. The methods of improving our fortune, which it principally recommends to us, are those which expose to no loss or hazard; real knowledge and skill in our trade or profession, assiduity and industry in the exercise of it, frugality, and even some degree of parsimony, in all our expences.

7   The prudent man always studies seriously and earnestly to understand whatever he professes to understand, and not merely to persuade other people that he understands it; and though his talents may not always be very brilliant, they are always perfectly genuine. He neither endeavours to impose upon you by the cunning devices of an artful impostor, nor by the arrogant airs of an assuming pedant, nor by the confident assertions of a superficial and imprudent pretender. He is not ostentatious even of the abilities which he really possesses. His conversation is simple and modest, and he is averse to all the quackish arts by which other people so frequently thrust themselves into public notice and reputation. For reputation in his profession he is naturally disposed to rely a good deal upon the solidity of his knowledge and abilities; and he does not always think of cultivating the favour of those little clubs and cabals, who, in the superior arts and sciences, so often erect themselves into the supreme judges of merit; and who make

ᶜ⁻ᶜ conveniences 6 7

[1] I.iii.1.8. For the economic implications of prudence, cf. WN II. iii, note 22.

it their business to celebrate the talents and virtues of one another, and to decry whatever can come into competition with them. If he ever connects himself with any society of this kind, it is merely in self-defence, not with a view to impose upon the public, but to hinder the public from being imposed upon, to his disadvantage, by the clamours, the whispers, or the intrigues, either of that particular society, or of some other of the same kind.

8   The prudent man is always sincere, and feels horror at the very thought of exposing himself to the disgrace which attends upon the detection of falsehood. But though always sincere, he is not always frank and open; and though he never tells any thing but the truth, he does not always think himself bound, when not properly called upon, to tell the whole truth. As he is cautious in his actions, so he is reserved in his speech; and never rashly or unnecessarily obtrudes his opinion concerning either things or persons.

9   The prudent man, though not always distinguished by the most exquisite sensibility, is always very capable of friendship. But his friendship is not that ardent and passionate, but too often transitory affection, which appears so delicious to the generosity of youth and inexperience. It is a sedate, but steady and faithful attachment to a few well-tried and well-chosen companions; in the choice of whom he is not guided by the giddy admiration of shining accomplishments, but by the sober esteem of modesty, discretion, and good conduct. But though capable of friendship, he is not always much disposed to general sociality. He rarely frequents, and more rarely figures in those convivial societies which are distinguished for the jollity and gaiety of their conversation. Their way of life might too often interfere with the regularity of his temperance, might interrupt the steadiness of his industry, or break in upon the strictness of his frugality.

10   But though his conversation may not always be very sprightly or diverting, it is always perfectly inoffensive. He hates the thought of being guilty of any petulance or rudeness. He never assumes impertinently over any body, and, upon all common occasions, is willing to place himself rather below than above his equals. Both in his conduct and conversation, he is an exact observer of decency, and respects with an almost religious scrupulosity, all the established decorums and ceremonials of society. And, in this respect, he sets a much better example than has frequently been done by men of much more splendid talents and virtues; who, in all ages, from that of Socrates and Aristippus,[2] down to that of Dr. Swift and Voltaire, and from that of Philip and Alexander the Great, down to that of the great Czar Peter of Moscovy, have too often distinguished themselves by the

---

[2] Aristippus of Cyrene, a companion of Socrates, noted for a combination of sensuality and self-control. He is often said to be the founder of the Cyrenaic philosophy of hedonism, but modern scholars think this is probably a confusion with his grandson of the same name.

most improper and even insolent contempt of all the ordinary decorums of life and conversation, and who have thereby set the most pernicious example to those who wish to resemble them, and who too often content themselves with imitating their follies, without even attempting to attain their perfections.

11   In the steadiness of his industry and frugality, in his steadily sacrificing the ease and enjoyment of the present moment for the probable expectation of the still greater ease and enjoyment of a more distant but more lasting period of time, the prudent man is always both supported and rewarded by the entire approbation of the impartial spectator, and of the representative of the impartial spectator, the man within the breast. The impartial spectator does not feel himself worn out by the present labour of those whose conduct he surveys; nor does he feel himself solicited by the importunate calls of their present appetites. To him their present, and what is likely to be their future situation, are very nearly the same: he sees them nearly at the same distance, and is affected by them very nearly in the same manner. He knows, however, that to the persons principally concerned, they are very far from being the same, and that they naturally affect *them* in a very different manner. He cannot therefore but approve, and even applaud, that proper exertion of self-command, which enables them to act as if their present and their future situation affected them nearly in the same manner in which they affect him.

12   The man who lives within his income, is naturally contented with his situation, which, by continual, though small accumulations, is growing better and better every day. He is enabled gradually to relax, both in the rigour of his parsimony and in the severity of his application; and he feels with double satisfaction this gradual increase of ease and enjoyment, from having felt before the hardship which attended the want of them. He has no anxiety to change so comfortable a situation, and does not go in quest of new enterprises and adventures, which might endanger, but could not well increase, the secure tranquillity which he actually enjoys. If he enters into any new projects or enterprises, they are likely to be well concerted and well prepared. He can never be hurried or drove into them by any necessity, but has always time and leisure to deliberate soberly and coolly concerning what are likely to be their consequences.

13   The prudent man is not willing to subject himself to any responsibility which his duty does not impose upon him. He is not a bustler in business where he has no concern; is not a meddler in other people's affairs; is not a professed counsellor or adviser, who obtrudes his advice where nobody is asking it. He confines himself, as much as his duty will permit, to his own affairs, and has no taste for that foolish importance which many people wish to derive from appearing to have some influence in the management of those of other people. He is averse to enter into any party disputes, hates

faction, and is not always very forward to listen to the voice even of noble and great ambition. When distinctly called upon, he will not decline the service of his country, but he will not cabal in order to force himself into it, and would be much better pleased that the public business were well managed by some other person, than that he himself should have the trouble, and incur the responsibility, of managing it. In the bottom of his heart he would prefer the undisturbed enjoyment of secure tranquillity, not only to all the vain splendour of successful ambition, but to the real and solid glory of performing the greatest and most magnanimous actions.

14   Prudence, in short, when directed merely to the care of the health, of the fortune, and of the rank and reputation of the individual, though it is regarded as a most respectable and even, in some degree, as an amiable and agreeable quality, yet it never is considered as one, either of the most endearing, or of the most ennobling of the virtues. It commands a certain cold esteem, but seems not entitled to any very ardent love or admiration.

15   Wise and judicious conduct, when directed to greater and nobler purposes than the care of the health, the fortune, the rank and reputation of the individual, is frequently and very properly called prudence. We talk of the prudence of the great general, of the great statesman, of the great legislator. Prudence is, in all these cases, combined with many greater and more splendid virtues, with valour, with extensive and strong benevolence, with a sacred regard to the rules of justice, and all these supported by a proper degree of self-command. This superior prudence, when carried to the highest degree of perfection, necessarily supposes the art, the talent, and the habit or disposition of acting with the most perfect propriety in every possible circumstance and situation. It necessarily supposes the utmost perfection of all the intellectual and of all the moral virtues. It is the best head joined to the best heart. It is the most perfect wisdom combined with the most perfect virtue. It constitutes very nearly the character of the Academical or Peripatetic[3] sage, as the inferior prudence does that of the Epicurean.

16   Mere imprudence, or the mere want of the capacity to take care of one's-self, is, with the generous and humane, the object of compassion; with those of less delicate sentiments, of neglect, or, at worst, of contempt, but never of hatred or indignation. When combined with other vices, however, it aggravates in the highest degree the infamy and disgrace which would otherwise attend them. The artful knave, whose dexterity and address exempt him, though not from strong suspicions, yet from punishment or distinct detection, is too often received in the world with an indulgence which he by no means deserves. The awkward and foolish one, who, for want of this dexterity and address, is convicted and brought

---

[3] Platonic or Aristotelian.

to punishment, is the object of universal hatred, contempt, and derision. In countries where great crimes frequently pass unpunished, the most atrocious actions become almost familiar, and cease to impress the people with that horror which is universally felt in countries where an exact administration of justice takes place. The injustice is the same in both countries; but the imprudence is often very different. In the latter, great crimes are evidently great follies. In the former, they are not always considered as such. In Italy, during the greater part of the sixteenth century, assassinations, murders, and even murders under trust, seem to have been almost familiar among the superior ranks of people. Caesar Borgia invited four of the little princes in his neighbourhood, who all possessed little sovereignties, and commanded little armies of their own, to a friendly conference at Senigaglia, where, as soon as they arrived, he put them all to death.[4] This infamous action, though certainly not approved of even in that age of crimes, seems to have contributed very little to the discredit, and not in the least to the ruin of the perpetrator. That ruin happened a few years after from causes altogether disconnected with this crime. Machiavel, not indeed a man of the nicest morality even for his own times, was resident, as minister from the republic of Florence, at the court of Caesar Borgia when this crime was committed. He gives a very particular account of it,[5] and in that pure, elegant, and simple language which distinguishes all his writings. He talks of it very coolly; is pleased with the address with which Caesar Borgia conducted it; has much contempt for the dupery and weakness of the sufferers; but no compassion for their miserable and untimely death, and no sort of indignation at the cruelty and falsehood of their murderer. The violence and injustice of great conquerors are often regarded with foolish wonder and admiration; those of petty thieves, robbers, and murderers, with contempt, hatred, and even horror upon all occasions. The former, though they are a hundred times more mischievous and destructive, yet when successful, they often pass for deeds of the most heroic magnanimity. The latter are always viewed with hatred and aversion, as the follies, as well as the crimes, of the lowest and most worthless of mankind. The injustice of the former is certainly, at least, as great as that of the latter; but the folly and imprudence are not near so great. A wicked and worthless man of parts often goes through the world with much more credit than he deserves. A wicked and worthless fool appears always, of all mortals, the most hateful, as well as the most contemptible. As prudence combined with other virtues, constitutes the noblest; so imprudence combined with other vices, constitutes the vilest of all characters.

[4] Two were strangled at Senigallia on the night of their arrival, 31 December 1502; the other two at the castle of Pieve on 18 January 1503.
[5] Machiavelli, *Descrizione del modo tenuto dal duca Valentino nello ammazzare Vitellozzo Vitelli, Oliverotto da Fermo, il signor Pagolo e il duca di Gravina Orsini.*

SECTION II

Of the Character of the Individual, so far as it can affect the
Happiness of other People

INTRODUCTION

1 THE character of every individual, so far as it can affect the happiness of
other people, must do so by its disposition either to hurt or to benefit
them.

2   Proper resentment for injustice attempted, or actually committed, is the
only motive which, in the eyes of the impartial spectator, can justify our
hurting or disturbing in any respect the happiness of our neighbour. To do
so from any other motive is itself a violation of the laws of justice, which
force ought to be employed either to restrain or to punish. The wisdom of
every state or commonwealth endeavours, as well as it can, to employ the
force of the society to restrain those who are subject to its authority, from
hurting or disturbing the happiness of one another. The rules which it
establishes for this purpose, constitute the civil and criminal law of each
particular state or country. The principles upon which those rules either
are, or ought to be founded, are the subject of a particular science, of all
sciences by far the most important, but hitherto, perhaps, the least cultivated, that of natural jurisprudence; concerning which it belongs not to
our present subject to enter into any detail. A sacred and religious regard
not to hurt or disturb in any respect the happiness of our neighbour, even
in those cases where no law can properly protect him, constitutes the
character of the perfectly innocent and just man; a character which,
when carried to a certain delicacy of attention, is always highly respectable
and even venerable for its own sake, and can scarce ever fail to be accompanied with many other virtues, with great feeling for other people, with
great humanity and great benevolence. It is a character sufficiently understood, and requires no further explanation. In the present section I shall
only endeavour to explain the foundation of that order which nature seems
to have traced out for the distribution of our good offices, or for the direction and employment of our very limited powers of beneficence: first,
towards individuals; and secondly, towards societies.

3   The same unerring wisdom, it will be found, which regulates every
other part of her conduct, directs, in this respect too, the order of her
recommendations; which are always stronger or weaker in proportion as
our beneficence is more or less necessary, or can be more or less useful.

CHAP. I

Of the Order in which Individuals are recommended by Nature to our care and attention

1   EVERY man, as the Stoics used to say, is first and principally recommended to his own care; and every man is certainly, in every respect, fitter and abler to take care of himself than of any other person. Every man feels his own pleasures and his own pains more sensibly than those of other people. The former are the original sensations; the latter the reflected or sympathetic images of those sensations. The former may be said to be the substance; the latter the shadow.

2   After himself, the members of his own family, those who usually live in the same house with him, his parents, his children, his brothers and sisters, are naturally the objects of his warmest affections. They are naturally and usually the persons upon whose happiness or misery his conduct must have the greatest influence. He is more habituated to sympathize with them. He knows better how every thing is likely to affect them, and his sympathy with them is more precise and determinate, than it can be with the greater part of other people. It approaches nearer, in short, to what he feels for himself.

3   This sympathy too, and the affections which are founded on it, are by nature more strongly directed towards his children than towards his parents, and his tenderness for the former seems generally a more active principle, than his reverence and gratitude towards the latter. In the natural state of things, it has already been observed,[1] the existence of the child, for some time after it comes into the world, depends altogether upon the care of the parent; that of the parent does not naturally depend upon the care of the child. In the eye of nature, it would seem, a child is a more important object than an old man; and excites a much more lively, as well as a much more universal sympathy. It ought to do so. Every thing may be expected, or at least hoped, from the child. In ordinary cases, very little can be either expected or hoped from the old man. The weakness of childhood interests the affections of the most brutal and hard-hearted. It is only to the virtuous and humane, that the infirmities of old age are not the objects of contempt and aversion. In ordinary cases, an old man dies without being much regretted by any body. Scarce a child can die without rending asunder the heart of somebody.

4   The earliest friendships, the friendships which are naturally contracted when the heart is most susceptible of that feeling, are those among brothers and sisters. Their good agreement, while they remain in the same family, is necessary for its tranquillity and happiness. They are capable

---

[1] III.3.13

of giving more pleasure or pain to one another than to the greater part of other people. Their situation renders their mutual sympathy of the utmost importance to their common happiness; and, by the wisdom of nature, the same situation, by obliging them to accommodate to one another, renders that sympathy more habitual, and thereby more lively, more distinct, and more determinate.

5   The children of brothers and sisters are naturally connected by the friendship which, after separating into different families, continues to take place between their parents. Their good agreement improves the enjoyment of that friendship; their discord would disturb it. As they seldom live in the same family, however, though of more importance to one another, than to the greater part of other people, they are of much less than brothers and sisters. As their mutual sympathy is less necessary, so it is less habitual, and therefore proportionably weaker.

6   The children of cousins, being still less connected, are of still less importance to one another; and the affection gradually diminishes as the relation grows more and more remote.

7   What is called affection, is in reality nothing but habitual sympathy. Our concern in the happiness or misery of those who are the objects of what we call our affections; our desire to promote the one, and to prevent the other; are either the actual feeling of that habitual sympathy, or the necessary consequences of that feeling. Relations being usually placed in situations which naturally create this habitual sympathy, it is expected that a suitable degree of affection should take place among them. We generally find that it actually does take place; we therefore naturally expect that it should; and we are, upon that account, more shocked when, upon any occasion, we find that it does not. The general rule is established, that persons related to one another in a certain degree, ought always to be affected towards one another in a certain manner, and that there is always the highest impropriety, and sometimes even a sort of impiety, in their being affected in a different manner. A parent without parental tenderness, a child devoid of all filial reverence, appear monsters, the objects, not of hatred only, but of horror.

8   Though in a particular instance, the circumstances which usually produce those natural affections, as they are called, may, by some accident, not have taken place, yet respect for the general rule will frequently, in some measure, supply their place, and produce something which, though not altogether the same, may bear, however, a very considerable resemblance to those affections. A father is apt to be less attached to a child, who, by some accident, has been separated from him in its infancy, and who does not return to him till it is grown up to manhood. The father is apt to feel less paternal tenderness for the child; the child, less filial reverence for the father. Brothers and sisters, when they have been educated in distant

countries, are apt to feel a similar diminution of affection. With the dutiful and the virtuous, however, respect for the general rule will frequently produce something which, though by no means the same, yet may very much resemble those natural affections. Even during the separation, the father and the child, the brothers or the sisters, are by no means indifferent to one another. They all consider one another as persons to and from whom certain affections are due, and they live in the hopes of being some time or another in a situation to enjoy that friendship which ought naturally to have taken place among persons so nearly connected. Till they meet, the absent son, the absent brother, are frequently the favourite son, the favourite brother. They have never offended, or, if they have, it is so long ago, that the offence is forgotten, as some childish trick not worth the remembering. Every account they have heard of one another, if conveyed by people of any tolerable good nature, has been, in the highest degree, flattering and favourable. The absent son, the absent brother, is not like other ordinary sons and brothers; but an all-perfect son, an all-perfect brother; and the most romantic hopes are entertained of the happiness to be enjoyed in the friendship and conversation of such persons. When they meet, it is often with so strong a disposition to conceive that habitual sympathy which constitutes the family affection, that they are very apt to fancy they have actually conceived it, and to behave to one another as if they had. Time and experience, however, I am afraid, too frequently undeceive them. Upon a more familiar acquaintance, they frequently discover in one another habits, humours, and inclinations, different from what they expected, to which, from want of habitual sympathy, from want of the real principle and foundation of what is properly called family-affection, they cannot now easily accommodate themselves. They have never lived in the situation which almost necessarily forces that easy accommodation, and though they may now be sincerely desirous to assume it, they have really become incapable of doing so. Their familiar conversation and intercourse soon become less pleasing to them, and, upon that account, less frequent. They may continue to live with one another in the mutual exchange of all essential good offices, and with every other external appearance of decent regard. But that cordial satisfaction, that delicious sympathy, that confidential openness and ease, which naturally take place in the conversation of those who have lived long and familiarly with one another, it seldom happens that they can completely enjoy.

9   It is only, however, with the dutiful and the virtuous, that the general rule has even this slender authority. With the dissipated, the profligate, and the vain, it is entirely disregarded. They are so far from respecting it, that they seldom talk of it but with the most indecent derision; and an early and long separation of this kind never fails to estrange them most com-

pletely from one another. With such persons, respect for the general rule can at best produce only a cold and affected civility (a very slender semblance of real regard); and even this, the slightest offence, the smallest opposition of interest, commonly puts an end to altogether.

10   The education of boys at distant great schools, of young men at distant colleges, of young ladies in distant nunneries and boarding-schools, seems, in the higher ranks of life, to have hurt most essentially the domestic morals, and consequently the domestic happiness, both of France and England.[2] Do you wish to educate your children to be dutiful to their parents, to be kind and affectionate to their brothers and sisters? put them under the necessity of being dutiful children, of being kind and affectionate brothers and sisters: educate them in your own house. From their parent's house they may, with propriety and advantage, go out every day to attend public schools: but let their dwelling be always at home. Respect for you must always impose a very useful restraint upon their conduct; and respect for them may frequently impose no useless restraint upon your own. Surely no acquirement, which can possibly be derived from what is called a public education, can make any sort of compensation for what is almost certainly and necessarily lost by it. Domestic education is the institution of nature; public education, the contrivance of man. It is surely unnecessary to say, which is likely to be the wisest.

11   In some tragedies and romances, we meet with many beautiful and interesting scenes, founded upon, what is called, the force of blood, or upon the wonderful affection which near relations are supposed to conceive for one another, even before they know that they have any such connection. This force of blood, however, I am afraid, exists no-where but in tragedies and romances. Even in tragedies and romances, it is never supposed to take place between any relations, but those who are naturally bred up in the same house; between parents and children, between brothers and sisters. To imagine any such mysterious affection between cousins, or even between aunts or uncles, and nephews or nieces, would be too ridiculous.

12   In pastoral countries, and in all countries where the authority of law is not alone sufficient to give perfect security to every member of the state, all the different branches of the same family commonly chuse to live in the neighbourhood of one another. Their association is frequently necessary for their common defence. They are all, from the highest to the lowest, of more or less importance to one another. Their concord strengthens their necessary association; their discord always weakens, and might destroy it. They have more intercourse with one another, than with the members of any other tribe. The remotest members of the same tribe claim some con-

---

[2] In WN V.i.f.36 (written before Part VI of TMS) Smith is equally critical of foreign travel as a substitute for university education.

nection with one another; and, where all other circumstances are equal, expect to be treated with more distinguished attention than is due to those who have no such pretensions. It is not many years ago that, in the High-lands of Scotland, the Chieftain used to consider the poorest man of his clan, as his cousin and relation. The same extensive regard to kindred is said to take place among the Tartars, the Arabs, the Turkomans, and, I believe, among all other nations who are nearly in the same state of society in which the Scots Highlanders were about the beginning of the present century.

13   In commercial countries, where the authority of law is always perfectly sufficient to protect the meanest man in the state, the descendants of the same family, having no such motive for keeping together, naturally separate and disperse, as interest or inclination may direct. They soon cease to be of importance to one another; and, in a few generations, not only lose all care about one another, but all remembrance of their common origin, and of the connection which took place among their ancestors. Regard for remote relations becomes, in every country, less and less, according as this state of civilization has been longer and more completely established. It has been longer and more completely established in England than in Scotland; and remote relations are, accordingly, more considered in the latter country than in the former, though, in this respect, the difference between the two countries is growing less and less every day. Great lords, indeed, are, in every country, proud of remembering and acknowledging their connection with one another, however remote. The remembrance of such illustrious relations flatters not a little the family pride of them all; and it is neither from affection, nor from any thing which resembles affection, but from the most frivolous and childish of all vanities, that this remembrance is so carefully kept up. Should some more humble, though, perhaps, much nearer kinsman, presume to put such great men in mind of his relation to their family, they seldom fail to tell him that they are bad genealogists, and miserably ill-informed concerning their own family history. It is not in that order, I am afraid, that we are to expect any extraordinary extension of, what is called, natural affection.

14   I consider what is called natural affection as more the effect of the moral than of the supposed physical connection between the parent and the child. A jealous husband, indeed, notwithstanding the moral connection, not-withstanding the child's having been educated in his own house, often regards, with hatred and aversion, that unhappy child which he supposes to be the offspring of his wife's infidelity. It is the lasting monument of a most disagreeable adventure; of his own dishonour, and of the disgrace of his family.

15   Among well-disposed people, the necessity or conveniency of mutual accommodation, very frequently produces a friendship not unlike that

which takes place among those who are born to live in the same family. Colleagues in office, partners in trade, call one another brothers; and frequently feel towards one another as if they really were so. Their good agreement is an advantage to all; and, if they are tolerably reasonable people, they are naturally disposed to agree. We expect that they should do so; and their disagreement is a sort of a small scandal. The Romans expressed this sort of attachment by the word *necessitudo*, which, from the etymology, seems to denote that it was imposed by the necessity of the situation.[3]

16   Even the trifling circumstance of living in the same neighbourhood, has some effect of the same kind. We respect the face of a man whom we see every day, provided he has never offended us. Neighbours can be very convenient, and they can be very troublesome, to one another. If they are good sort of people, they are naturally disposed to agree. We expect their good agreement; and to be a bad neighbour is a very bad character. There are certain small good offices, accordingly, which are universally allowed to be due to a neighbour in preference to any other person who has no such connection.

17   This natural disposition to accommodate and to assimilate, as much as we can, our own sentiments, principles, and feelings, to those which we see fixed and rooted in the persons whom we are obliged to live and converse a great deal with, is the cause of the contagious effects of both good and bad company. The man who associates chiefly with the wise and the virtuous, though he may not himself become either wise or virtuous, cannot help conceiving a certain respect at least for wisdom and virtue; and the man who associates chiefly with the profligate and the dissolute, though he may not himself become profligate and dissolute, must soon lose, at least, all his original abhorrence of profligacy and dissolution of manners. The similarity of family characters, which we so frequently see transmitted through several successive generations, may, perhaps, be partly owing to this disposition, to assimilate ourselves to those whom we are obliged to live and converse a great deal with. The family character, however, like the family countenance, seems to be owing, not altogether to the moral, but partly too to the physical connection. The family countenance is certainly altogether owing to the latter.

18   But of all attachments to an individual, that which is founded altogether upon the esteem and approbation of his good conduct and behaviour, confirmed by much experience and long acquaintance, is, by far, the most respectable. Such friendships, arising not from a constrained sympathy, not from a sympathy which has been assumed and rendered habitual for the sake of *a*conveniency*a* and accommodation; but from a natural sympathy,

a-a convenience 6 7   *See Introduction, 50.*

---

[3] The Latin word means (1) necessity or need, (2) close connection or relationship.

from an involuntary feeling that the persons to whom we attach ourselves
are the natural and proper objects of esteem and approbation; can exist
only among men of virtue. Men of virtue only can feel that entire confidence in the conduct and behaviour of one another, which can, at all
times, assure them that they can never either offend or be offended by
one another. Vice is always capricious: virtue only is regular and orderly.
The attachment which is founded upon the love of virtue, as it is certainly,
of all attachments, the most virtuous; so it is likewise the happiest, as well
as the most permanent and secure. Such friendships need not be confined
to a single person, but may safely embrace all the wise and virtuous, with
whom we have been long and intimately acquainted, and upon whose
wisdom and virtue we can, upon that account, entirely depend. They who
would confine friendship to two persons, seem to confound the wise security
of friendship with the jealousy and folly of love. The hasty, fond, and
foolish intimacies of young people, founded, commonly, upon some slight
similarity of character, altogether unconnected with good conduct, upon a
taste, perhaps, for the same studies, the same amusements, the same
diversions, or upon their agreement in some singular principle or opinion,
not commonly adopted; those intimacies which a freak begins, and which a
freak puts an end to, how agreeable soever they may appear while they last,
can by no means deserve the sacred and venerable name of friendship.

19   Of all the persons, however, whom nature points out for our peculiar
beneficence, there are none to whom it seems more properly directed than
to those whose beneficence we have ourselves already experienced. Nature,
which formed men for that mutal kindness, so necessary for their happiness,
renders every man the peculiar object of kindness, to the persons to whom
he himself has been kind. Though their gratitude should not always correspond to his beneficence, yet the sense of his merit, the sympathetic
gratitude of the impartial spectator, will always correspond to it. The
general indignation of other people, against the baseness of their ingratitude, will even, sometimes, increase the general sense of his merit. No
benevolent man ever lost altogether the fruits of his benevolence. If he does
not always gather them from the persons from whom he ought to have
gathered them, he seldom fails to gather them, and with a tenfold increase,
from other people. Kindness is the parent of kindness; and if to be beloved
by our brethren be the great object of our ambition, the surest way of
obtaining it is, by our conduct to show that we really love them.

20   After the persons who are recommended to our beneficence, either by
their connection with ourselves, by their personal qualities, or by their past
services, come those who are pointed out, not indeed to, what is called, our
friendship, but to our benevolent attention and good offices; those who are
distinguished by their extraordinary situation; the greatly fortunate and the
greatly unfortunate, the rich and the powerful, the poor and the wretched.

The distinction of ranks, the peace and order of society, are, in a great measure, founded upon the respect which we naturally conceive for the former. The relief and consolation of human misery depend altogether upon our compassion for the latter. The peace and order of society, is of more importance than even the relief of the miserable. Our respect for the great, accordingly, is most apt to offend by its excess; our fellow-feeling for the miserable, by its defect. Moralists exhort us to charity and compassion. They warn us against the fascination of greatness. This fascination, indeed, is so powerful, that the rich and the great are too often preferred to the wise and the virtuous. Nature has wisely judged that the distinction of ranks, the peace and order of society, would rest more securely upon the plain and palpable difference of birth and fortune, than upon the invisible and often uncertain difference of wisdom and virtue. The undistinguishing eyes of the great mob of mankind can well enough perceive the former: it is with difficulty that the nice discernment of the wise and the virtuous can sometimes distinguish the latter. In the order of all those recommendations, the benevolent wisdom of nature is equally evident.

21   It may, perhaps, be unnecessary to observe, that the combination of two, or more, of those exciting causes of kindness, increases the kindness. The favour and partiality which, when there is no envy in the case, we naturally bear to greatness, are much increased when it is joined with wisdom and virtue. If, notwithstanding that wisdom and virtue, the great man should fall into those misfortunes, those dangers and distresses, to which the most exalted stations are often the most exposed, we are much more deeply interested in his fortune than we should be in that of a person equally virtuous, but in a more humble situation. The most interesting subjects of tragedies and romances are the misfortunes of virtuous and magnanimous kings and princes. If, by the wisdom and manhood of their exertions, they should extricate themselves from those misfortunes, and recover completely their former superiority and security, we cannot help viewing them with the most enthusiastic and even extravagant admiration. The grief which we felt for their distress, the joy which we feel for their prosperity, seem to combine together in enhancing that partial admiration which we naturally conceive both for the station and the character.

22   When those different beneficent affections happen to draw different ways, to determine by any precise rules in what cases we ought to comply with the one, and in what with the other, is, perhaps, altogether impossible. In what cases friendship ought to yield to gratitude, or gratitude to friendship; in what cases the strongest of all natural affections ought to yield to a regard for the safety of those superiors upon whose safety often depends that of the whole society; and in what cases natural affection may, without impropriety, prevail over that regard; must be left altogether to the decision of the man within the breast, the supposed impartial spectator, the great

judge and arbiter of our conduct. If we place ourselves completely in his situation, if we really view ourselves with his eyes, and as he views us, and listen with diligent and reverential attention to what he suggests to us, his voice will never deceive us. We shall stand in need of no casuistic rules to direct our conduct. These it is often impossible to accommodate to all the different shades and gradations of circumstance, character, and situation, to differences and distinctions which, though not imperceptible, are, by their nicety and delicacy, often altogether undefinable. In that beautiful tragedy of Voltaire, the Orphan of China,[4] while we admire the magnanimity of Zamti, who is willing to sacrifice the life of his own child, in order to preserve that of the only feeble remnant of his ancient sovereigns and masters; we not only pardon, but love the maternal tenderness of Idame, who, at the risque of discovering the important secret of her husband, reclaims her infant from the cruel hands of the Tartars, into which it had been delivered.

CHAP. II

Of the order in which Societies are by nature recommended to our Beneficence

1 THE same principles that direct the order in which individuals are recommended to our beneficence, direct that likewise in which societies are recommended to it. Those to which it is, or may be of most importance, are first and principally recommended to it.

2   The state or sovereignty in which we have been born and educated, and under the protection of which we continue to live, is, in ordinary cases, the greatest society upon whose happiness or misery, our good or bad conduct can have much influence. It is accordingly, by nature, most strongly recommended to us. Not only we ourselves, but all the objects of our kindest affections, our children, our parents, our relations, our friends, our benefactors, all those whom we naturally love and revere the most, are commonly comprehended within it; and their prosperity and safety depend in some measure upon its prosperity and safety. It is by nature, therefore, endeared to us, not only by all our selfish, but by all our private benevolent affections. Upon account of our own connexion with it, its prosperity and glory seem to reflect some sort of honour upon ourselves. When we compare it with other societies of the same kind, we are proud of its superiority, and mortified in some degree, if it appears in any respect below them. All the illustrious characters which it has produced in former times (for against those of our own times envy may sometimes prejudice

---

[4] *L'Orphelin de la Chine*, produced in 1755. Smith praises it also in his 'Letter to the Editors of the *Edinburgh Review*' (now published in EPS), 17.

us a little), its warriors, its statesmen, its poets, its philosophers, and men of letters of all kinds; we are disposed to view with the most partial admiration, and to rank them (sometimes most unjustly) above those of all other nations. The patriot who lays down his life for the safety, or even for the vain-glory of this society, appears to act with the most exact propriety. He appears to view himself in the light in which the impartial spectator naturally and necessarily views him, as but one of the multitude, in the eye of that equitable judge, of no more consequence than any other in it, but bound at all times to sacrifice and devote himself to the safety, to the service, and even to the glory of the greater number. But though this sacrifice appears to be perfectly just and proper, we know how difficult it is to make it, and how few people are capable of making it. His conduct, therefore, excites not only our entire approbation, but our highest wonder and admiration, and seems to merit all the applause which can be due to the most heroic virtue. The traitor, on the contrary, who, in some peculiar situation, fancies he can promote his own little interest by betraying to the public enemy that of his native country; who, regardless of the judgment of the man within the breast, prefers himself, in this respect so shamefully and so basely, to all those with whom he has any connexion; appears to be of all villains the most detestable.

3   The love of our own nation often disposes us to view, with the most malignant jealousy and envy, the prosperity and aggrandisement of any other neighbouring nation. Independent and neighbouring nations, having no common superior to decide their disputes, all live in continual dread and suspicion of one another. Each sovereign, expecting little justice from his neighbours, is disposed to treat them with as little as he expects from them. The regard for the laws of nations, or for those rules which independent states profess or pretend to think themselves bound to observe in their dealings with one another, is often very little more than mere pretence and profession. From the smallest interest, upon the slightest provocation, we see those rules every day, either evaded or directly violated without shame or remorse. Each nation foresees, or imagines it foresees, its own subjugation in the increasing power and aggrandisement of any of its neighbours; and the mean principle of national prejudice is often founded upon the noble one of the love of our own country. The sentence with which the elder Cato is said to have concluded every speech which he made in the senate, whatever might be the subject, '*It is my opinion likewise that Carthage ought to be destroyed,*'[1] was the natural expression of the savage patriotism of a strong but coarse mind, enraged almost to madness against a foreign nation from which his own had suffered so much. The more humane sentence with which Scipio Nasica is said to have concluded all

[1] Plutarch, *Lives*, Marcus Cato (Cato the Elder), 27, reports the practice both of Cato and of Scipio.

his speeches, '*It is my opinion likewise that Carthage ought not to be destroyed*,'[1] was the liberal expression of a more enlarged and enlightened mind, who felt no aversion to the prosperity even of an old enemy, when reduced to a state which could no longer be formidable to Rome. France and England may each of them have some reason to dread the increase of the naval and military power of the other; but for either of them to envy the internal happiness and prosperity of the other, the cultivation of its lands, the advancement of its manufactures, the increase of its commerce, the security and number of its ports and harbours, its proficiency in all the liberal arts and sciences, is surely beneath the dignity of two such great nations. These are all real improvements of the world we live in. Mankind are benefited, human nature is ennobled by them. In such improvements each nation ought, not only to endeavour itself to excel, but from the love of mankind, to promote, instead of obstructing the excellence of its neighbours. These are all proper objects of national emulation, not of national prejudice or envy.

4   [2]The love of our own country seems not to be derived from the love of mankind. The former sentiment is altogether independent of the latter, and seems sometimes even to dispose us to act inconsistently with it. France may contain, perhaps, near three times the number of inhabitants which Great Britain contains.[3] In the great society of mankind, therefore, the prosperity of France should appear to be an object of much greater importance than that of Great Britain. The British subject, however, who, upon that account, should prefer upon all occasions the prosperity of the former to that of the latter country, would not be thought a good citizen of Great Britain. We do not love our country merely as a part of the great society of mankind: we love it for its own sake, and independently of any such consideration. That wisdom which contrived the system of human affections, as well as that of every other part of nature, seems to have judged that the interest of the great society of mankind would be best promoted by directing the principal attention of each individual to that particular portion of it, which was most within the sphere both of his abilities and of his understanding.

5   National prejudices and hatreds seldom extend beyond neighbouring

---

[2] Here and in § 11 Smith may possibly be criticizing Richard Price's celebrated sermon on 'The Love of our Country', preached on 4 November 1789, welcoming the French Revolution. See note to § 12 below. In Letter 251 addressed to George Chalmers, dated 22 December 1785, Smith wrote of Price: 'I have always considered him as a factious citizen, a most superficial Philosopher and by no means an able calculator.'

[3] In WN V.ii.k.78 (published in 1776) Smith cites the Abbé Expilly and Necker for an estimate of the population of France as 23 or 24 million, 'three times the number perhaps contained in Great Britain'. Richard Price, in an appendix to his sermon, calculated the population of France as 30 million, a figure that others thought too high. Modern scholars estimate the population of France in 1789 as about 27 million and that of Great Britain about 9 million.

nations. We very weakly and foolishly, perhaps, call the French our natural enemies; and they perhaps, as weakly and foolishly, consider us in the same manner. Neither they nor we bear any sort of envy to the prosperity of China or Japan. It very rarely happens, however, that our good-will towards such distant countries can be exerted with much effect.

6 The most extensive public benevolence which can commonly be exerted with any considerable effect, is that of the statesmen, who project and form alliances among neighbouring or not very distant nations, for the preservation either of, what is called, the balance of power, or of the general peace and tranquillity of the states within the circle of their negotiations. The statesmen, however, who plan and execute such treaties, have seldom any thing in view, but the interest of their respective countries. Sometimes, indeed, their views are more extensive. The Count d'Avaux, the plenipotentiary of France, at the treaty of Munster, would have been willing to sacrifice his life (according to the Cardinal de Retz,[4] a man not over-credulous in the virtue of other people) in order to have restored, by that treaty, the general tranquillity of Europe. King William seems to have had a real zeal for the liberty and independency of the greater part of the sovereign states of Europe; which, perhaps, might be a good deal stimulated by his particular aversion to France, the state from which, during his time, that liberty and independency were principally in danger. Some share of the same spirit seems to have descended to the first ministry of Queen Anne.[5]

7 Every independent state is divided into many different orders and societies, each of which has its own particular powers, privileges, and immunities. Every individual is naturally more attached to his own particular order or society, than to any other. His own interest, his own vanity, the interest and vanity of many of his friends and companions, are commonly a good deal connected with it. He is ambitious to extend its privileges and immunities. He is zealous to defend them against the encroachments of every other order or society.

8 Upon the manner in which any state is divided into the different orders and societies which compose it, and upon the particular distribution which has been made of their respective powers, privileges, and immunities, depends, what is called, the constitution of that particular state.

9 Upon the ability of each particular order or society to maintain its own powers, privileges, and immunities, against the encroachments of every

---

[4] *Mémoires*, under September 1650: Pléiade ed. (Paris, 1956), 370 (372 in recent printings); *Oeuvres*, ed. A. Feillet and others (Paris, 1870–1920), iii.104. The Peace of Westphalia was concluded by treaties signed at Münster and Osnabrück on 24 October 1648.
[5] William of Orange, both before and after he came to the British throne, fostered a grand alliance of European states against Louis XIV of France. The policy was maintained in the first years of Queen Anne's reign by continuing the War of the Spanish Succession under the leadership of the Duke of Marlborough.

other, depends the stability of that particular constitution. That particular constitution is necessarily more or less altered, whenever any of its subordinate parts is either raised above or depressed below whatever had been its former rank and condition.

10   All those different orders and societies are dependent upon the state to which they owe their security and protection. That they are all subordinate to that state, and established only in subserviency to its prosperity and preservation, is a truth acknowledged by the most partial member of every one of them. It may often, however, be hard to convince him that the prosperity and preservation of the state require any diminution of the powers, privileges, and immunities of his own particular order or society. This partiality, though it may sometimes be unjust, may not, upon that account, be useless. It checks the spirit of innovation. It tends to preserve whatever is the established balance among the different orders and societies into which the state is divided; and while it sometimes appears to obstruct some alterations of government which may be fashionable and popular at the time, it contributes in reality to the stability and permanency of the whole system.

11   The love of our country seems, in ordinary cases, to involve in it two different principles; first, a certain respect and reverence for that constitution or form of government which is actually established; and secondly, an earnest desire to render the condition of our fellow-citizens as safe, respectable, and happy as we can. He is not a citizen who is not disposed to respect the laws and to obey the civil magistrate; and he is certainly not a good citizen who does not wish to promote, by every means in his power, the welfare of the whole society of his fellow-citizens.

12   [6] In peaceable and quiet times, those two principles generally coincide and lead to the same conduct. The support of the established government seems evidently the best expedient for maintaining the safe, respectable, and happy situation of our fellow-citizens; when we see that this government actually maintains them in that situation. But in times of public discontent, faction, and disorder, those two different principles may draw different ways, and even a wise man may be disposed to think some alteration necessary in that constitution or form of government, which, in its actual condition, appears plainly unable to maintain the public tranquillity. In such cases, however, it often requires, perhaps, the highest effort of political

[6] It seems likely that Smith had the French Revolution in mind when writing this and the succeeding paragraphs. His remarks in §§ 15 and 17 about a 'spirit of system' and 'the man of system' may refer to the constitution-makers of 1789, or perhaps to the rationalist philosopher Richard Price again (cf. editorial note 2 to § 4 above), especially if Smith is echoing d'Alembert's disparaging use of the phrase 'the spirit of system' to describe rationalism in the Preliminary Discourse of the *Encyclopédie*. In Letter 287 addressed to Thomas Cadell, dated 31 March 1789, Smith says he has written a complete new Part VI for TMS; but since, according to Stewart, V.9, the manuscript was sent to the press at 'the beginning of the [following] winter', Smith doubtless made changes after March.

wisdom to determine when a real patriot ought to support and endeavour to re-establish the authority of the old system, and when he ought to give way to the more daring, but often dangerous spirit of innovation.

13   Foreign war and civil faction are the two situations which afford the most splendid opportunities for the display of public spirit. The hero who serves his country successfully in foreign war gratifies the wishes of the whole nation, and is, upon that account, the object of universal gratitude and admiration. In times of civil discord, the leaders of the contending parties, though they may be admired by one half of their fellow-citizens, are commonly execrated by the other. Their characters and the merit of their respective services appear commonly more doubtful. The glory which is acquired by foreign war is, upon this account, almost always more pure and more splendid than that which can be acquired in civil faction.

14   The leader of the successful party, however, if he has authority enough to prevail upon his own friends to act with proper temper and moderation (which he frequently has not), may sometimes render to his country a service much more essential and important than the greatest victories and the most extensive conquests. He may re-establish and improve the constitution, and from the very doubtful and ambiguous character of the leader of a party, he may assume the greatest and noblest of all characters, that of the reformer and legislator of a great state; and, by the wisdom of his institutions, secure the internal tranquillity and happiness of his fellow-citizens for many succeeding generations.

15   Amidst the turbulence and disorder of faction, a certain spirit of system is apt to mix itself with that public spirit which is founded upon the love of humanity, upon a real fellow-feeling with the ^{a}inconveniencies^a and distresses to which some of our fellow-citizens may be exposed. This spirit of system commonly takes the direction of that more gentle public spirit; always animates it, and often inflames it even to the madness of fanaticism. The leaders of the discontented party seldom fail to hold out some plausible plan of reformation which, they pretend, will not only remove the ^{b}inconveniencies^b and relieve the distresses immediately complained of, but will prevent, in all time coming, any return of the like ^{c}inconveniencies^c and distresses. They often propose, upon this account, to new-model the constitution, and to alter, in some of its most essential parts, that system of government under which the subjects of a great empire have enjoyed, perhaps, peace, security, and even glory, during the course of several centuries together. The great body of the party are commonly intoxicated with the imaginary beauty of this ideal system, of which they have no experience, but which has been represented to them in all the most dazzling colours in which the eloquence of their leaders could paint it. Those leaders

---

$^{a-a}$ inconveniences *6 7   See Introduction, 50.* $^{b-b}$ inconveniences *6 7*
$^{c-c}$ inconveniences *6 7*

themselves, though they originally may have meant nothing but their own aggrandisement, become many of them in time the dupes of their own sophistry, and are as eager for this great reformation as the weakest and foolishest of their followers. Even though the leaders should have preserved their own heads, as indeed they commonly do, free from this fanaticism, yet they dare not always disappoint the expectation of their followers; but are often obliged, though contrary to their principle and their conscience, to act as if they were under the common delusion. The violence of the party, refusing all palliatives, all temperaments, all reasonable accommodations, by requiring too much frequently obtains nothing; and those ᵈinconvenienciesᵈ and distresses which, with a little moderation, might in a great measure have been removed and relieved, are left altogether without the hope of a remedy.

16   The man whose public spirit is prompted altogether by humanity and benevolence, will respect the established powers and privileges even of individuals, and still more those of the great orders and societies, into which the state is divided. Though he should consider some of them as in some measure abusive, he will content himself with moderating, what he often cannot annihilate without great violence. When he cannot conquer the rooted prejudices of the people by reason and persuasion, he will not attempt to subdue them by force; but will religiously observe what, by Cicero, is justly called the divine maxim of Plato,⁷ never to use violence to his country no more than to his parents. He will accommodate, as well as he can, his public arrangements to the confirmed habits and prejudices of the people; and will remedy as well as he can, the ᵉinconvenienciesᵉ which may flow from the want of those regulations which the people are averse to submit to. When he cannot establish the right, he will not disdain to ameliorate the wrong; but like Solon, when he cannot establish the best system of laws, he will endeavour to establish the best that the people can bear.⁸

17   The man of system, on the contrary, is apt to be very wise in his own conceit; and is often so enamoured with the supposed beauty of his own

---

ᵈ⁻ᵈ inconveniences 6 7   ᵉ⁻ᵉ inconveniences 6 7

---

⁷ Plato's maxim is in *Crito*, 51 c. Cicero cites it in *Epistulae ad Familiares*, I.ix.18, 'vim neque parenti neque patriae afferri oportere', but does not call it 'divine'. Earlier in the same letter, I.ix.12, Cicero uses the word 'divinitus' of another maxim of Plato, 'Quales in republica principes essent, tales reliquos solere esse cives' (usually taken, with some hesitation, to be a very free rendering of a passage in Plato, *Laws*, 711 c). Smith refers again to 'the divine maxim of Plato' in § 18 below, and Eckstein (ii.579) thinks that there he apparently has in mind the maxim about leaders and citizens. It seems to us more probable that Smith is still thinking of the use of violence. In LJ(A) v.124 and LJ(B) 15 (Cannan ed., 11) Smith says that the Tory principle of authority equates rebellion against government with rebellion against a parent ('father' in LJ(A)).

⁸ Plutarch, *Lives*, Solon, 15.

ideal plan of government, that he cannot suffer the smallest deviation from any part of it. He goes on to establish it completely and in all its parts, without any regard either to the great interests, or to the strong prejudices which may oppose it. He seems to imagine that he can arrange the different members of a great society with as much ease as the hand arranges the different pieces upon a chess-board. He does not consider that the pieces upon the chess-board have no other principle of motion besides that which the hand impresses upon them; but that, in the great ʄchess-boardʄ of human society, every single piece has a principle of motion of its own, altogether different from that which the legislature might chuse to impress upon it. If those two principles coincide and act in the same direction, the game of human society will go on easily and harmoniously, and is very likely to be happy and successful. If they are opposite or different, the game will go on miserably, and the society must be at all times in the highest degree of disorder.

18   Some general, and even systematical, idea of the perfection of policy and law, may no doubt be necessary for directing the views of the statesman. But to insist upon establishing, and upon establishing all at once, and in spite of all opposition, every thing which that idea may seem to require, must often be the highest degree of arrogance. It is to erect his own judgment into the supreme standard of right and wrong. It is to fancy himself the only wise and worthy man in the commonwealth, and that his fellow-citizens should accommodate themselves to him and not he to them. It is upon this account, that of all political speculators, sovereign princes are by far the most dangerous. This arrogance is perfectly familiar to them. They entertain no doubt of the immense superiority of their own judgment. When such imperial and royal reformers, therefore, condescend to contemplate the constitution of the country which is committed to their government, they seldom see any thing so wrong in it as the obstructions which it may sometimes oppose to the execution of their own will. They hold in contempt the divine maxim of Plato,[9] and consider the state as made for themselves, not themselves for the state. The great object of their reformation, therefore, is to remove those obstructions; to reduce the authority of the nobility; to take away the privileges of cities and provinces, and to render both the greatest individuals and the greatest orders of the state, as incapable of opposing their commands, as the weakest and most insignicant.

ʄ–ʄ 7   chess board 6 *Cf. the two preceding instances.*

---

[9] See § 16 above.

CHAP. III
Of universal Benevolence

1   THOUGH our effectual good offices can very seldom be extended to any wider society than that of our own country; our good-will is circumscribed by no boundary, but may embrace the immensity of the universe. We cannot form the idea of any innocent and sensible being, whose happiness we should not desire, or to whose misery, when distinctly brought home to the imagination, we should not have some degree of aversion. The idea of a mischievous, though sensible, being, indeed, naturally provokes our hatred: but the ill-will which, in this case, we bear to it, is really the effect of our universal benevolence. It is the effect of the sympathy which we feel with the misery and resentment of those other innocent and sensible beings, whose happiness is disturbed by its malice.

2   This universal benevolence, how noble and generous soever, can be the source of no solid happiness to any man who is not thoroughly convinced that all the inhabitants of the universe, the meanest as well as the greatest, are under the immediate care and protection of that great, benevolent, and all-wise Being, who directs all the movements of nature; and who is determined, by his own unalterable perfections, to maintain in it, at all times, the greatest possible quantity of happiness. To this universal benevolence, on the contrary, the very suspicion of a fatherless world, must be the most melancholy of all reflections; from the thought that all the unknown regions of infinite and incomprehensible space may be filled with nothing but endless misery and wretchedness. All the splendour of the highest prosperity can never enlighten the gloom with which so dreadful an idea must necessarily over-shadow the imagination; nor, in a wise and virtuous man, can all the sorrow of the most afflicting adversity ever dry up the joy which necessarily springs from the habitual and thorough conviction of the truth of the contrary system.

3   The wise and virtuous man is at all times willing that his own private interest should be sacrificed to the public interest of his own particular order or society. He is at all times willing, too, that the interest of this order or society should be sacrificed to the greater interest of the state or sovereignty, of which it is only a subordinate part. He should, therefore, be equally willing that all those inferior interests should be sacrificed to the greater interest of the universe, to the interest of that great society of all sensible and intelligent beings, of which God himself is the immediate administrator and director. If he is deeply impressed with the habitual and thorough conviction that this benevolent and all-wise Being can admit into the system of his government, no partial evil which is not necessary for the universal good, he must consider all the misfortunes which may befal

himself, his friends, his society, or his country, as necessary for the prosperity of the universe, and therefore as what he ought, not only to submit to with resignation, but as what he himself, if he had known all the connexions and dependencies of things, ought sincerely and devoutly to have wished for.

4   Nor does this magnanimous resignation to the will of the great Director of the universe, seem in any respect beyond the reach of human nature. Good soldiers, who both love and trust their general, frequently march with more gaiety and alacrity to the forlorn station, from which they never expect to return, than they would to one where there was neither difficulty nor danger. In marching to the latter, they could feel no other sentiment than that of the dulness of ordinary duty: in marching to the former, they feel that they are making the noblest exertion which it is possible for man to make. They know that their general would not have ordered them upon this station, had it not been necessary for the safety of the army, for the success of the war. They cheerfully sacrifice their own little systems to the prosperity of a greater system. They take an affectionate leave of their comrades, to whom they wish all happiness and success; and march out, not only with submissive obedience, but often with shouts of the most joyful exultation, to that fatal, but splendid and honourable station to which they are appointed. No conductor of an army can deserve more unlimited trust, more ardent and zealous affection, than the great Conductor of the universe. In the greatest public as well as private disasters, a wise man ought to consider that he himself, his friends and countrymen, have only been ordered upon the forlorn station of the universe; that had it not been necessary for the good of the whole, they would not have been so ordered; and that it is their duty, not only with humble resignation to submit to this allotment, but to endeavour to embrace it with alacrity and joy. A wise man should surely be capable of doing what a good soldier holds himself at all times in readiness to do.

5   The idea of that divine Being, whose benevolence and wisdom have, from all eternity, contrived and conducted the immense machine of the universe, so as at all times to produce the greatest possible quantity of happiness, is certainly of all the objects of human contemplation by far the most sublime. Every other thought necessarily appears mean in the comparison. The man whom we believe to be principally occupied in this sublime contemplation, seldom fails to be the object of our highest veneration; and though his life should be altogether contemplative, we often regard him with a sort of religious respect much superior to that with which we look upon the most active and useful servant of the commonwealth. The Meditations of Marcus Antoninus,[1] which turn principally

---

[1] Marcus Aurelius.

upon this subject, have contributed more, perhaps, to the general admiration of his character, than all the different transactions of his just, merciful, and beneficent reign.

6   The administration of the great system of the universe, however, the care of the universal happiness of all rational and sensible beings, is the business of God and not of man. To man is allotted a much humbler department, but one much more suitable to the weakness of his powers, and to the narrowness of his comprehension; the care of his own happiness, of that of his family, his friends, his country: that he is occupied in contemplating the more sublime, can never be an excuse for his neglecting the more humble department; and he must not expose himself to the charge which Avidius Cassius is said to have brought, perhaps unjustly, against Marcus Antoninus;[2] that while he employed himself in philosophical speculations, and contemplated the prosperity of the universe, he neglected that of the Roman empire. The most sublime speculation of the contemplative philosopher can scarce compensate the neglect of the smallest active duty.

SECTION III
Of Self-command

1   THE man who acts according to the rules of perfect prudence, of strict justice, and of proper benevolence, may be said to be perfectly virtuous. But the most perfect knowledge of those rules will not alone enable him to act in this manner: his own passions are very apt to mislead him; sometimes to drive him and sometimes to seduce him to violate all the rules which he himself, in all his sober and cool hours, approves of. The most perfect knowledge, if it is not supported by the most perfect self-command, will not always enable him to do his duty.

2   Some of the best of the ancient moralists seem to have considered those passions as divided into two different classes: first, into those which it requires a considerable exertion of self-command to restrain even for a single moment; and secondly, into those which it is easy to restrain for a single moment, or even for a short period of time; but which, by their continual and almost incessant solicitations, are, in the course of a life, very apt to mislead into great deviations.

---

[2] In a letter reported by Vulcacius Gallicanus, *Life of Avidius Cassius*, xiv.5 (in *Scriptores Historiae Augustae*). Smith gives a paraphrase, not a translation; the letter says nothing of 'the prosperity of the universe'.

3   Fear and anger, together with some other passions which are mixed or connected with them, constitute the first class. The love of ease, of pleasure, of applause, and of many other selfish gratifications, constitute the second. Extravagant fear and furious anger, it is often difficult to restrain even for a single moment. The love of ease, of pleasure, of applause, and other selfish gratifications, it is always easy to restrain for a single moment, or even for a short period of time; but, by their continual solicitations, they often mislead us into many weaknesses which we have afterwards much reason to be ashamed of. The former set of passions may often be said to drive, the latter, to seduce us from our duty. The command of the former was, by the ancient moralists above alluded to, denominated fortitude, manhood, and strength of mind; that of the latter, temperance, decency, modesty, and moderation.

4   The command of each of those two sets of passions, independent of the beauty which it derives from its utility; from its enabling us upon all occasions to act according to the dictates of prudence, of justice, and of proper benevolence; has a beauty of its own, and seems to deserve for its own sake a certain degree of esteem and admiration. In the one case, the strength and greatness of the exertion excites some degree of that esteem and admiration. In the other, the uniformity, the equality and unremitting steadiness of that exertion.

5   The man who, in danger, in torture, upon the approach of death, preserves his tranquillity unaltered, and suffers no word, no gesture to escape him which does not perfectly accord with the feelings of the most indifferent spectator, necessarily commands a very high degree of admiration. If he suffers in the cause of liberty and justice, for the sake of humanity and the love of his country, the most tender compassion for his sufferings, the strongest indignation against the injustice of his persecutors, the warmest sympathetic gratitude for his beneficent intentions, the highest sense of his merit, all join and mix themselves with the admiration of his magnanimity, and often inflame that sentiment into the most enthusiastic and rapturous veneration. The heroes of ancient and modern history, who are remembered with the most peculiar favour and affection, are, many of them, those who, in the cause of truth, liberty, and justice, have perished upon the scaffold, and who behaved there with that ease and dignity which became them. Had the enemies of Socrates suffered him to die quietly in his bed, the glory even of that great philosopher might possibly never have acquired that dazzling splendour in which it has been beheld in all succeeding ages. In the English history, when we look over the illustrious heads which have been engraven by Vertue and Howbraken,[1] there is

---

[1] Smith is thinking of a book of engravings with some letterpress: Thomas Birch, *The Heads of Illustrious Persons of Great Britain, engraven by Mr. Houbraken, and Mr. Vertue. With their Lives and Characters* (1743).

scarce any body, I imagine, who does not feel that the axe, the emblem of having been beheaded, which is engraved under some of the most illustrious of them; under those of the Sir Thomas Mores, of the Rhaleighs, the Russels, the Sydneys,[2] etc. sheds a real dignity and interestingness over the characters to which it is affixed, much superior to what they can derive from all the futile ornaments of heraldry, with which they are sometimes accompanied.

6   Nor does this magnanimity give lustre only to the characters of innocent and virtuous men. It draws some degree of favourable regard even upon those of the greatest criminals; and when a robber or highwayman is brought to the scaffold, and behaves there with decency and firmness, though we perfectly approve of his punishment, we often cannot help regretting that a man who possessed such great and noble powers should have been capable of such mean enormities.

7   War is the great school both for acquiring and exercising this species of magnanimity. Death, as we say, is the king of terrors; and the man who has conquered the fear of death, is not likely to lose his presence of mind at the approach of any other natural evil. In war, men become familiar with death, and are thereby necessarily cured of that superstitious horror with which it is viewed by the weak and unexperienced. They consider it merely as the loss of life, and as no further the object of aversion than as life may happen to be that of desire. They learn from experience, too, that many seemingly great dangers are not so great as they appear; and that, with courage, activity, and presence of mind, there is often a good probability of extricating themselves with honour from situations where at first they could see no hope. The dread of death is thus greatly diminished; and the confidence or hope of escaping it, augmented. They learn to expose themselves to danger with less reluctance. They are less anxious to get out of it, and less apt to lose their presence of mind while they are in it. It is this habitual contempt of danger and death which ennobles the profession of a soldier, and bestows upon it, in the natural apprehensions of mankind, a rank and dignity superior to that of any other profession. The skilful and successful exercise of this profession, in the service of their country, seems to have constituted the most distinguishing feature in the character of the favourite heroes of all ages.

8   Great warlike exploit, though undertaken contrary to every principle of justice, and carried on without any regard to humanity, sometimes interests us, and commands even some degree of a certain sort of esteem for the very worthless characters which conduct it. We are interested even in the ex-

[2] Sir Thomas More was beheaded in 1535, having been declared guilty of high treason; Sir Walter Raleigh in 1618, having been condemned to death in 1603 on a charge of conspiracy against James I; William, Lord Russell, and Algernon Sidney (or Sydney), both in 1683 for complicity in the Rye House plot.

ploits of the Buccaneers;[3] and read with some sort of esteem and admiration, the history of the most worthless men, who, in pursuit of the most criminal purposes, endured greater hardships, surmounted greater difficulties, and encountered greater dangers, than, perhaps, any which the ordinary course of history gives an account of.

9   The command of anger appears upon many occasions not less generous and noble than that of fear. The proper expression of just indignation composes many of the most splendid and admired passages both of ancient and modern eloquence. The Philippics of Demosthenes,[4] the Catalinarians of Cicero,[5] derive their whole beauty from the noble propriety with which this passion is expressed. But this just indignation is nothing but anger restrained and properly attempered to what the impartial spectator can enter into. The blustering and noisy passion which goes beyond this, is always odious and offensive, and interests us, not for the angry man, but for the man with whom he is angry. The nobleness of pardoning appears, upon many occasions, superior even to the most perfect propriety of resenting. When either proper acknowledgments have been made by the offending party; or, even without any such acknowledgments, when the public interest requires that the most mortal enemies should unite for the discharge of some important duty, the man who can cast away all animosity, and act with confidence and cordiality towards the person who had most grievously offended him, seems justly to merit our highest admiration.

10   The command of anger, however, does not always appear in such splendid colours. Fear is contrary to anger, and is often the motive which restrains it; and in such cases the meanness of the motive takes away all the nobleness of the restraint. Anger prompts to attack, and the indulgence of it seems sometimes to shew a sort of courage and superiority to fear. The indulgence of anger is sometimes an object of vanity. That of fear never is. Vain and weak men, among their inferiors, or those who dare not resist them, often affect to be ostentatiously passionate, and fancy that they show, what is called, spirit in being so. A bully tells many stories of his own insolence, which are not true, and imagines that he thereby renders himself, if not more amiable and respectable, at least more formidable to his audience. Modern manners, which, by favouring the practice of duelling, may be said, in some cases, to encourage private revenge, contribute, perhaps, a good deal to render, in modern times, the restraint of anger by fear still more contemptible than it might otherwise appear to be. There is always something dignified in the command of fear, whatever may be the motive upon which it is founded. It is not so with the command of anger.

---

[3] The pirates who operated off the Spanish Main in the seventeenth century.
[4] Demosthenes' speeches urging the Athenians to resist Philip of Macedon.
[5] Cicero's speeches accusing Catiline of conspiracy in 63 B.C.

Unless it is founded altogether in the sense of decency, of dignity, and propriety, it never is perfectly agreeable.

11   To act according to the dictates of prudence, of justice, and proper beneficence, seems to have no great merit where there is no temptation to do otherwise. But to act with cool deliberation in the midst of the greatest dangers and difficulties; to observe religiously the sacred rules of justice in spite both of the greatest interests which might tempt, and the greatest injuries which might provoke us to violate them; never to *a*suffer*a* the benevolence of our temper to be damped or discouraged by the malignity and ingratitude of the individuals towards whom it may have been exercised; is the character of the most exalted wisdom and virtue. Self-command is not only itself a great virtue, but from it all the other virtues seem to derive their principal lustre.

12   The command of fear, the command of anger, are always great and noble powers. When they are directed by justice and benevolence, they are not only great virtues, but increase the splendour of those other virtues. They may, however, sometimes be directed by very different motives; and in this case, though still great and respectable, they may be excessively dangerous. The most intrepid valour may be employed in the cause of the greatest injustice. Amidst great provocations, apparent tranquillity and good humour may sometimes conceal the most determined and cruel resolution to revenge. The strength of mind requisite for such dissimulation, though always and necessarily contaminated by the baseness of falsehood, has, however, been often much admired by many people of no contemptible judgment. The dissimulation of Catharine of Medicis is often celebrated by the profound historian Davila;[6] that of Lord Digby, afterwards Earl of Bristol, by the grave and conscientious Lord Clarendon;[7] that of the first Ashley Earl of Shaftesbury, by the judicious Mr. Locke.[8] Even Cicero seems to consider this deceitful character, not indeed as of the highest dignity, but as not unsuitable to a certain flexibility of manners, which, he thinks, may, notwithstanding, be, upon the whole, both agreeable and respectable. He exemplifies it by the characters of Homer's Ulysses, of the Athenian Themistocles, of the Spartan Lysander, and of the Roman Marcus Crassus.[9] This character of dark and deep dissimulation occurs most commonly in times of great public disorder; amidst the

a-a 7 suffer 6

[6] Enrico Caterino Davila, *Historia delle guerre civili di Francia* (1630). Smith's copy of this work was of an edition published in London in 1755 (Bonar, *Catalogue 2*, 54). In that edition see e.g. vol. i, 66–7, 99, 641–2.

[7] Edward Hyde, 1st Earl of Clarendon, *History of the Rebellion and Civil Wars in England*; e.g. Book IV, §§ 127, 154–5, 193.

[8] John Locke, 'Memoirs relating to the Life of Anthony, first Earl of Shaftesbury'; *Works* (London, 1777), iv.233–43.

[9] Smith is referring to *De Officiis*, I.xxx.107–9, where Cicero, discussing general and particular propriety, distinguishes between universal and individual human characters.

violence of faction and civil war. When law has become in a great measure impotent, when the most perfect innocence cannot alone insure safety, regard to self-defence obliges the greater part of men to have recourse to dexterity, to address, and to apparent accommodation to whatever happens to be, at the moment, the prevailing party. This false character, too, is frequently accompanied with the coolest and most determined courage. The proper exercise of it supposes that courage, as death is commonly the certain consequence of detection. It may be employed indifferently, either to exasperate or to allay those furious animosities of adverse factions which impose the necessity of assuming it; and though it may sometimes be useful, it is at least equally liable to be excessively pernicious.

13 The command of the less violent and turbulent passions seems much less liable to be abused to any pernicious purpose. Temperance, decency, modesty, and moderation, are always amiable, and can seldom be directed to any bad end. It is from the unremitting steadiness of those gentler exertions of self-command, that the amiable virtue of chastity, that the respectable virtues of industry and frugality, derive all that sober lustre which attends them. The conduct of all those who are contented to walk in the humble paths of private and peaceable life, derives from the same principle the greater part of the beauty and grace which belong to it; a beauty and grace, which, though much less dazzling, is not always less pleasing than those which accompany the more splendid actions of the hero, the statesman, or the legislator.

14 After what has already been said, in several different parts of this discourse, concerning the nature of self-command, I judge it unnecessary to enter into any further detail concerning those virtues. I shall only observe at present, that the point of propriety, the degree of any passion which the impartial spectator approves of, is differently situated in different passions. In some passions the excess is less disagreeable than the defect; and in such passions the point of propriety seems to stand high, or nearer to the excess than to the defect. In other passions, the defect is less disagreeable than the excess; and in such passions the point of propriety seems to stand low, or nearer to the defect than to the excess. The former are the passions which the spectator is most, the latter, those which he is least disposed to sympathize with. The former, too, are the passions of which the immediate

---

Listing types of individual character, Cicero writes of shrewdness with an ability to conceal and dissimulate, citing Themistocles among his examples. He then speaks of a more extreme craftiness, with Marcus Crassus and Lysander as two of his examples. Cicero does not cite Ulysses in this chapter, though in xxxi.113 he describes Ulysses as an example of endurance. In III.xxvi.97, however, he refers to the dissimulation of Ulysses in feigning madness to escape military service. Smith, writing from memory, has probably confused this last with what Cicero says, at I.xxx.108, of Solon, who is classed with Themistocles and is called 'especially crafty and shrewd in having feigned madness in order to save his life' and serve the state.

feeling or sensation is agreeable to the person principally concerned; the latter, those of which it is disagreeable. It may be laid down as a general rule, that the passions which the spectator is most disposed to sympathize with, and in which, upon that account, the point of propriety may be said to stand high, are those of which the immediate feeling or sensation is more or less agreeable to the person principally concerned: and that, on the contrary, the passions which the spectator is least disposed to sympathize with, and in which, upon that account, the point of propriety may be said to stand low, are those of which the immediate feeling or sensation is more or less disagreeable, or even painful, to the person principally concerned. This general rule, so far as I have been able to observe, admits not of a single exception. A few examples will at once, both sufficiently explain it and demonstrate the truth of it.

15   The disposition to the affections which tend to unite men in society, to humanity, kindness, natural affection, friendship, esteem, may sometimes be excessive. Even the excess of this disposition, however, renders a man interesting to every body. Though we blame it, we still regard it with compassion, and even with kindness, and never with dislike.[10] We are more sorry for it than angry at it. To the person himself, the indulgence even of such excessive affections is, upon many occasions, not only agreeable, but delicious. Upon some occasions, indeed, especially when directed, as is too often the case, towards unworthy objects, it exposes him to much real and heartfelt distress. Even upon such occasions, however, a well-disposed mind regards him with the most exquisite pity, and feels the highest indignation against those who affect to despise him for his weakness and imprudence. The defect of this disposition, on the contrary, what is called hardness of heart, while it renders a man insensible to the feelings and distresses of other people, renders other people equally insensible to his; and, by excluding him from the friendship of all the world, excludes him from the best and most comfortable of all social enjoyments.

16   The disposition to the affections which drive men from one another, and which tend, as it were, to break the bands of human society; the disposition to anger, hatred, envy, malice, revenge; is, on the contrary, much more apt to offend by its excess than by its defect. The excess renders a man wretched and miserable in his own mind, and the object of hatred, and sometimes even of horror, to other people. The defect is very seldom complained of. It may, however, be defective. The want of proper indignation is a most essential defect in the manly character, and, upon many occasions, renders a man incapable of protecting either himself or his friends from insult and injustice. Even that principle, in the excess and improper direction of which consists the odious and detestable passion

---

[10] Cf. Hume, *Enquiry concerning the Principles of Morals*, VII; ed. Selby-Bigge, § 208.

of envy, may be defective. Envy is that passion which views with malignant dislike the superiority of those who are really entitled to all the superiority they possess. The man, however, who, in matters of consequence, tamely suffers other people, who are entitled to no such superiority, to rise above him or get before him, is justly condemned as mean-spirited. This weakness is commonly founded in indolence, sometimes in good nature, in an aversion to opposition, to bustle and solicitation, and sometimes, too, in a sort of ill-judged magnanimity, which fancies that it can always continue to despise the advantage which it then despises, and, therefore, so easily gives up. Such weakness, however, is commonly followed by much regret and repentance; and what had some appearance of magnanimity in the beginning frequently gives place to a most malignant envy in the end, and to a hatred of that superiority, which those who have once attained it, may often become really entitled to, by the very circumstance of having attained it. In order to live comfortably in the world, it is, upon all occasions, as necessary to defend our dignity and rank, as it is to defend our life or our fortune.

17 Our sensibility to personal danger and distress, like that to personal provocation, is much more apt to offend by its excess than by its defect. No character is more contemptible than that of a coward; no character is more admired than that of the man who faces death with intrepidity, and maintains his tranquillity and presence of mind amidst the most dreadful dangers. We esteem the man who supports pain and even torture with manhood and firmness; and we can have little regard for him who sinks under them, and abandons himself to useless outcries and womanish lamentations. A fretful temper, which feels, with too much sensibility, every little cross accident, renders a man miserable in himself and offensive to other people. A calm one, which does not allow its tranquillity to be disturbed, either by the small injuries, or by the little disasters incident to the usual course of human affairs; but which, amidst the natural and moral evils infesting the world, lays its account and is contented to suffer a little from both, is a blessing to the man himself, and gives ease and security to all his companions.

18 Our sensibility, however, both to our own injuries and to our own misfortunes, though generally too strong, may likewise be too weak. The man who feels little for his own misfortunes must always feel less for those of other people, and be less disposed to relieve them. The man who has little resentment for the injuries which are done to himself, must always have less for those which are done to other people, and be less disposed either to protect or to avenge them. A stupid insensibility to the events of human life necessarily extinguishes all that keen and earnest attention to the propriety of our own conduct, which constitutes the real essence of virtue. We can feel little anxiety about the propriety of our own actions,

when we are indifferent about the events which may result from them. The man who feels the full distress of the calamity which has befallen him, who feels the whole baseness of the injustice which has been done to him, but who feels still more strongly what the dignity of his own character requires; who does not abandon himself to the guidance of the undisciplined passions which his situation might naturally inspire; but who governs his whole behaviour and conduct according to those restrained and corrected emotions which the great inmate, the great demi-god within the breast prescribes and approves of; is alone the real man of virtue, the only real and proper object of love, respect, and admiration. Insensibility and that noble firmness, that exalted self-command, which is founded in the sense of dignity and propriety, are so far from being altogether the same, that in proportion as the former takes place, the merit of the latter is, in many cases, entirely taken away.

19   But though the total want of sensibility to personal injury, to personal danger and distress, would, in such situations, take away the whole merit of self-command, that sensibility, however, may very easily be too exquisite, and it frequently is so. When the sense of propriety, when the authority of the judge within the breast, can control this extreme sensibility, that authority must no doubt appear very noble and very great. But the exertion of it may be too fatiguing; it may have too much to do. The individual, by a great effort, may behave perfectly well. But the contest between the two principles, the warfare within the breast, may be too violent to be at all consistent with internal tranquillity and happiness. The wise man whom Nature has endowed with this too exquisite sensibility, and whose too lively feelings have not been sufficiently blunted and hardened by early education and proper exercise, will avoid, as much as duty and propriety will permit, the situations for which he is not perfectly fitted. The man whose feeble and delicate constitution renders him too sensible to pain, to hardship, and to every sort of bodily distress, should not wantonly embrace the profession of a soldier. The man of too much sensibility to injury, should not rashly engage in the contests of faction. Though the sense of propriety should be strong enough to command all those sensibilities, the composure of the mind must always be disturbed in the struggle. In this disorder the judgment cannot always maintain its ordinary acuteness and precision; and though he may always mean to act properly, he may often act rashly and imprudently, and in a manner which he himself will, in the succeeding part of his life, be for ever ashamed of. A certain intrepidity, a certain firmness of nerves and hardiness of constitution, whether natural or acquired, are undoubtedly the best preparatives for all the great exertions of self-command.

20   Though war and faction are certainly the best schools for forming every man to this hardiness and firmness of temper, though they are the best

remedies for curing him of the opposite weaknesses, yet, if the day of trial should happen to come before he has completely learned his lesson, before the remedy has had time to produce its proper effect, the consequences might not be agreeable.

21   Our sensibility to the pleasures, to the amusements and enjoyments of human life, may offend, in the same manner, either by its excess or by its defect. Of the two, however, the excess seems less disagreeable than the defect. Both to the spectator and to the person principally concerned, a strong propensity to joy is certainly more pleasing than a dull insensibility to the objects of amusement and diversion. We are charmed with the gaiety of youth, and even with the playfulness of childhood: but we soon grow weary of the flat and tasteless gravity which too frequently accompanies old age. When this propensity, indeed, is not restrained by the sense of propriety, when it is unsuitable to the time or to the place, to the age or to the situation of the person, when, to indulge it, he neglects either his interest or his duty; it is justly blamed as excessive, and as hurtful both to the individual and to the society. In the greater part of such cases, however, what is chiefly to be found fault with is, not so much the strength of the propensity to joy, as the weakness of the sense of propriety and duty. A young man who has no relish for the diversions and amusements that are natural and suitable to his age, who talks of nothing but his book or his business, is disliked as formal and pedantic; and we give him no credit for his abstinence even from improper indulgences, to which he seems to have so little inclination.

22   The principle of self-estimation may be too high, and it may likewise be too low. It is so very agreeable to think highly, and so very disagreeable to think meanly of ourselves, that, to the person himself, it cannot well be doubted, but that some degree of excess must be much less disagreeable than any degree of defect. But to the impartial spectator, it may perhaps be thought, things must appear quite differently, and that to him, the defect must always be less disagreeable than the excess. And in our companions, no doubt, we much more frequently complain of the latter than of the former. When they assume upon us, or set themselves before us, their self-estimation mortifies our own. Our own pride and vanity prompt us to accuse them of pride and vanity, and we cease to be the impartial spectators of their conduct. When the same companions, however, suffer any other man to assume over them a superiority which does not belong to him, we not only blame them, but often despise them as mean-spirited. When, on the contrary, among other people, they push themselves a little more forward, and scramble to an elevation disproportioned, as we think, to their merit, though we may not perfectly approve of their conduct, we are often, upon the whole, diverted with it; and, where there is no envy in the case, we are almost always much less displeased with them, than we

should have been, had they suffered themselves to sink below their proper station.

23   In estimating our own merit, in judging of our own character and conduct, there are two different standards to which we naturally compare them. The one is the idea of exact propriety and perfection, so far as we are each of us capable of comprehending that idea. The other is that degree of approximation to this idea which is commonly attained in the world, and which the greater part of our friends and companions, of our rivals and competitors, may have actually arrived at. We very seldom (I am disposed to think, we never) attempt to judge of ourselves without giving more or less attention to both these different standards. But the attention of different men, and even of the same man at different times, is often very unequally divided between them; and is sometimes principally directed towards the one, and sometimes towards the other.

24   So far as our attention is directed towards the first standard, the wisest and best of us all, can, in his own character and conduct, see nothing but weakness and imperfection; can discover no ground for arrogance and presumption, but a great deal for humility, regret and repentance. So far as our attention is directed towards the second, we may be affected either in the one way or in the other, and feel ourselves, either really above, or really below, the standard to which we compare ourselves.

25   The wise and virtuous man directs his principal attention to the first standard; the idea of exact propriety and perfection. There exists in the mind of every man, an idea of this kind, gradually formed from his observations upon the character and conduct both of himself and of other people. It is the slow, gradual, and progressive work of the great demigod within the breast, the great judge and arbiter of conduct. This idea is in every man more or less accurately drawn, its colouring is more or less just, its outlines are more or less exactly designed, according to the delicacy and acuteness of that sensibility, with which those observations were made, and according to the care and attention employed in making them. In the wise and virtuous man they have been made with the most acute and delicate sensibility, and the utmost care and attention have been employed in making them. Every day some feature is improved; every day some blemish is corrected. He has studied this idea more than other people, he comprehends it more distinctly, he has formed a much more correct image of it, and is much more deeply enamoured of its exquisite and divine beauty. He endeavours as well as he can, to assimilate his own character to this archetype of perfection. But he imitates the work of a divine artist, which can never be equalled. He feels the imperfect success of all his best endeavours, and sees, with grief and affliction, in how many different features the mortal copy falls short of the immortal original. He remembers, with concern and humilation, how often, from want of attention, from want of judgment,

from want of temper, he has, both in words and actions, both in conduct and conversation, violated the exact rules of perfect propriety; and has so far departed from that model, according to which he wished to fashion his own character and conduct. When he directs his attention towards the second standard, indeed, that degree of excellence which his friends and acquaintances have commonly arrived at, he may be sensible of his own superiority. But, as his principal attention is always directed towards the first standard, he is necessarily much more humbled by the one comparison, than he ever can be elevated by the other. He is never so elated as to look down with insolence even upon those who are really below him. He feels so well his own imperfection, he knows so well the difficulty with which he attained his own distant approximation to rectitude, that he cannot regard with contempt the still greater imperfection of other people. Far from insulting over their inferiority, he views it with the most indulgent commiseration, and, by his advice as well as example, is at all times willing to promote their further advancement. If, in any particular qualification, they happen to be superior to him (for who is so perfect as not to have many superiors in many different qualifications?), far from envying their superiority, he, who knows how difficult it is to excel, esteems and honours their excellence, and never fails to bestow upon it the full measure of applause which it deserves. His whole mind, in short, is deeply impressed, his whole behaviour and deportment are distinctly stamped with the character of real modesty; with that of a very moderate estimation of his own merit, and, at the same time, of a full sense of the merit of other people.

26   In all the liberal and ingenious arts, in painting, in poetry, in music, in eloquence, in philosophy, the great artist feels always the real imperfection of his own best works, and is more sensible than any man how much they fall short of that ideal perfection of which he has formed some conception, which he imitates as well as he can, but which he despairs of ever equalling. It is the inferior artist only, who is ever perfectly satisfied with his own performances. He has little conception of this ideal perfection, about which he has little employed his thoughts; and it is chiefly to the works of other artists, of, perhaps, a still lower order, that he deigns to compare his own works. Boileau, the great French poet (in some of his works, perhaps not inferior to the greatest poet of the same kind, either ancient or modern), used to say, that no great man was ever completely satisfied with his own works. His acquaintance Santeuil (a writer of Latin verses, and who, on account of that schoolboy accomplishment, had the weakness to fancy himself a poet), assured him, that he himself was always completely satisfied with *his* own. Boileau replied, with, perhaps, an arch ambiguity, *b*that*b* he certainly was the only great man that ever was so.[11] Boileau, in

b–b That *6 7*

---

[11] Jean de Santeul (1630–97) had some reputation in his own day as a writer of liturgical

judging of his own works, compared them with the standard of ideal perfection, which, in his own particular branch of the poetic art, he had, I presume, meditated as deeply, and conceived as distinctly, as it is possible for man to conceive it. Santeuil, in judging of *his* own works, compared them, I suppose, chiefly to those of the other Latin poets of his own time, to the greater part of whom he was certainly very far from being inferior. But to support and finish off, if I may say so, the conduct and conversation of a whole life to some resemblance of this ideal perfection, is surely much more difficult than to work up to an equal resemblance any of the productions of any of the ingenious arts. The artist sits down to his work undisturbed, at leisure, in the full possession and recollection of all his skill, experience, and knowledge. The wise man must support the propriety of his own conduct in health and in sickness, in success and in disappointment, in the hour of fatigue and drowsy indolence, as well as in that of the most awakened attention. The most sudden and unexpected assaults of difficulty and distress must never surprise him. The injustice of other people must never provoke him to injustice. The violence of faction must never confound him. All the hardships and hazards of war must never either dishearten or appal him.

27   Of the persons who, in estimating their own merit, in judging of their own character and conduct, direct by far the greater part of their attention to the second standard, to that ordinary degree of excellence which is commonly attained by other people, there are some who really and justly feel themselves very much above it, and who, by every intelligent and impartial spectator, are acknowledged to be so. The attention of such persons, however, being always principally directed, not to the standard of ideal, but to that of ordinary perfection, they have little sense of their own weaknesses and imperfections; they have little modesty; are often assuming, arrogant, and presumptuous; great admirers of themselves, and great contemners of other people. Though their characters are in general much less correct, and their merit much inferior to that of the man of real and modest virtue; yet their excessive presumption, founded upon their own excessive self-admiration, dazzles the multitude, and often imposes even upon those who are much superior to the multitude. The frequent, and often wonderful, success of the most ignorant quacks and imposters, both civil and religious, sufficiently demonstrate how easily the multitude are imposed upon by the most extravagant and groundless pretensions. But when those pretensions are supported by a very high degree of real and solid merit, when they are displayed with all the splendour which ostentation can bestow upon them, when they are supported by high rank and great power, when they have

hymns and other sacred poems in Latin. He appears as a character in Boileau's *Dialogue des poètes*, which makes fun of French authors who write in Latin. We cannot trace the source of Smith's anecdote.

often been successfully exerted, and are, upon that account, attended by
the loud acclamations of the multitude; even the man of sober judgment
often abandons himself to the general admiration. The very noise of those
foolish acclamations often contributes to confound his understanding, and
while he sees those great men only at a certain distance, he is often disposed
to worship them with a sincere admiration, superior even to that with which
they appear to worship themselves. When there is no envy in the case, we all
take pleasure in admiring, and are, upon that account, naturally disposed,
in our own fancies, to render complete and perfect in every respect the characters which, in many respects, are so very worthy of admiration. The excessive self-admiration of those great men is well understood, perhaps, and
even seen through, with some degree of derision, by those wise men who
are much in their familiarity, and who secretly smile at those lofty pretensions, which, by people at a distance, are often regarded with reverence,
and almost with adoration. Such, however, have been, in all ages, the greater
part of those men who have procured to themselves the most noisy fame,
the most extensive reputation; a fame and reputation, too, which have often
descended to the remotest posterity.

28   Great success in the world, great authority over the sentiments and
opinions of mankind, have very seldom been acquired without some degree of this excessive self-admiration. The most splendid characters, the
men who have performed the most illustrious actions, who have brought
about the greatest revolutions, both in the situations and opinions of mankind; the most successful warriors, the greatest statesmen and legislators,
the eloquent founders and leaders of the most numerous and most successful sects and parties; have many of them been, not more distinguished for
their very great merit, than for a degree of presumption and self-admiration
altogether disproportioned even to that very great merit. This presumption
was, perhaps, necessary, not only to prompt them to undertakings which a
more sober mind would never have thought of, but to command the submission and obedience of their followers to support them in such undertakings. When crowned with success, accordingly, this presumption has
often betrayed them into a vanity that approached almost to insanity and
folly. Alexander the Great appears, not only to have wished that other
people should think him a God, but to have been at least very well disposed to fancy himself such. Upon his death-bed, the most ungodlike of all
situations, he requested of his friends that, to the respectable list of Deities,
into which himself had long before been inserted, his old mother Olympia
might likewise have the honour of being added.[12] Amidst the respectful

---

[12] Quintus Curtius, *History of Alexander*, IX.vi.26, reports Alexander as asking his
friends to 'consecrate' Olympias 'to immortality' if he himself should die before doing so.
This was not on his death-bed, however, but after recovery from a wound that had led to
reports of his death.

admiration of his followers and disciples, amidst the universal applause of
the public, after the oracle, which probably had followed the voice of that
applause, had pronounced him the wisest of men,[13] the great wisdom of
Socrates, though it did not suffer him to fancy himself a God, yet was not
great enough to hinder him from fancying that he had secret and frequent
intimations from some invisible and divine Being.[14] The sound head of
Caesar was not so perfectly sound as to hinder him from being much
pleased with his divine genealogy from the goddess Venus; and, before the
temple of this pretended great-grandmother, to receive, without rising
from his seat, the Roman Senate, when that illustrious body came to present
him with some decrees conferring upon him the most extravagant honours.[15] This insolence, joined to some other acts of an almost childish
vanity, little to be expected from an understanding at once so very acute
and comprehensive, seems, by exasperating the public jealousy, to have
emboldened his assassins, and to have hastened the execution of their
conspiracy. The religion and manners of modern times give our great
men little encouragement to fancy themselves either Gods or even Pro-
phets. Success, however, joined to great popular favour, has often so far
turned the heads of the greatest of them, as to make them ascribe to themselves both an importance and an ability much beyond what they really
possessed; and, by this presumption, to precipitate themselves into many
rash and sometimes ruinous adventures. It is a characteristic almost peculiar
to the great Duke of Marlborough, that ten years[16] of such uninterrupted
and such splendid success as scarce any other general could boast of, never
betrayed him into a single rash action, scarce into a single rash word or
expression. The same temperate coolness and self-command cannot, I
think, be ascribed to any other great warrior of later times; not to Prince
Eugene,[17] not to the late King of Prussia,[18] not to the great Prince of
Conde,[19] not even to Gustavus Adolphus.[20] Turrenne[21] seems to have

---

[13] Cf. Plato, *Apology of Socrates*, 21 a.

[14] Socrates often spoke of his δαιμόνιον, a divine sign or voice that warned him not to
do certain actions.

[15] Cf. Suetonius, *Lives of the Caesars*, I.78.

[16] Smith presumably has in mind the ten years of Britain's participation in the War of
the Spanish Succession, 1702–12, though the Duke of Marlborough was deprived of his
offices at the end of 1711.

[17] Prince Eugène of Savoy (1663–1736), commander of the Austrian army in the War
of the Spanish Succession.

[18] Frederick the Great, who died in 1786, about three years before Smith composed this
passage for ed. 6.

[19] Louis II de Bourbon, Prince of Condé (1621–86), known as 'the Great Condé',
victor at the battles of Rocroy (1643) and Lens (1648).

[20] King of Sweden, 1611–32, commander of the Protestant forces in the Thirty Years'
War.

[21] Henri de La Tour d'Auvergne, Vicomte de Turenne (1611–75), marshal of France,
rival of Condé, noted for his simple, honest character as well as for his military genius.

approached the nearest to it; but several different transactions of his life sufficiently demonstrate that it was in him by no means so perfect as in the great Duke of Marlborough.

29   In the humble projects of private life, as well as in the ambitious and proud pursuits of high stations, great abilities and successful enterprise, in the beginning, have frequently encouraged to undertakings which necessarily led to bankruptcy and ruin in the end.

30   The esteem and admiration which every impartial spectator conceives for the real merit of those spirited, magnanimous, and high-minded persons, as it is a just and well-founded sentiment, so it is a steady and permanent one, and altogether independent of their good or bad fortune. It is otherwise with that admiration which he is apt to conceive for their excessive self-estimation and presumption. While they are successful, indeed, he is often perfectly conquered and overborne by them. Success covers from his eyes, not only the great imprudence, but frequently the great injustice of their enterprises; and, far from blaming this defective part of their character, he often views it with the most enthusiastic admiration. When they are unfortunate, however, things change their colours and their names. What was before heroic magnanimity, resumes its proper appellation of extravagant rashness and folly; and the blackness of that avidity and injustice, which was before hid under the splendour of prosperity, comes full into view, and blots the whole lustre of their enterprise. Had Caesar, instead of gaining, lost the battle of Pharsalia,[22] his character would, at this hour, have ranked a little above that of Catiline,[23] and the weakest man would have viewed his enterprise against the laws of his country in blacker colours, than, ᶜperhaps,ᶜ even Cato,[24] with all the animosity of a party-man, ever viewed it at the time. His real merit, the justness of his taste, the simplicity and elegance of his writings, the propriety of his eloquence, his skill in war, his resources in distress, his cool and sedate judgment in danger, his faithful attachment to his friends, his unexampled generosity to his enemies, would all have been acknowledged; as the real merit of Catiline, who had many great qualities, is acknowledged at this day. But the insolence and injustice of his all-grasping ambition would have darkened and extinguished the glory of all that real merit. Fortune has in this, as well as in some other respects already mentioned, great influence over the moral sentiments of mankind, and, according as she is either favourable or adverse, can render the same character the object,

ᶜ⁻ᶜ 7   ∼ₐ 6

---

[22] Caesar's defeat of Pompey at the battle of Pharsalus (48 B.C.) decided the outcome of the Civil War.

[23] The conspiracy of Catiline in 63 B.C., shown up by Cicero, met with universal reprobation.

[24] Marcus Porcius Cato Uticensis (95–46 B.C.), a leader of the aristocratic party, consistently opposed Caesar.

either of general love and admiration, or of universal hatred and contempt. This great disorder in our moral sentiments is by no means, however, without its utility; and we may on this, as well as on many other occasions, admire the wisdom of God even in the weakness and folly of man.[25] Our admiration of success is founded upon the same principle with our respect for wealth and greatness, and is equally necessary for establishing the distinction of ranks and the order of society. By this admiration of success we are taught to submit more easily to those superiors, whom the course of human affairs may assign to us; to regard with reverence, and sometimes even with a sort of respectful affection, that fortunate violence which we ᵈareᵈ no longer capable of resisting; not only the violence of such splendid characters as those of a Caesar or an Alexander, but often that of the most brutal and savage barbarians, of an Attila, a Gengis,[26] or a Tamerlane. To all such mighty conquerors the great mob of mankind are naturally disposed to look up with a wondering, though, no doubt, with a very weak and foolish admiration. By this admiration, however, they are taught to acquiesce with less reluctance under that government which an irresistible force imposes upon them, and from which no reluctance could deliver them.

31   Though in prosperity, however, the man of excessive self-estimation may sometimes appear to have some advantage over the man of correct and modest virtue; though the applause of the multitude, and of those who see them both only at a distance, is often much louder in favour of the one than it ever is in favour of the other; yet, all things fairly computed, the real balance of advantage is, perhaps in all cases, greatly in favour of the latter and against the former. The man who neither ascribes to himself, nor wishes that other people should ascribe to him, any other merit besides that which really belongs to him, fears no humiliation, dreads no detection; but rests contented and secure upon the genuine truth and solidity of his own character. His admirers may neither be very numerous nor very loud in their applauses; but the wisest man who sees him the nearest and who knows him the best, admires him the most. To a real wise man the judicious and well-weighed approbation of a single wise man, gives more heartfelt satisfaction than all the noisy applauses of ten thousand ignorant though enthusiastic admirers. He may say with Parmenides, who, upon reading a philosophical discourse before a public assembly at Athens, and observing, that, except Plato, the whole company had left him, continued, notwithstanding, to read on, and said that Plato alone was audience sufficient for him.[27]

ᵈ⁻ᵈ 7   ear 6

[25] Cf. the final words of II.iii.3.2 above.   [26] Genghis Khan.

[27] Smith's memory has misled him. Cicero, *Brutus*, li.91, tells the story about Antimachus reading a long poem before an audience that eventually consisted only of Plato.

32   It is otherwise with the man of excessive self-estimation. The wise men
who see him the nearest, admire him the least. Amidst the intoxication of
prosperity, their sober and just esteem falls so far short of the extravagance
of his own self-admiration, that he regards it as mere malignity and envy.
He suspects his best friends. Their company becomes offensive to him.
He drives them from his presence, and often rewards their services, not
only with ingratitude, but with cruelty and injustice. He abandons his
confidence to flatterers and traitors, who pretend to idolize his vanity and
presumption; and that character which in the beginning, though in some
respects defective, was, upon ᵉtheᵉ whole, both amiable and respectable,
becomes contemptible and odious in the end. Amidst the intoxication of
prosperity, Alexander killed Clytus, for having preferred the exploits of
his father Philip to his own; put Calisthenes to death in torture, for having
refused to adore him in the Persian manner; and murdered the great
friend of his father, the venerable Parmenio, after having, upon the most
groundless suspicions, sent first to the torture and afterwards to the scaffold the only remaining son of that old man, the rest having all before died
in his own service.[28] This was that Parmenio of whom Philip used to say,
that the Athenians were very fortunate who could find ten generals every
year, while he himself, in the whole course of his life, could never find one
but Parmenio.[29] It was upon the vigilance and attention of this Parmenio
that he reposed at all times with confidence and security, and, in his hours
of mirth and jollity, used to say, Let us drink, my friends, we may do it
with safety, for Parmenio never drinks.[30] It was this same Parmenio, with
whose presence and counsel, it had been said, Alexander had gained all his
victories; and without whose presence and counsel, he had never gained a
single victory.[31] The humble, admiring, and flattering friends, whom
Alexander left in power and authority behind him, divided his empire
among themselves, and after having thus robbed his family and kindred of

ᵉ⁻ᵉ 7 *om.* 6

The philosopher Parmenides (even if in his old age he met the young Socrates, as Plato's
dialogue *Parmenides* supposes) must have died before Plato was born.

[28] Alexander killed Cleitus at a banquet in 328 B.C., when both were the worse for
drink. Callisthenes died of torture or disease after being imprisoned in 327 B.C. for alleged
complicity in a plot to assassinate Alexander. Parmenion's son Philotas was accused in
330 B.C. of conspiring against Alexander, and under torture he implicated his father also,
whereupon Alexander had both of them put to death.

[29] Plutarch, *Apophthegmata* (*Moralia*, Book III), 177 c.

[30] Smith's memory has misled him. He seems to be conflating two similar remarks made
by Philip, not about Parmenion, but about another of his generals, Antipater. One is reported by Athenaeus, *Deipnosophistae*, 435 d: 'We must drink; it is enough that Antipater
is sober.' The other by Plutarch, *Apophthegmata*, 179 b: 'I was asleep with safety, for
Antipater was awake.'

[31] Presumably a reference to the exaggerated comment of Quintus Curtius, *History of
Alexander*, VII.ii.33: 'Multa sine rege prospere, rex sine illo nihil magnae rei gesserat.'

their inheritance, put, one after another, every single surviving individual of them, whether male or female, to death.

33   We frequently, not only pardon, but thoroughly enter into and sympathize with the excessive self-estimation of those splendid characters in which we observe a great and distinguished superiority above the common level of mankind. We call them spirited, magnanimous, and high-minded; words which all involve in their meaning a considerable degree of praise and admiration. But we cannot enter into and sympathize with the excessive self-estimation of those characters in which we can discern no such distinguished superiority. We are disgusted and revolted by it; and it is with some difficulty that we can either pardon or suffer it. We call it pride or vanity; two words, of which the latter always, and the former for the most part, involve in their meaning a considerable degree of blame.

34   Those two vices, however, though resembling, in some respects, as being both modifications of excessive self-estimation, are yet, in many respects, very different from one another.

35   The proud man is sincere, and, in the bottom of his heart, is convinced of his own superiority; though it may sometimes be difficult to guess upon what that conviction is founded. He wishes you to view him in no other light than that in which, when he places himself in your situation, he really views himself. He demands no more of you than, what he thinks, justice. If you appear not to respect him as he respects himself, he is more offended than mortified, and feels the same indignant resentment as if he had suffered a real injury. He does not even then, however, deign to explain the grounds of his own pretensions. He disdains to court your esteem. He affects even to despise it, and endeavours to maintain his assumed station, not so much by making you sensible of his superiority, as of your own meanness. He seems to wish, not so much to excite your esteem for *himself*, as to mortify ʃthatʃ for *yourself*.

36   The vain man is not sincere, and, in the bottom of his heart, is very seldom convinced of that superiority which he wishes you to ascribe to him. He wishes you to view him in much more splendid colours than those in which, when he places himself in your situation, and supposes you to know all that he knows, he can really view himself. When you appear to view him, therefore, in different colours, perhaps in his proper colours, he is much more mortified than offended. The grounds of his claim to that character which he wishes you to ascribe to him, he takes every opportunity of displaying, both by the most ostentatious and unnecessary exhibition of the good qualities and accomplishments which he possesses in some tolerable degree, and sometimes even by false pretensions to those which he either possesses in no degree, or in so very slender a degree that he may well enough be said to possess them in no degree. Far from despising your

ʃ-ʃ *ital. 6   7 Probably an error in the MS.*

esteem, he courts it with the most anxious assiduity. Far from wishing to mortify your self-estimation, he is happy to cherish it, in hopes that in return you will cherish his own. He flatters in order to be flattered. He studies to please, and endeavours to bribe you into a good opinion of him by politeness and complaisance, and sometimes even by real and essential good offices, though often displayed, perhaps, with unnecessary ostentation.

37   The vain man sees the respect which is paid to rank and fortune, and wishes to usurp this respect, as well as that for talents and virtues. His dress, his equipage, his way of living, accordingly, all announce both a higher rank and a greater fortune than really belong to him; and in order to support this foolish imposition for a few years in the beginning of his life, he often reduces himself to poverty and distress long before the end of it. As long as he can continue his expence, however, his vanity is delighted with viewing himself, not in the light in which you would view him if you knew all that he knows; but in that in which, he imagines, he has, by his own address, induced you actually to view him. Of all the illusions of vanity this is, perhaps, the most common. Obscure strangers who visit foreign countries, or who, from a remote province, come to visit, for a short time, the capital of their own country, most frequently attempt to practise it. The folly of the attempt, though always very great and most unworthy of a man of sense, may not be altogether so great upon such as upon most other occasions. If their stay is short, they may escape any disgraceful detection; and, after indulging their vanity for a few months or a few years, they may return to their own homes, and repair, by future parsimony, the waste of their past profusion.

38   The proud man can very seldom be accused of this folly. His sense of his own dignity renders him careful to preserve his independency, and, when his fortune happens not to be large, though he wishes to be decent, he studies to be frugal and attentive in all his expences. The ostentatious expence of the vain man is highly offensive to him. It outshines, perhaps, his own. It provokes his indignation as an insolent assumption of a rank which is by no means due; and he never talks of it without loading it with the harshest and severest reproaches.

39   The proud man does not always feel himself at his ease in the company of his equals, and still less in that of his superiors. He cannot lay down his lofty pretensions, and the countenance and conversation of such company overawe him so much that he dare not display them. He has recourse to humbler company, for which he has little respect, which he would not willingly chuse; and which is by no means agreeable to him; that of his inferiors, his flatterers, and dependants. He seldom visits his superiors, or, if he does, it is rather to show that he is entitled to live in such company, than for any real satisfaction that he enjoys in it. It is as Lord Clarendon

says of the Earl of Arundel, that he sometimes went to court, because he could there only find a greater man than himself; but that he went very seldom, because he found there a greater man than himself.[32]

40   It is quite otherwise with the vain man. He courts the company of his superiors as much as the proud man shuns it. Their splendour, he seems to think, reflects a splendour upon those who are much about them. He haunts the courts of kings and the levees of ministers, and gives himself the air of being a candidate for fortune and preferment, when in reality he possesses the much more precious happiness, if he knew how to enjoy it, of not being one. He is fond of being admitted to the tables of the great, and still more fond of magnifying to other people the familiarity with which he is honoured there. He associates himself, as much as he can, with fashionable people, with those who are supposed to direct the public opinion, with the witty, with the learned, with the popular; and he shuns the company of his best friends whenever the very uncertain current of public favour happens to run in any respect against them. With the people to whom he wishes to recommend himself, he is not always very delicate about the means which he employs for that purpose; unnecessary ostentation, groundless pretensions, constant assentation, frequently flattery, though for the most part a pleasant and a sprightly flattery, and very seldom the gross and fulsome flattery of a parasite. The proud man, on the contrary, never flatters, and is frequently scarce civil to any body.

41   Notwithstanding all its groundless pretensions, however, vanity is almost always a sprightly and a gay, and very often a good-natured passion. Pride is always a grave, a sullen, and a severe one. Even the falsehoods of the vain man are all innocent falsehoods, meant to raise himself, not to lower other people. To do the proud man justice, he very seldom stoops to the baseness of falsehood. When he does, however, his falsehoods are by no means so innocent. They are all mischievous, and meant to lower other people. He is full of indignation at the unjust superiority, as he thinks it, which is given to them. He views them with malignity and envy, and, in talking of them, often endeavours, as much as he can, to extenuate and lessen whatever are the grounds upon which their superiority is supposed to be founded. Whatever tales are circulated to their disadvantage, though he seldom forges them himself, yet he often takes pleasure in believing them, is by no means unwilling to repeat them, and even sometimes with some degree of exaggeration. The worst falsehoods of vanity are all what we call white lies: those of pride, whenever it condescends to falsehood, are all of the opposite complexion.

42   Our dislike to pride and vanity generally disposes us to rank the persons whom we accuse of those vices rather below than above the common level.

---

[32] Clarendon, *History of the Rebellion and Civil Wars in England*, Book I, § 119.

In this judgment, however, I think, we are most frequently in the wrong, and that both the proud and the vain man are often (perhaps for the most part) a good deal above it; though not near so much as either the one really thinks himself, or as the other wishes you to think him. If we compare them with their own pretensions, they may appear the just objects of contempt. But when we compare them with what the greater part of their rivals and competitors really are, they may appear quite otherwise, and very much above the common level. Where there is this real superiority, pride is frequently attended with many respectable virtues; with truth, with integrity, with a high sense of honour, with cordial and steady friendship, with the most inflexible firmness and resolution. Vanity, with many amiable ones; with humanity, with politeness, with a desire to oblige in all little matters, and sometimes with a real generosity in great ones; a generosity, however, which it often wishes to display in the most splendid colours that it can. By their rivals and enemies, the French, in the last century, were accused of vanity; the Spaniards, of pride; and foreign nations were disposed to consider the one as the more amiable; the other, as the more respectable people.

43   The words *vain* and *vanity* are never taken in a good sense. We sometimes say of a man, when we are talking of him in good humour, that he is the better for his vanity, or that his vanity is more diverting than offensive; but we still consider it as a foible and a ridicule in his character.

44   The words *proud* and *pride*, on the contrary, are sometimes taken in a good sense. We frequently say of a man, that he is too proud, or that he has too much noble pride, ever to suffer himself to do a mean thing. Pride is, in this case, confounded with magnanimity. Aristotle, a philosopher who certainly knew the world, in drawing the character of the magnanimous man, paints him with many features which, in the two last centuries, were commonly ascribed to the Spanish character: that he was deliberate in all his resolutions; slow, and even tardy, in all his actions; that his voice was grave, his speech deliberate, his step and motion slow; that he appeared indolent and even slothful, not at all disposed to bustle about little matters, but to act with the most determined and vigorous resolution upon all great and illustrious occasions; that he was not a lover of danger, or forward to expose himself to little dangers, but to great dangers; and that, when he exposed himself to danger, he was altogether regardless of his life.[33]

45   The proud man is commonly too well contented with himself to think that his character requires any amendment. The man who feels himself all-perfect, naturally enough despises all further improvement. His self-sufficiency and absurd conceit of his own superiority, commonly attend him

[33] Cf. Aristotle, *Nicomachean Ethics*, 1125^{a}13–14, 1124^{b}7–8.

from his youth to his most advanced age; and he dies, as Hamlet says, with all his sins upon his head, unanointed, unanealed.[34]

46   It is frequently otherwise with the vain man. The desire of the esteem and admiration of other people, when for qualities and talents which are the natural and proper objects of esteem and admiration, is the real love of true glory; a passion which, if not the very best passion of human nature, is certainly one of the best. Vanity is very frequently no more than an attempt prematurely to usurp that glory before it is due. Though your son, under five-and-twenty years of age, should be but a coxcomb; do not, upon that account, despair of his becoming, before he is forty, a very wise and worthy man, and a real proficient in all those talents and virtues to which, at present, he may only be an ostentatious and empty pretender. The great secret of education is to direct vanity to proper objects. Never suffer him to value himself upon trivial accomplishments. But do not always discourage his pretensions to those that are of real importance. He would not pretend to them if he did not earnestly desire to possess them. Encourage this desire; afford him every means to facilitate the acquisition; and do not take too much offence, although he should sometimes assume the air of having attained it a little before the time.

47   Such, I say, are the distinguishing characteristics of pride and vanity, when each of them acts according to its proper character. But the proud man is often vain; and the vain man is often proud. Nothing can be more natural than that the man, who thinks much more highly of himself than he deserves, should wish that other people should think still more highly of him: or that the man, who wishes that other people should think more highly of him than he thinks of himself, should, at the same time, think much more highly of himself than he deserves. Those two vices being frequently in the same character, the characteristics of both are necessarily confounded; and we sometimes find the superficial and impertinent ostentation of vanity joined to the most malignant and derisive insolence of pride. We are sometimes, upon that account, at a loss how to rank a particular character, or whether to place it among the proud or among the vain.

48   Men of merit considerably above the common level, sometimes under-rate as well as over-rate themselves. Such characters, though not very dignified, are often, in private society, far from being disagreeable. His companions all feel themselves much at their ease in the society of a man

---

[34] Smith is misquoting from memory. It is the Ghost, not Hamlet, who speaks thus of his own death:

> Cut off even in the blossoms of my sin,
> Unhousell'd, disappointed, unaneled;
> No reckoning made, but sent to my account
> With all my imperfections on my head:

> (*Hamlet*, I.v.76–9.)

so perfectly modest and unassuming. If those companions, however, have not both more discernment and more generosity than ordinary, though they may have some kindness for him, they have seldom much respect; and the warmth of their kindness is very seldom sufficient to compensate the coldness of their respect. Men of no more than ordinary discernment never rate any person higher than he appears to rate himself. He seems doubtful himself, they say, whether he is perfectly fit for such a situation or such an office; and immediately give the preference to some impudent blockhead who entertains no doubt about his own qualifications. Though they should have discernment, yet, if they want generosity, they never fail to take advantage of his simplicity, and to assume over him an impertinent superiority which they are by no means entitled to. His good-nature may enable him to bear this for some time; but he grows weary at last, and frequently when it is too late, and when that rank, which he ought to have assumed, is lost irrecoverably, and usurped, in consequence of his own backwardness, by some of his more forward, though much less meritorious companions. A man of this character must have been very fortunate in the early choice of his companions, if, in going through the world, he meets always with fair justice, even from those whom, from his own past kindness, he might have some reason to consider as his best friends; and a youth, too unassuming and too unambitious, is frequently followed by an insignificant, complaining, and discontented old age.

49   Those unfortunate persons whom nature has formed a good deal below the common level, seem sometimes to rate themselves still more below it than they really are. This humility appears sometimes to sink them into idiotism. Whoever has taken the trouble to examine idiots with attention, will find that, in many of them, the faculties of the understanding are by no means weaker than in several other people, who, though acknowledged to be dull and stupid, are not, by any body, accounted idiots. Many idiots, with no more than ordinary education, have been taught to read, write, and account tolerably well. Many persons, never accounted idiots, notwithstanding the most careful education, and notwithstanding that, in their advanced age, they have had spirit enough to attempt to learn what their early education had not taught them, have never been able to acquire, in any tolerable degree, any one of those three accomplishments. By an instinct of pride, however, they set themselves upon a level with their equals in age and situation; and, with courage and firmness, maintain their proper station among their companions. By an opposite instinct, the idiot feels himself below every company into which you can introduce him. Ill-usage, to which he is extremely liable, is capable of throwing him into the most violent fits of rage and fury. But no good usage, no kindness or indulgence, can ever raise him to converse with you as your equal. If you can bring him to converse with you at all, however, you will frequently find

his answers sufficiently pertinent, and even sensible. But they are always stamped with a distinct consciousness of his own great inferiority. He seems to shrink and, as it were, to retire from your look and conversation; and to feel, when he places himself in your situation, that, notwithstanding your apparent condescension, you cannot help considering him as immensely below you. Some idiots, perhaps the greater part, seem to be so, chiefly or altogether, from a certain numbness or torpidity in the faculties of the understanding. But there are others, in whom those faculties do not appear more torpid or benumbed than in many other people who are not accounted idiots. But that instinct of pride, necessary to support them upon an equality with their brethren, seems totally wanting in the former and not in the latter.

50   That degree of self-estimation, therefore, which contributes most to the happiness and contentment of the person himself, seems likewise most agreeable to the impartial spectator. The man who esteems himself as he ought, and no more than he ought, seldom fails to obtain from other people all the esteem that he himself thinks due. He desires no more than is due to him, and he rests upon it with complete satisfaction.

51   The proud and the vain man, on the contrary, are constantly dissatisfied. The one is tormented with indignation at the unjust superiority, as he thinks it, of other people. The other is in continual dread of the shame which, he foresees, would attend upon the detection of his groundless pretensions. Even the extravagant pretensions of the man of real magnanimity, though, when supported by splendid abilities and virtues, and, above all, by good fortune, they impose upon the multitude, whose applauses he little regards, do not impose upon those wise men whose approbation he can only value, and whose esteem he is most anxious to acquire. He feels that they see through, and suspects that they despise his excessive presumption; and he often suffers the cruel misfortune of becoming, first the jealous and secret, and at last the open, furious, and vindictive enemy of those very persons, whose friendship it would have given him the greatest happiness to enjoy with unsuspicious security.

52   Though our dislike to the proud and the vain often disposes us to rank them rather below than above their proper station, yet, unless we are provoked by some particular and personal impertinence, we very seldom venture to use them ill. In common cases, we endeavour, for our own ease, rather to acquiesce, and, as well as we can, to accommodate ourselves to their folly. But, to the man who under-rates himself, unless we have both more discernment and more generosity than belong to the greater part of men, we seldom fail to do, at least, all the injustice which he does to himself, and frequently a great deal more. He is not only more unhappy in his own feelings than either the proud or the vain, but he is much more liable to every sort of ill-usage from other people. In almost all cases, it is better

to be a little too proud, than, in any respect, too humble; and, in the sentiment of self-estimation, some degree of excess seems, both to the person and to the impartial spectator, to be less disagreeable than any degree of defect.

53   In this, therefore, as well as in every other emotion, passion, and habit, the degree that is most agreeable to the impartial spectator is likewise most agreeable to the person himself; and according as either the excess or the defect is least offensive to the former, so, either the one or the other is in proportion least disagreeable to the latter.

CONCLUSION *of the* SIXTH PART

1   CONCERN for our own happiness recommends to us the virtue of prudence: concern for that of other people, the virtues of justice and beneficence; of which, the one restrains us from hurting, the other prompts us to promote that happiness. Independent of any regard either to what are, or to what ought to be, or to what upon a certain condition would be, the sentiments of other people, the first of those three virtues is originally recommended to us by our selfish, the other two by our benevolent affections. Regard to the sentiments of other people, however, comes afterwards both to enforce and to direct the practice of all those virtues; and no man during, either the whole of his life, or that of any considerable part of it, ever trod steadily and uniformly in the paths of prudence, of justice, or of proper beneficence, whose conduct was not principally directed by a regard to the sentiments of the supposed impartial spectator, of the great inmate of the breast, the great judge and arbiter of conduct. If in the course of the day we have swerved in any respect from the rules which he prescribes to us; if we have either exceeded or relaxed in our frugality; if we have either exceeded or relaxed in our industry; if, through passion or inadvertency, we have hurt in any respect the interest or happiness of our neighbour; if we have neglected a plain and proper opportunity of promoting that interest and happiness; it is this inmate who, in the evening, calls us to an account for all those omissions and violations, and his reproaches often make us blush inwardly both for our folly and inattention to our own happiness, and for our still greater indifference and inattention, perhaps, to that of other people.

2   But though the virtues of prudence, justice, and beneficence, may, upon different occasions, be recommended to us almost equally by two different principles; those of self-command are, upon most occasions, principally and almost entirely recommended to us by one; by the sense of propriety, by regard to the sentiments of the supposed impartial spectator. Without the restraint which this principle imposes, every passion would, upon most

occasions, rush headlong, if I may say so, to its own gratification. Anger would follow the suggestions of its own fury; fear those of its own violent agitations. Regard to no time or place would induce vanity to refrain from the loudest and most impertinent ostentation; or voluptuousness from the most open, indecent, and scandalous indulgence. Respect for what are, or for what ought to be, or for what upon a certain condition would be, the sentiments of other people, is the sole principle which, upon most occasions, overawes all those mutinous and turbulent passions into that tone and temper which the impartial spectator can enter into and sympathize with.

3   Upon some occasions, indeed, those passions are restrained, not so much by a sense of their impropriety, as by prudential considerations of the bad consequences which might follow from their indulgence. In such cases, the passions, though restrained, are not always subdued, but often remain lurking in the breast with all their original fury. The man whose anger is restrained by fear, does not always lay aside his anger, but only reserves its gratification for a more safe opportunity. But the man who, in relating to some other person the injury which has been done to him, feels at once the fury of his passion cooled and becalmed by sympathy with the more moderate sentiments of his companion, who at once adopts those more moderate sentiments, and comes to view that injury, not in the black and atrocious colours in which he had originally beheld it, but in the much milder and fairer light in which his companion naturally views it; not only restrains, but in some measure subdues, his anger. The passion becomes really less than it was before, and less capable of exciting him to the violent and bloody revenge which at first, perhaps, he might have thought of inflicting.

4   Those passions which are restrained by the sense of propriety, are all in some degree moderated and subdued by it. But those which are restrained only by prudential considerations of any kind, are, on the contrary, frequently inflamed by the restraint, and sometimes (long after the provocation given, and when nobody is thinking about it) burst out absurdly and unexpectedly, and with tenfold fury and violence.

5   Anger, however, as well as every other passion, may, upon many occasions, be very properly restrained by prudential considerations. Some exertion of manhood and self-command is even necessary for this sort of restraint; and the impartial spectator may sometimes view it with that sort of cold esteem due to that species of conduct which he considers as a mere matter of vulgar prudence; but never with that affectionate admiration with which he surveys the same passions, when, by the sense of propriety, they are moderated and subdued to what he himself can readily enter into. In the former species of restraint, he may frequently discern some degree of propriety, and, if you will, even of virtue; but it is a propriety and virtue

of a much inferior order to those which he always feels with transport and admiration in the latter.

6   The virtues of prudence, justice, and beneficence, have no tendency to produce any but the most agreeable effects. Regard to those effects, as it originally recommends them to the actor, so does it afterwards to the impartial spectator. In our approbation of the character of the prudent man, we feel, with peculiar complacency, the security which he must enjoy while he walks under the safeguard of that sedate and deliberate virtue. In our approbation of the character of the just man, we feel, with equal complacency, the security which all those connected with him, whether in neighbourhood, society, or business, must derive from his scrupulous anxiety never either to hurt or offend. In our approbation of the character of the beneficent man, we enter into the gratitude of all those who are within the sphere of his good offices, and conceive with them the highest sense of his merit. In our approbation of all those virtues, our sense of their agreeable effects, of their utility, either to the person who exercises them, or to some other persons, joins with our sense of their propriety, and constitutes always a considerable, frequently the greater part of that approbation.

7   But in our approbation of the virtues of self-command, complacency with their effects sometimes constitutes no part, and frequently but a small part, of that approbation. Those effects may sometimes be agreeable, and sometimes disagreeable; and though our approbation is no doubt stronger in the former case, it is by no means altogether destroyed in the latter. The most heroic valour may be employed indifferently in the cause either of justice or of injustice; and though it is no doubt much more loved and admired in the former case, it still appears a great and respectable quality even in the latter. In that, and in all the other virtues of self-command, the splendid and dazzling quality seems always to be the greatness and steadiness of the exertion, and the strong sense of propriety which is necessary in order to make and to maintain that exertion. The effects are too often but too little regarded.

PART VII
Of Systems of MORAL PHILOSOPHY
Consisting of Four Sections

SECTION I

ᵃOf the Questions which ought to be examined in a Theory of Moral Sentimentsᵃ

1 IF we examine the most celebrated and remarkable of the different theories which have been given concerning the nature and origin of our moral sentiments, we shall find that almost all of them coincide with some part or other of that which I have been endeavouring to give an account of; and that if every thing which has already been said be fully considered, we shall be at no loss to explain what was the view or aspect of nature which led each particular author to form his particular system. From some one or other of those principles which I have been endeavouring to unfold, every system of morality that ever had any reputation in the world has, perhaps, ultimately been derived. As they are all of them, in this respect, founded upon natural principles, they are all of them in some measure in the right. But as many of them are derived from a partial and imperfect view of nature, there are many of them too in some respects in the wrong.

2 ¹In treating of the principles of morals there are two questions to be considered. First, wherein does virtue consist? Or what is the tone of temper, and tenour of conduct, which constitutes the excellent and praise-worthy character, the character which is the natural object of esteem, honour, and approbation? And, secondly, by what power or faculty in the mind is it, that this character, whatever it be, is recommended to us? Or in other words, how and by what means does it come to pass, that the mind prefers one tenour of conduct to another, denominates the one right and the other wrong; considers the one as the object of approbation, honour, and reward, and the other of blame, censure, and punishment?

3 We examine the first question when we consider whether virtue consists in benevolence, as Dr. Hutcheson imagines;² or in acting suitably to the different relations we stand in, as Dr. Clarke supposes;³ or in the wise and

---

ᵃ⁻ᵃ Of the questions . . . theory of moral sentiments *1-5* *Of the Questions which ought to be examined in a Theory of Moral Sentiments 6 7*

¹ It seems likely that the first version of Smith's lectures on ethics began at this point, with a systematic survey of earlier theories before developing Smith's own views in the light of his criticisms of Hutcheson and Hume.

² Francis Hutcheson (1694–1746), Professor of Moral Philosophy at the University of Glasgow, 1730–46. For his view that virtue consists essentially in benevolence, see especially *Inquiry concerning Moral Good and Evil*, III.i; Raphael, *British Moralists 1650–1800*, § 328.

³ Samuel Clarke, 1675–1729. For his view that right or obligatory action (rather than

prudent pursuit of our own real and solid happiness, as has been the opinion of others.

4 We examine the second question, when we consider, whether the virtuous character, whatever it consists in, be recommended to us by self-love, which makes us perceive that this character, both in ourselves and others, tends most to promote our own private interest; or by reason, which points out to us the difference between one character and another, in the same manner as it does that between truth and falsehood; or by a peculiar power of perception, called a moral sense, which this virtuous character gratifies and pleases, as the contrary disgusts and displeases it; or last of all, by some other principle in human nature, such as a modification of sympathy, or the like.

5 I shall begin with considering the systems which have been formed concerning the first of these questions, and shall proceed afterwards to examine those concerning the second.

SECTION II

^aOf the different Accounts which have been given of the Nature
of Virtue^a

INTRODUCTION

1 THE different accounts which have been given of the nature of virtue, or of the temper of mind which constitutes the excellent and praise-worthy character, may be reduced to three different classes. According to some, the virtuous temper of mind does not consist in any one species of affections, but in the proper government and direction of all our affections, which may be either virtuous or vicious according to the objects which they pursue, and the degree of ^bvehemence^b with which they pursue them. According to these authors, therefore, virtue consists in propriety.

2 According to others, virtue consists in the judicious pursuit of our own private interest and happiness, or in the proper government and direction

---

^{a–a} Of . . . accounts . . . nature of virtue *1–5* *Of the different Accounts which have been given of the Nature of Virtue 6 7*
   ^{b–b} violence *1*

virtue) is acting suitably to the different relations of things, see *Discourse of Natural Religion*, I; Raphael, *British Moralists*, §§ 225–6, 230–2.

of those selfish affections which aim solely at this end. In the opinion of these authors, therefore, virtue consists in prudence.

3   Another set of authors make virtue consist in those affections only which aim at the happiness of others, not in those which aim at our own. According to them, therefore, disinterested benevolence is the only motive which can stamp upon any action the character of virtue.

4   The character of virtue, it is evident, must either be ascribed indifferently to all our affections, when under proper government and direction; or it must be confined to some one class or division of them. The great division of our affections is into the selfish and the benevolent. If the character of virtue, therefore, cannot be ascribed indifferently to all our affections, when under proper government and direction, it must be confined either to those which aim directly at our own private happiness, or to those which aim directly at that of others. If virtue, therefore, does not consist in propriety, it must consist either in prudence or in benevolence. Besides these three, it is scarce possible to imagine that any other account can be given of the nature of virtue. I shall endeavour to show hereafter how all the other accounts, which are seemingly different from any of these, coincide at bottom with some one or other of them.

CHAP. I
Of those Systems which make Virtue consist in Propriety

1   ACCORDING to Plato, to Aristotle, and to Zeno, virtue consists in the propriety of conduct, or in the suitableness of the affection from which we act to the object which excites it.

2   I.   In the system of Plato* the soul is considered as something like a little state or republic, composed of three different faculties or orders.

3   The first is the judging faculty, the faculty which determines not only what are the proper means for attaining any end, but also what ends are fit to be pursued, and what degree of relative value we ought to put upon each. This faculty Plato called, as it is very properly called, reason, and considered it as what had a right to be the governing principle of the whole. Under this appellation, it is evident, he comprehended not only that faculty by which we judge of truth and falsehood, but that by which we judge of the propriety or impropriety of desires and affections.

4   The different passions and appetites, the natural subjects of this ruling principle, but which are so apt to rebel against their master, he reduced to two different classes or orders. The first consisted of those passions, which

*See Plato de Rep. lib iv.

are founded in pride and resentment, or in what the schoolmen called the irascible part of the soul; ambition, animosity, the love of honour, and the dread of shame, the desire of victory, superiority, and revenge; all those passions, in short, which are supposed either to rise from, or to denote what, by a metaphor in our language, we commonly call spirit or natural fire. The second consisted of those passions which are founded in the love of pleasure, or in what the schoolmen called the concupiscible part of the soul. It comprehended all the appetites of the body, the love of ease and security, and of all sensual gratifications.

5   It rarely happens that we break in upon that plan of conduct, which the governing principle prescribes, and which in all our cool hours we had laid down to ourselves as what was most proper for us to pursue, but when prompted by one or other of those two different sets of passions; either by ungovernable ambition and resentment, or by the importunate solicitations of present ease and pleasure. But though these two orders of passions are so apt to mislead us, they are still considered as necessary parts of human nature: the first having been given to defend us against injuries, to assert our rank and dignity in the world, to make us aim at what is noble and honourable, and to make us distinguish those who act in the same manner; the second, to provide for the support and necessities of the body.

6   In the strength, acuteness, and perfection of the governing principle was placed the essential virtue of prudence,[1] which, according to Plato, consisted in a just and clear discernment, founded upon general and scientific ideas, of the ends which were proper to be pursued, and of the means which were proper for attaining them.

7   When the first set of passions, those of the irascible part of the soul, had that degree of strength and firmness, which enabled them, under the direction of reason, to despise all dangers in the pursuit of what was honourable and noble; it constituted the virtue of fortitude and magnanimity. This order of passions, according to this system, was of a more generous and noble nature than the other. They were considered upon many occasions as the auxiliaries of reason, to check and restrain the inferior and brutal appetites. We are often angry at ourselves, it was observed, we often become the objects of our own resentment and indignation, when the love of pleasure prompts to do what we disapprove of; and the irascible part of our nature is in this manner called in to assist the rational against the concupiscible.

8   When all those three different parts of our nature were in perfect concord with one another, when neither the irascible nor concupiscible passions ever aimed at any gratification which reason did not approve of, and when reason never commanded any thing, but what these of their own accord were willing to perform: this happy composure, this perfect and com-

---

[1] Smith is here translating the word σοφία, usually rendered 'wisdom'.

plete harmony of soul, constituted that virtue which in their language is expressed by a word[2] which we commonly translate temperance, but which might more properly be translated good temper, or sobriety and moderation of mind.

9   Justice, the last and greatest of the four cardinal virtues, took place, according to this system, when each of those three faculties of the mind confined itself to its proper office, without attempting to encroach upon that of any other; when reason directed and passion obeyed, and when each passion performed its proper duty, and exerted itself towards its proper object easily and without reluctance, and with that degree of force and energy, which was suitable to the value of what it pursued. In this consisted that complete virtue, that perfect propriety of conduct, which Plato, after some of the ancient Pythagoreans, denominated Justice.

10   The word, it is to be observed, which expresses justice in the Greek language,[3] has several different meanings; and as the correspondent word in all other languages, so far as I know, has the same, there must be some natural affinity among those various significations. In one sense we are said to do justice to our neighbour when we abstain from doing him any positive harm, and do not directly hurt him, either in his person, or in his estate, or in his reputation. This is that justice which I have treated of above, the observance of which may be extorted by force, and the violation of which exposes to punishment.[4] In another sense we are said not to do justice to our neighbour unless we conceive for him all that love, respect, and esteem, which his character, his situation, and his connexion with ourselves, render suitable and proper for us to feel, and unless we act accordingly. It is in this sense that we are said to do injustice to a man of merit who is connected with us, though we abstain from hurting him in every respect, if we do not exert ourselves to serve him and to place him in that situation in which the impartial spectator would be pleased to see him. The first sense of the word coincides with what Aristotle and the Schoolmen call commutative justice, and with what Grotius[5] calls the *justitia expletrix*, which consists in abstaining from what is another's, and in doing voluntarily whatever we can with propriety be forced to do. The second sense of the word coincides with what some have called distributive justice*, and with the *justitia attributrix* of Grotius, which consists in

---

* The distributive justice of Aristotle is somewhat different. It consists in the proper distribution of rewards from the public stock of a community. See Aristotle Ethic. Nic. l.5.c.2 [1130^{b}31–2].

---

[2] σωφροσύνη. For the doctrine described here, cf. Plato, *Republic*, 430 e, 442 c–d.

[3] δικαιοσύνη. Its different meanings are discussed by Aristotle, *Nicomachean Ethics*, V.i–ii.

[4] Cf. II.ii.1.5 above.

[5] *De Jure Belli ac Pacis*, I.i.8.

proper beneficence, in the becoming use of what is our own, and in the applying it to those purposes either of charity or generosity, to which it is most suitable, in our situation, that it should be applied. In this sense justice comprehends all the social virtues. There is yet another sense in which the word justice is sometimes taken, still more extensive than either of the former, though very much a-kin to the last; and which runs too, so far as I know, through all languages. It is in this last sense that we are said to be unjust, when we do not seem to value any particular object with that degree of esteem, or to pursue it with that degree of ardour which to the impartial spectator it may appear to deserve or to be naturally fitted for exciting. Thus we are said to do injustice to a poem or a picture, when we do not admire them enough, and we are said to do them more than justice when we admire them too much. In the same manner we are said to do injustice to ourselves when we appear not to give sufficient attention to any particular object of self-interest. In this last sense, what is called justice means the same thing with exact and perfect propriety of conduct and behaviour, and comprehends in it, not only the offices of both commutative and distributive justice, but of every other virtue, of prudence, of fortitude, of temperance. It is in this last sense that Plato evidently understands what he calls justice, and which, therefore, according to him, comprehends in it the perfection of every sort of virtue.

11   Such is the account given by Plato of the nature of virtue, or of that temper of mind which is the proper object of praise and approbation. It consists, according to him, in that state of mind in which every faculty confines itself within its proper sphere without encroaching upon that of any other, and performs its proper office with that precise degree of strength and vigour which belongs to it. His account, it is evident, coincides in every respect with what we have said above concerning the propriety of conduct.

12   II. Virtue, according to Aristotle*, consists in the *a*habit of mediocrity*a* according to right reason. Every particular virtue, according to him, lies in a kind of middle between two opposite vices, of which the one offends from being too much, the other from being too little affected by a particular species of objects. Thus the virtue of fortitude or courage lies in the middle between the opposite vices of cowardice and of presumptuous rashness, of which the one offends from being too much, and the other

*See Aristotle Ethic. Nic. l.2.c.5. et seq. et l.3.c.5. et seq.[6]

a-a habitual mediocrity of the affections *1*

[6] The definition quoted by Smith comes at *Nicomachean Ethics*, II.vi.15 (1106^{b}36–1107^{a}1). Smith's rendering, 'the habit of mediocrity', is a little misleading, perhaps more so than the earlier version of ed. 1. It would be more accurate to say: 'Virtue is a disposition (or state of character), concerned with choice, consisting of a mean that is determined by reason.'

from being too little affected by the objects of fear. Thus too the virtue of frugality lies in a middle between avarice and profusion, of which the one consists in an excess, the other in a defect of the proper attention to the objects of self-interest. Magnanimity, in the same manner, lies in a middle between the excess of arrogance and the defect of pusillanimity, of which the one consists in too extravagant, the other in too weak a sentiment of our own worth and dignity. It is unnecessary to observe that this account of virtue corresponds too pretty exactly with what has been said above concerning the propriety and impropriety of conduct.

13   According to Aristotle*, indeed, virtue did not so much consist in those moderate and right affections, as in the habit of this moderation. In order to understand this, it is to be observed, that virtue may be considered either as the quality of an action, or as the quality of a person. Considered as the quality of an action, it consists, even according to Aristotle, in the reasonable moderation of the affection from which the action proceeds, whether this disposition be habitual to the person or not. Considered as the quality of a person, it consists in the habit of this reasonable moderation, in its having become the customary and usual disposition of the mind. Thus the action which proceeds from an occasional fit of generosity is undoubtedly a generous action, but the man who performs it, is not necessarily a generous person, because it may be the single action of the kind which he ever performed. The motive and disposition of heart, from which this action was performed, may have been quite just and proper: but as this happy mood seems to have been the effect rather of accidental humour than of any thing steady or permanent in the character, it can reflect no great honour on the performer. When we denominate a character generous or charitable, or virtuous in any respect, we mean to signify that the disposition expressed by each of those appellations is the usual and customary disposition of the person. But single actions of any kind, how proper and suitable soever, are of little consequence to show that this is the case. If a single action was sufficient to stamp the character of any virtue upon the person who performed it, the most worthless of mankind might lay claim to all the virtues; since there is no man who has not, upon some occasions, acted with prudence, justice, temperance, and fortitude. But though single actions, how laudable soever, reflect very little praise upon the person who performs them, a single vicious action performed by one whose conduct is usually very regular, greatly diminishes and sometimes destroys altogether our opinion of his virtue. A single action of this kind sufficiently shows that his habits are not perfect, and that he is less to be depended upon, than, from the usual train of his behaviour, we might have been apt to imagine.

*See Aristotle Ethic. Nic. lib. ii. ch. 1, 2, 3, and 4.

14   Aristotle too*, when he made virtue to consist in practical habits, had it probably in his view to oppose the doctrine of Plato, who seems to have been of opinion that just sentiments and reasonable judgments concerning what was fit to be done or to be avoided, were alone sufficient to constitute the most perfect virtue. Virtue, according to Plato, might be considered as a species of science,[7] and no man, he thought, could see clearly and demonstratively what was right and what was wrong, and not act accordingly. Passion might make us act contrary to doubtful and uncertain opinions, not to plain and evident judgments. Aristotle, on the contrary, was of opinion, that no conviction of the understanding was capable of getting the better of inveterate habits, and that good morals arose not from knowledge but from action.

15   III. According to Zeno†, the founder of the Stoical doctrine, every animal was by nature recommended to its own care, and was endowed with the principle of self-love, that it might endeavour to preserve, not only its existence, but all the different parts of its nature, in the best and most perfect state of which they were capable.

16   The self-love of man embraced, if I may say so, his body and all its different members, his mind and all its different faculties and powers, and desired the preservation and maintenance of them all in their best and most perfect condition. Whatever tended to support this state of existence was, therefore, by nature pointed out to him as fit to be chosen; and whatever tended to destroy it, as fit to be rejected. Thus health, strength, agility and ease of body as well as the external [b]conveniencies[b] which could promote these; wealth, power, honours, the respect and esteem of those we live with; were naturally pointed out to us as things eligible, and of which the possession was preferable to the want. On the other hand, sickness, infirmity, unwieldiness, pain of body, as well as all the external [c]inconveniencies[c] which tend to occasion or bring on any of them; poverty, the want of authority, the contempt or hatred of those we live with; were, in the same manner, pointed out to us as things to be shunned and avoided. In each of those two opposite classes of objects, there were some which appeared to be more the objects either of choice or rejection, than others in the same class. Thus, in the first class, health appeared evidently preferable to strength, and strength to agility; reputation to power, and power to riches. And thus too, in the second class, sickness was more to be avoided

---

*See Aristotle Mag. Mor. lib. i. ch. 1.
†See Cicero de finibus, lib. iii.; also Diogenes Laertius in Zenone, lib. vii. segment 84[f].

[b-b] *1-5 7* conveniences *6*   [c-c] *1-5* inconveniences *6 7*

---

[7] i.e. exact knowledge.

than unwieldiness of body, ignominy than poverty, and poverty than the
*d*loss of power.*d* Virtue and the propriety of conduct consisted in choosing and rejecting all different objects and circumstances according as they
were by nature rendered more or less the objects of choice or rejection;
in selecting always from among the several objects of choice presented to
us, that which was most to be chosen, when we could not obtain them all;
and in selecting too, out of the several objects of rejection offered to us,
that which was least to be avoided, when it was not in our power to avoid
them all. By choosing and rejecting with this just and accurate discernment, by thus bestowing upon every object the precise degree of attention
it deserved, according to the place which it held in this natural scale of
things, we maintained, according to the Stoics, that perfect rectitude of
conduct which constituted the essence of virtue. This was what they called
to live consistently, to live according to nature, and to obey those laws and
directions which nature, or the Author of nature, had prescribed for our
conduct.

17   So far the Stoical idea of propriety and virtue is not very different from
that of Aristotle and the ancient Peripatetics.[8]*e*

---

d-d want of authority. *1-5*
e At this point, eds. *1-5* continue with a short passage that was withdrawn in ed. 6. We give
the text of ed. *1* with the variants of eds. *2-5* below. The first part of the passage runs on from
§ 17, and the second part, beginning a fresh paragraph, runs on into § 18.

What chiefly distinguished those two systems from one another was the different degrees
of self-command which they required. The peripatetics [Peripatetics *5*] allowed of some
degree of perturbation as suitable to the weakness of human nature, and as useful to so
imperfect a creature as man. If his own misfortunes [*1E 2-5* misfortune *1*] excited no
passionate grief, if his own injuries called forth no violent [lively *2-5*] resentment, reason,
or a regard to the general rules which determined what was right and fit to be done,
would commonly, they thought, be too weak to prompt him to avoid the one or to beat off
the other. The Stoics, on the contrary, demanded the most perfect apathy, and regarded
every emotion that [which *2-5*] could in the smallest degree disturb the tranquility
[tranquillity *5*] of the mind, as the effect of levity and folly. The Peripatetics seem to
have thought that no passion exceeded the bounds of propriety as long as the spectator,
by the utmost effort of humanity, could sympathize with it. The stoics, [Stoics, *2-5*] on
the contrary, appear to have regarded every passion as improper, which made any demand upon the sympathy of the spectator, or required him to alter in any respect the natural
and ordinary state of his mind, in order to keep time with the vehemence of its [his *5*
an error, not a correction] emotions. A man of virtue, they seem to have thought, ought not
to depend upon the generosity of those he lives with for pardon or approbation.
According to the stoics [Stoics, *2-5*] every event ought, to a wise man, to [event should,
to a wise man, *2-5*] appear indifferent, and what for its own sake could be the object
neither of desire, [desire *5*] nor aversion, neither of joy, [joy *5*] nor sorrow. If he preferred
some events to others, if some situations were the objects of his choice, and others of his
rejection*, it was not, because he regarded the one as [as, *2-5*] in themselves, in any

---

*Some of these expressions sound a little aukward [awkward *5*] in the English language:
they are literal translations of the [translations of *2 3*] technical terms of the stoics. [Stoics.
2-5]

---

[8] The followers of Aristotle.

18   *Among those primary objects which nature had recommended* to us
as eligible, was the prosperity of our family, of our relations, of our friends,
of our country, of mankind, and of the universe in general. Nature, too,
had taught us, that as the prosperity of two was preferable to that of one,
that of many, or of all, must be infinitely more so. That we ourselves were
but one, and that consequently wherever our prosperity was inconsistent
with that, either of the whole, or of any considerable part of the whole, it
ought, even in our own choice, to yield to what was so vastly preferable.
As all the events in this world were conducted by the providence of a wise,
powerful, and good God, we might be assured that whatever happened
tended to the prosperity and perfection of the whole. If we ourselves,
therefore, were in poverty, in sickness, or in any other calamity, we ought,
first of all, to use our utmost endeavours, so far as justice and our duty
to others would allow, to rescue ourselves from this disagreeable circumstance. But if, after all we could do, we found this impossible, we ought
to rest satisfied that the order and perfection of the universe required that
we should in the mean time continue in this situation. And as the prosperity
of the whole should, even to us, appear preferable to so insignificant a part
as ourselves, our situation, whatever it was, ought from that moment to
become the object of our *liking,* if we would maintain that complete
propriety and rectitude of sentiment and conduct in which consisted the
perfection of our nature. If, indeed, any opportunity of extricating ourselves
should offer, it became our duty to embrace it. The order of the universe,
it was evident, no longer required our continuance in this situation, and
the great Director of the world plainly called upon us to leave it, by so
clearly pointing out the road which we were to follow. It was the same case
with the adversity of our relations, our friends, our country. If, without
violating any more sacred obligation, it was in our power to prevent or put
an end to their calamity, it undoubtedly was our duty to do so. The propriety of action, the rule which Jupiter had given us for the direction of our
conduct, evidently required this of us. But if it was altogether out of our
power to do either, we ought then to consider this event as the most fortunate which could possibly have happened; because we might be assured
that it tended most to the prosperity and order of the whole, which was
what we ourselves, if we were wise and equitable, ought most of all to

respect better than the other, or thought that his own happiness would be more compleat
[complete 4 5] in what is called [in, what is called, 2–5] the fortunate, than in what is
commonly regarded as the distressful situation; but because the propriety of action, the
rule which the gods had given him for the direction of his conduct, required him to choose
and reject in this manner. Among the primary objects of natural inclination, or among
those things which nature had originally recommended to us as eligible, . . .
    f–f . . . Among the primary objects of natural inclination, or among those things which
nature had originally recommended *1–5*
        g–g choice, and even of our desire, *1–5*

desire. *ʰIt was our own final interest considered as a part of that whole, of which the prosperity ought to be, not only the principal, but the sole object of our desire.ʰ*

19   *ʲ'In what sense,'* says Epictetus,[9] 'are some things said to be according to our nature, and others contrary to it? It is in that sense in which we consider ourselves as separated and detached from all other things. For thus it may be said to be according to the nature of the foot to be always clean. But if you consider it as a foot, and not as something detached from the rest of the body, it must behove it sometimes to trample in the dirt, and sometimes to tread upon thorns, and sometimes, too, to be cut off for the sake of the whole body; and if it refuses this, it is no longer a foot. Thus, too, ought we to conceive with regard to ourselves. What are you? A man. If you consider yourself as something separated and detached, it is agreeable to your nature to live to old age, to be rich, to be in health. But if you consider yourself as a man, and as a part of a whole, upon account of that whole, it will behove you sometimes to be in sickness, sometimes to be exposed to the inconveniency of a sea voyage, sometimes to be in want; and at last, perhaps, to die before your time. Why then do you complain? Do not you know that by doing so, as the foot ceases to be a foot, so you cease to be a man*?'ᵏ*

*Arrian. lib. ii.c.5. [Arrian's *Discourses of Epictetus.*]

ʰ⁻ʰ *om. 1–5*

ʲ *No new paragraph in eds. 1–5*

ᵏ *At this point, eds. 1–5 contain a further paragraph, withdrawn in ed. 6. We give the text of ed. 1 with the variants of eds. 2–5 below.*

The footnote at the end of § 19, giving the reference to Arrian, appeared in eds. 1–5 but was omitted in ed. 6 (and therefore in ed. 7 also). This omission was no doubt inadvertent. When revising a copy of ed. 4 for the preparation of ed. 6, Smith presumably cancelled the paragraph to be withdrawn, and failed to notice that the footnote, appearing at the bottom of the relevant page, ought to be retained as belonging to the preceding paragraph.

This submission to the order of the universe, this entire indifference with regard to whatever concerns ourselves, when put into the balance with the interest of the whole, could derive its propriety, it is evident, from no other principle besides that [that, *4*] upon which I have endeavoured to show that the [show, the *4* show the *5*] propriety of justice was founded. As long as we view our own interests with our own eyes, it is scarce possible that we should willingly acquiesce in their being thus sacrificed to the interests of the whole. It is only when we view those opposite interests with the eyes of others [others, *4 5*] that what concerns ourselves can appear to be so contemptible in the comparison, as to be resigned without any reluctance. To every body but the person principally concerned [concerned, *4 5*] nothing can appear more agreeable to reason and propriety [propriety, *5*] than that the part should give place to the whole. But what is agreeable to the reason of all other men, ought not to appear contrary to his. He himself therefore ought to approve of this sacrifice [sacrifice, *2–5*] and acknowledge its conformity to reason. But all the affections of a wise man, according to the stoics, [Stoics, *5*] are perfectly agreeable to reason and propriety, and of their own accord coincide with whatever these ruling principles prescribe. A wise man, therefore, could never feel any reluctance to comply with this disposition of things.

Eds. 1–5 then proceed to VII.ii.1.48: IV. Besides these ancient, . . .

[9] *Discourses*, II.v.24–6.

20 [1]'A wise man never complains of the destiny of Providence, nor thinks the universe in confusion when he is out of order. He does not look upon [m]himself[m] as a whole, separated and detached from every other part of nature, to be taken care of by itself and for itself. He regards himself in the light in which he imagines the great genius of human nature, and of the world, regards him. He enters, if I may say so, into the sentiments of that divine Being, and considers himself as an atom, a particle, of an immense and infinite system, which must and ought to be disposed of, according to the conveniency of the whole. Assured of the wisdom which directs all the events of human life, whatever lot befalls him, he accepts it with joy, satisfied that, if he had known all the connections and dependencies of the different parts of the universe, it is the very lot which he himself would have wished for. If it is life, he is contented to live; and if it is death, as nature must have no further occasion for his presence here, he willingly goes where he is appointed. I accept, said a [n]cynical philosopher, whose doctrines were in this respect the same as those of the Stoics,[10] I accept,[n] with equal joy and satisfaction, whatever fortune can befall me. Riches or poverty, pleasure or pain, health or sickness, all is alike: nor would I desire that the Gods should in any respect change my destination. If I was to ask of them any thing beyond what their bounty has already bestowed, it should be that they would inform me before-hand what it was their pleasure should be done with me, that I might of my own accord place myself in this situation, and demonstrate the cheerfulness with which I embraced their allotment. If I am going to sail, says Epictetus,[11] I chuse the best ship and the best pilot, and I wait for the fairest weather that my circumstances and duty will allow. Prudence and propriety, the principles which the Gods have given me for the direction of my conduct, require this of me; but they require no more: and if, notwithstanding, a storm arises, which neither the strength of the vessel nor the skill of the pilot are likely to withstand,

---

[1] § 20 (*with* He *in place of* A wise man) *appears in eds. 1–5 as the latter part of a paragraph in a special chapter on the Stoical Philosophy. In ed. 1 this is Part I, sect. iv, chap. 3, and in eds. 2–5 it is Part I, sect. iii, chap. 3. See what is now I.iii.2.9, textual note* [c–c] *and editorial note 7. See also VII.ii.1.23, textual note* [r], *below.*

[m–m] himself, according to what self-love would suggest, *1–5*

[n–n] stoical philosopher, *1–5*

---

[10] As Eckstein (ii.586) suggests, Smith is probably referring to a statement of Demetrius the Cynic, reported by Seneca, *De Providentia* (*Dialogues*, Book I), v.5: 'I have only one complaint to make of you, immortal gods, that you did not make your will known to me before; for I should then have come the sooner to the state in which I now am after summons.' Seneca was a close friend and warm admirer of Demetrius, who lived in Rome under the emperors Gaius, Nero, and Vespasian. When Smith wrote 'a stoical philosopher' for ed. 1, he will have recalled simply that the passage was quoted by the Stoic Seneca and illustrated Stoic attitudes. His revision in ed. 6 is a correct statement of Demetrius' position.

[11] Cf. *Discourses*, II.v.10–14. Smith's words here are a paraphrase rather than a translation.

I give myself no trouble about the consequence. All that I had to do is done already. The directors of my conduct never command me to be miserable, to be anxious, desponding, or afraid. Whether we are to be drowned, or to come to a harbour, is the business of Jupiter, not mine. I leave it entirely to his determination, nor ever break my rest with considering which way he is likely to decide it, but receive whatever comes with equal indifference and security.[o]

21 [p]From this perfect confidence in that benevolent wisdom which governs the universe, and from this entire resignation to whatever order that wisdom might think proper to establish, it necessarily followed, that, to the Stoical wise man, all the events of human life must be in a great measure indifferent. His happiness consisted altogether, first, in the contemplation of the happiness and perfection of the great system of the universe, of the good government of the great republic of Gods and men, of all rational and sensible beings; and, secondly, in discharging his duty, in acting properly in the affairs of this great republic whatever little part that wisdom had assigned to him. The propriety or impropriety of his endeavours might be of great consequence to him. Their success or disappointment could be of none at all; could excite no passionate joy or sorrow, no passionate desire or aversion. If he preferred some events to others, if some situations were the objects of his choice and others of his rejection, it was not because he regarded the one as in themselves in any respect better than the other, or thought that his own happiness would be more complete in what is called the fortunate than in what is regarded as the distressful situation; but because the propriety of action, the rule which the Gods had given him for the direction of his conduct, required him to chuse and reject in this manner. All his affections were absorbed and swallowed up in two great affections; in that for the discharge of his own duty, and in that for the greatest possible happiness of all rational and sensible beings. For the gratification of this latter affection, he rested with the most perfect security upon the wisdom and power of the great Superintendant of the universe. His sole anxiety was about the gratification of the former; not about the event, but about the propriety of his own endeavours. Whatever the event might be, he trusted to a superior power and wisdom for turning it to promote that great end which he himself was most desirous of promoting.

22 This propriety of chusing and rejecting, though originally pointed out to us, and as it were recommended and introduced to our acquaintance by the things, and for the sake of the things, chosen and rejected; yet when we

---

[o] *At this point, eds. 1–5 proceed with a fresh paragraph,* Such was the philosophy of the stoics . . ., *which leads into what is now the second sentence of I.iii.2.9. See the final part of the variant printed in note* [c-c] *at that place.*

[p] *§§ 21–2 were added in ed. 6. They replace the first part of the second paragraph (beginning* It was upon this account that, according to the stoical philosophy, . . .) *of the chapter on the Stoical Philosophy in eds. 1–5. See note* [c-c] *at I.iii.2.9.*

had once become thoroughly acquainted with it, the order, the grace, the beauty which we discerned in this conduct, the happiness which we felt resulted from it, necessarily appeared to us of much greater value than the actual obtaining of all the different objects of choice, or the actual avoiding of all those of rejection. From the observation of this propriety arose the happiness and the glory; from the neglect of it, the misery and the disgrace of human nature.

23 ᵠBut to a wise man, to one whose passions were brought under perfect subjection to the ruling principles of his nature, the exact observation of this propriety was equally easy upon all occasions. Was he in prosperity, he returned thanks to Jupiter for having joined him with circumstances which were easily mastered, and in which there was little temptation to do wrong. Was he in adversity, he equally returned thanks to the director of this spectacle of human life, for having opposed to him a vigorous athlete, over whom, though the contest was likely to be more violent, the victory was more glorious, and equally certain. Can there be any shame in that distress which is brought upon us without any fault of our own, and in which we behave with perfect propriety? There can, therefore, be no evil, but, on the contrary, the greatest good and advantage. A brave man exults in those dangers in which, from no rashness of his own, his fortune has involved him. They afford an opportunity of exercising that heroic intrepidity, whose exertion gives the exalted delight which flows from the consciousness of superior propriety and deserved admiration. One who is master of all his exercises has no aversion to measure his strength and activity with the strongest. And, in the same manner, one who is master of all his passions, does not dread any circumstance in which the Superintendant of the universe may think proper to place him. The bounty of that divine Being has provided him with virtues which render him superior to every situation. If it is pleasure, he has temperance to refrain from it; if it is pain, he has constancy to bear it; if it is danger or death, he has magnanimity and fortitude to despise it.ʳ The events of human life can never find him unprepared, or at a loss how to maintain that propriety of sentiment and conduct which, in his own apprehension, constitutes at once his glory and his happiness.

24 Human life the Stoics appear to have considered as a game of great

---

ᵠ *§ 23, apart from the last sentence, which was added in ed. 6, is a revision of a passage which, in eds. 1–5, formed the latter part of the second paragraph in the chapter on the Stoical Philosophy. There it began (see note* ᶜ⁻ᶜ *at I.iii.2.9):*

. . . To a wise man, on the contrary, to one whose passions were all brought under perfect subjection to the ruling principles of his nature, to reason and the love of propriety, to act so as to deserve approbation was equally easy upon all occasions.

ʳ *At this point, eds. 1–5 proceed, without a fresh paragraph,* He never complains of the destiny of providence, . . . *and continue as in VII.ii.1.20 above. The last sentence of § 23, and the whole of §§ 24–47, were added in ed. 6.*

skill; in which, however, there was a mixture of chance, or of what is vulgarly understood to be chance. In such games the stake is commonly a trifle, and the whole pleasure of the game arises from playing well, from playing fairly, and playing skilfully. If notwithstanding all his skill, however, the good player should, by the influence of chance, happen to lose, the loss ought to be a matter, rather of merriment, than of serious sorrow. He has made no false stroke; he has done nothing which he ought to be ashamed of; he has enjoyed completely the whole pleasure of the game. If, on the contrary, the bad player, notwithstanding all his blunders, should, in the same manner, happen to win, his success can give him but little satisfaction. He is mortified by the remembrance of all the faults which he committed. Even during the play he can enjoy no part of the pleasure which it is capable of affording. From ignorance of the rules of the game, fear and doubt and hesitation are the disagreeable sentiments that precede almost every stroke which he plays; and when he has played it, the mortification of finding it a gross blunder, commonly completes the unpleasing circle of his sensations. Human life, with all the advantages which can possibly attend it, ought, according to the Stoics, to be regarded but as a mere two-penny stake; a matter by far too insignificant to merit any anxious concern. Our only anxious concern ought to be, not about the stake, but about the proper method of playing. If we placed our happiness in winning the stake, we placed it in what depended upon causes beyond our power, and out of our direction. We necessarily exposed ourselves to perpetual fear and uneasiness, and frequently to grievous and mortifying disappointments. If we placed it in playing well, in playing fairly, in playing wisely and skilfully; in the propriety of our own conduct in short; we placed it in what, by proper discipline, education, and attention, might be altogether in our own power, and under our own direction. Our happiness was perfectly secure, and beyond the reach of fortune. The event of our actions, if it was out of our power, was equally out of our concern, and we could never feel either fear or anxiety about it; nor ever suffer any grievous, or even any serious disappointment.

25   Human life itself, as well as every different advantage or disadvantage which can attend it, might, they said, according to different circumstances, be the proper object either of our choice or of our rejection. If, in our actual situation, there were more circumstances agreeable to nature than contrary to it; more circumstances which were the objects of choice than of rejection; life, in this case, was, upon the whole, the proper object of choice, and the propriety of conduct required that we should remain in it. If, on the other hand, there were, in our actual situation, without any probable hope of amendment, more circumstances contrary to nature than agreeable to it; more circumstances which were the objects of rejection than of choice; life itself, in this case, became, to a wise man, the object of rejection, and he was not only at liberty to remove out of it, but the propriety of conduct,

the rule which the Gods had given him for the direction of his conduct, required him to do so. I am ordered, says Epictetus,[12] not to dwell at Nicopolis. I do not dwell there. I am ordered not to dwell at Athens. I do not dwell at Athens. I am ordered not to dwell in Rome. I do not dwell in Rome. I am ordered to dwell in the little and rocky island of Gyarae. I go and dwell there. But the house smokes in Gyarae. If the smoke is moderate, I will bear it, and stay there. If it is excessive, I will go to a house from whence no tyrant can remove me. I keep in mind always that the door is open, that I can walk out when I please, and retire to that hospitable house which is at all times open to all the world; for beyond my undermost garment, beyond my body, no man living has any power over me. If your situation is upon the whole disagreeable; if your house smokes too much for you, said the Stoics, walk forth by all means. But walk forth without repining; without murmuring or complaining. Walk forth calm, contented, rejoicing, returning thanks to the Gods, who, from their infinite bounty, have opened the safe and quiet harbour of death, at all times ready to receive us from the stormy ocean of human life; who have prepared this sacred, this inviolable, this great asylum, always open, always accessible; altogether beyond the reach of human rage and injustice; and large enough to contain both all those who wish, and all those who do not wish to retire to it: an asylum which takes away from every man every pretence of complaining, or even of fancying that there can be any evil in human life, except such as he may suffer from his own folly and weakness.

26   The Stoics, in the few fragments of their philosophy which have come down to us, sometimes talk of leaving life with a gaiety, and even with a levity, which, were we to consider those passages by themselves, might induce us to believe that they imagined we could with propriety leave it whenever we had a mind, wantonly and capriciously, upon the slightest disgust or uneasiness. 'When you sup with such a person,' says Epictetus,[13] 'you complain of the long stories which he tells you about his Mysian wars. "Now my friend, says he, having told you how I took possession of an eminence at such a place, I will tell you how I was besieged in such another place." But if you have a mind not to be troubled with his long stories, do not accept of his supper. If you accept of his supper, you have not the least pretence to complain of his long stories. It is the same case with what you call the evils of human life. Never complain of that of which it is at all times in your power to rid yourself.' Notwithstanding this gaiety and even levity of expression, however, the alternative of leaving life, or of remaining in it, was, according to the Stoics, a matter of the most serious and import-

---

[12] *Discourses*, I.xxv.18–21. Smith has put together two remarks about smoke that are separated in the original. See also editorial note 38 below.

[13] Cf. *Discourses*, I.xxv.15–17. The latter part of Smith's quotation is a paraphrase rather than a translation.

ant deliberation. We ought never to leave it till we were distinctly called upon to do so by that superintending power which had originally placed us in it. But we were to consider ourselves as called upon to do so, not merely at the appointed and unavoidable term of human life. Whenever the providence of that superintending Power had rendered our condition in life upon the whole the proper object rather of rejection than of choice; the great rule which he had given us for the direction of our conduct, then required us to leave it. We might then be said to hear the awful and bene-volent voice of that divine Being distinctly calling upon us to do so.

27   It was upon this account that, according to the Stoics, it might be the duty of a wise man to remove out of life though he was perfectly happy; while, on the contrary, it might be the duty of a weak man to remain in it, though he was necessarily miserable. If, in the situation of the wise man, there were more circumstances which were the natural objects of rejection than of choice, the whole situation became the object of rejection, and the rule which the Gods had given him for the direction of his conduct, re-quired that he should remove out of it as speedily as particular circum-stances might render convenient. He was, however, perfectly happy even during the time that he might think proper to remain in it. He had placed his happiness, not in obtaining the objects of his choice, or in avoiding those of his rejection; but in always choosing and rejecting with exact propriety; not in the success, but in the fitness of his endeavours and exertions. If, in the situation of the weak man, on the contrary, there were more circum-stances which were the natural objects of choice than of rejection; his whole situation became the proper object of choice, and it was his duty to remain in it. He was unhappy, however, from not knowing how to use those circumstances. Let his cards be ever so good, he did not know how to play them, and could enjoy no sort of real satisfaction, either in the progress, or in the event of the game, in whatever manner it might happen to turn out*.

28   The propriety, upon some occasions, of voluntary death, though it was, perhaps, more insisted upon by the Stoics, than by any other sect of ancient philosophers, was, however, a doctrine common to them all, even to the peaceable and indolent Epicureans. During the age in which flourished the founders of all the principal sects of ancient philosophy; during the Peloponnesian war and for many years after its conclusion, all the different republics of Greece were, at home, almost always distracted

---

*See Cicero de finibus, lib. 3. ªc.18.ª Olivet's edition.

ª⁻ª c.13. *6 7 Misprint*¹⁴

---

¹⁴ The first sentence of § 27 is a translation of a sentence in Cicero, *De Finibus*, III.xviii.60. The misprint of '13' for '18' was undetected by Smith and even by Eckstein, who notes (ii.587) that the reference seems irrelevant.

by the most furious factions; and abroad, involved in the most sanguinary wars, in which each sought, not merely superiority or dominion, but either completely to extirpate all its enemies, or, what was not less cruel, to reduce them into the vilest of all states, that of domestic slavery, and to sell them, man, woman, and child, like so many herds of cattle, to the highest bidder in the market. The smallness of the greater part of those states, too, rendered it, to each of them, no very improbable event, that it might itself fall into that very calamity which it had so frequently, either, perhaps, actually inflicted, or at least attempted to inflict upon some of its neighbours. In this disorderly state of things, the most perfect innocence, joined to both the highest rank and the greatest public services, could give no security to any man that, even at home and among his own relations and fellow-citizens, he was not, at some time or another, from the prevalence of some hostile and furious faction, to be condemned to the most cruel and ignominious punishment. If he was taken prisoner in war, or if the city of which he was a member was conquered, he was exposed, if possible, to still greater injuries and insults. But every man naturally, or rather necessarily, familiarizes his imagination with the distresses to which he foresees that his situation may frequently expose him. It is impossible that a sailor should not frequently think of storms and shipwrecks, and foundering at sea, and of how he himself is likely both to feel and to act upon such occasions. It was impossible, in the same manner, that a Grecian patriot or hero should not familiarize his imagination with all the different calamities to which he was sensible his situation must frequently, or rather constantly expose him. As an American savage prepares his death-song, and considers how he should act when he has fallen into the hands of his enemies, and is by them put to death in the most lingering tortures, and amidst the insults and derision of all the spectators;[15] so a Grecian patriot or hero could not avoid frequently employing his thoughts in considering what he ought both to suffer and to do in banishment, in captivity, when reduced to slavery, when put to the torture, when brought to the scaffold. But the philosophers of all the different sects very justly represented virtue; that is, wise, just, firm, and temperate conduct; not only as the most probable, but as the certain and infallible road to happiness even in this life. This conduct, however, could not always exempt, and might even sometimes expose the person who followed it to all the calamities which were incident to that unsettled situation of public affairs. They endeavoured, therefore, to show that happiness was either altogether, or at least in a great measure, independent of fortune; the Stoics, that it was so altogether; the Academic and Peripatetic philosophers,[16] that it was so in a great measure. Wise, prudent, and good conduct was, in the first place, the conduct most likely to ensure

---

[15] Cf. V.2.9 above.   [16] The followers of Plato and Aristotle respectively.

success in every species of undertaking; and secondly, though it should fail
of success, yet the mind was not left without consolation. The virtuous
man might still enjoy the complete approbation of his own breast; and
might still feel that, how untoward soever things might be without, all was
calm and peace and concord within. He might generally comfort himself,
too, with the assurance that he possessed the love and esteem of every
intelligent and impartial spectator, who could not fail both to admire his
conduct, and to regret his misfortune.

29   Those philosophers endeavoured, at the same time, to show, that the
greatest misfortunes to which human life was liable, might be supported
more easily than was commonly imagined. They endeavoured to point out
the comforts which a man might still enjoy when reduced to poverty,
when driven into banishment, when exposed to the injustice of popular
clamour, when labouring under blindness, under deafness, in the extremity
of old age, upon the approach of death. They pointed out, too, the considerations which might contribute to support his constancy under the
agonies of pain and even of torture, in sickness, in sorrow for the loss of
children, for the death of friends and relations, etc. The few fragments which
have come down to us of what the ancient philosophers had written upon
these subjects, form, perhaps, one of the most instructive, as well as one of
the most interesting remains of antiquity. The spirit and manhood of their
doctrines make a wonderful contrast with the desponding, plaintive, and
whining tone of some modern systems.[17]

30   But while those ancient philosophers endeavoured in this manner to
suggest every consideration which could, as Milton says,[18] arm the obdured
breast with stubborn patience, as with triple steel; they, at the same time,
laboured above all to convince their followers that there neither was nor
could be any evil in death; and that, if their situation became at any time
too hard for their constancy to support, the remedy was at hand, the door
was open, and they might, without fear, walk out when they pleased. If
there was no world beyond the present, death, they said, could be no evil;
and if there was another world, the Gods must likewise be in that other,
and a just man could fear no evil while under their protection. Those philosophers, in short, prepared a death-song, if I may say so, which the Grecian
patriots and heroes might make use of upon the proper occasions; and, of all
the different sects, the Stoics, I think it must be acknowledged, had prepared by far the most animated and spirited song.

31   Suicide, however, never seems to have been very common among the

---

[17] Cf. 'whining and melancholy moralists', III.3.9 above; also Letter 163 addressed to
Alexander Wedderburn, dated 14 August 1776, in which Smith says that Hume is facing
death 'with more real resignation . . .than any Whining Christian ever dyed with pretended
resignation to the will of God'.
[18] *Paradise Lost*, II.568–9.

Greeks. Excepting Cleomenes,[19] I cannot at present recollect any very illustrious either patriot or hero of Greece, who died by his own hand. The death of Aristomenes[20] is as much beyond the period of true history as that of Ajax.[21] The common story of the death of Themistocles,[22] though within that period, bears upon its face all the marks of a most romantic fable. Of all the Greek heroes whose lives have been written by Plutarch, Cleomenes appears to have been the only one who perished in this manner. Theramines, Socrates, and Phocion,[23] who certainly did not want courage, suffered themselves to be sent to prison, and submitted patiently to that death to which the injustice of their fellow-citizens had condemned them. The brave Eumenes allowed himself to be delivered up, by his own mutinous soldiers, to his enemy Antigonus, and was starved to death, without attempting any violence.[24] The gallant Philopoemen suffered himself to be taken prisoner by the Messenians, was thrown into a dungeon, and was supposed to have been privately poisoned.[25] Several of the philosophers, indeed, are said to have died in this manner; but their lives have been so very foolishly written, that very little credit is due to the greater part of the tales which are told of them. Three different accounts have been given of the death of Zeno the Stoic. One is, that after enjoying, for ninety-eight years, the most perfect state of health, he happened, in going out of his school, to fall; and though he suffered no other damage than that of breaking or dislocating one of his fingers, he struck the ground with his hand, and, in the words of the Niobe of Euripides, said, *I come,*

[19] The suicide of Cleomenes, King of Sparta, in 220/19 B.C. is described by Plutarch, *Lives*, Cleomenes, 37.

[20] Smith has confused Aristomenes with Aristodemus, both legendary heroes of Messene. Aristodemus fought in the first war against Sparta (eighth century B.C.), Aristomenes in the second war (seventh century). Pausanias, IV.13, writes of the suicide of Aristodemus; in IV.24 he mentions the death of Aristomenes as a natural event following illness.

[21] Ajax, son of Telamon, one of the leaders of the Greeks in Homer's *Iliad*. Later poets tell the story that he went mad, killed a flock of sheep thinking they were his enemies, and then killed himself.

[22] Athenian statesman, commander of the fleet that defeated the Persians at the battle of Salamis, 480 B.C. In later political dispute Themistocles was exiled from Athens and died in Asia Minor. Thucydides, I.138, says his death was the result of illness but also reports a tale of suicide.

[23] All three were sentenced to death at Athens, where capital punishment took the form of drinking hemlock. Theramenes, one of the 'Thirty Tyrants' of 404 B.C., was charged with treason. Socrates was charged in 399 with impiety and corrupting the youth. Phocion, general and statesman who favoured collaboration with the Macedonians, was sentenced in 317 on a charge of treason.

[24] Eumenes and Antigonus governed parts of Asia after the death of Alexander the Great. Antigonus defeated Eumenes and had him put to death in 316 B.C. Smith is referring to Plutarch, *Lives*, Eumenes, 17–19, but has forgotten that, after being starved, Eumenes was in the end forcibly killed.

[25] Philopoemen of Megalopolis, eight times general of the Achaean Confederacy, was captured by the Messenians in 182 B.C. and given poison to drink. Smith is referring to Plutarch, *Lives*, Philopoemen, 18–20.

why doest thou call me? and immediately went home and hanged himself.[26]
At that great age, one should think, he might have had a little more patience.
Another account is, that, at the same age, and in consequence of a like
accident, he starved himself to death.[27] The third account is, that, at
seventy-two years of age, he died in the natural way; by far the most
probable account of the three, and supported too by the authority of a
cotemporary, who must have had every opportunity of being well informed;
of Persaeus,[28] originally the slave, and afterwards the friend and disciple
of Zeno. The first account is given by Apollonius of Tyre,[29] who flourished
about the time of Augustus Caesar, between two and three hundred years
after the death of Zeno. I know not who is the author of the second account.
Apollonius, who was himself a Stoic, had probably thought it would do
honour to the founder of a sect which talked so much about voluntary death,
to die in this manner by his own hand. Men of letters, though, after their
death, they are frequently more talked of than the greatest princes or
statesmen of their times, are generally, during their life, so obscure and
insignificant that their adventures are seldom recorded by cotemporary
historians. Those of after-ages, in order to satisfy the public curiosity,
and having no authentic documents either to support or to contradict their
narratives, seem frequently to have fashioned them according to their own
fancy; and almost always with a great mixture of the marvellous. In this
particular case the marvellous, though supported by no authority, seems to
have prevailed over the probable, though supported by the best. Diogenes
Laertius plainly gives the preference to the story of Apollonius. Lucian
and Lactantius appear both to have given credit to that of the great age
and of the violent death.[30]

32   This fashion of voluntary death appears to have been much more pre-
valent among the proud Romans, than it ever was among the lively,
ingenious, and accommodating Greeks. Even among the Romans, the
fashion seems not to have been established in the early and, what are called,
the virtuous ages of the republic. The common story of the death of Regulus,[31] though probably a fable, could never have been invented, had it been

[26] Diogenes Laertius, VII.28, but the end of the story is that Zeno throttled (not
hanged) himself. The lost play *Niobe*, from which Zeno quotes, was probably by Timo-
theus (Nauck, *Trag. Graec. Fragmenta*, 51), not Euripides.

[27] Lucian, *Macrobioi*, 19; cf. Diogenes Laertius, VII.31.

[28] Persaeus is reported by Diogenes Laertius, VII.28, to say simply that Zeno came to
Athens at the age of 22 and died at 72.

[29] Diogenes Laertius reports Apollonius as saying that Zeno presided over his school for
58 years (in contrast to the figures given by Persaeus), but does not explicitly attribute to
Apollonius the account of Zeno's death at 98.

[30] Lucian, *Macrobioi*, 19, supports the story of self-starvation at 98, not that of a
'violent' death. Lactantius, *Institutes*, III.18, and *Epitome*, 34(39), includes Zeno in a list
of ancient philosophers who committed suicide; he says nothing about age and his words
do not necessarily imply violent death.

[31] Marcus Atilius Regulus, commander of the Roman army against Carthage in the

supposed that any dishonour could fall upon that hero, from patiently submitting to the tortures which the Carthaginians are said to have inflicted upon him. In the later ages of the republic some dishonour, I apprehend, would have attended this submission. In the different civil wars which preceded the fall of the commonwealth, many of the eminent men of all the contending parties chose rather to perish by their own hands, than to fall into those of their enemies. The death of Cato, celebrated by Cicero, and censured by Caesar,[32] and become the subject of a very serious controversy between, perhaps, the two most illustrious advocates that the world had ever beheld, stamped a character of splendour upon this method of dying which it seems to have retained for several ages after. The eloquence of Cicero was superior to that of Caesar. The admiring prevailed greatly over the censuring party, and the lovers of liberty, for many ages afterwards, looked up to Cato as to the most venerable martyr of the republican party. The head of a party, the Cardinal de Retz observes, may do what he pleases; as long as he retains the confidence of his own friends, he can never do wrong;[33] a maxim of which his Eminence had himself, upon several occasions, an opportunity of experiencing the truth. Cato, it seems, joined to his other virtues that of an excellent bottle companion. His enemies accused him of drunkenness, but, says Seneca, whoever objected this vice to Cato, will find it much easier to prove that drunkenness is a virtue, than that Cato could be addicted to any vice.[34]

33   Under the Emperors this method of dying seems to have been, for a long time, perfectly fashionable. In the epistles of Pliny[35] we find an account of several persons who chose to die in this manner, rather from vanity

First Punic War. After striking successes he was defeated and taken prisoner in 255 B.C. According to a dubious later tradition, he was sent to Rome by the Carthaginians in 250 to propose terms for peace or the exchange of prisoners, but he dissuaded the Senate from accepting the proposals and voluntarily returned to Carthage, where he was tortured and killed.

[32] Marcus Porcius Cato Uticensis (95–46 B.C.) committed suicide after the defeat by Julius Caesar of the republican forces in Africa. Cicero wrote a eulogy in his pamphlet *Cato*, and Caesar replied with his *Anticato*.

[33] Smith is mistaken; de Retz did not say this, though he did make several other observations (some not altogether unlike this one, others tending to contradict it) about parties and their heads.

[34] Seneca, *De Tranquillitate Animi* (*Dialogues*, Book IX), xvii.9.

[35] Pliny writes in *Letters*, I.12, of Corellius Rufus, who committed suicide when suffering from an incurable disease; in III.16, of Arria, who, when her husband Paetus had been condemned to death, stabbed herself and urged him to follow her, saying 'Paetus, it does not hurt'; and in VI.24, of an aged couple who drowned themselves at the instigation of the wife because the husband was afflicted with ulcers in his private parts. Eckstein (ii.589) cites these passages as possible references but thinks that they do not fit Smith's disparaging comments. Smith is certainly referring to at least the last two instances; hence his remark about 'the ladies' in the next sentence. He is quite likely to think that none of these suicides had 'proper or necessary' reasons and that Arria's famous last words were 'vanity and ostentation'. Some of Pliny's own comments on the first two instances can be taken to imply a view not altogether dissimilar.

and ostentation, it would seem, than from what would appear, even to a sober and judicious Stoic, any proper or necessary reason. Even the ladies, who are seldom behind in following the fashion, seem frequently to have chosen, most unnecessarily, to die in this manner; and, like the ladies in Bengal, to accompany, upon some occasions, their husbands to the tomb. The prevalence of this fashion certainly occasioned many deaths which would not otherwise have happened. All the havock, however, which this, perhaps the highest exertion of human vanity and impertinence, could occasion, would, probably, at no time, be very great.

34   The principle of suicide, the principle which would teach us, upon some occasions, to consider that violent action as an object of applause and approbation, seems to be altogether a refinement of philosophy.[36] Nature, in her sound and healthful state, seems never to prompt us to suicide. There is, indeed, a species of melancholy (a disease to which human nature, among its other calamities, is unhappily subject) which seems to be accompanied with, what one may call, an irresistible appetite for self-destruction. In circumstances often of the highest external prosperity, and sometimes too, in spite even of the most serious and deeply impressed sentiments of religion, this disease has frequently been known to drive its wretched victims to this fatal extremity. The unfortunate persons who perish in this miserable manner, are the proper objects, not of censure, but of commiseration. To attempt to punish them, when they are beyond the reach of all human punishment, is not more absurd than it is unjust. That punishment can fall only on their surviving friends and relations, who are always perfectly innocent, and to whom the loss of their friend, in this disgraceful manner, must always be alone a very heavy calamity. Nature, in her sound and healthful state, prompts us to avoid distress upon all occasions; upon many occasions to defend ourselves against it, though at the hazard, or even with the certainty of perishing in that defence. But, when we have neither been able to defend ourselves from it, nor have perished in that defence, no natural principle, no regard to the approbation of the supposed impartial spectator, to the judgment of the man within the breast, seems to call upon us to escape from it by destroying ourselves. It is only the consciousness of our own weakness, of our own incapacity to support the calamity with proper manhood and firmness, which can drive us to this resolution. I do not remember to have either read or heard of any

[36] Probably a reference to Hume's essay *Of Suicide*, published after his death in unauthorized editions, anonymously in 1777 and with ascription to Hume in 1784 and 1789. Smith's discussion of suicide in this chapter was written for ed. 6 of TMS. Bonar, *Catalogue 1*, 53 (repeated in *Catalogue 2*, 90), suggests, and Eckstein, ii.589, firmly endorses, a description of it as a 'reply' to Hume. This is true of Smith's denial that suicide may be praiseworthy, but not otherwise. Smith is following Hume when he says that suicide is commonly due to melancholy and when he urges (contrary to contemporary opinion and practice, as Eckstein notes) that suicide should not be considered criminal.

American savage, who, upon being taken prisoner by some hostile tribe, put himself to death, in order to avoid being afterwards put to death in torture, and amidst the insults and mockery of his enemies. He places his glory in supporting those torments with manhood, and in retorting those insults with tenfold contempt and derision.

35   This contempt of life and death, however, and, at the same time, the most entire submission to the order of Providence; the most complete contentment with every event which the current of human affairs could possibly cast up, may be considered as the two fundamental doctrines upon which rested the whole fabric of Stoical morality. The independent and spirited, but often harsh Epictetus, may be considered as the great apostle of the first of those doctrines: the mild, the humane, the benevolent Antoninus,[37] of the second.

36   The emancipated slave of Epaphriditus, who, in his youth, had been subjected to the insolence of a brutal master, who, in his riper years, was, by the jealousy and caprice of Domitian, banished from Rome and Athens, and obliged to dwell at Nicopolis, and who, by the same tyrant, might expect every moment to be sent to Gyarae, or, perhaps, to be put to death;[38] could preserve his tranquillity only by fostering in his mind the most sovereign contempt of human life. He never exults so much, ᵗaccordinglyᵗ his eloquence is never so animated as when he represents the futility and nothingness of all its pleasures and all its pains.

37   The good-natured Emperor, the absolute sovereign of the whole civilized part of the world, who certainly had no peculiar reason to complain of his own allotment, delights in expressing his contentment with the ordinary course of things, and in pointing out beauties even in those parts of it where vulgar observers are not apt to see any. There is a propriety and even an engaging grace, he observes,[39] in old age as well as in youth; and the weakness and decrepitude of the one state are as suitable to nature as the bloom and vigour of the other. Death, too, is just as proper a termination of old age, as youth is of childhood, or manhood of youth. As we frequently say, he remarks upon another occasion,[40] that the physician has ordered to such a man to ride on horseback, or to use the cold bath, or to

ᵗ⁻ᵗ 7 acordingly; 6

---

[37] Marcus Aurelius.

[38] Epictetus was the slave, then the freedman, of Epaphroditus, freedman and secretary of Nero. In writing of 'a brutal master' (which need not necessarily refer to Epaphroditus), Smith is thinking of the (dubious) tale of Celsus (Origen, *Against Celsus*, VII.53) that Epictetus had his leg broken by his master. When the emperor Domitian banished the philosophers from Rome in A.D. 89, Epictetus went to live in Nicopolis (Aulus Gellius, XV.11). There is no reason to think that he was 'obliged' to live there, was banished from Athens as well as Rome, or was in danger of being sent to Gyaros (an island used by the Roman emperors as a place of banishment). Smith is reading too much into the quotation from Epictetus at § 25 above.

[39] Cf. Marcus Aurelius, *Meditations*, III.2, IX.3.   [40] V.8

walk barefooted; so ought we to say, that Nature, the great conductor and physician of the universe, has ordered to such a man a disease, or the amputation of a limb, or the loss of a child. By the prescriptions of ordinary physicians the patient swallows many a bitter potion; undergoes many a painful operation. From the very uncertain hope, however, that health may be the consequence, he gladly submits to all. The harshest prescriptions of the great Physician of nature, the patient may, in the same manner, hope will contribute to his own health, to his own final prosperity and happiness: and he may be perfectly assured that they not only contribute, but are indispensably necessary to the health, to the prosperity and happiness of the universe, to the furtherance and advancement of the great plan of Jupiter. Had they not been so, the universe would never have produced them; its all-wise Architect and Conductor would never have suffered them to happen. As all, even the smallest of the co-existent parts of the universe, are exactly fitted to one another, and all contribute to compose one immense and connected system; so all, even apparently the most insignificant of the successive events which follow one another, make parts, and necessary parts, of that great chain of causes and effects which had no beginning, and which will have no end; and which, as they all necessarily result from the original arrangement and contrivance of the whole; so they are all essentially necessary, not only to its prosperity, but to its continuance and preservation. Whoever does not cordially embrace whatever befals him, whoever is sorry that it has befallen him, whoever wishes that it had not befallen him, wishes, so far as in him lies, to stop the motion of the universe, to break that great chain of succession, by the progress of which that system can alone be continued and preserved, and, for some little conveniency of his own, to disorder and discompose the whole machine of the world. 'O world,' says he, in another place,[41] 'all things are suitable to me which are suitable to thee. Nothing is too early or too late to me which is seasonable for thee. All is fruit to me which thy seasons bring forth. From thee are all things; in thee are all things; for thee are all things. One man says, O beloved city of Cecrops.[42] Wilt not thou say, O beloved city of God?'

38   From these very sublime doctrines the Stoics, or at least some of the Stoics, attempted to deduce all their paradoxes.

39   The Stoical wise man endeavoured to enter into the views of the great Superintendant of the universe, and to see things in the same light in which that divine Being beheld them. But, to the great Superintendant of the universe, all the different events which the course of his providence may bring forth, what to us appear the smallest and the greatest, the bursting of a bubble, as Mr. Pope says,[43] and that of a world, for example,

[41] IV.23   [42] Athens, said to have been founded by Cecrops.
[43] *Essay on Man,* I.90.

were perfectly equal, were equally parts of that great chain which he had predestined from all eternity, were equally the effects of the same unerring wisdom, of the same universal and boundless benevolence. To the Stoical wise man, in the same manner, all those different events were perfectly equal. In the course of those events, indeed, a little department, in which he had himself some little management and direction, had been assigned to him. In this department he endeavoured to act as properly as he could, and to conduct himself according to those orders which, he understood, had been prescribed to him. But he took no anxious or passionate concern either in the success, or in the disappointment of his own most faithful endeavours. The highest prosperity and the total destruction of that little department, of that little system which had been in some measure committed to his charge, were perfectly indifferent to him. If those events had depended upon him, he would have chosen the one, and he would have rejected the other. But as they did not depend upon him, he trusted to a superior wisdom, and was perfectly satisfied that the event which happened, whatever it might be, was the very event which he himself, had he known all the connections and dependencies of things, would most earnestly and devoutly have wished for. Whatever he did under the influence and direction of those principles was equally perfect; and when he stretched out his finger, to give the example which they commonly made use of, he performed an action in every respect as meritorious, as worthy of praise and admiration, as when he laid down his life for the service of his country. As, to the great Superintendant of the universe, the greatest and the smallest exertions of his power, the formation and dissolution of a world, the formation and dissolution of a bubble, were equally easy, were equally admirable, and equally the effects of the same divine wisdom and benevolence; so, to the Stoical wise man, what we would call the great action required no more exertion than the little one, was equally easy, proceeded from exactly the same principles, was in no respect more meritorious, nor worthy of any higher degree of praise and admiration.

40   As all those who had arrived at this state of perfection, were equally happy; so all those who fell in the smallest degree short of it, how nearly soever they might approach to it, were equally miserable. As the man, they said, who was but an inch below the surface of the water, could no more breathe than he who was an hundred yards below it; so the man who had not completely subdued all his private, partial, and selfish passions, who had any other earnest desire but that for the universal happiness, who had not completely emerged from that abyss of misery and disorder into which his anxiety for the gratification of those private, partial, and selfish passions had involved him, could no more breathe the free air of liberty and independency, could no more enjoy the security and happiness of the wise man, than he who was most remote from that situation. As all the

actions of the wise man were perfect, and equally perfect; so all those of the man who had not arrived at this supreme wisdom were faulty, and, as some Stoics pretended, equally faulty. As one truth, they said, could not be more true, nor one falsehood more false than another; so an honourable action could not be more honourable, nor a shameful one more shameful than another. As in shooting at a mark, the man who missed it by an inch had equally missed it with him who had done so by a hundred yards; so the man who, in what to us appears the most insignificant action, had acted improperly and without a sufficient reason, was equally faulty with him who had done so in, what to us appears, the most important; the man who has killed a cock, for example, improperly and without a sufficient reason, with him who had murdered his father.

41   If the first of those two paradoxes should appear sufficiently violent, the second is evidently too absurd to deserve any serious consideration. It is, indeed, so very absurd that one can scarce help suspecting that it must have been in some measure misunderstood or misrepresented. At any rate, I cannot allow myself to believe that such men as Zeno or Cleanthes,[44] men, it is said, of the most simple as well as of the most sublime eloquence, could be the authors, either of these, or of the greater part of the other Stoical paradoxes, which are in general mere impertinent quibbles, and do so little honour to their system that I shall give no further account of them. I am disposed to impute them rather to Chrysippus,[45] the disciple and follower, indeed, of Zeno and Cleanthes, but who, from all that has been delivered down to us concerning him, seems to have been a mere dialectical pedant, without taste or elegance of any kind. He may have been the first who reduced their doctrines into a scholastic or technical system of artificial definitions, divisions, and subdivisions; one of the most effectual expedients, perhaps, for extinguishing whatever degree of good sense there may be in any moral or metaphysical doctrine. Such a man may very easily be supposed to have understood too literally some animated expressions of his masters in describing the happiness of the man of perfect virtue, and the unhappiness of whoever fell short of that character.

42   The Stoics in general seem to have admitted that there might be a degree of proficiency in those who had not advanced to perfect virtue and happiness. They distributed those proficients into different classes, according to the degree of their advancement; and they called the imperfect virtues which they supposed them capable of exercising, not rectitudes, but proprieties, fitnesses, decent and becoming actions, for which a plausible or probable reason could be assigned, what Cicero expresses by the Latin word *officia*, and Seneca, I think more exactly, by that of *convenientia*. The doctrine of those imperfect, but attainable virtues, seems to have

[44] Cleanthes succeeded Zeno as head of the Stoic school of philosophy.
[45] The third head of the Stoic school.

constituted what we may call the practical morality of the Stoics. It is the subject of Cicero's Offices;[46] and is said to have been that of another book written by Marcus Brutus, but which is now lost.[47]

43   The plan and system which Nature has sketched out for our conduct, seems to be altogether different from that of the Stoical philosophy.

44   By Nature the events which immediately affect that little department in which we ourselves have some little management and direction, which immediately affect ourselves, our friends, our country, are the events which interest us the most, and which chiefly excite our desires and aversions, our hopes and fears, our joys and sorrows. Should those passions be, what they are very apt to be, too vehement, Nature has provided a proper remedy and correction. The real or even the imaginary presence of the impartial spectator, the authority of the man within the breast, is always at hand to overawe them into the proper tone and temper of moderation.

45   If, notwithstanding our most faithful exertions, all the events which can affect this little department, should turn out the most unfortunate and disastrous, Nature has by no means left us without consolation. That consolation may be drawn, not only from the complete approbation of the man within the breast, but, if possible, from a still nobler and more generous principle, from a firm reliance upon, and a reverential submission to, that benevolent wisdom which directs all the events of human life, and which, we may be assured, would never have suffered those misfortunes to happen, had they not been indispensably necessary for the good of the whole.

46   Nature has not prescribed to us this sublime contemplation as the great business and occupation of our lives. She only points it out to us as the consolation of our misfortunes. The Stoical philosophy prescribes it as the great business and occupation of our lives. That philosophy teaches us to interest ourselves earnestly and anxiously in no events, external to the good order of our own minds, to the propriety of our own choosing and rejecting, except in those which concern a department where we neither have nor ought to have any sort of management or direction, the department of the great Superintendant of the universe. By the perfect apathy which it prescribes to us, by endeavouring, not merely to moderate, but to eradicate all our private, partial, and selfish affections, by suffering us to feel for whatever can befall ourselves, our friends, our country, not even the sympathetic and reduced passions of the impartial spectator, it endeavours to render us altogether indifferent and unconcerned in the suc-

---

[46] *De Officiis.*

[47] Marcus Junius Brutus, who joined in the murder of Julius Caesar, is reported by Seneca, *Epistles* (Book XV), 95.45, to have written a book entitled περὶ καθήκοντος ('On Propriety'). Two later grammarians, Charisius and Priscianus, cite it by the Latin equivalent, *De Officiis.*

cess or miscarriage of every thing which Nature has prescribed to us as the proper business and occupation of our lives.

47   The reasonings of philosophy, it may be said, though they may confound and perplex the understanding, can never break down the necessary connection which Nature has established between causes and their effects. The causes which naturally excite our desires and aversions, our hopes and fears, our joys and sorrows, would no doubt, notwithstanding all the reasonings of Stoicism, produce upon each individual, according to the degree of his actual sensibility, their proper and necessary effects. The judgments of the man within the breast, however, might be a good deal affected by those reasonings, and that great inmate might be taught by them to attempt to overawe all our private, partial, and selfish affections into a more or less perfect tranquillity. To direct the judgments of this inmate is the great purpose of all systems of morality. That the Stoical philosophy had very great influence upon the character and conduct of its followers, cannot be doubted; and that though it might sometimes incite them to unnecessary violence, its general tendency was to animate them to actions of the most heroic magnanimity and most extensive benevolence.

48   "IV.   Besides these ancient, there are some modern systems, according to which virtue consists in propriety; or in the suitableness of the affection from which we act, to the cause or object which excites it. The system of Dr. Clark,[48] which places virtue in acting according to the relations of things, in regulating our conduct according to the fitness or incongruity which there may be in the application of certain actions to certain things, or to certain relations: that of Mr. Woollaston,[49] which places it in acting according to the truth of things, according to their proper nature and essence, or in treating them as what they really are, and not as what they are not: that of my Lord Shaftesbury,[50] which places it in maintaining a proper balance of the affections, and in allowing no passion to go beyond its proper sphere; are all of them more or less inaccurate descriptions of the same fundamental idea.

---

[u] *Ed. 6 here reverts to the text of eds. 1–5. See note* [k] *at the end of VII.ii.1.19.*

[48] Samuel Clarke; see VII.i.3, note 3.
[49] William Wollaston (1660–1724), *Religion of Nature delineated*, I; Raphael, *British Moralists 1650–1800*, §§ 274–90.
[50] Anthony Ashley Cooper, 3rd Earl of Shaftesbury (1671–1713). His account specifically of virtue is given in *Inquiry concerning Virtue*, I.ii.3; Raphael, *British Moralists*, §§ 200–2. Smith's interpretation of Shaftesbury's view is questionable. It is perhaps due to a misunderstanding of Shaftesbury's formal definition of virtue at *Inquiry*, I.iii.1, as 'a certain just disposition, or proportionable affection of a rational creature towards the moral objects of right and wrong'. Here 'proportionable affection' means an affection proportionable or suitable to the moral objects, but Smith may have taken it to refer to a balance of one affection to others.

49   *v*None of those systems either give, or *w*even pretend to*w* give, any precise or distinct measure by which this fitness or propriety of affection can
be ascertained or judged of. That precise and distinct measure can be
found nowhere but in the sympathetic feelings of the impartial and well-
informed spectator.*v*

50   The description of *x*virtue, besides,*x* which is either given, or at least
meant and intended to be given in each of those systems, for some of the
modern authors are not very fortunate in their manner of expressing themselves, is no doubt quite just, so far as it goes. There is no virtue without
propriety, and wherever there is propriety some degree of approbation is
due. But still this description is imperfect. For though propriety is an
essential ingredient in every virtuous action, it is not always the sole ingredient. Beneficent actions have in them another quality by which they
appear not only to deserve approbation but recompense. None of those
systems account either easily or sufficiently for that superior degree of
esteem which seems due to such actions, or for that diversity of sentiment
which they naturally excite. Neither is the description of vice more complete. For, in the same manner, though impropriety is a necessary ingredient
in every vicious action, it is not always the sole ingredient; and there is
often the highest degree of absurdity and impropriety in very harmless and
insignificant actions. Deliberate actions, of a pernicious tendency to those
we live with, have, besides their impropriety, a peculiar quality of their
own by which they appear to deserve, not only disapprobation, but punishment; and to be the objects, not of dislike merely, but of resentment and
revenge: and none of those systems easily and sufficiently account for that
superior degree of detestation which we feel for such actions.

CHAP. II

Of those Systems which make Virtue consist in Prudence

1   THE most ancient of those systems which make virtue consist in prudence,
and of which any considerable remains have come down to us, is that of
Epicurus, who is said, however, to have borrowed all the leading principles
of his philosophy from some of those who had gone before him, particularly from Aristippus;[1] though it is very probable, notwithstanding this
allegation of his enemies, that at least his manner of applying those principles was altogether his own.

---

v–v *om.* *1–5*   *w–w* 7 even to pretend to *6*   *x–x* virtue *1–5*

---

[1] Founder of the Cyrenaic school of philosophy, which regarded pleasure as the sole
end of action.

2   According to Epicurus*, bodily pleasure and pain were the sole ultimate
objects of natural desire and aversion. That they were always the natural
objects of those passions, he thought required no proof. Pleasure might,
indeed, appear sometimes to be avoided; not, however, because it was
pleasure, but because, by the enjoyment of it, we should either forfeit some
greater pleasure, or expose ourselves to some pain that was more to be
avoided than this pleasure was to be desired. Pain, in the same manner,
might appear sometimes to be eligible; not, however, because it was pain,
but because by enduring it we might either avoid a still greater pain, or
acquire some pleasure of much more importance. That bodily pain and
pleasure, therefore, were always the natural objects of desire and aversion,
was, he thought, abundantly evident. Nor was it less so, he imagined, that
they were the sole ultimate objects of those passions. Whatever else was
either desired or avoided, was so, according to him, upon account of its
tendency to produce one or other of those sensations. The tendency to
procure pleasure rendered power and riches desirable, as the contrary
tendency to produce pain made poverty and insignificancy the objects of
aversion. Honour and reputation were valued, because the esteem and love
of those we live with were of the greatest consequence both to procure
pleasure and to defend us from pain. Ignominy and bad fame, on the contrary, were to be avoided, because the hatred, contempt and resentment of
those we lived with, destroyed all security, and necessarily exposed us to
the greatest bodily evils.

3   All the pleasures and pains of the mind were, according to Epicurus,
ultimately derived from those of the body. The mind was happy when it
thought of the past pleasures of the body, and hoped for others to come:
and it was miserable when it thought of the pains which the body had formerly endured, and dreaded the same or greater thereafter.

4   But the pleasures and pains of the mind, though ultimately derived from
those of the body, were vastly greater than their originals. The body felt
only the sensation of the present instant, whereas the mind felt also the
past and the future, the one by remembrance, the other by anticipation,
and consequently both suffered and enjoyed much more. When we are
under the greatest bodily pain, he observed, we shall always find, if we
attend to it, that it is not the suffering of the present instant which chiefly
torments us, but either the agonizing remembrance of the past, or the yet
more horrible dread of the future. The pain of each instant, considered
by itself, and cut off from all that goes before and all that comes after it, is a
trifle, not worth the regarding. Yet this is all which the body can ever be
said to suffer. In the same manner, when we enjoy the greatest pleasure,
we shall always find that the bodily sensation, the sensation of the present
instant, makes but a small part of our happiness, that our enjoyment

*See Cicero de finibus, lib. i. Diogenes Laert. l. x.

chiefly arises either from the cheerful recollection of the past, or the still more joyous anticipation of the future, and that the mind always contributes by much the largest share of the entertainment.

5   Since our happiness and misery, therefore, depended chiefly on the mind, if this part of our nature was well disposed, if our thoughts and opinions were as they should be, it was of little importance in what manner our body was affected. Though under great bodily pain, we might still enjoy a considerable share of happiness, if our reason and judgment maintained their superiority. We might entertain ourselves with the remembrance of past, and with the hopes of future pleasure; we might soften the rigour of our pains, by recollecting what it was which, even in this situation, we were under any necessity of suffering. That this was merely the bodily sensation, the pain of the present instant, which by itself could never be very great. That whatever agony we suffered from the dread of its continuance, was the effect of an opinion of the mind, which might be corrected by juster sentiments; by considering that, if our pains were violent, they would probably be of short duration; and that if they were of long continuance, they would probably be moderate, and admit of many intervals of ease; and that, at any rate, death was always at hand and within call to deliver us, which as, according to him, it put an end to all sensation, either of pain or pleasure, could not be regarded as an evil. When we are, said he, death is not; and when death is, we are not; death therefore can be nothing to us.

6   If the actual sensation of positive pain was in itself so little to be feared, that of pleasure was still less to be desired. Naturally the sensation of pleasure was much less pungent than that of pain. If, therefore, this last could take so very little from the happiness of a well-disposed mind, the other could add scarce any thing to it. When the body was free from pain and the mind from fear and anxiety, the superadded sensation of bodily pleasure could be of very little importance; and though it might diversify, could not properly be said to increase the happiness of *ªtheª* situation.

7   In ease of body, therefore, and in security or tranquillity of mind, consisted, according to Epicurus, the most perfect state of human nature, the most complete happiness which man was capable of enjoying. To obtain this great end of natural desire was the sole object of all the virtues, which, according to him, were not desirable upon their own account, but upon account of their tendency to bring about this situation.

8   Prudence, for example, though, according to this philosophy, the source and principle of all the virtues, was not desirable upon its own account. That careful and laborious and circumspect state of mind, ever watchful and ever attentive to the most distant consequences of every action, could

---

ª⁻ª 5 this *1–4* 6 7   *The revision in ed. 5 was probably made by the author, chiefly in order to avoid the repetition of* this situation *at the end of* § 7.

not be a thing pleasant or agreeable for its own sake, but upon account of its tendency to procure the greatest goods and to keep off the greatest evils.

9   To abstain from pleasure too, to curb and restrain our natural passions for enjoyment, which was the office of temperance, could never be desirable for its own sake. The whole value of this virtue arose from its utility, from its enabling us to postpone the present enjoyment for the sake of a greater to come, or to avoid a greater pain that might ensue from it. Temperance, in short, was nothing but prudence with regard to pleasure.

10   To support labour, to endure pain, to be exposed to danger or to death, the situations which fortitude would often lead us into, were surely still less the objects of natural desire. They were chosen only to avoid greater evils. We submitted to labour, in order to avoid the greater shame and pain of poverty, and we exposed ourselves to danger and to death in defence of our liberty and property, the means and instruments of pleasure and happiness; or in defence of our country, in the safety of which our own was necessarily comprehended. Fortitude enabled us to do all this cheerfully, as the best which, in our present situation, could possibly be done, and was in reality no more than prudence, good judgment, and presence of mind in properly appreciating pain, labour, and danger, always choosing the less in order to avoid the greater.

11   It is the same case with justice. To abstain from what is another's was not desirable on its own account, and it could not surely be better for you, that I should possess what is my own, than that you should possess it. You ought, however, to abstain from whatever belongs to me, because by doing otherwise you will provoke the resentment and indignation of mankind. The security and tranquillity of your mind will be entirely destroyed. You will be filled with fear and consternation at the thought of that punishment which you will imagine that men are at all times ready to inflict upon you, and from which no power, no art, no concealment, will ever, in your own fancy, be sufficient to protect you. That other species of justice which consists in doing proper good offices to different persons, according to the various relations of neighbours, kinsmen, friends, benefactors, superiors, or equals, which they may stand in to us, is recommended by the same reasons. To act properly in all these different relations procures us the esteem and love of those we live with; as to do otherwise excites their contempt and hatred. By the one we naturally secure, by the other we necessarily endanger our own ease and tranquillity, the great and ultimate objects of all our desires. The whole virtue of justice, therefore, the most important of all the virtues, is no more than discreet and prudent conduct with regard to our neighbours.

12   Such is the doctrine of Epicurus concerning the nature of virtue. It may seem extraordinary that this philosopher, who is described as a person of the most amiable manners, should never have observed, that, whatever

may be the tendency of those virtues, or of the contrary vices, with regard to our bodily ease and security, the sentiments which they naturally excite in others are the objects of a much more passionate desire or aversion than all their other consequences; that to be amiable, to be respectable, to be the proper object of esteem, is by every well-disposed mind more valued than all the ease and security which love, respect, and esteem can procure us; that, on the contrary, to be odious, to be contemptible, to be the proper object of indignation, is more dreadful than all that we can suffer in our body from hatred, contempt, or indignation; and that consequently our desire of the one character, and our aversion to the other, cannot arise from any regard to the effects which either of them is likely to produce upon the body.

13   This system is, no doubt, altogether inconsistent with that which I have been endeavouring to establish. It is not difficult, however, to discover from what phasis, if I may say so, from what particular view or aspect of nature, this account of things derives its probability. By the wise contrivance of the Author of nature, virtue is upon all ordinary occasions, even with regard to this life, real wisdom, and the surest and readiest means of obtaining both safety and advantage. Our success or disappointment in our undertakings must very much depend upon the good or bad opinion which is commonly entertained of us, and upon the general disposition of those we live with, either to assist or to oppose us. But the best, the surest, the easiest, and the readiest way of obtaining the advantageous and of avoiding the unfavourable judgments of others, is undoubtedly to render ourselves the proper objects of the former and not of the latter. 'Do you desire,' said Socrates,[2] 'the reputation of a good musician? The only sure way of obtaining it, is to become a good musician. Would you desire in the same manner to be thought capable of serving your country either as a general or as a statesman? The best way in this case too is really to acquire the art and experience of war and government, and to become really fit to be a general or a statesman. And in the same manner if you would be reckoned sober, temperate, just, and equitable, the best way of acquiring this reputation is to become sober, temperate, just, and equitable. If you can really render yourself amiable, respectable, and the proper object of esteem, there is no fear of your not soon acquiring the love, the respect, and esteem of those you live with.' Since the practice of virtue, therefore, is in general so advantageous, and that of vice so contrary to our interest, the consideration of those opposite tendencies undoubtedly stamps an additional beauty and propriety upon the one, and a new deformity and impropriety upon the other. Temperance, magnanimity, justice, and beneficence, come thus to be

---

[2] Smith is presumably recalling a report of Xenophon, *Memorabilia*, I.7, but the supposed quotation (not printed as such in eds. 1–5) is a very free paraphrase, not a translation.

approved of, not only under their proper characters, but under the additional character of the highest wisdom and most real prudence. And in the same manner, the contrary vices of intemperance, pusillanimity, injustice, and either malevolence or sordid selfishness, come to be disapproved of, not only under their proper characters, but under the additional character of the most short-sighted folly and weakness. Epicurus appears in every virtue to have attended to this species of propriety only. It is that which is most apt to occur to those who are endeavouring to persuade others to regularity of conduct. When men by their practice, and perhaps too by their maxims, manifestly show that the natural beauty of virtue is not like to have much effect upon them, how is it possible to move them but by representing the folly of their conduct, and how much they themselves are in the end likely to suffer by it?

14   By running up all the different virtues too to this one species of propriety, Epicurus indulged a propensity, which is natural to all men, but which philosophers in particular are apt to cultivate with a peculiar fondness, as the great means of displaying their ingenuity, the propensity to account for all appearances from as few principles as possible. And he, no doubt, indulged this propensity still further, when he referred all the primary objects of natural desire and aversion to the pleasures and pains of the body. The great patron of the atomical philosophy, who took so much pleasure in deducing all the powers and qualities of bodies from the most obvious and familiar, the figure, motion, and arrangement of the small parts of matter, felt no doubt a similar satisfaction, when he accounted, in the same manner, for all the sentiments and passions of the mind from those which are most obvious and familiar.

15   The system of Epicurus agreed with those of Plato, Aristotle, and Zeno, in making virtue consist in acting in the most suitable manner to obtain ᵇtheᵇ *primary objects of natural desire. It differed from all of them in two other respects; first, in the account which it gave of those primary objects of natural desire; and secondly, in the account which it gave of the excellence of virtue, or of the reason why that quality ought to be esteemed.

16   The primary objects of natural desire consisted, according to Epicurus, in bodily pleasure and pain, and in nothing else: whereas, according to the other three philosophers, there were many other objects, such as knowledge, such as the happiness of our relations, of our friends, of our country, which were ultimately desirable for their own sakes.

17   Virtue too, according to Epicurus, did not deserve to be pursued for its own sake, nor was itself one of the ultimate objects of natural appetite, but was eligible only upon account of its tendency to prevent pain and to

---

*Prima naturae.

ᵇ⁻ᵇ *1–5 om. 6 7 Printer's error*

procure ease and pleasure. In the opinion of the other three, on the contrary, it was desirable, not merely as the means of procuring the other primary objects of natural desire, but as something which was in itself more valuable than them all. Man, they thought, being born for action, his happiness must consist, not merely in the agreeableness of his passive sensations, but also in the propriety of his active exertions.

CHAP. III

Of those Systems which make Virtue consist in Benevolence

1 THE system which makes virtue consist in benevolence, though I think not so ancient as all of those which I have already given an account of, is, however, of very great antiquity. It seems to have been the doctrine of the greater part of those philosophers who, about and after the age of Augustus, called themselves Eclectics, who pretended to follow chiefly the opinions of Plato and Pythagoras, and who upon that account are commonly known by the name of the later Platonists.[1]

2 In the divine nature, according to these authors, benevolence or love was the sole principle of action, and directed the exertion of all the other attributes. The wisdom of the Deity was employed in finding out the means for bringing about those ends which his goodness suggested, as his infinite power was exerted to execute them. Benevolence, however, was still the supreme and governing attribute, to which the others were subservient, and from which the whole excellency, or the whole morality, if I may be allowed such an expression, of the divine operations, was ultimately derived. The whole perfection and virtue of the human mind consisted in some resemblance or participation of the divine perfections, and, consequently, in being filled with the same principle of benevolence and love which influenced all the actions of the Deity. The actions of men which flowed from this motive were alone truly praise-worthy, or could claim any merit in the sight of the Deity. It was by actions of charity and love only that we could imitate, as became us, the conduct of God, that we could express our humble and devout admiration of his infinite perfections, that by fostering in our own minds the same divine principle, we could bring our own affections to a greater resemblance with his holy attributes, and thereby become more proper objects of his love and esteem; till at last we

[1] In a note to Ancient Logics, 3, Smith writes similarly of 'that eclectic philosophy, from which the later Platonists arose'. But it is hard to say what writers he has in mind in §§ 1–2 of the present chapter. Later *Stoics* such as Seneca, Epictetus, and Marcus Aurelius, stressed benevolence. The Neoplatonists advocated an imitation of God but did not associate this with love or benevolence. Smith may be reading back into them the doctrines of Christian thinkers who were influenced by Neoplatonism in other respects.

arrived at that immediate converse and communication with the Deity to which it was the great object of this philosophy to raise us.

3   This system, as it was much esteemed by many ancient fathers of the Christian church, so after the Reformation it was adopted by several divines of the most eminent piety and learning and of the most amiable manners; particularly, by Dr. Ralph Cudworth, by Dr. Henry More, and by Mr. John Smith of Cambridge.[2] But of all the patrons of this system, ancient or modern, the late Dr. Hutcheson was undoubtedly, beyond all comparison, the most acute, the most distinct, the most philosophical, and what is of the greatest consequence of all, the soberest and most judicious.[3]

4   That virtue consists in benevolence is a notion supported by many appearances in human nature. It has been observed already, that proper benevolence is the most graceful and agreeable of all the affections, that it is recommended to us by a double sympathy, that as its tendency is necessarily beneficent, it is the proper object of gratitude and reward, and that upon all these accounts it appears to our natural sentiments to possess a merit superior to any other. It has been observed too, that even the weaknesses of benevolence are not very disagreeable to us, whereas those of every other passion are always extremely disgusting. Who does not abhor excessive malice, excessive selfishness, or excessive resentment? But the most excessive indulgence even of partial friendship is not so offensive. It is the benevolent passions only which can exert themselves without any regard or attention to propriety, and yet retain something about them which is engaging. There is something pleasing even in mere instinctive good-will which goes on to do good offices without once reflecting whether by this conduct it is the proper object either of blame or approbation. It is not so with the other passions. The moment they are deserted, the moment they are unaccompanied by the sense of propriety, they cease to be agreeable.

5   As benevolence bestows upon those actions which proceed from it, a beauty superior to all others, so the want of it, and much more the contrary inclination, communicates a peculiar deformity to whatever evidences such a disposition. Pernicious actions are often punishable for no other

---

[2] All three were members of the group of seventeenth-century philosophers known as the Cambridge Platonists. The main ethical work of Ralph Cudworth (1617–88) is *Treatise concerning Eternal and Immutable Morality*; of Henry More (1614–87), *Enchiridion Ethicum*, translated into English by Edward Southwell as *An Account of Virtue*; and of John Smith (1618–52), *Select Discourses*.

[3] Francis Hutcheson (1694–1746) was Professor of Moral Philosophy at the University of Glasgow from 1730 to 1746 and so Adam Smith's teacher. His most important works on ethics are *Inquiry concerning Moral Good and Evil* (Treatise II of *Inquiry into Beauty and Virtue*); *Essay on the Passions and Affections. With Illustrations on the Moral Sense*; and *System of Moral Philosophy*. Smith eulogizes him again in Letter 274 addressed to Archibald Davidson, Principal of Glasgow University, dated 16 November 1787, accepting the office of Lord Rector. Smith there writes of having been appointed to the Chair of Moral Philosophy, 'to which the abilities and Virtues of the never to be forgotten Dr Hutcheson had given a superior degree of illustration'.

reason than because they shew a want of sufficient attention to the happiness of our neighbour.

6   Besides all this, Dr. Hutcheson* observed that whenever in any action, supposed to proceed from benevolent affections, some other motive had been discovered, our sense of the merit of this action was just so far diminished as this motive was believed to have influenced it. If an action, supposed to proceed from gratitude, should be discovered to have arisen from an expectation of some new favour, or if what was apprehended to proceed from public spirit, should be found out to have taken its origin from the hope of a pecuniary reward, such a discovery would entirely destroy all notion of merit or praise-worthiness in either of these actions. Since, therefore, the mixture of any selfish motive, like that of a baser alloy, diminished or took away altogether the merit which would otherwise have belonged to any action, it was evident, he imagined, that virtue must consist in pure and disinterested benevolence alone.

7   When those actions, on the contrary, which are commonly supposed to proceed from a selfish motive, are discovered to have arisen from a benevolent one, it greatly enhances our sense of their merit. If we believed of any person that he endeavoured to advance his fortune from no other view but that of doing friendly offices, and of making proper returns to his benefactors, we should only love and esteem him the more. And this observation seemed still more to confirm the conclusion, that it was benevolence only which could stamp upon any action the character of virtue.

8   Last of all, what, he imagined, was an evident proof of the justness of this account of virtue, in all the disputes of casuists concerning the rectitude of conduct, the public good, he observed, was the standard to which they constantly referred; thereby universally acknowledging that whatever tended to promote the happiness of mankind was right and laudable and virtuous, and the contrary, wrong, blamable, and vicious. In the late debates about passive obedience and the right of resistance, the sole point in controversy among men of sense was, whether universal submission would probably be attended with greater evils than temporary insurrections when privileges were invaded. Whether what, upon the whole, tended most to the happiness of mankind, was not also morally good, was never once, he said, made a question.[4]

9   Since benevolence, therefore, was the only motive which could bestow upon any action the character of virtue, the greater the benevolence which was evidenced by any action, the greater the praise which must belong to it.

*See Inquiry concerning Virtue, sect. 1. and 2. [The reference is presumably to Sect. II.iii; Raphael, *British Moralists 1650–1800*, §§ 318–19.]

[4] Cf. Hutcheson, *Inquiry concerning Moral Good and Evil* (or *Inquiry concerning . . . Virtue . . .*), III.iii; Selby-Bigge, *British Moralists*, § 112.

10   Those actions which aimed at the happiness of a great community, as they demonstrated a more enlarged benevolence than those which aimed only at that of a smaller system, so were they, likewise, proportionally the more virtuous. The most virtuous of all affections, therefore, was that which embraced as its object the happiness of all intelligent beings. The least virtuous, on the contrary, of those to which the character of virtue could in any respect belong, was that which aimed no further than at the happiness of an individual, such as a son, a brother, a friend.

11   In directing all our actions to promote the greatest possible good, in submitting all inferior affections to the desire of the general happiness of mankind, in regarding one's self but as one of the many, whose prosperity was to be pursued no further than it was consistent with, or conducive to that of the whole, consisted the perfection of virtue.

12   Self-love was a principle which could never be virtuous in any degree or in any direction. It was vicious whenever it obstructed the general good. When it had no other effect than to make the individual take care of his own happiness, it was merely innocent, and though it deserved no praise, neither ought it to incur any blame. Those benevolent actions which were performed, notwithstanding some strong motive from self-interest, were the more virtuous upon that account. They demonstrated the strength and vigour of the benevolent principle.

13   Dr. Hutcheson* was so far from allowing self-love to be in any case a motive of virtuous actions, that even a regard to the pleasure of self-approbation, to the comfortable applause of our own consciences, according to him, diminished the merit of a benevolent action.[5] This was a selfish motive, he thought, which, so far as it contributed to any action, demonstrated the weakness of that pure and disinterested benevolence which could alone stamp upon the conduct of man the character of virtue. In the common judgments of mankind, however, this regard to the approbation of our own minds is so far from being considered as what can in any respect diminish the virtue of any action, that it is rather looked upon as the sole motive which deserves the appellation of virtuous.

14   Such is the account given of the nature of virtue in this amiable system, a system which has a peculiar tendency to nourish and support in the human heart the noblest and the most agreeable of all affections, and not

---

*Inquiry concerning virtue, sect. 2. art. 4. also Illustrations on the moral sense, sect. 5. last paragraph.

---

    [5] Hutcheson does not in fact say that it diminishes merit. In *Inquiry*, II.iv (Raphael, *British Moralists 1650–1800*, § 322), he says that a virtuous benevolence cannot be produced by the desire for self-approbation; and in *Illustrations*, V, last paragraph, he says that the pleasure of self-approbation helps us to be constant in virtue but does not add to merit.

only to check the injustice of self-love, but in some measure to discourage that principle altogether, by representing it as what could never reflect any honour upon those who were influenced by it.

15   As some of the other systems which I have already given an account of, do not sufficiently explain from whence arises the peculiar excellency of the supreme virtue of beneficence, so this system seems to have the contrary defect, of not sufficiently explaining from whence arises our approbation of the inferior virtues of prudence, vigilance, circumspection, temperance, constancy, firmness. The view and aim of our affections, the beneficent and hurtful effects which they tend to produce, are the only qualities at all attended to in this system. Their propriety and impropriety, their suitableness and unsuitableness, to the cause which excites them, are disregarded altogether.

16   Regard to our own private happiness and interest, too, appear upon many occasions very laudable principles of action. The habits of oeconomy, industry, discretion, attention, and application of thought, are generally supposed to be cultivated from self-interested motives, and at the same time are apprehended to be very praise-worthy qualities, which deserve the esteem and approbation of every body. The mixture of a selfish motive, it is true, seems often to sully the beauty of those actions which ought to arise from a benevolent affection. The cause of this, however, is not that self-love can never be the motive of a virtuous action, but that the benevolent principle appears in this particular case to want its due degree of strength, and to be altogether unsuitable to its object. The character, therefore, seems evidently imperfect, and upon the whole to deserve blame rather than praise. The mixture of a benevolent motive in an action to which self-love alone ought to be sufficient to prompt us, is not so apt indeed to diminish our sense of its propriety, or of the virtue of the person who performs it. We are not ready to suspect any person of being defective in selfishness. This is by no means the weak side of human nature, or the failing of which we are apt to be suspicious. If we could really believe, however, of any man, that, was it not from a regard to his family and friends, he would not take that proper care of his health, his life, or his fortune, to which self-preservation alone ought to be sufficient to prompt him, it would undoubtedly be a failing, though one of those amiable failings, which render a person rather the object of pity than of contempt or hatred. It would still, however, somewhat diminish the dignity and respectableness of his character. Carelessness and want of oeconomy are universally disapproved of, not, however, as proceeding from a want of benevolence, but from a want of the proper attention to the objects of self-interest.

17   Though the standard by which casuists frequently determine what is right or wrong in human conduct, be its tendency to the welfare or disorder of society, it does not follow that a regard to the welfare of society should be

the sole virtuous motive of action, but only that, in any competition, it ought to cast the balance against all other motives.[6]

18   Benevolence may, perhaps, be the sole principle of action in the Deity, and there are several, not improbable, arguments which tend to persuade us that it is so. It is not easy to conceive what other motive an independent and all-perfect Being, who stands in need of nothing external, and whose happiness is complete in himself, can act from. But whatever may be the case with the Deity, so imperfect a creature as man, the support of whose existence requires so many things external to him, must often act from many other motives. The condition of human nature were peculiarly hard, if those affections, which, by the very nature of our being, ought frequently to influence our conduct, could upon no occasion appear virtuous, or deserve esteem and commendation from any body.

19   Those three systems, that which places virtue in propriety, that which places it in prudence, and that which makes it consist in benevolence, are the principal accounts which have been given of the nature of virtue. To one or other of them, all the other descriptions of virtue, how different soever they may appear, are easily reducible.

20   That system which places virtue in obedience to the will of the Deity, may be counted either among those which make it consist in prudence, or among those which make it consist in propriety. When it is asked, why we ought to obey the will of the Deity, this question, which would be impious and absurd in the highest degree, if asked from any doubt that we ought to obey him, can admit but of two different answers. It must either be said that we ought to obey the will of the Deity because he is a Being of infinite power, who will reward us eternally if we do so, and punish us eternally if we do otherwise: or it must be said, that independent of any regard to our own happiness, or to rewards and punishments of any kind, there is a congruity and fitness that a creature should obey its creator, that a limited and imperfect being should submit to one of infinite and incomprehensible perfections. Besides one or other of these two, it is impossible to conceive that any other answer can be given to this question. If the first answer be the proper one, virtue consists in prudence, or in the proper pursuit of our own final interest and happiness; since it is upon this account that we are obliged to obey the will of the Deity. If the second answer be the proper one, virtue must consist in propriety, since the ground of our obligation to obedience is the suitableness or congruity of the sentiments of humility and submission to the superiority of the object which excites them.

21   That system which places virtue in utility,[7] coincides too with that which

---

[6] The view expressed in the last clause of this sentence is an unusual one for an opponent of utilitarianism to accept.

[7] The following sentence shows that Smith has Hume in mind. Cf. IV.2.3 above.

makes it consist in propriety. According to this system, all those qualities of the mind which are agreeable or advantageous, either to the person himself or to others, are approved of as virtuous, and the contrary disapproved of as vicious. But the agreeableness or utility of any affection depends upon the degree which it is allowed to subsist in. Every affection is useful when it is confined to a certain degree of moderation; and every affection is disadvantageous when it exceeds the proper bounds. According to this system therefore, virtue consists not in any one affection, but in the proper degree of all the affections. The only difference between it and that which I have been endeavouring to establish, is, that it makes utility, and not sympathy, or the correspondent affection of the spectator, the *ᵃnatural and originalᵃ* measure of this proper degree.

CHAP. IV

Of licentious Systems

1 ALL those systems, which I have hitherto given an account of, suppose that there is a real and essential distinction between vice and virtue, whatever these qualities may consist in. There is a real and essential difference between the propriety and impropriety of any affection, between benevolence and any other principle of action, between real prudence and shortsighted folly or precipitate rashness. In the main too all of them contribute to encourage the praise-worthy, and to discourage the blamable disposition.

2 It may be true, perhaps, of some of them, that they tend, in some measure, to break the balance of the affections, and to give the mind a particular bias to some principles of action, beyond the proportion that is due to them. The ancient systems, which place virtue in propriety, seem chiefly to recommend the great, the awful, and the respectable virtues, the virtues of self-government and self-command; fortitude, magnanimity, independency upon fortune, the contempt of all outward accidents, of pain, poverty, exile, and death. It is in these great exertions that the noblest propriety of conduct is displayed. The soft, the amiable, the gentle virtues, all the virtues of indulgent humanity are, in comparison, but little insisted upon, and seem, on the contrary, by the Stoics in particular, to have been often regarded as mere weaknesses which it behoved a wise man not to harbour in his breast.

3 The benevolent system, on the other hand, while it fosters and encourages all those milder virtues in the highest degree, seems entirely to neglect the more *ᵃawfulᵃ* and respectable qualities of the mind. It even

ᵃ⁻ᵃ *om.* *1–3*

ᵃ⁻ᵃ *1–5* lawful *6 7*

denies them the appellation of virtues. It calls them moral abilities, and treats them as qualities which do not deserve the same sort of esteem and approbation, that is due to what is properly denominated virtue. All those principles of action which aim only at our own interest, it treats, if that be possible, still worse. So far from having any merit of their own, they diminish, it pretends, the merit of benevolence, when they co-operate with it: and prudence, it is asserted, when employed only in promoting private interest, can never even be imagined a virtue.

4   That system, again, which makes virtue consist in prudence only, while it gives the highest encouragement to the habits of caution, vigilance, sobriety, and judicious moderation, seems to degrade equally both the amiable and respectable virtues, and to strip the former of all their beauty, and the latter of all their grandeur.

5   But notwithstanding these defects, the general tendency of each of those three systems is to encourage the best and most laudable habits of the human mind: and it were well for society, if, either mankind in general, or even those few who pretend to live according to any philosophical rule, were to regulate their conduct by the precepts of any one of them. We may learn from each of them something that is both valuable and peculiar. If it was possible, by precept and exhortation, to inspire the mind with fortitude and magnanimity, the ancient systems of propriety would seem sufficient to do this. Or if it was possible, by the same means, to soften it into humanity, and to awaken the affections of kindness and general love towards those we live with, some of the pictures with which the benevolent system presents us, might seem capable of producing this effect. We may learn from the system of Epicurus, though undoubtedly the *b*most imperfect*b* of all the three, how much the practice of both the amiable and respectable virtues is conducive to our own interest, to our own ease and safety and quiet even in this life. As Epicurus placed happiness in the attainment of ease and security, he exerted himself in a particular manner to show that virtue was, not merely the best and the surest, but the only means of acquiring those invaluable possessions. The good effects of virtue, upon our inward tranquillity and peace of mind, are what other philosophers have chiefly celebrated. Epicurus, without neglecting this topic, has chiefly insisted upon the influence of that amiable quality on our outward prosperity and safety. It was upon this account that his writings were so much studied in the ancient world by men of all different philosophical parties. It is from him that Cicero, the great enemy of the Epicurean system, borrows his most agreeable proofs that virtue alone is sufficient to secure happiness. Seneca, though a Stoic, the sect most opposite to that of Epicurus, yet quotes this philosopher more frequently than any other.

b-b worst *1-5*

6   ᶜThere is, however, another system which seemsᶜ to take away altogether the distinction between vice and virtue, and of which the tendency
is, upon that account, wholly pernicious: I mean ᵈthe system of Dr.
Mandeville. Though the notions of this authorᵈ are in almost every respect
erroneous, there are, however, some appearances in human nature, which,
when viewed in a certain manner, seem at first sight to favour them.
ᵉThese, described and exaggerated by the lively and humorous, though
coarse and rustic eloquence of Dr. Mandeville, have thrown upon his
doctrinesᵉ an air of truth and probability which is very apt to impose upon
the unskilful.[1]

7   ᶠDr. Mandevilleᶠ considers whatever is done from a sense of propriety,
from a regard to what is commendable and praise-worthy, as being done
from a love of praise and commendation, or as he calls it from vanity.
Man, he observes, is naturally much more interested in his own happiness
than in that of others, and it is impossible that in his heart he can ever
really prefer their prosperity to his own. Whenever he appears to do so, we
may be assured that he imposes upon us, and that he is then acting from
the same selfish motives as at all other times. Among his other selfish passions, vanity is one of the strongest, and he is always easily flattered and
greatly delighted with the applauses of those about him. When he appears
to sacrifice his own interest to that of his companions, he knows that
ᵍhisᵍ conduct will be highly agreeable to their self-love, and that they will
not fail to express their satisfaction by bestowing upon him the most extravagant praises. The pleasure which he expects from this, over-balances, in
his opinion, the interest which he abandons in order to procure it. His
conduct, therefore, upon this occasion, is in reality just as selfish, and arises
from just as mean a ʰmotive,ʰ as upon any other. He is flattered, however,
and he flatters ʲhimself,ʲ with the belief that it is entirely disinterested;

ᶜ⁻ᶜ There are, however, some other systems which seem *1–5*
ᵈ⁻ᵈ the systems of the duke of Rochefaucault [Rochefoucault *4 5*] and Dr. Mandeville.
Tho' [Though *2–5*] the notions of both these authors *1–5*
ᵉ⁻ᵉ These, first slightly sketched out with the elegance and delicate precision of the duke
of Rochefaucault, [Rochefoucault, *4 5*] and afterwards more fully represented with the
lively and humourous, tho' [humorous, though *2–5*] coarse and rustic eloquence of Dr.
Mandeville, have thrown upon their doctrines *1–5*
ᶠ⁻ᶠ Dr. Mandeville, the most methodical of those two authors, *1–5*
ᵍ⁻ᵍ *5* this *1–4 6 7*   *The revision in ed. 5 was probably a correction (it is certainly an
improvement) made by the author, and overlooked in the preparation of ed. 6 from the pages
of ed. 4.*
ʰ⁻ʰ *5* ∼ₐ *1–4 6 7*   *See preceding note*
ʲ⁻ʲ *5* ∼ₐ *1–4 6 7*

   [1] Smith's omission in ed. 6 of the references to La Rochefoucauld was a result of correspondence with Louis Alexandre, Duc de La Rochefoucauld d'Anville (1743–92),
whom Smith had met in 1765 at Geneva. In Letter 194 from the Duke, dated 3 March
1778, there is a mild protest about 'le mal que vous avez dit' of his ancestor. Letter 199
from the Duke, dated 6 August 1779, shows that Smith had written on 15 May and had
mentioned a new edition of TMS, presumably adding that it would revise or omit the

since, unless this was supposed, it would not seem to merit any commendation either in his own eyes or in those of others. All public spirit,
therefore, all preference of public to private interest, is, according to him,
a mere cheat and imposition upon mankind; and that human virtue which
is so much boasted of, and which is the occasion of so much emulation
among men, is the mere offspring of flattery begot upon pride.[2]

8   Whether the most generous and public-spirited actions may not, in
some sense, be regarded as proceeding from self-love, I shall not at present
examine. The decision of this question is not, I apprehend, of any importance towards establishing the reality of virtue, since self-love may frequently be a virtuous motive of action. I shall only endeavour to show that
the desire of doing what is honourable and noble, of rendering ourselves
the proper objects of esteem and approbation, cannot with any propriety
be called vanity. Even the love of well-grounded fame and reputation, the
desire of acquiring esteem by what is really estimable, does not deserve
that name. The first is the love of virtue, the noblest and the best passion
[k]in[k] human nature. The second is the love of true glory, a passion inferior
no doubt to the former, but which in dignity appears to come immediately
after it. He is guilty of vanity who desires praise for qualities which are
either not praise-worthy in any degree, or not in that degree in which he
expects to be praised for them; who sets his character upon the frivolous
ornaments of dress and equipage, or upon the equally frivolous accomplishments of ordinary behaviour. He is guilty of vanity who desires praise for
what indeed very well deserves it, but what he perfectly knows does not
belong to him. The empty coxcomb who gives himself airs of importance
which he has no title to, the silly liar who assumes the merit of adventures
which never happened, the foolish plagiary[3] who gives himself out for the
author of what he has no pretensions to, are properly accused of this passion. He too is said to be guilty of vanity who is not contented with the

[k-k] 5 of 1–4 6 7

statements about La Rochefoucauld. (Smith may or may not have meant ed. 5, which
appeared in 1781, but this in fact contained only very minor revision.) In Letter 248
addressed to the Duke, dated 1 November 1785, Smith repeats his 'promise' relating
to a new edition of TMS, which he hopes 'to execute before the end of the ensuing winter'.
He also commissioned Dugald Stewart (*Works*, vi.256, x.46), when visiting Paris in 1789,
to express to the Duke 'his sincere regret for having introduced the name of his ancestor
and that of Dr. Mandeville in the same sentence' and to say that this would be remedied 'in
the future editions of his *Theory*'. Ed. 6 appeared in 1790. Smith has inadvertently left
unaltered, in the title of the chapter, the plural term 'Systems'.

   Although Smith coupled La Rochefoucauld with Mandeville in the general remarks of
§ 6, the specific criticisms made in the remainder of the chapter were confined, even in
the original version, to tenets of Mandeville.

   [2] '. . . the Moral Virtues are the Political Offspring which Flattery begot upon Pride.'
Mandeville, *Enquiry into the Origin of Moral Virtue*; in *Fable of the Bees*, ed. Kaye, i.51.

   [3] Rae, *Life*, 32–3, 63–5, 269–70, discusses, with justified scepticism, reports of Smith's
fear of plagiarism. There is no reason to suppose that in the present passage (written for
ed. 1) Smith has stronger feelings about the plagiary than about the coxcomb or the liar.

silent sentiments of esteem and approbation, who seems to be fonder of
their noisy expressions and acclamations than of the sentiments themselves,
who is never satisfied but when his own praises are ringing in his ears, and
who solicits with the most anxious importunity all external marks of respect,
is fond of titles, of compliments, of being visited, of being attended, of
being taken notice of in public places with the appearance of deference and
attention. This frivolous passion is altogether different from either of the
two former, and is the passion of the lowest and the least of mankind, as
they are of the noblest and the greatest.

9   But though these three passions, the desire of rendering ourselves the
proper objects of honour and esteem; or of becoming what is honourable
and estimable; the desire of acquiring honour and esteem by really deserving those sentiments; and the frivolous desire of praise at any rate, are
widely different; though the two former are always approved of, while the
latter never fails to be despised; there is, however, a certain remote affinity
among them, which, exaggerated by the humorous and diverting eloquence
of this lively author, has enabled him to impose upon his readers. There
is an affinity between vanity and the love of true glory, as both these passions aim at acquiring esteem and approbation. But they are different in
this, that the one is a just, reasonable, and equitable passion, while the
other is unjust, absurd, and ridiculous. The man who desires esteem for
what is really estimable, desires nothing but what he is justly entitled to,
and what cannot be refused him without some sort of injury. He, on the
contrary, who desires it upon any other terms, demands what he has no
just claim to. The first is easily satisfied, is not apt to be jealous or suspicious that we do not esteem him enough, and is seldom solicitous about
receiving many external marks of our regard. The other, on the contrary,
is never to be satisfied, is full of jealousy and suspicion that we do not
esteem him so much as he desires, because he has some secret consciousness that he desires more than he deserves. The least neglect of ceremony,
he considers as a mortal affront, and as an expression of the most determined contempt. He is restless and impatient, and perpetually afraid that
we have lost all respect for him, and is upon this account always anxious
to obtain new expressions of esteem, and cannot be kept in temper but by
continual attention and adulation.

10   There is an affinity too between the desire of becoming what is honourable and estimable, and the desire of honour and esteem, between the love of
virtue and the love of true glory. They resemble one another not only in
this respect, that both aim at really being what is honourable and noble,
but even in that respect in which the love of true glory resembles what is
properly called vanity, some reference to the sentiments of others. The man
of the greatest magnanimity, who desires virtue for its own sake, and is
most indifferent about what actually are the opinions of mankind with

regard to him, is still, however, delighted with the thoughts of what they should be, with the consciousness that though he may neither be honoured nor applauded, he is still the proper object of honour and applause, and that if mankind were cool and candid and consistent with themselves, and properly informed of the motives and circumstances of his conduct, they would not fail to honour and applaud him. Though he despises the opinions which are actually entertained of him, he has the highest value for those which ought to be entertained of him. That he might think himself worthy of those honourable sentiments, and, whatever was the idea which other men might conceive of his character, that when he should put himself in their situation, and consider, not what was, but what ought to be their opinion, he should always have the highest idea of it himself, was the great and exalted motive of his conduct. As even in the love of virtue, therefore, there is still some reference, though not to what is, yet to what in reason and propriety ought to be, the opinion of others, there is even in this respect some affinity between it, and the love of true glory. There is, however, at the same time, a very great difference between them. The man who acts solely from a regard to what is right and fit to be done, from a regard to what is the proper object of esteem and approbation, though these sentiments should never be bestowed upon him, acts from the most sublime and godlike motive which human nature is even capable of conceiving. The man, on the other hand, who while he desires to merit approbation is at the same time anxious to obtain it, though he too is laudable in the main, yet his motives have a greater mixture of human infirmity. He is in danger of being mortified by the ignorance and injustice of mankind, and his happiness is exposed to the envy of his rivals and the folly of the public. The happiness of the other, on the contrary, is altogether secure and independent of fortune, and of the caprice of those he lives with. The contempt and hatred which may be thrown upon him by the ignorance of mankind, he considers as not belonging to him, and is not at all mortified by it. Mankind despise and hate him from a false notion of his character and conduct. If they knew him better, they would esteem and love him. It is not him whom, properly speaking, they hate and despise, but another person whom they mistake him to be. Our friend, whom we should meet at a masquerade in the garb of our enemy, would be more diverted than mortified, if under that disguise we should vent our indignation against him. Such are the sentiments of a man of real magnanimity, when exposed to unjust censure. It seldom happens, however, that human nature arrives at this degree of firmness. Though none but the weakest and most worthless of mankind are much delighted with false glory, yet, by a strange inconsistency, false ignominy is often capable of mortifying those who appear the most resolute and determined.

11   Dr. Mandeville is not satisfied with representing the frivolous motive of

vanity, as the source of all those actions which are commonly accounted virtuous. He endeavours to point out the imperfection of human virtue in many other respects. In every case, he pretends, it falls short of that complete self-denial which it pretends to, and, instead of a conquest, is commonly no more than a concealed indulgence of our passions. Wherever our reserve with regard to pleasure falls short of the most ascetic abstinence, he treats it as gross luxury and sensuality. Every thing, according to him, is luxury which exceeds what is absolutely necessary for the support of human nature, so that there is vice even in the use of a clean shirt, or of a convenient habitation. The indulgence of the inclination to sex, in the most lawful union, he considers as the same sensuality with the most hurtful gratification of that passion, and derides that temperance and that chastity which can be practised at so cheap a rate. The ingenious sophistry of his reasoning, is here, as upon many other occasions, covered by the ambiguity of language. There are some of our passions which have no other names except those which mark the disagreeable and offensive degree. The spectator is more apt to take notice of them in this degree than in any other. When they shock his own sentiments, when they give him some sort of antipathy and uneasiness, he is necessarily obliged to attend to them, and is from thence naturally led to give them a name. When they fall in with the natural state of his own mind, he is very apt to overlook them altogether, and either gives them no name at all, or, if he give them any, it is one which marks rather the subjection and restraint of the passion, than the degree which it still is allowed to subsist in, after it is so subjected and restrained. Thus the common names* of the love of pleasure, and of the love of sex, denote a vicious and offensive degree of those passions. The words temperance and chastity, on the other hand, seem to mark rather the restraint and subjection which they are kept under, than the degree which they are still allowed to subsist in. When he can show, therefore, that they still subsist in some degree, he imagines, he has entirely demolished the reality of the virtues of temperance and chastity, and shown them to be mere impositions upon the inattention and simplicity of mankind. Those virtues, however, do not require an entire insensibility to the objects of the passions which they mean to govern. They only aim at restraining the violence of those passions so far as not to hurt the individual, and neither disturb nor offend the society.

12   It is the great fallacy of Dr. Mandeville's book† to represent every passion as wholly vicious, which is so in any degree and in any direction. It is thus that he treats every thing as vanity which has any reference, either to what are, or to what ought to be the sentiments of others: and it is by means of this sophistry, that he establishes his favourite conclusion, that private

*Luxury and lust.
†Fable of the Bees.

vices are public benefits.[4] If the love of magnificence, a taste for the elegant arts and improvements of human life, for whatever is agreeable in dress, furniture, or equipage, for architecture, statuary, painting, and music, is to be regarded as luxury, sensuality, and ostentation, even in those whose situation allows, without any inconveniency, the indulgence of those passions, it is certain that luxury, sensuality, and ostentation are public benefits: since without the qualities upon which he thinks proper to bestow such opprobrious names, the arts of refinement could never find encouragement, and must languish for want of employment. Some popular ascetic doctrines which had been current before his time, and which placed virtue in the entire extirpation and annihilation of all our passions, were the real foundation of this licentious system. It was easy for Dr. Mandeville to prove, first, that this entire conquest never actually took place among men; and secondly, that, if it was to take place universally, it would be pernicious to society, by putting an end to all industry and commerce, and in a manner to the whole business of human life. By the first of these propositions he seemed to prove that there was no real virtue, and that what pretended to be such, was a mere cheat and imposition upon mankind; and by the second, that private vices were public benefits, since without them no society could prosper or flourish.

13   Such is the system of Dr. Mandeville, which once made so much noise in the world, and which, though, perhaps, it never gave occasion to more vice than what would have been without it, at least taught that vice, which arose from other causes, to appear with more effrontery, and to avow the corruption of its motives with a profligate audaciousness which had never been heard of before.

14   But how destructive soever this system may appear, it could never have imposed upon so great a number of persons, nor have occasioned so general an alarm among those who are the friends of better principles, had it not in some respects bordered upon the truth. A system of natural philosophy may appear very plausible, and be for a long time very generally received in the world, and yet have no foundation in nature, nor any sort of resemblance to the truth. The vortices of Des Cartes were regarded by a very ingenious nation, for near a century together, as a most satisfactory account of the revolutions of the heavenly bodies. Yet it has been demonstrated, to the conviction of all mankind, that these pretended causes of those wonderful effects, not only do not actually exist, but are utterly impossible, and if they did exist, could produce no such effects as are ascribed to them.[5] But it is otherwise with systems of moral philosophy, and an author who pretends to account for the origin of our moral sentiments,

---

[4] The full title of Mandeville's work is *The Fable of the Bees: or, Private Vices, Publick Benefits.*

[5] Smith discusses Descartes's theory of vortices at some length in Astronomy, IV.61–6.

cannot deceive us so grossly, nor depart so very far from all resemblance
to the truth. When a traveller gives an account of some distant country,
he may impose upon our credulity the most groundless and absurd fictions
as the most certain matters of fact. But when a person pretends to inform
us of what passes in our neighbourhood, and of the affairs of the very parish
which we live in, though here too, if we are so careless as not to examine
things with our own eyes, he may deceive us in many respects, yet the greatest falsehoods which he imposes upon us must bear some resemblance to
the truth, and must even have a considerable mixture of truth in them. An
author who treats of natural philosophy, and pretends to assign the causes
of the great phaenomena of the universe, pretends to give an account of the
affairs of a very distant country, concerning which he may tell us what he
pleases, and as long as his narration keeps within the bounds of seeming
possibility, he need not despair of gaining our belief. But when he proposes
to explain the origin of our desires and affections, of our sentiments of
approbation and disapprobation, he pretends to give an account, not only of
the affairs of the very parish that we live in, but of our own domestic concerns. Though here too, like indolent masters who put their trust in a
steward who deceives them, we are very liable to be imposed upon, yet we
are incapable of passing any account which does not preserve some little
regard to the truth. Some of the articles, at least, must be just, and even
those which are most overcharged must have had some foundation, otherwise the fraud would be detected even by that careless inspection which we
are disposed to give. The author who should assign, as the cause of any
natural sentiment, some principle which neither had any connexion with
it, nor resembled any other principle which had some such connexion,
would appear absurd and ridiculous to the most injudicious and unexperienced reader.

SECTION III

Of the different Systems which have been formed concerning the
Principle of Approbation

INTRODUCTION

1 AFTER the inquiry concerning the nature of virtue, the next question of
importance in Moral Philosophy, is concerning the principle of approbation,
concerning the power or faculty of the mind which renders certain characters agreeable or disagreeable to us, makes us prefer one tenour of con-

duct to another, denominate the one right and the other wrong, and consider the one as the object of approbation, honour, and reward; the other as that of blame, censure, and punishment.

2   Three different accounts have been given of this principle of approbation. According to some, we approve and disapprove both of our own actions and of those of others, from self-love only, or from some view of their tendency to our own happiness or disadvantage: according to others, reason, the same faculty by which we distinguish between truth and falsehood, enables us to distinguish between what is fit and unfit both in actions and affections: according to others this distinction is altogether the effect of immediate sentiment and feeling, and arises from the satisfaction or disgust with which the view of certain actions or affections inspires us. Self-love, reason, and sentiment, therefore, are the three different sources which have been assigned for the principle of approbation.

3   Before I proceed to give an account of those different systems, I must observe, that the determination of this second question, though of the greatest importance in speculation, is of none in practice. The question concerning the nature of virtue necessarily has some influence upon our notions of right and wrong in many particular cases. That concerning the principle of approbation can possibly have no such effect. To examine from what contrivance or mechanism within, those different notions or sentiments arise, is a mere matter of philosophical curiosity.

CHAP. I

Of those Systems which deduce the Principle of Approbation from Self-love

1   THOSE who account for the principle of approbation from self-love, do not all account for it in the same manner, and there is a good deal of confusion and inaccuracy in all their different systems. According to Mr. Hobbes, and many of his followers*, man is driven to take refuge in society, not by any natural love which he bears to his own kind, but because without the assistance of others he is incapable of subsisting with ease or safety. Society, upon this account, becomes necessary to him, and whatever tends to its support and welfare, he considers as having a remote tendency to his own interest; and, on the contrary, whatever is likely to disturb or destroy it, he regards as in some measure hurtful or pernicious to himself. Virtue is the great support, and vice the great disturber of human society. The former, therefore, is agreeable, and the latter offensive to every man; as from the one he foresees the prosperity, and from the other the ruin and disorder of what is so necessary for the comfort and security of his existence.

*Puffendorff, Mandeville.

2   That the tendency of virtue to promote, and of vice to disturb the order of society, when we consider it coolly and philosophically, reflects a very great beauty upon the one, and a very great deformity upon the other, cannot, as I have observed upon a former occasion,[1] be called in question. Human society, when we contemplate it in a certain abstract and philosophical light, appears like a great, an immense machine, whose regular and harmonious movements produce a thousand agreeable effects. As in any other beautiful and noble machine that was the production of human art, whatever tended to render its movements more smooth and easy, would derive a beauty from this effect, and, on the contrary, whatever tended to obstruct them would displease upon that account: so virtue, which is, as it were, the fine polish to the wheels of society, necessarily pleases; while vice, like the vile rust, which makes them jar and grate upon one another, is as necessarily offensive. This account, therefore, of the origin of approbation and disapprobation, so far as it derives them from a regard to the order of society, runs into that principle which gives beauty to utility, and which I have explained upon a former occasion;[2] and it is from thence that this system derives all that appearance of probability which it possesses. When those authors describe the innumerable advantages of a cultivated and social, above a savage and solitary life; when they expatiate upon the necessity of virtue and good order for the maintenance of the one, and demonstrate how infallibly the prevalence of vice and disobedience to the laws tend to bring back the *a*other,*a* the reader is charmed with the novelty and grandeur of those views which they open to him: he sees plainly a new beauty in virtue, and a new deformity in vice, which he had never taken notice of before, and is commonly so delighted with the discovery, that he seldom takes time to reflect, that this political *b*view,*b* having never occurred to him in his life before, cannot possibly be the ground of that approbation and disapprobation with which he has always been accustomed to consider those different qualities.

3   When those authors, on the other hand, deduce from self-love the interest which we take in the welfare of society, and the esteem which upon that account we bestow upon virtue, they do not mean, that when we in this age applaud the virtue of Cato, and detest the villany of Catiline, our sentiments are influenced by the notion of any benefit we receive from the one, or of any detriment we suffer from the other. It was not because the prosperity or subversion of society, in those remote ages and nations, was apprehended to have any influence upon our happiness or misery in the present times; that according to those philosophers, we esteemed the virtu-

---

a-a *1-5 7* othet, *6*   *b-b* *1-5* ~∧ *6 7*

[1] IV.2.1–2 above. For Smith's use of the word 'occasion' here and later in the paragraph, cf. IV.2.7 and 9.

[2] IV.1.2

ous, and blamed the disorderly characters. They never imagined that our sentiments were influenced by any benefit or damage which we supposed actually to redound to us, from either; but by that which might have redounded to us, had we lived in those distant ages and countries; or by that which might still redound to us, if in our own times we should meet with characters of the same kind. The idea, in short, which those authors were groping about, but which they were never able to unfold distinctly, was that indirect sympathy which we feel with the gratitude or resentment of those who received the benefit or suffered the damage resulting from such opposite characters: and it was this which they were indistinctly pointing at, when they said, that it was not the thought of what we had gained or suffered which prompted our applause or indignation, but the conception or imagination of what we might gain or suffer if we were to act in society with such associates.

4   Sympathy, however, cannot, in any sense, be regarded as a selfish principle. When I sympathize with your sorrow or your indignation, it may be pretended, indeed, that my emotion is founded in self-love, because it arises from bringing your case home to myself, from putting myself in your situation, and thence conceiving what I should feel in the like circumstances. But though sympathy is very properly said to arise from an imaginary change of situations with the person principally concerned, yet this imaginary change is not supposed to happen to me in my own person and character, but in that of the person with whom I sympathize. When I condole with you for the loss of your only son, in order to enter into your grief I do not consider what I, a person of such a character and profession, should suffer, if I had a son, and if that son was unfortunately to die: but I consider what I should suffer if I was really you, and I not only change circumstances with you, but I change persons and characters. My grief, therefore, is entirely upon your account, and not in the least upon my own. It is not, therefore, in the least selfish. How can that be regarded as a selfish passion, which does not arise even from the imagination of any thing that has befallen, or that relates to myself, in my own proper person and character, but which is entirely occupied about what relates to you? A man may sympathize with a woman in child-bed; though it is impossible that he should conceive himself as suffering her pains in his own proper person and character. That whole account of human nature, however, which deduces all sentiments and affections from self-love, which has made so much noise in the world, but which, so far as I know, has never yet been fully and distinctly explained, seems to me to have arisen from some confused misapprehension of the system of sympathy.

CHAP. II

Of those Systems which make Reason the Principle of Approbation

1 IT is well known to have been the doctrine of Mr. Hobbes, that a state of nature is a state of war; and that antecedent to the institution of civil government there could be no safe or peaceable society among men. To preserve society, therefore, according to him, was to support civil government, and to destroy civil government was the same thing as to put an end to society. But the existence of civil government depends upon the obedience that is paid to the supreme magistrate. The moment he loses his authority, all government is at an end. As self-preservation, therefore, teaches men to applaud whatever tends to promote the welfare of society, and to blame whatever is likely to hurt it; so the same principle, if they would think and speak consistently, ought to teach them to applaud upon all occasions obedience to the civil magistrate, and to blame all disobedience and rebellion. The very ideas of laudable and blamable, ought to be the same with those of obedience and disobedience. The laws of the civil magistrate, therefore, ought to be regarded as the sole ultimate standards of what was just and unjust, of what was right and wrong.

2 It was the avowed intention of Mr. Hobbes, by propagating these notions, to subject the consciences of men immediately to the civil, and not to the ecclesiastical powers, whose turbulence and ambition, he had been taught, by the example of his own times, to regard as the principal source of the disorders of society. His doctrine, upon this account, was peculiarly offensive to theologians, who accordingly did not fail to vent their indignation against him with great asperity and bitterness. It was likewise offensive to all sound moralists, as it supposed that there was no natural distinction between right and wrong, that these were mutable and changeable, and depended upon the mere arbitrary will of the civil magistrate. This account of things, therefore, was attacked from all quarters, and by all sorts of weapons, by sober reason as well as by furious declamation.

3 In order to confute so odious a doctrine, it was necessary to prove, that antecedent to all law or positive institution, the mind was naturally endowed with a faculty, by which it distinguished in certain actions and affections, the qualities of right, laudable, and virtuous, and in others those of wrong, blamable, and vicious.

4 Law, it was justly observed by Dr. Cudworth*, could not be the original source of those distinctions; since upon the supposition of such a law, it must either be right to obey it, and wrong to disobey it, or indifferent whether we obeyed it, or disobeyed it. That law which it was indifferent whether we obeyed or disobeyed, could not, it was evident, be the source

*Immutable Morality, l.1.

of those distinctions; neither could that which it was right to obey and wrong to disobey, since even this still supposed the antecedent notions or ideas of right and wrong, and that obedience to the law was conformable to the idea of right, and disobedience to that of wrong.[1]

5   Since the mind, therefore, had a notion of those distinctions antecedent to all law, it seemed necessarily to follow, that it derived this notion from reason, which pointed out the difference between right and wrong, in the same manner in which it did that between truth and falsehood: and this conclusion, which, though true in some respects, is rather hasty in others, was more easily received at a time when the abstract science of human nature was but in its infancy, and before the distinct offices and powers of the different faculties of the human mind had been carefully examined and distinguished from one another. When this controversy with Mr. Hobbes was carried on with the greatest warmth and keenness, no other faculty had been thought of from which any such ideas could possibly be supposed to arise. It became at this time, therefore, the popular doctrine, that the essence of virtue and vice did not consist in the conformity or disagreement of human actions with the law of a superior, but in their conformity or disagreement with reason, which was thus considered as the original source and principle of approbation and disapprobation.

6   That virtue consists in conformity to reason, is true in some respects, and this faculty may very justly be considered as, in some sense, the source and principle of approbation and disapprobation, and of all solid judgments concerning right and wrong. It is by reason that we discover those general rules of justice by which we ought to regulate our actions: and it is by the same faculty that we form those more vague and indeterminate ideas of what is prudent, of what is decent, of what is generous or noble, which we carry constantly about with us, and according to which we endeavour, as well as we can, to model the tenor of our conduct. The general maxims of morality are formed, like all other general maxims, from experience and induction. We observe in a great variety of particular cases what pleases or displeases our moral faculties, what these approve or disapprove of, and, by induction from this experience, we establish those general rules. But induction is always regarded as one of the operations of reason. From reason, therefore, we are very properly said to derive all those general maxims and ideas. It is by these, however, that we regulate the greater part of our moral judgments, which would be extremely uncertain and precarious if they depended altogether upon what is liable to so many variations as immediate sentiment and feeling, which the different states of health and humour are capable of altering so essentially. As our most solid

---

[1] Smith has in mind *Treatise concerning Eternal and Immutable Morality*, I.ii.3–4; Raphael, *British Moralists 1650–1800*, §§ 122–3. Cudworth's argument is not quite as Smith represents it, but in principle Smith's view of Cudworth's position is sound enough.

judgments, therefore, with regard to right and wrong, are regulated by maxims and ideas derived from an induction of reason, virtue may very properly be said to consist in a conformity to reason, and so far this faculty may be considered as the source and principle of approbation and disapprobation.

7 But though reason is undoubtedly the source of the general rules of morality, and of all the moral judgments which we form by means of them; it is altogether absurd and unintelligible to suppose that the first perceptions of right and wrong can be derived from reason, even in those particular cases upon the experience of which the general rules are formed. These first perceptions, as well as all other experiments upon which any general rules are founded, cannot be the object of reason, but of immediate sense and feeling. It is by finding in a vast variety of instances that one tenor of conduct constantly pleases in a certain manner,[2] and that another as constantly displeases the mind, that we form the general rules of morality. But reason cannot render any particular object either agreeable or disagreeable to the mind for its own sake. Reason may show that this object is the means of obtaining some other which is naturally either pleasing or displeasing, and in this manner may render it either agreeable or disagreeable for the sake of something else. But nothing can be agreeable or disagreeable for its own sake, which is not rendered such by immediate sense and feeling. If virtue, therefore, in every particular instance, necessarily pleases for its own sake, and if vice as certainly displeases the mind, it cannot be reason, but immediate sense and feeling, which, in this manner, reconciles us to the one, and alienates us from the other.

8 Pleasure and pain are the great objects of desire and aversion: but these are distinguished not by reason, but by immediate sense and feeling. If virtue, therefore, be desirable for its own sake, and if vice be, in the same manner, the object of aversion, it cannot be reason which originally distinguishes those different qualities, but immediate sense and feeling.

9 As reason, however, in a certain sense, may justly be considered as the principle of approbation and disapprobation, these sentiments were, through inattention, long regarded as originally flowing from the operations of this faculty. Dr. Hutcheson had the merit of being the first who distinguished with any degree of precision in what respect all moral distinctions may be said to arise from reason, and in what respect they are founded upon immediate sense and feeling. In his illustrations upon the moral sense[3] he has explained this so fully, and, in my opinion, so *a*un-

---

a-a 2–5 7 ∼∧ *1* unanswerably, 6

[2] The phrase recalls Hume: 'All morality depends upon our sentiments; and when any action, or quality of the mind, pleases us *after a certain manner*, we say it is virtuous; . . .' *Treatise of Human Nature*, III.ii.5; ed. Selby-Bigge, 517. The argument of the latter part of the paragraph is derived from *Treatise*, III.i.1–2.
[3] I–IV

answerably,ᵃ that, if any controversy is still kept up about this subject, I can impute it to nothing, but either to inattention to what that gentleman has written, or to a superstitious attachment to certain forms of expression, a weakness not very uncommon among the learned, especially in subjects so deeply interesting as the present, in which a man of virtue is often loath to abandon, even the propriety of a single phrase which he has been accustomed to.

CHAP. III
Of those Systems which make Sentiment the Principle of Approbation

1 THOSE systems which make sentiment the principle of approbation may be divided into two different classes.

2   I. According to some the principle of approbation is founded upon a sentiment of a peculiar nature, upon a particular power of perception exerted by the mind at the view of certain actions or affections; some of which affecting this faculty in an agreeable and others in a disagreeable manner, the former are stamped with the characters of right, laudable, and virtuous; the latter with those of wrong, blamable, and vicious. This sentiment being of a peculiar nature distinct from every other, and the effect of a particular power of perception, they give it a particular name, and call it a moral sense.

3   II. According to others, in order to account for the principle of approbation, there is no occasion for supposing any new power of perception which had never been heard of before: Nature, they imagine, acts here, as in all other cases, with the strictest oeconomy, and produces a multitude of effects from one and the same cause; and sympathy, a power which has always been taken notice of, and with which the mind is manifestly endowed, is, they think, sufficient to account for all the effects ascribed to this peculiar faculty.

4   I. Dr. Hutcheson* had been at great pains to prove that the principle of approbation was not founded on self-love. He had demonstrated too that it could not arise from any operation of reason. Nothing remained, he thought, but to suppose it a faculty of a peculiar kind, with which Nature had endowed the human mind, in order to produce this one particular and important effect. When self-love and reason were both excluded, it did not occur to him that there was any other known faculty of the mind which could in any respect answer this purpose.

5   This new power of perception he called a moral sense, and supposed it to

*Inquiry concerning Virtue.

be somewhat analogous to the external senses. As the bodies around us, by affecting these in a certain manner, appear to possess the different qualities of sound, taste, odour, colour; so the various affections of the human mind, by touching this particular faculty in a certain manner, appear to possess the different qualities of amiable and odious, of virtuous and vicious, of right and wrong.

6   The various senses or powers of perception*, from which the human mind derives all its simple ideas, were, according to this system, of two different kinds, of which the one were called the direct or antecedent, the other, the reflex or consequent senses. The direct senses were those faculties from which the mind derived the perception of such species of things as did not presuppose the antecedent perception of any other. Thus sounds and colours were objects of the direct senses. To hear a sound or to see a colour does not presuppose the antecedent perception of any other quality or object. The reflex or consequent senses, on the other hand, were those faculties from which the mind derived the perception of such species of things as presupposed the antecedent perception of some other. Thus harmony and beauty were objects of the reflex senses. In order to perceive the harmony of a sound, or the beauty of a colour, we must first perceive the sound or the colour. The moral sense was considered as a faculty of this kind.[2] That faculty, which Mr. Locke calls reflection, and from which he derived the simple ideas of the different passions and emotions of the human mind, was, according to Dr. Hutcheson, a direct internal sense. That faculty again by which we perceived the beauty or deformity, the virtue or vice of those different passions and emotions, was a reflex, internal sense.

7   Dr. Hutcheson endeavoured still further to support this doctrine, by shewing that it was agreeable to the analogy of nature, and that the mind was endowed with a variety of other reflex senses exactly similar to the moral sense; such as a sense of beauty and deformity in external objects; a public sense, by which we sympathize with the happiness or misery of our fellow-creatures; a sense of shame and honour, and a sense of ridicule.

8   But notwithstanding all the pains which this ingenious philosopher has taken to prove that the principle of approbation is founded in a peculiar power of perception, somewhat analogous to the external senses, there are some consequences, which he acknowledges to follow from this doctrine,

---

*Treatise of the Passions.[1]

[1] Smith's memory has misled him. Hutcheson's distinction between '*direct* and *antecedent*' perceptions and '*reflex* or *subsequent*' perceptions is not in the *Essay on the . . . Passions and Affections* (to which Smith's note refers), but in a later work, *Short Introduction to Moral Philosophy* (or, in its original Latin form, *Philosophiae Moralis Institutio Compendiaria*), I.i.3.

[2] Consequently not analogous to the external senses, as Smith has suggested in § 5 above.

that will, perhaps, be regarded by many as a sufficient confutation of it. The qualities he allows*, which belong to the objects of any sense, cannot, without the greatest absurdity, be ascribed to the sense itself. Who ever thought of calling the sense of seeing black or white, the sense of hearing loud or low, or the sense of tasting sweet or bitter? And, according to him, it is equally absurd to call our moral faculties virtuous or vicious, morally good or evil. These qualities belong to the objects of those faculties, not to the faculties themselves. If any man, therefore, was so absurdly constituted as to approve of cruelty and injustice as the highest virtues, and to disapprove of equity and humanity as the most pitiful vices, such a constitution of mind might indeed be regarded as inconvenient both to the individual and to the society, and likewise as strange, surprising, and unnatural in itself; but it could not, without the greatest absurdity, be denominated vicious or morally evil.

9   Yet surely if we saw any man shouting with admiration and applause at a barbarous and unmerited execution, which some insolent tyrant had ordered, we should not think we were guilty of any great absurdity in denominating this behaviour vicious and morally evil in the highest degree, though it expressed nothing but depraved moral faculties, or an absurd approbation of this horrid action, as of what was noble, magnanimous, and great. Our heart, I imagine, at the sight of such a spectator, would forget for a while its sympathy with the sufferer, and feel nothing but horror and detestation, at the thought of so execrable a wretch. We should abominate him even more than the tyrant who might be goaded on by the strong passions of jealousy, fear, and resentment, and upon that account be more excusable. But the sentiments of the spectator would appear altogether without cause or motive, and therefore most perfectly and completely detestable. There is no perversion of sentiment or affection which our heart would be more averse to enter into, or which it would reject with greater hatred and indignation than one of this kind; and so far from regarding such a constitution of mind as being merely something strange or inconvenient, and not in any respect vicious or morally evil, we should rather consider it as the very last and most dreadful stage of moral depravity.

10   Correct moral sentiments, on the contrary, naturally appear in some degree laudable and morally good. The man, whose censure and applause are upon all occasions suited with the greatest accuracy to the value or unworthiness of the object, seems to deserve a degree even of moral approbation. We admire the delicate precision of his moral sentiments: they lead our own judgments, and, upon account of their uncommon and surprising justness, they even excite our wonder and applause. We cannot indeed be always

---

*Illustrations upon the Moral Sense, sect. 1. p. 237, et seq.; third edition [Raphael, *British Moralists 1650-1800*, § 364].

sure that the conduct of such a person would be in any respect correspondent to the precision and accuracy of his judgments concerning the conduct of others. Virtue requires habit and resolution of mind, as well as delicacy of sentiment; and unfortunately the former qualities are sometimes wanting, where the latter is in the greatest perfection. This disposition of mind, however, though it may sometimes be attended with imperfections, is incompatible with any thing that is grossly criminal, and is the happiest foundation upon which the superstructure of perfect virtue can be built. There are many men who mean very well, and seriously purpose to do what they think their duty, who notwithstanding are disagreeable on account of the coarseness of their moral sentiments.

11   It may be said, perhaps, that though the principle of approbation is not founded upon any power of perception that is in any respect analogous to the external senses, it may still be founded upon a peculiar sentiment which answers this one particular purpose and no other. Approbation and disapprobation, it may be pretended, are certain feelings or emotions which arise in the mind upon the view of different characters and actions; and as resentment might be called a sense of injuries, or gratitude a sense of benefits, so these may very properly receive the name of a sense of right and wrong, or of a moral sense.

12   But this account of things, though it may not be liable to the same objections with the foregoing, is exposed to others which are equally unanswerable.

13   First of all, whatever variations any particular emotion may undergo, it still preserves the general features which distinguish it to be an emotion of such a kind, and these general features are always more striking and remarkable than any variation which it may undergo in particular cases. Thus anger is an emotion of a particular kind: and accordingly its general features are always more distinguishable than all the variations it undergoes in particular cases. Anger against a man is, no doubt, somewhat different from anger against a woman, and that again from anger against a child. In each of those three cases, the general passion of anger receives a different modification from the particular character of its object, as may easily be observed by the attentive. But still the general features of the passion predominate in all these cases. To distinguish these, requires no nice observation: a very delicate attention, on the contrary, is necessary to discover their variations: every body takes notice of the former; scarce any body observes the latter. If approbation and disapprobation, therefore, were, like gratitude and resentment, emotions of a particular kind, distinct from every other, we should expect that in all the variations which either of them might undergo, it would still retain the general features which mark it to be an emotion of such a particular kind, clear, plain, and easily distinguishable. But in fact it happens quite otherwise. If we attend to what

we really feel when upon different occasions we either approve or disapprove, we shall find that our emotion in one case is often totally different from that in another, and that no common features can possibly
be discovered between them. Thus the approbation with which we view
a tender, delicate, and humane sentiment, is quite different from that with
which we are struck by one that appears great, daring, and magnanimous.
Our approbation of both may, upon different occasions, be perfect and
entire; but we are softened by the one, and we are elevated by the other,
and there is no sort of resemblance between the emotions which they excite
in us. But according to that system which I have been endeavouring to
establish, this must necessarily be the case. As the emotions of the person
whom we approve of, are, in those two cases, quite opposite to one another,
and as our approbation arises from sympathy with those opposite emotions,
what we feel upon the one occasion, can have no sort of resemblance to
what we feel upon the other. But this could not happen if approbation consisted in a peculiar emotion which had nothing in common with the sentiments we approved of, but which arose at the view of those sentiments,
like any other passion at the view of its proper object. The same thing
holds true with regard to disapprobation. Our horror for cruelty has no
sort of resemblance to our contempt for mean-spiritedness. It is quite a
different species of discord which we feel at the view of those two different
vices, between our own minds and those of the person whose sentiments
and behaviour we consider.

14   Secondly, I have already observed,[3] that not only the different passions
or affections of the human mind which are approved or disapproved of,
appear morally good or evil, but that proper and improper approbation
appear, to our natural sentiments, to be stamped with the same characters.
I would ask, therefore, how it is, that, according to this system, we approve or disapprove of proper or improper approbation? To this question
there is, I imagine, but one reasonable answer, which can possibly be given.
It must be said, that when the approbation with which our neighbour
regards the conduct of a third person coincides with our own, we approve
of his approbation, and consider it as, in some measure, morally good;
and that, on the contrary, when it does not coincide with our own sentiments, we disapprove of it, and consider it as, in some measure, morally
evil. It must be allowed, therefore, that, at least in this one case, the coincidence or opposition of sentiments, between the observer and the person
observed, constitutes moral approbation or disapprobation. And if it does
so in this one case, I would ask, why not in every other? *Or to* what
purpose imagine a new power of perception in order to account for those
sentiments?

---

a-a *2E* or to *1* to *2–7*

[3] §§ 9–10 above.

15   Against every account of the principle of approbation, which makes it
depend upon a peculiar sentiment, distinct from every other, I would object; that it is strange that this sentiment, which Providence undoubtedly
intended to be the governing principle of human nature, should hitherto
have been so little taken notice of, as not to have got a name in any language.
The word moral sense is of very late formation, and cannot yet be considered as making part of the English tongue. The word approbation has
but within these few years been appropriated to denote peculiarly any
thing of this kind. In propriety of language we approve of whatever is
entirely to our satisfaction, of the form of a building, of the contrivance of
a machine, of the flavour of a dish of meat. The word conscience does not
immediately denote any moral faculty by which we approve or disapprove.
Conscience supposes, indeed, the existence of some such faculty, and
properly signifies our consciousness of having acted agreeably or contrary
to its directions. When love, hatred, joy, sorrow, gratitude, resentment,
with so many other passions which are all supposed to be the subjects of
this principle, have made themselves considerable enough to get titles
to know them by, is it not surprising that the sovereign of them all should
hitherto have been so little heeded, that, a few philosophers excepted,
nobody has yet thought it worth while to bestow a name upon ᵇit?ᵇ

16   When we approve of any character or action, the sentiments which we
feel, are, according to the foregoing system, derived from four sources,
which are in some respects different from one another. First, we sympathize
with the motives of the agent; secondly, we enter into the gratitude of
those who receive the benefit of his actions; thirdly, we observe that his
conduct has been agreeable to the general rules by which those two sympathies generally act; and, last of all, when we consider such actions as
making a part of a system of behaviour which tends to promote the happiness either of the individual or of the society, they appear to derive a
beauty from this utility, not unlike that which we ascribe to any well-
contrived machine. After deducting, in any one particular case, all that must
be acknowledged to proceed from some one or other of these four principles,
I should be glad to know what remains, and I shall freely allow this overplus to be ascribed to a moral sense, or to any other peculiar faculty, provided any body will ascertain precisely what this overplus is. It might be
expected, perhaps, that if there was any such peculiar principle, such as
this moral sense is supposed to be, we should feel it, in some particular
cases, separated and detached from every other, as we often feel joy,
sorrow, hope, and fear, pure and unmixed with any other emotion. This
however, I imagine, cannot even be pretended. I have never heard any
instance alleged in which this principle could be said to exert itself alone

ᵇ⁻ᵇ ~. *1–7*

and unmixed with sympathy or antipathy, with gratitude or resentment, with the perception of the agreement or disagreement of any action to an established rule, or last of all with that general taste for beauty and order which is excited by inanimated as well as by animated objects.

17   II. There is another system which attempts to account for the origin of our moral sentiments from sympathy, distinct from that which I have been endeavouring to establish. It is that which places virtue in utility, and accounts for the pleasure with which the spectator surveys the utility of any quality from sympathy with the happiness of those who are affected by it. This sympathy is different both from that by which we enter into the motives of the agent, and from that by which we go along with the gratitude of the persons who are benefited by his actions. It is the same principle with that by which we approve of a well-contrived machine. But no machine can be the object of either of those two last mentioned sympathies. I have already, in the fourth part of this discourse,[4] given some account of this system.

SECTION IV

Of the Manner in which different Authors have treated of the practical Rules of Morality

1   IT was observed in the third part of this discourse,[1] that the rules of justice are the only rules of morality which are precise and accurate; that those of all the other virtues are loose, vague, and indeterminate; that the first may be compared to the rules of grammar; the others to those which critics lay down for the attainment of what is sublime and elegant in composition, and which present us rather with a general idea of the perfection we ought to aim at, than afford us any certain and infallible directions for acquiring it.

2   As the different rules of morality admit such different degrees of accuracy, those authors who have endeavoured to collect and digest them into systems have done it in two different manners; and one set has followed through the whole that loose method to which they were naturally directed by the consideration of one species of virtues; while another has as universally endeavoured to introduce into their precepts that sort of accuracy of which only some of them are susceptible. The first have wrote like critics, the second like grammarians.

---

[4] IV.2.3 ff. The 'system' referred to is that of Hume. Smith's distinction between the type of sympathy that enters into Hume's ethics and the two types that he himself has used is entirely just.

[1] III.6.9–11

3   I. The first, among whom we may count all the ancient moralists, have contented themselves with describing in a general manner the different vices and virtues, and with pointing out the deformity and misery of the one disposition as well as the propriety and happiness of the other, but have not affected to lay down many precise rules that are to hold good unexceptionably in all particular cases. They have only endeavoured to ascertain, as far as language is capable of ascertaining, first, wherein consists the sentiment of the heart, upon which each particular virtue is founded, what sort of internal feeling or emotion it is which constitutes the essence of friendship, of humanity, of generosity, of justice, of magnanimity, and of all the other virtues, as well as of the vices which are opposed to them: and, secondly, what is the general way of acting, the ordinary tone and tenor of conduct to which each of those sentiments would direct us, or how it is that a friendly, a generous, a brave, a just, and a humane man, would, upon ordinary occasions, chuse to act.

4   To characterize the sentiment of the heart, upon which each particular virtue is founded, though it requires both a delicate and an accurate pencil, is a task, however, which may be executed with some degree of exactness. It is impossible, indeed, to express all the variations which each sentiment either does or ought to undergo, according to every possible variation of circumstances. They are endless, and language wants names to mark them by. The sentiment of friendship, for example, which we feel for an old man is different from that which we feel for a young: that which we entertain for an austere man different from that which we feel for one of softer and gentler manners: and that again from what we feel for one of gay vivacity and spirit. The friendship which we conceive for a man is different from that with which a woman affects us, even where there is no mixture of any grosser passion. What author could enumerate and ascertain these and all the other infinite varieties which this sentiment is capable of undergoing? But still the general sentiment of friendship and familiar attachment which is common to them all, may be ascertained with a sufficient degree of accuracy. The picture which is drawn of it, though it will always be in many respects incomplete, may, however, have such a resemblance as to make us know the original when we meet with it, and even distinguish it from other sentiments to which it has a considerable resemblance, such as good-will, respect, esteem, admiration.

5   To describe, in a general manner, what is the ordinary way of acting to which each virtue would prompt us, is still more easy. It is, indeed, scarce possible to describe the internal sentiment or emotion upon which it is founded, without doing something of this kind. It is impossible by language to express, if I may say so, the invisible features of all the different modifications of passion as they show themselves within. There is no other way of marking and distinguishing them from one another, but

by describing the effects which they produce without, the alterations which they occasion in the countenance, in the air and external behaviour, the resolutions they suggest, the actions they prompt to. It is thus that Cicero, in the first book of his Offices, endeavours to direct us to the practice of the four cardinal virtues, and that Aristotle in the practical parts of his Ethics, points out to us the different habits by which he would have us regulate our behaviour, such as liberality, magnificence, magnanimity, and even jocularity and good-humour, qualities which that indulgent philosopher has thought worthy of a place in the catalogue of the virtues,[2] though the lightness of that approbation which we naturally bestow upon them, should not seem to entitle them to so venerable a name.

6   Such works present us with agreeable and lively pictures of manners. By the vivacity of their descriptions they inflame our natural love of virtue, and increase our abhorrence of vice: by the justness as well as delicacy of their observations they may often help both to correct and to ascertain our natural sentiments with regard to the propriety of conduct, and suggesting many nice and delicate attentions, form us to a more exact justness of behaviour, than what, without such instruction, we should have been apt to think of. In treating of the rules of morality, in this manner, consists the science which is properly called Ethics, a science which, though like criticism it does not admit of the most accurate precision, is, however, both highly useful and agreeable. It is of all others the most susceptible of the embellishments of eloquence, and by means of them of bestowing, if that be possible, a new importance upon the smallest rules of duty. Its precepts, when thus dressed and adorned, are capable of producing upon the flexibility of youth, the noblest and most lasting impressions, and as they fall in with the natural magnanimity of that generous age, they are able to inspire, for a time at least, the most heroic resolutions, and thus tend both to establish and confirm the best and most useful habits of which the mind of man is susceptible. Whatever precept and exhortation can do to animate us to the practice of virtue, is done by this science delivered in this manner.

7   II. The second set of moralists, among whom we may count all the casuists of the middle and latter ages of the christian church, as well as all those who in this and in the preceding century have treated of what is called natural jurisprudence, do not content themselves with characterizing in this general manner that tenor of conduct which they would recommend to us, but endeavour to lay down exact and precise rules for the direction of every circumstance of our behaviour. As justice is the only virtue with regard to which such exact rules can properly be given; it is this

[2] Cf. *Nicomachean Ethics*, IV.1–3, 5, 8.

virtue, that has chiefly fallen under the consideration of those two different sets of writers. They treat of it, however, in a very different manner.

8   Those who write upon the principles of jurisprudence, consider only what the person to whom the obligation is due, ought to think himself entitled to exact by force; what every impartial spectator would approve of him for exacting, or what a judge or arbiter, to whom he had submitted his case, and who had undertaken to do him justice, ought to oblige the other person to suffer or to perform. The casuists, on the other hand, do not so much examine what it is, that might properly be exacted by force, as what it is, that the person who owes the obligation ought to think himself bound to perform from the most sacred and scrupulous regard to the general rules of justice, and from the most conscientious dread, either of wronging his neighbour, or of violating the integrity of his own character. It is the end of jurisprudence to prescribe rules for the decisions of judges and arbiters. It is the end of casuistry to prescribe rules for the conduct of a good man. By observing all the rules of jurisprudence, supposing them ever so perfect, we should deserve nothing but to be free from external punishment. By observing those of casuistry, supposing them such as they ought to be, we should be entitled to considerable praise by the exact and scrupulous delicacy of our behaviour.

9   It may frequently happen that a good man ought to think himself bound, from a sacred and conscientious regard to the general rules of justice, to perform many things which it would be the highest injustice to extort from him, or for any judge or arbiter to impose upon him by force. To give a trite example; a highwayman, by the fear of death, obliges a traveller to promise him a certain sum of money. Whether such a promise, extorted in this manner by unjust force, ought to be regarded as obligatory, is a question that has been very much debated.

10   If we consider it merely as a question of jurisprudence, the decision can admit of no doubt. It would be absurd to suppose that the highwayman can be entitled to use force to constrain the other to perform. To extort the promise was a crime which deserved the highest punishment, and to extort the performance would only be adding a new crime to the former. He can complain of no injury who has been only deceived by the person by whom he might justly have been killed. To suppose that a judge ought to enforce the obligation of such promises, or that the magistrate ought to allow them to sustain action at law, would be the most ridiculous of all absurdities. If we consider this question, therefore, as a question of jurisprudence, we can be at no loss about the decision.

11   But if we consider it as a question of casuistry, it will not be so easily determined. Whether a good man, from a conscientious regard to that most sacred rule of justice, which commands the observance of all serious promises, would not think himself bound to perform, is at least much more

doubtful. That no regard is due to the disappointment of the wretch who brings him into this situation, that no injury is done to the robber, and consequently that nothing can be extorted by force, will admit of no sort of dispute. But whether some regard is not, in this case, due to his own dignity and honour, to the inviolable sacredness of that part of his character which makes him reverence the law of truth and abhor every thing that approaches to treachery and falsehood, may, perhaps, more reasonably be made a question. The casuists accordingly are greatly divided about it. One party, with whom we may count Cicero among the ancients, among the moderns, Puffendorf, Barbeyrac his commentator, and above all the late Dr. Hutcheson, one who in most cases was by no means a loose casuist, determine, without any hesitation, that no sort of regard is due to any such promise, and that to think otherwise is mere weakness and superstition.[3] Another party, among whom we may reckon *some of the ancient fathers of the church, as well as some very eminent modern casuists, have been of another opinion, and have judged all such promises obligatory.

12   If we consider the matter according to the common sentiments of mankind, we shall find that some regard would be thought due even to a promise of this kind; but that it is impossible to determine how much, by any general rule that will apply to all cases without exception. The man who was quite frank and easy in making promises of this kind, and who violated them with as little ceremony, we should not chuse for our friend and companion. A gentleman who should promise a highwayman five pounds and not perform, would incur some blame. If the sum promised, however, was very great, it might be more doubtful, what was proper to be done. If it was such, for example, that the payment of it would entirely ruin the family of the promiser, if it was so great as to be sufficient for promoting the most useful purposes, it would appear in some measure criminal, at least extremely improper, to throw it, for the sake of a punctilio, into such worthless hands. The man who should beggar himself, or who should throw away an hundred thousand pounds, though he could afford that vast sum, for the sake of observing such a parole with a thief, would appear to the common sense of mankind, absurd and extravagant in the highest degree. Such profusion would seem inconsistent with his

---

*St. Augustine, La Placette.[4]

---

[3] Cicero, *De Officiis*, I.x.32; III.xxix.107. Samuel Pufendorf, *De Jure Naturae et Gentium*, III.vi.11–13; IV.ii.8: *De Officio Hominis et Civis*, I.ix.15.3. Jean Barbeyrac, French translator and editor of Pufendorf, agrees with the latter's view in notes to the first two of the passages cited, especially the second, where Barbeyrac also opposes the contrary opinion of Jean La Placette, a French Protestant theologian and moralist, as given in *Traité du serment* (1701), II.21. Francis Hutcheson, *Philosophiae Moralis Institutio Compendiaria* (English version, *Short Introduction to Moral Philosophy*), II.ix.9: *System of Moral Philosophy*, II.ix.5.

[4] Cf. St. Augustine, *Letters*, 125.3. For La Placette see preceding note.

duty, with what he owed both to himself and others, and what, therefore, regard to a promise extorted in this manner, could by no means authorise. To fix, however, by any precise rule, what degree of regard ought to be paid to it, or what might be the greatest sum which could be due from it, is evidently impossible. This would vary according to the characters of the persons, according to their circumstances, according to the solemnity of the promise, and even according to the incidents of the rencounter: and if the promiser had been treated with a great deal of that sort of gallantry, which is sometimes to be met with in persons of the most abandoned characters, more would seem due than upon other occasions. It may be said in general, that exact propriety requires the observance of all such promises, wherever it is not inconsistent with some other duties that are more sacred; such as regard to the public interest, to those whom gratitude, whom natural affection, or whom the laws of proper beneficence should prompt us to provide for. But, as was formerly taken notice of, we have no precise rules to determine what external actions are due from a regard to such motives, nor, consequently, when it is that those virtues are inconsistent with the observance of such promises.

13   It is to be observed, however, that whenever such promises are violated, though for the most necessary reasons, it is always with some degree of dishonour to the person who made them. After they are made, we may be convinced of the impropriety of observing them. But still there is some fault in having made them. It is at least a departure from the highest and noblest maxims of magnanimity and honour. A brave man ought to die, rather than make a promise which he can neither keep without folly, nor violate without ignominy. For some degree of ignominy always attends a situation of this kind. Treachery and falsehood are vices so dangerous, so dreadful, and, at the same time, such as may so easily, and, upon many occasions, so safely be indulged, that we are more jealous of them than of almost any other. Our imagination therefore attaches the idea of shame to all violations of faith, in every circumstance and in every situation. They resemble, in this respect, the violations of chastity in the fair sex, a virtue of which, for the like reasons, we are excessively jealous; and our sentiments are not more delicate with regard to the one, than with regard to the other. Breach of chastity dishonours irretrievably. No circumstances, no solicitation can excuse it; no sorrow, no repentance atone for it. We are so nice in this respect that even a rape dishonours, and the innocence of the mind cannot, in our imagination, wash out the pollution of the body. It is the same case with the violation of faith, when it has been solemnly pledged, even to the most worthless of mankind. Fidelity is so necessary a virtue, that we apprehend it in general to be due even to those to whom nothing else is due, and whom we think it lawful to kill and destroy. It is to no purpose that the person who has been guilty of the breach of it,

urges that he promised in order to save his life, and that he broke his promise because it was inconsistent with some other respectable duty to keep it. These circumstances may alleviate, but cannot entirely wipe out his dishonour. He appears to have been guilty of an action with which, in the imaginations of men, some degree of shame is inseparably connected. He has broke a promise which he had solemnly averred he would maintain; and his character, if not irretrievably stained and polluted, has at least a ridicule affixed to it, which it will be very difficult entirely to efface; and no man, I imagine, who had gone through an adventure of this kind would be fond of telling the story.

14   This instance may serve to show wherein consists the difference between casuistry and jurisprudence, even when both of them consider the obligations of the general rules of justice.

15   But though this difference be real and essential, though those two sciences propose quite different ends, the sameness of the subject has made such a similarity between them, that the greater part of authors whose professed design was to treat of jurisprudence, have determined the different questions they examine, sometimes according to the principles of that science, and sometimes according to those of casuistry, without distinguishing, and, perhaps, without being themselves aware when they did the one, and when the other.

16   The doctrine of the casuists, however, is by no means confined to the consideration of what a conscientious regard to the general rules of justice would demand of us. It embraces many other parts of Christian and moral duty. What seems principally to have given occasion to the cultivation of this species of science was the custom of auricular confession, introduced by the Roman Catholic superstition, in times of barbarism and ignorance. By that institution, the most secret actions, and even the thoughts of every person, which could be suspected of receding in the smallest degree from the rules of Christian purity, were to be revealed to the confessor. The confessor informed his penitents whether, and in what respect they had violated their duty, and what penance it behoved them to undergo, before he could absolve them in the name of the offended Deity.

17   The consciousness, or even the suspicion of having done wrong, is a load upon every mind, and is accompanied with anxiety and terror in all those who are not hardened by long habits of iniquity. Men, in this, as in all other distresses, are naturally eager to disburthen themselves of the oppression which they feel upon their thoughts, by unbosoming the agony of their mind to some person whose secrecy and discretion they can confide in. The shame, which they suffer from this acknowledgment, is fully compensated by that alleviation of their uneasiness which the sympathy of their confident seldom fails to occasion. It relieves them to find that they are not altogether unworthy of regard, and that however their past conduct

may be censured, their present disposition is at least approved of, and is perhaps sufficient to compensate the other, at least to maintain them in some degree of esteem with their friend. A numerous and artful clergy had, in those times of superstition, insinuated themselves into the confidence of almost every private family. They possessed all the little learning which the times could afford, and their manners, though in many respects rude and disorderly, were polished and regular compared with those of the age they lived in. They were regarded, therefore, not only as the great directors of all religious, but of all moral duties. Their familiarity gave reputation to whoever was so happy as to possess it, and every mark of their disapprobation stamped the deepest ignominy upon all who had the misfortune to fall under it. Being considered as the great judges of right and wrong, they were naturally consulted about all scruples that occurred, and it was reputable for any person to have it known that he made those holy men the confidents of all such secrets, and took no important or delicate step in his conduct without their advice and approbation. It was not difficult for the clergy, therefore, to get it established as a general rule, that they should be entrusted with what it had already become fashionable to entrust them, and with what they generally would have been entrusted, though no such rule had been established. To qualify themselves for confessors became thus a necessary part of the study of churchmen and divines, and they were thence led to collect what are called cases of conscience, nice and delicate situations in which it is hard to determine whereabouts the propriety of conduct may lie. Such works, they imagined, might be of use both to the directors of consciences and to those who were to be directed; and hence the origin of books of casuistry.

18   The moral duties which fell under the consideration of the casuists were chiefly those which can, in some measure at least, be circumscribed within general rules, and of which the violation is naturally attended with some degree of remorse and some dread of suffering punishment. The design of that institution which gave occasion to their works, was to appease those terrors of conscience which attend upon the infringement of such duties. But it is not every virtue of which the defect is accompanied with any very severe compunctions of this kind, and no man applies to his confessor for absolution, because he did not perform the most generous, the most friendly, or the most magnanimous action which, in his circumstances, it was possible to perform. In failures of this kind, the rule that is violated is commonly not very determinate, and is generally of such a nature too, that though the observance of it might entitle to honour and reward, the violation seems to expose to no positive blame, censure, or punishment. The exercise of such virtues the casuists seem to have regarded as a sort of works of supererogation, which could not be very strictly exacted, and which it was therefore unnecessary for them to treat of.

19   The breaches of moral duty, therefore, which came before the tribunal of the confessor, and upon that account fell under the cognizance of the casuists, were chiefly of three different kinds.

20   First and principally, breaches of the rules of justice. The rules here are all express and positive, and the violation of them is naturally attended with the consciousness of deserving, and the dread of suffering punishment both from God and man.

21   Secondly, breaches of the rules of chastity. These in all grosser instances are real breaches of the rules of justice, and no person can be guilty of them without doing the most unpardonable injury to some other. In smaller instances, when they amount only to a violation of those exact decorums which ought to be observed in the conversation of the two sexes, they cannot indeed justly be considered as violations of the rules of justice. They are *ᵃgenerally,ᵃ* however, violations of a pretty plain rule, and, at least in one of the sexes, tend to bring ignominy upon the person who has been guilty of them, and consequently to be attended in the scrupulous with some degree of shame and contrition of mind.

22   Thirdly, breaches of the rules of veracity. The violation of truth, it is to be observed, is not always a breach of justice, though it is so upon many occasions, and consequently cannot always expose to any external punishment. The vice of common lying, though a most miserable meanness, may frequently do hurt to nobody, and in this case no claim of vengeance or satisfaction can be due either to the persons imposed upon, or to others. But though the violation of truth is not always a breach of justice, it is always a breach of a very plain rule, and what naturally tends to cover with shame the person who has been guilty of it.ᵇ

23   There seems to be in young children an instinctive disposition to believe whatever they are told. Nature seems to have judged it necessary for their preservation that they should, for some time at least, put implicit confidence in those to whom the care of their childhood, and of the earliest and most necessary parts of their education, is intrusted. Their credulity, accordingly, is excessive, and it requires long and much experience of the falsehood of mankind to reduce them to a reasonable degree of diffidence and distrust. In grown-up people the degrees of credulity are, no doubt, very different. The wisest and most experienced are generally the least credulous. But the man scarce lives who is not more credulous than he ought to be, and who does not, upon many occasions, give credit to tales, which not only turn out to be perfectly false, but which a very moderate degree of reflection and attention might have taught him could not well

---

ᵃ⁻ᵃ *1–5* ~ₐ *6 7*
ᵇ *At this point, eds. 1–5 continue, without a fresh paragraph,* The great pleasure of conversation, and indeed of society, arises from . . ., *and then proceed as in* § 28. §§ 23–7, *and the beginning of* § 28, *were added in ed. 6.*

be true. The natural disposition is always to believe. It is acquired wisdom and experience only that teach incredulity, and they very seldom teach it enough. The wisest and most cautious of us all frequently gives credit to stories which he himself is afterwards both ashamed and astonished that he could possibly think of believing.

24   The man whom we believe is necessarily, in the things concerning which we believe him, our leader and director, and we look up to him with a certain degree of esteem and respect. But as from admiring other people we come to wish to be admired ourselves; so from being led and directed by other people we learn to wish to become ourselves leaders and directors. And as we cannot always be satisfied merely with being admired, unless we can at the same time persuade ourselves that we are in some degree really worthy of admiration; so we cannot always be satisfied merely with being believed, unless we are at the same time conscious that we are really worthy of belief. As the desire of praise and that of praise-worthiness, though very much a-kin, are yet distinct and separate desires; so the desire of being believed and that of being worthy of belief, though very much a-kin too, are equally distinct and separate desires.

25   The desire of being believed, the desire of persuading, of leading and directing other people, seems to be one of the strongest of all our natural desires. It is, perhaps, the instinct upon which is founded the faculty of speech, the characteristical faculty of human nature. No other animal possesses this faculty, and we cannot discover in any other animal any desire to lead and direct the judgment and conduct of its fellows. Great ambition, the desire of real superiority, of leading and directing, seems to be altogether peculiar to man, and speech is the great instrument of ambition, of real superiority, of leading and directing the judgments and conduct of other people.

26   It is always mortifying not to be believed, and it is doubly so when we suspect that it is because we are supposed to be unworthy of belief and capable of seriously and wilfully deceiving. To tell a man that he lies, is of all affronts the most mortal. But whoever seriously and wilfully deceives is necessarily conscious to himself that he merits this affront, that he does not deserve to be believed, and that he forfeits all title to that sort of credit from which alone he can derive any sort of ease, comfort, or satisfaction in the society of his equals. The man who had the misfortune to imagine that nobody believed a single word he said, would feel himself the outcast of human society, would dread the very thought of going into it, or of presenting himself before it, and could scarce fail, I think, to die of despair. It is probable, however, that no man ever had just reason to entertain this humiliating opinion of himself. The most notorious liar, I am disposed to believe, tells the fair truth at least twenty times for once that he seriously and deliberately lies; and, as in the most cautious the disposition to believe

is apt to prevail over that to doubt and distrust; so in those who are the most regardless of truth, the natural disposition to tell it prevails upon most occasions over that to deceive, or in any respect to alter or disguise it.

27   We are mortified when we happen to deceive other people, though unintentionally, and from having been ourselves deceived. Though this involuntary falsehood may frequently be no mark of any want of veracity, of any want of the most perfect love of truth, it is always in some degree a mark of want of judgment, of want of memory, of improper credulity, of some degree of precipitancy and rashness. It always diminishes our authority to persuade, and always brings some degree of suspicion upon our fitness to lead and direct. The man who sometimes misleads from mistake, however, is widely different from him who is capable of wilfully deceiving. The former may safely be trusted upon many occasions; the latter very seldom upon any.

28   Frankness and openness conciliate confidence. We trust the man who seems willing to trust us. We see clearly, we think, the road by which he means to conduct us, and we abandon ourselves with pleasure to his guidance and direction. Reserve and concealment, on the contrary, call forth diffidence. We are afraid to follow the man who is going we do not know where. ᶜThe great pleasure of conversation and society, besides, arisesᶜ from a certain correspondence of sentiments and opinions, from a certain harmony of minds, which like so many musical instruments coincide and keep time with one another. But this most delightful harmony cannot be obtained unless there is a free communication of sentiments and opinions. We all desire, upon this account, to feel how each other is affected, to penetrate into each other's bosoms, and to observe the sentiments and affections which really subsist there. The man who indulges us in this natural passion, who invites us into his heart, who, as it were, sets open the gates of his breast to us, seems to exercise a species of hospitality more delightful than any other. No man, who is in ordinary good temper, can fail of pleasing, if he has the courage to utter his real sentiments as he feels them, and because he feels them. It is this unreserved sincerity which renders even the prattle of a child agreeable. How weak and imperfect soever the views of the open-hearted, we take pleasure to enter into them, and endeavour, as much as we can, to bring down our own understanding to the level of their capacities, and to regard every subject in the particular light in which they appear to have considered it. This passion to discover the real sentiments of others is naturally so strong, that it often degenerates into a troublesome and impertinent curiosity to pry into those secrets of our neighbours which they have very justifiable reasons for concealing; and, upon many occasions, it requires prudence and

ᶜ⁻ᶜ The great pleasure of conversation, and indeed of society, arises *1–5   Ed. 6 has here rejoined the text of the earlier editions. See note ᵇ at § 22 above.*

a strong sense of propriety to govern this, as well as all the other passions of human nature, and to reduce it to that pitch which any impartial spectator can approve of. To disappoint this curiosity, however, when it is kept within proper bounds, and aims at nothing which there can be any just reason for concealing, is equally disagreeable in its turn. The man who eludes our most innocent questions, who gives no satisfaction to our most inoffensive inquiries, who plainly wraps himself up in impenetrable obscurity, seems, as it were, to build a wall about his breast. We run forward to get within it, with all the eagerness of harmless curiosity; and feel ourselves all at once pushed back with the rudest and most offensive violence.*d*

29   *e*The man of reserve and concealment, though seldom a very amiable character, is not disrespected or despised. He seems to feel coldly towards us, and we feel as coldly towards him. He is not much praised or beloved, but he is as little hated or blamed. He very seldom, however, has occasion to repent of his caution, and is generally disposed rather to value himself upon the prudence of his reserve. Though his conduct, therefore, may have been very faulty, and sometimes even hurtful, he can very seldom be disposed to lay his case before the casuists, or to fancy that he has any occasion for their acquittal or approbation.

30   It is not always so with the man, who, from false information, from inadvertency, from precipitancy and rashness, has involuntarily deceived. Though it should be in a matter of little consequence, in telling a piece of common news, for example, if he is a real lover of truth, he is ashamed of his own carelessness, and never fails to embrace the first opportunity of making the fullest acknowledgments. If it is in a matter of some consequence, his contrition is still greater; and if any unlucky or fatal consequence has followed from his misinformation, he can scarce ever forgive himself. Though not guilty, he feels himself to be in the highest degree, what the ancients called, piacular,[5] and is anxious and eager to make every

---

d *At this point, eds. 1–5 continue the paragraph with four further sentences, withdrawn in ed. 6. We give the text of ed. 1 with the variants of eds. 2–5 below.*

If to conceal is so disagreeable, to attempt to deceive us is still more disgusting, even tho' [though 2–5] we could possibly suffer nothing by the success of the fraud. If we see that our companion wants to impose upon us, if the sentiments and opinions which he utters appear evidently not to be his own, let them be ever so fine, we can derive no sort of entertainment from them; and if something of human nature did not now and then transpire through all the covers which falshood [falsehood 4 5] and affectation are capable of wraping [wrapping 4 5] around it, a puppet of wood would be altogether as pleasant a companion as a person who never spoke as he was affected. No man ever deceives, with regard to the most insignificant matters, who is not conscious of doing something like an injury to those he converses with; and who does not inwardly blush and shrink back with shame and confusion even at the secret thought of a detection. Breach of veracity, therefore, being always attended with some degree of remorse and self-condemnation, naturally fell under the cognizance of the casuists.

e *§§ 29–31 were added in ed. 6.*

[5] Cf. II.iii.4–5, a passage likewise added in ed. 6.

sort of atonement in his power. Such a person might frequently be disposed to lay his case before the casuists, who have in general been very
favourable to him, and though they have sometimes justly condemned
him for rashness, they have universally acquitted him of the ignominy of
falsehood.

31   But the man who had the most frequent occasion to consult them, was
the man of equivocation and mental reservation, the man who seriously
and deliberately meant to deceive, but who, at the same time, wished to
flatter himself that he had really told the truth. With him they have dealt
variously. When they approved very much of the motives of his deceit,
they have sometimes acquitted him, though, to do them justice, they have
in general and much more frequently condemned him.

32   The chief subjects of the works of the casuists, therefore, were the conscientious regard that is due to the rules of justice; how far we ought to
respect the life and property of our neighbour; the duty of restitution; the
laws of chastity and modesty, and wherein consisted what, in their language,
are called the sins of concupiscence; the rules of veracity, and the obligation of oaths, promises, and contracts of all kinds.

33   It may be said in general of the works of the casuists that they attempted,
to no purpose, to direct by precise rules what it belongs to feeling and sentiment only to judge of. How is it possible to ascertain by rules the exact
point at which, in every case, a delicate sense of justice begins to run into a
frivolous and weak scrupulosity of conscience? When it is that secrecy and
reserve begin to grow into dissimulation? How far an agreeable irony may
be carried, and at what precise point it begins to degenerate into a detestable lie? What is the highest pitch of freedom and ease of behaviour which
can be regarded as graceful and becoming, and when it is that it first
begins to run into a negligent and thoughtless licentiousness? With regard to all such matters, what would hold good in any one case would
scarce do so exactly in any other, and what constitutes the propriety and
happiness of behaviour varies in every case with the smallest variety of
situation. Books of casuistry, therefore, are generally as useless as they are
commonly tiresome. They could be of little use to one who should consult
them upon occasion, even supposing their decisions to be just; because,
notwithstanding the multitude of cases collected in them, yet upon account
of the still greater variety of possible circumstances, it is a chance, if
among all those cases there be found one exactly parallel to that under consideration. One, who is really anxious to do his duty, must be very weak,
if he can imagine that he has much occasion for them; and with regard to
one who is negligent of it, the style of those writings is not such as is
likely to awaken him to more attention. None of them tend to animate us
to what is generous and noble. None of them tend to soften us to what
is gentle and humane. Many of them, on the contrary, tend rather to teach

us to chicane with our own consciences, and by their vain subtilties serve to authorise innumerable evasive refinements with regard to the most essential articles of our duty. That frivolous accuracy which they attempted to introduce into subjects which do not admit of it, almost necessarily betrayed them into those dangerous errors, and at the same time rendered their works dry and disagreeable, abounding in abtruse and metaphysical distinctions, but incapable of exciting in the heart any of those emotions which it is the principal use of books of morality to excite.

34   The two useful parts of moral philosophy, therefore, are Ethics and Jurisprudence: casuistry ought to be rejected altogether; and the ancient moralists appear to have judged much better, who, in treating of the same subjects, did not affect any such nice exactness, but contented themselves with describing, in a general manner, what is the sentiment upon which justice, modesty, and veracity are founded, and what is the ordinary way of acting to which those virtues would commonly prompt us.

35   Something, indeed, not unlike the doctrine of the casuists, seems to have been attempted by several philosophers. There is something of this kind in the third book of Cicero's Offices, where he endeavours like a casuist to give rules for our conduct in many nice cases, in which it is difficult to determine whereabouts the point of propriety may lie. It appears too, from many passages in the same book, that several other philosophers had attempted something of the same kind before him. Neither he nor they, however, appear to have aimed at giving a complete system of this sort, but only meant to show how situations may occur, in which it is doubtful, whether the highest propriety of conduct consists in observing or in receding from what, in ordinary cases, are the rules of duty.

36   Every system of positive law may be regarded as a more or less imperfect attempt towards a system of natural jurisprudence, or towards an enumeration of the particular rules of justice. As the violation of justice is what men will never submit to from one another, the public magistrate is under a necessity of employing the power of the commonwealth to enforce the practice of this virtue. Without this precaution, civil society would become a scene of bloodshed and disorder, every man revenging himself at his own hand whenever he fancied he was injured. To prevent the confusion which would attend upon every man's doing justice to himself, the magistrate, in all governments that have acquired any considerable authority, undertakes to do justice to all, and promises to hear and to redress every complaint of injury. In all well-governed states too, not only judges are appointed for determining the controversies of individuals, but rules are prescribed for regulating the decisions of those judges; and these rules are, in general, intended to coincide with those of natural justice. It does not, indeed, always happen that they do so in every instance. Sometimes what is called the constitution of the state, that is, the interest of the government; some-

times the interest of particular orders of men who tyrannize the government, warp the positive laws of the country from what natural justice would prescribe. In some countries, the rudeness and barbarism of the people hinder the natural sentiments of justice from arriving at that accuracy and precision which, in more civilized nations, they naturally attain to. Their laws are, like their manners, gross and rude and undistinguishing. In other countries the unfortunate constitution of their courts of judicature hinders any regular system of jurisprudence from ever establishing itself among them, though the improved manners of the people may be such as would admit of the most accurate. In no country do the decisions of positive law coincide exactly, in every case, with the rules which the natural sense of justice would dictate. Systems of positive law, therefore, though they deserve the greatest authority, as the records of the sentiments of mankind in different ages and nations, yet can never be regarded as accurate systems of the rules of natural justice.

37   It might have been expected that the reasonings of lawyers, upon the different imperfections and improvements of the laws of different countries, should have given occasion to an inquiry into what were the natural rules of justice independent of all positive institution. It might have been expected that these reasonings should have led them to aim at establishing a system of what might properly be called natural jurisprudence, or a theory of the general principles which ought to run through and be the foundation of the laws of all nations.[6] But though the reasonings of lawyers did produce something of this kind, and though no man has treated systematically of the laws of any particular country, without intermixing in his work many observations of this sort; it was very late in the world before any such general system was thought of, or before the philosophy of law was treated of by itself, and without regard to the particular institutions of any one nation. In none of the ancient moralists, do we find any attempt towards a particular enumeration of the rules of justice. Cicero in his Offices, and Aristotle in his Ethics, treat of justice in the same general manner in which they treat of all the other virtues. In the laws of Cicero and Plato,[7] where we might naturally have expected some attempts towards an enumeration of those rules of natural equity, which ought to be enforced by the positive laws of every country, there is, however, nothing of this kind. Their laws are laws of police, not of justice.[8] Grotius seems to have been the first who

---

[6] Cf. LJ(B) 1 (Cannan ed., 1): 'Jurisprudence is that science which inquires into the general principles which ought to be the foundation of the laws of all nations.' See note 9 below.

[7] i.e. Plato's *Laws* and Cicero's *De Legibus*.

[8] For Smith's distinction between justice and 'police' cf. LJ(A) I.1–4, VI.1–2; LJ(B) 5, 203 (Cannan ed., 3, 154); especially the last passage, where Smith explains that the function of police in relation to security is 'the execution of justice, so far as it regards regulations for preventing crimes, or the method of keeping a city guard'. In the present

attempted to give the world any thing like a system of those principles which ought to run through, and be the foundation of the laws of all nations: and his treatise of the laws of war and peace, with all its imperfections, is perhaps at this day the most complete work that has yet been given upon this subject.[9] I shall in another discourse endeavour to give an account of the general principles of law and government, and of the different revolutions they have undergone in the different ages and periods of society, not only in what concerns justice, but in what concerns police, revenue, and arms, and whatever else is the object of law.[10] I shall not, therefore, at present enter into any further detail concerning the history of jurisprudence.

THE END

context he is evidently distinguishing between general principles of justice and detailed laws and institutions for giving effect to those principles.

[9] Cf. LJ(B) 1 (Cannan ed., 1): 'Grotius seems to have been the first who attempted to give the world any thing like a regular system of natural jurisprudence, and his treatise on the laws of war and peace, with all its imperfections, is perhaps at this day the most compleat work on this subject.' The correspondence here and at note 6 above is so close as to suggest that the form of LJ(B) represents Smith's draft of a version of his jurisprudence lectures that would be fit for publication.

[10] Cf. § 2 of the Advertisement with which ed. 6 begins.

Appendix I

MINOR VARIANTS

The numerals in roman type preceding an entry denote page and line. The numerals in italic type following a variant denote the editions in which the variant occurs. *1E* and *2E* denote the Errata lists of editions 1 and 2.

9.1   PART I] THE / THEORY / OF / MORAL SENTIMENTS / PART I *6 7*
9.3   Consisting . . . Sections] *om.* *1* Consisting of three Sections *2–5*
9.5–6 Of the . . . CHAP. I] *om.* *1*
9.7   Of] *rom.* *1*
9.14   others,] ~ₐ *1–3* a matter of fact] *om.* *1*
9.24   did, . . . can,] ~ₐ~ₐ *1–5*
9.25   person,] persons, *1 2*
9.28   own,] ~ₐ *1*
9.31   body,] ~ₐ *1–5*
9.32   the same . . . him,] him, *1–5*
10.10 if] *om.* *1* (*corr.* *1E*)
10.11 fibres,] ~, *5*
10.11–12 bodyₐ complain,] ~, ~ₐ *1–5*
10.12 which] that *1*
10.24 delicate,] ~ₐ *1–5*
10.27 analogous] analagous *1 2*
10.37 imaginesₐ] ~, *1–5*
11.1   merely] meerly *1–3*
11.8   cheerful] chearful *1–5*
11.10 universally, or with] universally with *1* universallyₐ or with *2*
11.11 passions] *om.* *1*
11.20 part] party *1–3* *Probably author's emendation; cf.* part *in* 11.34
11.37 lamentations,] ~ₐ *5*
11.38 inquire] enquire *1–4*
11.40 which] that *1* Till] 'Till *1 2*
11.41 though] tho' *1–5*
12.6   because,] ~ₐ *1–5*
12.16 wretch,] ~ₐ *5*
12.23 mother,] ~ₐ *1–5*
12.27 these,] ~ₐ *1–3*
12.30 future,] ~ₐ *1–5*
12.31 foresight,] ~ₐ *1–5*
12.33 will, in vain, . . . it,] ~ₐ~ₐ~ₐ *1–5*
12.39 grave,] ~ₐ *1–3*
12.40–1 obliterated, . . . time, . . . affections, . . . memory,] ~ₐ~ₐ~ₐ~ₐ *1–5*
13.2   now,] ~ₐ *1–3*
13.3   body;] ~: *1–3*
13.8   love,] ~ₐ *1–3* lamentations] lamentation *1*
13.18–20 It is from . . . to us, and that] It is this very illusion of the imagination which renders the foresight of our own dissolution so terrible to us, and *1*
13.26–7 CHAP. II / *Of . . . mutual Sympathy*] SECT. II / Of the sentiment by

which we approve or disapprove of the passions and affections of other men, as suitable or unsuitable to their objects / CHAP. I / Of the pleasure of mutual SYMPATHY *1*

13.34	weakness,] ∼ₐ *1–5*
14.5	nobody] no-body *1–3* no body *4 5*
14.15–16	surprise] surprize *1–4*
14.17	presentsₐ] ∼, *7*
14.18	him,] ∼ₐ *1*
14.24	though] tho' *1*
14.29	sympathy,] ∼ₐ *5*
14.30	joy:] ∼; *1 2*
14.31	enliven] enlieven *1*
15.2	disagreeableₐ] ∼, *7*
15.24	disagreeableₐ passion;] ∼, ∼: *1–3* ∼,∼; *4 5*
15.27	little] but little *1*
15.30	sympathizing] sympathising *1–3*
15.34	awkward] aukward *1–5*
15.35	they live] *om. 1*
15.41	sympathize] sympathise *5*
16.1–2	the conversation . . . sympathize with,] conversing with a man whom we can entirely sympathise with in all his passions, *1*
16.13	joy;] ∼, *1–5*
16.17	CHAP. III] CHAP. II *1*
16.18–19	*Of the manner . . . our own*] rom. *1*
16.27	thingₐ] ∼, *1 2* entirely] intirely *1*
16.36	who,] ∼ₐ *2 3*
17.4	heartily when] heartily at what *1*
17.8	disapprobation:] approbation: *2* (*corr. 2E*)
17.16	othersₐ] ∼, *5*
18.1	entirely] intirely *1–4*
18.6	situation,] ∼ₐ *1 7*
18.7	sympathize] sympathise *5*
18.11–12	what our sentiments . . . other occasions,] what, upon most occasions, our sentiments would correspond with, correct *1*
18.17–19	cause which . . . motive which . . . end which . . . effect which] cause that . . . motive that . . . end that . . . effect that *1*
18.37	say;] ∼, *5*
18.43	occasion to,] ∼ₐ *1*
19.2	objects;] ∼: *1 2*
19.9	CHAP. IV] CHAP. III *1*
19.10	*The . . . continued*] rom. *1*
19.19	entirely] intirely *1–4*
19.25	all] in a word, all *1*
19.26	regardₐ] ∼, *1–5*
19.30	these,] ∼ₐ *1 2*
20.2	praise or admiration] praise of admiration *1*
20.9	heightened] heightned *1–3*
20.16	perceptibleₐ] ∼, *1–5*
20.21	admiration,] ∼ₐ *1–5*
20.31	delicate,] ∼ₐ *2 3*
20.36–7	andₐ at the same time,] ∼, ∼, *5*

21.33　render‸] ～, *1–3*
22.3　principally] *om. 1 (corr. 1E)*
22.3–4　and‸ at the same time‸] ～, ～, *1 2 5* ～, ～‸ *3 4*
22.4　complete] compleat *1–3*
23.10　only] merely *1*
23.13　strangers‸] ～, *7* an acquaintance.] a mere acquaintance. *1*
23.22　CHAP. V] CHAP. IV *1*
23.23　*Of . . . virtues*] rom. *1*
23.28　the gentle, the amiable] the gentle and the amiable *1*
24.19　swelling] swellings *5*
25.6　Christianity,] christianity, *1–5*
25.22　surprises] surprizes *4*
25.37　actions‸] ～, *1–5*
26.15　for ever] forever *1*
26.25　and‸] ～, *1*
27.1　SECTION II] SECTION III *1*
27.2　Degrees . . . Passions . . . Propriety] degrees . . . passions . . . propriety *1–5*
27.5　lie,] lye, *1–3*
27.10　weakness‸] ～, *1 2*
27.11　defect‸] ～, *2–5*
27.23　decent,] ～‸ *7*
27.24　sympathize] sympathise *1–3*
27.26　*Of . . . body*] rom. *1* *Passions*] passions *1* *passions 2–5*
27.29　sympathize] sympathise *1–3*
28.1　sympathize] sympathise *1–3*
28.2　occasions‸] ～, *1*
28.6　sympathize] sympathise *1–3*
28.8　sympathize] sympathise *1–3*
28.9　Nature] nature *1–3*
28.12　complete indulgence‸] compleat indulgence, *1* compleat indulgence‸ *2–5*
28.17　intire] entire *5*
28.21　ancient] antient *1–5*
28.22　connexion] connection *1–3*
28.25　even] and even *1*
28.27　body‸] ～, *1 2*
29.6　arm:] ～; *1–5*
29.8　out-cry,] outcry, *5*
29.10　body:] ～; *1*
29.24　sympathize] sympathise *1–3*
29.33　gone‸] ～, *7*
30.2　sympathize] sympathise *1–3*
30.6　gout‸] ～, *1 2* though] tho' *1*
30.7　though] tho' *1*
30.12　manner‸] ～, *1–5*
30.22　objects] object *3–5*
30.32　foresee] forsee *1*
30.35　colic!] cholic. *1–3* colic. *4*
31.2　entirely] intirely *1–3*
31.7　surprise,] surprize, *1–3*

31.11–12   *Of those . . . Imagination*] rom. *1*   *Passions . . . Imagination*] passions . . . imagination *1* *passions . . . imagination* 2–5
31.15   sympathized] sympathised *1–3*
31.18–19   always, . . . measure,] ~ₐ ~ₐ *1–5*
31.24   sympathize] sympathise *1–3*
31.25   he is] he his *1*
31.37   style] stile *1–3*
32.1   style] stile *1–3*
32.6   though] tho' *1*
32.7   though] tho' *1*
32.13   interest] interests *2 3* (*corr. 2E*)
32.13–14   kind: in] ~: In *1*
32.15   Though] Tho' *1*
32.19   the violence] violence *2 3*
33.16   violent;] ~: *1–5*
33.21   though] tho' *1*
33.22   though] tho' *1*
33.23   though] tho' *1*
33.32   though] tho' *1*
33.33   though] tho' *1*
33.35   fame,] ~ₐ *7*
34.6   *Of . . . Passions*] rom. *1*   *Passions*] passions *1* *passions* 2–5
34.7   which, though] ~ₐ tho' *1* ~ₐ though *2–5*
34.10   are,] ~ₐ *1–5*
34.12   feels them,] ~ₐ *1–5*
34.30   at] for *1*
34.31   though] tho' *1*
35.3   by itₐ] ~, *1–5*
35.8   sympathize] sympathise *1–3*
35.9   his] the *1* (*corr. 1E*)
35.14   public,] publick, *1–5*
35.26   public] publick *1–5*
35.34   agreeable;] ~: *1 2*
35.35   public.] publick. *1–5*
35.37   pleasure,] ~ₐ *1–3*
35.40   music] musick *1–3 5*
36.2–3   dissectingₐ and amputation-knives,] ~, ~; *1–3*
36.9   though] tho' *1*
36.11–12   no sympathy. With regard] ~; and, with regard *1*
36.16   ancient] antient *1 2*
36.36   forces] force *2 3* (*corr. 2E*)
37.3   though] tho' *1*
37.9   nobody,] no body, *1–5*
37.14   Nature,] nature, *1–3*
38.2   constitute,] constitutes, *1–4*
38.3   which] that *1*
38.5   completely] compleatly *1–5*   sympathize] sympathise *1*
38.17   coolₐ] ~, *1–3*
38.20   stile] style *5 7*
38.31   *Of . . . Passions*] rom. *1*   *Passions*] passions *1* *passions* 2–5
38.32–3   the whole . . . mentioned,] this whole set of passions, *1*

39.6–7   sympathize] sympathise *1–3*
39.13   happiness,] ~ˌ *1–5*
39.15   dissension] dissention *1–3*
39.20   other's] others *1–5*
39.27–8   feels it. It] ~, it *1*
39.35   where] in which *1*
39.38   raillery ˌ] ~, *1–5*
39.39   interest] interests *1–3*
39.41   cheerfulness,] chearfulness, *1–5*   contentment?] ~. *1–3*
40.4   imposes?] ~. *1–3*
40.10   love,] ~; *7*
40.19   falsehood,] falshood, *1–4*
40.27   *Of . . . Passions*] *rom. 1*   *Passions*] passions *1* *passions 2–5*
40.35   objects,] ~ˌ *1–5*
40.38   sympathize] sympathise *1–3*
40.39   The man ˌ who,] ~, ~ˌ *1–3* ~, ~, *4 5*   fortune,] ~ˌ *1*
41.5   sympathizing] sympathising *1–3*   judgment,] ~ˌ *1–5*
41.22   atone] attone *1–3*
41.23   provoked,] ~ˌ *1*
41.35   sympathize] sympathise *1–3*
41.42   cheerfulness,] chearfulness, *1–5*
42.1   sympathize] sympathise *1–3*
42.6   though] tho' *1*
42.24   dulness] dullness *1–5*
42.27   sympathize] sympathise *1–3*
42.33   sympathizing] sympathising *1–3*
42.40   good-breeding] good breeding *1*
42.41   them;] ~, *1 2*
43.1   acquired ˌ] ~, *5*
43.15   are] *om. 1*
43.17   SECTION III] SECTION IV *1*
43.18–20   Effects . . . Prosperity . . . Adversity . . . Judgment . . . Mankind . . .
           Propriety . . . Action . . . Approbation] effects . . . prosperity . . . ad-
           versity . . . judgment . . . mankind . . . propriety . . . action . . . appro-
           bation *1–5*
43.22–4   *That . . . concerned*] *rom. 1*
43.31   Nobody,] No body, *1* No-body, *2–4 Eds. 6 and 7 read* No-/body,
           but the practice of ed. 6 elsewhere shows that this = Nobody.
44.3   complete] compleat *1–5*
44.7   entirely] intirely *1–4*
44.16   shew] show *1–5*
44.27   sympathize] sympathise *1–3*
44.33   is,] ~ˌ *1–4*
44.34   sympathize] sympathise *1–3*
44.35   sympathize] sympathise *1–3*
45.2   sympathize] sympathise *1–3*
45.3   sympathize] sympathise *1–3*
45.9   complete] compleat *1–5*
45.13   entirely] intirely *1*
45.18–19   entirely] intirely *1–4*
45.22   superfluous;] ~: *1 2*

45.31	Though] Tho' *1*
45.33	on] upon *1*
45.34	state,] ~ₐ *5*
45.36	sympathize] sympathise *1-3*
45.39	that ₐ] ~, *1-5*
45.43	sympathize] sympathise *1-3*
46.8	afraid,] ~ₐ *1-5*
46.15	completest] compleatest *1-5*
46.16	announce] enounce *1-3*
46.19	meₐ] ~, *5*
46.20	agreeable] agreable *draft of 1759*
46.20-1	admit any disagreeable] allow of any disagreable *draft*
46.21	answer,] ~ₐ *draft*
46.24	himself,] ~ₐ *draft*
46.25	agreeable] agreable *draft*
46.26	agreeable or disagreeable] agreable or disagreable *draft*
47.14	christeningₐ] ~, *1*
47.24	feel?] ~! *5*
47.30	theirs?] ~! *5* sensible,] ~ₐ *7*
47.33	on] upon *1*
47.36	for ever.] forever. *1-4*
47.42	cheerfulness] chearfulness *1-5*
48.4	entirely.] intirely. *1-4*
48.8	on] upon *1*
48.13	complete] compleat *1-5*
48.34	gayest] gaiest *1 2* cheerful] chearful *1-5*
49.7	complete] compleat *1-5*
49.13	victory he] victory that he *1*
49.37	himselfₐ] ~, *5*
49.39	Biron,] Byron, *1*
50.4	*Of . . . Ranks*] rom. *1* *Ambition, . . . Ranks*] ambition, . . . ranks *1* ambition, . . . ranks *2-5*
50.5	sympathize] sympathise *1-3*
50.15	clothing,] cloathing, *1-5*
50.17	conveniencies,] conveniences, *7*
50.21	higher] highest *1 (corr. 1E)*
50.23	clothed] cloathed *1-5*
50.24	sounderₐ] ~, *7*
50.27	nobody] no-/body *1* no body *2-5*
50.31	complacency,] ~ₐ *1-3*
50.34	attention] atention *7*
51.8	or, thatₐ] ~, ~, *4 5*
51.13	notice of,] ~ₐ *4 5*
51.15	crowd] croud *1-5*
51.22	miseryₐ] ~, *1-5*
51.31	andₐ if] ~, if *1*
51.34	which,] ~ₐ *2-4*
51.40	for ever] forever *1*
52.3	those] these *1*
52.7	think,] ~ₐ *3 4* Natureₐ] nature, *1-3* Nature, *4 5*
52.8	stationsₐ] ~, *1-3*

52.11	befals] befalls *7*
52.28	terrible₍₎] ~, *7* higher] high *1 2*
52.36	completing] ocmpleating *1–5*
52.38	recompense] recompence *1–3 5 7*
53.3	of Nature.] of nature. *1–3*
53.4	them₍₎] ~, *1–5*
53.7	were] was *1–5*
53.12	hatred,] ~₍₎ *1–3*
53.13	them:] ~; *5*
53.26	Revolution,] revolution, *1–3 7*
53.33	fellow-citizens,] fellow citizens, *1–3*
54.3	at. These] ~: these *1–5*
54.6–7	preheminence,] pre-eminence, *7*
54.22	embarrassment] embarassment *1–3*
54.34	valour,] ~₍₎ *1–3*
55.3	it] *om. 5*
55.16	public] publick *1*
55.20	characterize] characterise *1–3*
55.27	undesirable.] undesireable. *1–3*
55.30	wished-for] wished for *1–4*
55.38	public] publick *1–3*
55.42	public] publick *1–3*
56.7	conducted,] ~₍₎ *1–5*
56.9	though] tho' *1* resentment,] ~₍₎ *1–5*
56.16	king] King *1–5*
56.21	king] King *1–5*
56.26	entirely] intirely *1*
56.41	king] King *1–5*
57.3	'Love,' says . . ., 'is] 'Love, says . . ., is *1–5* Rochfaucault,] Rochefaucault, *1* Rochfoucault, *5 7*
57.5	entire] intire *1–3*
57.13	enjoyment,] ~₍₎ *1–5*
57.14	satisfaction,] ~₍₎ *1–5*
57.16	court,] Court, *1–5*
57.17	independent?] independant? *1–3*
57.32	pre-eminence,] preeminence, *1* pre-/eminence, *2–5*
57.37	though] tho' *1*
57.39	entirely] intirely *1–3*
60.2	public₍₎] publick, *1–5*
60.3	though] tho' *1*
60.6	case,] case, therefore, *1–5*
60.16	punishments,] ~₍₎ *4 5*
60.28	consciousness₍₎] ~, *7*
61.2	if there] if There *1*
61.8	the erect] erect *1*
61.14	'Great dangers,' says . . . 'have] 'Great dangers, says . . . have *1–5* Cardinal] cardinal *1*
61.18	just now observing₍₎] observing just now, *1* just now observing, *2*
61.20	utmost] remotest *1* (*corr. 1E*)
65.20	gaudy] gawdy *7*

67.1	PART II] THE / THEORY / OF / MORAL SENTIMENTS / PART II 6 7
67.3	Consisting . . . Sections] *om. 1* Consisting of three Sections *2–5*
67.5	Of . . . Demerit] Of the sense of merit and demerit *1–5*
67.10	Merit and Demerit,] merit and demerit, *1–5*
67.15	relations: first,] ~: First, *1*
67.27–9	*That whatever . . . punishment*] *rom. 1*
68.25	obligations,] ~∧ *7*
68.37	Though] Tho'/ *2–5*
68.42	though] tho' *1*
69.10	though] tho' *1*
69.17	through] thro' *1*
69.28	*Of the . . . resentment*] *rom. 1*
69.33–4	entirely sympathizes] intirely sympathises *1–3*
69.34	entirely] intirely *1–3*
70.1	sympathize] sympathise *1–3*
70.2	deserve reward,] ~∧ *7*
70.4	punishment,] ~∧ *7*
70.6	sympathize] sympathise *2 3*
70.12	though] tho' *1*
70.21	sympathize] sympathise *2 3*
70.24	entirely] intirely *1*
70.27	sympathize] sympathise *2 3*
71.2	sympathize] sympathise *2 3*
71.4	that] *om. 7*
71.15	would feel,] ~∧ *7*
71.23	Nature,] nature, *1–3*
71.23–4	reflections] reflexions *1–3*
71.28–31	*That where . . . suffers it*] *rom. 1*
72.4	sympathize] sympathise *2 3*
72.11	recompense.] recompence. *5*
72.25	prodigality∧] ~, *1 2*
72.26	nobody] no body *1* no/body *2–4* no-/body *5*
72.32	entirely] intirely *1–3*
72.36	entirely] intirely *1–3*
73.13	*Recapitulation . . . chapters*] *rom. 1*
73.14	sympathize] sympathise *2 3*
73.17	entirely] intirely *1–3*
73.19	entirely] intirely *1–3* sympathize] sympathise *2 3*
73.23	recompense.] recompence. *1–3 5*
73.25	entirely] intirely *1–3* sympathize] sympathise *2 3*
73.27	account,] ~∧ *1–3*
73.30	recompense.] recompence. *5* entirely] intirely *1–3*
73.32	entirely] intirely *1–3* sympathize] sympathise *2 3*
73.35	directed,] ~∧ *1–5*
73.37	sympathize] sympathise *2 3*
74.12	entirely] intirely *1–3* sympathize] sympathise *2 3*
74.14	entirely] intirely *1*
74.16	entirely] intirely *1–3*
74.17	sympathize] sympathise *2 3*

74.23	*The analysis . . . Demerit*] rom. *1* *Merit and Demerit*] merit and demerit *1* *merit and demerit* *2–5*
75.11	sympathizes] sympathises *2 3*
75.20	breast] breasts *1*
75.28	beforehand] before-hand *1* before-/hand *2–5*
76.14	lively,] ~ᴧ *5*
76.39	counterparts to] counterparts of *1* (*corr. 1E*)
76.42	though,] tho', *1*
76.44	entirely] intirely *1*
76.45	entirely] intirely *1–3*
76.46	sufferer,] ~; *5*
76.47	own,] ~; *5*
77.1	time to,] ~; *5*
77.2–3	this account] his account *1*
77.3	inflicting,] ~; *5* impossibleᴧ] ~, *1 2*
77.4	entirely] intirely *1*
77.6	this moderation,] his moderation, *1* (*corr. 1E*)
77.22–3	wholly and in] wholly in *2–5* (*corr. 2E*)
77.32	inquiry] enquiry *2 3*
77.41	Author] author *1 2* entrusted] intrusted *1*
77.51	Nature] nature *1–3*
77.54	intire] entire *5*
77.55	though] tho' *1*
78.4	Director] director *1–3*
78.9	though] tho' *1*
78.14	entirely] intirely *1–4*
78.17	myself,] himself, *2* (*corr. 2E*)
78.22	thatᴧ] ~, *1–3*
78.28	Of . . . Beneficence] Of justice and beneficence *1–5*
78.30	*Comparison . . . virtues*] rom. *1*
78.31	tendency,] ~ᴧ *1–3* motives,] ~ᴧ *1–3*
78.32	reward;] a reward; *7*
78.37–8	mere . . . punishment; . . . mere] meer . . . punishment: . . . meer *1–3*
78.42	recompense] recompence *1–3*
79.1	positive] posiive *1* body. He] ~; he *1*
79.6	gratitude, therefore,] ~ᴧ ~ᴧ *7*
79.7	in gratitude] ingratitude *1* (*corr. 1E*)
79.14	complete] compleat *1–3 5*
79.18	mere] meer *1–3*
79.27	mere] meer *1–3*
79.38	approve ofᴧ] ~, *1–5*
80.1	use of,] ~ᴧ *1–3*
80.8	last mentioned] last-mentioned *5*
80.10	tied,] tyed, *1–3*
80.11–12	propriety,] ~ᴧ *3–5*
80.14	blamable,] blameable, *1–3 5*
80.16	blamable] blameable *1–3 5*
80.19	blamable] blameable *1–3 5*
80.23	properᴧ] ~, *1–3*
80.24	contraryᴧ] ~, *1*

80.25	blamable] blameable *1-3 5*
81.15	occasions,] ~_∧ *1*
81.16	another,] ~_∧ *2*
81.20	civilized] civilised *5*
81.28	merely] meerly *1*
81.29	what, . . . orders,] ~_∧ ~_∧ *1*
81.30	blamable] blameable *1-3 5*
81.34	that which] what *1 2*
81.39	mere] meer *1-3*
81.43	observance] observation *1 (corr. 1E)*
82.4	Mere] Meer *1-3*
82.13	Nature.] nature. *1-3*
82.14	beneficent.] benificent. *1*
82.17	desert] desart *1-3*
82.18	nobody] no-body *1-5* inquire] enquire *1-3*
82.23	merely] meerly *1-3*
82.27	*Of the sense . . . Merit*] rom. 1 Justice, . . . Remorse, . . . Merit] justice, . . . remorse, . . . merit *1 justice, . . . remorse, . . . merit 2-5*
82.31	merely] meerly *1-3*
82.32	merely] meerly *1-3*
82.36	man_∧ is,] ~, ~_∧ *1* nature, first_∧] ~_∧ ~, *1*
83.3	connexion,] connection, *1-3*
83.5	though] tho' *1*
83.11	Though] Tho' *1*
83.13	Though] Tho' *1*
83.15	Though] Tho' *1*
83.30	wealth,] ~_∧ *3 4*
83.38	sympathize] sympathise *2 3*
83.43	higher;] ~, *1-5*
84.18	shame,] ~_∧ *1-3*
84.21-2	sympathizing] sympathising *2 3*
84.32	greatest_∧] ~, *1-5*
85.13	and,] ~_∧ *1*
85.15	backward_∧] ~, *7*
85.20	cheerfulness,] chearfulness, *1-3*
85.27	*Of the . . . Nature*] rom. 1 Nature] nature *1 nature 2-5*
85.30	others] other's *7*
85.32	friendship,] ~_∧ *1-5*
85.36	though] tho' *1*
86.1	though] tho' *1*
86.3	though] tho' *1*
86.5	though] tho' *1*
86.18	though] tho' *1* beneficence;] ~: *7*
86.20	Though] Tho' *1* Nature,] nature, *1-3*
86.29	Nature,] nature, *1-3*
86.30	In order to] To *1*
86.31	Nature] nature *1-3*
86.34	chastise] chastize *1-3* though] tho' *1*
86.36	connexion,] connection, *1-3*
87.5	propagation] propogation *1*
87.19	though,] tho', *1*

87.23	ends,] ~ˏ *7*
87.27	view,] ~ˏ *1–5*
88.2	though] tho' *1*
88.5	Its] It's *1* 'Tis *2* (*corr. 2E*)
88.11	hatedˏ] ~, *1–3*
88.22	true,] ~ˏ *1–3*
88.24	punishment,] ~ˏ *1–3*
88.32	punishment,] ~ˏ *1–3*
88.36	humanityˏ] ~, *1*
89.1	enlarged compassionˏ] ~, *1–3*
89.9	though] tho' *1*
89.21	us,] ~ˏ *1–5*
89.41–2	multitude:] ~; *1 2*
90.2	us,] ~ˏ *1–4*
90.4	injured, or destroyed,] ~ˏ~ˏ *1–5*
90.9	esteem,] ~ˏ *1–3*
90.11	this,] ~ˏ *1–5*
90.16	though] tho' *1*
90.36	blamable,] blameable, *1–3 5*
91.15	Nature] nature *1–3*
91.16	authorises] authorizes *4 5*
92.1	SECTION III] SECT. III *1*
92.2–3	Influence . . . Fortune . . . Sentiments . . . Mankind, . . . Merit . . . Demerit . . . Actions] influence . . . fortune . . . sentiments . . . mankind, . . . merit . . . demerit . . . actions *1–5*
92.8	or,] ~ˏ *1–5* lastly, to] last, to all *1–5* last of all, to *2E*
92.15	blameable] blamable *4*
93.3	trigger] tricker *1–5*
93.10	someway] some way *1–3* some-/way *4 5*
93.14	disapprobation,] ~ˏ *2 3*
93.17	nobody] no body *1–4* Its] It's *1–5*
93.19	thatˏ] ~, *1 2*
93.24	or of] or *5* *The reading of ed. 5 might well be a revision by the author, since it accords with Smith's usual practice.*
93.34	nobody] no body *1–5*
93.38	Author] author *1*
94.2	*Of the . . . Fortune*] rom. *1* *Influence . . . Fortune*] influence . . . fortune *1* influence . . . fortune *2–5*
94.19	shipwreck,] shipwreek, *2 3*
95.8	officer,] ~ˏ *1*
95.9	the horse] he horse *1* (*corr. 1E*)
95.10	across] a-cross *1–4*
95.14	complete] compleat *1–3 5*
95.19	satisfy himˏ] ~, *1–3*
96.19	complete] compleat *1–3*
96.24	approved of] approved or *1* (*corr. 1E*)
96.28	not only necessary . . . satisfaction, but] both necessary . . . satisfaction, and *1–5* complete] compleat *1–3*
96.38	benevolenceˏ] ~, *1*
96.39	blameable] blamable *4* other;] ~, *1*
97.4	Fortune,] fortune, *1–3* mankindˏ] ~, *1–5*

97.7   *Of the . . . Fortune*] rom. *1*   *Influence . . . Fortune*] influence . . .
        fortune *1* *influence . . . fortune 2–5*

97.10   blamable] blameable *1–3* 5

97.15   1.] I. *1–5 Contrast* 2. *in all eds. at* §6

97.16   beneficent, . . . hand, . . . malevolent,] ∼ᴧ∼, ∼ᴧ 5

97.18   incomplete] incompleat *1–3*

97.20   consequences] consequence *1* (*corr. 1E*)

97.23   solicits,] sollicits, *2 3*

97.24   entitled] intitled *1–3*

97.26   first:] ∼; *1*

97.27   into] in *1* (*corr. 1E*)

98.4   complete:] compleat: *1–3*

98.16   since,] ∼ᴧ *1–4*

98.22   him,] ∼ᴧ *1*

98.42   complete] compleat *1–3*

99.3   complete] compleat *1–3*

99.8   completely] compleatly *1–3*

99.20   splendour] splendor *1–5*

99.21   has] have *1–4*

99.34   into] into it *3 4*

99.36   punishmentsᴧ] ∼, 5

100.1   though] tho' *1*

100.7   saidᴧ] ∼, 7

100.12   man,] ∼ᴧ *2 3*

100.13   enemyᴧ] ∼, *1–5*

100.15   though] tho' *1–3*

100.16   assassin] assassine *1–3*

100.18   committing it,] ∼ᴧ *1–3*

100.28   though] tho' *1*

100.29   mischief,] ∼ᴧ *1–3*

100.30   him,] ∼ᴧ *1–3*

100.36   disciplineᴧ] ∼, 7

101.14   though] tho' *1*

101.17   though] tho' *1*

101.31   though] tho' *1*

102.1   entitled] intitled *1–3*

102.5   chagrin] chagrine *1–3*

102.6   king] King *1–5*

102.13   authorize] authorise *2 3*

102.16   though] tho' *1*

102.17   though] tho' *1*

102.18   gratification,] ∼ᴧ *1–3*

102.19   person,] ∼ᴧ 5   directed,] ∼ᴧ *3–5*

102.24   would] will *2–5* (*corr. 2E*)

102.27   chastisementᴧ] ∼, 5   though] tho' *1*

102.31   though] tho' *1*

102.36   fellow-creatures] fellow creatures *1*

103.5   above-mentioned,] above mentioned, *1 5*

103.7   though] tho' *1*

103.10–11   Nothing, however,] ∼ᴧ∼ᴧ *1–5*

103.35   blamable] blameable *1–3 5*   negligence,] ∼ᴧ *1–5*

104.6	this] the *2 3* (*corr. 2E*)
104.8	who‸] ~, *5*
104.15	events,] effects, *1*
104.31	*Of the . . . Sentiments*] rom. *1* Irregularity . . . Sentiments] irregularity . . . sentiments *1* irregularity . . . sentiments *2–5*
104.34	Fortune,] fortune, *1–3*
105.27	Actions, therefore,] ~‸~‸ *1–5*
105.29	Author] author *1*
105.40	Author,] author, *1–3*
106.5	mere] meer *1–3*
106.12	Nature] nature *1–3*
106.20	justest,] justness, *2* (*corr. 2E*) entitled] intitled *1–3*
106.21	though] tho' *1* inutility] utility *2* (*corr. 2E*)
106.24	entitle] intitle *1–3* recompense?] recompence? *1–3 5*
106.28	though] tho' *1*
106.34	slow,] ~‸ *1–3*
106.39	which, he feels,] ~‸~‸ *1–5*
106.40	should, without design,] ~‸~‸ *1–5*
107.23	resentment,] ~‸ *7*
108.3	Nature] nature *1–5*
108.6	maxim, That] ~, that *1–5* *Cf.* That *introducing maxims in the first lines of II.i.3.2 and 3*
108.6–7	conduct,] ~‸ *1–5*
108.11	appear,] ~‸ *1*
108.14	entirely] intirely *1–3*
109.1	PART III] THE / THEORY / OF / MORAL SENTIMENTS / PART III *6 7*
109.2–3	Foundation . . . Judgments . . . Sentiments . . . Conduct, . . . Sense . . . Duty] foundation . . . judgments . . . sentiments . . . conduct, . . . sense . . . duty *1–5*
109.12	conduct,] ~‸ *7*
110.10	reference,] ~‸ *1–5*
110.10–11	or to what, upon . . . condition, would be, or to what, we imagine,] ~‸~‸~, ~‸~‸ *1–5*
110.13–14	If, . . . situation,] ~‸~‸ *1–4*
110.15	approve of it,] ~‸ *1–5*
110.16	disapprobation,] ~‸ *1–5*
110.18	Were] Was *1–5*
110.19	place,] ~‸ *1–5*
110.23	look at,] ~; *2–5*
110.28	disapprove of‸] ~, *5*
110.33	sorrows,] ~‸ *1*
110.34	though] tho' *1*
111.3	though] tho' *1*
111.6	some of them,] ~‸ *1*
111.8	sorrows,] ~‸ *1–5*
111.9–10	now, therefore,] ~‸~‸ *1–5*
111.13–14	sensible,] ~‸ *1*
111.17	our persons] our own persons *1–5*
112.3	If, . . . examination,] ~‸~‸ *1–5*
112.5	others. If,] ~: if, *1–5*

112.9   unsupportable] insupportable *1–5*
112.12   connexion] connection *1–3*
112.15   other people] others *1–5*
112.19   begin, . . . account,] ~ₐ ~ₐ *1–5*
112.23   looking-glass] looking glass *3*
112.24   other people,] others, *1–5*
112.27   secure that,] ~ₐ *1*
112.29–30 often, . . . account,] ~ₐ ~ₐ *1–5*
113.2   upon it,] ~ₐ *draft of 1759*
113.3   persons;] ~, *draft 2–5*
113.6   spectator,] ~ₐ *draft*
113.8   to me,] ~ₐ *draft 2–5*
113.11   opinion] oppinion *draft*   the second ₐ] ~, *draft*
113.15   amiable ₐ] ~; *5*   meritorious;] ~, *1 draft 2–5*
113.16   virtue;] ~, *1 draft 2–5*
113.16–17 and to be odious and punishable,] and the contrary ₐ *1*   all] both *1*
113.18   amiable,] ~ₐ *1 draft 2–5*
113.19   love, or . . . gratitude;] ~ₐ ~, *1*   ~ₐ ~; *draft*
113.21   regards,] ~ₐ *1 draft 2–5*
113.22   self-satisfaction] self satisfaction *draft*
113.24   happiness ₐ] ~, *1*
113.25   misery ₐ] ~, *1*
114.35   sufficient ₐ that,] ~, ~ₐ *1–5*
114.36   should, in some way or other,] ~ₐ some way or other ₐ *1–5*
115.1   and that ₐ] ~, *1 2*
115.2   were] was *1–5*   different] opposite *1–5*
115.8   reflections, the reflection of] reflexions, the reflexion upon *1–3*
           reflections, the reflection upon *4 5*
115.18   liar,] lyar, *1 2* lyer, *3* lier, *4*
115.20   existence;] ~, *1–5*   coxcomb,] ~ₐ *1–5*
115.22   pretensions to;] ~, *1–5*
115.36   examination,] ~; *5*
115.37   though] tho' *1*
115.40   pleased,] ~ₐ *1–5*
116.4   though] tho'/ *2 3*
116.8   behaviour. When] ~; when *1–5*
116.9–10   influenced it. He] ~; he *1–5*
116.11   though] tho' *1*
116.12   himself,] ~ₐ *1–5*
116.13   to that ₐ] ~, *1–5*
116.16   sentiments,] ~ₐ *1–5*
116.21   follow] flow *1–5*
116.23   in future times] thereafter *1–5*
116.25   ears; the] ~. The *1–3*
116.30   which, indeed,] ~ₐ ~ₐ *1–5*
116.31   would be bestowed,] ~ₐ *1–5*
117.41   case,] ~ₐ *7*
118.4   through] thro' *1–5*
118.5   though] tho' *1* tho'/ *2–5*
118.6   for ever] forever *1*
118.16   suffer,] ~ₐ *1–5*

118.17   merely] meerly *1*
118.21   though] tho' *1*
118.24   life: he] ~: He *1–5*
118.25   and, if] ~∧ if *1–5 7*
118.27   manner∧] ~, *1–3*
118.30   affrighted] afrighted *1*
118.30–1   furies, which, . . . life,] ~∧ ~∧ ~∧ *1–5*
118.35   complete] compleat *1–3*
118.39   driven,] ~∧ *1–3*   discover,] ~∧ *1–5*
118.42   fellow-citizens, and,] citizens, ~∧ *1–5*
119.1   had become] were become *1–5*   hoped,] ~∧ *1–5*
119.3   mankind;] ~, *1–5*
119.4   resentment; to atone, . . . measure,] ~, to attone∧ ~∧ *1–3*   ~, to atone∧ ~∧ *4 5*
122.14   falsehood] fasehood *7*
125.18   Perreault] Perrault *7*
127.6   desire,] ~∧ *7*
134.27   within,] ~∧ *draft of 1759*
134.28   dimensions;] ~, *draft 2–5*
134.29   people.] men. *draft 2–5*
134.30   body,] ~∧ *draft*
135.2   to∧ what may be called∧] ~, ~, *draft The commas are added in Smith's own hand.*
135.5   lawns, and woods,] ~∧ ~∧ *draft*
135.11   judgment] judgement *draft*
135.17   manner,] ~∧ *draft*
135.21   connexion] connection *draft*   interests,] ~∧ *draft*
135.22   balance] ballance *draft 2 3*
135.25   interests,] ~∧ *draft*
135.26   own place∧] ~, *draft 2–5*   own eyes∧] ~, *2*
135.27   the place,] ~∧ *2–5*
135.28   connexion] connection *draft 2 3*   either,] ~∧ *draft*
135.29   Here,] ~∧ *draft 2–5*   too,] ~∧ *draft*
136.1   do this] this *2 (corr. 2E)*   readily,] ~∧ *draft*
136.2   reflection,] ~∧ *draft*
136.3   philosophy,] ~∧ *draft 2–4*
136.9   connexion] connection *2 3*
136.20   diversion,] ~∧ *2 3*
136.24   but,] ~∧ *2–5*
137.1   paltry] paultry *2–5*
137.2   paltry] paultry *2–5*   himself,] ~∧ *2–4*
137.7   When our] when our *7*
137.14   Nature] nature *2 3*
137.15   self-love.] ~? *2–4*
137.18   It is he∧] ~, *2–5*
137.19   to us,] ~∧ *2–5*
137.29   others,] ~; *7*
137.33   affection,] ~∧ *2–4*
137.34   occasions;] ~, *2–5*   grandeur,] ~∧ *2 3*
138.25   befal] befall *7*
138.33   connexion] connection *2 3*

139.4	others,] ~; *5*
139.8	feelings;] ~, *2–5*
139.11	increase] encrease *2 3*
139.12	another,] ~‸ *2–5*
139.13–14	ourselves‸] ~, *2–5*
139.27	Winter:] ~: *5*
140.1	misfortunes‸] ~, *2–5*
140.13	possessed] was possessed of *2–5*
140.14	connexion,] connection, *2 3*
140.18	entitled] intitled *2 3*
140.24	Nature;] nature; *2 3*
140.32	moralists‸] ~, *2–5*
140.35	Stoics.] stoics. *2–5* Stoics,] stoics, *2–5*
140.39	interest should] interests should *2*
141.1	befalls] befals *2 3*
141.2	befalls] befals *2 3*
141.3	befalls] befals *2* neighbour,'] neighbour, *draft of 1759*
141.4	wife,] ~‸ *draft 2–5* nobody] no body *draft 2–4*
141.6	things; but,] ~. But, *draft* ~: ~, *2–5*
142.27	them,] ~‸ *7*
151.40	Joanna] Johanna *7*
152.5	revival] rivival *7*
157.4	authorising.] authorizing. *draft 4 5*
157.5	occasions‸] ~, *2–5*
157.7	it: first,] ~; ~, *1* ~. First, *draft 2–5* act; and‸ secondly,] ~ ~‸ ~, *1* ~; ~‸ ~‸ *draft* ~; ~, ~, *2–5*
157.8	cases;] ~, *1–5*
157.12	doing,] ~‸ *1–5* with] when *7*
157.15	us‸] ~, *1–5* light in which] light which *1 (corr. 1E)*
157.17	calls] call *2 (corr. 2E)*
157.19	them,] ~‸ *1*
157.21	and which, . . . last,] ~‸ ~‸ *1–4*
157.24	complete] compleat *1–3*
157.25	Malebranche] Malebranch *1–3*
157.26	reasonable‸] ~, *1–5*
157.29	into the sentiments] into sentiments *2–5*
157.30	interested us‸] ~, *1–5*
158.7	importance‸ in comparison of what] ~, compared to what *1–5*
158.8	regret‸ . . . repentance;] ~, ~, *1–5*
158.9	in time to come.] for the future. *1–5*
158.11	character‸] ~, *1–5*
158.23	purpose,] ~‸ *1*
159.28	because,] ~‸ *2 3*
159.30	formed,] ~‸ *1–5*
159.41	blamable] blameable *1–3 5*
160.12–13	excite for the person . . . of the spectator.] excite the love, the respect, or the horror of the spectator, for the person who performs them. *1–5*
161.6	yet,] ~‸ *1–3*
161.10	himself‸] ~, *1* through] thro' *1*
161.13–14	forebodes,] forbodes, *1–3*
161.31	though] tho' *1*

161.38–9	*Of the influence . . . Deity*] rom. *1* Rules . . . Morality, . . . Laws] rules . . . morality, . . . laws *1* *rules . . . morality, . . . laws* 2–5
162.3	through] thro' *1*
162.12	Though] Tho' *1* Tho'/ 2–5
162.19	blamable] blameable *1–3 5*
162.31	though] tho' *1*
162.35	Though] Tho' *1*
162.39	mould] mold *1–3* suiting,] ~ₐ *1–3*
163.4	through] thro' *1*
163.9	on] upon *1*
163.10	through] thro' *1* tenour] tenor *1–3*
163.11	other,] ~ₐ 5
163.20	were] was *1–5* though] tho' *1*
163.27	But,] ~, 5
163.38	morality,] ~, *1–4*
163.43	happen,] ~ₐ *1–3* objects] object *1* (*corr. 1E*)
164.7	ascribed] ascribe 2
164.12	resemblance of] resemblance to *1*
164.23	gods] Gods *1–3*
165.23	soothes] sooths *1–5*
165.30	fit,] ~ₐ *1–3* unfit,] ~ₐ *1–3*
165.32	words,] ~ₐ *1*
165.36	prescribe,] ~, *1–4*
166.2	them,] ~, 5
166.3	men:] ~; *1* 2
166.7	contrary,] ~ₐ *1*
166.7–8	tranquillity] tranquility *1* 2
166.11–12	Author of nature,] Author of Nature, *1* author of Nature, 2 3
166.22	nature] Nature *1–3*
166.32	recompense] recompence 5
166.38–9	recompense, . . . recompense] recompence, . . . recompence *1–3 5*
166.43	believed,] ~; 5 recompenses] recompences *1–3 5*
167.11	justice,] ~ₐ 7 humanity,] ~, *1–5* acquiring,] ~, 5
167.19	manner,] ~ₐ *1–4*
167.27	though] tho' *1*
167.33	recompenses] recompences *1–3 5* qualities,] ~ₐ *1–5*
167.38	justice,] ~ₐ *1–5*
167.43	rouses] rouzes *1–3*
168.12	traitor,] traitour, *1–3*
168.14	Nature] nature *1–3*
168.24	abhorrence,] ~ₐ *1–3*
168.29	though] tho' *1*
168.30	though,] tho', *1*
168.31	gods] Gods *1–3*
168.32	and, like them,] ~ₐ~, *1–5*
168.33–4	to accelerate] accelerates *1–5*
168.37	controlled] controuled *1–5*
168.38	though] tho' *1*
168.41	men,] ~, *1–4*
169.1	enterprise] enterprize *1–3*
169.3	Nature] nature *1–3*

169.5	rousing] rouzing *1–3*
169.6	when,] ~∧ *1–3*
169.7	what] What *1*
169.10	enraged∧] ~, *1–4*
169.13	Author] author *1–3*
169.14	us∧] ~, *1*
169.16	complete] compleat *1–3*
169.35–7	I can no longer . . . fidelity.] can I any longer . . . fidelity? *1*
169.40	leisure∧] ~, *1–5*
170.2	regarded∧] ~, *1–5*
170.6	Deity∧] ~, *1–5*
170.7	nobody] no body *1–4* no-/body *5*
170.12	though] tho' *1*
170.13	violation.] ~! *7*
170.23	tie,] tye, *1–5*
170.25	action,] ~∧ *1–5*
170.36	sacrifices,] ~∧ *1–3*
171.2–3	*In what . . . motives*] rom. *1* *Sense . . . Duty*] sense . . . duty *1* sense . . . duty *2–5*
171.13	conduct, . . . respect,] ~∧~∧ *1–5*
171.15	public-spirited] public spirited *1*
171.28	question,] ~∧ *3 4*
171.37	and, secondly,] ~∧~, *1–5*
171.38	inaccuracy,] ~∧ *1–5*
172.1	ought to] should *1*
172.10	Though] Tho' *1*
172.14	though] tho' *1*
172.34	than for what] than what *2–5*
172.35	though] tho' *1*
172.36	allow] allow of *1*
172.40	hold, . . . respects,] ~∧~∧ *1–5*
173.1	little,] ~∧ *2 3*
173.4	awkward,] aukward, *1–3*
173.10–11	severe oeconomy∧] ~, *1–5*
173.12	proceed,] ~∧ *1–5*
173.14	tenor] tenour *4 5* to-day] to day *1*
173.15	three-pence] three pence *1*
173.16–17	ten-pence] ten pence *1*
173.22	sake;] ~: *1 2*
173.35	between] betwixt *1*
173.36	enterprise] enterprize *1–3*
173.37	loss or] loss of *2–5* (*corr. 2E*)
173.39	which∧] ~, *5*
173.43	heroes and conquerors, . . . statesmen,] Heroes and Conquerors, . . . Statesmen, *1–5*
174.1	though] tho' *1*
174.29	When . . . lend him?] When . . . lend it him? *1*
174.32–3	yours, . . . yours,] your's, . . . your's, *1*
175.11	Though] Tho' *1* awkward] aukward *1–3*
175.19	tenor] tenour *4 5*

175.22   stedfastness‿] ~, *1–4*
175.24   Though] Tho' *1*
175.26   though] tho' *1*
175.40   critics] criticks *1–5*
175.42   indispensable.] indispensible. *1–3*
176.5   writing;] ~, *1–5* ~: *7* though] tho' *1*
176.7   perfections. And] ~: and *1–5*
176.9   beneficence: though] ~. Tho' *1* ~. Though *2–5*
176.38   though] tho' *1*
177.8   nature. A] ~: a *1–5*
177.12   though] tho' *1*
177.16   indispensableness] indispensibleness *1–3*
177.33   though] tho' *1*
177.35   complete] compleat *1–3*
177.36   bigoted] bigotted *1–5*
177.38   Protestants,] protestants, *1–4*
177.40   complete] compleat *1–3*
178.6   who‿] ~, *5*
178.9   laugh‿] ~, *1*
178.12   properly‿] ~, *1 2*
179.1   PART IV] THE / THEORY / OF / MORAL SENTIMENTS / PART IV *6 7*
179.2   Sentiment . . . Approbation] sentiment . . . approbation *1–5*
179.5–6   *Of the beauty . . . Beauty*] rom. *1*
179.6   *Beauty*] beauty *1 beauty 2–5*
179.33   art,] ~‿ *1*
180.1   pleasure,] ~‿ *5*
180.26   men,] ~‿ *1*
180.28   knowledge,] ~‿ *1*
180.29   which] that *1*
180.32   which] that *1*
180.34   clothes] cloaths *1–3*
180.37   Jew's-box,] Jews-box, *1–5*
181.5   him,] ~‿ *1–5*
181.19   afford,] ~‿ *1–5*
181.33   galled] gauled *1–3*
181.39   too,] ~‿ *1–3*
182.2   great,] ~‿ *1–5*
182.8   conveniency] convenience *3–5*
182.14   doubt, perhaps, . . . palace,] ~‿ ~‿ ~‿ *1*
182.19   concerned,] concern'd, *1*
182.29   But in] ¶ But in *1* disease‿] ~, *1–5*
182.31   one, . . . situation,] ~‿ ~‿ *1*
182.34   for ever,] forever, *1*
182.36   In this] ¶ In this *1*
182.37   man‿] ~, *5*
182.40   machines‿] ~, *1–3* trifling] triffling *1*
183.6   that] who *1*
183.12   though] tho' *1*
183.23   separated] seperated *1* arrangement] arangement *1*
183.30   grand‿ . . . beautiful‿] ~, ~, *5*

184.18	inhabitants₍∧₎] ~, *1–5*
184.21–2	though . . . though] tho'. . . tho' *1*
185.5	Providence] providence *1–3*
185.15	institutions₍∧₎] ~, *1–5*
185.17	those₍∧₎] ~, *1–3*
185.19	public-spirited] public spirited *1*
185.20	premiums] praemiums *1–3*
185.21	linen] linnen *1*
185.23	manufacturer₍∧₎] ~, *1–5*
185.30–1	encumber] incumber *1–3*
185.32	proportion₍∧₎] ~, *1–4*
185.41	to have] to bave *1*
186.3	spirit,] ~₍∧₎ *1*
186.4	well-natured James the First of Great Britain] well natured James the first of Great-Britain *1–3* well natured James the First of Great-Britain *4* well-natured James the First of Great-Britain *5*
186.5	seems, . . . contrary,] ~₍∧₎~₍∧₎ *1* glory₍∧₎] ~, *1–4*
186.6	man₍∧₎] ~, *1–5*
186.17	him,] ~₍∧₎ *1*
186.19	of him₍∧₎] ~, *1–5*
186.23	clothed,] cloathed, *1–3*
186.26	connexions] connections *1–3*
187.4	men,] ~₍∧₎ *3 4* rouse] rouze *1–3*
187.7–9	*Of the beauty . . . approbation*] rom. *1*
187.7	*Utility*] utility *1* utility *2–5*
187.13	resolute,] ~₍∧₎ *1–3*
187.15	effeminate,] ~₍∧₎ *1–3*
187.16	contrary, forebodes] ~₍∧₎ forbodes *1* ~, forbodes *2–4*
187.19	second,] ~₍∧₎ *1–5*
187.20	awkward] aukward *1–3*
187.26	men?] ~. *1–4*
187.31	consider,] ~₍∧₎ *1*
187.33	himself,] ~₍∧₎ *1*
188.1	merit or] merit and *1*
188.8–9	contrary,] ~₍∧₎ *1*
188.18	And₍∧₎ Nature,] ~, nature, *1* ~₍∧₎ nature, *2 3*
188.28	of all,] ~₍∧₎ *1*
188.30	well-contrived] well contrived *1–4*
188.33	secondly,] ~₍∧₎ *1*
189.3	are, . . . all,] ~₍∧₎~₍∧₎ *1*
189.5	foreseeing] forseeing *1 2*
189.11	on] upon *1*
189.12	occasion,] ~₍∧₎ *1*
189.13	merely] meerly *1–3*
189.17	prove it,] ~₍∧₎ *1–4*
189.25	appetites,] ~₍∧₎ *1*
189.25–6	occasion, is approved of,] ~₍∧₎~₍∧₎ *1*
189.26	propriety, ~₍∧₎ *1*
189.27	manner,] ~₍∧₎ *1*
189.29	solicitations] sollicitations *1 2*
189.36	interested] interests *3–5*

189.38 experience,] ~ₐ 5
189.39 self-command,] ~ₐ *1*
190.1 industry,] ~ₐ *1–3*
190.14 tenour] tenor *1–3*
190.16 to-day,] to day, *1*
190.18 the one] one *3–5*
190.23 generosity,] ~ₐ *1–3*
190.32 fair-sex,] fair sex, *1–5*
190.34 donations,] ~ₐ *1–4*
190.36 concerned,] ~ₐ *1*
191.5 otherwise] otherways *1*
191.9 becauseₐ] ~, *1*
191.13 interests,] ~ₐ *1–5*
191.15 bystander, ~ₐ *1* by-stander, *5*
191.16 than their own;] ~, *1*
191.18 sacrifice their own,] ~; *1–3*
191.23 his own;] ~, *1*
191.26–7 feels, . . . himself,] ~ₐ~ₐ *1*
191.33 is notₐ] ~, *1–5*
191.34 is, to himself,] ~ₐ~ₐ *1* desireable] desirable *2–5*
191.37 lightₐ] ~, *1–3*
191.38 in thatₐ] ~, *1–3*
191.42 if, . . . it,] ~ₐ~ₐ *1*
192.1 thwarting,] ~ₐ *1*
192.3 who, . . . station,] ~ₐ~ₐ *1*
192.4 guinea,] ~ₐ *1*
192.6 timesₐ] ~, *1–3*
192.15 character,] ~ₐ *1* tie,] tye, *1–5*
192.16 with them;] ~, *1*
192.20 noble,] ~ₐ *1–3*
192.21 them, undoubtedly,] ~ₐ~ₐ *1*
192.31 on] upon *1*
192.32 temperance,] ~ₐ *1–3*
192.33 behaviour: he] ~: He *1–5*
192.34–5 well-contrived] well contrived *1–4*
192.36 awkward] aukward *1–3*
193.1 merely] meerly *1–3*
193.6–7 connexion . . . connexion.] connection . . . connection. *1–3*
193.14 conduct,] ~ₐ *1*
193.15 conceive,] ~ₐ *1*
194.2–3 Sentiments of Moral Approbation and Disapprobation] sentiments of moral approbation and disapprobation *1–5*
194.6 *Of the . . . Deformity*] rom. *1* *Influence of Custom and Fashion . . . Notions of Beauty and Deformity*] Influence of custom and fashion . . . notions of beauty and deformity *1* *influence of custom and fashion . . . notions of beauty and deformity* *2–5*
194.7 principlesₐ] ~, *1 2*
194.10 blameable] blamable *4 5*
194.11 praise-worthy.] praise worthy. *1*
194.16 appear,] appearsₐ *1* appears, *2 3*
194.18 Though,] Tho'ₐ *1*

194.20   awkward] aukward *1–3*
194.23   clothes,] cloaths, *1–3*
194.25   awkwardness] aukwardness *1–3*
194.28   Those‿] ~, *2 3*
194.29   taste,] ~‿ *1*
194.30   awkward.] aukward. *1–3*
194.31   diminishes,] ~‿ *1*   altogether,] ~‿ *1*
194.33   dress‿] ~, *5*
194.34   strangers,] ~‿ *1*
194.37   easy,] ~‿ *1–3*
195.4   though] tho' *1*
195.5   seems,] ~‿ *1*
195.7   grace,] ~‿ *5*   before, and‿] ~; ~, *5*
195.9   awkwardness.] aukwardness. *1–3*
195.13   taste,] ~‿ *1*
195.17   Clothes] Cloaths *1–3*
195.18   well-fancied] well fancied *1–4*   twelve-month,] twelve month, *1–3*
195.19   which] what *2 3*
195.21   durable. In five‿] ~, In five, *1*
195.26   well-contrived] well contrived *1–4*
195.27   through] thro' *1*
195.27–8   generations: a well-written] ~: A well written *1*   ~: a well written *2–4*
195.28   world;] ~, *1*
195.29   continue‿] ~, *2*   style,] stile, *1–3*
195.36   allow,] ~‿ *1–5*
195.41–2   satisfy them,] ~‿ *1*
195.42   furniture,] ~‿ *1*
196.3   Ionic] Jonic *1*
196.10   ancients] antients *1–3*
196.13   though,] tho'‿ *1*
196.21   clothes] cloaths *1–3*
196.22   though] tho' *1*
196.25   though] tho' *1*
196.27   ancient] antient *1–3*   rhetoricians,] ~‿ *1*
196.29   sentiment,] ~‿ *1–3*
196.33   though] tho' *1*
196.34   English, is] english‿ is *1* English‿ is *2–5*
196.36   verse with,] ~‿ *1*
197.1   contrary,] ~‿ *1*
197.3   sublimity,] ~‿ *1–3*
197.4   flippant,] ~‿ *1–3*
197.5   English,] ~‿ *1–5*
197.13   style] stile *1–3*
197.20   though] tho' *1* tho'/ *2–5*
197.20–1   reputation, . . . pretended,] ~‿ ~‿ *1*
197.21   style,] stile, *1–3*   which‿] ~, *5*   though] tho' *1*
197.24   possess,] ~‿ *1–5*
198.1   author,] ~‿ *1–5*
198.3   rhyme,] Rhyme, *1*
198.6   Addison,] ~‿ *1*

198.12   things?] ~! 5
198.20   middle,] ~ₐ 1–5
198.22   straight,] streight, 1–3
198.24   Nature] nature 1–3
198.28   though] tho' 1
198.31   which] that 1 though] tho' 1
198.34   manner,] ~ₐ 1
199.10   climates,] ~ₐ 1–4
199.13   Moorish] moorish 1
199.15   countenance?] ~! 5
199.19   ugliness.] uggliness. 1
199.20   North-America] North America 5
199.25   savages,] ~ₐ 1
199.26   endeavouring,] ~ₐ 1
199.28   And that,] ~ₐ 1–4
199.32   Father,] father, 1–5
199.39   to us,] ~ₐ 1–4
200.3   though] tho' 1
200.6   please,] ~ₐ 1 customₐ] ~, 5 7
200.7–8   things: or] ~: Or 1
200.11   *Of . . . Sentiments*] rom. 1 *Influence . . . Custom . . . Fashion . . .*
          Moral Sentiments] influence . . . custom . . . fashion . . . moral senti-
          ments 1 *influence . . . custom . . . fashion . . . moral sentiments* 2–5
200.16   There is,] ~ₐ 1
200.24   education: but] ~: But 1
200.26   though] tho' 1
200.28   fashionₐ] ~, 1–5
200.37   Those,] ~ₐ 1
200.39   falsehood,] falshoodₐ 1–3 injustice;] ~, 5
201.2   or of . . . punishment due] and of . . . punishment that is due 1
201.4   as, . . . called,] ~ₐ ~ₐ 1
201.5   may, . . . practised,] ~ₐ . . . practicedₐ 1
201.7   tooₐ] ~, 1
201.8   and,] ~ₐ 1–4
201.12–13 puritan. Severity] ~; severity 1–5
201.17   many superior] many superiour 3–5
201.19   humanity,] ~ₐ 1–3
201.31–2 which, . . . feature,] ~ₐ ~ₐ 1–5
201.33   which nature] that nature 1
201.40   worn-out] worn out 1–3
202.1   unpractised] unpracticed 1
202.4   immovable] immoveable 3
202.19   ourselves,] ~ₐ 1–5
202.25   sympathize] sympathise 2 3
202.27   blameₐ] ~, 1–5
202.29   safety,] ~ₐ 2–5
202.37   clergyman,] ~ₐ 1–5
202.38   manₐ] ~, 1
202.40   announce] anounce 1–3
203.8   clergymanₐ] ~, 1–5
203.18   profession. Yet,] ~: yet, 1–5

203.20	mind$_\wedge$] ~, *1–5*
203.22	danger,] ~; *1–5*
203.38	lose$_\wedge$] ~, *5*
203.38–9	amusements$_\wedge$] ~, *1–5*
204.2	fellow-citizens.] fellow citizens. *1*
204.17	embarrassed,] embarassed, *1–3*
204.21	countries$_\wedge$] ~, *1–5* apt,] ~$_\wedge$ *1*
204.24	blamable$_\wedge$] blameable$_\wedge$ *1–3* blamable, *4*
204.24–5	vary, . . . degree$_\wedge$] ~$_\wedge$ ~, *1–5*
204.29	nobleman,] ~$_\wedge$ *1*
204.33	varies,] ~$_\wedge$ *1*
205.5	politeness,] ~$_\wedge$ *1–5*
205.7	it$_\wedge$ therefore$_\wedge$] ~, ~, *1–3* ~$_\wedge$~, *4 5*
205.8	pleasure$_\wedge$] ~, *1–5*
205.13	danger: he] ~: He *1–5*
205.20	neighbour: and] ~: And *1–5*
205.30	love,] ~$_\wedge$ *1 2*
205.35	control.] controul. *1–5*
205.36	exception,] ~$_\wedge$ *1*
205.38–9	complete] compleat *1–3*
205.39	whom,] ~$_\wedge$ *1–5*
205.42	marriage,] ~$_\wedge$ *1–5*
205.43	connexion] connection *1–3*
206.2	houses] house *1*
206.6–7	bear, . . . countrymen,] ~$_\wedge$ ~$_\wedge$ *1–5*
206.7	insults,] ~$_\wedge$ *1–5*
206.14	ingenuity$_\wedge$] ~, *1–5*
206.24	smoke] smoak *3*
206.26–7	this dreadful] the dreadful *1 2* (*corr. 2E*)
206.33	imagination$_\wedge$] ~, *1*
207.1	brutality,] ~$_\wedge$ *1–3*
207.3	firmness,] ~$_\wedge$ *1*
207.11	though] tho' *1*
207.11–12	countenance, . . . behaviour,] ~$_\wedge$ ~$_\wedge$ *1–5*
207.22	behaviour,] ~$_\wedge$ *1*
207.25	the Italians,] Italians, *1*
207.27	surprise] surprize *1–3*
207.28	and who,] ~$_\wedge$ *1*
207.30	example] examples *1*
207.32	abbot] abbot of *2 3* Dû] Dù *5* on being] upon being *1*
207.33	shillings,] ~$_\wedge$ *1* on receiving] upon receiving *1*
208.1	Scipios, . . . Leliuses,] Scipio's, . . . Lelius's, *1–3*
208.2	ancient] antient *1–3*
208.3	themselves$_\wedge$] ~, *1–5* gravity,] ~$_\wedge$ *1–3* judgment;] ~, *1–3*
208.6	Crassus,] ~$_\wedge$ *1–3*
208.13	way,] ~$_\wedge$ *1* measure,] ~$_\wedge$ *1*
208.14	open,] ~$_\wedge$ *1–3*
208.16	falsehood] falshood *1–3*
208.17	nations,] ~$_\wedge$ *1*
208.19	and that,] ~$_\wedge$ *1*
208.23	though] tho' *1* lie] lye *1–3*

208.25 Though] Tho' *1*
208.29 tranquillity] tranquility *1*   mind: but] ~: But *1-5*
208.33 passion,] ~‸ *1* passions‸ *2-5*   except,] ~‸ *1*
209.3 satisfaction,] ~‸ *1*
209.7 inconsiderable,] ~‸ *1-5*
209.9 style] stile *1-3*
209.16 small] smaller *1 2*
209.18 show us,] ~‸ *1*
209.21 Though] Tho' *1*
209.29 and, perhaps,] ~‸~‸ *1*
209.30 destroys‸] ~, *1*
209.31 general, ... style] ~‸ ... stile *1-3*
209.37 style] stile *1-3*
209.38 authorises] authorizes *1-5*
209.39 usages,] ~‸ *1-4*
209.40-1 establishing, ... blameless,] ~‸~‸ *1 2*
209.41 actions,] ~‸ *1*
209.43-210.1 infant? Its ... its ... its] infant? it's ... it's ... it's *1*
210.2 age‸] ~, *5*
210.4 imagine‸] ~, *1 2*   parent‸] ~, *5*
210.5 violate? Yet] violate? yet *1*
210.6 new-born] new born *1-3*
210.7 Greece,] ~‸ *1*   Athenians;] ~, *1*
210.13 its] it's *1*
210.19 case‸] ~, *5*
210.20 One‸ who,] ~‸~‸ *1-4* ~, ~, *5*   enemy,] ~‸ *1 5*
210.22 since, ... save it,] ~‸~‸ *1*
210.23 dying with] dying along with *1-3*
210.25 surprise] surprize *1-3*
210.28 had‸ ... time‸] ~, ~, *5*   authorised] authorized *1-5*
210.29 tolerated] tollerated *1*
210.31 this,] ~‸ *1-3*
210.32 abuse,] ~‸ *1*
210.33 far-fetched] far fetched *1-3*   public] publick *1*
210.39 authorise.] authorize. *1-5*
210.41 what, in itself,] ~‸~‸ *1 2*
211.2 style] stile *1-3*
211.3-4 unlawfulness] unlawfullness *1*
211.5 moment,] ~‸ *1 2*   men's] mens *1-4*
211.6 have] *om. 1-5*
231.34 which,] ~‸ *7*
233.2 aggrandisement,] aggrandizement, *7*
242.7 supposes] imposes *7 This cannot be an author's revision, since, apart from the general improbability of such revision of ed. 6 (see Introduction, 4(a), p. 35), imposes makes far less good sense.*
242.33 are the] ar ethe *7*
246.23 indulgences,] indulgencies, *7*
248.39 poet), assured him,] ~‸~‸ *7*
251.29 Turrenne] Turenne *7*
253.36 who,] ~‸ *7*
254.26 counsel,] ~‸ *7*

258.20   good humour,] good-humour, 7
261.40   fail͜] ~, 7
262.5   passion,] ~͜ 7
265.1   PART VII] *sic 1 See note* ᵃ⁻ᵃ *at beginning of V.2* PART VI *1E*
           2–5 THE / THEORY / OF / MORAL SENTIMENTS / PART VII
           6 7
265.3   Consisting . . . Sections] *om. 1* Consisting of four Sᴇᴄᴛɪᴏɴs *2–5*
265.4   SECTION I] SECT. I *1*
265.12   nature͜] ~, *5*
265.16   respect,] ~͜ *1*
265.21   consist? Or] ~; or *1*
265.22   tenour] tenor *1–3*
265.23   honour,] ~͜ *1–3*
265.24   And, secondly,] and͜~, *1–5*
265.25   character,] ~͜ *1* Or in] or in *1*
265.27   tenour] tenor *1–3* right͜] ~, *5*
265.28   honour,] ~͜ *1–3*
265.29   censure,] ~͜ *1–3*
265.31   Hutcheson] Hutchison *2 3*
265.32   Clarke] Clark *1–3 5*
266.2   others.] ~? *1–3*
266.8   falsehood;] falshood; *1–3*
266.16   SECTION] SECT. *1*
266.25   vicious] vitious *1–3*
267.2   therefore,] ~͜ *1–3*
267.8   affections,] ~͜ *1* direction;] ~, *1*
267.11   virtue, therefore,] ~͜~͜ *1*
267.11–12 affections,] ~͜ *1*
267.21   *Of those . . . Propriety*] rom. *1* Systems . . . Virtue . . . Propriety]
           systems . . . virtue . . . propriety 1 systems . . . virtue . . . propriety 2–5
267.22   Aristotle,] ~͜ *1–3*
267.26   republic,] republick, *1*
267.33   falsehood,] falshood, *1–3*
267.35   subjects] subject *2–5 (corr. 2E)*
267.38   Rep. lib. iv.] rep. lib. 4. *1–3*
268.2   honour,] ~͜ *1–3*
268.3   superiority,] ~͜ *1–3*
268.4   rise] arise *1–3*
268.5   what, . . . language,] ~͜~͜ *1–3*
268.10   conduct,] ~͜ *1*
268.14   solicitations] sollicitations *1–3*
268.15   though] tho' *1*
268.17   nature: the] ~: The *1*
268.20   second,] ~͜ *1–5*
268.21   acuteness,] ~͜ *1–3*
268.24   ideas,] ~͜ *2 3*
268.27   firmness,] ~͜ *7*
268.32   reason, to check͜] ~͜~, *1*
268.35   prompts to] prompts us to *1–3 The revision was probably due to the*
           author, since he often uses the expression prompts to.
268.42–269.1 complete] compleat *1–3*

269.1	soul,] ~∧ *1*
269.6	mind∧] ~, *1*
269.7	its] it's *1*
269.12	complete] compleat *1–3*
269.13	ancient] antient *1–3*
269.15	language,] ~∧ *1–3*
269.23	respect,] ~∧ *1–3*
269.24	connexion] connection *1–3*
269.27	though] tho' *1* tho'/ *2–4*
269.28	serve him∧] ~, *5*
269.32	another's,] anothers, *1–3*
269.37	public] publick *1* See] see *1*
270.3	suitable, . . . situation,] ~∧~∧ *1*
270.6	though] tho' *1* a-kin] *sic 2–7 with no line division (cf. 336.17)* akin *1*
270.20	therefore,] ~∧ *1*
270.30	according to Aristotle*,] *according to Aristotle, *1–3*
270.37	See Aristotle∧] ~, *7*
271.18	its] it's *1*
271.26	on] upon *1*
271.27	generous∧] ~, *1–3*
271.34	temperance,] ~∧ *1–3*
271.35	though] tho' *1*
271.36	vicious] vitious *1–3*
271.40	upon, than, . . . behaviour,] ~∧~∧~∧ *1*
271.42	See Aristotle∧] ~, *7* ch. 1, 2, 3, and 4.] ch. 1. 2. 3 and 4. *1–5*
272.11	and that] and the *2*
272.13	Stoical] stoical *4 5*
272.14	endowed] indowed *1–3*
272.15	self-love,] ~∧ *1* self love, *3*
272.23	agility∧] ~, *4 5*
272.24	body∧] ~, *1–5*
272.25	these;] ~, *1–5*
272.26	with;] ~, *1–5*
272.27	the want.] the contrary. *1–5*
272.28	unwieldiness,] unweildiness, *1 7* body,] ~∧ *7*
272.29	tend] tended *1–5* them;] ~, *1–5*
272.30	were,] ~∧ *1–3*
272.32	of objects,] ~∧ *1–5*
272.33	rejection,] ~∧ *1–5*
272.34	Thus,] ~∧ *1–3* class,] ~∧ *1 2*
272.35	to power,] ~∧ *1*
272.37	See Aristotle∧] ~, *7*
272.38	lib. iii.;] lib. iii.∧ *1–5* segment∧] ~. *1*
273.1	unwieldiness] unweildeness *1* unwieldiness *2 7*
273.3	circumstances∧] ~, *5*
273.5	choice presented] choice which were presented *1*
273.6	obtain them all;] ~: *1–5*
273.7	too,] ~∧ *1–5* rejection offered] rejection which might be offered *1*
273.8	avoided,] ~∧ *1*

273.11   it deserved,] that was due to it, *1*

273.15   nature, or the Author of nature,] ~ₐ or the author of nature ₐ *1*
~, or the author of nature, *2–4*

273.18   ancient] antient *1–5*   Peripatetics.] peripatetics. *1–4*

274.2   prosperityₐ] ~, *4 5*

274.3   Nature, too,] ~ₐ~ₐ *1–5*

274.4   taught us,] ~ₐ *1–4*

274.5   many, . . . all,] ~ₐ~ₐ *1–5*

274.7   with that,] ~ₐ *1*

274.10   powerful,] ~ₐ *1–5*   happenedₐ] ~, *1–5*

274.12–13   ought, first of all,] ~ₐ~ₐ *1*

274.15   But if,] ~ₐ *1–4*

274.20   complete] compleat *1–3*

274.21–2   consisted . . . nature.] the perfection of our nature consists. *1–5*

274.25   Director] director *1–4*

274.27   If,] ~ₐ *1–4*

274.28   or put] or to put *1–5*

274.33   happened; because] ~: Because *1–5*

274.34   whole,] ~; *1* ~: *2–5*

275.4   sense,' says Epictetus, 'are] sense, says Epictetus, are *1–5*

275.9   behove] behoove *1*

275.10   sometimes, too,] ~ₐ~ₐ *1–5*

275.12   Thus, too,] ~ₐ~ₐ *1–5*

275.15   as a man,] ~ₐ *1*   that whole,] ~ₐ *1–5*

275.16   behove] behoove *1–5*

275.19   Do not] Don't *1–5*

275.20   man*?] ~. *1–5*

275.21   lib. ii.] lib. 2. *3*

276.1   Providence,] providence, *1–5*

276.4   by itselfₐ] ~, *1–5*

276.5   genius] Genius *1–5*

276.6   world,] ~ₐ *1–3*

276.7   divine] Divine *1–5*

276.8   mustₐ] ~, *1–5*

276.10   befalls] befals *5*

276.11   connections] connexions *1–5*

276.13   live;] ~: *1–5*   nature] Nature *4 5*

276.17   befall] befal *1–5*

276.19   Gods] gods *4 5*

276.20   thingₐ] ~, *1–5*   should beₐ] ~, *5*

276.21   before-hand] beforehand *1* before-/hand *2–5*

276.23   cheerfulness] chearfulness *1–5*

276.24   shipₐ] ~, *1–5*

276.26   Gods] gods *4 5*

276.29   vesselₐ] ~, *1–5*   pilotₐ] ~, *5*

277.1   to doₐ] ~, *1–5*

277.5   entirely] intirely *1–3*

277.36   chusing] choosing *7*

278.15   though] tho' *1*

278.20   dangersₐ] ~, *1–5*

278.25   And,] ~ₐ *1–5*

278.26   circumstance] circumstances *2–5*
278.26–7   Superintendant] superintendent *1–3* superintendant *4 5*
278.28   divine] Divine *4 5*   Being] being *1–3*
281.2   power] Power *7*
281.12   in it,] ~; *7*
281.20   his happiness,] this happiness, *7*
284.2   illustrious⌃] ~, *7*
291.15   absurd⌃] ~, *7*
293.19   ancient,] antient, *1–3*
293.21   act,] ~⌃ *1–3*
293.22   Clark,] Clarke, *3*
293.25   relations: that] ~: That *1–5*   Woollaston,] Woolaston, *5*
293.28   Lord] lord *1–5*
293.29   allowing⌃] ~, *1*
293.30   sphere;] ~: *1–3*
294.10   is propriety⌃] ~, *1–5*
294.11   though] tho' *1*
294.14   recompense.] recompence. *1–3 5*
294.17–18   complete.] compleat. *1–3*
294.18   For,] ~⌃ *2–5*   though] tho' *1*
294.19   vicious] vitious *1–3*   ingredient;] ~, *1–5*
294.25   account] accounts *1*
294.28   *Of . . . Prudence*] rom. *1*   *Systems . . . Virtue . . . Prudence*] systems virtue . . . prudence *1* systems . . . virtue . . . prudence *2–5*
294.29   ancient] antient *1–3*
294.30   to us,] ~⌃ *1*
294.31   said,] ~⌃ *1 5*
294.33   though] tho' *1*
295.1   Epicurus*,] ~⌃ *1–3*
295.2   objects] object *2*
295.3   thought⌃] ~, *1*   Pleasure⌃ might,] ~, ~⌃ *1*
295.14   avoided,] ~⌃ *1–5*
295.16   desirable,] desireable, *1 2*
295.21   contempt⌃] ~, *4 5*
295.22   lived] live *1*   with,] ~⌃ *1–5*   exposed] expose *2* (*corr. 2E*)
295.29   though] tho' *1*
295.38   after it,] ~⌃ *1*
295.40   In] For *1*
295.42   instant,] ~⌃ *1–5*
296.1   cheerful] chearful *1–3*   past,] ~⌃ *1*
296.4   on] upon *1*
296.7   Though] Tho' *1*
296.12   merely] meerly *1*
296.14–15   continuance,] ~⌃ *1–5*
296.16   that, . . . violent,] ~⌃ ~⌃ *1*
296.20   sensation,] ~⌃ *5*
296.21   could] would *5*
296.32   tranquillity] tranquility *1 2*
296.34   complete] compleat *1–3*
296.36   desirable] desireable *1–3*
296.38   though,] tho', *1* though⌃ *3–5*

296.39   desirable] desireable *1*
297.2   procure] *om. 1 (corr. 1E)*
297.4–5   desirable] desireable *1–3*
297.11   were chosen] are chosen *1*
297.12   submitted] submit *1*
297.13   exposed] expose *1*
297.15   was] is *1*
297.16   enabled] enables *1*   cheerfully,] chearfully, *1–3*
297.17   could] can *1*   and was] and is *1*
297.18   judgment,] ~‸ *1–3*
297.19   labour,] ~‸ *1–3*   choosing] chusing *1–3*
297.21   another's] anothers *1*   was] is *1*
297.22   desirable] desireable *1–3*   on] upon *1*   could not] cannot *1*
297.24   ought,] ~‸ *2–4*
297.26   tranquillity] tranquility *1–3*
297.29–30   ever, . . . fancy,] ~‸ ~‸ *1–3*
297.32   superiors,] ~‸ *1–3*
297.36–7   endanger‸] ~, *1*
297.37   tranquillity,] tranquility, *1–3*
298.1   vices,] ~‸ *1*
298.4   consequences; that] ~; That *1–5*
298.6   respect,] ~‸ *1–3*
298.6–7   us; that] ~; That *1–5*
298.8   dreadful] dreaded *1 2*
298.9   contempt,] ~‸ *1–3*
298.15   nature,] ~‸ *1*
298.17   Author] author *1–3*
298.22   easiest,] ~‸ *1–3*
298.23   and of] and *1*
298.25–6   desire,' said Socrates, 'the] desire, said Socrates, the *1–5*
298.32–3   just, . . . just,] ~‸ ~‸ *1*
298.35   respect,] ~‸ *1*
298.40   justice,] ~‸ *1–3*
299.3   manner,] ~‸ *1–5*
299.4   selfishness,] ~‸ *1*
299.9   practice,] ~‸ *1*
299.10   like] likely *1 2*   *The revision was probably made by the author, to avoid the repetition of* likely *at the end of the sentence.*
299.23   motion,] ~‸ *1–3*
299.29   all of them] all them *5*
299.32   virtue,] ~‸ *1*
299.33   Epicurus,] ~‸ *1*
299.37   desirable] desirable *1–3*   sakes.] sake. *1 2*
299.39   ultimate] primary *1 (corr. 1E)*
300.2   desirable, not merely] desireable, not meerly *1–3*
300.5   merely] meerly *1–3*
300.8   *Of . . . Benevolence*] rom. *1*   *Systems . . . Virtue . . . Benevolence*] systems . . . virtue . . . benevolence *1*   systems . . . *virtue* . . . *benevolence* *2–5*
300.9   though] tho' *1*
300.10   ancient] antient *1–3*

300.14	who∧ . . . account∧] ~, ~, *7*
300.15	later] latter *1*
300.18	Deity] deity *1–3*
300.27	Deity.] deity. *1–5*
300.29	Deity.] deity. *1–5*
300.31–2	that∧ by] ~, by *5*
301.1	Deity] deity *1–5*
301.3	ancient] antient *1–3*
301.4	Christian . . . Reformation] christian . . . reformation *1–5*
301.5	learning∧] ~, *5*
301.7	ancient] antient *1–3*
301.8	Hutcheson∧] ~, *1–5* undoubtedly,] ~∧ *1 3–5*
301.12	already,] ~∧ *1–5*
301.13	affections, that] ~, That *1* (*corr. 1E*)
301.15	beneficent,] beneficent, *1*
301.17	too,] ~∧ *1–5*
301.19	abhor∧] ~, *1*
301.29	from it,] ~∧ *1*
301.31	inclination,] ~∧ *1*
302.1	shew] show *1–5*
302.3	this,] ~∧ *1*
302.6	action,] ~∧ *1*
302.27	referred;] ~, *1*
302.29	contrary,] ~∧ *1* blamable, and vicious.] blameable∧ and vitious. *1* blameable, and vicious. *2 3* blameable, and vicious. *5*
302.30	resistance,] resistence, *1*
302.33	what,] ~∧ *1*
302.39	Inquiry . . . Virtue,] enquiry . . . virtue∧ *1* Enquiry . . . virtue, *2 3* Inquiry . . . virtue, *4*
303.11	one's self] ourselves *1 2* ones self *3 4*
303.12	consistent with,] ~∧ *1*
303.15	vicious] vitious *1–3*
303.17	merely] meerly *1–3* though] tho' *1* tho'/ *2–4* though/ *5*
303.25	to him,] ~∧ *1*
303.28	man] men *1*
303.36	art. 4. also Illustrations] art. 4. also illustrations *1* art. 4. also illustrations *2*
304.12	unsuitableness,] ~∧ *1*
304.14	interest,] ~∧ *1–5*
304.16	attention,] ~∧ *1–3 7*
304.31	man,] ~∧ *1–3*
304.35	though] tho' *1* tho'/ *2–4* though/ *5* failings,] ~∧ *7*
304.41	Though] Tho' *1*
304.43	society,] ~; *1–3*
305.3	Deity,] deity, *1–3*
305.6	Being,] being, *1–5* external,] ~∧ *1*
305.7	complete] compleat *1–3*
305.8	Deity,] deity, *1–3*
305.19	Deity,] deity, *1–3*
305.22	Deity,] deity, *1–3*
305.25	Deity] deity *1–3* Being] being *1–5*

305.26   do so,] ~ₐ *1*
305.27   otherwise: or] ~: Or *1–5*   that ₐ] ~, *5*
305.31   two,] ~ₐ *1–5*
305.33   prudence,] ~ₐ *1*
305.35   Deity.] deity. *1–3*
305.40   utility,] ~ₐ *1–5*
306.1   system,] ~ₐ *1–5*
306.3   others,] ~ₐ *1*
306.4   vicious.] vitious. *1–3*
306.6–7   degree of moderation; . . . the proper bounds.] degree of violence; . . .
            the bounds of moderation. *1*
306.8   consists ₐ] ~, *1–5*
306.14   *Of . . . Systems*] rom. *1*   *Systems*] systems *1*   systems *2–5*
306.19–20   short-sighted] short sighted *1*
306.21   blamable] blameable *1–3 5*
306.22–3   tend, . . . measure,] ~ₐ~ₐ *1*
306.23   balance] ballance *1 2*
306.24   bias] biass *1–3*   action,] ~ₐ *1*
306.25   ancient] antient *1–3*
306.26   awful,] ~ₐ *1–3*
306.29   exile,] ~ₐ *1–3*
306.31–2   are, . . . comparison, . . . seem,] ~ₐ~ₐ~ₐ *1*
306.33   mere] meer *1–3*
307.1   abilities,] ~ₐ *1*
307.3   approbation, that] ~ₐ which *1*
307.11   sobriety,] ~ₐ *1–3*
307.12   beauty,] ~ₐ *1*
307.16   society, if,] ~ₐ~ₐ *1* ~, ~ₐ *5*
307.21   ancient] antient *1–3*
307.22   means,] ~ₐ *1*
307.26   though] tho' *1*
307.28   ease ₐ and safety ₐ] ~, ~, *5*
307.31   merely] meerly *1*
307.33   tranquillity] tranquility *1–3*
307.37   ancient] antient *1–3*
307.40   though] tho' *1*   Stoic,] stoic, *1–3*
308.5   nature,] ~ₐ *1–5*
308.24   over-balances,] overbalances, *1* over-/balances, *2–5*
308.26   occasion,] ~ₐ *1*
309.3   public to] public or *2* (*corr. 2E*)
309.4   mere] meer *1–3*
309.6   mere] meer *1–3*
309.7   public-spirited] public spirited *1–5*
309.7–8   not, . . . sense,] ~ₐ~ₐ *1*
309.8   self-love,] ~ₐ *1*
309.13   approbation,] ~ₐ *1*
309.16   the best] best *1*
309.22   or upon] or *1–5*
310.4   solicits] sollicits *1–3*
310.8   lowest ₐ] ~, *1–5*   mankind,] ~ₐ *1*
310.10   though] tho' *1*

310.14	though] tho' *1* approved of,] ~ˏ *1*
310.16	them,] ~ˏ *1*
310.20	reasonable,] ~ˏ *1–3*
310.21	absurd,] ~ˏ *1–3*
310.26	solicitous] sollicitous *1–3*
310.31	considersˏ . . . affront,] ~, ~ˏ *1*
310.32	impatient,] ~ˏ *1*
310.35	attention] attendance *1–5*
310.43	indifferent] indiffernt *7*
311.2	though] tho' *1*
311.6	Though] Tho' *1* Tho'/ *2 3* Though/ *4 5*
311.7	he has] yet he has *1*
311.14	though] tho' *1*
311.19	though] tho' *1*
311.22	approbationˏ] ~, *1 2*
311.23	though] tho' *1*
311.26	rivalsˏ] ~, *1–5* public.] publick. *1*
311.32	better,] ~ˏ *1*
311.37	magnanimity,] ~; *1*
311.39	Though] Tho' *1*
312.3–4	complete] compleat *1–3*
312.9	nature,] ~; *5*
312.25	names* of the love] names of the *love *1–5*
312.25–6	pleasure, . . . sex,] ~, ~ˏ *1–3* ~ˏ~, *5*
312.26	vicious] vitious *1–3*
312.27	chastity,] ~ˏ *1*
312.28	under,] ~ˏ *1*
312.32	mere] meer *1–3*
312.38	vicious,] vitiousˏ *1* vitious, *2 3*
312.39–40	reference, . . . what are,] ~ˏ~ˏ *1*
312.40	or to what] or what *2*
312.41	sophistry,] ~ˏ *1*
313.3	painting,] ~ˏ *1–3*
313.4	as luxury, sensuality,] ~, ~ˏ *1–5*
313.6	that luxury, sensuality,] ~, ~ˏ *1–3*
313.7	sinceˏ] ~, *1–5*
313.13–14	andˏ secondly, that,] ~, ~, ~, *1–4* ~, ~, ~ˏ *5*
313.14	take placeˏ] ~, *1–3*
313.18	such,] ~ˏ *1* mere] meer *1–3*
313.22	though, perhaps,] tho'ˏ ~ˏ *1*
313.23–4	vice, which . . . causes,] ~ˏ~ˏ *1*
313.31	plausible,] ~ˏ *1*
313.35–6	demonstrated, . . . mankind,] ~ˏ~ˏ *1*
313.39	philosophy,] ~; *5*
314.2	gives] gives us *1*
314.6	though] tho' *1*
314.8	falsehoods] falshoods *1–3*
314.18	Though] Tho' *1*
314.25–6	connexion . . . connexion,] connection . . . connection, *1–3*
314.30–1	Systems . . . Principle . . . Approbation] systems . . . principle . . . approbation *1–5*

314.36   tenour] tenor *1–3*
315.2   honour,] ~ₐ *1–3*
315.3   censure,] ~ₐ *1–3*
315.8   falsehood,] falshood, *1–3*
315.13   reason,] ~ₐ *1 2*
315.22   mere] meer *1–3*
315.24   *Of those . . . Self-love*] rom. *1   Principle . . . Approbation . . . Self-love*]
           principle . . . approbation . . . self-love *1 principle . . . approbation . . .*
           self-love 2–5
315.27   Hobbes,] Hobbs, *1–3*
315.29–30 because ₐ . . . others ₐ] ~, ~, *5*
315.33   interest;] ~, *1–5*
315.35   support,] ~ₐ *1 2 7*   former,] ~ₐ *1 2*
315.36   agreeable,] ~ₐ *7*
315.39   Puffendorff,] Puffendorf. *1* Puffendorff. *2–5*
316.6   machine,] ~ₐ *1*
316.13   jar] jarr *1–3*
316.24   to him:] ~; *1–3*
316.33   mean,] ~ₐ *5*
316.34   villany] villainy *1–3*
316.36   one,] ~ₐ *1*
316.39   that ₐ according] ~, according *5*
317.1   characters.] character. *1–5*
317.3   to us,] ~ₐ *1*
317.20   though] tho' *1*
317.26   die:] ~, *1*
317.31–2   passion, . . . befallen, . . . myself,] ~ₐ~ₐ~ₐ *1*
317.33   you?] ~. *1–5*
317.36   person ₐ] ~, *1–3*
318.2   *Of those . . . Approbation*] rom. *1   Systems . . . Reason . . . Principle*
           . . . Approbation] systems . . . reason . . . principle . . . approbation *1*
           systems . . . reason . . . principle . . . approbation 2–5
318.3   Hobbes,] Hobbs, *1–3*
318.4   nature ₐ] ~, *1–4*   and that ₐ] ~, *5*
318.5   government ₐ] ~, *4 5*
318.15   blamable,] blameable, *1–3 5*
318.16   obedience ₐ] ~, *7*
318.19   Hobbes,] Hobbs, *1–3*
318.24   theologians,] Theologians, *1–5*
318.27   changeable,] ~ₐ *1 2*
318.28   mere] meer *1–3*
318.29   quarters,] ~ₐ *1 7*
318.31   doctrine,] ~ₐ *1*
318.33   endowed] indowed *1–3*   faculty,] ~ₐ *1*   distinguished ₐ] ~, *5*
318.34   affections,] ~ₐ *1*   laudable,] ~ₐ *1–3*
318.35   blamable,] blameable ₐ *1–3* blameable, *5*   vicious.] vitious. *1–3*
318.37   since ₐ] ~, *7*
318.41   Morality,] morality. *1* morality, *2 3*
319.9   which, though] ~ₐ tho' *1* ~ₐ though *2–5*
319.14   Hobbes] Hobbs *1–3*
319.21   reason,] ~ₐ *1 2*

319.22	considered∧ as,] ~, ~∧ *1-4* ~, ~, *5*
319.28	us,] ~∧ *4*
319.29	tenor] tenour *4 5*
320.1	wrong,] ~∧ *1-3*
320.6	though] tho' *1*
320.14	tenor] tenour *4 5*
320.21	own sake,] ~∧ *1 2*
320.24	which,] ~∧ *1 2*
320.27	reason,] ~∧ *1 2*
320.28	therefore, be] ~, is *1-5* desirable] desireable *1* vice be,] vice is, *1-5*
320.29	manner,] ~∧ *1 2*
320.32-3	were, through] ~∧ thro' *1*
321.3	attachment to] attachment for *1-3*
321.9	*Of those . . . Approbation*] rom. *1* Systems . . . Sentiment . . . Principle . . . Approbation] systems . . . sentiment . . . principle . . . approbation *1* systems . . . sentiment . . . principle . . . approbation *2-5*
321.15	agreeable∧] ~, *5*
321.16	former] first *1* stamped] stampt *1-5*
321.17	latter] last *1* blamable,] blameable∧ *1-3* blamable∧ *4* blameable, *5* vicious.] vitious. *1-3*
321.23	Nature,] nature, *1-3*
321.30	too∧] ~, *5*
321.32	Nature] nature *1-3*
321.38	Inquiry . . . Virtue.] Enquiry . . . virtue. *1-3*
322.1-2	us, . . . manner,] ~∧ ~∧ *1*
322.3	mind,] ~∧ *1 2*
322.5	vicious,] vitious, *1-3*
322.9	one∧] ~, *2 3*
322.10	other,] ~∧ *1*
322.13-14	sound∧ . . . colour∧] ~, ~, *5*
322.25	emotions,] ~∧ *1 2* reflex,] ~∧ *1*
322.30	moral sense;] ~, *1 2*
322.31	public sense,] ~∧ *1*
322.37	Passions.] passions. *1-3*
323.2	sense, cannot,] ~∧ ~∧ *1*
323.3	absurdity,] ~∧ *1 2* Who ever] Whoever *1*
323.5	bitter? And,] ~? and, *1*
323.12	surprising,] ~∧ *1-3*
323.14	vicious∧] ~, *5*
323.15	Yet∧ surely∧] ~, ~, *5*
323.19	though] tho' *1*
323.20	magnanimous,] ~∧ *1-3*
323.23	detestation,] ~∧ *5*
323.25	fear,] ~∧ *1-3*
323.27	completely] compleatly *1-3*
323.30	kind;] ~, *1 2*
323.31	merely] meerly *1-3*
323.32	vicious] vitious *1-3*
323.35	man,] ~∧ *1*
323.39	surprising] surprizing *1-3*

323.41   Moral Sense, sect.] moral sense. Sect. *1–3* Moral Sense. Sect.
          4 5 p.] page *1 2* seq.; third edition.] seq. Third Edition. *1–5*
324.4   sentiment;] ∼, *1*
324.6   though] tho' *1*
324.6–7   imperfections,] ∼∧ *1*
324.9   well,] ∼∧ *1* purpose] propose *1 2*
324.10   who∧ notwithstanding∧] ∼, ∼, *5*
324.12   said, perhaps, ... though] ∼∧∼∧ ... tho' *1*
324.15   purpose∧] ∼, *5*
324.21   though] tho' *1*
324.30   man∧] ∼, *1–5*
324.37   former;] ∼: *1–5*
324.40   that∧] ∼, *5*
324.42   plain,] ∼∧ *1–3*
325.1   feel∧] ∼, *5*
325.5   delicate,] ∼∧ *1–3*
325.6   daring,] ∼∧ *1–3*
325.7   may, ... occasions,] ∼∧∼∧ *1*
325.8   entire;] intire; *1–3*
325.10   But∧] ∼, *1–5*
325.12   of, are, in those two cases, quite] of∧ are quite *1* of, are quite *2 3*
          another,] ∼∧ *1*
325.25   disapproved of,] ∼∧ *4 5*
325.27   appear, ... sentiments,] ∼∧∼∧ *1* stamped] stampt *1–5* char-
          acters.] ∼? *5 The question mark was presumably intended for the
          next sentence; see next entry.*
325.29   approbation?] ∼. *1–5* To this question∧] ∼, *1–5*
325.30   there is, I imagine,] I imagine∧ there is∧ *1* answer,] ∼∧ *5*
325.31   said,] ∼∧ *1 2*
325.33   his approbation, ... as, ... measure, ... good;] ∼∧∼∧∼∧∼, *1*
325.34   that, ... contrary,] ∼∧∼∧ *1* ∼∧∼, *2–5*
325.35   as, in some measure,] ∼∧∼∧ *1*
325.37   sentiments,] ∼∧ *1*
326.1–2   approbation, ... sentiment,] ∼∧∼∧ *1*
326.3   Providence] providence *1–3*
326.18   surprising] surprizing *1–3*
326.20   nobody] no body *1–5*
326.30–1 well-contrived] well contrived *1–4*
326.39   hope,] ∼∧ *1–3* This∧] ∼, *5*
326.41   alleged] alledged *1 2*
327.3   rule, or∧ last of all∧] ∼; ∼, ∼, *5*
327.9   from sympathy∧] ∼, *5*
327.12   gratitude of] gratitude to *5 Clearly a printer's error, although a
          change in a substantive*
327.13   well-contrived] well contrived *1–4*
327.18–19 Manner ... Authors ... Rules ... Morality] manner ... authors ...
          rules ... morality *1–5*
327.26   aim at,] ∼∧ *1*
327.30   manners;] ∼, *1* through] thro'/ *2–5*
327.33   precepts∧] ∼, *5*
328.1   ancient] antient *1–3 5*

328.4   disposition_∧ ... the other,] ~, ~; *5*

328.11   virtues,] ~_∧ *1 2*   them:] ~? *5*

328.12   secondly, what] ~, What *1–5*

328.13   tenor] tenour *4 5*

328.15   act.] ~? *5*

328.17   though] tho' *1*

328.22–3   old man_∧] ~, *5*

328.24   austere man_∧] ~, *5*

328.28   What author] Who *1*

328.30   friendship_∧] ~, *5*

328.30–1   attachment which] attachment that *1*

328.32   picture which] picture that *1*   though] tho' *1*

328.33   incomplete,] incompleat, *1–3*

328.38–40   is, indeed, ... founded,] ~_∧~_∧~_∧~_∧ *1*

329.4   Offices,] offices, *1*

329.5   virtues, ... Aristotle_∧] ~; ~, *5*

329.6   Ethics,] ethics, *1 2*

329.8   good-humour, qualities_∧] good humour, ~, *1–5*

329.10   though] tho' *1*

329.14–15   justness_∧ ... observations_∧] ~, ~, *5*

329.20   Ethics,] ethics, *1–3*

329.20–1   science_∧ which, though like criticism_∧ it] ~, ~_∧ tho' like criticism, it
1 ~, ~_∧ though like criticism, it *2–4* ~_∧~, though like criticism,
it *5*

329.25   adorned,] ~_∧ *1*

329.26   youth,] ~_∧ *1 5*

329.34   church,] ~_∧ *1*

329.35   preceding] preceeding *1*

329.37   tenor] tenour *4 5*

330.3   Those_∧] ~, *2 3*   jurisprudence,] Jurisprudence_∧ *1* Jurisprudence, *2 3*

330.4   what_∧] ~, *2 3*

330.4–5   due, ... force;] ~_∧~, *1*

330.6   arbiter,] ~_∧ *1*

330.8–10   casuists, ... hand, ... is, ... force, as what it is,] ~_∧~_∧~_∧~, ~_∧ *1*

330.22   justice,] ~_∧ *4*

330.25   highwayman,] highway-man, *1–3*

330.29   merely] meerly *1–3*

330.30   suppose_∧] ~, *5*   highwayman] highway-man *1–3*

330.32   which] that *1*

330.38–9   jurisprudence,] ~_∧ *1 2*

330.41   man,] ~_∧ *1*   to that] to the *5*

331.6   truth_∧] ~, *5*

331.7   falsehood,] falshood, *2 3*

331.9   ancients,] antients, *1–3*

331.13   mere] meer *1–3*

331.14   ancient] antient *1–3*

331.20   rule_∧] ~, *7*

331.22   chuse] choose *4 5*

331.23   highwayman] highway-man *1–3*

331.24   perform,] ~_∧ *1 2*

331.31	an hundred ... though] a hundred ... tho' *1*
331.33	appear_∧] ~, *2 3* mankind,] ~_∧ *1*
331.35	La] la *1-5*
332.2	authorise.] authorize. *1-5*
332.20	though] tho' *1*
332.25-6	folly, ... ignominy.] ~_∧ ... Ignominy. *1*
332.27	falsehood_∧] ~, *1* falshood_∧ *2 3*
332.27-8	dreadful, and,] ~, ~_∧ *1-3*
332.35	irretrievably.] irretriveably. *1 2*
332.36	solicitation] sollicitation *1-3*
333.2	promise_∧] ~, *5*
333.9	through] thro' *1* kind_∧] ~, *1-5*
333.12	casuistry_∧] ~, *1-3*
333.14	though ... though] tho'. ... tho' *1*
333.16	authors_∧] ~, *5*
333.19-20	distinguishing, and, perhaps,] ~_∧ ~_∧ ~_∧ *1* ~_∧ ~, ~, *2*
333.23	justice_∧] ~, *1-4*
333.24	Christian] christian *1-3*
333.29	receding] receeding *1*
333.30	Christian] christian *1-3* purity,] ~_∧ *1 2*
333.32	penance] pennance *1 2* behoved] behooved *1*
333.33	Deity.] deity. *1 2*
333.35	terror] terrour *4 5*
333.37	disburthen] disburden *1*
334.5	family. They] ~, They *1*
334.6	though] tho' *1*
334.7	regular_∧] ~, *5*
334.19	though] tho' *1*
334.30	remorse_∧] ~, *5*
334.32	terrors] terrours *4 5*
334.38	too,] ~_∧ *1* that_∧] ~, *5*
334.39	though] tho' *1*
334.40	censure,] ~_∧ *1-3*
334.43	was_∧ therefore_∧] ~, ~, *1 2*
335.6	suffering_∧] ~, *1-3*
335.19	though] tho' *1*
335.20	cannot] can/not *1 Perhaps a misprint for* can-/not
335.21	though] tho' *1*
335.22	nobody,] no person, *1-5*
335.23	upon,] ~_∧ *1*
337.22-3	which_∧ ... instruments_∧] ~, ~, *5*
337.26	other's] others *1-3* bosoms,] ~_∧ *1*
337.31	pleasing,] ~_∧ *1*
337.36	understanding_∧] ~, *1*
337.40	neighbours_∧] ~, *5*
337.41	concealing;] ~, *1-4*
338.9	curiosity;] ~, *1-5*
339.17	concupiscence;] ~: *1-5* veracity,] ~_∧ *1 2*
339.18	promises,] ~_∧ *1-3*
339.20	rules] Rules *1 2*
339.31	behaviour_∧] ~, *5*

339.40	style] stile *1–3*
340.2	authorise] authorize *4 5*
340.5	errors,] errours, *3–5*
340.10	altogether;] ~, *1–5*
340.13	describing,] ~_∧ *1*
340.14	modesty,] ~_∧ *1–3*
340.18	Offices,] offices, *1 2*
340.23	complete] compleat *1–3*
340.26	receding] receeding *1*
340.30	public] publick *1 2*
340.38	too,] ~_∧ *1*
341.5	civilized] civilised *1–3*
341.6	are, . . . manners,] ~_∧~_∧ *1–3* rude_∧] ~, *5*
341.9	though] tho' *1*
341.11	exactly, . . . case,] ~_∧~_∧ *1*
341.13	though_∧ . . . authority,] tho'_∧ ~_∧ *1*
341.16	lawyers,] ~_∧ *1*
341.18	inquiry] enquiry *1–3*
341.19	justice_∧] ~, *1*
341.22–3	through_∧ . . . foundation of_∧] ~, ~, *5*
341.23	But though] But tho' *1–5*
341.30–1	Offices, . . . Ethics,] offices, . . . ethics, *1 2*
341.35	there is,] ~_∧ *4*
341.36	police,] ~_∧ *1* first_∧] ~, *2–5*
342.2	through,] thro', *1*
342.4	complete] compleat *1–3*
342.9	revenue,] ~_∧ *1–3*
342.12	THE END] FINIS *1 2 om. 5*

for its own sakes and without any further view Duty, as it does to us, the natural and proper object of ... before the Lover and ... and Vice of hatred and punishment ... we which cannot surely be satisfied with demanding some atonement, some expiation for the Offences of man..., and Revelation teaches us that this atonement has not only been demanded but has been paid for, at least, the more valuable part of Mankind

When some occasions indeed we banish ... from a View to the general interest of ... which ... we imagine cannot be otherwise suffered. The punishments, for Example, which military discipline prescribes are all inflicted from this motive, and a Sentinel who falls asleep upon his Watch suffers death by the ... and Laws of War because such carelessness might endanger the whole Army. In our hearts we cannot blame this necessary severity. Nothing can be more just than that one man should be sacrificed to the security of thousands. But do we regard this punishment in the same light in which we look upon that of an ungrateful murderer or parricide? Does our heart naturally applaud the same Ardor with which it goes along with the other? We look upon the one as an unfortunate Victim who indeed must be devoted to the interest of Numbers but whom in our hearts we would be glad to save, & we are only sorry that the Interests of many should oppose it. If the other should escape from punishment it would excite our highest indignation & we should call upon God to avenge, in another world, that Crime which the injustice of Mankind had neglected to chastise upon Earth.

The violation of Justice is what Mankind will never submit to from their Equals. It provokes the Resentment of the injured and incites them to take vengeance upon the Offender. They feel that Mankind applaud

First page of manuscript described in Appendix II

Appendix II

THE PASSAGE ON ATONEMENT, AND A MANUSCRIPT FRAGMENT
ON JUSTICE

TMS II.ii.3 criticizes the view that the idea of justice arises solely from utility. In editions 1–5, the chapter ends with a paragraph of orthodox theological doctrine on retributive justice. The paragraph is unusual for Smith, both in its concluding firm endorsement of Christian revelation, and in the 'high-flying' rhetoric of an earlier pious phrase ('neither can he see any reason why the divine indignation should not be let loose without restraint, upon so vile an insect, as he is sensible that he himself must appear to be '—slightly toned down for edition 3). In edition 6, the paragraph was removed and replaced by a single dry sentence: 'In every religion, and in every superstition that the world has ever beheld, accordingly, there has been a Tartarus as well as an Elysium; a place provided for the punishment of the wicked, as well as one for the reward of the just.'

This important change, made in 1788–9, would naturally lead one to think that Smith had become more sceptical about orthodox religion; or perhaps that he felt less inclination or obligation to express pious sentiments once he had quitted a Professorship of Moral Philosophy. (It is clear from the Advertisement to edition 6 that some of the revisions then made had been contemplated long before.) There has in fact been a curious controversy about possible reasons for Smith's withdrawal of the paragraph.

William Magee, Archbishop of Dublin, published in 1801 a volume of *Discourses on the Scriptural Doctrines of Atonement and Sacrifice*. In edition 2, 1809, he added a number of Illustrations and Explanatory Dissertations, and in one of these (No. XXII) he quoted part of Adam Smith's paragraph on divine justice, taking great satisfaction in the thought that the orthodox view of the Christian doctrine of Atonement was endorsed by a distinguished philosopher, 'and he too the familiar friend of David Hume'. Elsewhere in edition 2 of his book (Dissertation No. LXIX), Magee attacked Hume along with Bolingbroke and expressed his astonishment that '*such a man as Adam Smith*' could describe Hume, after the latter's death, as having come as near as possible 'to the idea of a PERFECTLY WISE AND VIRTUOUS MAN'. The emphasis of capital letters is of course Magee's own addition to the words that Smith had used of Hume.

What happened next is pleasantly recounted by Rae, *Life*, 428–9. (Rae's first quotation from Magee is not entirely accurate.) Magee had ended his illustration from TMS by saying that the views which Smith had supported 'as the natural suggestions of reason' were nevertheless 'the scoff of sciolists and witlings'. 'The sciolists and witlings', writes Rae, 'were not slow in returning the scoff, and pointing out that while Smith was, no doubt, as an intellectual authority all that the Archbishop claimed for him, his authority really ran against the Archbishop's view and not in favour of it, inasmuch as he had withdrawn the passage relied on from the last edition of his work.' Magee tried to extricate himself from his discomfiture by adding a footnote in edition 3 of his own book, 1812, attributing Smith's withdrawal to 'the infection of David Hume's society . . . one proof more . . . of the danger, even to the most enlightened, from a familiar contact with infidelity'; and then Magee referred again to Smith's obituary praise of Hume which had shocked so many of the conventionally religious. Rae himself joins in 'returning the scoff' with the comment that Smith's 'intercourse with Hume was at its closest when he first published the passage in 1759, whereas Hume was fourteen years in his grave when the passage was omitted'. But Magee was under a misapprehension. He thought (and, as we shall see, he was not the only one to think) that the passage had been withdrawn long before edition 6. In the added footnote in which he refers to the influence of Hume, Magee writes: 'The fact is, that in the later editions of the *Theory of Moral Sentiments*, no one sentence appears of the extract which has been cited above, and which I had derived from the first edition, the only one that I possessed.'

Rae goes on to say that 'there is no reason to believe that Smith's opinion about the atonement was anywise different in 1790 from what it was in 1759, or for doubting his own explanation of the omission, which he is said to have given to certain Edinburgh friends, that he thought the passage unnecessary and misplaced'. The report of this explanation is in vol. ii, 40, of *Memoirs of the Life and Works of Sir John Sinclair* (1837) by his son, the Rev. John Sinclair. What Archdeacon Sinclair actually says of Smith is this:

In the second edition of his Theory of Moral Sentiments, he omitted, on the suggestion, as is supposed, of his sceptical friend, a splendid passage, referred to by Archbishop Magee as among the ablest illustrations of the doctrine of Atonement. In the suspicion thus excited, my father did not participate. He was anxious to think favourably of a venerated friend. Smith himself justified the omission alluded to, not on the ground that the doctrine of Atonement was unfounded, but that the paragraph was unnecessary and misplaced.

When Archdeacon Sinclair states that the passage was omitted in edition 2, he is obviously just following what he took to be the natural sense of Magee's footnote and has not himself looked at the relevant editions of TMS. Sinclair goes on to evoke a moving image of Smith on his knees at his mother's deathbed, praying to the Redeemer whom he was alleged to have rejected. This is supposed to be evidence either that the withdrawal of the passage on the Redeemer did not imply any loss of faith or that the faith was later regained. In fact Smith's mother died (in 1784) several years before the withdrawal in edition 6. It is not clear from Archdeacon Sinclair's account whether Smith's reasons for the omission of the paragraph were given directly to Sir John Sinclair himself or, as Rae apparently infers, to others in Edinburgh. Presumably Archdeacon Sinclair was told the story by his father. If Smith did give the explanation to anyone, it must have been within the short space of time that intervened between the publication of edition 6 and his death. That would have happened only if this particular revision (a minor one, compared with others) had been noted and had excited remark very soon after publication. Oddly enough, Rae himself, despite the reference to Sinclair on p. 429 of the *Life*, says on p. 428 that 'the suppression of the passage about the atonement escaped notice for twenty years' until Magee quoted it.

After mentioning Sinclair's report, Rae then writes:

As if taking an odd revenge for its suppression, the original manuscript of this particular passage seems to have reappeared from between the leaves of a volume of Aristotle in the year 1831, when all the rest of the MS. of the book and of Smith's other works had long gone to destruction.

At the end of this sentence we are referred to a footnote, which simply says 'Add. MSS., 32,574', and so suggests that the manuscript which came to light in 1831 is now in the British Library (the British Museum). In fact this is not so. Additional Manuscript 32,574 in the British Library is Volume XVI of the Notebooks of the Rev. John Mitford (1781–1859), and it is the source of Rae's information. The first entry in this volume is signed 'J. Mitford' and is dated '1855. Sept. 26.' On leaf number 64, there is the following note:

on Adam Smith's Moral Sentiments. 'I am sorry to find sd Bp. Bathurst, that his Splendid Passage on the necessity of a Redeemer, was omitted in the Second Edition.' The omission probably owing to his Acquaintance with Hume.
B^p Bathurst and Chalmers. +

'Second Edition' and 'Splendid Passage' show that Bathurst was simply relying on Sinclair's book. The sign + at the end of Mitford's original entry was presumably added later, together with this note on the facing verso of leaf 63:

+
A. Smith's injunctions to his Executors to destroy all his loose Mss. were strictly followed. but that Passage so long[?] preserved, reappeared from between the folds of a Volume of Aristotle in 1831.

Discovered by Revd W. B. Cunningham of Preston Pans into whose hands Dr Smith's Library had passed

The Rev. W. B. Cunningham of Prestonpans was the husband of one of the two daughters of David Douglas, Lord Reston, the cousin to whom Adam Smith bequeathed his books and other possessions. On the death of Lord Reston, Adam Smith's library was divided between the two daughters. (See Bonar, *Catalogue 2*, intro. xvi–xvii.)

W. R. Scott, *ASSP*, 57–9, describes one of four manuscripts in the possession of the Glasgow University Library. This particular manuscript consists of one folio sheet of four pages, and the four documents together contain fifteen pages of writing. Scott says:

The date of these four documents is of great importance. The many avocations of Adam Smith during the first eight years he was at Glasgow [i.e. 1751–9] make it highly improbable, if not impossible, that they could have been written then, and thus they may be assigned to the Edinburgh period [i.e. 1748–51].

The one manuscript which is relevant to the present discussion is taken by Scott to be 'introductory to a group of lectures' on jurisprudence, delivered in Edinburgh and corresponding to the Glasgow lectures on jurisprudence, a Report of which was published by Edwin Cannan in 1896. Scott describes the manuscript as follows:

There had been a very brief account of moral obligation, and the surviving manuscript begins with the statement that 'duty, for its own sake and without any further view, is the natural and proper object of love and reward, and vice of hatred and punishment'. Here follow the sentences on the Atonement, which appeared in the first five editions of the *Theory of Moral Sentiments* with small alterations. At this point in the *Theory* a chapter ends, and in the next a different aspect of the subject is begun. Here [i.e. in the manuscript] the discussion continues with material rewards and punishments. The sentry found asleep at his post is discussed, then the argument passes on to the institution of the civil magistrate. The authority of custom or statute law is traced back to the natural principles of justice, and the study of the rules which express it constitutes Natural Jurisprudence or the Theory of the General Principles of Law. Adam Smith indicates that he will give a particular discourse upon that subject. The concluding part of this paper discusses the relation between Justice and Benevolence and between the latter and resentment and punishment. No doubt the lectures went on (as indicated) to discuss how far these principles find expression in existing legal systems.

In footnote 2 to p. 58, Scott writes:

This manuscript may be that which was found in a volume of Aristotle in 1831 (Rae, *Life*, p. 261 [error for p. 429]) and described as that of a part of the *Theory of Moral Sentiments*. The beginning of it very closely resembles the corresponding part of the *Theory*. The remainder is quite different.

In footnote 5 to p. 320 of his book, Scott refers again to what he calls 'the celebrated sentences on the Atonement', and writes:

There is no reason to doubt Adam Smith's own statement that they were withdrawn in the sixth edition of the *Theory* (1790) because they were misplaced. Rae mentions (*Life*, p. 429) that the manuscript, containing the sentences, was found in a volume of Aristotle in the year 1831. Whether Rae intended it or not, this has been taken to mean that the fragment discovered was a part of the *Theory*. It was not, being the part of the Edinburgh Lectures which is described in Part I, Chapter V [i.e. pp. 57–9]. This MS. begins with the conclusion of a discussion which is that 'duty for its own sake' is 'the natural and proper object of love and reward'. As first written this lecture went on to examine in some detail the principles of legal sanctions. At an early revision the sentences on the Atonement were inserted. This obviously was not a happy arrangement. In the *Theory* the passage was expanded and made to close Part II, Section ii, Chapter iii. Then follows Section iii, which discusses the influence of fortune upon the sentiments of mankind, which is far from being an ideal collocation.

Scott did not print the text of the manuscript described in these quotations. It is given below, but first some comment needs to be made on several points in Scott's account.

(1) Scott's ground for assigning this and the other three short manuscripts (amounting in all to fifteen pages) to the period of the Edinburgh lectures is extraordinarily flimsy. Since Smith had the time, between 1751 and 1759, not only to write TMS but to compose courses of lectures which extended beyond the subject-matter of that book to natural theology, jurisprudence, and economics, why should it be supposed that his 'many avocations' made it 'highly improbable, if not impossible,' for him to compose these pieces which are all concerned with subjects that were included in his lectures as Professor of Moral Philosophy?

(2) Scott's assertion that the initial words of the manuscript had been preceded by 'a very brief account of moral obligation' (how did he know that it was 'very brief'?) is a figment of his imagination, produced by a misreading of the first word of the manuscript, which is 'Deity', but which Scott took to be 'Duty'. In

any case, Smith would never have said that *duty* is 'the natural object of love and reward, and vice of hatred and punishment'. Obviously *virtue* is what corresponds to vice in this connection. The manuscript begins with words that do not make a complete sentence: 'Deity, as it does to us, for its own sake and without any further view the natural and proper object of Love and Reward and Vice of hatred and punishment.' Scott must have supposed that the word 'is' had been inadvertently omitted before 'the natural and proper object', and he conveniently ignored the phrase 'as it does to us'. Clearly the word 'Deity' will have been preceded by some such words as 'Virtue appears to the'. In editions 1–2 of TMS, the paragraph that was withdrawn from edition 6 contains the following sentence (in editions 3–5, the first words are revised to 'Our untaught, natural sentiments, all'):

All our natural sentiments prompt us to believe, that as perfect virtue is supposed necessarily to appear to the Deity, as it does to us, for its own sake, and without any further view, the natural and proper object of love and reward, so must vice, of hatred and punishment.

(3) In the footnote to his p. 58, Scott says that the manuscript 'may be' that which was found in a volume of Aristotle in 1831, though in the footnote to p. 320 he takes for granted that it was. Scott evidently did not look up Rae's reference to the British Library manuscript, but there is in fact positive proof that the Glasgow manuscript is the one referred to in Mitford's second note. Mitford says the manuscript was 'Discovered by Revd W. B. Cunningham of Preston Pans'. In the margin of the first page of the Glasgow manuscript, there is written, in a later hand:

W.B.C. Free Church Manse
Prestonpans.

(4) In the footnote to his p. 320, Scott says there is no reason to doubt Smith's own statement that the paragraph of editions 1–5 was withdrawn because it was 'misplaced'. This gives only half of the reason as reported by Sinclair and Rae, namely that Smith thought the passage 'unnecessary and misplaced'. The addition of 'unnecessary' makes a difference.

(5) Judging from what Scott says in the note to his p. 320, he appears to think that the manuscript 'as first written' did not contain anything about the Atonement. 'At an early revision the sentences on the Atonement were inserted.' In fact, the manuscript 'as first written' had this as its second sentence:

The Justice of the Deity we think cannot surely be satisfied with [error for 'without'] demanding some attonement, some expiation for the Offences of Mankind, and Revelation teaches us that this attonement has not only been demanded but has been paid for, at least, the more valuable part of Mankind.

Later, two sentences, corresponding to further words in the paragraph of editions 1–5 of TMS, were inserted before the sentence just quoted, but they are about our consciousness of human imperfection in the sight of God rather than about the idea of atonement.

(6) The remainder of the manuscript, that is to say, by far the greater part of it, does not correspond to anything in the so-called paragraph on 'atonement'; but many of the later words of the manuscript correspond to *other* passages in

the printed texts of TMS, and on the second page there occur the very words 'the Theory of moral Sentiments'. Consequently some caution is needed before accepting Scott's hasty conclusion that the manuscript was not a part of TMS but belonged to the Edinburgh lectures.

Having cleared Scott's preconceptions from our path, it will be best to describe the manuscript anew, and to give its full text, before discussing further its relation to the printed editions of TMS.

The manuscript (Glasgow University Library, MS. Gen. 1035/227) was originally a single folio sheet (the two halves of which have now come apart) of four pages. The watermarks, briefly mentioned by Scott in a footnote ending on his p. 266, are similar to two of those which Scott describes on his p. 322, one of them being illustrated in Plate XV which faces that page. One half of the sheet has as its watermark 'G.R.' within a circular emblem and surmounted by a crown, with the word 'DURHAM' beneath. The other half-sheet has the watermark of Britannia within a picket fence, and the motto 'PRO PATRIA', as illustrated in Scott's Plate XV, but in reverse; that is to say, Britannia is sitting on the left and facing right, with the motto at her right, while in Scott's plate she is sitting on the right and facing left, with the motto at her left. The writing on the manuscript covers the whole of the first three pages, and three-quarters of the fourth page, indicating that it then came to an end. Catchwords at the foot of the first three pages make quite clear the order in which they were written. Each of the pages has a margin at the left, and the top half of the margin on the first page contains a lengthy insertion, preceded by a figure 2 or a sign resembling it, which Adam Smith was evidently accustomed to use for this purpose, as can be seen from two of the other manuscripts which were reproduced in facsimile by Scott (*ASSP*, 381, 383, 385). The place, in the original writing, at which the addition is to be inserted, is likewise indicated by a figure 2. The bottom half of the margin of the first page contains the later entry made by Mr. Cunningham. The margins on the other three sheets are left blank.

In the text of the manuscript, the words originally written, and most of the revisions and insertions, are in the hand of an amanuensis. Two or three of the revisions, however, are in the hand of Adam Smith himself; e.g. the word 'men' substituted for 'Mankind' in the first paragraph; and the figure 2 at the end of the first sentence, though not the corresponding figure 2 that precedes the inserted passage in the margin. Some of the remaining revisions are written above the relevant line. Others, however, are written on the same line as, and immediately after, cancelled words, showing that Smith made some changes as he dictated the piece. This feature of the document is one piece of evidence for the conclusion that it was written before the manuscript actually used for edition 1 of TMS.

In the text that follows, square brackets enclose words or letters that are struck out or over-written in the manuscript, while angle brackets enclose words or letters that constitute revisions of cancelled material or later insertions. It will be recalled that the manuscript begins in the middle of a sentence.

Deity, as it does to us, ⟨for its own sake and without any further view⟩ the natural and proper object of Love and Reward and Vice of hatred and punishment.⟨2⟩ ⟨2. Nay vice we are apt to fear should appear before the holiness of God more worthy of punishment than the imperfection of human Virtue can ever be of Reward.

Man when about to appear before a Being of such perfect Sanctity can feel but little Confidence in his own merit[.]⟨;⟩ [But the divine Justice etc.] and when he remembers the numberless blemishes and imperfections in his own Conduct must dread punishment rather than hope for Reward. The divine Justice etc.⟩ The ⟨divine⟩ Justice [of the Deity] we think cannot surely be satisfied with⟨out⟩ demanding some attonement, some expiation for the Offences of [Mankind]⟨men⟩, and Revelation teaches us that this attonement has not only been demanded but has been paid for, at least, the more valuable part of Mankind.

[There are indeed] Upon some occasions indeed we punish meerly from a View to the general interest of Society which [cann] we imagine cannot be otherwise supported. The punishments, for Exemple, which military discipline prescribes are all inflicted from this motive, and a Centinel who falls asleep upon his Watch [is] suffers death by the Laws of War because such carelessness might endanger the whole Army. In our hearts we cannot blame this necessary Severity. Nothing can be more just, than that one man [can]⟨should⟩ be sacrificed to the security of thousands. But do we regard th[e]⟨is⟩ punishment in the same light in which we look upon that of an ungrateful murderer or parricide[;]⟨?⟩ Does our heart naturally applaud[1] the same Ardor with which it goes along with the other? We look upon the one as an unfortunate Victime who indeed must be devoted to the interest of Numbers but whom in our hearts we would be glad to save, and we are only sorry that the Interests of [others] many should oppose it. If the other should escape from punishment it would excite our highest indignation and we [w]⟨sh⟩ould call upon God to avenge ⟨in another world⟩ that Crime which the injustice of Mankind had neglected to chastise upon Earth.

The violation of Justice is what Mankind will never submit to from their Equals. It provokes the Resentment of the injured and incites them to take vengeance upon the Offender. They feel that Mankind applaud and go along with ⟨t⟩h[i]⟨e⟩m when they punish him,[2] and they imagine that they become contemptible when they do not. That civil Society may not be a Scene of Bloodshed ⟨confusion⟩ and disorder every man revenging himself at his own hand whenever he fancies himself injured, the Magistrates in all Governments that have acquired considerable Authority employs the power of the commonwealth to enforce the practice of Justice, and to give Satisfaction to the injured either by punishing the offender or by obliging him to compensate the wrong that has been done. The magistrate promises to hear all complaints of injustice, to enquire diligently into the circumstances alledged upon both Sides, and to give that redress which to any impartial person shall appear to be just and equitable. Hence the origin of both civil and criminal Jurisdiction. The Rules by which the magistrate[s] in [all] ⟨each⟩ countries actually regu[l]lates all his discisions of this kind [which]⟨whether⟩ established upon express Statute, upon acc[o--?]⟨iden⟩tal custom or upon their own evident equity constitute the civil and criminal Jurisprudence of that Country. The Rules by which it is most suitable to the natural principles of Justice, or to the Analogy of those Sentiments upon which our Sense of it is founded that such descisions should be regulated, const[-?]⟨i⟩tute what is called Natural Jurisprudence, or the Theory of the general principles of Law. they make a very important part of the Theory of moral Sentiments. I shall not at present, however, stop to analyse them, as I intend hereafter to give a particular discourse upon that Subject.

When our benevolence to each particular person is exactly proportioned to the

---

[1] The word 'with' has presumably been omitted.

[2] In the final word of this clause, the amanuensis appears to have begun to write 'th' (i.e. 'them'?) and then changed it to 'h'.

importance of those circumstances which point them out to our favourable regard, we are, by a metaphor, said to do them Justice[:]⟨;⟩ and we are said to do them injustice when it is otherwise. When we chuse [-?]⟨r⟩ather, for exemple, to do a good Office to a new acquaintance than to an Old friend we are said to do Injustice to the latter. This, however, is a different Species of Injustice from that which we have been treating of above. It does not consist in doing hurt, but in not doing good according to the most perfect propriety. In the Schools it has been distinguished by the name of d[e?]⟨i⟩stributive Justice, as the former, which can alone properly be called Justice, has been denominated commutat[--?]⟨iv⟩e Justice. In the observation of distributive Justice consists the proper exercise of all the social and beneficent Virtues. It cannot be extorted by force. The violation of it does no positive harm, and therefor, exposes to no punishment. The Rules which determine the external actions which it prescribes, are loose and unaccurate and fall short of that exact pre[s]⟨c⟩ision, which, as I shall show hereafter, is peculiar to the Rules of what is properly called Justice. The Rules of punishment have been by most Writers referred to distributive Justice as well as the Rules of Beneficence, and they seem to have imagined that improper vengea[--?]⟨nc⟩e was an impropriety of the same kind with improper Benevolence. There is indeed a certain degree of looseness and inaccuracy [of] in what may be called the natural principles of punishment. What is the extent of the Right which is violated, and wherein consists its v[e?]⟨i⟩olation, can in almost all cases be determined with exact precision. But what degree of Resentment or punishment is due for this violation cannot easily be fixed exactly by general Rules which have any great foundation in nature; but varies with every variety of Circumstances: And so far the principles and rules of punishments resemble those of Beneficence. But they differ from them in another Circumstance which is much more essential, and which those Writers have not perhaps, sufficiently attended to. Improper punishment, punishment which is either not due at all or which exceeds the demerit of the Crime, is an injury to the Criminal, may and ought to be opposed by force, and if inflicted, exposes the person who inflicts it to punishment in his turn. But meer improper Beneficence cannot be opposed by force and exposes the person who exercises it to no punishment.

Compare the following set of extracts from TMS. References are given to the arrangement of chapters and paragraphs in the present (and so in the sixth) edition, but since the manuscript is earlier than any of the printed texts, the actual words and punctuation of the quotations are taken (except for the sixth extract) from edition 1.

All our natural sentiments prompt us to believe, that as perfect virtue is supposed necessarily to appear to the Deity, as it does to us, for its own sake, and without any further view, the natural and proper object of love and reward, so must vice, of hatred and punishment. . . . If we consult our natural sentiments, we are apt to fear, lest before the holiness of God, vice should appear to be more worthy of punishment than the weakness and imperfection of human virtue can ever seem to be of reward. Man, when about to appear before a being of infinite perfection, can feel but little confidence in his own merit, . . . he can easily conceive, how the numberless violations of duty, of which he has been guilty, should render him the proper object of aversion and punishment; . . . Some other intercession, some other sacrifice, some other atonement, he imagines, must be made for him, beyond what he himself is capable of making, before the purity of the divine justice can be reconciled to his manifold offences. The doctrines of revelation . . . show us . . . that the most powerful intercession has been made, and that the most dreadful atonement has been paid for our manifold transgressions and iniquities. (II.ii.3, final paragraph —the one suppressed in edition 6)

Upon some occasions, indeed, we both punish and approve of punishment, merely from a view to the general interest of society, which, we imagine, cannot otherwise be secured. Of this kind are all the punishments inflicted for breaches of what is called either civil police, or military discipline. . . . A centinel, for example, who falls asleep upon his watch, suffers death by the laws of war, because such carelessness might endanger the whole army. This severity may, upon many occasions, appear necessary, and, for that reason, just and proper. When the preservation of an individual is inconsistent with the safety of a multitude, nothing can be more just than that the many should be preferred to the one. Yet this punishment, how necessary soever, always appears to be excessively severe. The natural atrocity of the crime seems to be so little, and the punishment so great, that it is with great difficulty that our heart can reconcile itself to it. . . . A man of humanity . . . must make an effort . . . before he can . . . go along with it . . . It is not, however, in this manner, that he looks upon the just punishment of an ungrateful murderer or parricide. His heart, in this case, applauds with ardour, and even with transport, the just retaliation which seems due to such detestable crimes, . . . He looks upon the centinel as an unfortunate victim, who, indeed, must, and ought to be, devoted to the safety of numbers, but whom still, in his heart, he would be glad to save; and he is only sorry, that the interest of the many should oppose it. But if the murderer should escape from punishment, it would excite his highest indignation, and he would call upon God to avenge, in another world, that crime which the injustice of mankind had neglected to chastise upon earth.   (II.ii.3.11)

There is, however, another virtue, . . . of which the violation exposes to resentment, and consequently to punishment. This virtue is justice: the violation of justice is injury: . . . It is, therefore, the proper object of resentment, and of punishment, . . . As mankind go along with, and approve of, the violence employed to avenge the hurt which is done by injustice, so they much more go along with, and approve of, that which is employed to prevent and beat off the injury, . . .

(II.ii.1.5)

Among equals each individual is naturally . . . regarded as having a right both to defend himself from injuries, and to exact a certain degree of punishment . . .

(II.ii.1.7)

As the violation of justice is what men will never submit to from one another, the publick magistrate is under a necessity of employing the power of the commonwealth to enforce the practice of this virtue. Without this precaution, civil society would become a scene of bloodshed and disorder, every man revenging himself at his own hand whenever he fancied he was injured. To prevent the confusion which would attend upon every man's doing justice to himself, the magistrate, in all governments that have acquired any considerable authority, undertakes to do justice to all, and promises to hear and to redress every complaint of injury. In all well-governed states too not only judges are appointed for determining the controversies of individuals, but rules are prescribed for regulating the decisions of those judges; and these rules are, in general, intended to coincide with those of natural justice. . . . In no country do the decisions of positive law coincide exactly in every case with the rules which the natural sense of justice would dictate.

(VII.iv.36)

The wisdom of every state or commonwealth endeavours . . . to restrain those who are subject to its authority, from hurting or disturbing the happiness of one another. The rules which it establishes for this purpose, constitute the civil and criminal law of each particular state or country. The principles upon which those rules either are, or ought to be founded, are the subject of a particular science, of all sciences by far the most important, but hitherto, perhaps, the least cultivated, that of natural jurisprudence; concerning which it belongs not to our present subject to enter into any detail. (VI.ii.intro.2. This passage was first added in edition 6.)

It might have been expected that the reasonings of lawyers . . . should have led them to aim at establishing a system of what might properly be called natural jurisprudence, or a theory of the general principles which ought to run through and be the foundation of the laws of all nations. . . . I shall in another discourse endeavour to give an account of the general principles of law and government, . . . I shall not, therefore, at present enter into any further detail concerning the history of jurisprudence. (VII.iv.37)

In one sense we are said to do justice to our neighbour when we abstain from doing him any positive harm, and do not directly hurt him, . . . This is that justice which I have treated of above, the observance of which may be extorted by force, and the violation of which exposes to punishment. In another sense we are said not to do justice to our neighbour unless we conceive for him all that love, respect and esteem, which his character, his situation, and his connection with ourselves, render suitable and proper for us to feel, and unless we act accordingly. It is in this sense that we are said to do injustice to a man of merit who is connected with us, tho' we abstain from hurting him in every respect, if we do not exert ourselves to serve him . . . The first sense of the word coincides with what Aristotle and the Schoolmen call commutative justice, and with what Grotius calls the *justitia expletrix*, which consists in abstaining from what is anothers, and in doing voluntarily whatever we can with propriety be forced to do. The second sense of the word coincides with what some have called distributive justice [Added footnote: 'The distributive justice of Aristotle is somewhat different . . .'], and with the *justitia attributrix* of Grotius, which consists in proper beneficence, in the becoming use of what is our own, and in the applying it to those purposes either of charity or generosity, to which it is most suitable in our situation that it should be applied. In this sense justice comprehends all the social virtues. There is yet another sense in which the word justice is sometimes taken, . . . Thus we are said to do injustice to a poem or a picture, when we do not admire them enough, . . . In the same manner we are said to do injustice to ourselves when we appear not to give sufficient attention to any particular object of self-interest. In this last sense, what is called justice means the same thing with exact and perfect propriety of conduct and behaviour, . . .
(VII.ii.1.10)

The decision of this question . . . will depend . . . secondly, upon the precision and exactness, or the looseness and inaccuracy of the general rules themselves.
(III.6.2)

Secondly, I say, it will depend partly upon the precision and exactness, or the looseness and inaccuracy of the general rules themselves, . . . (III.6.8)

The general rules of almost all the virtues . . . are in many respects loose and inaccurate, . . . (III.6.9)

There is, however, one virtue of which the general rules determine with the greatest exactness every external action which it requires. This virtue is justice.
(III.6.10)

Beneficence is always free, it cannot be extorted by force, the meer want of it exposes to no punishment: . . .
(II.ii.1.3)

The printed editions of TMS do not contain several sentences found towards the end of the manuscript, concerning the difference between improper vengeance or punishment and improper benevolence. It may be thought that this is because Adam Smith wanted to reserve the topic for his projected book on jurisprudence, but a more likely explanation is that he had changed his view by the time he came to publish TMS. Two points require notice.

(1) In the manuscript, Smith says, of the natural principles of punishment, that the extent and character of the violation of a right can be determined with precision, but not the degree of resentment or punishment due, since this latter varies with circumstances. Now there is evidence in the manuscript that, at the time when Smith dictated it, he had not yet thought out his theory of the impartial spectator (a theory which underwent considerable development between the publication of editions 1 and 6 of TMS, as can be seen in the elaboration of the account of conscience in Part III, first for edition 2 and then again for edition 6). When discussing the function of the magistrate, the manuscript says that he 'promises to hear all complaints of injustice, . . . and to give that redress which to any impartial person shall appear to be just and equitable'. TMS reproduces this simply as 'promises to hear and to redress every complaint of injury'. If Smith had included at this time the reference to 'any impartial person', he would certainly have written of the impartial 'spectator' instead. Once he had formulated his theory of the impartial spectator, he of course took the view that the proper degree of resentment or punishment was that which had the sympathy of the impartial spectator, as we can see from II.ii.2 of TMS. This chapter relates to resentment. That Smith would hold the same view of punishment is obvious enough, but can be confirmed from the two extant Reports of his lectures on jurisprudence. LJ(A), a full Report of lectures delivered in 1762–3, contains the following sentences at ii.89–90.

Now in all cases the measure of the punishment to be inflicted on the delinquent is the concurrence of the impartial spectator with the resentment of the injured. If the injury is so great as that the spectator can go along with the injured person in revenging himself by the death of the offender, this is the proper punishment, and what is to be exacted by the offended person or the magistrate in his place who acts in the character of an impartial spectator. . . . In all cases a punishment appears equitable in the eyes of the [unconcerned spectator] ⟨rest of mankind⟩ when it is such that the spectator would concur with the offended person in exacting.

In LJ(B), a summarized version of lectures delivered in 1763–4, the corresponding passage is at 181 (Cannan ed., 136): 'Injury naturaly excites the resentment of the spectator, and the punishment of the offender is reasonable as far as the indifferent spectator can go along with it. This is the natural measure of punishment.'

Consequently Smith would no longer accept the view that the rules of punishment resemble those of beneficence in being imprecise. That is why the relevant sentences of the manuscript are not reproduced in TMS, either at II.ii.1, where justice and beneficence are compared, or at III.6.8–10, where Smith distinguishes the precision of the rules of justice from the looseness of the rules of other virtues.

(2) Having noted an apparent similarity between improper punishment and improper benevolence, the manuscript goes on to contrast them, in that improper punishment may and ought to be opposed by force and renders the inflicter of it liable to punishment in his turn as having done an injury, while improper beneficence cannot be opposed by force and exposes to no punishment. The conclusion about 'improper' (i.e. want of proper) beneficence is reproduced in TMS at II.ii.1.3, but not that about improper punishment. It is indeed surprising that nowhere in TMS does Smith repeat the statement in the manuscript that 'Improper punishment, punishment which is either not due at all or which exceeds the demerit of the Crime, is an injury to the Criminal'. This is not only a sound expression of what Smith would call our 'natural moral sentiments'; it is a point which one would expect Smith, as an upholder of the retributive or desert theory of punishment, to include in his criticism of the utilitarian account of justice. Why does he not do so?

The fact is that Smith found himself in a cleft stick on this issue and had not thought out his position consistently. In the manuscript he says that the sentinel is punished for reasons of utility ('meerly from a View to the general interest of Society'), but he then writes: 'In our hearts we cannot blame this necessary Severity. *Nothing can be more just* [our italics], than that one man should be sacrificed to the security of thousands.' In the printed text of TMS, the sentences just quoted are modified and elaborated.

This severity may, upon many occasions, appear necessary, and, for that reason, just and proper. When the preservation of an individual is inconsistent with the safety of a multitude, nothing can be more just than that the many should be preferred to the one. Yet this punishment, how necessary soever, always appears to be excessively severe. The natural atrocity of the crime seems to be so little, and the punishment so great, that it is with great difficulty that our heart can reconcile itself to it. Though such carelessness appears very blameable, yet the thought of this crime does not naturally excite any such resentment, as would prompt us to take such dreadful revenge.

Smith is still prepared to say it is 'just' (as well as 'proper') to inflict, for utilitarian reasons, a punishment whose severity exceeds the 'natural atrocity' of the crime. But in these circumstances he could not say elsewhere, as the manuscript does, that 'punishment . . . which exceeds the demerit of the Crime, is an injury to the Criminal', for 'injury' means a breach of justice.

The extant Reports of the lectures on jurisprudence quote Smith as again using the example of the sentinel. In LJ(B) 182 (Cannan ed., 136), he is still prepared to call the punishment 'just': 'if a centinel be put to death for leaving[3]

---

[3] Perhaps Smith in fact said 'sleeping at' and was misheard by the student whose report is copied in LJ(B). The sentinel would have been more culpable if he had deliberately left his post.

his post, tho' the punishment be just and the injury that might have ensued be very great, yet mankind can never enter into this punishment as if he had been a thief or a robber.' But in LJ(A) ii.92, Smith expresses himself more cautiously:

In the same manner the military laws punish a centinell who falls asleep upon guard with death. This is intirely founded on the consideration of the publick good; and tho we *may perhaps* [our italics] approve of the sacrificing one person for the safety of a few, yet such a punishment when it is inflicted affects us in a very different manner from that of a cruel murtherer or other attrocious criminall.

Apart from the few sentences comparing improper punishment with improper benevolence, the whole of the substance of our manuscript fragment, often with the self-same words, is included in different parts of TMS. It is interesting to observe that, even when writing new material for edition 6, Smith was prepared to repeat some of the thought of the manuscript fragment, and even to introduce a brief phrase (but perhaps only by chance) that had occurred in the manuscript and that he had not previously used in TMS.

There can be no doubt that the manuscript is earlier than edition 1 of the book. As we have already observed, some of the corrections in the manuscript were made at the first dictation of the material, and it is the revised words, together with insertions made subsequently, that find a place in edition 1 of TMS. Often, too, the version in the printed text expands and improves upon the thought of the manuscript. The discussion of the sentinel is one, but not the only, clear instance of such improvement. Then again there is the evidence already cited that in the manuscript the theory of the impartial spectator has not yet been explicitly formulated.

Having established that the manuscript preceded the one submitted to the printer for edition 1 of the TMS, we can now consider for what purpose it was written. There are two possibilities, (1) that it was part of an early draft of the book, and (2) that it was part of a lecture. The first hypothesis receives some support from one piece of evidence, namely the occurrence in the manuscript of the very words 'the Theory of moral Sentiments'. As against that, however, there are two considerations which point, one of them strongly, to the alternative hypothesis of a lecture.

First, in the manuscript Smith states his intention 'hereafter to give a particular discourse' on natural jurisprudence or the theory of the general principles of law. In the last paragraph of TMS he says he will endeavour 'in another discourse' to give an account of the general principles of law and government, and of the history of jurisprudence. Here 'another discourse' means, of course, another book; but that cannot be the meaning of the words in the manuscript, 'I intend hereafter to give a particular discourse'. To *give* a *particular* discourse can only mean to deliver a lecture, or possibly a series of lectures.

The second consideration is less compelling, though worth mentioning. The manuscript stops before the end of a page, as do the two manuscripts of similar length reproduced in facsimile by Scott in *ASSP*, 379–85. Scott mentions (58) that these three manuscripts differ from the larger 'early draft of part of *The Wealth of Nations*' (the text of which he prints on pp. 322–53) in that a new chapter, in the latter work, follows on from the previous one, on the same page, if there is room, instead of beginning on a fresh page. The first printed versions of TMS and WN often begin a new chapter on the same page as the end of the previous chapter, if there is adequate space left, and one can infer that this was Smith's practice in the manuscripts for those books, since the printers of the first editions appear to have followed their copy closely in other respects. We can therefore agree with Scott that the blank space at the end of three of the short manuscripts, including the one discussed here, is a reason for regarding them as the final portions of lectures.

Whatever may be said, however, of the two other fragments, which deal with economics,[4] there is no reason to assign our particular manuscript to Smith's Edinburgh lectures, which, so far as we know, did not deal with ethics. Scott attributed this lecture to the Edinburgh period because he took it to be an introduction to lectures on law and because he thought Smith must have been too busy, during his first years in Glasgow, to write about law and economics. Since it is now perfectly clear that this particular manuscript covers the subject-matter of parts of TMS, the obvious conclusion is that it comes from one of the lectures which he gave as Professor of Moral Philosophy at Glasgow.

The lecture was, of course, on justice, and the single sentence about the Christian doctrine of the Atonement is relatively incidental. Smith's retention of this sheet cannot possibly have been due to any desire he might have had to re-arrange the position in TMS of the paragraph on divine justice. If he did have that purpose, he would have kept the whole paragraph, not just a sheet which begins in the middle of it; and in any event he would have used the fuller version of the paragraph that was printed in editions 1–5, and not the shorter version that he had originally written for his lecture course. It is perhaps idle to speculate on the reasons why this particular sheet happened to be placed in one of Smith's books and so preserved, but if conjecture may be allowed, one can hazard a different suggestion.

We have already noted that certain sentences at the end of the manuscript were not used in TMS, partly because Smith had altered his view on one point and partly because he would have seen a difficulty in his position on another. Now in these sentences of the manuscript, he is discussing what he takes to be the scholastic view of distributive justice, as distinguished from commutative justice, which, he has said, can alone properly be called justice. The distinction between different senses of the term 'justice' is described in TMS at VII.ii.1.10. We are there told that one sense 'coincides with what *Aristotle and the Schoolmen* call commutative justice', and that a second sense 'coincides with what *some* have called distributive justice' [our italics]. At this point Smith inserts a footnote to explain that 'The distributive justice of Aristotle is somewhat different'. The note goes on to give a succinct explanation of Aristotle's view and ends with a reference to the *Nicomachean Ethics*. Now Mitford's information was that Mr. Cunningham found the manuscript in a volume of Aristotle, and it is not too fanciful in the circumstances to suppose that the volume was, or included, Aristotle's *Ethics*. In preparing his earlier thoughts for publication, Smith would have checked many of his statements, and in this instance he would have found, by reference to

---

[4] Ronald L. Meek and Andrew S. Skinner, 'The Development of Adam Smith's Ideas on the Division of Labour', *Economic Journal*, lxxxiii (1973), 1094–1116 (especially 1104–6), give reasons for assigning these two fragments to an even later period, the 1760s.

Aristotle, that some qualification was needed to the bare statement in the lecture that 'in the Schools' the name of distributive justice was used for the proper allocation of beneficence. Following up this line of thought, one can even suggest an identification of the particular volume in which the manuscript was found. Adam Smith had a copy of the Works of Aristotle in Greek and Latin, edited by du Val and published in four folio volumes at Paris in 1629. (Bonar, *Catalogue 2*, 10, incorrectly gives the date as 1729.) Apart from this, he had separate editions of the *Rhetoric* and of the *Poetics* but no separate edition of the *Ethics*. Volume III of the du Val edition includes Aristotle's ethical writings, and it is quite likely that this volume was the one in which the manuscript was found. Smith's copy of the du Val Aristotle was certainly among the books that were bequeathed to Mrs. Cunningham, and it is now in the Library of the Queen's University of Belfast. It would be pleasant to be able to report that Volume III shows some line of discoloration as the result of having secreted a folded sheet of paper for some seventy years, either at the relevant part of the *Nicomachean Ethics* or in the end-papers, but the Sub-Librarian at the Queen's University tells us that there is no such trace.

Returning from these speculations to the fairly solid facts established earlier, there are some further inferences that may be drawn from the manuscript. To those who know the content of TMS, the title of the book seems a little strange, for the basic concepts of Smith's distinctive theory are sympathy and the impartial spectator, not moral sentiments. In the manuscript, Smith uses the phrase 'the Theory of moral Sentiments' as parallel to 'the Theory of the general principles of Law', and from this we can see that the title of his book is not meant to describe his own individual contribution to ethics but is his name for the scope of the subject in general (just as more recent writers have entitled their books *The Theory of Good and Evil* or *The Theory of Morals*, meaning that they are writing essays *in* ethical theory, not that their own views alone can properly be called 'the' theory). Once we realize that Smith's title is his name for the *subject*, it no longer seems strange. He was first taught ethics by Hutcheson, but Hume was the thinker who stimulated him to form a theory of his own. In Smith's eyes Hume had demonstrated conclusively that moral judgement and action are not based on reason but on 'sentiment' or feeling. Hume had further suggested that the 'peculiar sentiment of morals' is mediated by sympathy; and Smith found this suggestion attractive in principle but over-simplified in its assumption that there was a single, 'peculiar', moral sentiment to be explained. He therefore elaborated a more complex account of sympathy, that would explain the distinction between several different forms of moral sentiment, the 'sense of propriety', of virtue, of merit, of duty. Hence he regards the task of ethical theory as that of giving an account of 'moral sentiments' in the plural.

Another inference from the manuscript that can be made with confidence is this. It has always been supposed, from hearsay and intrinsic probability, that Smith worked up TMS from his lectures on ethics. The manuscript provides definite proof that he did so, even to the extent of repeating many of the very words of his lectures in their written form. Some, slightly hazardous, internal evidence pointing in this direction can be found in the book itself, as is mentioned in section 1(*a*) of our Introduction (p. 4) and in editorial footnotes at II.i.1,

IV.2.7 and 9, and VII.iii.1.2. But comparison of the manuscript with relevant parts of the printed texts puts the matter beyond any doubt.

This leads to yet another point. Rae (*Life*, 260–1) reports the opinion of J. R. McCulloch that Smith dictated WN to an amanuensis but wrote the manuscript of TMS in his own hand, and that this accounts for a difference in the style of the two works. Rae is sceptical, since there is no evidence that McCulloch had anything more to go on than his own impression that the style of WN is more diffuse than that of TMS, and Rae himself does not share that impression. We can be fairly certain, from our knowledge of Smith's extensive use of amanuenses, that WN was indeed dictated. Now if Smith was using an amanuensis even for his lectures, it seems likely that he would have done so for the manuscript of TMS.[5] Evidence from another quarter, however, makes this less certain. A comparison of details of antique spellings in edition 1 of WN with corresponding details in letters written in Smith's own hand, shows clearly enough that he himself did not write the manuscript used by the printers. A similar scrutiny of details of spelling and contractions in edition 1 of TMS, on the other hand, shows little deviation from, and indeed a good deal of correspondence with, Smith's practice in his letters. So it is possible that he did write the manuscript of his first book in his own hand. Nevertheless, we have already seen that much of the actual phraseology and construction of sentences repeats material in the lectures, which he had dictated to an amanuensis. If, as McCulloch believed, dictation produced a more diffuse style, the effect should be apparent in TMS too. One can of course account for differences of style in the two books, if differences there be, simply by the difference in Smith's age at the respective dates of composition. Certainly the passages added in edition 6 of TMS tend to be more diffuse than the writing of the original book, but the simplest explanation of this is that in 1759 Smith was a man in his thirties, while in 1788–9 he was in his sixties.

So much for the manuscript fragment. A good deal can be learned from it about the composition of TMS, but nothing about the reasons why Smith withdrew the paragraph on divine justice. In returning to this question, we want to suggest that Archbishop Magee was not so silly as Rae supposed, but we must state clearly at the outset that our suggestion on this issue is to a certain extent speculative.

The paragraph withdrawn from edition 6 occurred at the end of a chapter that considers the extent to which the sense of justice depends on utility. Earlier in the chapter, Smith gives partial support to a utilitarian theory of justice, and speaks of 'the account commonly given of our approbation of the punishment of injustice' (II.ii.3.7). In LJ(A) ii.90, he again discusses utilitarian theories of 'the originall measure of punishments', which, he says, have been held by 'Grotius and other writers'. But if one thinks of a utilitarian account of justice in general, Smith must surely have regarded Hume as the main contemporary proponent. His description of the utilitarian account in TMS II.ii.3.6 seems to refer particularly to Hume's view that utility pleases through sympathy. Writing in the 1750s, Smith was bound to recall that Hume, in the *Enquiry concerning the Principles of Morals* (1751), had argued strongly for the view that justice, unlike

---

[5] The draft revision of 1759, sent to Sir Gilbert Elliot, is in the hand of an amanuensis.

benevolence, arises *solely* from utility. Consequently, even though Smith's criticism of the utilitarian view of justice may have been aimed originally at a wider target, in the particular context of TMS II.ii.3 it must have seemed, and indeed have been intended, to be primarily directed against Hume, as are Smith's criticisms of utilitarianism elsewhere in the book.

This conclusion is confirmed by a couple of minor revisions of the disputed paragraph that were introduced in edition 3. Editions 1 and 2 state that a utilitarian view of divine justice 'is not the doctrine of nature, but of an artificial, though ingenious, refinement of philosophy', and that 'All our natural sentiments prompt us' to take a non-utilitarian view. In edition 3, the first phrase becomes 'is not the doctrine of untaught nature but of an artificial refinement of reason and philosophy', and the second phrase becomes 'Our untaught, natural sentiments, all prompt us'. The addition of 'untaught' in both sentences plainly takes account of Hume's distinction between different senses of the term 'natural' (*Treatise of Human Nature*, III.i.2, III.ii.1; ed. Selby-Bigge, 474-5, 484).

It is likely that Hume would have discussed with Smith in conversation their radical difference of opinion on the place of utility in moral judgement, and the minor revision noted above may be due to Hume's criticism. It is also possible that Hume may have teased Smith about his acceptance of conventional orthodoxy on theological matters. However that may be, edition 3 of TMS contains some further minor revisions of the paragraphs on divine justice, and of later remarks on the character of the clergyman, toning down the categorical affirmations of the original version. Editions 1 and 2 said that a non-retributive view of divine justice 'can, by no means, be so easily admitted'; edition 3 alters this to 'seems repugnant to some very natural feelings'. Editions 1 and 2 stated firmly that man can see no reason why he should not be the subject of divine indignation; edition 3 says 'he thinks he can see no reason'. In editions 1 and 2, man 'is sensible' that he appears to God to be a vile insect, and 'is conscious' that he is undeserving of happiness; in edition 3, he only 'imagines' the first and 'suspects' the second. In editions 1 and 2, repentance, sorrow, humiliation, and contrition 'are' the sentiments which become him; in edition 3, they 'seem' so. A similar problematic note is struck by a revision in the preceding paragraph (II.ii.3.12) of 'religion authorises' to 'religion, we suppose, authorises'. Then again, at V.2.5, the clergyman, who in editions 1 and 2 'is' the messenger of serious tidings and 'is' continually occupied with the grand and solemn, becomes in edition 3 one who 'seems to be' the former and 'is supposed to be' the latter. It is of course possible that the more cautious statements of edition 3 represent Smith's original views, the expression of which he felt would be injudicious as coming from a Professor of Moral Philosophy but which honesty obliged him to make clear after he had quitted his Chair. At any rate we ought to note that, in Smith's revision of TMS, the withdrawal of the paragraph on divine justice in edition 6 was not the first suggestion that he might have moved away from orthodox theology.

Whether or not the changes made in edition 3 were influenced by discussion with Hume, there is no doubt that the criticism of utilitarianism which ends with the paragraph on divine justice was first and foremost a criticism of Hume. In the light of this, let us consider what Smith might have been ready to say in 1759 and reluctant to let stand after the death of Hume in 1776. (Edition 5 of TMS appeared in 1781, but at *this* juncture we can properly say that Smith's 'many avocations' prevented him for a long time from making the radical revisions that he had contemplated.) It will be recalled that Magee had been shocked by Smith's estimate of Hume's character, and in this Magee was not alone. The phrase that Magee quoted had given great offence to the faithful at the time of its original publication. It came in the last sentence of Letter 178 addressed to William Strahan, dated 9 November 1776, soon after Hume's death. The letter was written for publication along with Hume's short autobiography. Smith knew very well that he was stirring up a hornet's nest, but although he was temperamentally averse from public controversy on matters of religion, he deliberately ended his letter with the statement that Hume had come as near to perfect virtue as human frailty allowed. It was written with the deepest sincerity, on the death of Smith's greatest friend, whom the world called an 'atheist'. When Smith came to revise his book on ethics, he must surely have felt some revulsion from concluding a criticism of Hume with a paragraph whose language echoed the sermons of those 'high-flying' preachers who had been the bitterest detractors of Hume. It is no wonder, if Archdeacon Sinclair's report is authentic, that Smith should have thought the paragraph 'unnecessary and misplaced'. It was unnecessary because the preceding criticism of utilitarian theory stood firmly enough on its own ground of appeal to our 'natural sentiments'. It was misplaced because it was (after 1776, at least) quite the wrong spirit in which to end a polemic directed as much against his dead friend as against anyone else. So instead of Christian doctrine about expiation and atonement, Smith made his own atonement by substituting a sentence so Humean in tone that it might almost be called a libation to Hume's ghost: 'In every religion, and in every superstition that the world has ever beheld, accordingly, there has been a Tartarus as well as an Elysium; a place provided for the punishment of the wicked, as well as one for the reward of the just.'

Rae concludes his account of the controversy by saying (*Life*, 429–30) that 'Smith gives a fresh expression to his belief in a future state and an all-seeing Judge in one of the new passages he wrote' for edition 6, showing 'that he died as he lived, in the full faith of those doctrines of natural religion which he had publicly taught'. Certainly Smith never abandoned *natural* religion. The new passages (there are in fact two of them, at III.2.12 and III.2.33) about the all-seeing Judge seem at first sight to be very near in doctrine to the suppressed paragraph, and indeed one might wonder why, if Smith really wanted to retain the paragraph in another place, he did not insert it there. Yet a closer look at the 'all-seeing Judge' passages gives a different impression. Rae quotes from the first of them but does not mention that Smith reverts to the idea more fully towards the end of the same chapter. The new passages, like the suppressed paragraph, are about the doctrine of divine reward and punishment in an afterlife, but Smith does not now give unqualified support to the doctrine as preached by Christians. The notion of heavenly reward, says Smith, is the only comfort for unrecognized innocence and virtue, but it has too often been taught in a form that contradicts our moral sentiments by confining divine salvation to the religious. He quotes and derides an address of Massillon to the effect that soldiers cannot hope for the heaven which one day of penance and mortification in a monk's cell can bring. 'To compare, in this manner, the futile mortifications of a monastery, to the ennobling hardships and hazards of war . . . is surely contrary to all our moral sentiments'. A paragraph of support for theology is followed by two paragraphs of scorn for 'monks and friars' as contrasted with 'heroes, . . . statesmen and lawgivers, . . . poets and philosophers . . . all the great protectors, instructors, and benefactors of mankind; all those to whom our natural sense of praise-worthiness forces us to ascribe the highest merit and most exalted virtue'. Smith then ends his chapter by quoting Voltaire's satirical couplet on the Christian concept of hell:

> Vous y grillez sage et docte Platon,
> Divin Homère, éloquent Cicéron.

If Smith had added to this honours list of the ancients a similar one for the moderns, he would have put Hume at the head of it to correspond to Plato (and Plato's Socrates). Smith's derision of 'monks and friars' and 'the futile mortifications of a monastery' has a familiar ring. It was Hume who wrote (*Enquiry concerning the Principles of Morals*, IX.i; ed. Selby-Bigge, §219) that 'penance, mortification, . . . and the whole train of monkish virtues . . . are . . . everywhere rejected by men of sense'. And it was Adam Smith who deliberately imitated the last sentence of Plato's *Phaedo* by ending his epitaph to Hume with the judgement that Hume had approached 'as nearly to the idea of a perfectly wise and virtuous man, as perhaps the nature of human frailty will permit'.

Addendum to Introduction, pp. *32-3*

A second Japanese translation was published in 1973 :

Dōtoku-kanjōron, translated by Hiroshi Mizuta from ed. 1, with notes of revisions made in subsequent editions; Tokyo, 1973.

Index